Integrated Language Arts for Emerging Literacy

Walter E. Sawyer
Jean C. Sawyer

Delmar Publishers Inc.

NOTICE TO THE READER

Cover design by Nancy Gwork
Cover photo by Michael Upright

Delmar staff

Administrative Editor: Jay Whitney
Project Editor: Theresa M. Bobear
Production Coordinator: James Zayicek
Design Coordinator: Karen Kunz Kemp
Art Coordinator: Megan Keane DeSantis

For information, address Delmar Publishers Inc.
3 Columbia Circle, Box 15-015
Albany, New York 12212-5015

Copyright 1993 by Delmar Publishers Inc.

Printed in the United States of America
Published simultaneously in Canada
by Nelson Canada,
a division of The Thomson Corporation

1 2 3 4 5 6 7 8 9 10 XXX 99 98 97 96 95 94 93

Library of Congress Cataloging-in-Publication Data

Sawyer, Walter.
   Integrated language arts for emerging literacy / Walter E. Sawyer,
Jean C. Sawyer.
      p. cm.
   Includes bibliographical references and index.
   ISBN 0-8273-4609-3
   1. Language arts (Elementary)—United States. 2. Literacy—United
States. 3. Language experience approach in education—United
States. I. Sawyer, Jean C. II. Title.
LB1576.S313 1993
372.6'0973—dc20

Table of Contents

SECTION 1 AN INTEGRATED APPROACH

SECTION 2 LEARNING ABOUT THE WORLD

SECTION 3 EMERGING LANGUAGE AND LITERACY

SECTION 4 COMPONENTS OF A PROGRAM

SECTION 5 SPECIAL NEEDS

SECTION 6 ENHANCING CREATIVITY

SECTION 7 PARENT AND SCHOOL PARTNERSHIPS

Dedication

To our parents, our first and most influential teachers, who started each of us on the road to literacy:

Rose D. Sawyer (1906–1989)
Walter E. Sawyer, Sr. (1904–1971)
Norma L. Handschur
Charles F. Handschur

WES
JCS

Preface

Integrated Language Arts for Emerging Literacy responds to the most current thinking, research, and practices in early childhood literacy programs. It presents a whole language approach to literacy development instruction for children from birth through the primary grades. The whole language approach has its roots in the educational programs of New Zealand and Australia, as well as the United States. The approach is increasingly being implemented in schools throughout the United States and Canada. It is a well thought out approach, supported by both research and common sense, and it is causing both states and provinces to rethink the process of becoming literate. The book makes a compelling case for the need to integrate language arts instruction for all children, in all programs in the community.

This book is needed because of its comprehensive approach to literacy development with young children. It may be the only book that presents a plan to integrate disabled children, parents, community resources, and the total curriculum into the regular classroom literacy development program. Whole language is not a specific set of activities, but is a system of beliefs about the interaction of a child's language modes and how educators can use the child's language to foster further growth. The approach emphasizes the use of whole pieces of language and texts rather than focusing on isolated bits and pieces of language. As a result, the emphasis is on using an abundance of children's literature as well as ample opportunities for using oral language and writing abilities. In order for teachers to be effective with the approach, they need to learn to make decisions about their instruction rather than relying on a teacher's manual or program guidebook for instructional practices. This book provides teachers with the background and practices needed to become effective decision-makers in the classroom.

A number of outstanding features of this book will help teachers become more effective in the classroom. The overall organization of the book enables readers to see the broad picture of education and how different parts of instruction fit into the broad picture. The seven major sections each introduce a general idea. Each section begins with a related statement from a well-known children's book author. These ideas can be discussed with others, prior to the reading of the units within the section, and used as motivators for seeking answers and understandings. Each unit begins with goals and a preview. The goals enable the reader to understand what should be acquired as a result of reading the section. The preview provides additional ideas and questions for consideration as the reading proceeds. Questions and activities for review and discussion follow each unit. These help the reader determine whether or not the goals for the unit have been achieved. They can serve as excellent ideas for classroom discussion as well as written responses.

The content of each unit includes a number of additional special features. Several hundred children's storybooks are cited, described, and used as examples. This helps the reader become familiar with a wide range of both classical and contemporary books for young children. Another special feature of the book is complete sections addressing the involvement of parents and exceptional children in the regular instructional program.

Several examples of thematic units are provided both in individual units and in the appendices of the book. Thematic units are essential building blocks for developing literacy through a whole language approach. Those described here can be readily transferred to actual classroom practice. Finally, a wide range of procedures, formats, checklists, and planning sheets are illustrated throughout the book. They cover virtually all aspects of a literacy development program. These two can be readily applied to actual classroom practice as they are presented or with local adaptations.

An instructor's guide is available for use with the program. The guide contains correct answers to the objective questions at the end of each unit as well as model responses to the more open-ended essay and discussion questions that are also found at the end of each unit. Also included in the instructor's guide is a set of additional activities that can be used with individuals or groups of pre-service or in-service teachers seeking to become more effective instructors.

Walter Sawyer is a graduate of Siena College, Assumption College, and the State University of New York at Albany. He holds B.A., M.A., and EdD degrees. He is certified in and has worked at all levels of education from nursery school through graduate school. Currently he is an administrator for the Waterford-Halfmoon School District in upstate New York and teaches graduate courses in reading and writing at Russell Sage College. He has been an active member at all levels of the International Reading Association and is past president of a local reading council. He has a deep personal interest in storytelling and has conducted storytelling workshops. He is the author of over forty publications in the field of literacy, including the Delmar publication, *Growing Up with Literature.*

Jean Sawyer is a graduate of the State University of New York. She holds a B.A. degree in Latin and an M.A. degree in developmental reading. She has worked with children from preschool through secondary school. While much of her current time is spent advocating for the education and literacy development of children with disabilities within regular educational programs, she continues an interest in classics through her membership in the Classical Association of the Empire State. Jean and Walter Sawyer have developed and implemented a lending library in their own school district that provides both related children's trade books and books on advocacy for parents of children with disabilities. They also review books for children and young adults for *Maine in Print,* the publication of the Maine Writer's and Publisher's Alliance.

The authors would like to acknowledge and thank the many individuals who have provided their knowledge and support to make this a better book: to Jay Whitney, our editor at Delmar, who gave us unwavering support and inspiration throughout the project; to our children, Andrew and Emily, who shared so many of the literacy experiences described in this book; to Frank Hodge, who constantly inspires us to see the world in new ways through his insights and the children's books that he loves and shares; to Melanie Stracuzzi, for her help with some of the illustrations appearing here; to the authors and publishers of children's books who provided comments, photographs, and books for use with this project; to our reviewers, whose valuable insights have strengthened the entire book:

Leanna Manna
Villa Maria College of Buffalo

Judith Brivic
San Antonio College

J. Amos Hatch
The University of Tennessee, Knoxville

Nancy Winter
Greenfield Community College

Billie A. Coffman
Pennsylvania College of Technology

Nancy H. Phillips
Lynchburg College

Carol Sharpe
Santa Barbara City College

Mary McKnight-Taylor
Hofstra University

Section 1
An Integrated Approach

Carol Carrick

"I was one of those lucky children to have a mother who read to me every day. I remember that even at the age of three I was trying, unsuccessfully, to decode my parents' novels. I was so anxious to read my own books that I spelled out the letters to my mother as she ironed, and thereby learned how to read.

It is clear to me that a child can do anything if he is motivated. Children will learn to read what interests them. What seven-year-old who is exposed to dinosaurs cannot read and spell *tyrannosaurus?*

Editors of basal readers have told me at the outset that they want good stories, but they can't mean this. The very qualities that make good literature—the development of interesting characters, provocative subject matter, and vivid descriptions are not allowed. I know it is impossible to write a compelling story with such constraints put on the writer. Given these limitations of vocabulary, subject matter, and length, the assignment becomes merely an exercise, a challenging puzzle."

Text courtesy of Carol Carrick. Photograph courtesy of Jules Worthington.

TO THE READER:

One of the most exciting and amazing adventures you will ever undertake may be about to begin. Watching, observing, and helping young children learn to use language can be one of the most important things a person can do. Teaching language skills will require you to be patient, understanding, and knowledgeable. You will need to be patient because all children grow at different rates. You must be willing to allow children to grow at these individual rates. As a teacher, understanding will also be an invaluable personal asset. Young children have many needs. They may not be ready to learn the things you would like to share with them on any given day. These needs are to be seen as opportunities rather than obstacles. You will need to have knowledge to assist you in making decisions about what constitutes a developmentally appropriate approach to developing language skills in young children.

The first section of this book will provide you with a basic understanding of language arts for young children. The approach shared in this section makes use of the ideas of many educators and early childhood specialists. It is a decidedly human approach, which is often referred to as whole language. The units in this section provide an integrated approach to oral language, writing, reading, and literature. You will notice that individual units may cover more than one language mode or major concept. For example, listening and speaking are addressed together in a unit on oral language rather than in two separate units on listening and speaking. This is because both listening and speaking occur simultaneously in natural environments. Reading and literature are also addressed in a single unit. This is because children don't simply read; children read written pieces, or literature. This view of the interwoven nature of language modes is a fundamental belief of the position taken in this text.

The ideas and strategies you will learn in this section will provide you with a firm knowledge base that you can rely on when making language arts instructional decisions. While the reader will find many practical ideas in this first section, the focus is on helping you to become a proactive teacher. That is, the knowledge presented here will help you to make decisions when a program is going smoothly and also when events in a program become less routine. Early childhood educators must be able to respond when children, programs, and classroom routines are not always predictable.

UNIT 1

What Is Whole Language?

UNIT GOALS

After completing this unit, the reader should:

- understand what is meant by "emergent literacy."
- be aware of the characteristics of whole language.
- become aware of the general history of whole language.
- possess a knowledge of the research supporting a whole language approach.
- understand the necessity for whole language teachers to develop a personal knowledge base.
- become aware of the criticisms of a whole language approach.

PREVIEW

Language surrounds us throughout our lives. From the moment we are born, our worlds are filled with conversation, laughter, signs, billboards, media messages, books, magazines, songs, and discussions. Our constant immersion in this environment enables us to acquire language in early childhood. Few individuals learn oral language through educational programs in schools. Rather, they learn it by listening to others speak and by attempting to communicate.

An integrated language arts program recognizes these facts. Further, it takes advantage of the natural abilities and tendencies of children to acquire language within their natural surroundings. This unit contributes to an understanding of this approach by developing a solid understanding of a variety of key features of language and learning. Some of the key features addressed by this chapter are:

- The concept of emerging literacy
- The concept of an integrated language arts program
- A description of whole language
- Assumptions held by whole language teachers
- Characteristics of whole language
- A history of the whole language movement
- Research supporting a whole language approach
- The importance of developing a knowledge base
- The criticisms of whole language

INTRODUCTION

To understand the concept of whole language, you must first comprehend the nature of literacy. This unit discusses literacy as a general idea, with emergent literacy as a focal point. The unit provides a definition of literacy that is derived from the purposes of literacy. While the purposes may differ from individual to individual, they usually include communication, achieving personal needs, deriving pleasure, developing social relationships, understanding the culture, and learning the rituals of society. Each need is discussed in the unit as it relates to literacy.

From that point, the framework of an integrated language arts program is constructed. The basic assumption of the approach is that the whole is greater than the sum of its parts. That is, the distinct facets of language cannot be separated from each other and retain the meaning that they have as a whole. Therefore, an integrated language arts program is comprised not only of different ideas and concepts, but also of the ways those ideas and concepts interact with each other. Among the components of such a program are communication modes, the thinking process, the concept of meaningfulness, the importance of processes, an understanding of human differences, and the role of evaluation.

An integrated language arts program is an extension of a whole language approach. A whole language approach to the language arts is best described as a philosophy rather than a set of activities. The philosophy is based on important assumptions about language, learning, children, and literature. A whole language approach is characterized by the use of whole texts, a literature-based approach to language learning, a child-centered atmosphere, cooperative activities, and parent involvement. Each of these is described in this unit.

In order for teachers to make appropriate classroom decisions, they need to understand the whole language approach. To do this they must be willing to continue to be students themselves. It is important that teachers become aware of the history of the development of the approach, its theoretical foundation, and the research that supports whole language. In addition, they need to continually expand this knowledge base through participation in workshops, exchanging ideas with other teachers, and reading relevant professional literature. Finally, they should become aware of the major criticisms of the approach. This knowledge will help teachers to continue to make valid classroom decisions and to grow professionally.

FIGURE 1-1 Children enjoy the language of books at a very young age.

EMERGING LITERACY

Defining literacy is a monumental task; defining emerging literacy becomes an even greater one. Over time, these subjects have been the focus of numerous professional articles and books. A fascinating look at the arguments is presented in a recent International Reading Association panel discussion (Aaron, Chall, Durkin, Goodman, and Strickland 1990). Though the participants disagreed about the quantity of language ability required to indicate that an individual is literate, they agreed that literacy refers to the ability to read and write. The argument about quantity concerned how well an individual had to read and write in order to be considered a literate individual in modern day life.

Literacy Defined

For the purpose of this book, literacy is defined as the ability to read and write at a level that enables an individual to function effectively as a productive member of society and that the individual finds satisfactory. If an individual does not read and write well enough to hold basic employment, participate in citizenship activities, or pursue social functions that require literacy, the individual cannot be considered literate. Beyond that, if individuals feel that they do not possess the reading and writing skills necessary to function effectively in modern day life, such individuals should be seen as needing further literacy instruction. The beliefs of the individual have a role in determining whether or not that person possesses literacy.

Purposes Of Literacy

To define emerging literacy, one must look even more closely at literacy and at the purposes of literacy. While literacy is usually seen as the ability to read and write, it must also be acknowledged that the ability to receive and express ideas, thoughts, and feelings plays an important role in developing reading and writing ability. Speaking ability, listening ability, sign language, and other forms of communication must therefore be included as important literacy skills. Listening, speaking, reading, and writing are closely interrelated. They work in conjunction with each other.

By acknowledging the critical roles of listening and speaking in the total literacy development process, understanding the purposes of literacy becomes easier. As children grow in early childhood, one can observe them exploring the purposes of literacy on a daily basis. While many purposes can be stated, six of the most important ones are described here.

The first purpose of literacy is communication. When a child points to a teddy bear on a shelf and says "bear," the communication is usually quite clear to a parent. The child is saying, "Give me my teddy bear." This is closely tied to, and perhaps overlaps, a second purpose of literacy: meeting the needs of the individual. A baby who makes a certain cry when hungry is communicating a need to meet nutritional needs. A child who excitedly tells an older sibling about the exciting field trip in nursery school that day is satisfying a need to share information with another person. Again, this too is closely tied with the major purpose of communication.

The third and fourth purposes of literacy are closely related: pleasure and developing friendships. Obviously these two are related, since children experience such a definite sense of pleasure the first few times they establish a friendship. Young children elicit pleasure from telling jokes, answering questions, laughing at funny stories, and talking to a new friend on the telephone for the first time. It is usually through language and play, of course, that young children develop friendships. The informal discus-

FIGURE 1-2 Young children attempt to communicate through their drawings.

sions that evolve from cooperative play activities are often the beginnings of friendships. Children discover through language and play that they share common interests and enjoy many of the same activities. This process builds many friendships.

The fifth and sixth purposes of literacy also are related to each other: understanding the culture and learning rituals. As children watch the world around them they begin to understand that some parts of life and certain activities have their own importance. It is through language that parents and teachers can help children understand the culture. The importance of work, play, citizenship, grieving, and celebrating are all explained through language. Through the common language shared by a society, the younger members learn such things as why certain holidays are celebrated and why it is necessary for individuals to abide by the rules of society. Many cultural concepts are actually demonstrated through rituals. This might include Independence Day fireworks displays, participation at a wedding as a ring bearer or flower girl, worshipping at a church, temple, mosque or synagogue, singing "Happy Birthday" at a birthday party, or learning an African folksong for an intercultural fair. Some of these rituals are explained by adults through language. At other times, the words recited within the rituals explain themselves. Rituals are an important and cherished part of any society. They tie us together as human beings and celebrate our humanity.

The purposes of literacy described here are not all-inclusive. They encompass, however, the major categories under which other purposes of literacy can be grouped. As young children go about the process of achieving these purposes, they do so mainly through listening and speaking. However, as they do this they are acquiring many concepts about language that will transfer to reading and writing. Written language can be used for all of these major purposes. Children may see the words to the "Happy Birthday" song written on a greeting card. They may receive a written copy of the words to the song they are learning even though they cannot yet read it. They may have books that contain some of the prayers they use during worship services. Greeting cards for birthdays, weddings, and other occasions contain language that reinforces the spoken words connected with them. They may also see a copy of a historic written document displayed at a patriotic celebration. Parents and teachers may share books, words, and sentences associated with any of these purposes. As this occurs, children begin to notice many things about written language. These pieces of information are referred to as concepts about print. The entire process of listening, speaking, acquiring concepts about print, and finally learning to read and write in a conventional sense is referred to as emerging literacy. The process begins at birth, perhaps even before, and extends throughout early childhood. This period of a child's life is a time of tremendous language growth. As such it is one of life's most exciting periods.

Concepts About Print

As children grow in the early childhood years, they make many discoveries about language. One of these discoveries is that oral and written language are related. They engage in experiments and attempts at written language through their drawing and by their attempts to write their names and perhaps that of a favorite animal, character, or toy. They also discover

FIGURE 1-3 Children make discoveries about language through their drawings.

things about written language through sharing stories. Each of these discoveries aids children as they progress in their reading and writing abilities. Concepts about print have been studied by a number of educators (Clay 1972, 1979; Strickland 1990). They have discovered a number of different concepts and several ways of describing them. For the purposes of this discussion, they will be described under the categories of physical aspects of a book, printed text and illustrations, attitudes toward print, and aspects of comprehension.

Physical Aspects of a Book.

Concepts within this category refer to the actual book and its physical features that are important to reading. Children acquire understandings in this area as they realize that a book must be held right side up in order to read it and that you turn the pages from front to back. They also may learn that various people are responsible for creating the book. Books often have an author and an illustrator, whose names may appear on the cover and title page. Identifying the front and back covers and knowing that one reads the left hand page before the right hand page are also concepts about the physical aspects of a book.

Printed Text and Illustrations.

Concepts within this category are based upon the idea that the markings and figures on the page represent meaning. Children learn that the different marks on the page mean different things and that being able to identify them correctly helps one get meaning from the book. As children acquire these concepts, they learn that there is a difference between letters, words, sentences, punctuation, and capitals. They may not understand what all of the differences mean, but they become aware that there are differences and that they do mean something. Other ideas that emerge include the fact that illustrations enhance the meaning of the text, lines are read from left to right and from the top to the bottom of the page, and that sounds can be used to represent many of the symbols on the page.

Attitude Toward Print.

A critically important set of concepts about print for the emergent reader deals with how children feel about reading and about themselves as readers. Among the concepts in this category are whether or not children identify favorite authors, select books for storytime, show an interest in listening to stories, seek to "read" stories independently after they have been read, and engage in talking about books and stories. Other concepts include whether children request books by favorite authors, request favorite books to be read, and recite predictable lines along with the text.

Aspects of Comprehension.

Concepts in the category of comprehension refer to the degree of understanding children possess about books that have been read or shared with them. Concepts that children can acquire in this area include the ability to talk about general ideas and specific details of a story, the ability to retell or dramatize a story, and the ability to compare the story to another story. More sophisticated concepts include the ability to predict words or upcoming events in the story, to identify cause and effect relationships in a story, and to generate possible events that might occur after the ending of a story.

While these concepts generally refer to the acts of reading and writing, these two acts are not necessarily distinguished as different subjects as they so often are in the minds of adults. Actually, this is a natural way of looking at language. Distinguishing between reading and writing is created by adults for the convenience of adults. In view of this, teachers might better take advantage of the natural aspects of how children approach reading and writing: as an integrated activity. In fact, language is not just integrated within itself. Language is integrated with all of life.

INTEGRATED LANGUAGE ARTS

Integration refers to the fact that many parts are related to each other so that the parts cannot be separated. This suggests that the language modes of listening, speaking, reading, and writing exist in such a way that each supports and derives meaning from the others. The view of integrated language arts used here, however, goes beyond that. It views language as a part of life itself. Language is integrated into the daily existence of all people. It is integrated into all aspects of their lives. Whether it involves a simple shopping trip or studying content area subjects, language is an intrinsic part of human reality. While the view of language here is a whole language view, it extends even further. Key characteristics of this view are evident when considering its relationship to such concepts as communication, thinking, meaningfulness, process, content areas, human differences, and evaluation.

Communication Modes

Harste et al. (1984) suggests that young children do not approach communication as adults do. Adults tend to rely primarily on words, resorting to other means such as illustrations and graphs only when words do not suffice. Children use all of the modes of communication available to them. They do not draw clear distinctions between oral language, music,

I Like The Part When
The I cat look Down at
Matt Then She Jumps
Higher

FIGURE 1-4 Children use a combination of writing and drawing to make their intended meaning clear.

drama, and art. Research supports the view that children use these systems to communicate and that they use knowledge from one system to support understanding in another system (Karnowski 1985, 1986).

Oral language is used for several functions (Halliday 1973; Tough 1976). It is used to plan and clarify written information as well as to aid other communication modes. Many three-year-olds understand the difference between writing and drawing (Lavine 1972; Hiebert 1978; Harste et al. 1984). However, most young children use the two in combination to make their intended meaning clear to the reader. Music and drama are also used by young children to help clarify the meaning of what they have written. As a result, teachers need to redefine traditional definitions of communication in order to encourage children to make full use of their communication potential (Karnowski 1986).

Thinking Processes

Thinking underlies all language use. It is inseparable from language in meaningful language. Developmental psychologists disagree about the relationship between language and thinking. Some feel that language precedes thinking, while others hold that the reverse is true. These views are discussed later. For the present, an integrated view of language arts holds that thinking is inextricably related to each of the language modes.

Whole language teachers agree that the thinking process is particularly related to oral social language. In social language, one must not only think about one's message, but about the recipient of the message as well. While this is true of all meaningful communications, social language has an immediacy to it. The receiver of the oral message is present. A speaker must frame the message in a way that the listener will understand. If understanding does not take place, this can be communicated instantaneously. The speaker must then quickly make decisions about how to best handle the situation: Do I try again? Is my message worth the effort? Is there a better way of stating this?

Meaningfulness

The purpose of communication is to make sense and to share that meaning with others. If something doesn't make sense, it is hard to explain the concept to someone else. If the information is meaningful, children will use assorted tools and strategies to communicate that meaning. For this reason, helping and guiding children grasp the meaning inherent in language should always be a high priority for those who work with young children. Language concepts and structures, therefore, are best learned and understood when they are taught within whole pieces of text. Isolating language from meaning usually makes learning language more difficult.

Processes

Language processes are closely related to meaning in language. An integrated language arts approach does not view language as a set of products. It does not see literacy as a state to be attained. While products of language such as oral statements and written stories are often produced, it is only through processes that meaning can be seen.

Literacy is a continually developing process. It involves language processes that become more and more sophisticated. Individuals acquire language skills and strategies that enable them to acquire greater and greater understandings about the world. Meaning does not exist by itself. Meaning comes with the successful use of a language process that allows the language user to understand a message. Until an individual grasps the meaning within the words, there is no meaning.

Content Areas

In view of the fact that understanding and meaning are so closely connected to language, it seems clear that learning results largely from the ability of learners to understand language. Most educators readily agree that the traditional content areas of mathematics, science, literature, and social studies rely on language for learning. However, nearly all of the subjects taught in school rely on understanding language as well. These include art, music, homemaking, health, technology, nutrition, physical education, and so on.

The relationship between language and content areas is not one-directional. While language can support the content areas, content area instruction can reinforce language learning. For example, when explaining an activity in physical education class, the instructor can reinforce the language of basic concepts that may be used. Such terms may include up, down, left, right, walk, run, jump sit, and so forth.

Human Differences

An integrated language arts program does not view the walls of the traditional classroom as the limits within which learning occurs. Just as language learning is not restricted to language arts class, it should not be restricted to a narrow view of the world either. Language is integrated with life. Life, therefore, ought to be integrated within the classroom. Parents should share an active role in education both in and out of the classroom. The community should be seen as an extension of the classroom.

Regular classroom programs ought to be accessible to all. The regular classroom experience, with special service and support as needed, is seen as the best place for all children to receive an education. Isolating disabled, gifted, culturally deprived, and non-English-language-speaking children in segregated educational programs is viewed as a disservice to all children. Children experiencing language difficulties

FIGURE 1-5 Children can explore the diversity of the world through an integrated approach to language arts.

can gain much from being educated in the same classrooms with those for whom language skills have come easier. Children who have acquired more language skills can strengthen those skills and gain a better understanding of humanity by receiving their education with those experiencing more difficulty.

Evaluation

The evaluation of an integrated language arts program and the learning it produces in children should be implemented with the ideas upon which it is based. Since such a program does not view language as sets of isolated tasks and artificially segregated skills, traditional testing procedures are not appropriate. Rather, the evaluation should be more informal. The benchmark of success is how well the program has been able to help children progress in their ability to discover and create meaning for themselves and for others. Portfolios that include the anecdotal records of the teacher and examples of student work can be used for evaluation processes.

A WHOLE LANGUAGE APPROACH

An integrated language arts program is based upon a whole language approach. This approach has a long developmental history. It has been described as a spirit, a philosophy, and a movement rather than as a set of activities or a methodology. As such, it is fundamentally different from traditional approaches to language arts programs that greatly rely on such things as basal reading texts, workbooks, ditto sheets, drills, and learning skills in isolation. The characteristics of a whole language program can best be understood if the teacher is aware of the assumptions upon which it is based and previous attempts to define it.

Assumptions

Often the assumptions of traditional language arts programs are based on limited support from theory or research. Educators increasingly question these assumptions as they delve into a whole language approach. Lovitt (1990), in considering the role of a teacher in a whole language program, charges that many traditional assumptions are false. Rather than attempting to modify traditional assumptions, it seems more reasonable to clearly identify those assumptions incorporated into a whole language program. Lovitt's work can serve as a springboard for developing a set of general assumptions for a whole language approach.

First, it is assumed that children develop in different ways at different ages. In language, particularly, children seem to reach different levels of skill and understanding in different ways and at different chronological ages. Given this, it is important for teachers to be aware of the fact that a sequenced curriculum may not be appropriate for helping children develop literacy. Each classroom needs to have individualized objectives corresponding to the needs and interests of the children.

A second assumption is based on the need to see students as individual learners. It holds that commercially prepared language arts texts, kits, supplementary materials, and text should never supercede the judgment of the teacher. There is no way for a person working in a publisher's office 2,000 miles away from the children in a classroom to know what will meet their needs. Also, that individual cannot know how to best develop a test that will accurately assess the learning of those children. Since language learning is fundamentally a process, commercially available products that focus mainly on student generated products are

inadequate. For many years, teachers have accepted the decision-making of commercial materials producers as being correct. It is easy to get used to using programs where all of the thinking has been done for you ahead of time. With such programs, the teacher need only follow the directions in the teacher's manual concerning the ditto, workbook page, or lesson to assign next. This does not mean that commercial products must be excluded from the whole language classroom. It does mean that they will have a less important role than they enjoyed in traditional classrooms.

A third assumption is that the role of the teacher is as a participant in the literate environment rather than as the individual in charge of that environment. The first responsibility of any teacher is the protection and safety of the children. The concept of being in control of the classroom does not mean, however, that children must be sitting quietly while paying close attention to what the teacher is saying at all times. The teacher is not seen as the possessor of all the knowledge worth knowing. The teacher does possess much knowledge and can help children find the knowledge they need. However, when the teacher functions more as a coordinator, children show that they are capable of teaching much language to each other. In the process of this cooperative activity, the children develop valuable social skills.

A fourth assumption is that the language arts and language learning should not be subjects and activities set apart from the regular curriculum. Language is seen as the primary tool for thinking about and dealing with nearly every aspect of life. In school, the strategies for language learning work effectively with all of the content areas. Even areas such as mathematics are learned more effectively when children are engaged in activities where they are encouraged and allowed to read, write, think, and talk about the topic.

Defining Whole Language

Dorothy Watson (1989) addresses the difficult task of defining whole language by first identifying the need to possess such a definitiion. She contends that a definition is needed because educators need to talk to parents, colleagues, and administrators about whole language. When it is framed in a definition, it helps teachers identify the theory, practice, and research that support it. Finally, it helps teachers to monitor what materials are being used and how they are being used.

Several reasons for the difficulty in defining whole language are described by Watson (1989). First, most whole language teachers reject a dictionary term for it. Such definitions are too closely tied to behavioristic research that tends to approach education from an opposing viewpoint. Second, people both for and against whole language hold strong emotions. Teachers who use a whole language approach do not necessarily see themselves as crusaders. They use the approach, find that it is effective, and go about their lives. Once a dictionary definition is presented, it is then open to attacks by critics. Defending definitions is not a high priority for whole language teachers. A third reason is that whole language teachers, the true whole language experts, have never really been asked for a definition.

A number of educators have offered a variety of definitions of whole language over the years. Goodman (1986) defined whole language as a way of coordinating views of language, learning, children, and teachers. Weaver (1988) called it an approach to reading and writing that builds upon the language and experiences of the child. Anderson (1984) described it as the written and oral language in connected discourse found in meaningful contexts. Bird (1987) called it a way of thinking, living, and learning with the children in classrooms. Watson (1989) defined it as a view of education that is supported by certain beliefs about learning, teaching, language, and curriculum.

All of these definitions are basically defensible even though they may at first seem different. This is an important point. There are boundaries to a whole language approach, but there is no right or wrong definition within those boundaries. This allows teachers to continually evaluate their views and to redefine their positions within this framework. In a field such as education, it is important for teachers to constantly reflect upon their approach to teaching and learning. As they are discovered, new knowledge and more effective approaches can be used in an instructional program.

A narrow behavioral definition of whole language would not allow one to maintain the flexibility needed to operate as a whole language teacher. Therefore, any definition of whole language needs to be sufficiently broad to allow teachers to refine and improve

FIGURE 1-6   Children need opportunities to explore language on their own terms.

their view of education. The definition used in this text is that whole language is a set of beliefs about education, language, and learning, supported by theory, research, and practice, that advocates a mutually supportive and accepting relationship between teachers and learners in a natural environment.

Whole language is a set of beliefs. Some beliefs, such as mutual support between teachers and learners, are found elsewhere in the definition. Others must be inferred from terms such as natural environment. Natural environment might include real books and real discussions as opposed to basal reading texts and artificial oral language exercises. Whatever the case, the purpose is not merely to define a certain set of beliefs. The only reason for formulating beliefs is so that they might be used to guide classroom practice.

Whole language is based on theory, research, and practice. Each of these will be explored in the discussions of the history and research on whole language. A major approach to teaching should be supported by clear, logical thinking and appropriate supporting research. This is the case with whole language. Traditional behavioral research investigates discrete variables in a laboratory type setting. It is of limited use for studying whole language. The reason for this is the belief that language learning occurs mostly in natural environments that are always in a state of change. As a result, language learning cannot be carefully controlled in a laboratory. Ethnographic studies, research done in natural settings and which takes into account all that occurs in that setting, is more appropriate for studying whole language classrooms.

Characteristics of Whole Language

A whole is often more than the sum of its parts. This is true of whole language. It is true that distinct characteristics can be identified within a whole language classroom. Each of these characteristics can be fairly well defined and described according to their appearance and function. In some cases, this has been carefully done (Butler 1987; Robbins 1990). However, picking and choosing some of these characteristics for inclusion in a traditional classroom does not turn such an environment into a whole language classroom. The reason for this is that the underlying essence or spirit is missing. It must be remembered that a whole language approach is a set of beliefs based on knowledge that guides the teacher in making decisions about the classroom. This set of beliefs is critical in allowing the teacher to integrate the characteristics into a meaningful whole. Examples of these integrated characteristics and their related activities are further illustrated in the sections on thematic units. The characteristics found in whole language classrooms are described here.

Whole Texts.

Little value seen in isolating meaningless bits and pieces of language for children to study, underline, sound out, circle, copy, and memorize. The reading material used in a whole language program is most often contemporary and classic children's literature. High quality children's books are found in abundance. All skills, including phonics, are taught within whole pieces of meaningful language. Writing is also geared toward the production of whole texts. Drawing and oral language are viewed as intrinsic parts of

FIGURE 1-7 Beauty and the Beast Storytellers, Martha Hamilton and Mitch Weiss of Ithaca, New York, spend their lives showing children the relationships between stories, oral language, dramatization, and play. *Courtesy of Jon Crispin. Reprinted by permission of Martha Hamilton and Mitch Weiss.*

the writing development process. Spelling, sentence construction, and learning vocabulary words are all done within the context of the child's own writing process. Spelling workbooks, grammar drills, and handwriting practice sheets are largely absent. Invented spelling, where children attempt to use the sounds of letters as guides to spelling words in their stories, is both encouraged and tolerated.

Literature Based.

Children's literature is a fundamental part of the program. It is the content of reading, and it plays a major role throughout the instructional day. Reading books aloud to children occurs every day, usually several times a day. Children are encouraged to attempt to read books that have been read to them, to talk about the books and to dramatize those stories. Big books, high quality children's literature printed in poster-sized books, are used as a tool to include groups of students in a shared literature experience. Periods of sustained silent reading, where everyone, including the teacher, goes to a favorite reading spot and reads silently, is a daily activity.

Shared, guided, and independent reading activities are common as well. Shared readings are readings and rereadings of favorite stories, poems, and songs in which children are encouraged to participate. Guided reading is often, although not always, a part of the program. It entails the assignment of a certain book, or one of several books related to a common theme, to a group of children. The reading is usually followed by conferences with the teacher and other group members for the purpose of discussing the book. Independent reading, in which children select reading material based upon their own interests, is more likely to occur. While it may also include reading conferences, it preserves the ownership of the child of the reading process. The more ownership and emotional involvement children have in their own learning, the fewer behavior problems arise.

Child-centered Teaching.

Children are the focus of whole language classrooms. They are included in decision making about the rules and procedures of the classroom. Their interests and needs are key factors in developing programs. The curriculum is usually organized into broad themes within which individual children can investigate and satisfy their own needs. The thematic units tend to integrate the language learning with all of the other content areas in the total program. Rather than attempting to keep children attentively focused on paper and pencil tasks throughout the day, the program provides time for thought. Children need time to think about both their behavioral and cognitive actions. It is only through such opportunities that thay are able to self-correct and reconstruct their thinking about their learnings.

Cooperative Activities.

Since all of the language modes are related, it makes sense to insure that children have ample opportunities for interaction with each other. One way of accomplishing this is through the development of a variety of centers to be used within the classroom during the year. A center is simply a table or an area that contains the necessary supplies to engage in a specific type of activity. Often, the teacher has demonstrated beforehand how to proceed with the activity located in each center. Centers may change periodically to conform to various seasons and thematic units being used in the program. Centers may be built around such concepts as listening, music, house keeping, art, numbers, cooking, crafts, and clay.

FIGURE 1-8 Children can develop the ability to reflect upon their lives and their learning.

The point of having a center in a whole language classroom is to enable children to use language as part of a cooperative process in carrying out an activity at the center. Therefore, the teacher makes decisions about how best to structure the activity of a center so that it fosters cooperation and language. Cooperative activities are quite effective with young children. Through such activities, children discover that they can learn from each other and that there is more than one way to look at a problem.

Activities such as these require children to be able to move about the room. As they go to centers, choose partners to share a story, and select materials from the reading or writing center they experience the need for self-discipline. This doesn't just happen, however. Teachers must supply the children with guidelines, clear expectations, limits, and consistent responses within a safe and welcoming environment. As children understand these guidelines, they become able to operate within the bounds of the classroom expectations.

This self-discipline is the logical goal of a well-managed classroom. As children see that they are both competent language users and responsible members of the classroom their self-esteem grows. If a child does not seem to be developing this self-esteem, it is not seen as a deficiency. Instead, the teaching, the materials, and the activities of the program are assessed to determine if they are meeting the child's needs. The underlying question is not whether the child is ready for the program but whether the program is ready for the child.

Parent Involvement.

The parents of children in a whole language program are the best and strongest allies a teacher can have. They need to know the philosophy, procedures, and materials of the program so that they can relate to, extend, expand, and reinforce the learning that takes place in the classroom. A true integration of effort is best. Parents need teachers to listen to their ideas and questions. Parents deserve thoughtful responses and helpful information concerning the program. Whenever possible, parents ought to be included in the operation of the classroom.

Newsletters, informational meetings, conferences, and informal communications can all serve to enhance parent/teacher communication. Rearing young children is both a tiring and exciting experience. While both possibilities must be accepted, it should always be assumed that parents are willing to help and encourage their children to develop the skills of literacy.

HISTORY OF WHOLE LANGUAGE

Whole language began to develop as a major force in education many decades before it became widely used in early childhood and elementary school programs. Theoretical ideas and the research supporting those ideas developed over time. The influences from which whole language emerges are varied. There is no one definable starting point. Rather, a number of individuals from different educational specialties contributed ideas that, when combined with the ideas of others, evolved into the whole language approach. The major fields of influence are curriculum development, psychology, reading, and written expression.

Curriculum Development

John Dewey was one of the earlier educators who viewed the importance of approaching the curriculum as an integrated whole (1943). He contended that life is not divided into compartments of mathematics, history, and so forth. He believed that schools should correlate the various disciplines to one another the same way as they are correlated in life. Dewey saw language as one of the tools with which children could investigate and construct meaning in the classroom. Others in the field of curriculum development continue to develop the ideas of Dewey in constructing an integrated curriculum.

Taba (1962) recognized the increasing needs of children who came from ever more varied backgrounds. Through the 1950s increasing numbers of children were entering and remaining in schools. These children came from wider backgrounds in native language, socio-economic status, ethnic origin, and nationality. Taba identified the task as not only integrating the curriculum, but making the curriculum relevant to an increasingly diverse population of school children. The child-centered school was a concept supported by Taba, who identified the learning process as being primarily a social process.

The most prominent educators in the field of curriculum development did not tend to play a large role in the emergence of whole language beyond that time. Instead, many lesser known individuals moved to the forefront in the area of curriculum development: the teachers. Yetta Goodman (1989) argues persuasively that the work of individual teachers and groups of teachers solidified the concept of whole language. Goodman suggests that the movement grew out of a need to reject the forces of behaviorists, back-to-basics advocates, standardized tests, and rigid, prescribed, educational practices. She relates this current stand as not altogether different from the stand of those who supported the "progressive schools" movement of Dewey's time.

Dewey (1938), a principal architect of the progressive schools movement, charged that the traditional approaches of the day included rigid subject matter structures imposed by outsiders using adult standards. Children are not equipped to deal with or benefit from these structures. A similar scenario can be seen in the whole language classroom. Whole language educators are constantly seeking and discovering ways to integrate language arts and other curriculum areas in meaningful and developmentally appropriate ways. As a result, practices can be seen in

FIGURE 1-9 Children use their own play as a basis for their drawings.

whole language classrooms that differ markedly from traditional lecture approaches to learning. Students can be seen seeking solutions to problems through reading, writing, and oral language. Music, art, science, and literature can be seen within a single activity designed to help children discover new knowledge about a topic. Children construct meaning through the construction of models, stories, and replicas. Figures 1-9 and 1-10 illustrate how children combine play, art, and writing in order to create meaning. Whole language teachers support an emphasis on meeting the individual child's needs, seeing play as important to intellectual development and valuing the process of problem solving. These views are all shared by early childhood educators, thereby making a whole language approach particularly appealing.

M. A. K. Halliday (1975) has studied instructional situations as they relate to learning and language use. Through his study, he has concluded that as children use language they learn language, learn through the language and learn about the language. This idea supports the view of seeing language modes as integrated with each other. It also supports the principle that language is integrated with other content areas.

Psychology

Behavioral psychology has had a great influence on education during the twentieth century. Its influence is seen in such concepts and products as highly structured sets of behavioral objectives, standardized tests, mastery learning, and task analysis. It has had relatively little influence on the development of whole language. The whole language movement is, in many ways, a reaction to the ideas inherent in behavioral psychology. Behavioral psychology suggests that human behavior is the result of a living thing responding to a stimulus from the environment. Furthermore, it holds that learning is based solely upon these stimulus-response interactions.

Developmental psychology, on the other hand, has contributed significantly to the foundations of whole language. The work of Swiss psychologist Jean Piaget, for example, provides some key understandings about how children view the world. His beliefs held that children are not passive recipients of information. Children seek information and knowledge through their play and interactions with the environment. They categorize the world in ways that may or may not conform to the vision of the world held by adults. These different views of the world are important because children bring them to the classroom instructional situation (Duckworth 1987).

Lev Vygotsky, a Russian psychologist who was also a contemporary of Piaget, provides whole language educators with some key principles as well. His work concerning the relationship between the individual child and the social environment is particularly relevant (Vygotsky 1986). In addition to the importance of the social environment, Vygotsky also examined the role of play in the development of intellectual functioning. He contends that in play children per-

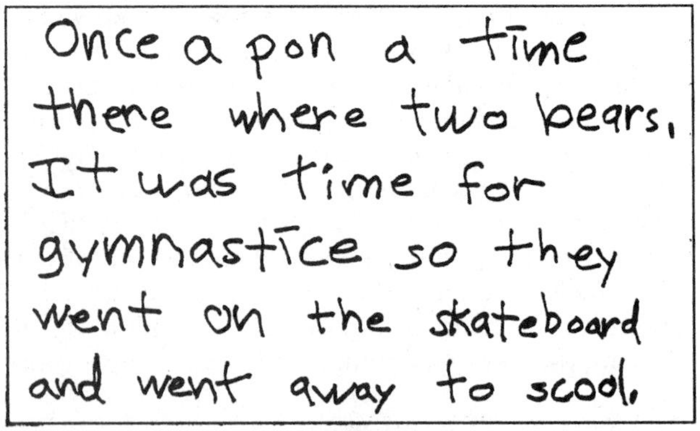

> Once a pon a time
> there where two bears,
> It was time for
> gymnastice so they
> went on the skateboard
> and went away to scool.

FIGURE 1-10 Children often use their own play as a basis for their writing.

form beyond the expectations of their ages; as such, play becomes a primary source of their development (Vygotsky 1978). Vygotsky refers to this gap between expectation and actual performance as the "zone of proximal development."

Reading

Some of the fundamental principles upon which the whole language approach rests can be traced to the first half of the twentieth century, to people such as Sylvia Ashton Warner and Louise Rosenblatt. Based upon some of the beliefs of John Dewey, Rosenblatt (1938/1976) was the first to describe reading as a transaction between the reader and the text. This established the basic principle that readers bring something of their own experience to the text and that they participate in the establishment of the meaning of that text. Sylvia Ashton Warner was a pioneering educator in New Zealand when she began to question the usefulness of a prepackaged state mandated program for the children she was teaching in the rural outreaches of the country (1963). Her work is increasingly cited as being far ahead of its time.

Lee and Lamoreaux (1943) provided educators working with young children an innovative tool for teaching reading called the language experience approach (LEA). The approach was updated two decades after its initial development (Lee and Allen 1963). LEA is an approach that provides a variety of experiences for children. The experiences may be field trips, storytelling sessions, or group activities dealing with literature, science, math, music, and so forth. The experiences are accompanied and followed by language that leads to the development of stories, charts, lists, and books. Teachers record these as they are generated orally by the children. These written documents then become the material that children can use for reading. Children can read them and are interested in reading them because they wrote them. While language experience can still be a useful tool, whole language goes far beyond it both in its views on child development and its instructional procedures.

A major detracting factor of LEA is the fact that it is largely a teacher controlled process. At this point, particularly, LEA and a whole language approach to reading proceed in different directions. Given the interrelationship between reading and writing, one might question how children develop their writing ability if the teacher does all the writing based upon the oral language of the children. After all, Read's (1975) discovery that children invent their own spellings to create written language provides support for a system that encourages children to generate their own writing. This is not within the context of an LEA approach. One might also question the different roles and functions oral and written language play. The question might be raised, "Is written language merely talk that has been written down?" Certainly not, for if it were, writing would be a much easier task for all of us.

Research in the field of reading has contributed to the development of the whole language approach as well. Frank Smith and Kenneth Goodman (1971) developed a view of reading that held it to be an interactive process between the reader, the text, and the language. This was in marked contrast to many of the views of the day that ranged from notions of reading as the simple decoding of letters into sounds to systems that held that reading was made up of a broad range of isolated subskills to be mastered.

Again, the scene shifts back to New Zealand. Donald Holdaway pioneered an approach to reading called the shared reading experience and encouraged the use of a literature based reading program (1970). The shared book experience involves a teacher working with a group of children, often using an easel with a big book. The big book is a book with print and illustrations large enough to be seen by all of the children in the group. Children are encouraged to discuss the possibilities of the story, predict events, and listen to confirm their predictions. The teacher reads the story, pointing to each word as it is read. Prior to the reading, the children's relevant background is explored, necessary vocabulary might be taught, and purposes for reading are set. Children are also encouraged to have personal responses to stories, engage in rereadings of stories, listen to additional storybook readings, and engage in choral readings of stories and poems. In short, children are immersed in a rich environment of language and literature within a classroom community of learners. The approach has a solid research base supporting its effectiveness (Clay 1972).

First Day of Spring

Sharon Gordon
Illustrated by Christine Willis

FIGURE 1-11 Children should be surrounded by literature on a variety of topics. *Courtesy of Troll Associates, Mahwah, New Jersey 07430.*

During the last half of the twentieth century, many experts in the field of children's literature testified to the power of using trade books as a major component in reading programs for children (Hodge 1990; Jacobs 1965). Others have also drawn similar conclusions concerning the importance of storybooks in the reading program (Huck and Kuhn 1968; King 1985; Martin, Jr. 1966/1974; Sawyer and Comer 1991). These views are supported by the research on storytelling, reading aloud, and the development of language in children (Applebee 1978; Rosen 1984; Wells 1986).

Written Expression

Many decades have passed since the earliest calls by Alvina Burrows for allowing children to express themselves in voices that are uniquely their own (Burrows, Jackson, and Saunders 1939/1984). During the 1970s and 1980s an explosion of discussion and research in the field of writing took place. Donald Graves (1983) continued to expand upon and to sup-

port the earlier work of Burrows. He clearly documented how writing development is enhanced when children have opportunities to write in a supportive environment.

Continuing this tradition, Calkins placed the writing of young children in its proper perspective (1986). She reminded us that writing as a formal subject of study is not what children need. Rather, children have a need to express their thoughts and to make themselves known. Adults have made writing development into a series of rules and assigned topics. To young children, writing is connected to art, music, and play.

The concept of using language as a tool for learning across the curriculum is an accepted component of a whole language approach. Educators in England are largely responsible for developing this approach (Bullock 1975). The concept has been adopted in other English-speaking countries and is becoming an effective tool in bilingual classrooms (Edelsky 1987).

RESEARCH SUPPORT FOR WHOLE LANGUAGE

The research related to the whole language approach is a fascinating mixture. Examining traditional research with an eye to how well it relates to whole language is fraught with problems. Educational research for the most part follows a behavioristic model that attempts to identify and control discrete variables in order to study one of them. The variables may range from the age and sex of the subjects being studied, to the types of instruction being provided, to different groups of children, to the achievement outcomes of the children following a period of experimental instruction. A major problem with behavioristic research is that it may not be particularly appropriate for examining whole language because of the multifaceted nature of that instructional approach.

Uniqueness of Whole Language

Whole language places a great emphasis on the environment or classroom setting as an important part of the learning situation. An environment that changes in order to support the needs of learners as their needs change is an intrinsic part of a whole language classroom. Since the behavioristic research model is based on the ability of the experiment to control such things as the classroom environment, there is a fundamental problem with using such a model to investigate whole language.

Kenneth Goodman (1989) contends that any research or researcher seeking to study whole language must begin by considering what whole language is and is not. He establishes the premise that a whole is greater than the sum of its parts. Whole language is a way teachers think about and practice what they do in the classroom (Rich 1983). As a result, Goodman (1989, 1990) contends that research findings, particularly experimental ones, cannot be easily applied to a whole language classroom since such studies seek to examine the world by investigating its discrete parts. Case study research on single children and ethnographic studies of individual classrooms seem to be more appropriate for the whole language classroom (Bissex and Bullock 1987). In the latter type of study, the researcher observes the environment rather than attempting to manipulate or control it. In view of this, each piece of research must be carefully considered for both its content and its appropriateness for examining whole language. For our purposes here, research is considered from three perspectives: the learner, the teacher's role in the classroom, and language and learning.

The Learner

Whole language is a child-centered approach. It holds as valid Dewey's (Dewey and Bentley 1949) notion that children are capable of learning and eager to learn. It further holds that much can be learned through watching and listening to children, as opposed to artificially controlling their environment.

An excellent example of how researchers can discover how children naturally learn language was demonstrated in the area of invented spelling. Although more interested in learning about the sense of phonology that children possess, Read (1971) became the first to examine the use of children's invented spellings. Through his observations, he discovered that children possess a remarkable sensitivity to the sounds of speech as clues for spelling. This was in marked contrast to the spelling strategies of adults, who tend to impose rules on what they do. This work was followed by the research of others (Y. Goodman

FIGURE 1-12 Children are eager to learn about themselves and their world.

and Wilde 1985; Milz 1982). These latter researchers demonstrated that young children move progressively toward conventional spelling over time without explicit instruction in spelling.

Another research area of interest is reading. From K. Goodman's (1984) research on mis-cue analysis came a transactional psycholinguistic theory of the reading process. It holds that readers predict as they read and use the reading to confirm or refute their predictions. Accordingly, whole language teachers learned that books for young children are easy or difficult for specific readers to the extent that they are predictable. Writers of books for young children, long in touch with their audiences, have shown a tendency over time to write books that are often predictable (K. Goodman 1990). Goodman (1984) demonstrated that this was a much more powerful concept for determining the readability of books for children than was the traditional readability formula. A readability formula assigns a grade level of difficulty for a particular text based on such things as sentence length and the number of unfamiliar words in the text. The major flaw of such formulas is that they don't include the motivation or interest of the reader as a factor in determining whether a book is too difficult or not.

The Role of the Teacher

A whole language approach accepts and values the differences of the learners within the classroom. This requires a special kind of teacher in a special role. While whole language teachers accept a major responsibility in planning a program, organizing a classroom, and providing resources, they do not view themselves as in charge of administering a prescribed program of instruction. Rather, they are guided by Vygotsky's perception of teachers as mediators (1978), helping and supporting learners as they attempt to understand the world.

Much of the research on whole language is being conducted not through large scale university and research foundations, but by teachers and others in the schools. A recent compilation of such research underscores the fact that by reasserting their control over the classroom program, teachers can reform education from within (Bissex and Bullock 1987). For example, Atwell (1987) notes the numerous research studies conducted by classroom teachers demonstrating the effectiveness of a whole language approach in writing development. The reports are supported with a variety of writing samples and vignettes.

Language and Learning

Whole language teachers understand language as having an interdependent relationship with learning and social bonds. They view it in the sense that Halliday (1975) presented it: people learn language, they learn through language and they learn about language at the same time. Further, such teachers understand that learning is best done in authentic social situations that include authentic projects and authentic literature and language as the medium for learn-

ing. They possess a realistic understanding of such things as the fallacy of providing instruction in phonics within rigidly controlled education materials.

Some prestigious researchers have placed a seal of approval on the direct teaching of phonics as the only road to reading (Anderson, Hiebert, Scott and Wilkinson 1985). Whole language teachers do not accept such a simplistic solution to the literacy problem. Yes, it would be nice if everyone could easily learn to read if they were given traditional direct instruction in phonics. This is not the case, however. Whole language teachers do support the learning of phonics to the extent that phonics can help provide a relationship between the sound system and the visual symbols of written language. K. Goodman demonstrates, however, that direct instruction in phonics does not produce readers. In fact, children come to understand phonic relationships most effectively as they learn to read (K. Goodman and Y. Goodman 1978) and to write (Y. Goodman and Wilde 1985).

The use of rigid sequential materials does not conform to research supporting a whole language approach. This is true whether the materials are instructional or evaluative. Schools consume a tremendous number of basal reading materials each year. They are easy to follow, have a seemingly logical sequence of instructional skills to follow, and require little decision making on the part of the user. Schools are not likely to give them up any time soon. This is true despite the fact that research shows that their use does not seem to rely on any rational model, let alone a child-centered model (Duffy and Ball 1986). In addition, a substantial body of research demonstrates that such an approach is developmentally inappropriate for young children (NAEYC 1987).

DEVELOPING A KNOWLEDGE BASE

While there is much theoretical, conceptual, and research support for a whole language approach, the role of the teacher as a seeker of knowledge and understanding is a never-ending one. Teachers must constantly be perceptive observers of children. They need to allow the behaviors of children to have an influence over the next actions they take. They need to become risk-takers in discovering what works best with each child at different moments in time.

FIGURE 1-13 There are many materials besides commercial programs that can be used to help children develop language abilities.

Whole language teachers take seriously the need to develop a knowledge base. One does not learn to be a teacher, after which learning is no longer necessary. Teachers need to continually examine both their own practices and the research and practices of others in their field. This can be accomplished in a variety of ways.

Professional Opportunities

Professional meetings are an effective tool for growth. It may be a conference, workshop, or building level meeting. It is always appropriate to schedule time for sharing professional knowledge. When this type of sharing is done, it is important to keep the characteristics of the sharing in perspective. It is not the "whats" that are so important. They are usually simple explanations of the activity or procedure. It is the "whys" and "hows" that are most important. Through them, teachers focus on the more critical aspects of the child, the language and the role of the teacher. It is usually a rather simple matter to implement a new activity. However, if one doesn't understand the reason for developing and using the new activity, its effectiveness becomes a random occurence.

Seeking new knowledge from the larger community is also most worthwhile. Sources of knowledge include discussions with parents, whole language support groups, reading/writing discussion groups, college courses, and professional literature. If these are not all available, those that are accessible should be sampled, examined, and visited. Consider starting a group of educators who can meet on a regular basis to discuss common interests. There are a number of relevant local, state, and national organizations. Membership can provide a wealth of reading material for professional growth. A key component of developing a knowledge base is understanding that it is something that is never totally accomplished.

Activities for Developing Understanding

In addition to professional opportunities, one can use individual activities that serve as tools for developing a better understanding of teaching, learning, and language. For example, teachers can interview other practicing teachers to get an idea of how they view their role as a teacher. Teachers might also recall the activities observed in education that did or did not seem to make sense at the time. Discussing each of these with a fellow educator can lead to new understandings.

Activities can center around personal reading and writing of teachers. For instance, compile a list of favorite books from your childhood. Try to identify the reasons for including each of these books on the list. Reread the books to see if the same things still hold true for you today. Taking a more recent approach, identify the last thing you read. Describe why you read it, the aspects of the text that made understanding it easy, and the aspects of the text that interfered with your understanding. Identify how these perceptions can be applied to teaching language to young children. Finally, identify the most recent piece of writing you did. Explain how you went about writing it, what caused difficulty in writing it, and how satisfied you were with the finished piece. Again, try to determine how these understandings can be applied to young children and language learning.

CRITICISMS OF WHOLE LANGUAGE

Despite the tremendous potential for enhancing literacy in a whole language approach, many educators voice skepticism about its value. Nearly all innovations are met with resistance by many of those who are more comfortable with the current state of affairs. This might be either a human characteristic of believing that we are doing the best that can be done or a more cynical lack of interest in making substantive changes in the system. Both can be costly in human terms. Consider, as an example, the Swiss watch industry. For years it rejected the use of electronic circuitry in its watches. Asian companies quickly and successfully integrated the new technology to the near destruction of the entire Swiss watch industry. Ironically, it was the Swiss who had originally developed the technology. It would do well for schools to learn from this example.

Much of the criticism of whole language originates with those who have a long-standing interest in continuing more traditional approaches. It is not surprising, therefore, that the arguments are often based on an inaccurate understanding of whole language. The arguments tend to assume that whole language is a rigid system to which advocates must conform. Some of the more frequently mentioned arguments against it suggest that whole language is merely a prescriptive set of specific activities, that its adherents are elitist, that it eliminates any active role for the teacher, and that it doesn't deal with the real world. While there are variations in the criticisms, they can usually be found under one of these categories. Each of these is examined on its merits.

Prescriptive Activities

If one were to observe a number of whole language classrooms at the preschool and early elementary school levels, a number of similar activities would be observed. It is likely that children would be seen listening to books read aloud by their teachers, engaging in drawing and writing, working on group projects, and participating in small group discussions about one topic or another. Unfamiliar observers might come away from these observations believing that a whole language classroom is merely one that includes a set number of specific activities for use with children.

The truth of the matter is that while activities may or may not be similar, the key to a whole language approach is the reasoning behind the teacher's decision. Each activity is selected for that group of children working on a certain theme and in consideration of the developmental factors operating within the group. The student can't learn about whole language

from the outside looking in. It is necessary to talk to and to listen to skilled whole language teachers describing how they go about making decisions for their classrooms at any given time. A knowledge base can be developed through wide reading of professional literature in this area. Finally, it is necessary to come to an understanding of education as having an emancipatory role. Education should help children to become independent individuals, capable of making a positive contribution to society.

Elitism

Whole language is sometimes criticized for elitism in two different ways. The first criticism is that whole language advocates see themselves as elitists. It is charged that they scorn anyone who does not fully "buy into" the system. It is somewhat difficult to substantiate this, as most teachers are too busy attending to the demands of their classrooms to engage in this type of superficial semantic argument. As will be seen, cooperation and sharing are two of the characteristics of a whole language program. A genuine whole language teacher might be the first to acknowledge that personal preferences and decisions must come from within the teacher. Tolerance of differences in others is an attribute that whole language teachers possess. This does not mean, however, that teachers can maintain traditional approaches to literacy and simply declare themselves whole language teachers.

The second charge relates to what is perceived as an unintentional elitism that works to the detriment of children who are from non-mainstream cultural backgrounds. As the argument goes, the program's acceptance of the natural language of the children, cooperative learning, and process approaches to language deny children access to the "power code" spoken and written by affluent whites (Delpit 1986, 1988; Pearson 1990). The criticism has three weaknesses. First, it confuses what is to be learned with how it is to be learned. While they are related, they are not the same thing. Learning within a cooperative setting does not limit the number of things one can learn. Second, the argument exhibits a traditional view of literacy instruction. It tends to see language instruction as focusing on the acquisition of specific skills. In this case, the skills are those language tools used by the power elite. Few whole language teachers would argue against assuring that all children acquire all of the language skills necessary to lead fulfilling lives. Third, the models of language within the books, poems, and fables found in children's literature provide broad exposure to mainstream language. In addition, whole language teachers would also defend the validity, power, and beauty of a student's natural language.

Role of Teachers

Teachers have traditionally been in control of the classroom. They have told the children where to sit, what to do, and how to do it. Some people believe that a whole language classroom is a loosely run ship, with no one in charge and with children making decisions about whether they will engage in learning or not. While children do participate in many of the decisions, a whole language classroom is not without a very definite structure. The teacher knows exactly what the goals are, what conditions and experiences will most likely help children toward those goals, and why everything in the classroom is happening as it is.

The idea of the teacher not standing in front of the class for much of the day providing direct instruction in short vowels, sight words, and alphabet activities sometimes makes unfamiliar teachers uncomfortable. The criticism holds that whole language teachers do not provide direct instruction or modeling of strategies. Whole language teachers do, however, provide specific instruction. It is often referred to as demonstration, and does have some of the characteristics of direct instruction and modeling. The difference, again, lies in the fact that it is not the activity that is most important, but the underlying reasons for the activity.

A traditional teacher might stand in front of a class and provide a direct instruction lesson on the long "e" sound. The teacher may even model a strategy to determine if a word contains the sound. A whole language teacher may provide a demonstration lesson with roughly the same content, but in a vastly different manner. First, the latter teacher would be unlikely to teach the lesson to the whole class. The children who would receive the instruction might range from a single child to a small group. Whatever the number, only those children who needed the skill, understood the

validity of learning the skill, and who would benefit from learning the skill at that point would be provided the instruction. The instruction would be geared toward making meaning and would use real texts for the learning. The logic is simple: provide a program that is developmentally appropriate for the child.

Real World

Whole language makes great use of the literature found in tradebooks written for children. It gives dignity to the early drawings and writings of young children as the wellspring from which later written expression will come. It encourages children to write about experiences they are comfortable with and feel confident discussing. In many cases, this takes the form of personal narrative writing. The criticism of such an approach suggests that most of the reading in the real world is not of the enjoyable books written for young children. The contention is that the real world is full of requirements to read such things as repair manuals, social service form instructions, and direction sheets. The argument continues to charge that the real world does not require one to write personal narratives. Rather, the real world demands that we write reports, sets of directions, and business letters.

Such arguments, besides again confusing the what and the how of instruction, reveal a disturbing view of humanity and the purposes of education. Yes, it is true that children's literature and personal writing are valued in a whole language program, particularly at the early childhood and elementary levels. However, this does not preclude children from learning other types of reading and writing. If we examine whole language programs, such learning will be seen at higher levels as it becomes meaningful to children. In any case, we should not lose sight of the beauty and power of literature simply because it is infrequently used in the work world. Similarly, many of the greatest individuals of all time are known to have kept journals in which they recorded their personal thoughts. Such a procedure has long been used as a means to better understand the world. Whole language views the real world as more than a place for work. There is a place in the real world for the beauty of the written word and the power of one's thoughts written down and preserved.

FIGURE 1-14 A lifelong love of reading for pleasure can begin at a very young age.

SUMMARY

An integrated language arts program is based on the fact that language fills the world around us. As human beings, we are constantly attempting to make sense of the world and all that we find in it. The young child's emerging literacy is, in effect, an attempt on the part of that child to understand the world. It begins with an awareness of sounds and proceeds to an understanding of a variety of concepts about print. At all stages the child is searching for meaning, trying to make sense out of each aspect.

An integrated language arts program is seen as a particularly effective approach for working with young children. An integrated approach holds that all of life is interconnected. The language modes, oral language, reading, and writing are all closely related. All people are connected through their language and their humanity. This is true for young, old, disabled, gifted, and native and non-English speakers.

It is somewhat difficult to define whole language. This is because it is primarily a set of beliefs by which teachers make classroom decisions rather than a rigid program or a set of activities. Whole language is a child-centered approach that operates within a natural environment using natural language and litera-
ture. Three fundamental characteristics are associated with a whole language approach. First is the belief that learning and language ought to be meaningful. Second, language is viewed as a process. It is something done rather than something produced or completed. Third, there is a belief that learning ought to include the active involvement of the learner. In relation to these factors, observers often see somewhat similar things occurring in whole language classrooms. In early childhood education it would be common to observe, among other things, such activities and materials as inventive spelling, big books, a preponderance of children's books, student drawing and writing, thematic units, and cooperative learning. This does not mean that the sum of these things adds up to a whole language classroom. It does not. The reasons behind the use of each of these is more important than the fact that they are there.

Whole language has a long and distinguished developmental history, originating in a number of places around the globe. John Dewey's beliefs about the learner, the content to be learned, and how learning should take place have played a prominent role. Followers of Dewey refined many of his ideas throughout the twentieth century. Their work also contributed to the development of whole language. At about the same time as Dewey, but on the other side of the globe, Sylvia Ashton Warner was taking such radical steps as rejecting prepackaged language arts programs for nontraditional students. In their place, she introduced student language and choice as part of language learning. She based her decisions on what was meaningful to the students. Individuals who followed her continued to develop other innovative ideas and practices such as the shared book experience.

As with the historical characteristics of whole language, the theory and research supporting it comes from a number of sources. Kenneth and Yetta Goodman are among the most productive of the many educators and researchers who have studied the approach over several decades. However, the pioneering work of others has also contributed much to support the approach. The theory and research provided by Lev Vygotsky (1978, 1986), a Russian psychologist, lend much support to the belief that adults facilitate the language learning of children, particularly in social environments. A variety of teacher researchers have provided volumes of case study and ethnographic research to support the effectiveness of a whole language approach.

Finally, to develop an adequate understanding of whole language, the reader needs to build a broad knowledge base of the literature surrounding it. A lack of understanding of the approach frequently explains many of the criticisms of it. While most progressive educators are adopting the approach, skeptics can be found. Among the most frequently cited criticisms are that it is a rigid system, it is elitist, it diminishes the role of the teacher, and it doesn't deal with the real world. Of course, teachers who have developed a substantial knowledge of whole language can easily identify the faulty assumptions upon which each of the criticisms is based.

Questions and Activities for Review and Discussion

Multiple Choice

1. Emergent literacy refers to
   a. learning phonics.
   b. memorizing the letters of the alphabet.
   c. period of time over which reading and writing are learned.
   d. learning to write in cursive.
2. Which basic process underlies all language processes?
   a. thinking
   b. writing
   c. seeing
   d. reading
3. Whole language is best described as
   a. a set of beliefs about language and learning.
   b. a set of skills required for learning to read.
   c. a series of reading texts used in primary grades.
   d. the history of reading instruction.
4. Which term is used to describe how something takes place?
   a. evaluation
   b. product
   c. process
   d. definition
5. Who is the twentieth century educator who first described reading as an interaction between the reader and the text?
   a. B. F. Skinner
   b. Walter Rugg
   c. John Dewey
   d. Louise Rosenblatt
6. Who is the psychologist who contends that children learn language from social interactions?
   a. Don Holdaway
   b. B. F. Skinner
   c. Jean Piaget
   d. Lev Vygotsky

7. Why are readability formulas limited in their usefulness?
   a. They don't take the reader into account.
   b. They can't be used with content area textbooks.
   c. They are too difficult for teachers to compute.
   d. They require a computer to use them.

True or False

T F 1. It is important for a whole language teacher to be familiar with the research supporting a whole language approach.

T F 2. The ability to predict what might happen in a story is not a useful concept for a young reader.

T F 3. A reading skills checklist is an adequate tool for evaluating learning in a whole language classroom.

T F 4. Big books are a useful tool for helping students share in a mutual language learning experience.

T F 5. It is impossible to define whole language.

Essay and Discussion

1. Describe what is meant by the phrase "concepts about print."
2. What do whole language teachers see as the relationship between thinking and language?
3. What are some of the differences between a traditional and a whole language approach to language learning?
4. Develop and explain a personal definition of whole language.
5. Describe how a whole language teacher can develop and increase a personal knowledge base.

References

Aaron, I.E., J.S. Chall, D. Durkin, K. Goodman, and D.S. Strickland. 1990. The panel of distinguished educators, Part I. *The Reading Teacher*. 43: 302–311.

Anderson, G. 1984. *The whole language approach to reading*. New York: University Press of America.

Anderson, R.C., E.H. Hiebert, J.A. Scott, and I.A. Williams. 1985. *Becoming a nation of readers: The report of the Commission on Reading*. Washington, D.C.: National Institute of Education.

Applebee, A. 1978. *The child's concept of story*. Chicago: University of Chicago Press.

Atwell, N. 1987. Wonderings to pursue: The writing teacher as researcher. Paper presented at the annual meeting of the National Council of Teachers of English, Los Angeles.

Bird, L. 1987. What is whole language? In Dialogue, edited by D. Jacobs. *Teachers networking: The whole language newsletter* 1:1. New York: Richard C. Owen.

Bissex, G., and R. Bullock, eds. 1987. *Seeing for ourselves*. Portsmouth, N.H.: Heinemann.

Bullock, A. 1975. *A language for life*. London: Her Majesty's Stationery Office.

Burrows, A., D. Jackson, and A. Saunders. 1939/1984. *They all want to write.* Hamden, Conn.: Library Professional Publication.

Butler, A. 1987. *The elements of whole language.* Crystal Lake, Ill.: Rigby.

Calkins, L.M. 1986. *The art of teaching writing.* Portsmouth, N.H.: Heinemann.

Clay, M. 1972/1979. *Reading: The patterning of complex behaviour.* Aukland, New Zealand: Heinemann.

Delpit, L.D. 1986. Skills and other dilemmas of a progressive black educator. *Harvard Educational Review* 56: 379–385.

Delpit, L.D. 1988. The silenced dialogue: Power and pedagogy in educating other people's children. *Harvard Educational Review* 58: 280–298.

Dewey, J. 1938. *Experience in education.* New York: Collier.

Dewey, J. 1943. *The child and the curriculum and the school and the society.* Chicago: University of Chicago Press.

Dewey, J., and L. Bentley. 1949. *Knowing and the known.* Boston: Beacon.

Duckworth, E. 1987. *The having of wonderful ideas.* New York: Teachers College Press.

Duffy, G.G., and D.L. Ball. 1986. Instructional decision making and reading teacher effectiveness. In *Effective Teaching of Reading: Research and Practice,* ed. J.V. Hoffman. Newark, Del.: International Reading Association.

Edelsky, C. 1987. *Habia una vey: Writing in a bilingual classroom.* Portsmouth, N.H.: Heinemann.

Ferreiro, E., and A. Teberosky. 1982. *Literacy before schooling.* Portsmouth, N.H.: Heinemann.

Goodman, K. 1984. Unity in reading. In *Becoming readers in a complex society,* ed. A. Purves and O. Niles. Chicago: University of Chicago Press.

Goodman, K. 1986. *What's whole in whole language.* Portsmouth, N.H.: Heinemann.

Goodman, K. 1989. Whole language research: Foundations and development. *Elementary School Journal.* 90: 207–221.

Goodman, K., and Y. Goodman. 1978. *Reading of American children whose language is a stable rural dialect of English or a language other than English* (Final Report). Washington, D.C.: National Institute of Education.

Goodman, K., and Y. Goodman. 1979. *A comprehension-centered whole language curriculum.* Tuczon, Ariz.: University of Arizona

Goodman, Y. 1989. Roots of the whole language movement. *Elementary School Journal* 90: 113–127.

Graves, D. 1983. *Writing: Teachers and children at work.* Portsmouth, N.H.: Heinemann.

Halliday, M.A.K. 1973. *Exploration in the function of language.* London: Edward Arnold.

Halliday, M.A.K. 1975. *Learning how to learn.* New York: Elsevier North-Holland.

Harste, J., V. Woodward, and C. Burke. 1984. *Language stories and literacy lessons.* Portsmouth, N.H.: Heinemann.

Hiebert, E.H. 1978. Preschool children's understanding of written language. *Child Development* 49: 1231–1234.

Hodge, F.P. 1990. Reading aloud: Listen to learn. *Instructor* C(3): 17–19.

Holdaway, D. 1979. *Foundations of literacy.* Sydney, Australia: Ashton Scholastic.

Huck, C., and D. Kuhn. 1968. *Children's literature in the elementary classroom.* New York: Holt, Rinehart, & Winston.

Jacobs, L. 1965. *Using literature with young children.* New York: Teachers College Press.

Karnowski, L. 1985. An observational study describing the composing behavior of three, four and five year olds during the writing process. Ph.D. diss., Miami Universlity, Oxford, Ohio.

Karnowski, L. 1986. How young writers communicate. *Educational Leadership* 44: 58–60.

King, M. 1985. Language and language learning for child watchers. In *Observing the language learning,* ed. A. Jaggar and M.T. Smith-Burke. Urbana, Ill.: National Council of Teachers of English; Newark, Del.: International Reading Association.

Lavine, L. 1972. The development of the perception of written language in pre-reading children: A cross-cultural study. Ph.D. diss., Cornell University, Ithaca, NY.

Lee, D., and R.V. Allen. 1943/1963. *Learning to read through experience.* New York: Appleton-Century Crofts.

Lovitt, Z. 1990. Rethinking my roots as a teacher. *Educational Leadership* 47: 6, 43–45.

Martin, B., Jr. 1966/1974. *Sounds of language.* New York: Holt, Rinehart, & Winston.

Milz, V. 1982. *Young children write: The beginnings.* Tucson, Ariz.: Program in Language and Literacy, University of Arizona.

National Association for the Education of Young Children. 1987. *Developmentally appropriate practices in early childhood programs children from birth through age 8.* Publication No. 24. Washington, D.C.: National Association for the Education of Young Children.

Pearson, P.D. 1990. Reading the whole language movement. *Elementary School Journal* 90: 231–241.

Read, C. 1971. Pre-school children's knowledge of English phonology. *Harvard Educational Review* 41: 1–34.

Read, C. 1975. *Children's categorization of speech sounds in English.* Urbana, Ill.: National Council of Teachers of English.

Rich, S. 1983. On becoming teacher experts: Teacher researchers. *Language Arts* 60: 892-894.

Robbins, P.A. 1990. Implementing whole language: Bridging children and books. *Educational Leadership* 47: 50–54.

Rosen, H. 1984. *Stories and meanings.* Sheffield, England: National Association for the Teaching of English; Upper Montclair, N.J.: Boynton/Cook.

Rosenblatt, L. 1938/1976. *Literature through exploration.* New York: Noble and Noble.

Sawyer, W.E., and D.E. Comer. 1991. *Growing up with literature.* Albany, N.Y.: Delmar Publishers Inc.

Smith, F., and K. Goodman. 1971. On the psycholinguistic method of teaching reading. *Elementary School Journal.* 71: 177–181.

Strickland, D., and L.M. Morrow. 1990. Sharing big books. *The Reading Teacher.* 43: 342–343.

Taba, H. 1962. *Curriculum development.* New York: Harcourt, Brace, & World.

Tough, J. 1976. *Listening to children talking*. London: Schools Council Publications.

Veatch, J. 1985. *How to teach reading with children's books*. New York: Owen.

Vygotsky, L. 1978. *Mind in society*. M. Cole, V. John-Steiner, S. Scribner, and E. Souberman, eds. Cambridge, Mass.: Harvard University Press.

Vygotsky, L.S. 1986. *Thought and language*. Cambridge, Mass.: M.I.T. Press.

Warner, S.A. 1963. *Teaching*. New York: Simon & Schuster.

Watson, D.J. 1989. Defining and describing whole language. *Elementary School Journal* 90: 2, 129–141.

Weaver, C. 1988. *Reading process and practice: From sociolinguistics to whole language*. Portsmouth, N.H.: Heinemann.

Wells, G. 1986. *The meaning makers*. Portsmouth, N.H.: Heinemann.

UNIT 2

Oral Language

UNIT GOALS

After completing this unit, the reader should:

- understand the importance of an oral language foundation for the development of literacy.
- understand how listening skills develop in the young child.
- understand how speaking skills develop in the young child.
- become aware of the range of skills and objectives that might be included in an early childhood program.
- become aware of a variety of activities that can be used to encourage the development of listening skills.
- become aware of a variety of activities that can be used to encourage the development of speaking skills.

PREVIEW

Oral language is the child's first contact with language. From the moment of birth, the child begins to hear the sounds and language of the world. The child also embarks on the road to speaking from the first time crying occurs. In fact, some people believe that unborn babies may be aware of the sound of their mother's heartbeat. For the first few years of life, listening and speaking comprise a large part of children's encounters with language. Throughout this period, language growth is nothing short of phenomenal. Children acquire language at an amazing rate. They also discover that oral language is used for a variety of purposes. Within this context, this unit will cover the following aspects of oral language:

- The importance of building an oral language foundation
- The purposes of listening
- The purposes of speaking
- The oral language skills and objectives for an early childhood program
- Activities for developing oral language in young children

INTRODUCTION

In traditional approaches to language arts, separate explanations are frequently presented for each of the four language modes: listening, speaking, reading, and writing. There is an implied assumption that each of these modes is a separate skill and that each

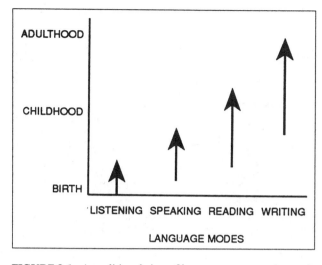

FIGURE 2-1 A traditional view of language suggests that each language mode develops independent of the others.

develops more or less independently of the other skills (Figure 2-1). However, there is also the belief that one mode develops only after a certain level of competence is achieved in a preceding mode. For example, a traditional approach to language arts contends that a child cannot learn to read until after the child learns to listen and to speak. Of course, this is not true. From the research on deaf individuals, it is known that people can learn to read without a high degree of physical ability to listen or speak.

The four modes of language are not independent of each other. Rather, they are closely interrelated and tend to develop, to a great extent, together (Figure 2-2). They support and reinforce each other. While it is possible for a deaf person to learn to read, this task is usually much easier for a person who has been able to listen to the language and sounds of the world for the first several years of life. The reason for this is, of course, that language embodies meaning. Language does not exist as an end in itself. Meaning connects one language mode to another. While this text may discuss one language mode at a time, it is always with the understanding that the "meaning connection" exists between that mode and the other modes.

ROLE OF ORAL LANGUAGE

Over 50 percent of a child's school day is spent listening. Students spend a great deal of time listen-

ing to teachers give directions, answers, and explanations. Therefore, a child with deficiencies in oral language ability is at a distinct disadvantage when engaged in classroom learning. A child with oral language deficiencies is also unlikely to be able to effectively engage in conversations, group discussions, or sharing activities with other students. Such learning activities are becoming increasingly important in progressive classrooms. Finally, children with oral language deficiencies are less likely to express their needs concerning learning that puzzles them. They may find themselves unable to phrase appropriate well-focused questions aimed at clarifying the messages they have heard.

Despite the obvious need for children to develop effective listening and speaking skills, these skills are often not taught. The importance of listening is often acknowledged by an admonition to children to "listen carefully." Speaking opportunities are often limited to brief, formal presentations such as book reports. It must be noted that while many adults do not spend much time reading and writing, nearly everyone en-

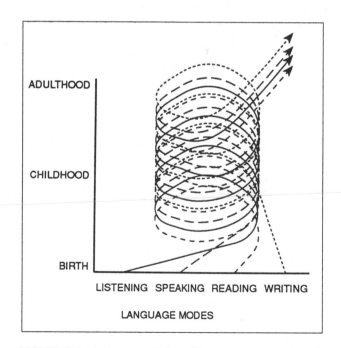

FIGURE 2-2 An integrated view of language suggests that all of the language modes are interrelated and that they develop in a related manner.

gages in conversation throughout the day. In view of this, it becomes increasingly clear that it is important to provide opportunities and activities for children to develop oral language. Children need opportunities to use oral language daily. Such opportunities need to make children aware of the uses of language as well as enhancing their appreciation for language.

Language as a Social Activity

Language learning is best viewed as a social activity. In this setting, discussion and sharing can be most easily encouraged to occur naturally. The environment can be structured so that listening and speaking are used for specific purposes. Within such a setting, children are more likely to take language use risks that they would not take in a more formal setting. New learning always entails risks and possible errors. A social learning situation operates best when it is non-threatening and supportive. Errors must be tolerated and expected as a normal part of the language learning process.

Different group sizes should be used for oral language activities. Pairs, small groups, and large groups each require different oral language, thinking, and problem-solving skills. These different structures provide children with a variety of opportunities for exploring the uses of language, problem solving, sharing, and responding to the thoughts of others. Within these group structures, a variety of members can be included. Adults, grandparents, older siblings, and younger children can provide further variety and opportunity for children to use different language skills. This variety of opportunities builds language tools for problem solving, positive attitudes, understanding, and self-expression. Each of these forms a portion of the foundation needed for reading, writing, thinking, and an understanding of literature.

Purposes for Oral Language

Understanding and creating meaning are the core purposes of language. Listening and speaking skills are learned in different social group sizes and for different purposes. The focus on using more informal social structures suggests that language is primarily a tool for sharing meaning in social situations both in the classroom and beyond the classroom. Therefore, listening and speaking skills are not learned as ends in

FIGURE 2-3   Children need a diversity of opportunities to use language as a communication tool.

themselves. They are seen as roads to an end. They are learned within the context of naturally occurring events. For example, the skill of arranging events in chronological order is best learned for the purpose of telling a story or retelling a personal recollection. The skill of receiving and providing information is learned for the purpose of interacting socially. Such learning reinforces the concept of language as a medium. Language is more readily perceived as having a validity and utility far beyond the classroom.

BUILDING AN ORAL LANGUAGE FOUNDATION

Since the development of a strong oral language foundation is closely related to other language modes and to learning, it is helpful to consider some of the ideas or concepts that can guide the teacher in building listening and speaking skills. Among these key ideas are modeling, story reading, storytelling, and oral language opportunities.

Modeling

The term *modeling* refers to showing a child how to do something by demonstrating it in a purposeful way. The goal is to show the child how to engage in the task or behavior so that the the child can repeat it independently. For example, the teacher may model or demonstrate how to do such things as throw a ball underhanded, draw a circle, walk up a flight of stairs, make a sad face, or tell a story. In so doing, the teacher might "talk through" the task by explaining each step and why it is done. The intent is to share the fundamental meaning and the appropriate steps for successfully engaging in the activity. Such modeling often needs to be repeated a number of times for children to fully grasp and replicate the task or behavior.

Modeling is an effective teaching tool for helping children to learn language. However, not all language skills can be taught to a child at any given age. The teacher must keep in mind that there are developmentally appropriate learnings for individual children at differing ages. The teacher must be aware of what a child is actually capable of at a given time and what the child has the potential for doing with appropriate modeling. Vygotsky (1978) uses the term "zone of proximal development" to describe the space between the child's actual and potential levels. He contends that human learning takes place in the space between what people can generate on their own and what they can understand when it is presented to them. The three critical aspects to be aware of here are the level of the child's actual understanding, the level of the child's potential understanding, and the appropriate model or guidance that needs to be presented to the child.

Story Reading and Storytelling

A wealth of literature is written for young children. Sharing stories is one of the most powerful language experiences in which a child can engage. The sense of language is reinforced each time a story is told or heard. Besides reading stories aloud to children, the art of oral storytelling can be used to provide language experiences to young children.

Storytelling is an oral sharing of a traditional, literary, or personal story, contends Peck (1989). In presenting a story in this manner, the teller does not recite a memorized version of the tale. Rather it is told in a natural flow of language using the essence of the tradition from where it comes. Storytelling is a shared experience between the teller and the listener. As such, it offers natural language opportunities for children. When students are regularly told stories, they are able to develop effective listening compre-

hension and critical listening skills. Stories that require active audience participation offer additional opportunities for listeners to focus on key parts of the story. When children are storytellers, they have opportunities to create and share meaning through speaking. As students tell stories to each other, they are engaged in both listening and speaking activities. As they do this, they develop a sense of the structure of stories. As this sense develops, more complex stories become more understandable.

Story reading and storytelling introduce children to different styles, authors, storytellers, and genres of literature. As they experience these variations, they begin to develop their own critical knowledge of literature. They begin to like certain types of stories, certain authors, and certain styles of presentation. They also begin to understand the concept of communication as an interaction between people. Children smile at certain points in the story. This gives feedback to the teller or reader. Children shiver with excitement as they sense and predict the approaching scary part of a story. All of these skills will later be applied when young children read and write stories on their own.

The oral language development that emerges through storytelling is a powerful factor in the development of literacy (Harste, Woodward, and Burke 1984). It provides a meaningful purpose for oral language in a natural social setting. In addition, it provides some useful tools for future reading and writing. Children will use their knowledge of stories as an aid to comprehending stories they read. When they write original stories, they will tend to use those story structures with which they are familiar (Sloan 1984).

Opportunities for Using Language

Certain steps are needed to develop a relative degree of competence with any human activity. Besides learning some of the basic points, children need to have the opportunity to practice the skill. So it is with emerging language. Within the context of opportunities, however, verbal support for the young child is needed. Trousdale (1990), in describing her interactive storytelling with a young child, referred to this support as scaffolding. She defines her scaffold as consisting of verbal support for the child's attempts to further a story line. This verbal scaffolding for chil-

FIGURE 2-4 Oral storytellers Peter and Mary Alice Amidon of Brattleboro, Vermont, provide a wealth of language experiences to children through their stories and music. *Photograph courtesy of Brooks Brown. Reprinted courtesy of Peter Amidon.*

dren developing oral language skills has been noted elsewhere, such as in the care-giver interactions observed with very young children (Bruner 1978). In Bruner's study, the interactions observed consisted of a dialogue sustained by the care-giver. The input of the care-giver was dependent upon the utterance of the child (Trousdale 1990). Lindfors (1987) noted that parents of young rapid language learners tended to allow the children to control the direction and content of the dialogue. That is, a high percentage of parental utterances were contingent upon the child's utterance. This behavior is not necessarily planned. It seems that it may occur somewhat naturally. Snow (1977) observed parental interactions with children at the babbling stage. It appeared that these parents tended to credit even these very young children with the intent to communicate. This suggests that early language development is encouraged when children receive support from those in their environment, when they have opportunities to practice dialogue, and when their utterances are given respect as meaningful language. As children gain in language competence, the less they need the support.

RESEARCH ON LISTENING AND SPEAKING DEVELOPMENT

An abundance of research supports an integrated approach to language and language arts instruction. At the infant level, a large body of research focuses on parent-child interaction. As children increase in age, the research includes more and more studies in daycare, preschool, and kindergarten programs. Much of the research involves observations of parents or other care-givers reading or telling stories to their children. In many of the studies, a great deal of verbal interaction is noted between parent and child. Much can be learned by considering the content of these interactions. Information and findings from a variety of these studies is included in the discussion that follows.

Function of Children's Questions and Comments

Much evidence supports the view that reading storybooks with young children provides them with many language conventions and structures (Cazden 1983; Chomsky 1972; Feitelson and Goldstein 1986; Hall 1987; Mason and Allen 1986; Sulzby and Teale 1987; Teale and Sulzby 1986; Wells 1986, 1987). Beyond this, the interaction between parent, child, and book has been viewed as one of the primary sources through which children acquire an understanding of the elements and purposes of reading and writing (Smith 1982; Wells 1986; Yaden, Smolkin, and Conlon 1989). Many of these studies focus on parent comments rather than child comments.

It is also important, however, to attend to the comments and questions of children during these sessions

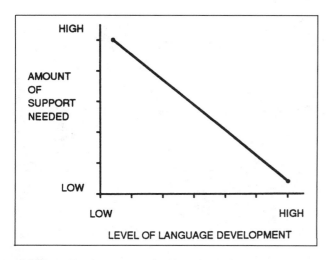

FIGURE 2-5 The amount of support needed decreases as children become more proficient language users.

Function of Adult Questions and Comments

The verbal interaction that accompanies the parent and child story sharing environment has been seen by Clay (1979) and Smith (1978) as helping children to learn many of the common features of and the differences between written and oral language. Research tends to support their view. Children who have frequently been read to have a better understanding of concepts about print: parts of a book, in which direction the print goes, and so forth (Baghban 1984; Doakes 1981; Hoffman 1982). Durkin (1974–1975) and Holdaway (1979) have established a connection between being read to at home and both a desire to learn to read and success in learning to read. Further, facility with more complex language structures and increased vocabulary are associated with being read to (Burroughs 1972; Chomsky 1972). Finally, experimental studies demonstrated that consistent story sharing over a period of time leads to significantly superior skills in decoding, vocabulary, and comprehension (Cohen 1968; Feitelson, Kita, and Goldstein 1986).

Despite the fact that story reading is generally seen as a positive force in literacy learning, Morrow (1988) contends that the mere act of being read to does not necessarily enhance literacy. There is support for this view. Studies have found that the reading style of the reader and the type of verbal interaction surrounding the story sharing has an effect on literacy development (Flood 1977; Heath 1982; Ninio 1980; Teale 1981) and children's comprehension of the story (Dunning and Mason 1984; Green and Harker 1982; Peterman, Dunning, and Mason 1985).

according to Yaden, Smolkin, and Conlon (1989). This is because many studies of early readers report that children constantly ask questions about the books being read (Clark 1976; Durkin 1966; Lass 1982; Plessas and Oakes 1964; Price 1976; Thomas 1985; Torrey 1973). Early readers are those children who learn to read before they receive formal reading instruction in school. The parents of these early readers reported in the studies attributed their children's reading ability to the questioning and interaction that takes place during story sharing sessions. Yaden, Smolkin, and Conlon (1989), contending that children's questions and comments are equally important to the development of literacy as the utterances of the parents, studied children's questions. They found that children most frequently ask questions about pictures, story meaning, and word meaning. Questions about letter forms, punctuation, and sentences occurred least frequently. They did note, however, that the reader's style and type of book did cause changes in the types of questions and comments children made. That is, books with spectacular illustrations or very large letters often generated questions directed toward those features. Likewise, a situation in which a parent or care-giver overly controlled the story sharing situation tended to result in fewer comments from the child.

Encouraging Oral Language

The question then is whether there are certain kinds of verbal interactions adults can encourage or provide to children in order to enhance language skills. Studies have shown that there are such practices. The conclusion of many of the studies is that the social interaction is most effective when the story reader and the listener are both actively constructing meaning based on the text (Bloome 1985; Heath 1982; Flood 1977; Ninio and Bruner 1978). The conversation and activities can take many forms, but most seem to focus on a cooperative attempt to make sense of the story in an active and enjoyable manner.

Brown (1975), Morrow (1985), and Pellegrini and Galda (1982) found that certain elements seem to enhance literacy skills. They found that when adults involved children in dramatizing, retelling, and illustrating stories that had been read to them, children were better able to relate the various parts of a story and to integrate information. Holdaway (1979) supports the view that children benefit most from story reading when there is an adult interacting with the child in a problem solving situation. That is, the child is encouraged to respond as much as possible while the adult supplies enough information to continue the dialogue. In this way, the adult and child actively attempt to construct meaning from the printed text. This is done by relating the new meaning to the experiences, background, and beliefs of the child.

Morrow (1988) discusses typical interactions between an adult story reader and a child listener in a sharing session. While reading, the reader often makes comments about the story. There is a tendency for these comments to generate questions or responses from the child. Children initiate questions or comments, which produce responses from the adult. While differences in interactive style do occur, the reading seems to be a collaborative effort aimed at constructing meaning from the printed text.

Verbal interactions surrounding story reading change as the child gets older. They also depend, to some extent, on the nature of the book being shared. Adults may ask questions, relate the story to their own experience, respond to questions, provide additional information, read sections of the story again, and offer praise. Cochran and Smith (1984) note that in addition to the interaction of listener and reader, understanding also depends on a two-way interaction between the text and the reader/listener. In one direction, the child's life experiences are used to make sense of the text. In the other direction, new information from the book is integrated into the child's view of the world so that it makes sense.

Adult Roles.

Three distinct roles for adult readers have been identified by Roser and Martinez (1985). As "co-

FIGURE 2-6   Books and story reading are important parts of oral language development. *Reprinted courtesy of Houghton Mifflin Company, nonexclusive and nontransferable.*

respondents," they begin discussions, relate the story to their own lives, and encourage children to do the same things. As "informers/monitors," they explain parts of a story that are not understood, expand upon the information in the story, and evaluate children's comprehension of the story. As "directors," they assume leadership over the session through such things as introducing and concluding the session. These roles become shared and interchangeable as children increase their participation in story sharing.

A tendency has been noted, not necessarily an appropriate one, for adults to encourage children to move away from an interactive approach to story reading as they get older. Heath (1980) observed this occurring with children as young as three years old. Up to that age, it appears that adults expect children to interrupt the reading with questions and comments. Beyond that age, children are often expected to keep still, listen to the story, and answer comprehension questions about the story in a traditional school lesson format. Heath noted that the questions posed by adults tended to differ according to the home of the child. Children from lower socio-economic status (SES) homes are most frequently asked lower cognitive level questions concerning what happened in the story and when it happened. Children from higher SES homes are more frequently asked higher level questions concerning why events in the story happened. This, of course, puts an already disadvantaged group at a still greater disadvantage when they are confronted with higher cognitive level questions in school.

Repeated Readings.

Listening to repeated readings of a story is effective in enhancing language and thinking. Most parents and teachers of young children are aware of the fact that children often request that favorite stories be read over again. This desire on the part of youngsters can be used as an effective tool for enhancing language skill by the parent or teacher.

From repeated readings, children are more able to discuss the literal meaning and make more interpretations about the meaning of stories (Snow 1983; Snow and Goldfield 1983). Higher cognitive level evaluative questions and interpretations were observed by Martinez and Roser (1985) and Yaden (1985) following repeated readings of a familiar book. Nonverbal interpretations of a story also seemed to increase with repeated readings of a story. Sulzby (1985) notes that dramatic reenactments of a story increase with additional readings. Repeated reading, therefore, is seen as an effective tool for developing additional understanding of a story for a child. It enhances meaning in a number of ways.

Readings and Repeated Readings

While repeated readings can be helpful to children, varied new single readings can provide different benefits. To study this, Morrow (1988) compared four year-olds in two groups in a daycare center. The first group was read a different story each week for ten weeks. Each story was read once. The second group was read one story the first week and three stories during the remaining nine weeks. With the latter group, each story was read three times. Morrow found that the first group tended to ask more questions in general and more detailed questions in particular. Their responses tended to focus more on details, relationships with their own experiences, and labeling. Over time, the second group gradually increased the complexity of the questions and com-

ments given. They tended to do more predicting and interpreting of the story. By the third reading the children were familiar enough with the story to make associations, elaborations, and evaluations of the story. The repeated readings seemed to be particularly beneficial to the low-ability children in the second group. They were observed to make more comments and ask more questions than higher ability children in the group.

The adults also appeared to change their management behaviors over the course of the study. During the ten weeks of the study, the management needs of the children decreased as they became more involved in discussing the story. As a result, over time the adults played a less dominant role. As children asked more questions, the adults had more opportunities to respond to children and to reinforce the appropriate behaviors of the children. A critically important finding of Morrow's study is that very young children, in this case four-year-olds, were capable of interpreting, evaluating, and making associations with stories. Typical traditional early childhood activities surrounding stories tend to focus on the mechanics of reading such as letter identification and sound-symbol relationships. Discussions about the meaning of a story sometimes never get beyond the literal level. As a result of Morrow's work, however, teachers of young children need to take into account the need to engage in a more interactive discussion of the meaning of stories. Since book sharing often needs to be done in one-to-one or small group situations, there is a need for early childhood educators to seek ways to involve parents, grandparents, older siblings, volunteers, and others in the day-to-day program.

LANGUAGE AS A PROCESS

Language is viewed here as a process rather than as a product. A product is a thing. A thing does not tend to change. It can be observed over time and will remain the same over time. The printed language on this page is a product. The reader can look at it now, tomorrow, and next week. It will still be here, and it will still say the same thing.

A process, on the other hand, is an activity or set of actions in which a person can engage. As one engages in the process of speaking or writing, things can

FIGURE 2-7 A skilled teacher uses oral language to help children deal with a range of feelings and experiences.

change from moment to moment and from week to week. Someone may say something one moment, obtain some new information about the topic a minute later, and make a very different statement about the original topic a moment later. For example, take the case of a daycare teacher observing a three-year-old fall out of a swing. The teacher might say something about the child being hurt. After examining the child and being assured by the child that there is no injury, the same teacher might then comment about the child not being hurt. Within a brief span of time, the teacher made two contradicting statements. Both, however, were valid in the context in which they were made.

The swing incident illustrates the fact that language is an ongoing process. As individuals acquire new information, the language they use to make sense of the world changes as the interpretation of the world changes. The information a person shares or receives is constantly being reviewed by the mind. As a result, meanings and perceptions can change.

Elements of the Process

Certain key elements are found in each of the four language modes: listening, speaking, reading, and writing. They are quite similar in both sequence and function. For each mode, people engage in some ac-

tion or actions prior to, during, and after the actual event (State Education Department 1989).

Listening.

Prior to actually listening, a child might become aware of a purpose for listening, be willing to listen, and be prepared to attend to the speaker even if distractions occur. During the actual act of listening, the listener might engage in such things as continuing to attend to the speaker, relating content to what one already knows, identifying areas not understood, and respecting the speaker. Following the listening, the listener might provide feedback to the speaker, attempt to clarify points not understood, and make judgments about what was heard.

Speaking.

Before speaking, one might determine the actual content of the message, how it should be presented, and what kind of audience will be hearing the message. During the speaking, the speaker must attend to such things as presenting a clear message, tone of voice, the correct vocabulary, possible responses, the environment, and nonverbal gestures that might enhance the message. Nonverbal gestures are movements like holding one's hands apart to show just how big the fish was. Following the speaking, the speaker should accept comments and constructive criticism, answer questions, and explain any points not understood by the listeners.

Reading.

Prior to reading a text, a reader might identify a purpose for reading, make predictions about the content of the text, and attempt to identify the author's intentions in writing the piece. During the reading, the effective reader self-monitors understanding of the text. Afterward, the reader might reread certain parts of the text to clarify meaning and respond to the text. Responding to the reading can take a variety of forms. A person can simply think about how the new information has changed previously held beliefs. Another response might be writing a summary statement in a notebook or having a discussion with someone who has also read the same piece.

FIGURE 2-8 The child who drew this picture told a story to go with it: "Jeremy has legs. Mommy has a skirt. Daddy has legs."

Writing.

Before actually writing a piece, an author might plan it by determining the ideas to include, how the ideas will be organized, and whether the piece will be a poem, a story, or a description. During the actual writing, the author might draft the message, revise the text, and read parts of the draft to make sure the meaning is clear. Following the writing, the author seeks to share the piece that was written. Part of the sharing is getting responses to the text by those who read it.

SKILLS AND BEHAVIORS

An integrated language arts program for young children cannot ignore the individual oral language skills and behaviors that must be acquired. Language skills are needed to enable youngsters to be competent at communicating their needs, thoughts, and ideas. Traditional language arts programs have long revolved around building specific skills. The deficiency of such programs is that the skills are taught in isolation, away from contexts that are meaningful to children. An integrated language arts program, on the other hand, seeks to enable children to acquire the skills through a variety of meaningful contexts: circle time, story sharing sessions, play, art, and so forth. Teaching skills in isolation versus skills in

meaningful contexts is a major difference between a traditional and an integrated language arts program.

By providing the skill learning in a natural language setting, the problem of transfer is greatly decreased. Teachers have long been frustrated with teaching a skill in an isolated setting and not having it transfer to other settings. Natural settings are particularly relevant to language learning, because it is in such settings that much language is used. Skills are needed for social language, the language used for learning, and the language used to develop deeper understandings of life. The oral language skills described here are viewed as a foundation, or base. They are not intended to be all-inclusive. Rather, they are key elements of effective listening and speaking that can be refined and strengthened. The skills described here are grouped into three categories: social interaction skills, information acquisition skills, and analysis and evaluation skills. There are, of course, other ways to group these skills. The grouping depends on the situation and the purpose of the teacher.

Social Interaction

Oral language is used by even very young children to communicate their wants and needs. Children and all other human beings are social by nature. Language is one of the most powerful tools children can use to satisfy their desire to meet others, develop friendships, and share the excitement of living. The following skills enable children to more fully use the powerful tool of language. Over the course of an early childhood program, it is important to help children develop the ability to demonstrate mastery of as many of these skills as possible. Of course, some skills are refined again and again, even into adulthood. The initial skills, however, are often acquired in childhood.

Distinguish Hearing from Listening.

Knowing the difference between hearing and listening enables the child to better monitor the environment. Hearing is the physical awareness of sounds and language. Listening includes hearing but demands a focused attention on the part of the listener. A child might be playing on a playground and hear the sounds of laughter, nearby automobile traffic, and perhaps an airplane flying overhead. The child's attention, however, is directed on the activity of the moment, perhaps riding on the swing. There is no need to attend to any of the sounds at the moment, so they are only heard. However, when the child's teacher calls to the students to line up to go inside for lunch, the child begins to listen. The child has a purpose for attending to what the teacher is saying. Most adults and many children engage in this skill without thinking about it. For many, the skill might not even need to be taught. It must, however, be used throughtout life.

Identify Listening Situations.

This is closely related to distinguishing between hearing and listening, but goes a step beyond. In this instance, the individual must be attuned to the characterisics of a situation in which it is important to listen to someone. Such a situation might be a social relationship using a toy telephone, a teacher reading a story to the group, or a classroom visitor explaining how to take care of a pet. On the other hand, it is not necessary for a child to attend to all conversations in the room. Such situations must be distinguished by the child as being appropriate listening opportunities.

Attend to the Speaker.

A listener needs to develop the practice of giving a speaker full attention. It is both a matter of politeness and the need to obtain all of the information being shared. For infants and toddlers this might mean turning the head in the direction of the person speaking. In older children it may mean stopping a current activity and actively listening to a teacher giving directions for an activity.

Identify a Purpose for Listening.

In order to acquire this skill, children must become aware of the environment in which they find themselves. They must also have some awareness of who the speaker is and think about possible meanings a message might have for themselves.

A child may listen attentively to the teacher on the playground giving directions for how to play a game. The child has decided to join in the game and realizes that participation depends on an understanding of the rules of the game. The desire to participate forms the child's purpose for listening.

Another child may eagerly listen to a parent reading a favorite book. The child likes the book because of the humorous repetition of a phrase throughout the book. The child knows when the phrase is coming and says it along with the reader. The child has identified a purpose for listening: the desire to enjoy the pleasure of the reading experience.

Respect the Speaker.

This skill serves as a useful social skill as well as the basis for being a good audience member in the future. To demonstrate the acquisiton of this skill, the child listens without interrupting, refrains from negative comments about oral language errors, maintains eye contact with the speaker, and responds appropriately. Responding may take place during and after the speaking. During the time the speaker is talking, the listener might smile at humorous comments and nod in agreement with points the speaker is making. After the speaker concludes, the listener might ask for clarification of a point, ask a question, or provide information related to what the speaker has said.

Use Appropriate Language and Ideas.

This skill entails the ability to remain focused on the topic being discussed. Children often volunteer any idea that occurs to them whether or not it is related to the topic being discussed. This is a natural part of development and must be both expected and tolerated. Gradually, however, children must develop the ability to focus more on the topic of discussion and provide information related to that topic. Teachers and other adults should constantly model and reinforce this behavior.

Respond to Listeners.

This skill enables the child to continue to develop social relationships and friendships with other children. It is a matter of both politeness and meaningfulness. Children must learn to allow others to have opportunities to speak after they have had their turn. They must also be attentive to whether or not their listeners understand them. If listeners look confused, the speaker must recognize that and attempt to clarify the meaning of the message.

FIGURE 2-9 Sharing a secret witha friend is an enjoyable way for children to focus on the context of language.

Focus on Content.

This skill applies to both listeners and speakers. The key function of communication is to share meaning. Children need to identify this as a part of their use of language. The primary reason for speaking is to share meaning. The primary reason for listening is to acquire meaning. Getting off on another topic while one is a speaker does not help the listeners understand the main point being shared. Listeners who daydream or focus primarily on the clothing the speaker is wearing are going to miss much of the content the speaker is trying to share.

Clarify Meaning.

Listeners and speakers both must develop this skill. It is highly related to the content of the communication. It requires the child to self-monitor understanding of the communication. Self-monitoring is assessing an understanding of the communciation. It is much like asking yourself whether something is understood or not. In speaking, it is an assessment of the audience's understanding. Are the listeners looking confused? Are they asking questions that don't seem necessary? Such cues indicate to a speaker or a listener whether or not it is necessary to explain something again or to seek more explanation.

Identify Key Points of a Story.

In early childhood education, much language will revolve around story sharing. Stories serve as a medium for learning new language and as a foundation for later learning to read. Familiarity with the key points of a story is necessary for understanding the story. While there are many aspects of literature, early childhood instruction should focus on such basic components as character, setting, plot, and theme. Character refers to the people, animals, or beings in the story. Setting refers to the place, time, and environment in which the story takes place. Plot refers to the problem presented in the story and the steps the characters take to overcome it. Theme refers to the underlying ideas that are important to the story. In literature for young children, the themes of family, friendship, love, and growing are common.

Uses Key Ideas for Telling a Story.

A useful tool for language growth is encouraging children to retell, reenact, and role play stories they make up about themselves as well as stories they have heard. The same key elements of stories can be encouraged in these activities. It is not realistic to consistently expect a high degree of sophistication with young children. While such literary components as plot and character are basic to understanding a story, they can become increasingly complex as one moves into more sophisticated literature. With young children, the teacher needs to be aware of their basic understandings. From that point on, the teacher can better comprehend the growth surrounding children's understanding of these concepts. Observing a child role play a sequence of three events from a familiar story when last month the child was only able to role play a sequence of two events represents growth in the child's understanding of plot.

Identify Language Used to Create an Emotional Response.

Most people like to hear or read a good story. What often makes a story good in a person's mind is whether or not he or she can relate to it. A feeling of empathy for a certain character pulls the reader into the story. Identifying with a similar situation or problem does likewise. Authors know this and use it to make the story enjoyable for the reader. Certain language is used to make the reader identify with the story and have an emotional response to the text. Each story is different, so there is no special list of words to locate in the story. Rather, the reader finds it in such things as the description of a character, a plot, or a problem familiar in one's own life. The reader identifies them and responds with comments like:

"I'm just like that character."
"I had a problem just like that once."
"I felt the same way when my pet cat died last year."
"I love being in a boat just like in this story."

Uses Language to Create an Emotional Response.

As children listen to stories they gain an understanding of the ways authors create an emotional response in readers and listeners. In telling their own stories, children can begin to use the same strategies in their language. Teachers can model this in the stories they tell and draw attention to it. It requires the storyteller to be aware of the audience. By having an understanding of the likes, dislikes, and beliefs of the audience, the storyteller can include things in the story that will appeal to that group. With young children, this needs to begin at a very basic level, perhaps using only one of the basic elements of a story. For example, if a child knows that the group is quite interested in dinosaurs, the child can make up a story that includes dinosaurs.

Identify Language Used to Create Images.

This skill, like the skill of creating emotional responses in an audience, is a higher level skill. It can be learned, however, at different levels of language sophistication. Language images are created with such things as alliteration, rhyme, and sounds. A number of other ways are used to create images, but these three are usually understood by young children. Alliteration is repeating the initial consonants of two or more words in a description. The phrase "cute cuddly cat" is an example of alliteration. Rhyme is usually created through ending sounds such as in the last words of the following lines:

"Old Barney was a jolly raccoon,
Who loved to dance by the light of the moon.
He danced with the knife the fork and the spoon.
He danced with them all the whole month of June."

The natural sounds of some words can create images in the mind of the reader because the sound of the word suggests the idea or object that the word represents. Examples of words that do this include: zip, whisper, pop, hiss, and bang.

Each of these image creating devices abound in the literature written for young children. Youngsters often like to anticipate and join in saying the line as it is reached in familiar stories. Lines that contain these devices are often the ones children remember best and tend to use in their reenactments of a story.

Use Language to Create Images.

As children learn to identify and appreciate the language used to create images in the stories they hear, their use can be modeled by teachers and parents in other language situations such as in writing their own personal stories. At first, children may tend to use these devices inaccurately. Rather than correcting their errors, children should be supported in their willingness to take risks and to use new language structures. Through increased use and familiarity with these devices, children often learn to use them more accurately in a natural manner.

Information Acquisition

As children go through their school years, they spend over half of their classroom time listening for information. They hear explanations by teachers. They listen to and watch filmstrips, movies, and videotapes. In addition, they learn much information from the listening and speaking that goes on in day-to-day conversations and interactions with family members and friends. Through speaking, children at a very young age are able to share their knowledge with others.

The skills needed for using oral language as a tool for language acquisition usually have both a receptive (listening) and expressive (speaking) component. Children must become aware of certain language characteristics when in a listening situation. However, it is equally important to develop the ability to use those same language characteristics when speaking.

FIGURE 2-10 The child who created these images read the story formed by the letters: "I like cats."

As children develop the following concepts, they increase the ability to acquire and share knowledge through the use of oral language.

Essential Information.

Children need to develop the ability to listen for and use key parts of the content of a message. Picture a group of young children visiting a pet shop. The owner may focus comments on the wide variety of animals people can choose as pets. Children may see and hear about things such as dog collars, water bottles for bird cages, and flea repellants for cats. While those can and should be recognized as details of some importance for pet owners, the main topic that should be recognized is that there are many different kinds of animals. It is often necessary to make sure children are focused on the main topic and that they recognize the other items as details.

Another type of essential information that can be drawn from this example is the fact that both the main topic and the details have a certain relationship.

The details mentioned above are supplies that one might need in order to care for a pet. Other details that children on the field trip may learn are such things as different breeds of dogs, varieties of fish, and birds that "talk."

When sharing information for others to acquire, children need to develop the ability to provide essential information when they are speaking. If a child wishes to talk about a new pet dog at circle time, the child needs to provide key information that the others in the group will need in order to have some understanding of this new pet. The main idea may be the fact that the child has a new pet dog. Details may include such things as dog collar, license, kennel, name, owner, color, veterinary shots, size, and procedures to be used in house breaking the dog. As bits of information presented randomly, they may not present a clear picture of the information the child is attempting to share.

It is more understandable for listeners if the speaker shares the information in ways that show the relationship of the information to the main topic. In the case of the child telling about a new pet, the child might describe the physical characteristics of the dog, followed by some of the things one needs to do in order to care for a pet. This requires at least the beginning of a sense of audience. A speaker must take into account the listeners. A judgment must be made about what kind of a presentation is needed for the listeners to benefit from what the speaker has to say.

Children do not necessarily do these things naturally. Although some may develop a facility for this simply by listening to and observing others, many children are helped by active modeling on the part of the teacher or other adult. The concept of meta-thinking can be a useful tool in this procedure.

Meta-thinking is thinking about thinking. It implies that a speaker can engage in thought about how to use language. For example, a speaker about to describe a new pet can consider the following questions prior to speaking:

"I wonder if my listeners all know what a pet is?"
"Should I first tell what my dog looks like?"
"Is it important to talk about the different foods for a pet?
"Is the name of the store where we bought the pet an important thing to tell?"

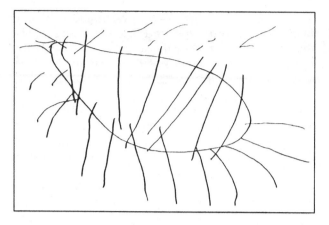

FIGURE 2-11   The child who drew this figure explained that it was a drawing of a pet cat.

An adult can model this process by thinking out loud and answering these questions prior to sharing some information. The use of a visual reinforcer such as a picture on a flannel board could reinforce the points. Numerous repetitions of modeling a process are often necessary for children to understand the procedure.

Directions and Descriptions.

In order for listeners to comprehend information, it is usually necessary to have all of the pieces presented in an understandable manner. A teacher explaining how to play a game describes the procedure using such tools as a sequence of steps or an organized set of rules. A child describing a favorite character from a picture book needs to be sure to include sufficient information in a logical manner. Again, the skill is needed for both listening and speaking. If the steps to a sequence are described out of order, the message may be rendered obscure or even meaningless. The message may be very clear in the mind of the speaker. For this reason, developing a concept of the needs of the audience is essential for young users of oral language.

Key Words.

Vocabulary is a critical part of any communication. Key words take on particular importance. They define the boundaries and the topic of the discussion.

The meaning of the entire interaction often hinges on a mutual understanding of key terms. They identify the main idea, provide details that are absolutely essential, and can even be the key that solves a riddle or makes a joke humorous. Listening for key words can spell the difference between understanding and confusion.

Listeners need to develop the ability to both recognize when they do not have an understanding of certain key words and to do something about it. This is another meta-thinking skill. That is, thinking about and coming to the conclusion that you do not understand one or two of the frequently used terms in a conversation is a valuable skill for a language user. The listener then has the opportunity to do something about it, such as asking the speaker to explain the terms. Another alternative might be to review a part of the discussion that makes the meaning of the term clear through the context.

For speakers, there is a need to determine whether or not the audience possesses an adequate knowledge of key terms. An adequate knowledge is the amount of information needed to understand the term in the context in which it is used. A young child may have spent yesterday afternoon in the backyard playing with a new pet dog named Jake. If the child begins to tell about the experience at circle time, the other children might follow along, thinking that Jake is a neighborhood friend of the child. Confusion would emerge when the child mentions that Jake got into trouble for tearing a towel on the clothesline with his teeth. Some children would use the context to make a guess that Jake was a dog and not another child. Not all children would be able to make that shift in understanding. Such examples provide material for teaching both good listening and speaking skills: for speaking, the necessity to adequately define key terms; and, for listening, the necessity of determining the understanding of the key terms.

Organization Patterns.

One of the basic purposes of language is communication of information. In order to aid this purpose, certain structures have developed in the language that help speakers explain and listeners understand. These structures, or organizational patterns, help the child to see the point of a message, make predictions, or focus on critical aspects of a message. The ability to both identify these patterns in listening and use them in speaking aids communication.

When the communication is a narrative or a story, the story schema pattern is indispensable. Most people learn such schemas naturally and take them for granted. Such things as phrases (e.g., "Once upon a time . . . and they lived happily ever after"), the introduction of the main characters, the unfolding of the problem, and the resolution of the plot are all part of the story schema. Using the familiar parts of a schema while telling a story aids the audience in understanding and appreciating the story. Identifying components while listening to a story helps to get beyond the words of the story and into the essence of the story.

Sequence is another important organizational pattern. It is especially useful for any kind of communication that attempts to explain how something happens. Whether the message is about how to make a peanut butter sandwich or what the wolf in the story does next, the use of a correct sequence is critical to the success or failure of the message. Other organizational patterns include generalizations supported by examples or details, cause and effect, and logical steps leading to a conclusion. There are other patterns, of course, as well as variations on each of these patterns.

Intonation.

Anyone who has ever listened to a speech delivered in a monotone voice will recognize that such a delivery does not help the speaker or listener communicate. Such a presentation is difficult to listen to because it is difficult for the audience to keep attending. It is also difficult to determine the most important parts of the message because everything seems to have equal emphasis. Intonation infuses the language with life and meaning by enabling the listener to identify key parts of the message while at the same time to be more captivated and involved in it.

Intonation uses several characteristics of sound to create interest in an oral message. Volume, or loudness, may be varied. This eliminates a monotonal quality and can signal that certain ideas are more important than others. Pitch, or the frequency of sound, can be used to make a message more serious (deeper pitch), more shrill (higher pitch), or a variety of qualities in between. Rate, or the speed of delivery, can give the message a lazy feeling (slow rate) or an imperative flavor (fast rate). All three of these characteristics are usually combined in language. They are used by everyone in daily conversations. Storytellers, story readers, and their messengers need to be especially aware of them. Emphasizing or de-emphasizing the characteristics of intonation can provide important clues as to the meaning of the story.

Creating Images.

By using different language tools, a speaker can create powerful images in listeners' minds. By identifying and understanding these images, listeners can develop a deeper understanding of the message a speaker is attempting to convey. Images are the mental pictures created in the mind to correspond to the verbal message.

Figurative language is one tool for creating images. In literal language, words mean exactly what they would seem to mean to most people. A dog is a dog, and happiness is happiness. With figurative language, the words can and do imply or represent something else. For example, the "American eagle" calls to mind something different than just a large bird. This particular bird is a symbol of a country and represents certain ideals and beliefs that other birds do not represent.

Similes and metaphors are words and terms that create unique pictures in the mind. A simile compares an actual thing with something that gives it a greater meaning. "Joey is like a clown at play time" is an example of a simile. The statement does not mean that Joey is actually a clown. Rather, it means that Joey does thing that remind one of the kinds of things a clown might do: act silly, fool around, and play tricks on others. The simile gets the point across in a colorful, effective, and efficient manner.

A metaphor implies that one thing is actually something else. "The computer has a powerful memory" and "Susan plows through books" are examples of metaphors. Computers don't really have memories in the same way humans do. They have electronic capabilities of storing and retrieving information. This gives rise to the use of the word memory. A powerful computer memory simply means that the computer

FIGURE 2-12   Folk and fairy tales can provide children with the figurative language they will use to create images. *Photo from "Muchie Lal," in* The Child's Fairy Tale Book, *by Kay Chorao, reprinted courtesy of E.P. Dutton.*

can store a large amount of information. However, a computer's memory and a human's memory are two very different things. Likewise, Susan does not really plow through a book in the same way that a farm implement turns dirt over in a field. The phrase about plowing through a book means that Susan is an avid reader who may spend long periods of time engaged in reading.

Idioms are colorful language phrases in which the meaning goes beyond the meaning of the individual words making up the phrase. Idioms include such phrases as "pulling my leg," "What's up?" and "down and out." These phrases have specific meanings within the culture, but those meanings can't be deter-

mined solely from the words within them. When idioms are understood, however, they convey a vivid image in a very few words.

Words that evoke feelings and emotions are also effective in creating images. Such words as hilarious, pitiful, terrified, ferocious, crying, mournful, and bouncy can all create special meanings because of the clarity of their meanings. Using and understanding colorful and vivid language adds much to the creation of meaning in oral language.

Nonverbal Cues.

In addition to all of the language tools the speaker can use to enhance meaning in oral language, nonverbal cues can also be recognized and used to add to meaning. Nonverbal cues include body language, facial expressions, and hand motions. Because these cues are so visual, they can be used with even very young children. Body language can include such things as strutting like a rooster, cowering fearfully in a corner, and slumping into a chair in an exhausted posture. Each can express feelings and emotions without words. Facial expressions can reveal happiness, sadness, fear, boredom, and excitement. They do this primarily through the eyes and mouth. Hand motions can express messages such as be quiet, come this way, stop, get down on the floor, hurry, and so forth. Nonverbal cues are used by most people in everyday living. When slightly exaggerated, they can be effective components of storytelling with young children.

Analysis and Evaluation

Life is often not an either/or situation. There are only a limited number of yes and no choices to be made. Even when it appears that there are only two alternatives, such as whether one will drink water or juice, there are often other things to consider before making even a seemingly easy decision. Is the water safe to drink? Where does it come from? Is it odorless? Does it have a sulphur smell? What kind of juice is it? Does it contain any added sugar? Whether one finally decides to have juice or water, it is quite possible that language skills related to oral language were used to analyze and evaluate the situation.

Analysis and evaluation skills become very sophisticated as one enters the difficult world of adult decision making. The foundation of those skills, however, begins in early childhood. While complex logical thinking skill is not usually present, young children can and do engage in making decisions based upon real reasons. Developing an awareness of these behaviors and improving the skills related to them can enhance the young child's ability to engage in analysis and evaluation skills. Some of the basic skills that can be developed are discussed here. The skills can be modeled by adults. It is equally important to reinforce children when they demonstrate the use of such skills in the context of their own listening and speaking.

Supporting Information.

Most children and adults accept standard definitions of things in the world as valid or true once they have learned them. For example, most people agree on what constitutes a cat, a table, gravity, the sun, and so forth. Disagreement occurs when subjective personal statements are expressed as though they were facts. They may of course be facts, but it is not as readily apparent. For example, there is often disagreement over such things as what is the best snack food, which restaurant makes the best pizza, or who will be a good president. Most people have opinions about such things, but there is not usually a consensus of opinion. Therefore, people often attempt to prove their belief as factual through a variety of language tools that use analysis and evaluation.

One of the most effective ways of convincing others of the truth of one's beliefs is through the use of supporting information. Supporting information often takes the form of ideas, examples, and reasons to support a general statement. A child may claim that a certain stuffed animal is the best toy. To support the statement, the child may mention such things as softness, fuzziness, color, characteristics of the face of the animal, and the fact that the toy was a gift from a grandparent. Not all of these reasons are logical, but they do constitute an understanding of supporting a statement.

Children need to recognize this skill in the oral language of others. Not everything that is spoken is true. Children seek evidence that something is in fact true. As they grow, they develop an awareness of the need to listen for reasons to believe something. Such a skill

FIGURE 2-13 Young children often enjoy explaining things to others.

has implications for situations ranging from child safety to making purchases in a store.

Relevant, Accurate, and Complete Information.

Moving beyond the simple inclusion of reasons or examples is the need to listen for and to use relevant, accurate, and complete information in oral language. Each of these can be viewed separately, but information that embodies all three characteristics is the most powerful.

Relevant information is directly related to the question or statement. An adult voter may cite the good looks and nice clothing of a political candidate as reasons to vote for that person. However, personal beauty and wardrobe do not provide an indication of how well the candidate will govern. Such information is not relevant. Similarly, a young child may say that a certain brand of a product is best because it has a name that rhymes with the child's first name.

Accurate information is free from error. An adult

may claim that a favorite baseball or football team is best because the team achieved a certain win/loss record this season. While the information provided may seem impressive, it must be correct. If it is found to be in error, the original claim is greatly diminished. In the childhood story about Chicken Little, the title character used inaccurate information in making the claim that the sky was falling.

Complete information contains all of the information needed by listeners and speakers. A young athlete may boast of greatness by virtue of finishing second in a hundred yard dash race. However, it may be that there were only two athletes in the race and that the second place runner posted a very slow time. The completeness of this new information decreases the importance of the original supporting information. It can work the other way as well. A young child may claim to be able to read at age four and as proof read a favorite book aloud. Those around the child may smile politely and assume that the child has simply memorized the story. Unbeknownst to everyone, the child may leave the room draw a picture and write a one sentence story about what just occurred. It is unlikely that the child could do the latter activity without having developed some reading skills. Because the child didn't provide more complete information, such as demonstrating some reading ability with a less familiar story, the original claim of being able to read was less powerful.

Voice and Speaking Patterns.

Listeners and speakers need to attend to how voice and speaking patterns are used. By emphasizing, pausing, raising the volume, and speaking softly, listeners are drawn to certain parts of the communication. These skills are learned in order to make clear the intended message. A reason for voting for a particular candidate may be made in a soft, low, reassuring voice. A reason for not voting for an opposing candidate may be made in a shrill whine with a sarcastic tone. As might be expected, given this example, voice and speaking pattern can persuade even when they are not totally relevant. A speaking pattern can and should draw attention to the meaning imbedded in the language. It should not take the place of the meaning in the language. Young children may not readily grasp such fine distinctions. The shrill, sarcas-

tic tones applied to opposing political candidates should not make us decide one way or another. We should simply view such advertisements as pointing to evidence that can and should be analyzed. The listener should make a decision based upon the accuracy of the evidence rather than the tone of delivery.

Making Judgments.

One of the most difficult thinking skills at any age is making judgments. This may be referred to as making a final evaluation, coming to a decision, or making a choice. It is basically the same process. While young children may not possess the more sophisticated logical reasoning skills of an adult, they do make decisions using whatever fundamental strategies they possess. At a basic level, children make judgments when they decide to accept, do, or believe something for some reason. From an adult point of view, the reasoning of a child may seem vague and often irrelevant. It is, however, reasoning that the child views as valid at that point in development.

Susan may like a story because she has a cat just like the cat in the book. Billy may not agree that carrots and celery sticks are a good snack because he prefers sweets. Tom and Nancy may believe in the tooth fairy because how else could that money get under their pillows at night. The reasons may be valid or not. Each of the reasons serves as a criterion for either accepting something as true or rejecting it as false.

The criteria, or reasons, for making decisions may come from within a person or from some outside source. Personal tastes in food provide certain criteria for deciding whether a food tastes good or not. These are criteria from within. On the other hand, training or religious beliefs may be used to make decisions about human behavior. A certain act is seen as wrong because it violates certain accepted rules that have been passed down in the culture. These rules serve as criteria from an outside source.

Finally, judgments can be made about the relevance, accuracy, and completeness of information used to support a statement. These judgments can be made about things that are said and heard. Young children will make many errors in developing these skills. Adults must be prepared to both tolerate the errors and to model the use of this skill.

ORAL LANGUAGE ACTIVITIES

There is no single set of oral language activities that can be seen as best for children at any age. Activities may be used in different ways with different age groups for many purposes. No set of activities should be seen as a program. A program is made up of the goals and objectives teachers hold for a group of children in a class. The activities serve as means to achieving those goals. The same activity may be reasonable at one time and inadvisable at another time.

None of the activities should be viewed as something to be done in an isolated manner. Teachers should select these and other activities for an integrated program that includes all of the language arts modes. The activities are intended to provide opportunities for children to explore language and thinking in order to meet the objectives outlined under the categories of social language, information acquisition, and analysis and judgment. Viewed in this manner, they can help provide a sound foundation for emerging literacy.

Learning about Oral Language.

This activity is actually a meta-thinking process. Children need to be taught to reflect upon their skills and abilities as language users. Some aspects of oral language are best learned from modeling by adults, while others can be taught through discussion. Care must be taken to correctly assess whether or not children are able to benefit from certain instruction at a given point in their development.

Learning about oral language can be done as a group activity. Teachers and children can engage in such things as developing standards for good listening and speaking. The group can also discuss any of the skills identified as being appropriate for the age and class. It is often a good idea to plan to cover topics several times over the course of the year to both re-teach and reinforce the skill. A briefer form of this activity can be useful in conjunction with any of the other activities. Such a session could focus on the purpose for listening or speaking within the specific activity being used.

Particularly relevant to this activity is the development of the concept of establishing purposes for listening. Teachers and parents need to be aware that children don't automatically understand that things

to listen for sometimes depend on the source of the message. There is a different purpose for listening to a story than there is for listening to a talk on fire safety. It is often helpful to children for adults to identify purposes before listening occurs. When this is done over time, children come to a realization of its importance.

Read Aloud.

One of the finest gifts any reader can give to a young child is a story read aloud in a dramatically exciting manner. Regardless of reading ability, most people usually enjoy such an experience. Besides sharing some of the excellent literature available for young children, a story read aloud can be used as a springboard for other activities that enhance oral language. The most obvious activity following a reading is group discussion of the book. Depending on the age level of the group, discussions could range from as basic a topic as what part of the story did children like best to consideration of the plot and theme of the book.

Young children who experience a story even once often incorporate parts of the story into their play. They may dramatize or pantomime the plot line. This is to be encouraged even if children are not totally accurate in their re-enactments. Children are constantly testing the boundaries of language and reality. They may be observed combining different parts of two or more stories they have heard.

Fingerplays.

Fingerplays have several formats and purposes. Fingerplays are a combination of story, poem, directions, song, and hand movements. Some are used for making transitions, perhaps between free play and circle time. Others are used as an introduction to a story or lesson. Still others are used just as an activity in themselves.

Most adults recall some of the more familiar fingerplays, such as "The Itsy Bitsy Spider," "Three Little Monkeys Jumping on the Bed," and "Here's the Church, and Here's the Steeple . . ." However, many fingerplays are made up by the teachers who use them. They are relatively easy to develop. They may or may not rhyme. All that is required is clarity of the language and some kind of hand movement that en-

FIGURE 2-14 Children may like a certain book for a number of different reasons. *Reprinted courtesy of Houghton Mifflin Company, nonexclusive and nontransferable.*

hances the message. Children can be encouraged to learn the words and the accompanying hand motions.

Fill in the Blank.

In order to engage children in this activity, one needs a story, book, or poem with fairly predictable content. A story that contains rich content with clear description is helpful. To do this activity, the teacher explains to the children that as the story or poem progresses they should think about what word goes best at the place where the story pauses. As the story unfolds, clues are given in the language. Children can be instructed to volunteer a response as individuals by raising their hands to be called on or by a group cho-

ral response. A choral response may be appropriate when there can be only one correct response. This does not mean that only that type of response should be sought. Stories can take fascinating and humorous directions by using tales that can have a variety of possible responses at the pauses. These are called mad-libs. Consider the following tale:

Once upon a time there was a girl named
_____. One day, she took some money and
a bag of food and set off to go to _____. On
the way through the deep, dark woods, she met a
big bad _____. He tried to gobble up the
girl. It didn't work though. She tricked him by
reaching into her bag of food and giving him

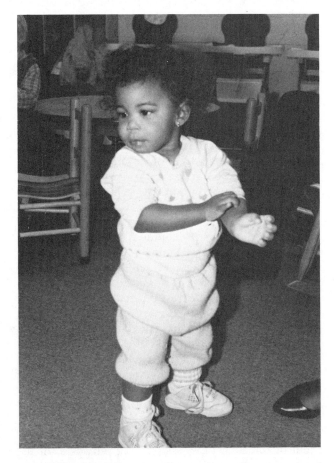

FIGURE 2-15 Children enjoy doing fingerplays created and modeled by the teacher.

_____. While he was busy trying to figure out what to do with it, the girl quietly tiptoed away and continued on her journey.

Some of this story has elements borrowed from the "Little Red Riding Hood" story. Children may or may not identify the big bad character as a wolf. Such an identification is logical, but not the only possible response. Other missing elements can be filled in with different responses. The responses may be discussed briefly with the children following the story. The point of an activity such as this is to have children provide information that makes sense within the context of the rest of the story. When this occurs, it demonstrates that the child is meaningfully interacting with language.

Predictable Book Sharing.

While this might be thought of as more of a reading activity, such an assumption simply reinforces the fact that it is impossible to isolate language modes from one another. In this case, the reading reinforces oral language. The activity is similar to the fill-in-the-blank activity described above. Here, however, the emphasis is more on a single correct response. The response may be a single word or a phrase. Often, the response is the same phrase repeated at different points in the book. Poster size books with large pictures and print are often used so that children can see the actual words as well as hear them being read. These large books are often referred to as "big books." This procedure may be seen as a transitional activity between oral language and reading. There is no need to put pressure on children to actually learn the written words by sight. Children for whom it is developmentally appropriate will actually learn to recognize and read the words with little pressure or assistance from adults. As with the fill-in-the-blank activity, the emphasis is on helping children discover that they have the power to use language by recreating it in ways that make sense.

Story Prediction.

Meaning does not exist on the page of a book or in the sounds that make up words. Meaning exists in the minds of the individuals who use language. This belief is put into practice with story prediction. To engage children in this activity the reader or teller of a story pauses from time to time. During the pauses, possible events are generated and discussed by the children. Here too, modeling by the teacher can be helpful to children. In framing predictions, it is important for the teacher to state the reasons for the prediction being made. In that way, the concept of this activity as a thinking activity is reinforced.

To engage in story prediction, children must have a basic understanding of what they have listened to up until that point. For example, in the "Little Red Riding Hood" story, the reader might pause at the point where the child proceeds on to Grandmother's house after meeting the wolf in the forest. In order for listeners to come up with meaningful predictions of what might happen next, they need to have come to an understanding that the child might be in danger, the wolf is up to no good, and something dreadful might be about to happen to Grandmother. With those facts, children can develop possible future events in the story. Again, the emphasis is not on coming up with the correct event, but generating reasonable possibilities. After all, this is what mature adult readers do when they read a novel. This activity is an enjoyable part of reading and literacy.

Visual Response.

Young children often engage in art activities as a means of both exploring and understanding their environment. This natural desire and activity can be used by children to help them understand the language they hear and use. Artwork should be seen as a natural part of writing and, hence, a natural part of language. Drawing pictures can be done before, during, and after a story is told. It can help a child form an image as well as help fill in the details. Unlike oral language that exists for only a moment in time, a drawing exists over time. It can be developed, changed, and removed by the child. It can be put aside and returned to later. It can have its meaning changed by the addition or deletion of a tiger, a baby, a fire engine, or a dinosaur.

Children enjoy talking about the art they create. Adults must learn to be attentive and patient listeners as children explain their illustrations. If the adult shares some of the same reality, perhaps having been the reader of the story the child is illustrating, questions that encourage the child to think about the story

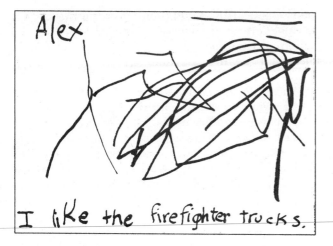

FIGURE 2-16 The child who drew this picture as a response to the environment dictated the story that was recorded by the teacher.

can be used. Criticism should be avoided. Keeping the child in charge of the conversation with questions that begin with the words *why* and *how* can help the child recreate through language what has been created with paper and crayon.

Language Identification.

In order to help children understand that they have power over language, language identification activities can be used. The focus of a language identification activity is to have children identify such things as figurative language before, during, or after it is used. For example, if the group is making up a story about a scary monster, children can contribute words that best describe such a monster before the story is developed. Of course, this activity could also be delayed until the monster is introduced in the story. After an oral story is created, the group might generate descriptive words about the monster as well.

While reading a story, a teacher might ask children to listen for words that help them create a picture of the story in their minds. Following the reading, children could share some of the words or phrases that helped them see the story unfold in their minds. An alternative might be to have children give a thumbs up sign to words and phrases that create clear images as they are read. Care should be taken here to not have constant interruptions to the flow of the story.

Storytelling.

Just because some young children haven't yet learned to read the words printed on a page doesn't mean that they cannot tell a good story. Children are aware of their experiences even though it may be from an egocentric point of view. As social beings, it is natural for children to want to share their experiences with others. While their stories may not have well defined characters, themes, settings, and plots, they are an important part of their lives. As such, they constitute the background they rely upon to understand the world. By encouraging sharing their stories, the teacher assists children in using language as a tool to further understand their environment.

Asking children to stand in front of a group to recite a story is an artificial and sometimes intimidating experience. Sharing is often best when it is informal and spontaneous. This can occur at circle time or during play time. Teachers can provide simple props, puppets, and flannel boards for use as aids in telling stories. Children may wish to engage in storytelling in small groups, in pairs, or alone, using a stuffed animal or a puppet as a prop.

Circle Time.

One of the fondest memories many adults have of their early education is the "Show And Tell" activity that occurs at circle time. Circle time has gone far beyond a single purpose. It is now an opportunity for children to share and learn a variety of concepts and ideas. It can provide a forum for discussion of classroom rules, a welcome back celebration for a classmate who has returned from a hospital stay, or an audience to share news about the arrival of a new baby. These and other activities are building blocks for oral language use. They provide an opportunity for language practice, a friendly audience, and a familiar, comforting structure.

Messenger.

While it may be a bit frightening the first time one does it, most youngsters enjoy the feeling of importance obtained from being the one chosen to carry an

FIGURE 2-17 This child is eager to share the story and picture she has created.

important message to the office, another classroom, the attendance clerk, or the kitchen. Whether the message is written on a piece of paper or spoken, it is a chance to demonstrate responsibility and dependability. When a teacher uses this activity, the idea that the purpose of the activity is communicating a message should be stressed.

Listening Games.

Although there are many books and articles filled with ideas for listening games, care should be taken in their use. When they are used as a language arts tool, the focus should be on language development. The game can provide a motivating vehicle for this, but it need not become the end in itself. The reason for this is that skills learned in one context do not always readily transfer to other contexts. Therefore, when

deciding to use a listening game, one would do well to integrate it within the context of the classroom program.

Take for example a unit on shapes and colors. The children may have colored a variety of circles, squares, triangles, and rectangles. They may have been asked to color one of each shape with the colors red, yellow, green, and blue. A teacher might now decide to have the children sit in a circle with their colored shapes in front of them for a game of "Simon Says." By structuring the activity this way, the teacher can now begin the game within the context of the shape and color lesson as follows:

Simon says, "Everybody sit up straight."
Simon says, "Hold up a red circle."
Simon says, "Put your red circle down."
Simon says, "Hold up a yellow square."
"Put your yellow square down. Uh-oh! Simon didn't say to put down your yellow square."

Telephone Call.

There is a certain etiquette to using a telephone. Most adults use the process without even thinking about it: dial a number, wait for the other party to pick up the telephone, listen for the greeting, identify yourself, ask to speak to a particular person, and so forth. The total procedure forms a schema that is logical but which is different than other informal and formal oral language procedures. As with many schemas, however, it is an important one to learn. By understanding it, one can better understand telephone conversations that take place in both real life and in stories in which only one half of the telephone conversation is heard.

In an early childhood program, the use of toy telephones can serve more than one purpose. Learning to use the telephone is, of course, an important skill to possess. Using a telephone also lends an added importance to a conversation for children. There is a tendency for children to attend more closely to the conversation when using a tool such as a telephone. While children using toy telephones will usually be able to see each other, the teacher can reinforce the concept that clear descriptions are needed on telephones because people can't really see each other. This idea can be made more concrete by visually separating the two children using the telephones with a screen of some type.

Role Playing.

Possessing a strong vocabulary is an effective tool for a language user. Understanding words in concrete terms can help children integrate vocabulary into their own language. While terms depicting concrete objects such as table, elephant, circus, house, and fire engine are fairly easily learned, terms dealing with emotions and feelings pose more difficulty. Modeling the emotion through pantomime and other forms of role playing can help children develop a clearer understanding of them.

Other children who do possess an understanding of these more abstract terms can be helpful in modeling them for others. A game type of format may be used. The teacher can tell a child a term to pantomime. The word could be an emotion or feeling: sad, happy, angry, excited, worried, boastful, eager, hungry, scared, and so on. Words can be chosen from the story currently being read in order to integrate this activity. As the word is being pantomimed, other children can take turns guessing the word. A teacher might ask the children with the correct answers what helped focus them on the right emotion being modeled. The game reinforces the vocabulary of both the actor and the audience. The discussion serves as a thinking out loud process that benefits other children. As children learn the new words, they can take turns demonstrating their meanings.

Decision Discussions.

Making decisions is a task everyone faces throughout life. Whether it is the color of a shirt, an item from a menu, or the type of vehicle one will purchase, life is a never-ending series of decisions. Sometimes, good decisions are made and all are happy with the result. At other times, it is clear that better decisions could have been made.

While it is true that not everything is always known prior to the actual decision, being careful to understand what is known at that point can help a person to make better decisions. Take, for example, the purchase of a used car. We should not make a decision to purchase based on the salesperson's smile and the shine on the car. Finding out as much as possible about the automobile will help us make a better decision. Look under the car to check for leaks. Check the odometer to see how many miles the car has already been driven. Have a mechanic check under the hood. Take it for a test drive over a variety of road surfaces. These are all things that may seem very clear to anyone who has purchased a used car that did not hold up very well. However, every day people make decisions such as this without learning enough beforehand.

The process can begin at a young age through decision discussions. By including children in some of the decisions made about the classroom or the home, they will see how the decision-making process works. Children will learn that information is needed to make better decisions. They will also learn that decisions have consequences. For example, if it is decided to go for a nature walk at 9:30 a.m. the weather should be checked to see if it looks like rain. By engaging in the decision-making, the children learn that their snack time has to be moved from 10:00 a.m. to 10:30 a.m., because walks usually take about an hour. While children like structure and routines, they can usually adapt to this type of time adjustment. In the process, their oral language skills are increased as they engage in these decision discussions.

Oral Language Center.

The language center is both a place and a set of beliefs. It can serve as a location for many of the other activities described here. The location of a center needs to be a quieter, less busy section of the classroom. It should accommodate half a dozen children and an adult in a comforatable seating arrangement with everyone able to see everyone else. Chairs or pillows arranged in a circle would be appropriate. It is essential that an adult be in the group to provide an appropriate model and to reinforce appropriate language skills as they are demonstrated.

Topics for discussion should always be developmentally appropriate. It is important to remember, however, that young children do not always clearly distinguish between fantasy and fact. The comments they offer may not always be realistic or presented in correct English. Children should not have these aspects of their contributions corrected. Doing so could diminish their self-confidence. Children are taking risks, trying to communicate, and attempting to make sense.

The adult role in the center is to coordinate and encourage rather than to control. Children must be encouraged to offer opinions, to listen to the ideas of others, to support the ideas of others, to offer alternative suggestions, and to justify their own statements. The teacher can foster these concepts by offering open-ended discussions. Discussions that are focused on finding the one correct answer are not appropriate. One of the most successful strategies is to relate discussions to other parts of the curriculum. In this way, all of the children are assured of having some knowledge of the topic that they can use to participate in the discussion.

SUMMARY

A traditional approach to language arts assumes that the language modes of listening, speaking, reading, and writing develop relatively independently of each other. For example, according to the traditional approach, a child cannot develop reading skills until after a fair amount of oral language skill has been acquired. An integrated curriculum, on the other hand, holds that all four language modes are closely related to each other. It further holds that all of the modes begin to develop early in life and in conjunction with each other.

Oral language is critically important to the development of the young child. The major underlying purpose of oral language is to create and acquire understanding of the world around us. A major part of every school day will be spent in listening. Oral language serves three roles: social interaction, information acquisition, and analysis and evaluation. Social interaction refers to the skills needed to develop relationships with others. Information acquisition refers to the skills required to share and learn new meanings. Analysis and evaluation refers to the ability to study and make decisions about people and information in the environment. Skills are needed in each of these three areas for a child to achieve literacy.

In an integrated curriculum, language learning is viewed as a social activity. The skills to be learned are best acquired in situations that involve many opportunities to use and practice language. There must be opportunities to both speak and listen in pairs and small groups. Teachers and other adults should be a part of the language environment. Rather than being in charge of the discussion, their role should be focused on providing opportunities, coordinating activities, encouraging participation, and modeling appropriate language skills. Helping children to develop meta-thinking skills is also a key feature of an integrated language arts curriculum. Meta-thinking refers to an awareness individuals develop about their own language skills and abilities.

Language skills are best learned in the contexts where they are most meaningful. Learning skills in an isolated setting, apart from the context in which they are to be used, or without any relationship to a meaningful situation is an inefficient procedure. Besides learning the skill in an isolated setting, the child is also expected to transfer the skill to new situations. In addition, the child is left to determine how the concept can be integrated into the new situation.

Finally, a wide range of activities should be provided for developing oral language skills. The activities, however, should not be seen as a program. Activities are a tool for achieving the goals of a program. The program should be centered around developmentally appropriate goals for individual children. Activities can and should make use of both storytelling and the good literature available for children.

Questions and Activities for Review and Discussion

Multiple Choice
   1. Traditional language arts instructional programs assume that language modes
      (e.g., listening, speaking, reading, writing) develop
      a. in conjunction with each other.

    b. separate from each other.

    c. only after a child begins to walk.

    d. at about age five.

2. Oral language skills are needed in order to

    a. participate in classroom discussions.

    b. engage in social conversations.

    c. express one's needs.

    d. all of the above

3. An integrated curriculum contends that the basic purpose of language is for

    a. understanding and creating meaning.

    b. answering questions in school.

    c. getting good grades in school.

    d. learning to read.

4. When children begin to write stories, they tend to

    a. only recopy stories they have listened to.

    b. make up everything in their heads.

    c. use story structures with which they are familiar.

    d. none of the above

5. Readers acting as "informer/monitors" would be most likely to

    a. explain parts of the story.

    b. relate the story to their own lives.

    c. bring a session to a conclusion.

    d. test the child's knowledge of the story just read.

6. Which children are particularly helped by repeated readings of a story?

    a. boys

    b. girls

    c. low-ability students

    d. high-ability students

7. The components that comprise the familiar language and structure of a story are referred to as

    a. plot outline.

    b. theme.

    c. character development.

    d. story schema.

True or False

  T   F 1. There are two language modes.

  T   F 2. Language learning should use a variety of group sizes.

  T   F 3. Modeling is an effective strategy language teaching.

  T   F 4. Reading aloud and discussing stories with young children has not been shown to influence language learning.

  T   F 5. Repeating the reading of a story to a child serves no language development purpose.

Essay and Discussion

1. Observe a group of children at play in a nursery school or a daycare center. Record the language used by the children. Summarize the language observation in a written statement.

2. Describe the various roles adults might take as readers of stories to young children. Using a children's book, identify some of the things one might do in each of these roles.
3. Describe what is meant by the phrase "language as a process."
4. What are the three basic elements of the language process associated with the language modes of listening, speaking, reading, and writing? Choose one mode and give an example of each of the three basic elements for that mode.
5. Explain how knowledge of a story schema can help listeners understand a story.

References

Baghban, M.J.M. 1984. *Our daughter learns to read and write: A case study from birth to three.* Newark, Del.: International Reading Association.

Bloome, D. 1985. Bedtime story reading as a social process. In J.A. Niles & R.V. Lalik, editors. *Issues in Literacy: A Research Perspective.* Thirty-fourth yearbook of the National Reading Conference. Rochester, N.Y.: National Reading Conference.

Brown, A. 1975. Recognition, reconstruction and recall of narrative sequences of preoperational children. *Child Development* 46: 155–166.

Bruner, J.S. 1978. The role of dialogue in language acquisition. In *The Child's Conception of Language,* ed. A. Sinclair, R.J. Jarvella, and W.J.M. Levelt. New York: Verlag.

Burroughs, M. 1972. *The stimulation of verbal behavior in culturally disadvantaged three year-olds.* Ph.D. diss., Michigan State University.

Cazden, C. 1983. Adult assistance to language development: Scaffolds, models and direct instruction. In *Developing Literacy: Young Children's Use of Language,* ed. C. Cazden. Newark, Del.: International Reading Association.

Chomsky, C. 1972. Stages in language development and reading exposure. *Harvard Educational Review* 42: 1–33.

Clark, M.M. 1976. *Young fluent readers.* Exeter, N.H.: Heinemann.

Clay, M.M. 1979. *Reading: The patterning of complex behavior.* Auckland: Heinemann.

Cochran-Smith, M. 1984. *The making of a reader.* Norwood, N.J.: Ablex.

Cohen, D. 1968. The effect of literature on vocabulary and reading achievement. *Elementary English* 45: 209–213, 217.

Doakes, D. 1981. *Book experiences and emergent reading behavior in preschool children.* Ph.D. diss., University of Alberta.

Dunning, D., and J. Mason. 1984. *An investigation of kindergarten children's expressions of story characters' intentions.* Paper presented at the annual meeting of the National Reading Conference, St. Petersburg, Fl.

Durkin, D. 1966. *Children who read.* New York: Columbia University, Teacher's College.

Durkin, D. 1974–1975. A six-year study of children who learned to read in school at the age of four. *Reading Research Quarterly* 10: 9–61.

Feitelson, D., and Z. Goldstein. 1986. Patterns of book ownership and reading to children in Israeli school-oriented and nonschool-oriented families. *The Reading Teacher* 39: 924–929.

Feitelson, D., B. Kita, and Z. Goldstein. 1986. Effects of listening to series stories on first graders' comprehension and use of language. *Research in the Teaching of English* 20: 339–356.

Flood, J. 1977. Parental styles in reading episodes with young children. *The Reading Teacher* 30: 846–867.

Green, J.L., and J.O. Harker. 1982. Reading to children: A communicative process. In *Reader Meets Author/Bridging the Gap: Psycholinguistic and Sociolinguistic Perspective*, ed. J.A. Langer and M.T. Smith-Burke. Newark, Del.: International Reading Association.

Hall, N. 1987. *The emergence of literacy.* Portsmouth, N.H.: Heinemann.

Harste, J., V. Woodward, and C. Burke. 1984. *Language stories and literacy lessons.* Portsmouth, N.H.: Heinemann.

Heath, S.B. 1980. The functions and uses of literacy. *Journal of Communication* 30: 123–133.

Heath, S.B. 1982. What no bedtime story means: Narrative skills at home and school. *Language in Society* 11: 49–76.

Hoffman, S.J. 1982. *Preschool reading-related behaviors: A parent diary.* Ph.D. diss., University of Pennsylvania.

Holdaway, D. 1979. *The foundations of literacy.* Sydney: Ashton Scholastic.

Lass, B. 1982. Portrait of my son as an early reader. *The Reading Teacher* 36: 20–29.

Lindfors, J.W. 1987. *Children's language and learning.* 2d ed. Englewood Cliffs, N.J.: Prentice-Hall.

Martinez, M., and N. Roser. 1985. Read it again: The value of repeated readings during storytime. *The Reading Teacher* 38: 782–786.

Mason, J.M., and J. Allen. 1986. A review of emergent literacy with implications for research and practice in reading. In *Review of Research in Education* 13: 3–47, ed. E.Z. Rothkopf. Washington, D.C.: American Educational Research Association.

Morrow, L.M. 1985. Retelling stories: A strategy for improving children's comprehension, concept of story structure and oral language complexity. *Elementary English* 85: 647–661.

Morrow, L.M. 1988. Young children's responses to one-to-one story readings in school settings. *Reading Research Quarterly* 23: 89–107.

Ninio, A. 1980. Picture-book reading in mother-infant dyads belonging to two subgroups in Israel. *Child Development* 51: 587–590.

Ninio, A., and J. Bruner. 1978. The achievement and antecedents of labeling. *Journal of Child Language* 5: 5–15.

Peck, J. 1989. Using storytelling to promote language and literacy development. *The Reading Teacher* 3: 138–141.

Pellegrini, A., and I. Galda. 1982. The effects of thematic-fantasy play training on the development of children's story comprehension. *American Educational Research Journal* 19: 443–452.

Peterman, C.L., D. Dunning, and J. Mason. 1985. *A storybook reading event: How a teacher's presentation effects kindergarten children's subsequent attemps to read from the text.* Paper presented at the annual meeting of the National Reading Conference, San Diego.

Plessas, G.P., and C.R. Oakes. 1964. Prereading experiences of selected early readers. *The Reading Teacher* 17: 241–245.

Price, E.H. 1976. How thirty-seven gifted children learned to read. *The Reading Teacher* 30: 44–48.

Roser, N., and M. Martinez. 1985. Roles adults play in preschoolers' response to literature. *Language Arts* 62: 485–490.

Sloan, G. 1984. *The child as critic.* New York: Teacher's College Press.

Smith, F. 1978. *Understanding reading.* 2d ed. New York: Holt, Rinehart & Winston.

Smith, F. 1982. *Understanding reading.* 3d ed. New York: Holt, Rinehart & Winston.

Snow, C.E. 1983. Literacy and language: Relationships during the preschool years. *Harvard Educational Review* 53: 165–189.

Snow, C.E. 1977. The development of conversation between mothers and babies. *Journal of Child Language* 4: 1–22.

Snow, C.E., and B.A. Goldfield. 1983. Turn the page, please: Situation-specific language acquisition. *Journal of Child Language* 10: 535–549.

State Education Department. 1989. *Listening and speaking in the English language arts.* Albany, N.Y.: New York State Education Department.

Sulzby, E. 1985. Children's emergent reading of favorite storybooks: A developmental study. *Reading Research Quarterly* 20: 458–481.

Sulzby, E., and W.H. Teale. 1987. Young children's storybook reading: A longitudinal study of parent-child interaction and children's independent functioning. (Final Report to the Spencer Foundation). Ann Arbor: The University of Michigan.

Teale, W.H., and E. Sulzby. 1986. *Emergent literacy: Writing and reading.* Norwood, N.J.: Ablex.

Thomas, K.F. 1985. Early reading as a social interaction process. *Language Arts* 62: 469–475.

Torrey, J. 1973. Learning to read without a teacher: A case study. In *Psycholinguistics and Reading,* ed. F. Smith. New York: Holt, Rinehart & Winston.

Trousdale, A.M. 1990. Interactive storytelling: Scaffolding children's early narratives. *Language Arts* 67: 164–173.

Vygotsky, L.S. 1978. *Mind in society: The development of higher psychological processes.* M. Cole, V. Johnsteiner, S. Scribner, and E. Souberman, editors and translators. Cambridge, Mass.: Harvard University Press.

Wells, G. 1986. *The meaning makers: Children learning language and using language to learn.* Portsmouth, N.H.: Heinemann.

Yade, D.B., Jr. 1985. Preschoolers' spontaneous inquiries about print and books. Paper presented at the annual meeting of the National Reading Conference, San Diego.

Yaden, D.B., Jr., L.B. Smolkin, and A. Conlon. 1989. Preschoolers' questions about pictures, print conventions and story text during reading aloud at home. *Reading Research Quarterly* 24: 188–214.

UNIT 3

In Writing

UNIT GOALS

After completing this unit, the reader should:

* understand the concept of writing competence.
* distinguish between a traditional approach and a process approach to writing.
* be able to identify children's writing while it is developing during the period from birth to age eight.
* develop an awareness of what constitutes the written products of young children.
* develop a knowledge of the skills and abilities young children can begin to develop.
* develop a repertoire of activities that can be used to encourage the development of writing skills in young children.

PREVIEW

The modern world is immersed in written words and visual images. Children are consistently exposed to print and pictures at a very young age. Newspapers, mail, posters, billboards, signs, and books are constantly seen by the young child.

Shortly after they are able to hold and move a crayon, marker, or other writing implement, children begin to make some of their own marks on paper, floors, walls, and doors. Adults may prefer that children confine most of their markings to paper. Children are less concerned about where they will use their crayons. Because adults seem to place some special importance on these markings that are known as

writing, children develop an interest in making sense of them.

All of these factors, early markings, drawings, and an interest in writing, are the beginnings of written expression for the young child. The development of writing ability begins in the first few years and can continue throughout life. This unit, which explores these early beginnings, develops the following key ideas:

* Concept of writing competence
* Traditional approach to teaching writing
* Process approach to teaching writing
* The role of the teacher and other adults

- Stages of writing development
- Observation of children as writers
- Skills and objectives of a writing program
- Activities for a writing program

INTRODUCTION

Language serves as a tool for helping children to learn and communicate. As with listening and speaking skills, children who are able to use writing as a tool for learning and communicating will expand their range of possibilities as human beings. Children grow in writing skill in developmental patterns that reflect their ability to make sense of the world and the writing process. Children vary widely in this development. Given these factors, however, it is believed that opportunities and instruction designed to facilitate growth are most effective when they take into consideration the integrated connections of all the language arts. That is, language is best learned in a natural manner that does not break it into isolated and artificially defined fragments.

Based on these assumptions about writing, the focus of the unit will be on a process approach to writing. Such an approach suggests instructional procedures, roles for teachers, and beliefs about the development of writing. These may differ from those that have traditionally been used in early childhood and elementary school programs.

WRITING COMPETENCE

In order to think about how to teach children to develop writing skills, it is necessary to come to an understanding of writing itself. If you were to ask a dozen people on the street what writing is, you would probably receive about a dozen different answers. Among the possibilities are:

> *"Writing is making neat letters and words."*
> *"Writing is telling a story."*
> *"Writing is putting your thoughts on paper."*
> *"Writing is talk written down."*
> *"Writing is a part of being literate."*
> *"Writing is hard work with a pencil and paper."*

While there may be some truth in some of these statements, they aren't particularly helpful to individuals who are attempting to help children develop writing skills.

Developing a broader philosophy about the meaning of schooling and learning is needed before deciding on what constitutes writing competence. That is, teachers must first answer the question, "What is the purpose of education?" This question must be answered because it forms the rationale for much of the writing children do in school. Given this, the answer also establishes the role of the teacher in teaching writing.

Mosenthal (1983) addresses the question as it relates to writing. His view establishes a variety of sociopolitical purposes of education. It is helpful to consider education from a sociological perspective since schools are a major social force. Since schools are frequently controlled, either directly or indirectly, by various political processes, it is necessary to understand this influence as well. For the purposes of this discussion, three potential purposes of education are examined. They correspond somewhat to the two extreme positions and the center position in the continuum developed by Mosenthal. They are identified here as cultural, developmental, and liberated purposes.

Cultural Purpose

Seeing education as having a purely cultural purpose suggests that the primary mission of a school or educational program is to pass important cultural knowledge from one generation to another. The teacher's role is as a keeper of the culture and dispenser of knowledge and skills. Learners are viewed as possessing little knowledge or ability of any relevance to the learning situation. The goal of education is to hone the skills of the learners until they are able to demonstrate correct knowledge, skills, and attitudes.

Within this purpose, writing might be seen as the ability to produce correct forms of letters, words, sentences, and pieces of writing. Writing instruction in early childhood and the lower grades would be largely confined to forming correct letters, spelling, punctuation, handwriting, and simple declarative sentences. In the upper grades, there would be a continuing emphasis on spelling and grammar with the addition of such things as correct phrasing and correct formats for different types of writing. Such a view tends to see students' writing as either correct or incorrect according to such things as the rules of grammar, spelling, usage, and letter formation.

Developmental Purpose

Viewing education as having mainly a developmental purpose gives the school the primary mission of helping children to grow intellectually by enhancing the child's interactions with the people and objects in the environment. Learning is not seen so much as the gathering of new facts. Rather, learning is viewed as an increase in the ability to deal with ideas that are increasingly complex. The role of the teacher is to provide opportunities for the child to deal with situations in which there is enough challenge to foster growth.

Writing instruction for this purpose would emphasize the growth of the writer. The teacher would not need to focus so much on the correctness of forms. Instead, teachers might encourage learners to break free from the concrete and to view objects, people, and events from different perspectives. As such, individual differences among young writers would be tolerated and accepted.

Liberated Purpose

Viewing the purpose of education as a liberating force gives schools the primary mission of changing the social order. This view of education recognizes that schools as they are currently set up are part of the existing social order and as such have an interest in maintaining that social order even if it means perpetuating such negative aspects of society as class distinctions. This view assumes that in traditional programs students of different social orders are taught differently in order to maintain class distinctions.

Writing instruction in this model would include instruction that enables all students to engage in higher level thinking and communication skills so that they might have the ability to effect changes in the social order. The specific instruction would be determined by the needs of the child. The goal, however, is to enable those who are historically the least well educated to achieve an equal social footing with those who, because of their social class, have been more educationally advantaged.

Most likely no school or program operates in total conformity with any of these purposes. Educators, like most people, tend to be eclectic. They choose ideas, concepts, and beliefs from a variety of sources to develop personal and institutional philosophies and policies. However, one can investigate these policies and practices in order to determine the basic beliefs about the purpose of education under which a specific school or program operates. In this way, one can identify the underlying beliefs of different programs as being on different places on a continuum.

The position taken by this text is between the developmental purposes and liberated purposes. The authors believe that children should be provided with instruction that is both developmentally appropriate and that enables them to continually grow in ways over which they have some control. Further, the authors believe that education should provide children with the ability to effectively participate in the future direction society will take. This means that the ability to think clearly, to look at situations from different angles, and to solve problems in new ways will be increasingly valuable. Education should not be seen solely as a process whereby children accumulate pieces of information. In the future, people will be able to survive or succeed based not only on what they know, but by how they deal with what they do not know.

LINEAR APPROACH TO WRITING

Traditionally, the approach used to teach writing in schools can best be described as a linear approach. This means that each of the steps in writing follows a straight line from a specific beginning to a specific end. The assumptions of the approach hold that young children do not really begin to learn to write until they reach the point where they can begin to be taught letter formation and the writing of some simple words. While this view is not the approach taken in this book, it is important to be aware of its characteristics, instructional procedures, and view concerning the role of the teacher. In this way, it can be identified accurately when it is confronted.

Characteristics

A traditional approach to writing holds that elements of writing are best learned separately, that children should master these skills independently, that writing is a subject onto itself, and that student writing should be evaluated primarily in terms of its mechanical accuracy. The approach is closely associated with a belief system that conforms to a cultural purpose philosophy of education. Each of the characteristics of the traditional approach is described here.

Separate elements.

For many years, children have been taught writing skills in ways that keep those elements isolated from each other. In preschool and kindergarten, children have been taught to identify and copy letters. The alphabet and children's names are often the only source of context. Children in the early primary grades study spelling, punctuation, and grammar as separate subjects. When these skills are addressed in contexts, it is often in sentences written by a textbook or workbook author rather than in sentences the children have written. While it is not often stated, the assumption is that children will somehow be able to integrate each of these separate skills into their own writing. This is often not the case, however.

Independent mastery.

In a traditional approach, children are expected to work independently. Sharing ideas and helping each other is not encouraged. There is an implied belief that in the real world people must be able to do these things by themselves. It is sometimes cited that in the middle school grades, high school, and college, students must be able to perform independently. As such, this argument is often used to justify the policy of maintaining independent work in writing in early childhood.

Separate subject.

In addition to teaching the elements of writing in a non-integrated manner, writing itself is usually viewed as a separate subject in a traditional language arts program. It is integrated with neither other language arts areas nor other content areas. Topics for writing are often assigned by a teacher without regard to the interests of the children and without regard to other subjects being studied at the time. While children may be asked to write as part of a reading or social studies program, they are ordinarily not taught how to write about reading or social studies. In addition, writing assignments are often confined to a limited number of forms such as essays and book reports.

Evaluation of the mechanics.

The approach to evaluation reinforces each of the other characteristics of a traditional approach to writing. Student writing is generally assessed in terms of how well it conforms to the norms of standard English spelling, handwriting, punctuation, capitalization, grammar, usage, and so forth. Quite often, mistakes are noted with red circles and coded with such comments as "sp" to denote a spelling error. Thoughtful considered responses by the teacher to the content of the writing are seldom provided to the children. In general, the only person to read the child's paper is the teacher. The teacher ordinarily neither reads nor assesses the child's writing until after it is completed.

Instructional Procedure

In keeping with the concept of a linear approach, the instructional procedure of a traditional writing program follows a simple step-by-step approach. There is little difference whether the child is five or fifteen years old. The procedure is basically the same. As seen in Figure 3-1, it involves a step-by-step process, with each step being started only after the previous step has been completed.

At the beginning of the procedure, a topic is usually assigned, and the writers outline their pieces. The usual format suggested is the traditional outline using numbers, Roman numerals, capital letters, and lowercase letters. While outlining thoughts can be helpful, the traditional outline is a device many children find less than helpful (Sawyer 1978).

After an outline is completed, students are instructed to compose a first draft in pencil. This entails writing sentences and paragraphs following the information contained in the formal outline.

When the first draft is completed, the writers are directed to edit their written work for mechanical errors and to copy it over in a final draft in neat handwriting. Both the first draft and the final draft are assigned as homework rather than as classroom activ-

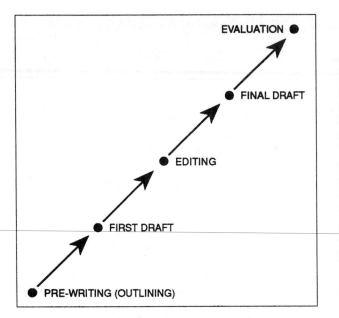

FIGURE 3-1 A linear approach sees writing as a series of steps to be accomplished one at a time.

ities. When the procedure is completed, the piece of writing is handed in to the teacher who corrects, grades, and returns the paper.

Role of the Teacher

In a traditional linear approach, the teacher is clearly the master of the learning environment. The teacher is in sole charge of assigning topics, teaching the skills of writing, setting timelines for completion of work, and evaluation of the writing. Instruction in the skills of writing is most often done through workbook pages and ditto sheets that are corrected by the teacher. The teacher serves as the primary audience for the majority of student writing.

Due to the necessity of assessing all of the papers, workbook pages, dittos, and other worksheets, the teacher's time is largely spent on clerical and administrative activities. There is little time left for the teacher to engage in writing. There is little time for sharing either student or teacher writing with the rest of the class. Since the teacher is responsible for the correction and evaluation of student writing, there is little need seen for such sharing.

PROCESS APPROACH TO WRITING

The integrated approach to language arts makes use of what is known as a process approach to writing. Whereas the traditional approach focuses on the products of student writing, the process approach focuses on the process of how students learn to write as having equal if not greater importance than the products of the writing. Paramount to this view is the belief that the finished products of student writing do not inform the teacher about how the students arrived at those products. Further, it is believed that only by becoming aware of that writing process can teachers design and implement effective instruction. As a result of these beliefs, the characteristics, instructional procedures, and roles of the teacher are strikingly distinct in a process approach to writing.

Characteristics

The characteristics of a process approach to writing tend to focus on how children go about the task of learning to write and improving their writing. In view of this, it should not be surprising that one might see children engaging in the writing process at a much earlier age than in the traditional classroom. The reason for this is the belief that children begin writing well before the point where they can produce a conventional written product whether that written product is a single letter or a ten-page essay. The actual steps in the development of writing is described later in the discussion on writing development. The following characteristics form the basic assumptions of a process approach.

Non-linear Sequence.

The first characteristic of a process approach to writing is the belief that writing does not follow a neat set of steps in a sequence. While it may sound logical to develop an outline, write a rough draft, edit it, and rewrite it in a final copy, true writers do not follow that process. When people write they may take notes and develop some outlines about their topic, but they do many other things as well. They may talk about the topic, wander around the room, take a walk, read about their topic, or simply think about it. They may draft a paragraph about it and then read or think about it some more. Anyone who has done a fair amount of writing can attest to the fact that it doesn't happen in the smooth, sequential way that the traditional approach to writing promotes.

Holistic View.

A process approach to writing views writing as a whole rather than a collection of small pieces. Content, organization, sentences, words, and mechanics only have relevance if they are seen as parts of a whole piece of writing. This does not negate the importance of any of these elements of writing. Rather it places them within a total view that may or may not stress them at various times during the writing process. For example, for much of the early phase of writing a piece, correct spelling of each word is not particularly important. No one but the writer is going to read it at this point. The writer, knowing the particular topic, will be able to continue working with the piece even though each word may not be spelled correctly. Likewise, at the final stage when the physical appearance of the piece is being polished, the focus on content will be diminished, and more stress will be placed on mechanics.

Authorship.

Children view themselves as authors in a process writing program. They see themselves as writing for a wide audience of peers and others, rather than just for their teacher. By interacting with their audience about their writing, children are motivated to revise their writing as a result of the audience feedback (Lamme 1989). By serving as both author and audience for others, children acquire the ability to be perceptive readers and writers (Hubbard 1985). By providing opportunities for children to participate in these roles, young writers learn how to discuss books and writing while they develop into a community of writers (Graves and Hansen 1983).

Three stages of understanding the concept of authorship have been identified in young children by Graves and Hansen (1983). The first stage focuses on the replication of familiar books and authors. Children view authors as people who write books that people enjoy. As such, children may imitate many of their favorite stories and writing styles. In the second stage, transition, children begin to see the possibility of

FIGURE 3-2 The writing process begins even before the child draws a picture and tells about it.

themselves as authors. They write stories that are accepted by others as meaningful pieces of literature. The stories are rightly placed next to the commercially published books in the room. The third stage, option awareness, occurs when children come to an understanding of themselves as responsible for making decisions about their writing. This stage emerges as a result of children having the opportunity to share their writings with an audience that provides feedback.

Conferencing.

One of the most critical characteristics of a process writing classroom is the provision for children to participate in conferences about their writing. While children may confer with the teacher about their work, it is essential that children also confer with the larger audience of their peers about their writing. These sessions may be called the "author's chair" or a peer conference, but the essence is still the same. The young writer has the opportunity to participate in the community of writers as both an author and as part of an audience.

A conference session typically contains a group of three to five students. Each student is given an opportunity to read or describe a piece currently being written. The piece may be in the form of notes, an illustration, or a draft. After sharing the piece, others in the group are given the opportunity to provide feedback to the author. The purpose of the conference is not to evaluate the piece. Therefore, neither negative comments nor statements about the relative quality of the piece are appropriate. Feedback should include information that helps the author determine whether the message is getting across and whether decisions need to be made about the writing in a revised draft. This process can and should be frequently modeled in both small and large groups by the teacher. Some of the appropriate responses to an author might begin with phrases such as:

> *"Your story seems to be saying . . ."*
> *"Why did the wolf ask the little girl . . ."*
> *"I didn't understand why the mother did . . ."*
> *"I would really like to know more about . . ."*
> *"What did the monster look like?"*
> *"What happened to . . ."*

The author of the story should not necessarily answer these questions orally at the conference. The comments should be viewed as feedback provided by an interested and supportive audience. They represent the kinds of questions others reading the story might also have. The author must make a decision about what to do with these questions. This entails deciding whether or not the piece is unclear, whether it needs more descriptive information, or whether the piece possibly includes irrelevant ideas. In a process writing program it is not unusual for children to write a number of revised drafts of a single piece, each time refining the piece based on audience feedback.

Younger children may not have actually written the words to their stories. Instead, they may be telling a story orally, based on a picture they have drawn. The feedback to the author is no less useful. Children should have many opportunities to share their developing authorship through language. The feedback serves the same purposes for a subsequent oral retelling as it does for a subsequent written draft.

Child-centered.

A process writing classroom sees child growth as a critical feature of the program. The purpose of the program is not to enable the child to produce technically correct words, sentences, and stories. Rather, the purpose is to provide developmentally appropriate activities that enable the child to experience growth in writing at the pace that is natural for that child. What is best for children in such a situation is an environment that provides a safe place for them to take risks with the language. As young authors, children need to make choices about the stories they will write or tell. They need to feel comfortable when they decide to attempt different literary forms such as poetry, advertisements, rhymes, and fantasy.

As children attempt to spell new words, teachers must accept their attempts. These attempts at spelling are often referred to as invented, inventive, developmental, or phonetic spelling. They are often based on words that have been seen in print or on the sounds children hear and match to letters. It is particularly important for adults not to go over these errors with a red pen, making corrections. Such actions can crush the confidence of a young child as a writer. The invented spellings are not wrong; they are merely incomplete. As children grow more accustomed to seeing the correct spellings in print, the invented spellings often disappear with little or no instruction or correction from adults.

Integration.

In a process writing classroom, writing is not a separate subject (DeGroff 1989; Goodman 1986; Smith 1982). It is integrated with reading, literature, other content areas, and the arts. Emergent literacy studies suggest that children's natural acquisition of literacy is related to an attachment to certain books, book authors, and the ownership they have over their own writing (Lamme 1989). When children read only basal readers, and only for the purpose of answering worksheet questions, they tend not to see the connection between reading and writing. Likewise, when they write only to provide something for the teacher to correct, the link between reading and writing is further obscured.

Responding to literature not only connects reading and writing, but can also provide a rich field of possibilities to write about. Children may respond to literature in writing, through illustration or by oral response. If it is done in writing, it can be done in a writing journal on a regular basis. Teacher reactions to the responses of children can encourage still further thinking about the story that was read. If children have not yet developed handwriting skills, their responses through illustration and oral discussion can serve the same purpose. Each type of response helps to link reading with writing and the other language arts. Each type of response helps children see that writing is done by real people for real reasons. Writers write to inform, entertain, and persuade their readers. By bringing these ideas into a discussion with young children, teachers can help youngsters make the reading/writing connection.

Instructional Procedures

The procedures for providing instruction in a process classroom are markedly different from the routines of a classroom following a linear approach. The classroom is a much less formal place. Children may be working on more than one piece of writing or illustration at any given time. Children will not all be writing on the same topic. Some children may be working independently while others are meeting in an author's chair or a conference group. There are few whole group lessons, but the teacher may frequently meet with small groups of children to teach a skill they may need at the time.

The view of writing held by teachers in a process classroom, while not visually observable in the room, is quite different from the view of teachers who use a linear model. In a process classroom, writing is seen as a recursive process. Figure 3-3 illustrates the basic framework that encompasses the recursive model. The recursive model usually includes the following stages in the process: planning, drafting, revising, editing/proofreading, and publishing. Each of these is described in the following sections.

Before describing the individual elements, however, it is necessary to have a fuller understanding of how a recursive model of writing operates. Figure 3-3 provides an outline, but it is incomplete. If it were complete, the recursive model would not be fundamentally different from a linear model, as illustrated in Figure 3-1. The major difference would be that one appears to be a straight line and the other a circle. The term "recursive" means to circle back. This is what provides an essential difference between the two models. At any point along the way, the writer can and should circle back to a previous stage as needed. All planning is not done prior to all drafting. All drafting is not completed prior to any revision. Writers do not operate in a neat, orderly manner. It is unrealistic to impose such a step-by-step model on emerging writers. As readers and writers who think, we constantly find the need to go back to re-read and re-write sections of a text. At times, we realize that we do not have enough information to justify a point or to provide sufficient examples. When that occurs, we may review our notes or illustrations again in order to re-plan our text. These same events naturally take place with emerging writers. Therefore, a more complete illustration of the recursive model is found in Figure 3-4. Each of the elements in a recursive model must be seen as having multiple occurrences as a child engages in writing.

Planning.

Activities that involve generating content, organizing content, and developing goals for writing are included in the planning process (Humes 1983). Whether the child is actually writing words, drawing an illustration, or developing a story orally makes no difference. As will be seen later, these are all developmentally related to writing.

Generating content includes anything the child does to provide material for possible inclusion in the piece. Observing the activities of the fire station in preparation for a language experience story (LEA) the group will write when they return to the classroom is a planning activity. Children talking about the pictures they will create to describe the story they have just heard are engaged in a planning activity. A five-year-old drawing a picture illustrating a favorite summer activity to accompany a story to be written using inventive spelling is engaged in planning. A teacher writing down

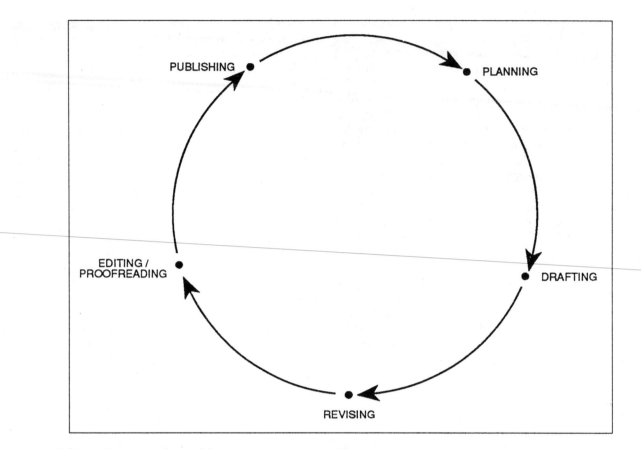

FIGURE 3-3 A recursive model sees writing as a process that circles back upon itself throughout the process.

ideas the children provide orally for a Thanksgiving story is actually engaging the children in a planning process. The child who is staring out the window while thinking about what to include in a story is engaged in planning. Clearly, this view is quite flexible when compared to the outline type of prewriting found in the more traditional linear approach to writing.

Organizing content refers to making decisions about the inclusion and structuring of the content. Young children often place pictures and words on a paper in a rather random order. This is content generation with little organization. As children discover how language works, they begin to engage in more organizational strategies. They decide that some content belongs on their paper and other content does not. They make a decision not to include a picture of a fire truck in the illustration showing their vacation

at the beach. In addition, they may decide to include only immediate family members in the beach picture despite the fact that there were hundreds of other people at the beach on that day. They also decide to draw the beach at the bottom of the picture and the sun up near the top. They may also decide to leave a space at the bottom of the illustration to label each of the people with their names. All of these actions are organizational. They are aimed at making the meaning of the message clear and conforming with the remembrance of the day in the writer's mind.

Setting goals refers to making decisions about how best to complete the overall task. Writers of all ages tend to set goals that address both content and procedures. Writers may decide to complete the task by including or not including illustrations, examples, descriptions, humor, and so forth. They may also decide

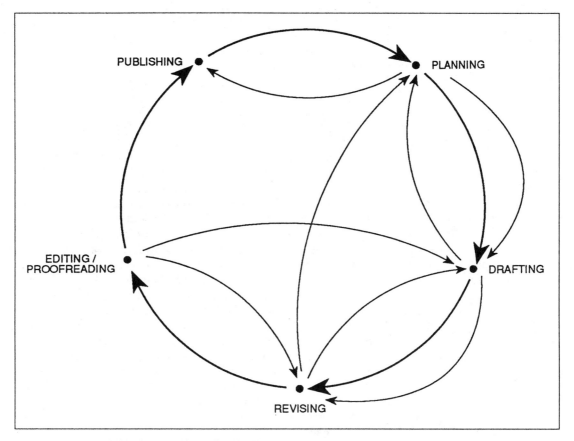

FIGURE 3-4 An expanded recursive model of writing shows how different stages of the writing process may occur several times before a piece is completed.

to use a narrative approach, poetry, or other genre to make their message clear.

Besides the three elements of planning, writers need to do two other things early in their piece. Both are best described as meta-writing elements. First, writers must be aware of the purpose of their writing. There is a world of difference between writing something because the teacher demands it and writing something because the writer wants to share an exciting incident that occurred over the weekend. In a process classroom, children take on much more of the reponsibility of developing their own topics. This leads to more ownership, emotional involvement, and motivation for writing. The second thing that writers must be aware of is the potential audience for the piece being written, illustrated, or developed for oral

retelling. Again, it makes a difference whether the audience is the teacher or the child's peers. In a process writing classroom there is an emphasis on writing for a wide range of potential audiences: peers, parents, cousins, children in other classes, etc.

Drafting.

Drafting is the process of placing on paper the ideas and images that evolved in the planning process. At times, drafting and planning are combined. That is, it is sometimes difficult to develop ideas without writing them down or making a picture or diagram of them. Two important elements are associated with the drafting process: learning and automaticity.

Whenever a child is engaged in content in a meaningful way, increased learning can take place. When a child is drawing a picture depicting the story that was just read aloud to the group, that child is engaged in drafting as part of the writing process. The illustration is a developmentally appropriate response to literature. To develop and complete the picture, the child must recall important details from the story. The child must re-create the story in the mind. Such re-creation is a meaningful interaction with the story. The more frequent these interactions, the greater the depth of knowledge about the story. As children recall more and more details, they may add things to the illustration.

Automaticity is a second element of importance to the drafting part of the writing process. Automaticity refers to the ability to do two things at once: one consciously and one subconsciously. People of all ages engage in various types of automatic behaviors. When walking down the street we automatically step over rocks and uneven edges of the sidewalk with virtually no conscious attention. When young children first begin to write letters and words it takes great effort and mental focus to do such things as stay on the line, form the letters correctly, spell the words, and leave spaces between words. As a result, children tend to focus more on the appearance of the writing than on the content of the writing. The same thing is true for younger children whose writing consists mostly of drawings. As they become more proficient, however, they are able to concentrate less on forming the actual letters and pictures and focus more attention on the content. When this occurs, they are developing more automaticity. They are able to form the words and pictures with the pencil or crayon, while at the same time making decisions about the content of the piece. It is a critical skill to develop. Traditional approaches to literacy spend much time on the correctness of the final product, often decreasing the amount of focus on content. An integrated approach places the correctness of the product in a more manageable perspective. By virtue of the fact that children in integrated process writing classrooms spend more time in actual writing, many of the mechanical aspects of writing become automatic, with much less teacher instruction.

Revision.

The process of revision involves making changes in a piece in order to make it conform to the intentions

of the author. During the planning and drafting stages, the writer must keep in mind the original intentions for the piece. It is possible for some of these intentions to change as the piece is developed. A child may add an incident to the text or delete a character from an illustration. During revision, there is more focus on the audience. The writer must make predictions about whether or not the piece will clearly convey the writer's intentions to the perceived audience. This is often done by stepping back and looking at the whole illustration or reading parts of the text.

A key facet of revision is the focus on meaning. A variety of procedures can be used to clarify meaning. Information can be added, deleted, or changed. Transitions can be made more clear. For example, a cause and effect relationship can be created to link two incidents in the story. Emotion-producing language can be added or deleted to emphasize or de-emphasize an element of the story. The case is similar when the child's writing consists mainly of drawings. In the pictures created by children, distinctive characters, large pointed teeth, bunnies, colored leaves, and monsters take the place of words. The changes that involve the revision of these pictures create the same effects as the changes made in a text written with words.

Editing and Proofreading.

Making sure that the mechanical details of the piece are correct and clear is best done near the completion of a piece. This, of course, is not always the point at which it is done. Writers can't seem to resist the urge to correct misspelled words, poorly formed letters, incorrect subject/verb agreement, and faulty punctuation as soon as such things are noticed. We all find ourselves doing it. The reason for this, of course, is that for years we have had this behavior reinforced in schools. The correctness of the written product has long been the benchmark of writing proficiency.

The correctness of the written product is seen as one of the goals of a process writing program. However, correctness of the written product is attended to at a time when it does not interfere with making the meaning of the piece clear. When a writer focuses on changing a misspelled word while writing a draft, it takes the writer's attention away from the content of the piece. After the word has been corrected, the writer must shift attention back to content. Unfortunately, the train of thought is broken along with any automaticity that was developed. Continued editing through the drafting phase results in a series of attention refocusing acts. It is ironic that the only one who really needs to read the initial draft is the actual writer, who could have read or understood the piece even with all of the mechanical errors included. Editing at the planning, drafting, and revising stages generally serves no useful purpose. Rather, it detracts from the whole writing process.

When a writer is approaching the point of being ready to share the story or picture with others, editing and proofreading become important. Correctness of the written product is done to show pride in completing the piece and to enable the audience to understand the piece. When done just prior to sharing, editing and proofreading enhance the product without distracting the writer from other stages of the process.

Basic skills.

Several basic skills assist children as they attempt to engage in the writing process. Children learn these skills at different times. There are few skills that are needed by all children at the same time. This does not mean that there should not be whole group instruction in language use.

When whole group instruction is used, it should be done with great care. Brief, clear, and well-focused lessons are best. The teacher needs to make a decision about whether or not the skill is, in fact, appropriate for most children in the group. At other times, minilessons with small groups of children are more appropriate. If five children are having difficulty holding a crayon or pencil, they can be instructed in such a way that it occurs within a meaningful context for them. Perhaps an art activity dealing with the topic the group has chosen for the week would serve as an appropriate task. Having children engage in meaningless activities such as drawing circles on a worksheet would not be appropriate. Such an activity sends a message to children that they are different and less able. It tells them that they do not possess the needed skills to do what the other children are doing. It is an unfortunate message that is too often sent to children.

FIGURE 3-5 Young writers need many opportunities to draw and write.

Role of the Teacher

In a process writing classroom, the role of the teacher is both challenging and fascinating. It is challenging because it requires the teacher to broaden the traditional ideas of what is involved in being a teacher. It is fascinating because the teacher becomes much more attuned to the thinking of children as writers. The role provides opportunities for self-renewal and professional growth right in the classroom. A teacher in a process writing classroom does not merely assign projects and evaluate them. In contrast to that traditional role, a process writing teacher provides opportunities, models the writing process, and assesses all aspects of the program.

Providing Opportunities.

Writing is often viewed as sharing ideas. The writer possesses an experience, story, or idea that is meaningful. Since human beings are social creatures, they have a natural inclination to share the experience. On the other hand, if children do not feel they have meaningful experiences worth sharing the teacher has a twofold role. The first role is to help children see that their lives do indeed have experiences that can serve as content for writing that is worth sharing. This can be done through group discussions, individual conferences, show and tell, and so forth. The second role is to provide additional experiences within the classroom that can be shared with parents, peers, and others.

Literature and sharing stories provide a rich and varied experience base for children. After listening to a story, children can re-create the story through an illustration or extend it through creating a new story that uses the same characters. Field trips and classroom visitors can serve as experiences for language experience stories in which the children orally retell the experience while the teacher writes their dictated thoughts on a chart. Encouraging children to reflect on their own experiences provides opportunities and topics for writing. Finally, time must be built into the program for writing. A regularly scheduled period each day should be allocated for children to engage in writing. While some children may possess the actual ability to form words and sentences, the time can also be used for planning, revising, drawing, and oral storytelling as parts of the writing process.

Modeling.

Another key ingredient of the process writing classroom is teacher involvement in the activities of the student. Modeling is the process of demonstrating how to do something. It is a powerful tool in language arts instruction. In developing the writing skills of young children, modeling is particularly effective, as it serves a variety of functions. By being involved and sharing one's own writing, a teacher sends a message that writing is a very important thing. By sharing writing with children and listening to their responses, teachers demonstrate key components of the process by which children can improve their own writing. The self-esteem of children is enhanced as they come to realize that they can help adults improve their writing by responding to it.

Finally, by modeling the writing process with their own writing, teachers can efficiently demonstrate key skills that they feel various children may need in their own writing. As this modeling of the process is done, it is often helpful for teachers to talk out loud about what they are doing and thinking. They may share why they are doing something, how they plan to change something, what a word means, and so forth. This reinforces the fact that writing is a thinking process and that it is necessary to reflect on one's writing.

Assessment.

Assessment refers to the act of collecting and gathering data in order to better understand something. As used here, it does not include the judgments made about the data in an evaluation process. The focus here is on understanding something. In a process writing classroom, one needs to assess several factors: the teacher's system of beliefs, the skills and needs of children, and the classroom environment.

The role of a teacher is that of a coordinator of opportunities. While direct teaching is involved, all children do not need the same instruction at the same time. Therefore, there is only a limited amount of whole group instruction. When it does occur, it is more geared to teaching about the process than about the product of writing. An assessment of the teacher's role can be done by responding to a series of statements. On a scale of 1 (never) to 5 (always), how would you respond to the following:

1. I read professional literature about writing.
2. I share ideas with my colleagues about writing.
3. I make writing a significant part of my classroom.
4. I demonstrate how writing can be a tool for understanding.
5. I involve my children in a variety of different kinds of writing.
6. I insure that students have opportunities to write for audiences other than myself.
7. I insure that students have opportunities to engage in writing that informs, entertains, and persuades.
8. I expect writing projects to take place over varying lengths of time.
9. I provide opportunities for students to share their ideas, illustrations, and writing with their peers.
10. I evaluate how the student writes as well as what the student writes.
11. I evaluate for content.
12. I individualize my writing instruction.
13. I respect student opinions that differ from my own.
14. I like to teach writing.
15. I am successful at teaching writing.

The last two questions are critical. The teacher does not have to be a great writer to either like to teach writing or to be successful at teaching writing. The teacher merely has to be a writer who enjoys the challenge of writing. Children can detect false enthusiasm. When they see that a teacher doesn't like writing, they get the message that writing is distasteful. When they see genuine enthusiasm, they get the message that writing can be meaningful and enjoyable. The more a teacher responds with "5's" to the above questions, the closer the teacher is to being a process writing teacher.

It is necessary to learn about the skills, abilities, and interests of children. By doing this, the teacher learns about the possible topics in which to engage the children. The teacher also gains an understanding of which skills to teach to which children. This information can be obtained from a variety of sources: child interviews, parent interviews, observation of children interacting with others, a collection of papers the child has done at home, and informal tasks given to the child in the classroom.

The classroom can be assessed to determine whether or not it is an appropriate environment for writing. While clean, flat surfaces are necessary, they do not have to be in the form of rows of desks. Tables, floors, and laptop boards all work just as well. Areas that provide a comfortable place for sharing are necessary. Display areas for completed papers and books are needed. These can be shelves, bulletin boards, or ropes stretched across the room to which student work is attached with clothespins. A well-lit area with various types of writing surfaces, pencils, crayons, markers, paints, scissors, tape, and glue must be accessible. Writing surfaces might include paper, poster board, cardboard, porcelain board, chalkboard, and fabric.

Assessment at this level should not be seen as evaluation other than as that needed to make some adjustments in the instruction. The purpose here is not to grade or place a value on student work. Instead, it is to help the teacher determine if the necessary pieces are in place to enhance the writing instruction and the learning of the children.

Writing Development

Children begin to engage in the process of writing well before they are given formal writing instruction in the early grades. Children learn early that the marks on a paper have some meaning. As they see adults attending carefully to those marks, they realize that the marks are important. They begin to make attempts at creating writing products soon after they can hold a writing tool.

Writing Products.

Figure 3-6 illustrates a typical example of early printing. In viewing this piece, note that some of the designs do tend to look like letters and punctuation marks. This may indicate that this child has noticed these in writing the child has seen. It is unlikely that the child could explain it in this way, however. Other children may or may not make early attempts at writing that look exactly like this. They may simply move a crayon back and forth on a paper, or make circles on a poster. While this particular example occurred with a child of about three years old, it could probably have occurred a year earlier or a year later. This concept should be kept in mind with all of the examples of children's writing depicted in this unit. While ages of the children who produced the examples may be given, other children may vary widely in the age at

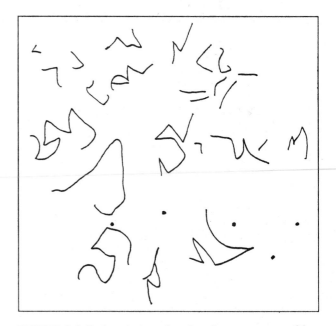

FIGURE 3-6 Early printing often has the appearance of letters.

which they could produce similar examples. In fact, other children may produce examples that do not seem anything like those presented here.

Figures 3-7 through 3-13 illustrate a progression of changes that occured in a child between the ages of three-and-one-half to about four-and-one-half years. Figure 3-7, drawn at about age three-and-one-half, is an illustration without written text accompanying it. This does not mean that there was not a language component to it. After completing this illustration, the child was asked to tell about the picture. The child responded that the picture contained, from left to right, "My Dad, my house, the grass, and me." The teacher showed wise judgment in asking the child to tell about the picture. Children are very emotionally attached to their art and writing. They believe that their pictures are clear and accurate. They are highly insulted with questions such as, "What's that a picture of?" Simply asking children to tell about their pictures alleviates the problem of not recognizing what the child has drawn.

Figure 3-8 was produced two months after Figure 3-7 and contains both an illustration and text. The text demonstrates an emerging awareness of letters.

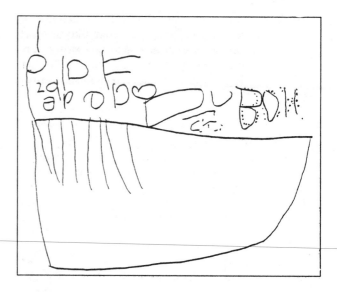

FIGURE 3-8 Children often attempt to add text to their drawings prior to going to kindergarten.

FIGURE 3-7 At about age three or four, children's writing often consists of a drawing with an oral statement by the child.

Rather than actually corresponding to specific words, these figures were placed on the paper because the child recognized that words and pictures are often found together. Some of the characters on the left side of the illustration are not actually letters, while some of the characters on the right have been adorned with dots. Children at this age do not tend to distinguish between art and writing. They see the two as being basically the same. Both are viewed as a means of self expression. In essence, the children are absolutely correct.

About one month after producing the piece in Figure 3-8, the child drew and labeled the self-portrait found in Figure 3-9. Increased control over the use of a pencil is seen. Some of the child's personal characteristics such as the happy smile and curly hair have been represented. The letters above the illustration are the child's attempt at spelling her name, Octavia. While not spelled completely, it was a successful attempt. Several of the actual letters of her name are present. At this point, spelling accuracy is not a problem. Much more important is the fact that the child has demonstrated a critically important aspect of early writing: the connection of symbol with reality. The child has demonstrated that the picture, which looks something like her, represents her. In addition,

FIGURE 3-9 Octavia's self-portrait

without any illustration. While the text is still difficult for an adult to interpret, it suggests that she has acquired the understanding that language can have meaning without illustrations or the presence of concrete objects.

The understanding that print can have meaning in and of itself did not deter Octavia from moving back and forth between the two mediums for the next several months. In Figure 3-10, she used a pencil to create a story with an accompanying illustration. In Figure 3-11, she used poster board and tempera paints as a medium. While one might have expected her to use such materials to create a picture, she confined her efforts just to text. However, she painted one of the best things an emerging writer can create: a picture of her name. In bright reds and greens, one can clearly see several of the letters of her name. While still not spelled completely, it is important to note that she has learned several things about language without

FIGURE 3-10 Octavia's house drawn at about age four

she has demonstrated that the word that spells her name also represents her. This is important because the letters of her name do not look like her at all. It is understood by the child that the visual symbols that make up her name are equated with her as a person.

Octavia drew the picture of her house (Figure 3-10) when she was about four years old. Several aspects of both the inside (television at the bottom of the picture) and the outside (windows with family members peering out) are evident. While only a limited number of letters are depicted, a piece that she produced at about the same time (Figure 3-11) contains text

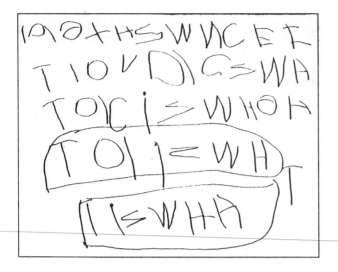

FIGURE 3-11 Octavia's early text without a drawing

any formal writing instruction. She has learned that letters in words come in a certain order, letters are on lines, letters go from left to right in words, letters have sounds, and letter sounds can sometimes be used as an aid to spelling. She is now using inventive spelling as an aid to creating meaning. The "E" painted at the end of her name has a sound that is like the sound created by the "i" in her name, Octavia.

Children engage in a variety of attempts to create meaning through their writing and drawing at the pre-kindergarten stage. Another child, Emily, created the pieces illustrated in Figures 3-14 through 3-16 just prior to entering kindergarten. Figure 3-14 is a self portrait. Like Octavia's self portrait it captures some of the characteristics (e.g., the bangs on the forehead) that distinguish her.

Figure 3-15 is not a story. Rather it is an example of something that might be seen as children discover their new power to express themselves in print. Having a limited writing vocabulary, Emily chose to write what she knew. That included her own name and most of the letters in her brother Andrew's name. Other letters she knew how to write are seen in various places around the page as well. As with Octavia, it is clear that Emily knows something about writing. She knows that writing is in lines, it goes from left to right, words are made up of letters, and letters have sounds.

Figure 3-16 demonstrates the true risks that emerging writers are willing to take in order to develop communication skills. While still not receiving any formal writing instruction, Emily did notice that other writers, adults and older siblings, connected their letters together. This type of writing is called cursive writing. Not being content with writing individual letters, or printed manuscript writing, Emily attempted to write in cursive. Clearly, she experienced some success. Although some of the letters are out of order, her name is clearly discernible at the left side of the piece. It is important to allow this kind of experimentation on the part of the young writer. It enhances the writer's self-confidence and builds the writer's trust in those who might respond to the writing. Such values will be quite useful in continuing the child's development as a writer.

As children enter kindergarten, they should have increased opportunities to engage in the writing process. At the very beginning of kindergarten, children are often able to write stories such as that found in Figure 3-17. The words state, "My dog makes cute sounds." Perceptive teachers in process writing classrooms take advantage of the skills, attitudes, and abilities children bring to writing. Among these is making use of the child's best sources of writing content: self, home, family, pets, play, and friends. Using these, children are given the confidence that they are writers from the first day of kindergarten. Shortly after entering kindergarten, children are able to write one-

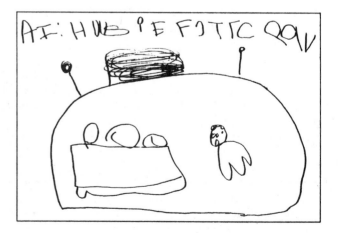

FIGURE 3-12 An early story in text and illustration by Octavia

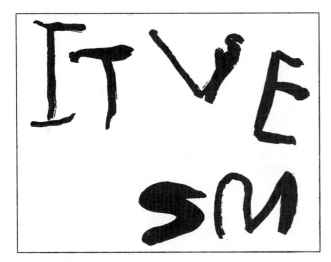

FIGURE 3-13 Children experiment with different materials to produce text.

guage is easily read and understood by others. The child has not mastered all of the mechanics of writing, but has made substantial progress through an ongoing interaction with books and writing. The child is writing in sentences, but doesn't punctuate them. The writing also demonstrates an understanding of the purpose of expository writing where an explanation is provided to the reader.

Figure 3-21 illustrates text and drawing done by a six-year-old near the end of first grade. They show further development in the writer's ability to handle narrative writing. Although all of the words are not clear to an adult, the writing uses character, setting,

sentence stories. Figure 3-18 provides such an example. The words from the story state, "I like when it's sunny out." Children may not always be able to form the letters and words. They should be encouraged to attempt the spellings as best they can. Some teachers ask the children to read aloud the words they have written while the teacher writes the words correctly below the child's words. Other teachers feel that this shouldn't be done, fearing that it takes ownership away from the children.

Later in kindergarten, children develop increasing control over their writing. Figure 3-19 illustrates a story written by a five-year-old. It states, "I like my Merry-go-round." By having daily opportunities to write, opportunities to share writing with others, and a wide exposure to books and children's literature, this child has acquired still more knowledge about writing. This child has an awareness that writing is done in lines just like in books and that conventional spellings can be included. These new skills are in addition to all of the other understandings about print observed in the writings of other young children described here.

By the middle of first grade, children are usually comfortable with the idea of writing about new things they are learning. Figure 3-20 shows a short essay and illustration written in conjunction with a lesson on street crossing safety. At this point, the written lan-

FIGURE 3-14 Emily's self-portrait at age four

FIGURE 3-15 Children write about things familiar to them such as their names and the names of their siblings.

FIGURE 3-16 Children need to be allowed to take risks with their language.

and plot in an appropriate manner. The story and illustration contain the themes of humor, danger, and friendship. For the most part, none of these more sophisticated aspects of literature were directly taught to the child. They were learned indirectly by the child

through writing opportunities, exposure to stories, and interacting with literature.

Writing process.

From the above illustrations, it is clear that much can be learned about children's writing abilities by examining the products of their writing. Such an examination, however, does not tell teachers all they need to know about children's writing. The products do not tell how children arrived at their current ability to write. Examining a piece of writing does not tell how the child went about putting that particular piece of writing together. The process of writing is particularly important to developing a good written product. To help children improve their writing ability, the teacher must help children improve their ability to engage in the writing process.

Observing the events that occur prior to the completion of a written product can inform the teacher of the strengths and needs of a writer, particularly at the planning and drafting stages (Sawyer 1978, 1987; Stallard 1974). It is particularly revealing to observe what children do before, during, and after they pause in their writing (Matsuhashi 1981; Sawyer 1988). Humes (1983) found that effective writers spend their time doing very different things than poor writers during the writing process. Effective writers spend more time

FIGURE 3-17 This kindergartener's story states, "My dog makes cute noises."

FIGURE 3-18 This kindergartener uses a story to express personal feelings by writing, "I like it when it's sunny out."

FIGURE 3-19 This kindergartener demonstrates increasing control over language.

According to Humes (1983), effective writers, because of their ability to focus on global content and ideas, tend to exhibit a higher degree of automaticity in their writing. They make fewer pauses in their writing and generally pause for longer periods of time. This is because they are engaged in such things as reviewing sections they have just written and planning the next sections they will write. In contrast, poorer writers make more frequent pauses for briefer periods of time for the purpose of attending to minor mechanical aspects such as spelling, handwriting, and punctuation. As a result, more effective writers tend to continually focus on the content of the writing, while poorer writers tended to constantly shift back and forth between mechanics and content. As a result, poorer writers become locked into a pattern that prevents them from improving their writing no matter how much they desire to increase the quality of their written products.

Therefore, process writing teachers carefully observe children at all stages of writing and record behaviors that provide them with the information to understand their needs as developing writers. This information can then be used to guide the teacher in

FIGURE 3-20 In the primary grades, children expand into writing that goes beyond personal narrative.

planning content and ideas, while poor writers spend more time focused on mechanical aspects of writing. This was found to be true at the planning, drafting, and revising stages of the writing process.

which students need assistance on various aspects of writing as well as what writing skills need to be modeled and reinforced during instructional mini-lessons. The following questions might be used as a guide for observing a young writer's behavior while that child is engaging in the writing process:

What does the writer do before beginning the first draft?

How often does the writer pause?

How long are the pauses?

What is the purpose of the pause?

What is the writer doing just before a pause occurs?

What does the writer do when resuming the draft after pausing?

Was writing frequently interrupted in order to correct minor mechanical errors?

When the writer stopped to re-read the piece was it to assess meaning or to locate mechanical errors?

Were revisions related to meaning or to mechanical errors?

SKILLS AND BEHAVIORS

Young children, just like older children and adults, engage in writing for a purpose. The purposes may vary from age group to age group and from child to child, but purpose is a common thread among all. Some children may write to amuse themselves, while others may write to share an exciting experience they recall. Since young children develop at widely varying rates, specific expectations should not be placed on them at certain ages. Related to this is the fact that much of the writing one does is constantly refined as one gains more and more control over the complexities of language. For example, seven-year-olds may write friendly letters as part of a primary grade curriculum. That does not mean that they have mastered the art of the friendly letter by the end of second grade. They continue to be exposed to refinements of writing friendly letters throughout their school years. Indeed, the friendly letters written by senior citizens who have spent their lives improving their ability to communicate through letters can be superior in quality to letters written by recent college graduates. The point is that it is difficult to assign skills and objectives to be mastered by the end of a certain grade or by the time a child reaches a certain age.

FIGURE 3-21 In the primary grades, children often include elements of character, setting, and plot in their writing.

The skills and behaviors described here are intended to serve as an outline for an individualized set of objectives for children. They are neither inclusive nor exclusive of all of the possible outcomes of an early childhood literacy program focused on writing. Objectives and activities should be used with children as it is developmentally appropriate to do so.

The writing skills that might be used with young children are grouped into three areas: narration, description, and explanation. A fourth type, persuasive writing, is generally not done with young children. This does not mean that young children cannot or should not experiment with persuasive writing. Each type of writing covers a wide range of possible communication activities. However, none of the three types of writing is usually found in a pure form. Each tends to be found in conjunction with the other types.

For example, a narrative story often contains descriptions of the setting and explanations of the characters' actions. The activities suggested to develop writing skills are, therefore, general in nature. Most of the activities can be adapted to focus on each of the types of writing. Finally, writers should keep in mind that writing covers a range of behaviors for the young child. While the term *writing* is often used in the description, the actual behavior the child may be engaged in could be oral language, illustration, role playing, or actual writing with paper and pencil.

Narrative Writing

Whenever we create or retell stories, we are engaged in narration. Storytelling is as old as humanity and is a powerful language tool. Most of us enjoy listening to a good story, and there is an urge in everyone to tell stories. The story may be a simple narration such as a news account or a narration with plot. A narration with plot employs conflict among human, natural, or supernatural forces. The plot proceeds to a climax of action and a resolution of the problem in some way. Plot is a sophisticated language device, yet young children often include the use of it as part of their stories. They develop an implicit knowledge of plot through their exposure to literature and storytelling.

When young children engage in narrative stories, the tales often involve themselves and their exploits. Given child development, this is to be expected. It provides a convenient opportunity to develop the ability to express themselves. Self-expression goes beyond a simple description of an individual. Self-expression also includes attitudes, feelings, beliefs, and values. Each child differs in these aspects of humanity. They are important to develop because they form the foundation of what will become the voice of the writer. A writer's voice is the intangible quality of the writing that makes it unique to the individual. Voice is the quality adults refer to when they say they can "read between the lines" or "get into the mind of the author." Ernest Hemingway, John Steinbeck, Mark Twain, Martin Luther King, and Taylor Caldwell all have distinctive voices that are recognizable and pleasurable to their readers. Voice is one of the qualities that gives ownership to a child's writing.

Identifies Experiences and Events.

At the most basic level, children must develop the ability to reflect upon themselves and their world. This reflection is not necessarily a philosophical reflection. Rather, it refers to the fact that events can be recalled, that they are distinct from other events, and that they can be shared through language. This may be done solely through oral language. A teacher might model the skill by simply describing a favorite childhood toy or activity. The child can then share a similar experience.

Selection of an Event.

When a child has developed an ability to reflect upon and recall events, the child might then decide that there is a specific event that might be shared. It may be the sharing of a secret, telling about a favorite toy, or making a wish for a birthday present. Whatever event has been selected has been done so for a reason. The child may not be able to articulate exactly why a certain event was chosen for sharing, but there was a reason. This is the beginning of using values and attitudes as a part of writing.

Inclusion of Relevant Information.

When children are excited about sharing something, they often leave out bits and pieces of the story. The listener is often puzzled by some of the information. This is to be expected with young children. Rather than correcting them, the perceptive teacher remains patient and continues the discussion with questions designed to seek additional information. Instead of saying, "I don't understand what it is you're talking about," a teacher would ask, "Who is Buffy? . . . Where are the trees? . . . Why did that happen?" This places the responsibility for clear communication with the child while at the same time providing helpful guidance to clarify the message.

Sequence Information.

Related to information relevance is the correct sequencing of information. This refers to sharing information in a sequence that makes the message understandable to the listener or reader. While time order sequence is often used, it is not the only accept-

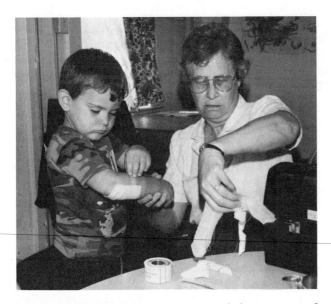

FIGURE 3-22 A common occurrence and the sequence of events associated with it often have the elements of a good story for children to retell.

able format. The content of the message can often dictate the sequence. A child telling about a fire that took place in the neighborhood may actually relate the story as follows (the numbers at the end of each sentence indicate the actual time order sequence):

"The house next door almost burned down yesterday."
(5)
"The firemen came and put it out." (4)
"The man in the house was smoking." (1)
"He fell asleep without putting out his cigarette." (2)
"His cigarette caught the sofa on fire." (3)

The story is very understandable even though the child uses a sequence that is not strictly in time order. The fact that the listener possesses a schema on how fires often start helps that individual to understand stories told out of time order. The schema helps us to rearrange the pieces and to fill in any missing details. The child telling the story may implicitly be assuming that the listener has this understanding.

Establish Point of View.

Point of view refers to the concept of who is telling the story. Is the story told in the first person with the teller being in the story? Is the story in the third person? Is it retelling of a story heard aloud? Whatever the case, encouraging children to maintain a consistent point of view will improve the clarity of their communications.

Uses Story Patterns.

Story patterns, or story grammars as they are sometimes called, refer to all of the aspects of language that help the reader understand that a story is being told and that parts of the story have definite relationships to other parts of the story. With literature for young children, familiar lines such as "Once upon a time . . . and they lived happily ever after" are a part of the story pattern. They tell us that a story is about to begin and that the story is over. Other devices that might be used include the repetition of certain key lines and descriptions of characters in ways that makes it clear that the character is either a hero or a villain.

Inclusion of Language Devices.

As children increase control over language and develop a repertoire of language and vocabulary, they may begin to take risks by using more sophisticated language. This may include poetic forms, rhyming words, dialogue, conversation, and figurative language. Many of these tools are learned through exposure to literature that uses such language devices and through the modeling of storytelling by teachers and other adults.

Use of Imaginary Characters.

Much of childhood deals with concrete experiences. However, since an abundance of literature shared with children involves fictional characters, youngsters do develop the ability to use fictional characters in their writing. At first, the characters may be borrowed from stories children have heard or read. Later, original fictional characters may be included. The stories using these fictional characters often contain real characters, such as the child, as well. Children often do not distinguish clearly between what is real and what is fantasy. It should be kept in mind that childhood is a time in which anything is possible.

Response to Stories and Events.

Most of us have responses to life events and stories. Comedians make us laugh. Some stories make us cry. Certain news events make us angry. Some of the things children say make us smile inside. Helping children to discover that they react to language develops an important awareness. When they understand the effect language has on them, they can consider ways in which they can use language to have similar effects on others. While children seem capable of responding to humor at a very young age, they can also surprise us by showing empathy for a sad story as well.

Records Experiences, Events, and Stories.

The skill of recording refers to the ability to dictate, illustrate, or write. As such, this skill can be combined with any of the other skills. Writing in childhood might be viewed as a development from observation to oral language to illustration to actual writing of words and sentences. There is a great overlap of each ability with both the one preceding it and the one subsequent to it. One form does not cease as the next emerges. Each can and should continue to develop. Children do not stop accompanying their stories with pictures because they outgrow the need or desire to draw. They stop drawing because school programs no longer encourage it or no longer allow enough time for it.

Descriptive Writing

While descriptive writing is often used to support narrative writing, the skills that develop it can be considered apart from narrative writing. Descriptive writing uses vocabulary that appeals to the senses in order to portray a person, animal, object, or idea. The vocabulary may be single words or words embedded in phrases, sentences, and paragraphs.

A piece of writing, an illustration, or an oral story may be planned to be descriptive. This can create additional demands on the young language user. With writing and illustration, the revision phase can be particularly focused on addressing the idea of increasing the descriptive aspects of the piece. Skills that can be addressed to help children use descriptive language tend to focus on words and sentences.

Using Sensory Words.

The first skill a child might learn in this type of language use includes the use of words that focus on physical descriptions. Activities for this can be concrete and aimed at inviting children to use their senses to experience the concept. For example, a cat, dog, or rabbit can be brought into the classroom for the children to meet. A teacher-led discussion can help the children to see that a number of words can be used to describe the animal. The animal in this example might be described as white, brown, grey, soft, fuzzy, fluffy, furry, warm, quiet, and so forth. If the children are in the four- to five-year-old age range, the teacher might encourage them to dictate a language experience story using a repeated line to develop a descriptive piece of writing that many children will be able to read. The story might unfold as follows.

"The Bunny"
The bunny is small.
The bunny is warm.
The bunny is white.
The bunny is fuzzy.
We like the bunny.

Appealing to the senses.

Children can be provided with a diversity of experiences to lead them to the realization that many senses can be appealed to through language. In the example with the bunny, the senses of touch and sight were targeted. From that point, children can explore the idea that objects can often appeal to a variety of senses. Serving a snack such as lemon sherbet can create an opportunity to experience a variety of senses as follows:

Sense Related Words

sight—yellow, rounded scoops
touch—smooth, wet, cold
taste—sweet, tart
smell—fruity, pleasant
sound—quiet, slurping

Each of the words identified can be discussed by the children. A description of the food can be created orally or in writing. The descriptive words may be used or not as decided by the group. Such an exercise provides a powerful reinforcement of the concept that language users have the power to make decisions about language while they are interacting with it.

Integrating descriptive words.

As was evident in the examples above, developing descriptive language with children is best done when it is integrated with whole pieces of text. It does youngsters little good to learn a group of descriptive words in isolation. They may be able to learn some of the words and what they mean, but they are limited in their ability to transfer them into their own speaking and writing vocabularies.

The goal of teaching descriptive language is to enable children to independently choose to make vocabulary selections as they move from oral language to dictated stories to stories written independently. One possible approach to this is to demonstrate how to plan a piece through the development of notes, drawings, and charts. By planning a piece in this way, the child interacts with specific words prior to using them. This can be helpful in developing automaticity in the drafting phase. The child will have just interacted with the terms prior to writing. As a result, the child will not have to shift away from content in order to try to come up with an appropriate word. The word will already be on the child's mind.

Explanatory Writing

Explanatory writing, also referred to as expository writing, seeks to provide clear, well-organized, and understandable factual information. While explanatory writing sometimes exists by itself, it also is found in conjunction with both descriptive and narrative writing. Since it relies on a broad knowledge of vocabulary, educational programs should provide a wide range of experiences and opportunities for children. In so doing, children will come in contact with a breadth of new words, ideas, and information that will serve as a base for their explanatory writing.

Vocabulary Development.

The building and use of a wide range of words is critical to expository writing. This development can be reinforced by helping children make the connec-

FIGURE 3-23 Descriptive language for writing can be built around the reading of a story. *Illustration from* The Pumpkin Patch, *by Elizabeth King. Reprinted courtesy of E.P. Dutton.*

tion between words as symbols and their actual concrete counterparts. It can be done with objects in the classroom and with the pictures and illustrations children create. Either orally or in writing, children and adults can label the objects found in the environment and in pictures. Using pictures found in children's literature enables teachers to bring experiences into the classroom that would not otherwise be possible. Children's books are rich with illustrations of other countries, buildings, vehicles, animals, clothing, and time periods. Children can respond to these stories orally, in writing, or through illustrations. Labels for the people, objects, and animals can be made clear and modeled by the teacher. If children are beginning to write with pencil and paper, they can use invented spelling for the words that are not familiar in print but that they know by sound.

Sentence Development.

Sentence development should not be seen as something that follows vocabulary development. It should be viewed as an outgrowth of it. Children often use single words or telegraphic phrases when they first

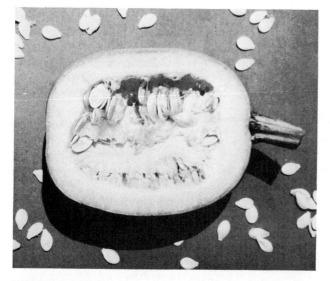

FIGURE 3-24A Vocabulary development for writing can be related to stories in very real ways. *Illustration from* The Pumpkin Patch, *by Elizabeth King. Reprinted courtesy of E.P. Dutton.*

FIGURE 3-24B The parts of a pumpkin and the words to identify them can be discovered following the reading of a story about pumpkins. *Illustration from* The Pumpkin Patch, *by Elizabeth King. Reprinted courtesy of E.P. Dutton.*

begin to write just as they do when they first begin to speak. Teachers can model the development of sentences by allowing children to dictate them orally. As children discover that they are capable of creating

such sentences orally, they can be encouraged to do the same thing in their writing. It is important to keep in mind that children will arrive at this capability at varying times. The best time to teach this or any other skill is when children need the skill to continue their own language growth.

Organizational Markers.

As children develop the ability to use oral and written expository language, they will discover a need to use language markers that help the reader better understand their message. Language markers are words that signal to the reader that the explanation is organized in a certain manner.

While there are a variety of possible markers, a limited number will enable most young language users to become more effective. Sequence markers suggest that there is a certain order to the way events occur in the explanation. Sequence markers include such terms as first, second, next, then, start, end, finish, last, finally, and so on. Directional and distance markers suggest ideas to readers that enable them to visualize spacial directions. Directional and distance markers include terms such as under, near, far, left, right, in front of, close, up, down, and so on. Other types of markers might be needed by specific children at certain times. Their use helps language users to give complete and understandable information.

Teachers can provide opportunities to develop the use of markers in the classroom. Activities such as drawing a map from the school to the firehouse can be used to develop direction and distance markers. Making snacks and craft projects can enable the teacher to constantly repeat the use of procedural and sequence markers. Classroom visitors such as firemen, nurses, bank clerks, florists, and bakers can use markers to describe and demonstrate the processes they use in performing their jobs.

Mechanical Skills

Mechanical skills are learned through a great deal of repetition of language use. In this way, they are used automatically each time they are needed. They can be useful when they involve language that is predictable. When choice is involved or a decision is to be made, skills are less useful. In those cases, strategies that enable children to plan and carry out a problem-solving activity may be more useful.

The mechanical skills of written language are those that have more to do with the rules of producing standard English than with the meaning of the written message. This is not to say that mechanical skills have nothing to do with the meaning of a written text. They do help to make the meaning clear by serving as cues to the reader. For example, punctuation tells the reader that there is a need to pause at the end of a sentence. Grammar enables the reader to realize that the action took place in the past. Spelling makes it clear that the cowboy jumped on a horse rather than a house. Capitalization informs the reader that the word Bob refers to a person rather than something done with apples at Halloween. Finally, legible handwriting enables the reader to focus on the meaning of the message rather than guessing at what a word might be.

The focus of instruction in mechanical skills should be on teaching the skills in context. There are a number of reason for this. First, it is only within context that mechanical skills have a function. A set of definitions of the grammatical parts of speech does not really enable the young writer to make use of them in a functional sense. Second, mechanical skills learned in isolation do not always transfer well to a contextual situation. Third, teaching mechanical skills in isolation is not the same as teaching writing. For many years, English language skills have been taught in isolation with no increase in overall writing ability on the part of students. Finally, learning mechanical skills in isolation tends to be a tedious activity, which suggests that writing is often a dull and boring activity.

Instruction in skills should be child centered and efficient. Child centered instruction assumes that the child is more important than the skill. The child should be a master of the skill rather than the other way around. Therefore, the instruction should reinforce the independence and autonomy of the child. The goal should not be to make the child demonstrate mastery over a set number of skills over a fixed period of time. This is where efficiency becomes important. Children have a need to learn and use certain skills at certain times. Other children may not have that need, or they may have already learned that particular skill. The instruction is made more efficient by teaching skills needed by the children. Since some children

often have a mastery of skills that other children need, their expertise can be used within the instructional program. It is quite possible for children to learn skills from each other. This enables the teacher to concentrate on teaching those skills that are new to all of the children to just those who need them.

Punctuation.

Punctuation is the system of symbols used to inform readers of meaningful aspects of the text not found in the written words. Research has demonstrated that children who are taught punctuation through their writing are able to identify and use punctuation far better than those who are taught punctuation through traditional methods (Composition in the English Language Arts Curriculum K-12, 1986). This is because the writers had an understanding of punctuation as it relates to meaning rather than a list of rules. As with any mechanical skill, the rules that govern the use of punctuation are far too numerous for most of us to keep in mind as we write.

How does punctuation relate to meaning? Think about the last time you were engaged in a discussion with a group of friends. Try to recall some of the body language and voice characteristics people in the group used to convey meaning to others. You may recall that changes in voice inflection may have indicated a question. An increase in volume may have indicated excitement. Counting out reasons for something on one's fingers may have suggested a series of items. Each of these visual clues to the oral message can be translated into writing through the use of punctuation.

Children use the same kinds of facial expressions and body language in their oral expressions that they see adults model in their discussions. As young children learn to write, they develop a need to translate this body language into writing. When children determine that the need exists, that is the time to teach that particular punctuation skill. Providing it at that time empowers children and gives them meaningful control over their language. Children will then grow in their writing ability with the understanding that punctuation serves to establish the writer's intentions. Children will not ask themselves, "What is the rule for using a . . .?" Rather, they will ask themselves, "How can I let the reader know . . .?"

Grammar.

Grammar is the study of how words are formed and the parts of speech (Moffett and Wagner, 1983). It has long held a major place in traditional English language arts classes in both elementary and secondary education. Over the last few decades, however, research has shown that the study of grammar in isolation fails to improve the writing skills of children (Elley, Barham, Lamb, and Wyllie 1976; Fraser and Hodson 1978; Hartwell 1985; Lundsteen 1976). More recently, George Hillocks, Jr. (1987), synthesizing research on all aspects of writing, concludes that traditional instruction in grammar results in significant decreases in writing ability.

Grammar is a highly abstract concept. The logical and conceptual thinking required to adequately deal with it is often not found in young children. Children do, however, begin to develop a natural intuitive oral grammar from the moment of birth. They make errors in grammar in their oral language, but they refine their language over time. Many of their grammatical errors in oral language disappear without any formal instruction in grammar.

The appropriate way to provide grammar instruction is during the writing process. Children should have ample opportunities to share their written pieces orally. They will then have an opportunity to compare their written grammatical structures to the intuitive criteria about the way the language should sound. In this way, grammar becomes a matter of decision making on the part of young writers. They need to decide if a statement is structured in such a way that the reader will understand it or not. From that point, the child's knowledge of grammar in writing can develop. That is, children develop criteria and guidelines from writing and the instruction that surrounds it, rather than by memorizing rules of grammar prior to applying them to their writing.

Spelling.

Spelling refers to the standard way of visually representing words. In education, spelling often takes on a life of its own. It is frequently viewed as a separate subject onto itself. It has its own sets of texts. It often receives its own place on the report cards of young children. Such a view of spelling is rejected in an integrated curriculum. Spelling has little or no importance other than within written language. Within written language it has a great deal of importance since it makes the individual words in a text recognizable and, therefore, comprehensible.

The English spelling system contains twenty-six graphemes, or letters. These letters represent about forty-four phonemes, or sounds. This latter number varies slightly depending on the linguistic viewpoint being used. In any case, this difference between the number of letters and the number of sounds causes many spelling difficulties due to the fact that there is not a one-to-one relationship betwen the two. Not only can some letters and letter combinations have more than one sound, but some sounds can be represented by a number of different letter combinations.

It is known that a list of about 100 words accounts for well over half of everything that is written in English. Words from the list often tend to have phonetically irregular spellings. That is, the letters used to spell them are not necessarily the letters that might be predicted based solely on the sound characteristics of the word. This causes these words to contain a large number of spelling errors when they are used.

Research has shown that children are more likely to spell correctly when spelling is taught through their writing (Composition in the Language Arts Curriculum K-12, 1986). Ironically, most children are given spelling words to learn from spelling workbooks. The words in the workbooks are often totally unrelated to the words children may be using in their writing. As a result, spelling instruction is of little value to a young writer and takes time away from more productive aspects of a language arts program.

Spelling instruction should be included within the writing process. It should be confined to the editing stages of the process. Children should be encouraged to not be concerned with correct spelling at the planning, drafting, and revising stages. Such concern is detrimental to the more appropriate focus on the comprehension of the content during those stages. It is far better to use invented spelling during those stages, even if all of the invented spellings are not corrected during the editing stage.

Within writing, spelling instruction should have two goals. First, children need to understand that they should focus on spelling primarily during the editing stages of writing. Spelling instruction is appropriate at that time. High-use words and words that the child tends to use as part of an individual writing style should be a major focus with child. The teacher needs to note these words and potential error patterns as part of the spelling instruction.

The second goal of spelling instruction is the development of a spelling independence. This includes the ability to recognize possible misspellings and strategies for dealing with misspellings. Ample opportunities for writing and using words is probably the best route to developing the ability to recognize possibly misspelled words. Children can take more control over how they deal with misspellings through such strategies as conferring with other children and by using beginning dictionaries at the editing stage. Each of these is preferable to requesting correct spellings from the teacher. The latter method simply reinforces dependence on someone else. Asking the teacher can be included in the total array of spelling strategies, but it should be viewed more as a last resort than anything else.

Capitalization.

Using upper case, or capital, letters to denote that a word is in a special position or that the word refers to something unique is referred to as capitalization. It is a skill that has a limited number of uses. The first word of a sentence is capitalized. The names of specific persons, places, and things are capitalized. Beyond that, there is very little else that is capitalized. As a writing convention, capitalization should be taught within the context of a child's own writing. Instruction can center around having children identify persons, places, and things in their own writing that require capitalization and explain the reasons for those capitalizations. The purpose of capitalization is to enable the reader to better understand the message of the writer.

Handwriting.

Handwriting, like spelling, has often tended to develop a life of its own in the education of young children. For decades children have practiced making lines, circles, and letters on dittos and workbook pages in the hope that they would develop a style similar to that presented in those workbooks. Does it work? An examination of the handwriting of a dozen adults chosen at random will quickly lead us to conclude that the large amount of time traditionally devoted to handwriting instruction in early childhood is largely an exercise in futility.

The goal of handwriting and handwriting instruction, whether manuscript or cursive, is to help the reader understand the meaning of the text by presenting it legibly and neatly. Most people have a handwriting style that is personal to them alone. As long as it is legible and reasonably neat it meets the needs of both readers and writers. According to Graves (1983), children go through several stages of developing handwriting, often in the first grade of school. They move through periods of wanting to simply write things on paper, to wanting their writing to be perfect the first time, to developing an understanding that the paper is only a draft that can be reworked. The more opportunity a child has to write, the more proficient the child will become in handwriting skill.

ACTIVITIES FOR DEVELOPING WRITING ABILITY

The activities that might be used in a process writing classroom are not based upon text, workbook, or ditto exercises. They tend to be closely related to the natural language of the children. Often, they deal with stories from the literature being used in the classroom. There is no age or grade level assigned to the activities, since most can be used with children over a wide span of years and grades. They should be used as they are seen to be appropriate to the children at the time.

Language Experience Approach

The language experience approach (LEA) has been used for many years to develop authentic stories by and with young children (Allen 1974; Stauffer 1980). Through the process of dictation, children learn that their experiences can be verbalized, written down, and read by others and themselves (Strickland and Morrow 1990). In general, an LEA story is developed following an experience that the children have engaged in firsthand. Using discussion, the children recreate the experience in words that are then written down by the teacher. The story is often transcribed on a chart or other large sheet of paper. The process can be done with individual students, small groups, or total classes. A major goal of LEA is to engage children in the use of language so that their facility with language increases.

While LEA will continue to remain a viable activity for developing writing skills, some educators question its use as a major tool (Strickland and Morrow 1990). Several questions have emerged as a result of research on LEA (Harste, Burke, and Woodward 1984). Will the dictation by the children decrease their opportunity to develop their own drafting skills? Does group writing interfere with a sense of authorship on the part of individual children? Will constant adult monitoring of correct writing decrease the willingness of children to take risks with their own writing? Is LEA a valid tool for a program that uses a whole language philosophy? The answers will differ depending on how LEA is used and the extent to which it serves as the primary activity for writing. Within certain limits, it should be seen as a tool for meeting some of the needs of an integrated language arts approach.

Chart Stories

A variation on LEA which allows for more individual writing is the use of chart stories. With this activity, a less structured approach is employed. The chart is seen more as just another source of information about print than as a writing product. Charts tend to be brief, spontaneous, and more varied than LEA stories (Strickland and Morrow 1990).

A chart may be used to record parts of a story, to model a concept about print, to record information, or to illustrate an experience. The procedure used to develop a chart has some of the characteristics of an LEA approach. Generally, students might be grouped around a chart at the beginning of a session. Depending on the objective of the instruction, the teacher develops ideas with the children and place key features identified on the chart. Following the development of the chart, children are encouraged to engage in their own writing process and to develop their own written products independently. They may select ideas from the chart or elsewhere if it serves

their purpose. This approach keeps much of the decision making about writing in the hands of the writers rather than in the power of the teacher. By providing time for sharing the written work developed from the use of the chart, children develop self-confidence and an increased sense of self-esteem.

Journals

Moving still another step away from the more structured LEA approach is a variety of activities involving the use of journals. A journal is a record of events, and it is usually written in daily. It is sometimes less personal than a diary. A diary might be used to record more personal thoughts. A journal, as used in a writing program, is used with the understanding that some entries might be further developed and shared with others in the group. While it should be a decision of the author about what entries to share, different types of journals might be expected to be shared more than other types. Journals can usually be used with children from pre-kindergarten through the elementary grades. The type of activities may depend on the type of journals used in a program.

Daily Journals.

The daily journal combines some of the characteristics of LEA and chart stories with greater writer independence. Strickland and Morrow (1990) outline a four-step process for using a daily journal. The first step, experiencing, is the acceptance of children's experiences as valid resources for ideas to write about. The experiences may be from the classroom or from outside it. They may be based upon an actual experience of the child or one that the child may have learned about through literature. The experience may be planned or spontaneous.

The second step is a group journal writing/reading activity. As the experience is discussed, the teacher serves as a scribe, model, motivator, and instructor for the writing. The focus is on having the children take the lead in developing language about the experience through their discussion and sharing. As the chart is completed, children are encouraged to echo the teacher's reading of the chart, story, or journal entry. Children are encouraged to note and talk

FIGURE 3-25 A visit to a scarecrow on a farm might be a good topic for an entry in a journal. *Illustration from* The Pumpkin Patch, *by Elizabeth King. Reprinted courtesy of E.P. Dutton.*

the story journal is to provide a vehicle for children to interpret stories through their art and writing. Many teachers prefer to use a set of four or five sheets of paper stapled together as a story journal for each book read aloud to the children. Not all stories will entail the use of a story journal, however.

The procedure outlined by Farris (1989) for using a story journal is similar to that used for other journal writing. It begins with the experience of the teacher reading a story aloud to the children. Following the reading, the children react to the story by noting such things as character, setting, and the language used by the author. Next, questions are asked about the story. The questions may deal with characters, plot, or things children didn't understand in the story.

about anything they find interesting in the written document.

Independent journal writing and drawing is the third step of the process. Children are free to use material developed in the group or other material of their own choosing to develop their own journal entry. Adults participate by making their own journal entries, responding to students and encouraging uniqueness, risk-taking, and invented spelling. The fourth step of the process is sharing. Opportunity must be provided for children to share their journal entries with teachers, peers, and parents. The entries may be letters, words, drawings, and so on. They can be displayed on a bulletin board, laminated, reread from time to time, or bound into a book containing other writing by the child.

Daily journals allow children to participate at the pace they find comfortable. The teacher can model a variety of writing concepts for the children to use if they are ready to incorporate the concept into their own writing. The writing of the children is valued and accepted. This approach allows for the integration of all children in a regular writing program that meets their needs.

Story Journals.

A story journal is a special type of journal used to connect literature and art with the writing process. According to Farris (1989), the primary purpose of

FIGURE 3-26 Fairy tales such as "Snow White" make good sources of literature for use with story journals. *Illustration from* The Child's Fairy Tale Book, *by Kay Chorao. Reprinted courtesy of E.P. Dutton.*

FIGURE 3-27 Children's book author Cynthia DeFelice

Following the discussion, children write about the story they have just experienced in their story journals. The writing may be text, illustration, or both. The writing may be an illustration of a favorite character, a statement about the setting, or other topics suggested by the teacher or students as appropriate. Some teachers encourage children to extend the story by creating new adventures (Sandmark and Coons 1988). The journal entries should be shared and displayed with others.

Literary Journals.

A more sophisticated type of story journal is the literary journal in which children experiment with various aspects of the story within their writing (Farris 1989). Topics or ideas for writing might include writing from the point of view of a story character, writing about being a character within the story, writing letters to characters in the story, writing reviews of the book, and writing about themes identified in the story.

Dialogue Journals.

One of the most effective tools for developing reading and writing skills through literature is the dialogue journal (Farris 1989). The actual journal can be made from a variety of options. Teacher-constructed journals of looseleaf and construction paper, commercially made blank books, composition books, and spiral bound notebooks are all appropriate as dialogue journal. The purpose of a dialogue journal is to enable children and teachers to have meaningful, ongoing, written dialogues about the books and literature they are reading.

In a dialogue journal, children write their thoughts on a regular basis (Five 1988). The types of writing can be similar to that found in story journals and literary journals. Teachers regularly read and respond to what the children have written. The procedure allows teachers to note the content, vocabulary, and mechanics the child has used. In their responses, teachers can provide feedback in terms of each of these areas to the students. Children get used to the idea of using the language and ideas modeled by the teacher to guide their subsequent writing. Such things as incorrect spelling, punctuation, and understandings of specific events in a story are addressed in a natural way while maintaining a focus on meaning.

Writing Workshop

A writing workshop is an activity that encourages children to increase their writing skills using a recursive approach to writing. Calkins (1987) contends that key elements of a successful writing workshop are simple and predictable schedules and expectations. By creating such an environment, young writers can evolve into effective writers because they know and understand what is happening, when it is going to happen, and why it will happen.

The environment is stuctured so that most of the time is spent by children in planning, drafting, revising, and editing. A short "author's meeting" is often held at the beginning of the period. At that time, the teacher may present a writing strategy or skill. Mini-lessons on topics ranging from identifying a topic to using quotation marks might be presented. The group often comes back together at the end of the period in order to share their pieces.

The floor plan, location of supplies, and furniture of the work area are particularly important. Writing tables, sharing areas, and comfortable places for engaging in writing will send the message that writing is an important activity that demands care and craftsmanship. By knowing what will happen when and by knowing where everything is located, children are able to take greater control of their writing. Supplies that might be included in a typical writing workshop area include an assortment of paper, pens, pencils, markers, tape, glue, safety scissors, and folders.

Children must know when activities can and will happen through a simple and predictable schedule. They need to know that they will have a certain time to write, share, discuss, plan, and revise their work. There is not one correct way to schedule or teach writing. Each group of children will have certain needs and strengths. Perceptive teachers will identify these and respond to them in a thoughtful considered manner.

Modeling.

Teachers can often provide the most powerful lessons by modeling appropriate writing behaviors, skills, and strategies in their own writing. By thinking out loud as they demonstrate how they solve problems in their own writing, teachers provide children with effective tools. They also reinforce the mutuality of the writing community within the classroom by being a part of the literate environment rather than in charge of that environment. Besides all of the skills and strategies of writing that can be modeled are the multitude of possible forms that writing can take. Writing is communication. It appears everywhere. Children need not confine their writing to stories, book reports, and essays. Among the possibilities of forms that can be shared with children are the following:

advertisements   autobiographies   awards
book covers   bumper stickers   cartoons
cereal boxes   couplets   definitions
descriptions   diaries   directions
explanations   fables   fairy tales
fortunes   good news/bad news   greeting cards
grocery lists   haiku   horoscopes
invitations   jokes   jump rope rhymes
labels   letters   memories
metaphors   menus   myths
newscasts   nursery rhymes   pattern stories
poems   postcards   posters
puns   questions   quotations
recipes   riddles   schedules
songs   superstitions   thank you notes
tongue twisters   travel brochures   want ads
warnings   weather reports   wish lists

These are but a few of the many possibilities. Checking one's mail, observing the environment, and becoming more watchful of print in daily life will make the supply of writing forms and ideas an endless one. The key to identifying appropriate writing forms is to place yourself in the position of a child. From this vantage point it is easier to determine the forms that are motivating and meaningful. Without that, there will be little reason for children to develop a sense of ownership over such writing activities. Even with such a list, children should be given wide discretion at an early age to make choices about the kinds of writing in which they will engage. Without choice, the sense of ownership is lost.

SUMMARY

In considering how to go about the task of helping children increase their writing ability, it is clear that teachers need to assess their views about education and its purposes. There are several ways to view the goals of education. On one end of the spectrum, education can be viewed as having the purely academic purpose of transmitting the culture to the next generation. Such a view sees writing as a matter of correctness of form with little emphasis on content. On the other end of the spectrum, education might be seen as having a purely liberating purpose. Such a view emphasizes the importance of enabling children to revise the social order as an outgrowth of their education. The position taken in this text is somewhere between this latter view and a middle view. Writing instruction should be developmentally appropriate for the children while at the same time encouraging them to take increasing control of their learning. Such control is viewed as a powerful tool that enables children to see themselves as competent learners.

There are two views of writing instruction. The traditional view sees writing as a linear process in which children complete prewriting, drafting, and editing in an orderly manner with each step coming at the completion of the previous step. On the other hand, a process approach sees writing as a circular or recursive process. In a process approach, writers recognize the need to repeat a number of the parts of a process as they go about the task of writing. It is a process characterized by such things as multiple drafts, a sense of authorship, a focus on content, and a tolerance for errors that occur as a result of young writers taking necessary language risks as a normal part of the learning process. The role of the teacher is markedly different in the two approaches. In a linear model, the teacher is clearly in charge of the writing process. In a process approach, the teacher is a fellow participant in the writing process.

An understanding of how children develop as writers comes not only from a study of the pieces children have written but also from observing how they go about composing the pieces they are writing. Children arrive at different stages of writing ability by way of a diverse set of paths. However, it was noted that children acquire a multitude of writing skills and strategies without any formal instruction in writing. Many of these are learned through the use of normal social language and through interaction with a broad range of children's books.

The skills that children develop can ordinarily be grouped under the categories of content, organization, language, sentence structure, and mechanics. While each can be discussed as a separate concept, it is most effective to develop the abilities needed for each within the context of whole pieces of text. The types of writing young children produce are mostly descriptive, expository, and narrative in nature. Most writing combines these types.

The activities that best enhance writing development are those that involve children in a supportive environment. Opportunities to write using different forms, to confer with peers, to receive constructive feedback, and to exercise some control over writing are viewed as most effective. Literature is seen as a key element for any writing program for young children. It provides language models, ideas for writing, and meaningful texts appropriate for young children.

Questions and Activities for Review and Discussion

Multiple Choice

1. A philosophy of education geared toward transferring cultural knowledge to the next generation would be most likely to include
   a. encouraging children to select their own writing topics.
   b. accepting invented spelling in young children's writing.
   c. the teaching of formal grammar as a subject.
   d. reading aloud by the teacher on a daily basis.
2. A process approach to writing tends to focus on
   a. how a piece of writing is developed.
   b. the correctness of the spelling in a written piece.
   c. the finished products of writing.
   d. editing as the key element of good writing.
3. Setting goals for the writing, generating content, and organizing content are all parts of
   a. drafting.
   b. revising.
   c. editing.
   d. planning.
4. In a process approach to writing, one of the roles of the teacher is to
   a. provide opportunities for writing.
   b. model parts of the writing process.

      c. share writing with children.

      d. all of the above.

5. Children begin to become writers

      a. shortly after entering kindergarten.

      b. when they have mastered narrative writing.

      c. shortly after they are born.

      d. at the end of the primary grades.

6. Automaticity refers to

      a. doing two things at the same time.

      b. self-motivation.

      c. the immediate response of the teacher.

      d. recall of a list of vocabulary words.

7. Narrative writing refers to writing that has as its main purpose

      a. persuading the reader of something.

      b. describing a person, place or thing.

      c. telling a story.

      d. explaining a process

True or False

    T   F 1. Writing is basically a combination of spelling, grammar, and hand-writing.

    T   F 2. Most writers write in a linear fashion.

    T   F 3. Listening to stories is of little help to an emerging writer.

    T   F 4. Writing or drawing a response to a story is a meaningful language arts activity.

    T   F 5. Mechanical writing skills are best taught within a text.

Essay and Discussion

1. Assuming that education has only a cultural transfer purpose, describe what an observer might see in a language arts program at the preschool level.
2. Compare and contrast the assumptions of the linear and process approaches to writing.
3. Describe the stages of authorship identified by Graves and Hansen.
4. Develop an activity that is aimed at helping children plan their writing and drawing.
5. Describe how pauses can help or hinder the process of drafting a piece.

References

Calkins, L.M., and S. Harwayne. 1987. *The writing workshop: A world of difference.* Portsmouth, N.H.: Heinemann.

Composition in the English language arts curriculum K–12. 1986. Albany, N.Y.: New York State Education Department.

Five, C.L. 1988. From workbook to workshop: Increasing children's involvement in the reading process. *The New Advocate* 1: 103–113.

DeGroff, L. 1989. Developing writing processes with children's literature. *The New Advocate* 2: 115–123.

Elley, W.B., I.H. Barham, H. Lamb, and M. Wyllie. 1976. The role of grammar in a secondary school English curriculum. *Research on the Teaching of English* 10: 1, 5–21.

Farris, P.J. 1989. Story time and story journals: Linking literature and writing. *The New Advocate* 2: 179–185.

Fraser, I.S., and L.M. Hodsen. 1978. Twenty-one kicks at the grammar horse. *English Journal* 50–51.

Goodman, K. 1986. *What's whole in whole language.* Portsmouth, N.H.: Heinemann.

Graves, D.H. 1983. *Writing: Teachers and children at work.* Portsmouth, N.H.: Heinemann.

Graves, D.H., and J. Hansen. 1983. The author's chair. *Language Arts* 60: 173–183.

Harste, J., C. Burke, and V. Woodward. 1989. *Language Stories and Literature Lessons.* Portsmouth, N.H.: Heinemann.

Hartwell, P. 1985. Grammar, grammars and the teaching of grammar. *College English* 47: 105–127.

Hillocks, G., Jr. 1987. Synthesis of research on teaching writing. *Educational Leadership* 44: 8, 71–82.

Hubbard, R. 1985. Second graders answer the question, Why publish? *The Reading Teacher* 38: 658–662.

Humes, A. 1983. Research in the composing process. *Review of Educational Research* 53: 201–216.

Lamme, L.L. 1989. Authorship: A key facet of whole language. *The Reading Teacher* 42: 704–710.

Lundsteen, S.W. 1976. *Children learn to communicate: Language arts through creative problem solving.* Englewood Cliffs, N.J.: Prentice-Hall.

Matsuhashi, A. 1981. Pausing and planning: The tempo of written discourse discussion. *Research on the Teaching of English* 15: 113–134.

Moffett, J., and B.J. Wagner. 1983. *Student-centered language arts and reading K–13.* Boston: Houghton-Mifflin.

Mosenthal, P. 1983. Defining classroom writing competence: A paradigmatic perspective. *Review of Educational Research* 53: 2, 217–251.

Sandmark, L., and G. Coons. 1988. Learning to read by writing about reading. *Teaching K–8* 18: 60–63.

Sawyer, W.E. 1978. How do the children write: Ask Heidi Seibert. *Language Arts* 55: 816–820.

Sawyer, W.E. 1987. Prewriting planning notation and sex of the writer as predictors of the quality of student writing. *New England Educator* 9–18.

Sawyer, W.E. 1988. The pause that regresses. *The English Record* 39: 2–8.

Smith, F. 1982. *Writing and the writer.* New York: Holt, Rinehart and Winston.

Stallard, C.K. 1974. An analysis of the behavior of good student writers. *Research in the Teaching of English* 8: 206–218.

Stauffer, R. 1980. *The language experience approach to teaching reading.* New York: Harper and Row.

Strickland, D.S., and L.M. Morrow. 1990. The daily journal: Using language experience strategies in an emergent literacy curriculum. *The Reading Teacher* 43: 422–423.

UNIT 4

Reading and Literature

U NIT GOALS

After completing this unit, the student should:

- become aware of the key understandings needed by emerging readers.
- understand the role of the teacher in enhancing the learning of reading.
- know the value of literature in a beginning reading program.
- be aware of the traditional approaches used to teach reading to young children.
- understand what is included in an integrated language arts program aimed at developing the reading ability of young children.
- possess an overall knowledge of the continuum of skills, objectives, and activities of a beginning reading program.
- be aware of the importance of the environment to a reading program.

PREVIEW

Reading is required in a multitude of activities of daily living. At the beginning of the twentieth century, when society was basically an agricultural society in the midst of change to an industrial society, it was possible for people to get along with little or no reading ability. This is no longer true. Contemporary society demands that its citizens have basic reading skills. Without such skills, people are severely limited in their employment opportunities as well as in their ability to participate in many other aspects of modern life.

The ability to read begins in early childhood. A weak foundation at that point can cause serious difficulties throughout a child's school career and even into adulthood. Most learning that occurs in other content areas in school depends to some extent on a child's ability to read effectively. An integrated language arts approach is seen as an effective approach to helping children best use their own interests and abilities to acquire the ability to read.

In this unit, the roles and understandings needed by teachers are explored. The elements of words, letters, sounds, phonics, comprehension, textbooks, workbooks, literature, and vocabulary are explained. Also included are discussions of how reading ability emerges, the relationship of reading to other content areas, and various approaches to reading instruction.

INTRODUCTION

For many years reading has been a cornerstone of primary school education. It usually consumes a major portion of the school day for children in kindergarten and the primary grades. In pre-kindergarten early childhood programs, reading readiness and language development activities usually have an equally prominent place. In spite of this, the development of reading ability continues to be a concern of educators, parents, and national leaders. The adult illiteracy rate in many developing countries is unacceptably high. Even many industrialized countries are frustrated by their own high rates of adult illiteracy.

Schools and educational programs are not the only factors that determine who will learn to read and who will not. Family support, preschool experiences, innate ability, and motivation all play a role in this outcome. However, much of what has passed as reading instruction in our schools is seen as less than effective in helping children learn to read. The possible reasons for the ineffectiveness are dealt with in another unit. For now it will only be necessary to understand what the traditional approaches are and how they are carried out with children. Along with that, this unit also describes a whole language approach to the teaching of reading, the skills, objectives, and activities that might be included in an effective program, and the importance of creating appropriate environments for beginning readers.

TRADITIONAL APPROACHES TO BEGINNING READING

For many decades, children have been taught to read using basal reading programs published by commercial publishers for use through the elementary grades. Basal reading programs usually include a set of texts keyed to specific grade levels, a set of accompanying workbooks, dittos, and corresponding teacher manuals. More recently, these programs have produced many additional supplementary materials for use with the reading texts. The supplementary materials include charts and checklists, vocabulary dittos, comprehension dittos, phonics worksheets, computerized management systems, skills checklists, placement tests, end-of-level tests, cumulative records, skills assessment sheets, enrichment activities, and resource kits. Each of the supplementary materials is usually keyed to specific skills on a scope and sequence chart used by the series. A scope and sequence chart is a grid that contains the sequence of reading skills taught by the series and such factors as the grade level at which it is taught and the materials used to teach it.

Publishers are under a lot of pressure to produce materials that will be seen favorably by those states that adopt texts on a statewide basis. As a result, there is not a great variety among the programs. In reviewing different programs, one can easily notice more similarities than differences. Most of the basal text series also produce a readiness version to be used in kindergarten to "get children ready" to begin using the actual series. Some publishers also produce an early childhood level of the program to be used with preschoolers. Other early childhood and readiness programs are available that are not associated with a specific basal reading series. Most are geared toward preparing children to enter a kindergarten readiness or a beginning reader program in grade one.

For several decades, debate has focused on the role of phonics as a central component of early reading programs. This is because word recognition has traditionally been the central focus of early reading instruction. Some series give much stress to phonics instruction. Others give more emphasis to recognition of whole words. This latter approach is often referred to as the "look-say" approach. More recently, the importance of comprehension has been emphasized as a part of early reading instruction. As a result, publishers have increased this aspect of their programs at the early levels. As whole language has become more prominent, publishers have revised their programs to include some of the activities frequently observed in whole language classrooms. As a result, most commercially produced programs have become an eclectic combination of each of these. It is helpful to understand the key aspects of readiness, phonics, looksay, and eclectic approaches even though there are probably no programs that fall purely into any of them.

Reading Readiness Programs

In a traditional approach to reading, the term *reading readiness* refers to the ability of the child to profit from beginning reading instruction. It is seen as including a combination of intellectual, maturational, motivational, social, and experiential factors. While the term is widely used, the concept is somewhat vague in terms of producing an agreed upon group of behaviors that identify children who are now ready to begin formal reading instruction.

Intellectual factors might be seen as including clear speech, knowledge of the alphabet and letter sounds, knowledge of basic concept words (e.g. up/down, left/right, color words), recognition of some words, and an understanding of basic word meanings. Maturational factors might include adequate physical development, normal speech, vision, and hearing, and the ability to do fine motor tasks (e.g., color within the lines, cut with scissors on the line). Motivational factors might include interest in stories and reading, desire to use books during free time, and the ability to remember events from a story. Social factors might include the ability to work within a group, the ability to share, and the ability to work independently. Experiential factors might include knowledge of colors, sizes, and shapes, an awareness of concepts (e.g., animals, foods, clothes), and the ability to talk about each of these.

Traditional readiness programs have tended to focus on reading by attempting to have children learn the letters of the alphabet in isolation. That is, entire weeks are spent studying the letters R, S, A, and so on. The letter is introduced by the teacher, and some words beginning with that letter are usually noted as well. During the next several lessons, children might say, identify, trace, color, and create sculptures of the letter for that week. Each week a new letter is introduced until the entire alphabet is covered. Commercial programs are available that focus solely on teaching the alphabet over the course of an entire academic year. Consonants are usually introduced

first. Vowels, due to the fact that they can have multiple sounds associated with them, are introduced later in the programs.

The tendency to focus on letters and letter sounds in readiness programs is based upon the belief that children need to master these skills in order to go on to the next level of language: words. Actually, it is the next level only in terms of quantity. That is, words are bigger than letters. In many ways, however, words may be easier for children to understand than letters because words have meaning attached to them whereas letters do not. Letters are highly abstract elements. They have sounds that, combined with other sounds, comprise words. Anderson (1964) has identified forty-two sounds, or phonemes, which correspond to the twenty-six graphemes, or letters, of the alphabet as follows:

Consonants

p as in pan	b as in bat	t as in ton	d as in dog
k as in kid	g as in go	f as in fan	v as in van
s as in see	z as in zoo	th as in then	th as in thin
ch as in chat	j as in jam	w as in way	wh as in whistle
sh as in shoe	zh as in measure	l as in lot	m as in man
n as in not	r as in run	y as in you	h as in him

Vowels

a as in at	a as in ate	e as in pen	e as in me
i as in it	i as in ice	o as in mop	o as in so
u as in up	u as in use	oo as in mood	oo as in foot
au as in auto	ou as in our	oi as in oil	ah as in ma
ai(r) as in pair			
e(r) as in her			

Complicating the matter further is the fact that a single sound may have a number of different spellings. Consider the sound of long "e" which can spelled e (as in me), ee (as in see), ei (as in either), ea (as in seat), ae (as in aegis), eo (as in people), ois (as in chamois), ey (as in key), i (as in ski), ay (as in quay), oe (as in amoeba), and y (as in baby). This problem repeats itself with all of the other vowels and many of the consonants as well. As a result, seeing reading readiness and initial reading instruction as mainly a phonetic awareness process places the teacher in an instructionally impossible situation with young children.

Reading readiness programs often stress perceptual development training as important, despite the absence of a body of research to support such a position. Perceptual development is typically described as auditory or visual. Auditory perception refers to the ability to obtain information from sounds, noise, speech, music, and so forth. Visual perception refers to the ability to obtain information such as shape, size, and color from the visual world. While such skills may have some use in reading and writing, little evidence suggests that they can be either efficiently increased through instruction or transferred to a reading situation by the child after they have been practiced in isolation. In spite of this, some educators continue to teach these skills in isolation as part of a reading readiness program.

Phonics Programs

The terms *phonics* and *phonetics* are frequently confused. Phonetics is the scientific study of speech sounds. Phonics has a number of meanings. First, it refers to any reading instructional approach that stresses sound-symbol relationships. This is especially true in beginning reading. Second, it can refer to a number of different approaches to the teaching of sound-symbol relationships as part of reading instruction. Third, it can refer to any type of materials and activities that are a part of an instructional program designed to teach phonic generalizations.

The two major approaches to teaching phonics are analytic and synthetic. Analytic phonics, also known as deductive phonics, uses an approach that proceeds from generalizations to specifics. With this approach, children are first taught a number of sight words followed by instruction in key phonic generalizations. The learners are then taught to apply these generalizations to other words in order to learn symbol-sound relationships.

Synthetic phonics, also known as inductive phonics, uses a part-to-whole approach. Children begin by learning the sounds represented by letters and combinations of letters. While learning to blend the sounds together to form words, learners are taught the generalizations to be applied in learning symbol-sound relationships.

The basic philosophy of a phonics approach to beginning reading assumes that the key to successfully learning to read is through the ability to master sound-symbol correspondence. Whether analytic or synthetic phonics approaches are used, sound-symbol correspondence as it applies to letters and words is held as the most important reading skill.

Phonics instruction traditionally takes place over several years in the elementary school. While there is some variation among programs, the sequence of major phonics skills cited by Anderson (1964) continues to be typical of many commercial programs:

1. Beginning sounds
2. Words that sound alike
3. Letter and word differences
4. Matching letters and words
5. Sound elements
6. Consonant sounds (e.g., d, l, m, p)
7. Speech consonants (e.g., sh, th) and consonant blends (e.g., sp, tw, fr)
8. Short vowels
9. Long vowels
10. Vowel blends (e.g., oi, au) and double vowels (e.g., ea, ee)
11. Silent letters (e.g., kn, gn)
12. Variant consonants (e.g., g, s)
13. Final e
14. Vowels followed by r
15. Prefixes
16. Suffixes

There are variations and subskills introduced under each of the above skill areas. Generally, children are taught to recognize sounds at the beginning of words, also referred to as the initial position. Later, recognition skills are learned for sounds found in the middle of words (medial position) and at the ends of words (final position). The grade at which the skills of a phonics program are taught varies from program to program. There is a tendency to move the instruction of these skills into increasingly lower grade levels, kindergarten, and even preschool programs.

Phonics skills are usually taught in isolation. That is, they are taught outside of any meaningful text or story. Often they appear on worksheets or dittos provided to each child. The children are instructed to write, copy, trace, recite, and identify the element being taught. This is often done by directing children to underline, circle, cross out, or print the correct answer to a series of tasks on a paper. Pictures and illustrations are often used to give children words to say that contain the actual sound-symbol relationships being studied at the time.

Basal readers are a part of the phonics program. Basal readers are books that contain a series of stories or brief essays. The stories are often written with a highly controlled vocabulary. Such a vocabulary consists mainly of words containing only the phonics elements the children have learned up to that point in their instruction. The intent of such stories is to provide opportunities for children to gain practice in using the phonic elements they have mastered at the time they are exposed to a particular story.

Look-Say Programs

The look-say method is also known as the analytic method or the word method. Essentially, it is an approach to beginning reading in which children are taught a substantial number of words prior to instruction in word analysis or word attack. It emerged as an approach around 1900 and has been used off and on throughout the twentieth century. It has often been attacked by those favoring a phonics approach.

Few programs can be called a pure look-say approach, just as few programs can be called a pure phonics approach. Those that lean toward a look-say methodology tend to approach initial reading instruction with materials and procedures that are rather similar to those used in a phonics program. The programs tend to break down the task of reading into separate skills that can be taught, practiced, and evaluated. Worksheets, dittos, and basals with controlled vocabulary are all staples of such programs.

Eclectic Approach

As noted previously, there are probably no initial reading programs that can be characterized as either a pure phonics or a pure look-say approach. Advocates of phonics programs attacked look-say methods as not addressing the needs of children to be able to decode unfamiliar words in their reading. Advocates of look-say programs attacked phonics methods as spending too much time on word attack skills while ignoring the fundamental need of children to be able to recognize words without going through a laborious decoding process for each word. Those who choose to use an eclectic approach in reading in the early childhood classroom give credence to both positions.

An eclectic approach is a system of teaching reading that takes pieces of a number of approaches and combines them in still another system. Most commercial readiness and early reading programs can best be described as eclectic approaches. Part of this is because there is some logic and validity to each of the views of early reading instruction. Some of the rationale for combining the programs is a response to marketing needs. Publishers must appeal to a variety of teachers and other educators if their programs are going to be successful.

An eclectic program is often cited as addressing the needs of children to have a fund of words that can be identified by sight while at the same time containing a strong phonics component. A major problem with such an approach is that by selecting different parts of disparate approaches, eclectic programs must often ignore some of the fundamental beliefs and assumptions supporting the different approaches. The approach can become no program at all since it lacks an overriding philosophy.

The eclectic approach, in spite of its obvious drawback of lacking a fundamental philosophy, is frequently cited as the method of choice. It allows teachers to take more control over what to include and exclude from classroom instruction. It also allows commercial publishers to include new ideas, methods, and activities within their materials. When educators become more concerned with comprehension as a part of the reading program, publishers expand programs to include more materials and activities in that area. The expansion of programs to include more materials directed toward comprehension essentially followed the process used to teach word and phonics skills. That is, comprehension is broken down into a set of discreet skills to be introduced, taught, practiced, and assessed individually. The skills are taught in isolation from other comprehension skills and often in isolation from whole pieces of text. Examples of such skills include:

1. Identifying the main idea of a paragraph or story
2. Recalling literal (factual) information
3. Understanding vocabulary
4. Identifying cause-effect relationships
5. Recalling a sequence of events
6. Drawing conclusions
7. Identifying implicit (unstated) information
8. Predicting outcomes

9. Identifying key terms
10. Distinguishing fact from opinion

As eclectic programs have included new ideas and the activities and materials needed to address them, older parts of the programs remained. As a result, teacher manuals, letter cards, word cards, basal readers, ditto sets, workbooks, skills practice books, assessment systems, and activity sheets needed to implement readiness and early reading instructional programs have reached a physical size that can best be described as massive.

WHOLE LANGUAGE APPROACH TO READING

A whole language approach to teaching reading is a fundamentally different approach. It has its own philosophy, assumptions, theoretical constructs, and research support. Responding to marketing pressures, commercial eclectic approaches have attempted to incorporate whole language into their array of materials and procedures. It hasn't been successful. A whole language approach is not a set of materials or a series of activities. While certain skills, objectives, materials, and activities might be observed in a whole language classroom, they do not constitute the essence of whole language. Adopting or adapting any of those aspects of whole language leaves the fundamental belief system behind. Three key beliefs of a whole language approach underlie what occurs in such a reading program. Those beliefs hold that reading instruction should be seen as a process, that it should be meaningful to children, and that there should be active involvement on the part of the learners.

Meaningfulness

The concept of meaningfulness holds that learning should be understandable to children and that it should make sense in their lives. The instruction should encompass materials and activities that can be related to the experiences they have acquired. Isolated skills taught in abstract ways are not appropriate. This does not mean that children do not need to learn the alphabet, phonics, and words. It does mean, however, that they need to learn these things in nat-

ural ways and within the context of real language and real literature written for children.

The concept of meaningfulness corresponds to those things that a child can comprehend. Comprehension refers to whether or not a child can relate new information or ideas to something already known in a way that makes sense to the child. As skills-based readiness and reading programs have been transplanted into nursery school and daycare programs, children are given increased instruction in isolated language skills having little meaning to them. In one study of preschool settings, children as young as three years old were observed completing developmental worksheets on the capital letter B. They were not allowed to engage in playtime until they had completed their worksheets (Hiebert, Stacy, and Jordan 1985). This type of developmentally inappropriate activity has drawn the criticism of many early childhood educators (Elkind 1987; Gallagher and Sigel 1987).

Preschool Experiences.

Instruction aimed at helping children grow toward the ability to read must take into account the experiences they have had and how instruction can be made meaningful within the context of that experience. One aspect to consider in determining preschoolers' knowledge of reading concepts is storybook reading. When asked to "read" a familiar storybook, three stages are observed (Pappas and Brown 1987; Sulzby 1985). At the first stage, children's responses consist primarily of labeling and commenting about the pictures on the page. At the second stage, children use the pictures to help tell the story. The language characterizing their tellings often has the rhythm and structure of written language. At the third stage, occurring primarily between three and six years of age, the tellings increasingly have the sound of formal speech. Children at this stage pay more attention to the language written on the page as well.

Besides familiarity with storybooks, children are more able to engage in early reading experiences if they are familiar with the culture in which they live. Visits to firehouses, stores, beaches, banks, parks, zoos, and so forth can provide children with a wealth of experiential background. Opportunities to learn about the not-so-familiar are beneficial as well since

FIGURE 4-1 Children create meaning by responding to stories in words and pictures.

many stories they will be exposed to will take place outside of their own neighborhoods. Therefore, participation in such experiences as multi-ethnic festivals and state fairs can broaden the range of background knowledge a child can bring to the reading experience.

Learning the Alphabet.

For years, teachers and parents have placed great value on children learning to recite the alphabet, letter identification, and letter formation as major parts of early schooling. Hiebert and Sawyer (1984) report that children entering kindergarten can name an average of fourteen letters. Letter identification has been seen as a predictor of success in learning to read (Durrell, 1958; Walsh, Price, and Gillingham, 1988). Children's knowledge of letters, however, does not mean that they understand the function of those letters. The same thing can be said about other early skills such as word recognition, phonemic awareness, and sound-symbol correspondence. Lomax and Mc-

Gee (1987) found that children at age three have often naturally learned to identify letters and several concepts about print. While they found that children did not seem to demonstrate much learning about such things as sound-symbol correspondence and word reading until age five or six, they did find that earlier learning was highly related to later learning. In fact, the earlier learning tended to continue to grow as new concepts and understandings begin to develop. This suggests a connectedness between each of the skills. That is, they underlie and support each other.

Besides letter recognition, letter production or writing is an important early reading development. Clay (1975) observed that preschoolers often created what she described as mock letters. These are letter-like figures containing many of the characteristics of letters. Once children know a few standard letters, they combine mock letters with the standard letters in their preschool writing and even into the first grade (Sulzby, Barnhart, and Hieshima 1989). Children seem to use what they know about letters to create their writing. It is often helpful for a teacher to listen to children discuss what they know about letters. This talk, or meta-knowledge about language, reveals the knowledge children possess about the form and function of language (McGee and Richgels 1989).

Children expand their knowledge of the form and function of language by learning to write their names (Clay 1975; Ferreiro 1986). This knowledge grows to include an understanding of the relationship between letters and sounds when children begin to use invented spelling in their writing (Ferreiro and Teberosky 1982). Much of the letter learning seems to have occurred in interactive dialogues and letter games between parent and child that followed predictable patterns (McGee and Richgels 1989). At the beginning of the routines, the parent or teacher assumes the bulk of the dialogue, often taking both the adult's and the child's role. After awhile, the child takes the child's role and eventually both the adult's and the child's role. This explanation is supported by Vygotsky's (1981) theory of development in which the child internalizes the structure of the activity until able to complete the activity independently.

Understanding how children come to learn the alphabet and the role that the adult must assume can help teachers better understand how and when to teach children about letters. Obviously, the teacher must be aware of the child's understanding of the form and function of letters. Simply introducing a letter to be learned each week is not appropriate. Young children may not be attending to letters and sounds at the time instruction is being provided in a formal program. Reading is, after all, primarily a meaning-making activity. It is more effective to invite children to participate in meaningful language activities in which they will have purposeful reasons for learning letters. McGee and Richgels (1989) identify a number of such activities:

- Inviting children to bring environmental print items (e.g., cereal boxes) to class for discussion and writing purposes
- Reading and writing the names of the children for display and identification purposes around the room
- Writing lists, thank-you notes, and stories as a part of the ongoing classroom activities
- Reading, writing, and talking about alphabet books
- Including alphabet rhymes, chants, and songs within the regular classroom program and activities

Phonics Instruction

A considerable body of theory and research supports a knowledge of phonics as an important reading skill (Anderson, Hiebert, Scott, and Wilkinson 1985; Chall 1983; Johnson and Baumann 1984; Pflaum, Walberg, Karegianes, and Rasher 1980; Williams 1985). On the other hand, some research demonstrates that while phonics can be taught as a totally isolated skill, such learning can have little effect on language understanding and learning to read (Lundberg, Frost, and Petersen 1988). A whole language approach advocates the use of whole stories with an emphasis on meaning. Are whole language and phonics instruction on opposing sides? No, not really. Are whole language and programs that teach phonics as skills isolated from meaningful texts on opposing sides? Yes, most definitely. Those who contend that whole language teachers are opposed to phonics are merely showing that they do not understand the whole language approach.

A basic tenet of the whole language philosophy is that children learn language that they hear, see, read, and use in meaningful ways (Cazden 1972; Chomsky 1972; Trachtenburg 1990; White 1984). In view of this, it makes sense to refrain from engaging children in activities that make little sense to them. They may learn some of the skills and be able to respond to test items administered in predictable situations. The ability of children to rapidly transfer those skills to other more meaningful contexts that are much less predictable than controlled worksheets, however, is highly suspect.

Whole language teachers address phonics, but within the context of meaningful literature. For young children, the phonics elements might include, initially, the sounds of the consonants. Such instruction can be a part of the activities described in the section on alphabet instruction above and through any number of storybooks found in most early childhood classrooms. Besides the consonant sounds, the vowel sounds might be introduced at times when it is developmentally appropriate for the children.

Vowel sounds can cause difficulty. When this occurs, it is often because instruction is presented to children before they are developmentally capable of benefiting from such instruction. When children can benefit, the instruction can usually be included as part of a literacy lesson using storybooks. While both short and long vowel sound instruction can be included using the following books, there are many others that could serve just as well (Trachtenburg 1990).

Vowel	Short/Long	Author/Title
a	short	Dr. Seuss, *The Cat in the Hat* (1957)
a	long	Kevin Henkes, *Sheila Rae, the Brave* (1987)
e	short	Paul Galdone, *The Little Red Hen* (1973)
e	long	Bill Martin, *Brown Bear, Brown Bear, What Do You See?*
i	short	Pat Hutchins, *Titch* (1971)
i	long	Barbara S. Hazen, *Tight Times* (1979)
o	short	Dr. Seuss, *Fox in Socks* (1965)
o	long	Brock Cole, *The Giant's Toe* (1986)

u	short	James Marshall, *The Cut-Ups* (1984)
u	long	Lore Segal, *Tell Me a Trudy* (1977)

The major point to be made is that phonics instruction can be provided at the developmentally appropriate time within the rich context of literature. If done in this way, it is meaningful for children, eliminates much of the problem of transfer and takes the tedium of completing worksheets out of the picture. Discussions about the role and function of the letters can arise naturally with the teacher and the child acting as a learning team.

Real Literature

The texts used as the medium for teaching about language in a whole language program consist of the literature that is specifically written as books for children. They were not written as texts for teaching a specific letter, sound, or word. Therefore they do not have a controlled vocabulary designed to include only those words that can be decoded using the rules and skills taught up to that point in the program. As a result, the authors of the literature are free to use the words they see as best conveying the meaning they envision in their minds. This leads to text that is of higher interest to children because it is free of artificial constraints that limit its vividness of language.

A traditional approach might, for example, attempt to teach the "short o" sound by first drilling the students on the sound that the "short o" makes. This might be followed by an identification task such as:

DIRECTIONS: Circle each of the following words that has the "short o" sound in it.

cat   cot   net   not   lot   let   log

This activity might be accompanied by a piece in a basal text that uses the "short o" sound in a number of words in the text. Such a piece might read something like this:

BOB'S TOP

Bob has a top.
It is a new top.
See Bob's new top.
Drop the top.
See Bob drop the top.
The top stops.

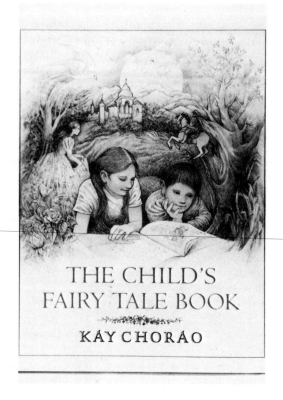

FIGURE 4-2 Real literature is used in abundance by the whole language teacher. *From* The Child's Fairy Tale Book, *by Kay Chorao. Reprinted courtesy of E.P. Dutton.*

While many children in the early stages of literacy development might be able to read this type of text, it does not meet their literacy needs. It is not a rich text. It is contrived, dull, and lacking in meaning. It is a story that is not going anywhere. It is a totally forgettable piece. Most of this type of writing is only published anonymously in basal series. The reason for its existence is to provide material for children to practice reading skills in controlled situations.

Using real literature, children are surrounded with print that contains the "short o" sound, but in the context of language that may contain other sounds and structures they may not have been formally taught as yet. There is nothing wrong with this. Most children have spent years listening to stories that contain sounds they have not learned to decode, words they are hearing for the first time, and ideas that are totally new to them. Rather than harming children, this provides them with new things to discover, a reason for attending, and grist for their curiosity. Using literature enables children to hear the "short o" sound in phrases such as "a dollop of jam," "lock the beast in the barn," and "a blue smock filled with boxes of colored chalk." The more vivid vocabulary found in these phrases accomplishes the goal of providing examples of language that uses the "short o" sound. In so doing, it also provides texts that have a heart and soul rather than texts that are merely hollow shells of language.

Process

Reading is a process rather than a product. A process is a systematic series of actions, activities, or procedures directed toward some end. The intended end result in reading is the arrival at the meaning of the written message. The process of reading is not merely a matter of decoding or identifying words. Being able to correctly say the words on the page does not mean that a child has an understanding of those words. There are different aspects to the process. There is a purpose to the process. There are some reliable procedures within the process that can help the child arrive at meaning. The teacher has a specific role in facilitating the process.

Components of the Process.

Reading involves constructive, selective, and strategic processes (State Education Department 1989). Each of these requires thought on the part of the reader in order to solve the problems presented to the reader by the text. As the reader solves these problems, the meaning of the text becomes clear.

In order to construct or build meaning from the text, the teacher must consider the reading task, the written text, and the reader. The reading task involves metacognition. That is, readers must be aware of themselves as readers. They must understand their purpose for reading, how much information they need to get from the text, and how they will decide that they have accomplished the task. With young children, this must be constantly modeled by the teacher. The teacher should always identify the purpose for reading. Discussions can also involve prediction of story events and various aspects of the story.

Readers need to consider the text material and the effect that its characteristics might have on meaning. Is the piece a narrative or a poem? Do the illustrations aid in understanding the story? Does the author use words and phrases that are particularly helpful or particularly confusing? Are the ideas in the story at the appropriate level of complexity for the children? The answers to each of these questions will play a role in the construction of meaning.

Readers need to be aware that they bring valuable background knowledge that can aid their comprehension. If the story takes place at the ocean, having had a vacation at the seashore will be helpful to understanding the story. In addition, interest, attending ability, and familiarity with the patterns of language used in the story all play a role in deriving meaning for the reader.

Readers must engage in the process of selecting behaviors that best aid their comprehension of text. With younger readers, such things as listening attentively, asking questions about word meanings and story actions, and requesting repeated readings may be useful. As children begin to read more independently, they need to use the appropriate phonemic (sound), semantic (meaning), and syntactic (structure) knowledge that they possess in order to make sense of what they are reading. Each of these terms is described later in this unit. One of the goals of reading instruction is to enable students to make rapid decisions about which of these cues to use for effective reading.

Another aspect of metacognition is the role of strategies as a part of the reading process. Readers must become aware of the fact that there are activities they can engage in before, during, and after reading that will enable them to better comprehend the text they are reading. By actively engaging in decisions about how to use the other processes, readers learn to better understand their texts.

Purpose for Reading.

Let us take a giant step back for a moment in order to get a total perspective on the purpose for reading. Setting purposes for reading is an important part of arriving at meaning. We may help children to see this by explaining that we are reading a story to find out if the big bad wolf did actually gobble down the three little pigs. We may also ask those children to find out if the story tells us anything about loving one's brothers as well. While each can be a legitimate purpose for reading, the second may be more important in the long term.

News reports have for years carried stories of how reading and thinking are critical to the survival of hostages and war prisoners. DeMott (1990) extends and explains this by relating it to the readers and writers who struggled behind the iron curtain for the better part of the twentieth century. While their government systematically attempted to control the truth through a large propaganda machine, entire generations of readers and writers strove to preserve that truth at great peril to their lives. DeMott concludes that in the total scheme of things, the fundamental reason for reading and writing is to connect ourselves to humanity and to extend the habit of telling the truth. While this may seem like a rather abstract concept to apply to young children, it can be seen in concrete terms anytime we read a book to a child. There is no mistaking the genuine laughter at the humorous antics of a character in a story. The tear that form in the child's eye when reading about the death of a pet in a storybook is real. Each enables the child to connect to truth, to humanity, and to life.

Reliable Procedures.

As children begin to engage in reading texts independently, they need to develop a repertoire of strategies and procedures to solve the problems they encounter in the text. The two major problems they are most likely to encounter are the identification of unfamiliar words and the comprehension of the text they are attempting to read. Strategies can be used by children who are making the transition from listening to stories to reading stories independently. Other strategies, particularly those dealing with comprehension, may be used by students who have not yet begun to make the transition.

For word identification, young readers need to make use of the three major cue systems: semantic, syntactic, and graphophonic. Semantic cues provide evidence from the general meaning of a text that aids the reader in identifying an unknown word. In a text about cowboys, a young reader might come across the word *horse*. If the text stated "The cowboy jumped on

FIGURE 4-3 A comfortable place for reading is like a doorway to the entire world.

the horse and rode across the field," the reader has evidence within the rest of the story to predict the actual word. It is less likely that a cowboy would ride a house than a horse. The young reader is more likely to read horse, since it makes sense within the context in which it is found.

Syntax provides evidence for identifying an unknown word from a knowledge of the rules and patterns of language. The young child may know the rules implicitly from language use rather than from being able to give definitions for the rules. Suppose a young reader came across a line in a storybook that reads "Billy drew a picture of his puppy," and could not identify the word *drew*. A knowledge of the structure of language would suggest that the word is a verb or an action word because there is the clear implication that something is going to be done regarding a picture. One can hang, destroy, paint, frame, or draw a picture. The child may be aided by some of the semantic features of the story at this point, such as the fact that Billy is an artist and is excited about getting a new puppy. The child might conclude at this point that the word is *drew*.

The child might have also used some graphophonic cues to aid in the identification of the word. Graphophonic cues include the visual characteristics and the sound characteristics of the letters. This is the least efficient tool of the three, but one that is sometimes needed for word identification. In this case, the young reader might have known the sound that *d* or *dr* makes and have concluded that the word could not be hang, destroy, paint, or frame.

Since semantic cues are an important part of the strategies used for word identification, it stands to reason that there is an overlap between word identification and comprehension strategies. Some of these overlapping strategies have been identified by Holdaway (1979):

- Re-run—Before making a proposal or correction, the reader begins the sentence again in an effort to determine a word.
- Read-on—Before making a proposal or correction, the reader continues reading to the end of the sentence, perhaps inserting the word *blank* for the unknown word.
- Picture—The reader uses the pictures or illustrations on the page to aid in understanding and thus to give clues about the unfamiliar word. Eventually a picture in the mind should replace the picture on the page.
- Identify—The reader might recall having seen the word in another place. If this procedure is used, a re-run should be used before proceeding on.
- Compare—The reader compares the word with a more familiar word in an attempt to provide clues about the new word.
- Ask—The reader simply asks someone. This is a favorite strategy of young children who teach themselves to read. When it is used, the teacher should simply supply the word and refrain from supplying a lesson. This enables the young reader to continue on with the meaning of the piece still fresh in mind.

Comprehension is a constructive process. The reader must participate in building meaning. There are many effective strategies for building meaning that can be implemented before, during, and after the actual act of reading the text. They all deal with building meaning, anticipating meaning, and re-creating meaning. Among the more effective strategies are:

- Predicting—The reader uses background knowledge, illustrations, and whatever text has been read to that point to construct hypotheses regarding the next sentence or action in the story. This can be done with small groups during story time, with bedtime or naptime reading, and when a child is engaged in independent reading. Finding out the degree of accuracy of the predictions is a powerful feedback communication for the child.
- Discussion—The obvious tool for understanding is simply talking about a story. It can be done at any point in the reading process. A teacher who participates in such a discussion can learn about what children do and don't understand, where they are confused, and how they go about the process of making sense of the language. The discussion can include prediction activities, reviews of what has been read, and imaginative activities.
- Imaginative activities—Holdaway (1979) suggests that stories are usually about the inner world of the emotions, intentions, behaviors, or human purposes. For the most part, these cannot be adequately expressed in words alone. The words must be backed up with feelings to have a true reality. By seeing actions in the story modeled, children can learn to use their own imaginations to become emotionally closer to the stories and the characters within those stories.
- Repetition—Whenever the meaning of the story is re-created in some way, understanding is reinforced. There are many ways to re-create the meaning of the story. For younger children, acting out the story, drawing pictures about the story, rereading the story, retelling the story, and reading related stories are all effective recreations of the meaning of the original story. For slightly older children, reading response journals can be added to the list. A reading response journal is a blank book in which children can write or draw a response to a story. It may be a summary of the story, questions about the story, a statement of how the story made them feel, or descriptions of how they wish the story had turned out.

Role of the Teacher.

Young children frequently learn to read and write naturally when they are immersed in a rich environment of meaningful texts (Staab 1990). This does not mean, however, that teachers have no role in reading development. They have a very definite role, but it is different from the traditional role of the teacher as the leader and center of the instructional process. In a whole language classroom, the teacher serves as a mediator and facilitator for children's learning. Newman (1985) calls this "leading from behind." This means that the teacher's role is to find out what the child is attempting to do and to help the child accomplish the task. Staab (1990) cautions that the mediation should be relevant to the child's task and in the context of meaningful learning. This does not mean that direct instruction is not provided. Rather, much of what used to be taught through direct instruction is now presented indirectly through mediation that might involve peer interaction, conferencing with the teacher, mini-lessons, modeling a strategy, and so on.

A classroom structured in such a way allows the teacher more opportunities to both learn about the needs of the children and develop mediation procedures to meet those needs. Goodman (1985) identifies these opportunities to engage in "kidwatching" as an important part of the planning, instructional, and assessment processes.

Active Involvement

Language learning is not a passive activity. It is not something done sitting in an easy chair while taking little or no initiative to participate in the process. Traditional approaches to teaching reading and writing have often leaned in this more passive direction. The teacher was seen as the source of knowledge, while children were viewed as passive recipients of that knowledge. The major activity of children was to read assigned texts, learn specified rules and complete worksheets as directed. A whole language approach sees all language learning as an active process. It sees it as an activity in which all members of the learning group share the responsibility for learning. Each of these ideas is further described here. In contrast, a passive activity is also explored. The relationship between television viewing and the reading development of young children is also described.

Shared Social Activity.

Children are actively involved in developing their reading ability long before they enter elementary

FIGURE 4-4 This teacher understands reading as a social activity.

school. They learn oral language, tell stories from the pictures in a book, learn letters, identify words, and even learn to read in some cases. They don't do any of these things by being passive. They accomplish each by actively reponding to their own curiosity and by attending to the world around them.

Teale and Sulzby (1989) have reviewed contemporary research on reading development. They have discovered a number of trends that indicate that researchers are attending to this early reading development. First, the age range of children studied has been extended downward to include children from almost the moment of birth. Second, literacy is increasingly being viewed as a social, language, and psychological process rather than as a simple cognitive process. Third, research on literacy is seen as closely tied to the child's environment. For this reason, more research is being conducted in both home and school settings.

Strickland (1990) has identified several of the findings revealed by this research on early literacy. First, much early language learning occurs naturally through interactions with people and the environment rather than as a result of direct instruction. Second, learning to read does not follow learning to talk. Oral language and reading development grow in an interdependent manner, each supporting the other. Oral language requires social contact. Third, learning to read requires meaningful activities with responsive others. Fourth, learning to read is particularly enhanced by shared book reading in which children acquire a sense of themselves as readers.

Shared Responsibility.

In a whole language classroom, children learn to take responsibility for their learning and reading development. Some children are more willing to accept this role than others. The more reluctant children need additional teacher support and mediation to move them in this direction. On the other hand, some teachers are reluctant to share the responsibility for student learning with the children themselves. This is particularly true of kindergarten and primary grade teachers when they are burdened with standardized tests and state mandated accountability programs.

To facilitate shared responsibility, a range of approaches has evolved for using tradebooks with children. There are, of course, those programs that advocate children's self selection of books for use in a reading instructional program (Veatch 1978). Some programs advocate cooperative student action in selecting books and activities (Stevens, Madden, Slavin, and Farnish 1987). Still others (Great Books 1984) include literature in a more traditional program of teacher-led discussions. A whole language approach, stressing the active involvement of learners, leans toward approaches that encourage student involvement. One of the primary aims of an educational program is to foster independent learning on the part of children. As long as children are forced to be dependent upon the teacher for learning decisions, independent learning behaviors will be delayed.

Television

Television viewing is a passive pursuit. The words, the pictures, and the sounds are all provided to the viewer. Most commercial television programs, particularly those aimed at a younger audience, contain simple plots, characters, settings, and themes. The presentations are largely done through pictures as opposed to language. The tendency for the viewers to play a passive role in watching television has long been criticized as having a negative effect on children.

Research studies conducted on young children support the belief that television has a negative effect on schooling in general and literacy development in particular. However, there is not a simple relationship between the two. That is, it cannot be stated categorically that the more television children watch the more their reading development will be slowed. There are different effects for different children. For some children, those who limit their viewing to an hour or so per day, there does not seem to be a negative effect associated with television viewing (Neuman, 1988). On the other hand, for heavy viewers the correlation between viewing time and reading development is always strongly negative (Beentjes and Van der Voort 1988).

The amount of television viewing has different effects on children depending on the type of shows they watch as well as their socio-economic status, intelligence, sex, and age. A negative relationship exists between reading development and entertainment types of shows such as cartoons and situation comedies (Degrosky 1981; Neuman 1981; Smyser-O'Sullivan 1981). A positive effect was found when children tend to view information-type programs such as news shows (Potter 1987). For light and moderate viewers, there is a negative effect for higher socio-ecomomic status children and a positive effect for lower socio-economic status children (Fetler 1984). Fetler suggested that this may be due to the fact that television may create some cultural opportunities for the latter group. There is conflicting evidence when comparing the viewing of girls and boys. A summary of research suggests that negative relationship may be stronger for girls than for boys (Williams, Haertel, Haertel, and Walberg 1982). Other studies found the opposite to be true (Morgan and Gross 1980; Smyser-O'Sullivan 1981).

While some studies have found that the negative

effect of television is stronger for older children (Neuman 1988), some studies have not found any differences based on age (Kohr 1979). Still other studies have found stronger relationships for both older and younger children (Corteen and Williams 1986). Corteen and Williams present a persuasive argument for believing that the strongest negative effects occur with the youngest children. They contend that young children are at the stage of language development that requires much practice to develop ease and fluency. The displacement of leisure time language and reading with television viewing has a twofold negative effect. First, young children do not improve their reading and language skills through practice. Second, they develop the habit of watching television rather than reading, which further decreases their opportunities to improve their reading ability.

In view of the research, one cannot compile a set of absolute truths about television viewing and its relationship to literacy development. It seems safe, however, to seriously question the advisability of allowing young children to spend large amounts of time in such a passive activity. This is especially true in view of the research supporting the need for active involvement on the part of children to learn language.

SKILLS AND OBJECTIVES FOR READING

The skills and objectives of an integrated language arts program are classified in this unit into four broad categories. These include early reading skills, reading for personal response, reading for information acquisition, and reading for evaluation and critical analysis. As with all of the language modes, there is substantial overlap between reading, writing, and oral language. The skills described here should not have age expectations placed on them. Children should begin to engage in the development of each as it is developmentally appropriate for them to do so. In addition to a lack of age expectations, there is no rigid sequence to these objectives and skills. Children get to whatever point they are in language development through a variety of different paths. Their needs must be considered by teachers who help them along those paths.

Early Reading Skills

Traditionally, the skills and concepts taught to children prior to the time they are able to read independently have been grouped in a category identified as reading readiness. The term *reading readiness* implies that there are things children need to know and do before they can begin to learn to read. Such a concept does not conform to the beliefs underlying a whole language approach. Rather, the fact that all language modes are interconnected suggests that children are learning important reading skills from the moment of birth. It is true that they are not ordinarily learning word decoding and sound-symbol correspondence at age two. However, we know that reading is based more on communicating sense than on mastering the mechanical skills associated with decoding unfamiliar words. As a result, early reading skills associated with a whole language early education program are in sharp contrast to traditional readiness skills that merely push beginning decoding skill learning downward. The early reading skills found here deal with language development and responding to the world of books, stories, and literature.

Oral Language Ability.

In order to have a background in which to integrate new information, children must develop their general language skills. A major part of this is done through informal opportunities to use listening and speaking. Through these opportunities, children build their vocabularies, develop social listening and speaking behaviors, and learn to express complete ideas for a variety of purposes. Experiencing success in this area provides them with a heightened sense of self-esteem. This, in turn, gives them the needed confidence to continue engaging in social communications and to take risks with language. Their success encourages still more success.

Responding to Literature.

The ability to respond to literature is usually a skill most children eagerly attempt. Most people enjoy a good story, especially if it is told in an enthusiastic manner. Regular read-aloud times throughout the day help children develop this ability. In responding to literature children expand their knowledge of vocabulary and basic concepts, become more aware of the rhythm of language, begin to recognize some words, and increase their understanding of letter-sound relationships. Further, they increase their awareness of the meaningfulness of language as they develop a sense of story, illustrations, and text. As they become increasingly involved in the stories they hear, they develop increased levels of observation, listening attention, and enjoyment of stories.

Connecting Reading and Writing.

As children become more attentive to the special marks on the pages of books, they develop an understanding of two things. First, they realize that the marks have something to do with the story being told. Second, they discover that they can make marks with their drawings that are much like the marks found on the pages of books. This connection of reading and writing provides the groundwork for a variety of other understandings for children. They continue to learn about the relationship between sounds and symbols, print conventions, and the function of written communications. By attempting to incorporate letters and words within their own drawings, children learn the value of planning, and the purpose of reading and writing. Figures 4–5 through 4–8 illustrate how a child responded to a story he had heard by creating a story in a similar style. It includes all of the elementas of a good narrative.

Selecting Reading Activities.

The desire to select reading as a leisure activity is critically important for young children to develop. As we have seen, it will help children to grow in language and learning well after they have completed their early childhood program. This goal has much to do with attitudes and its attainment can be seen by observing indications of certain attitudes through children's actions. Things to watch for include taking care of books, learning where books are kept, sharing books with others, adopting appropriate story time behaviors, and expressing preferences for certain authors or types of stories. Each of these is a statement that books are a source of pleasure and enjoyment.

Reading for Personal Response

As children progress in their early reading skills, they can gradually make the transition into acquiring

FIGURE 4-5 The scene and characters are well established.

reading skills that engage them in increasingly more independent reading. The read-aloud session should never be allowed to disappear from any classroom. As

FIGURE 4-6 The plot unfolds.

FIGURE 4-7 The climax of the story

children grow in skill, however, they will seek opportunities to practice their own reading skills and strategies independently. This is to be expected and encouraged. The objectives in this area deal with relating personally to the text on a very human level.

share those feelings. They may relate to a particular character in a story or to a problem being experienced by that character. Children will smile at humorous moments and feel sad at the situations that require a sympathetic response on the part of the reader.

Responding Creatively to the Text.

When children establish an emotional bond with a story, they will often demonstrate this through re-creations of the story. Some children may engage in dramatic role playing of the events contained in the story. Others may draw pictures or develop other artistic forms depicting scenes from the story. Children may include some of the language from the story in their illustrations through invented spellings of story characters or actions.

Identifying Important Language.

One of the benefits of using read-alouds in the early childhood classroom is the fact that children are constantly exposed to new and varied words, rhythms, and patterns of language. An evil character may be described with terms such as beast, ferocious, fearless, and tricky. A poem may contain a catchy line that children will remember. An interesting idiom or cliche such as "on pins and needles" may capture the interest of children. This language is often absorbed, thought about, and even used in the child's own language repertoire. Discussions about the stories can bring out the idea that authors use certain words and phrases because they seem just right for the story that is being told. Children can demonstrate their ability to identify key aspects of language in stories as they use some of the new terms and phrases in their drawings and in their play activities.

Reading for Information Acquisition

This area increases further active involvement in reading. Children must also begin to assume a monitoring role for their reading, making decisions about their understanding of what is being read. As information is acquired, children increase the use they make of that information. Each of the abilities acquired here makes children more powerful language users.

FIGURE 4-8 The problem is resolved.

Relating to the Text.

Students who are involved with stories will relate to them in a particularly human way and will most likely

Recalling Information.

Skill in this area is both an oral language skill and a reading skill. To demonstrate the skill, children remember a simple story in the order in which it was told. They are able to recall specific parts of the story and create alternative endings to the story. Children may also exhibit this skill when they demonstrate an ability to identify a number of words that have some meaning to them. This is the beginning of a sight word vocabulary. The words may be key words from the story or they may simply be words the child has seen and heard over and over in a number of stories. This is a skill that can easily be modeled by the teacher. It is an excellent example of how oral language and reading are intertwined.

Selecting Information.

At this level, children become more sophisticated in the way they view language from a story. They begin to select information based on a purpose. For example, a teacher might be discussing a fairy tale with the children following the reading of the tale. Rather than simply recalling information or the sequence of the story, children can demonstrate the ability to select information that demonstrates an understanding of the relationship of different aspects of the story. A child might determine that the wolf in the story did something for a certain reason. Another child links the fact that something happened to the tortoise because of something the hare had done. Establishing these relationships can be linked to other parts of a reading such as making predictions about story events before and during the actual reading.

Relating Information to Experience.

Developing the ability to relate information from the story to personal experiences allows children to grow in their ability to interpret and extend new information. Developing this skill may require regular modeling by the teacher. A teacher might, for example, recall how a problem in the story was solved in a way similar to a problem in real life. Directions from a recipe might be applied to the actual creation of the product (e.g., cookies, pudding, etc.). The story might also be extended through a discussion about

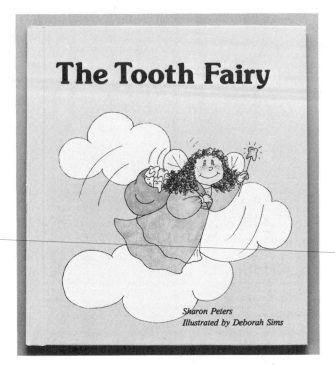

FIGURE 4-9 Many stories are related to the experiences of children. *Reprinted courtesy of Troll Associates, Mahwah, New Jersey 07430.*

what might happen next if the author had continued the story beyond the end of the book.

Using Key Language.

Authors use specific language for specific reasons. One of the major reasons is, of course, to tell the story just the way they intended it to be told. Another reason is to help the reader understand the story the way the author intended. For this to occur, children must learn to not only identify key language, but to use that language to aid their understanding of the story. Reading is an interaction between the author, the reader and the text. The reader needs to learn how the author includes certain words to evoke a feeling of scariness on the part of the reader. Readers must use illustrations and descriptions of characters and settings to help make predictions about subsequent events in the story. As each of these develops, better understanding of the whole text emerges.

Monitoring the Reading Process.

Monitoring is a metacognitive skill. It refers in this case to readers and listeners being aware of how they are going about the task of gaining an understanding of the text. It is a self-reflective skill that children develop at different ages. At the beginning stages, children become aware that there are reasons for reading and that they can do something about it when they feel they are not accomplishing the task. For example, a teacher might ask the children to listen to a story in order to find out what sometimes happens to people who are not willing to share. Children who are developing monitoring skills might recognize right away that they don't know the meaning of the word *share*. They may or may not do something about it. Children who are developing monitoring skills may ask the teacher for the meaning of the word or they may attempt to determine the meaning through the context of the story. Children who lack such monitoring skills may neither be aware of the fact that they do not know the meaning of the word nor understand that this lack of understanding will be a problem in the reading of the story.

Reading for Evaluation and Critical Analysis

Evaluation and critical analysis are the most sophisticated reading skills. They tend to develop over a lifetime of reading. Some may argue that they do not begin to develop until children are capable of using logical reasoning. Although logical reasoning skills may be helpful for these abilities, young children can often demonstrate the ability to evaluate texts in ways that are developmentally appropriate for them.

Making Personal Selections.

Anyone who has worked with young children and books will most likely be able to recall a child who wanted to read the same book over and over again. Another child may have wanted to read only books about trucks. Still another child may have constantly asked for Dr. Seuss books. Each of these actions suggests that the children have gone through some type of an evaluation process in arriving at their preferences. They may not have followed the reasoning and logic adults would have used, but they made their requests based on something. This is the beginning of evaluation. Something in the books, such as the rhyming patterns or the illustrations, captivated these children. Perhaps something within their own experiences drove them toward a specific type of literature. Teachers can foster an awareness of this ability by listening to children give their reasons for their choices.

Evaluating Literary Quality.

Writing is a very personal activity. Writers usually put their hearts and souls into what they are writing in the hopes that readers will find it enjoyable, instructive, entertaining, persuasive and so forth. These hopes of writers sometimes are fulfilled and sometimes are not fulfilled. Some books seem to be loved by all. Some books appeal to certain audiences. Some books seem to appeal to no one. Each of these possibilities exists. The ultimate consumers and users of children's books are the children themselves. As they grow in reading sophistication, children become more and more able to identify the aspects of a book that make it appealing to them. It may be such things as the rythmic language or the illustrations. Perhaps it is because the child can recognize most of the words in the story and can identify the rest through the use of context and picture clues. It might also be because the author uses believable characters with whom the reader easily identifies. An awareness of the reasons can help the child make future book selections and provide a powerful motivation toward reading independence.

READING ACTIVITIES

All of the reading activities in which children are involved should be planned with the ultimate goal of providing appropriate reading instruction. That goal is to develop readers who choose to read. Readers who choose to read do so in order to expand their understanding of the world and to enrich their lives. This goal can best be reached by developing activities that are meaningful, process oriented, and that accommodate the children's involvement. Meaningful activities will include language and materials that are relevant to the interests and developmental levels of the children. Activities that involve children in language processes aimed at making sense of the world will help to insure the active participation of the group. Finally, the teacher needs to stay within the role of coordinator and mediator. The teacher needs to become a participant in the learning environment rather than its caretaker. The following activities, when implemented on the basis of a whole language system of beliefs, allow for each of these conditions to be met.

Create Environments

Language growth does not take place in a vacuum. It takes place in classrooms, homes, and in many areas of the community. As children grow, they need to do so within environments that foster language stimulation. Such environments contain visual, sound, and human resources. Elkind (1975) states that thinking begins with the images and pictures children associate with earlier experiences.

The needs of the children can provide clues and criteria for deciding the type of environment to provide. A knowledge of child development suggests different things as children grow from birth through their early school years. As children become able to express their needs and preferences, their desires should be taken into account in constructing environments. In all cases, adults and the roles they assume should be seen as an intrinsic part of the environment.

Infant Environments.

Infants learn through their senses. Their environment should take this into account. Infants tend to be spontaneous in their play and activities. They move from toy to toy, spending a variety of time spans with each.

Sound experiences should be included. These might be the sounds of everyday life such as trains, car horns, musical toys, and real instruments such as the piano. The sound should also include the sounds of language. Poetry, chants, and songs should be evident throughout the day. With careful planning, this type of language can be used at story time, feeding time, nap time, and play time.

Visual experiences and the language that accompanies them should be present. Bright colors, signs, and symbols can serve to stimulate the infant. They can be talked about and described on a regular basis. Toys, stuffed animals, games, and puzzles are all part of the visual experience. They have the added benefit of providing motor stimulation.

Toddler Environments.

Play takes on increasing importance at this age. Toddlers develop a tremendous amount of language through their play. An environment for toddlers should replicate the world on a smaller scale. It should include child-oriented objects that are found in the real world. This includes books, furniture, puppets, clothing, tools, building materials, and so on. The room needs to include places for reading, writing, oral language, eating, playing, resting, and sharing. Language, reading, and writing should be in abundant supply in this environment. Adults in this environment should serve as readers, listeners, creators, providers, responders, writers, artists, singers, approvers, and supporters.

Preschool Environments.

While a preschool environment contains many of the aspects of earlier environments, some additions reflect the increasing sophistication of the children. Real materials are increasingly found. This might include ingredients for recipes, tape recorders that the children can operate independently, and writing tools used by grown-ups (e.g., pencils, typewriter, computer). It is important to provide more sophisticated art and building materials with which children can engage in representing and recreating stories.

Reading and writing by the children is much more visible here. As a result, there is an increasing variety of tradebooks, big books, and books made by the class. There are more spaces for displaying the art and writing of children. The children have more freedom here, but also attend to language activities for longer periods of time. At this age, children become increasingly aware of the relationships between art, music, writing, drama, role playing, and the concept that each of them has meaning.

In this environment, adults encourage the increasing independence of the child. Children are encouraged to make decisions regarding making sense of the world. Their decisions, artwork, writing attempts,

FIGURE 4-10 Mem Fox, children's book author, creates stories that help children understand their world. *Photo courtesy of Mem Fox.*

and value judgments are accepted. Language is used as a tool for helping children reflect upon each of these things.

Kindergarten Environments.

Children are often engaging in many reading and writing activities. This is true despite the fact that they probably have not been given any formal instruction in either in a traditional sense. At this age, children possess a number of language skills. They are often able to read their names and some other words. They are often able to write their names as well as some other familiar words. Their drawing and language abilities are sophisticated enough for them to begin writing their own books. They play games that involve language. They understand that language has meaning. They know the difference between oral and written language.

Environments for kindergarteners often provide special places for a variety of language and language related activities. Many teachers provide some of the activities that can be engaged in at some of these places or centers. Listening centers, reading centers, science centers, mathematics or counting centers, and art centers are only a few of the possibilities. In a whole language classroom, the activities at the centers are often developed with input from the children. The activities are often related to a particular theme, which relates the activities to one another. For example, the centers may all have activities dealing with a holiday, gardening, nutrition, or jobs in the community.

The role of the adults in this environment becomes increasingly more subtle. The adult must maintain the ability to observe children in order to diagnose needs and frustrations. The adult must serve as a fellow reader and writer along with the children. The adult also provides opportunities for reading, writing, acting out stories, and creating stories. At this stage, adults continue to provide the books, paper, and assorted materials needed for the increasingly complex language and play of the children.

Primary Grade Environments.

There can be a great similarity between the kindergarten environment and the environment found in the early grades. Many teachers, however, like to arrange early grade classrooms in rows of desks. There is little need for this, and it may be done more as a tradition than for any instructional reason. In fact, separating the early school years into separate grade levels seems to be more for the convenience of adults than for any reasons associated with childhood education.

The classroom needs to contain an increased variety of books, magazines, and other reading materials. The materials should be at a variety of difficulty levels to provide adequate challenge to a variety of readers. An assortment of writing tools needs to be provided as well. This includes the traditional types of lined and unlined paper used in primary grade writing activities, materials with which to make books, computers, and writing implements.

Children at this age can tend to develop some rigid behaviors. They may want to be the first ones finished with a project. They may want to produce a perfect paper. They may get frustrated when they are unable to read a sentence perfectly. They may only want to read a certain book again and again. The adults in the environment must be aware of this and take it into consideration in their roles as teachers. An important role for adults is to provide time for a variety of language activities to occur: dramatic recreation of stories, regular silent reading time, regular story times, regular writing times, activities which integrate learning, encouragement to take risks within the process of language learning, and opportunities for oral language.

Read-alouds

One of the foundation building blocks of an early childhood education program is reading stories with children. Literature is the content of the language arts program. Reading is a skill or ability which is developed through this content. Storybooks provide vocabulary, new language structures, rhythmic patterns, ideas for writing, and sources for creative play ideas for young children. A variety of stories should be read to children several times each day.

Books can serve as central features around which entire units and programs are built. They can serve as the central or related feature of units on everything from basic concepts to nutrition to fantasy to animal stories. Because of its versatility, reading stories can be combined with most of the other activities described here. In fact, most of the activities cannot be done without the use of such literature.

Book Discussions

Children and teachers can talk about the book or books they are reading at any time during the reading process. Discussions before the reading may deal with such things as setting a purpose for reading, establishing the background of the story, helping children to recall information that may assist them in understanding the story, making predictions about the story, and identifying any words they may need to know to understand the story. At pauses during the story the discussions may be used to clarify meanings of words and concepts, to review and refine predictions about the story content, and to assess understanding to that point. Discussions following a story may focus on a general understanding and appreciation of the story, a reassessment of the predictions

FIGURE 4-11 Patricia Reilly Giff, children's book author, creates books for young readers that are excellent for read alouds and discussions. *Courtesy of Tornberg Associates. Used by permission of Patricia Reilly Giff.*

made about the story, a review of purposes for reading, and relating the story to the lives of the readers.

Story Re-creation

Activities which re-create a story are powerful and effective tools for enhancing understanding. It is here that comprehension is truly developed because in order to engage in re-creation activities children have to manipulate the language and ideas of the story over and over again. Such manipulation helps children to make the story more a part of their lives. The re-creation can take many forms.

Re-creation through Play.

Play is a concrete way for children to relive the adventure they learned about in the story. While the

FIGURE 4-12 Frank Hodge, a noted reader, writer, story-teller, and teacher, shares a story.

FIGURE 4-13 A realistic play mat can encourage children to recreate stories through play.

entire story might not be acted out in play time, children are often observed taking the roles of characters from stories while imagining settings from the story within the familiar environment of the classroom. If such props as flannel boards or puppets are available, children may engage in directing the telling of the story using these props.

Re-creation through Language.

Stories may be re-created in a variety of ways through both written and oral language. Children may engage in retelling stories to the teacher, to their classmates, and to their parents. They may also choose to re-read the story by themselves. If they do not possess sufficient word recognition skills for an actual reading, children may choose to re-read the story by means of recall and picture clues.

If the story has been read several times, children can often be observed reading many of the words on each page through recognition while filling in the rest of the details from memory. There was a time when educators demeaned this activity as "not real reading, just memorizing some of the words on the page." However, it should be seen as a natural part of emerging literacy as children exert more confidence over the language and seek to see themselves as competent readers. This activity can be enhanced through the use of choral reading. As stories are read again, or as repetitive lines recur in stories, children can be encouraged to read along with the teacher. They may do this reading along by using either a recall of the lines or by recognizing key words on the actual page.

The stories children have heard may be re-created through written responses and drawings. Preschool children can own reading journals in which they draw and label favorite parts of the stories they hear. These can serve as a basis for talking about the story with parents and others at a later time. Such illustrations can also serve as a record of a child's growth in language. As time passes, one will note that the illustrations include additional information about the story as well as some words developed through invented spelling.

Independent Reading

Independent reading is how most adults engage in reading. They do not read because someone told them to do it. They do not read for the purpose of answering artificial questions at the end of each chapter. They do read for a variety of purposes: to be informed, to be entertained, to seek guidance. They do read because it provides something positive in their lives. So it is with children as well. They need to have time to read purely for the pleasure of discovering new worlds, finding adventure, and meeting new friends. Through regular silent reading times, children have an opportunity to re-create the story the teacher read that day, to practice the reading skills and strategies they are developing, and to gain a fuller understanding of the world. Too often, children spend too much time practicing the skills of reading in situations isolated from real books and too little time applying those skills in authentic texts and literature. Regular periods for silent reading are an important part of an early childhood education program.

SUMMARY

Reading and literature are inseparable in terms of their relationship with each other in a whole language early childhood program. Literature is the content of what children use as they go about the process of learning to read. Learning to read involves using the other language modes, oral language, and writing.

Traditional reading programs have tended to be characterized by approaches that emphasize either phonics or a look-say approach. As new knowledge and innovations emerged in the field of reading, they were added to the traditional program. As a result, these programs became increasingly eclectic. Most of the programs, however, maintain the use of scope and sequence charts of skills to be taught, graded basal reading texts, and a variety of supplementary materials. The supplementary materials include such things as workbooks, ditto masters, kits, testing materials, and computer assisted instructional programs.

Many commercially published reading programs publish separate readiness programs designed to be used in kindergarten or early childhood education programs. These programs have increasingly stressed topics which have formerly been taught in the primary grades. Letters, sounds, sight words, visual discrimination, auditory discrimination, and sound-symbol correspondence are frequently included in reading readiness programs.

Phonics has often been given a place of primary importance in beginning reading and reading readiness programs. The skills and understandings associated with phonics in such programs are frequently taught in isolation from real texts and literature. In order to maintain a fixed progression of skill instruction, traditional programs use graded basal reading texts. These texts contain practice materials in which children can practice reading using the skills they have been taught up until that point.

A whole language approach to reading addresses most of the skills formerly included in traditional reading programs. This includes phonics, sight word recognition, comprehension, and monitoring of one's reading. However, it addresses them in vastly different ways in to different degrees.

A whole language approach teaches reading as a process, as a meaningful activity, and as an activity in which children must be actively involved. Reading is a process in which children construct meaning by using a variety of strategies. It is a purposeful activity in which the traditional roles of the teacher and student are revised. The teacher shares the process with students by becoming more of a mediator instead of the individual in the room who has all of the answers. Reading is a meaningful activity because all of the language used in the instruction is taken from real texts written by real authors. Phonics, the alphabet, sight words, and comprehension are all taught through meaningful literature. Reading requires active involvement by young learners. Reading is seen as a shared social activity in which children assume more of the responsibility for their own growth in reading ability. As a result of this approach, children relate learning to their experience, learn to select appropriate literature, and choose to read as a leisure activity.

There are a variety of reading skills, strategies, and activities that are conducted in a whole language classroom. It is a mistake, however, to assume that they can be included in a traditional program in order to transform it into a whole language classroom. Whole language is a set of beliefs by which teachers make instructional decisions. To implement the activities without an understanding of why they are used is of limited value to young readers.

Questions and Activities for Review and Discussion

Multiple Choice

1. A traditional approach to reading instruction would suggest that before children learn to read they must master
   a. listening comprehension skills to the first grade level.
   b. reading readiness skills.
   c. the ability to sit quietly for ten minutes.
   d. an oral language vocabulary of at least 200 words.
2. Phonics refers to
   a. the meaning of words.
   b. how words are formed.
   c. the various parts of speech.
   d. the sounds of letters and letter combinations.
3. A whole language approach to reading includes the following as primary beliefs of materials.
   a. meaningfulness, skill worksheets, workbooks.
   b. workbooks, skills in isolation, process.
   c. process, skill worksheets, meaningfulness.
   d. meaningfulness, process, active involvement.
4. Preschool experiences are most helpful for emerging readers in the area of
   a. letter recognition.
   b. comprehension.
   c. phonics.
   d. alphabet learning.
5. A whole language approach generally provides phonics instruction
   a. through whole pieces of text.
   b. by means of a basal reader.
   c. using phonics worksheets.
   d. by isolating the skills from the text.
6. Being aware of one's ability as a reader is referred to as
   a. semantics.
   b. metacognition.
   c. syntactics.
   d. phonetics.
7. Responding to literature is often done in a whole language classroom
   a. following a read-aloud story.
   b. through comprehension worksheets.
   c. by writing book reports.
   d. using computer assisted instruction.

True or False

T   F   1. Letter recognition is often cited as a reading readiness skill.
T   F   2. Most important reading skills can be effectively taught through skill worksheets.
T   F   3. There is little difference between the writing found in basal readers and that found in tradebooks.

T   F   4. Educators have traditionally seen phonics and look-say reading approaches as fundamentally different.

T   F   5. In a whole language classroom, the teacher serves more as a mediator than as a lecturer.

Essay and Discussion
1. Compare and contrast the phonics approach and the look-say approach.
2. What are some of the differences found between the literature found in children's tradebooks and the writing found in basal readers?
3. Describe some of the procedures for word identification that might be observed in a whole language classroom.
4. What are the stages preschool children demonstrate as they attempt to read a familiar tradebook?
5. How is the teacher's role in the whole language classroom different from that of the teacher in a traditional classroom?

References

Anderson, P.S. 1964. *Language skills in elementary education*. New York: Macmillan.

Anderson, R.C., E.H. Hiebert, J.A. Scott, and I.A.G. Wilkinson. 1985. *Becoming a nation of readers*. Champaign, Ill.: Center for the Study of Reading.

Beentjes, J.W.J., and T.H.A. Van der Voort. 1988. Television's impact on children's reading skills: A review of research. *Reading Research Quarterly* 23: 389–413.

Cazden, C. 1972. *Child language and education*. New York: Holt.

Chall, J.S. 1983. *Stages of reading development*. New York: McGraw Hill.

Chomsky, C. 1972. Stages in language development and reading exposure. *Harvard Educational Review* 42: 1–33.

Clay, M.M. 1975. *What did I write?* Portsmouth, N.H.: Heinemann.

Corteen, R.S., and T.M. Williams. 1986. Television and reading skills. In *The Impact of Television: A Natural Experiment in Three Communities*, ed. T.M. Williams. Orlando, Fl.: Academic Press.

Degrosky, D.S. 1981. *Television viewing and reading achievement of seventh and eighth graders*. New Brunswick, N.J.: Rutgers University (ERIC Document Reproduction Service No. ED 215 291).

DeMott, B. 1990. Why we read and write. *Educational Leadership* 47: 6.

Durrell, D.D. 1958. Success in first grade reading. *Journal of Education* 140: 1–48.

Elkind, D. 1975. *A sympathetic understanding of the child: Birth to sixteen*. Boston: Allyn & Bacon.

Elkind, D. 1987. *Miseducation: Preschoolers at risk*. New York: Knopf.

Fetler, M. 1984. Television viewing and school achievement. *Journal of Communication* 34(2): 104–118.

Ferriero, E. 1986. The interplay between information and assimilation in beginning literacy. In *Emergent Literacy: Reading and Writing,* ed. W.H. Teale and E. Sulzby. Norwood, N.J.: Ablex.

Ferriero, E. and A. Teberosky. 1982. *Literacy before schooling.* Exeter, N.H.: Heinemann.

Gallagher, J.M., and I.E. Sigel, eds. 1987. Introduction to special issue: Hothousing of young children. *Early Childhood Research Quarterly* 2: 201–202.

Goodman, Y. 1985. Kidwatching: Observing children in the classroom. In *Observing the Language Learner,* ed. A. Jaggar and M.T. Smith-Burke. Newark, Del.: International Reading Association.

Great Books Program. 1984. Chicago, Ill.: Great Books.

Hiebert, E.H., B. Stacy, and L. Jordan. 1985. An analysis of literacy experiences in preschool settings. University of Kentucky.

Hiebert, E.H., and C.C. Sawyer. 1984. Young children's concurrent abilities in reading and spelling. Paper presented at the annual meeting of the American Educational Research Association, New Orleans.

Holdaway, D. 1979. *The foundations of literacy.* New York: Scholastic.

Johnson, D.D., and J.F. Baumann. 1984. Word identification. In *Handbook of Educational Research,* ed. P.D. Pearson. New York: Longman.

Kohr, R.L. 1979. The relationship of homework and television viewing to cognitive and noncognitive student outcomes. Paper presented at the annual meeting of the National Council for Measurement in Education, San Francisco.

Lomax, R.G., and L.M. McGee. 1987. Young children's concepts about print and reading: Toward a model of word reading acquisition. *Reading Research Quarterly* 22: 237–256.

Lundberg, I., J. Frost, and O. Petersen. 1988. Effects of an extensive program for stimulating awareness in preschool children. *Reading Research Quarterly* 23: 263–284.

McGee, L.M., and D.J. Richgels. 1989. "K is Kristen's": Learning the alphabet from a child's perspective. *The Reading Teacher* 43: 216–225.

Morgan, M., and L. Gross. 1980. Television and academic achievement. *Journal of Broadcasting* 24: 117–232.

Neuman, S.B. 1981. *The effects of television on reading behavior.* Willimantic, Conn.: Eastern Connecticut State College (ERIC Document Reproduction Service No. ED 205 941).

Neuman, S.B. 1988. The displacement effect: Assessing the relation between television viewing and reading performance. *Reading Research Quarterly* 23: 414–440.

Newman, J. 1985. Insights from reading and writing research and their implications for developing whole language curriculum. In *Whole Language: Theory and Use,* ed. J. Newman. Portsmouth, N.H.: Heinemann.

Pappas, C.C., and E. Brown, E. 1987. Learning to read by reading: Learning how to extend the functional potential of language. *Research in the Teaching of English* 21: 160–184.

Pflaum, S.W., H.J. Walberg, M.L. Karegianes, and P. Rasher. 1980. Reading instruction: A quantitative analysis. *Educational Researcher* 9(7): 12–18.

Potter, W.J. 1987. Does television viewing hinder academic achievement among adolescents? *Human Communication Research* 14: 27–46.

Smyser-O'Sullivan, S.W. 1981. A study of the relationship between television viewing habits and early reading achievement. *Dissertation Abstracts International* 41: 4972-A (University Microfilms No. AAD 81–11630).

Staab, C.F. 1990. Teacher mediation in one whole literacy classroom. *The Reading Teacher* 43: 548–552.

State Education Department. 1989. *Reading and literature in the English language arts curriculum K-12.* Albany, N.Y.: State Education Department.

Stevens, R., N. Madden, R. Slavin, and A. Farnish. 1987. Cooperative integrated reading and composition: Two field experiments. *Reading Research Quarterly* 22: 433–454.

Strickland, D.S. 1990. Emergent literacy: How young children learn to read. *Educational Leadership* 47: 6, 18–23.

Sulzby, E. 1985. Children's emergent reading of favorite storybooks: A developmental study. *Reading Research Quarterly* 20: 458–481.

Sulzby, E., J. Barnhart, and J. Hieshima. 1989. Forms of writing and rereading from writing: A preliminary report. In *Reading/Writing Connections: An Instructional Priority in Elementary School,* ed. J. Mason. Boston: Allyn & Bacon.

Teale, W., and E. Sulzby. 1989. Emergent literacy: New perspectives. In *Emerging Literacy: Young Children Learning to Read and Write,* ed. D.S. Strickland and L.M. Morrow. Newark, Del.: International Reading Association.

Trachtenburg, P. 1990. Using children's literature to enhance phonics instruction. *The Reading Teacher* 43: 648–654.

Veatch, J. 1978. *Reading in the elementary school.* New York: John Wiley.

Vygotsky, L.S. 1981. The genesis of higher mental functions. In J.V. Wertsch (Ed.), *The Concept of Activity in Soviet Psychology,* ed. J.V. Wertsch. White Plains, N.Y.: Sharpe.

Walsh, D.J., G.G. Price, and M.G. Gillingham. 1988. The critical but transitory importance of letter naming. *Reading Research Quarterly* 23: 108–122.

White, D. 1984. *Books before five.* Portsmouth, N.H.: Heinemann.

Williams, J.P. 1985. The case for explicit decoding instruction. In *Reading Education: Foundations for a Literate America,* ed. J. Osborn, P.T. Wilson, and R.C. Anderson. Lexington, Mass.: Lexington Books.

Williams, P.A., E.H. Haertel, G.D. Haertel, and H.J. Walberg. 1982. The impact of leisure time television on school learning: A research synthesis. *American Educational Research Journal* 19: 19–50.

Section 2
Learning about the World

Robert Munsch

"Reading and writing are like swimming. You learn them by doing them."

Photograph courtesy of Whitman Golden Canada Ltd. Text courtesy of Robert Munsch.

TO THE READER:

Isn't the world a delightful and exciting place? Isn't it even more so when seen through the eyes of a child? It is full of colors, objects, textures, shapes, smells, sights, and sounds. Exploring each and every one of these for the first time can be a thrilling discovery. When observing young children engage in these discoveries, it is fascinating to observe the child's interest flow from object to object and from idea to idea.

From the viewpoint of the young child, the world is not divided into parts and sections. What we grown-ups refer to as school subjects are actually integrated into the whole of experience for the child. Our dividing up the world into subjects is merely an arbitrary decision made for our own convenience. The world is an integration of many parts. In reality, no distinction is made between areas that will later become the separate school subjects of literature, science, social studies, art, and music. All are blended into a whole from the child's point of view.

This section contains two units. The first unit investigates the integration of language arts with other content areas as a natural way of viewing the world with young children. While different content areas are mentioned, it should be understood that in early childhood education, the content areas are nearly always addressed in an integrated manner. Content areas are mentioned only for the purpose of creating an example of a concept being discussed. Children come to know their world by interacting with it. Through talking, experiencing, and playing, children come to know about the things around them. Language is a critical part of this process.

The second unit in this section explores the world of literature for young children. Many times, children cannot learn everything from personal experience. A Native American child living in the Southwest might not be able to experience a large, northern, industrial city. An inner city child may not have the opportunity to experience the environment of the dairy farm. Storybooks for young children provide a powerful means to help these children bridge the gap between their own worlds and the worlds experienced by others. The power of literature does not end there. Through literature, young children can also explore the worlds of fantasy, make believe, and feelings. It is a wonderful journey. People who spend their time with young children are fortunate to be able to go on that journey again and again.

UNIT 5

Integrating Language Arts and the Content Areas

UNIT GOALS

After completing this unit, the reader should:

- understand how growth in language ability supports learning in the content areas.
- identify the content areas that can be supported through the integration of the language arts.
- develop an awareness of children's literature that addresses the content areas.
- become familiar with topics that might be included in a content area study unit.
- understand how content area information is ordinarily structured and organized.
- become familiar with the thematic unit as a tool for organizing content area study.

PREVIEW

For years, educators and schools have chosen to view language arts as a subject that stands alone. In the early elementary school grades, this view has long been the accepted position from which programs are organized. This pattern is continued and solidified in the secondary schools to the point where teachers are often certified in a single subject. They are allowed to teach that subject and no other.

This pattern has unfortunate consequences for children, since language skills are so important for learning science, mathematics, social studies, and so on. Every teacher providing instruction in any content subject expects, or at least hopes, that students will learn the material through reading, writing, and discussion. Teachers expect that the appropriate reading, writing, and oral language skills taught in the language arts portion of the educational program will provide the necessary skills and abilities to learn the other content areas. This is not something a teacher can always assume. Children often experience difficulty when they are expected to independently transfer skills from one area to another. In addition, it is likely that the appropriate language skills for dealing with science cannot be adequately addressed when providing instruction focused solely on literature. Some language and thinking skills may be more useful in some content areas than others.

An additional problem relates to the fact that in real life information and knowledge do not exist in neat, compartmentalized units. While attempting to operate within the context of modern life, children often have to draw on learnings from different areas for the solution to a single problem. In drawing on knowledge from these, language is the medium for thinking about and drawing on that knowledge.

It makes sense, therefore, to consider procedures by which language arts learning can occur within the context of all content areas. It is ineffective to delegate such instruction to the language arts program. This unit explores issues related to integrating language arts instruction with each of the content areas. Among the key concepts is an exploration of the relationship between language and learning content, a discussion of the general content areas found in early childhood education, and a description of how children's literature can support content learning. A major vehicle for organizing content area and language arts instruction, the thematic unit, is presented.

INTRODUCTION

The content areas are an artificial system of organizing knowledge about the topics people recognize as important. Obviously no one can know everything about each of the fields available for study. Indeed, it is impossible to know even one field completely. This is because knowledge has expanded greatly in most fields of study over the past century, the past decade, and even the past year. In addition, new knowledge will be constantly generated in the future. This prevents even the most studious of scholars from keeping up with the knowledge in more than a very narrow area of interest.

As a result of the vast amount of potential information to be learned, teachers are faced with the task of determining which information in a subject area is most important to know. This is a tremendous re-

sponsibility. Take the area of social studies, for example. Even at the preschool level, for instance, teachers must decide which community helpers youngsters need to know about. It may be reasonably easy to identify some key individuals within a given community, such as the policeman, the fireman, the teacher, and so forth. But given the ability of the children to acquire information, it quickly becomes apparent that choices must be made. Does the teacher include the owner of the corner store, the social worker, the volunteer Big Brother, or the doctor at the health clinic? Obviously, each of these is an important community member, but choices must be made.

In addition to making choices, the teacher must keep in mind that information must be presented to children so that it makes sense. Few individuals are adept at storing large amounts of random information. Young children are no exception. Because they are still learning to deal with language in general, they are even more limited in their ability to deal with isolated information. It makes sense, therefore, to provide instruction that presents knowledge in a way that is understandable to young children. The instruction should be structured so that learning in one area supports learning in another area. This efficiency will result in better understanding and retention in both areas.

In order to provide instruction in content areas that is most meaningful to children, it is first necessary to identify and describe some of the possible content areas that might be included in an early childhood educational program. Second, it is necessary to more fully understand how integrating language arts with content areas can be beneficial to both areas. A comprehensive understanding of the thematic unit can provide an effective tool for organizing instruction. Each of these topics is explored in this unit. In addition, a sample unit on the theme of "Trees and Forests" is provided.

THE CONTENT AREAS

Content is the "what" of education. It is the "stuff" or the material to be learned in a subject area. Traditionally, content has been grouped under a variety of subject area headings referred to as the disciplines. A discipline is a grouping of knowledge or content items for instructional purposes. For years, scholars in each of the disciplines have stressed the need to have students understand how knowledge is grouped or structured in a discipline as the appropriate way to learn that discipline. This approach is consistent with a view that sees the major purpose of education as the transfer of cultural knowledge from one generation to the next.

An integrated curriculum questions the value of viewing content areas in isolation. A number of troubling questions can be raised about providing content area instruction as isolated units for the purpose of learning large amounts of knowledge grouped under that discipline. Are the disciplines natural in the way they divide content areas from each other? How useful is learning a large amount of information in a discipline without knowing how that information is related to other information inside and outside that discipline? How useful is knowing the isolated information in the first place? Given the rate at which knowledge is changing, for how long will information within a content area be valid? Will knowing "what" be as useful as knowing "how"? This last question is most critical, because it takes a futuristic stance. After all, most children now in early childhood education programs will be using their education at some point in the future. Some people suggest that knowing how to deal with situations in which one doesn't have or doesn't know the answer may be more valuable than having the answers to questions that are never asked. With this in mind, let us look at some of the traditional content areas and what they might include for young learners. While these areas do not constitute a total early childhood program curriculum, they comprise a large number of the general areas under which many of the parts of the program could be grouped.

Literature

The content of the language arts is literature. Literature is the language that is written down for a variety of purposes. The purposes include informing, explaining, entertaining, and persuading. As children go through schools, this idea seems to get lost. Children spend large amounts of time engaged in learning lists of spelling words, grammar rules, sentence types, and punctuation. Each of these has a

FIGURE 5-1 Literature is a major portion of the content of the language arts. *From* Paul Revere's Ride, *by Henry Wadsworth Longfellow, illustrated by Ted Rand. Reprinted courtesy of E.P. Dutton.*

place and a value. However, their ultimate purpose is to enable the individual to communicate in writing. Similar problems are seen in reading instruction. Children spend much time learning lists of vocabulary words, completing phonics worksheets, and reading texts that are not literature, but rather passages designed to provide practice in an isolated skill.

In an integrated language arts approach, both fictional and nonfictional literature is used. It is often created by the teacher and the child. It is drawn from traditional sources. It is derived from contemporary storybooks for children. There is overlap between each of these sources. Much of the literature used with young children is drawn from the oral tradition and includes rhyme and song. Nursery rhymes, finger plays, chants, fables, fairy tales, and folk tales are all part of this tradition. In addition, classic and contemporary fiction specifically written for young children are included. Finally, informational nonfiction is included. While this includes biography, it also includes a variety of other materials that may fall into other content area categories as well.

FIGURE 5-2 Children's books about living things help to integrate science with the language arts. *From* The Secretive Timber Rattlesnake, *by Bianca Lavies. Reprinted courtesy of E.P. Dutton.*

Science

The field of science includes the study of living things and study of the physical world. In secondary education, separate subjects are established for a number of these areas: biology, physics, earth science, and chemistry. At the early childhood level, these separate subjects are often combined with each other. Selected aspects of science are chosen that are appropriate to the needs and interests of the children. Ordinarily, areas addressed include body awareness, cooking or food preparation, health, nutrition, nature, living things, computers, earth, and space. Science topics often engender enthusiasm, meaning, and purpose. The words used are often fascinating to children. The hands-on activities associated with science projects can provide motivating meaningful activities for young children.

Mathematics

Mathematics is the study of numbers and the quantification of our world. Recent developments in mathematics education have moved away from a primary focus on arithmetic computations and the memorization of facts. Mathematics is rightly being seen more as a tool for solving problems. In an increasingly technological society it is a necessary and useful tool. The ways in which mathematics has been included in early childhood programs have generally been appropriate from the view of mathematics as a problem-solving tool. The general areas of mathematics study for young children include counting, numbers, estimation, telling time, money, calender, computation, concept learning, and problem solving.

Social Studies

The social studies include all of the subjects that deal with the ways in which human beings relate to each other as part of the world community. They include a broad range of disciplines, some of which seem only slightly related. Among the disciplines that might be found under the general topic of social studies are geography, history, economics, sociology, political science, and anthropology.

At the early childhood level, social studies topics are usually geared to those areas of importance to the developing child. They tend to include concepts and ideas children can relate to and understand. Among the possible social studies topics for young children are self-esteem, independence, family, friendship, social skills, the community, local history, holidays, and folklore.

FIGURE 5-3 Number books help to integrate mathematics with the language arts. *From* When I Was One, *by Colin and Jacqui Hawkins. Reprinted courtesy of Viking Penguin.*

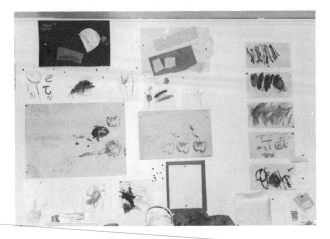

FIGURE 5-4 Children combine their study of nutrition and art with these vegetable prints.

Physical Education

Anyone who has ever worked with young children will verify the need for daily exercise and movement. Growing bodies need large amounts of healthy activity both to develop physical skills and to expend energy. The early childhood physical education program is both structured and unstructured. In the structured component, children learn activities to develop fine motor (small muscle) and large motor (large muscle) abilities, games, sports, and individual skills such as riding a tricycle. The unstructured component usually comprises a greater amount of time during the day. It consists of large amounts of free play time. The time is spent running, using playground equipment, actively recreating stories and practicing motor skills that might have been learned in the structured component.

Arts

The arts are nourishment for the soul. They include areas that celebrate the uniqueness of humanity. The arts are a reflection of the human condition. They portray in an aesthetic manner the joy, pain, happiness, and sorrow of life. Generally, anything that one might include under the topics of music, art, or drama is included. In early childhood programs, the arts have a special place because they have the ability to reach young people at a very basic level. A happy song is obviously happy. It is usually quite easy to identify a scary picture. In a theatrical performance for children the "good guys" are very good and the "bad guys" are very bad.

The arts should be an important part of an educational program for young children. In music, children should be exposed to musical performances, singing songs, and the original creation of songs. In art, children can experiment with a variety of media to create personal works: clay, paint, pencil, crayons, markers, wet sand, chocolate pudding, shaving cream, and so forth. In drama, children experience the world of theater as both audience and performer. Creative play and creative dramatics allow children to become actively involved in the creation of a reality. Attendance at children's plays, storytelling performances, and puppet shows helps children to experience the role of audience.

INTEGRATING CONTENT AREAS

While whole language is increasingly being used in schools, its use is often confined to an overly narrow portion of the program and the day. In a research study, Hiebert and Fisher (1990) identified three areas in which they felt whole language influence could be expanded or revised in reference to content area instruction: expository texts, integration of subject matter, and grouping strategies. They suggest that the practices of whole language could do much to facilitate the improvement of education if they were more broadly used.

Extending Whole Language Principles

Hiebert and Fisher (1990) refer to the need to expand a process approach to writing into expository texts as creating a balance between narrative and expository writing. As explained in the unit on writing, an integrated approach stresses the need to develop and encourage writing in descriptive, narrative, expository, and persuasive pieces. Hiebert and Fisher observed classrooms where the teachers were insufficiently prepared to provide instruction using a whole language approach. Young children, particularly, do not differentiate between various types of writing. They can often be observed combining a drawing, a narrative, and an expository piece. Indeed it is rather difficult to write in a manner that is purely narrative, descriptive, expository, or persuasive. Each type of writing is often found in combination with other types.

The second point made by Hiebert and Fisher is the need for teachers to integrate whole language principles with teaching other subject matters. Again, their observations found that some teachers had difficulty extending whole language principles beyond the boundaries of the language arts curriculum. Given the foundations upon which whole language is based, it is logical that whole language principles extend to all content areas and that themes or projects for study be derived from different areas. This does not mean a forced integration in which a story about a bug is combined with a lesson on bugs and followed up with a walk in the park to count bugs as a mathematics activity. Those are isolated activities forced together by an inadequate bond. Instead, integrated units need to be carefully planned. They must be correlated to the developmental needs and abilities of the learners, and they must be authentic and purposeful. Involving children in deciding what types of content on a given topic are worth knowing makes good sense here, despite the fact that they may not know of all the possibilities from which to choose. Young children often know enough about a number of topics to determine the kinds of things they would like to know more about. Such input creates tangible outcomes for them as well as allowing them to develop an ownership of the unit.

The third area of concern identified by Hiebert and Fisher was in the grouping patterns they observed in the classrooms. They noted a lack of small group work led by the teacher. They observed large group instruction and individual conferencing between student and teacher but no teacher-led small groups. However, whole language teachers do use a variety of grouping patterns depending on the needs of the unit or classwork. On the other hand, there is an avoidance in whole language classrooms of long-term ability grouping for the purpose of providing different types of instruction to different types of students. Instead, a variety of grouping patterns and teacher support are provided, depending on the needs of the students to complete tasks successfully.

Benefits of Integration

According to Dewey (1966), as children pursue learning for which they have an interest they develop a variety of skills as part of the process. Integrated units, in which children have an interest, provide such an opportunity (Strickland and Morrow 1990). Strickland and Morrow (1990) point out that the interdisciplinary approach emerged from the works of early educators and psychologists such as Pestalozzi, Froebel, Piaget, and Dewey. Each of these individuals believed that much of learning is based on student interest. As a result, the most effective instruction would be that which actively involves the child.

Strickland and Morrow (1990) also contend that integrated units based upon whole language principles can accomodate both children's interests and their individual needs. Such units provide positive settings for social interaction that will include appropriately modeled behaviors. Such units also provide authentic funtional experiences. They enable the teacher to use a variety of literacy activities throughout the day.

When children move into the middle school grades from traditional elementary school skill-based programs, a common problem is often noted. Simply stated, these students do not know how to deal with content materials (Applebee, Langer, and Mullis 1989). They do not read their content area texts with sufficient comprehension. They do not produce expository pieces that demonstrate an ability to deal with the subject matter. A major reason for this problem is the fact that these students have not had sufficient opportunities to use language skills to manipulate the material. Language skills, isolated from real pieces of text, are usually taught only in language arts classes. Content material is taught in content lessons. There is little or no integration. As a result, students become limited in their ability to learn. An awareness of the need to integrate language learning and content materials early in a child's education can pay big dividends for that child further down the educational road.

Ways of structuring expository material are described by several educators (McGee and Richgels 1985; Piccolo 1987). Armbruster, Anderson, and Ostertag (1989) reduce the possiblities to five types of expository text structures: description, sequence, cause-effect, compare/contrast, and problem-solution. No one would suggest teaching these formal structures to young children. However, activities and discussions that involve these structures could be introduced early and consistently used throughout the child's schooling. Consider the example of the pond, and picture the possibilities for discussions about a pond. Ask children what they see as they look at the pond (description). They can generate ideas about how water gets into the pond and where it goes when it leaves the pond (sequence). They can tell what might happen if people throw garbage into the pond (cause-effect). They could explain the difference between the pond and the ocean (compare/contrast). They could generate ideas for making the water in the pond cleaner (problem-solution). Each of these possibilities could be done as either a small group or large group activity. Each could be done through oral language, writing/drawing, or a combination of the two. The idea is not to have children come up with consistently accurate information, but rather to encourage them to use language to deal with an idea while gaining an awareness of the ways of viewing a natural object. As children became accustomed to dealing with content material, the understanding of these structures is reflected in their reading and writing.

Content Area Books

In days past, books for children that addressed content areas were often dull works filled with information presented in a straightforward, factual manner. They were written from a technical point of view with the importance of historical and scientific accuracy taking precedence over the needs and interests of the children using the books. While there is no need to sacrifice accuracy, books that include subject matter information can take into consideration the needs of the audience. Indeed, this is accomplished with a great many of the subject matter books for young children that have recently been published. In addition, teachers have come to realize that scientifically and historically accurate works of fiction can play an increasingly important role in children's learning. Authors of such works take great pains to research the background of their books. As a result, writers such as Carol Carrick and Joanna Cole present works of fiction that are totally accurate concerning the scientific and environmental backgrounds of the stories. As a result, content study for young children can include a variety of literature: nonfiction, biography, fiction, and poetry. Let us examine different areas in

FIGURE 5-5 Children can choose from a variety of scientifically and environmentally accurate books. *From* Dolphins and Porpoises, *by Sharon Gordon. Reprinted courtesy of Troll Associates, Mahwah, New Jersey 07430.*

which literature can be used as part of the unit. We can begin with the already mentioned topic of the pond.

Ponds.

Given a hypothetical unit on ponds, the teacher can choose from a variety of books that provide information about ponds, tell stories in which ponds have a prominent role, or are related to the topic of pond life. Not every book of course is appropriate for all age levels. The teacher must be aware of the needs, interests, and abilities of the children for whom the book is selected. For our purposes here, books with a range of applicability will be suggested. The final decision must be made by the teacher who knows the children and has specific reasons for selecting the book.

An excellent nonfiction work to begin with is *The Hidden Life of the Pond* (1988), by David M. Schwartz. Making fine use of Dwight Kuhn's accompanying photographs, the book chronicles the lives of the inhabitants of a northeastern freshwater pond throughout the seasons. A hydra, a mole, and a water lily are among the many living things featured. One of the high points of the book is the description of the life of a mosquito complete with stunning photographs. In a similar vein, Bianca Lavies's *Lily Pad Pond* (1989) presents a clear and simple description of the development of a tadpole into a frog. Just as important as the descriptive information are the photographs that accompany the book. This book is intended for five- to seven-year-olds. A related book for younger readers is Ron Hirschi's *Who Lives in . . . Alligator Swamp* (1987). In this work, photographs are used to help children learn about the animals and plants ordinarily found in this type of aquatic environment. From Europe comes Tilde Michels's *At the Frog Pond* (1989). Translated from the German by Nina Ignatowicz, the book features remarkable paintings by Reinhard Michl. Moving closer to a narrative is Jim Arnosky's poetic look at fresh water in *Come Out, Muskrats* (1989). While the book actually depicts life in a river, it is in a quiet section of river that shares much with pond life. The reader learns about muskrats, turtles, fish, frogs, and water bugs that live in or near the water.

Fictional stories that take place in or near ponds can be helpful as well. Carol Carrick's scientifically accurate story *Dark and Full of Secrets* (1984) details a young boy's dual feelings about the pond. On the one hand, he is curious and fascinated about the life that exists below the serene surface of the pond. On the other hand, he is aware that he needs to act in a safe manner when around water. The story has just the right amount of fear to capture the interest of youngsters without scaring them. As a result, they participate in learning the fascinating features of pond life.

Cities.

One of the most common social studies areas studied in early childhood programs is the community. It makes a great deal of sense to focus on community during these years, since it is the world the child knows best. Many elementary grade programs continue this focus through the second grade. Since the majority of people live in towns and cities, one might wish to build a unit around the subject of cities. A similar unit might be developed around country life or rural areas if preferred. In either case, young children should become familiar with the variety of locations in which people choose to live. As with the unit on ponds, both nonfiction books and fictional stories dealing with life in the city are selected. The levels of difficulty of the books chosen should be checked to determine their appropriateness for the children with whom they are to be used.

An excellent nonfiction choice to begin with is *Town and Country* (1985), by Alice Provensen and Martin Provensen. Aimed at five- to seven-year-olds, the book compares and contrasts town and country life through both its text and its finely detailed illustrations that were also created by the authors. The book provides information about the positive aspects of living in each location. If a unit on cities is being presented around the holiday season, the teacher should be sure to include Roxie Munro's *Christmastime in New York City* (1987). Through pictues and text, the reader is taken to all of the places that make New York City such a spectacular place to visit during the holiday season. At the end of the book is a brief history of the famous locations depicted. A sense of history can be added to the unit with *My Block* (1988), by Richard Rosenblum. While the text deals with a simple story, a young boy deciding on a job that will enable him to continue to live on his block forever, the book is basically nonfiction. The setting is New York City in the 1930s. The book presents a nostalgic, idealized view of life at the time. It also realistically depicts the jobs people held and the sense of neighborhood communities shared in that earlier day. An important lesson from the book is the fact that children were fundamentally the same then as they are today. This book is appropriate for children aged three years old and up.

Fictional stories that occur in cities and involve cities in their plots abound. What better place to start than Janet Stevens's adaptation of the Aesop fable *The Town Mouse and the Country Mouse* (1987). Intended for audiences in the four-to-seven age group, the story details the visits of each character to the other's environment. As a result of their visits, they come to the conclusion that they are each best suited to their own environments. Also written for the same age group is *Jason's Bus Ride* (1987), by Harriet Ziefert. This story provides an easy to read text with colorful illustrations to take the reader on a bus ride around the city. For slightly younger children, a fictional story taking place in New York City is Michael Foreman's *Cat and Canary* (1987). The cat in the story, having become entangled in a kite string, is unexpectedly whisked into the skies above the city. This provides the scene for the author's spectacular watercolor paintings of the famous Manhattan skyscrapers as seen from the cat's perspective.

For children in the three- to five-year-old age range, Anne Rockwell's *Come to Town* (1985) is a sure winner. The detailed illustrations provide a wealth of information about the buildings and locations found in a city. The story and illustrations motivate children to participate in the reading and to talk about the story. A good companion book for this one is Lenore Blegvad's *Anna Banana and Me* (1985). Locations such as the playground, the park, and an apartment are featured. The story concerns the attempts of a small

FIGURE 5-7 A content journal with hypotheses added

boy to keep up with the fearless antics of Anna Banana. An added bonus for using the book is the theme of overcoming fears.

While these books are among some of the best, they are by no means the only ones available in each of these areas. The same is true for most other content areas. A key tool for developing a resource of books for use in different content areas is wide reading in the topics to be studies. Bookstore owners and children's librarians are quite eager to provide help and assistance to anyone searching for children's books on a particular topic.

Content Journals

One of the most useful tools for helping children learn the terms, ideas, and processes of content subjects is the content journal or learning log. As chil-

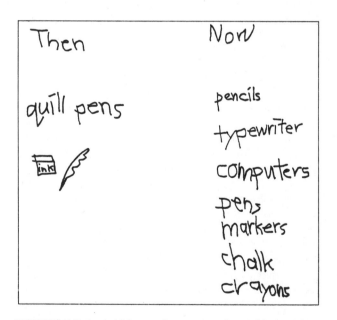

FIGURE 5-6 An initial entry in a content journal by a young child who was exposed to a unit about life in the eighteenth century.

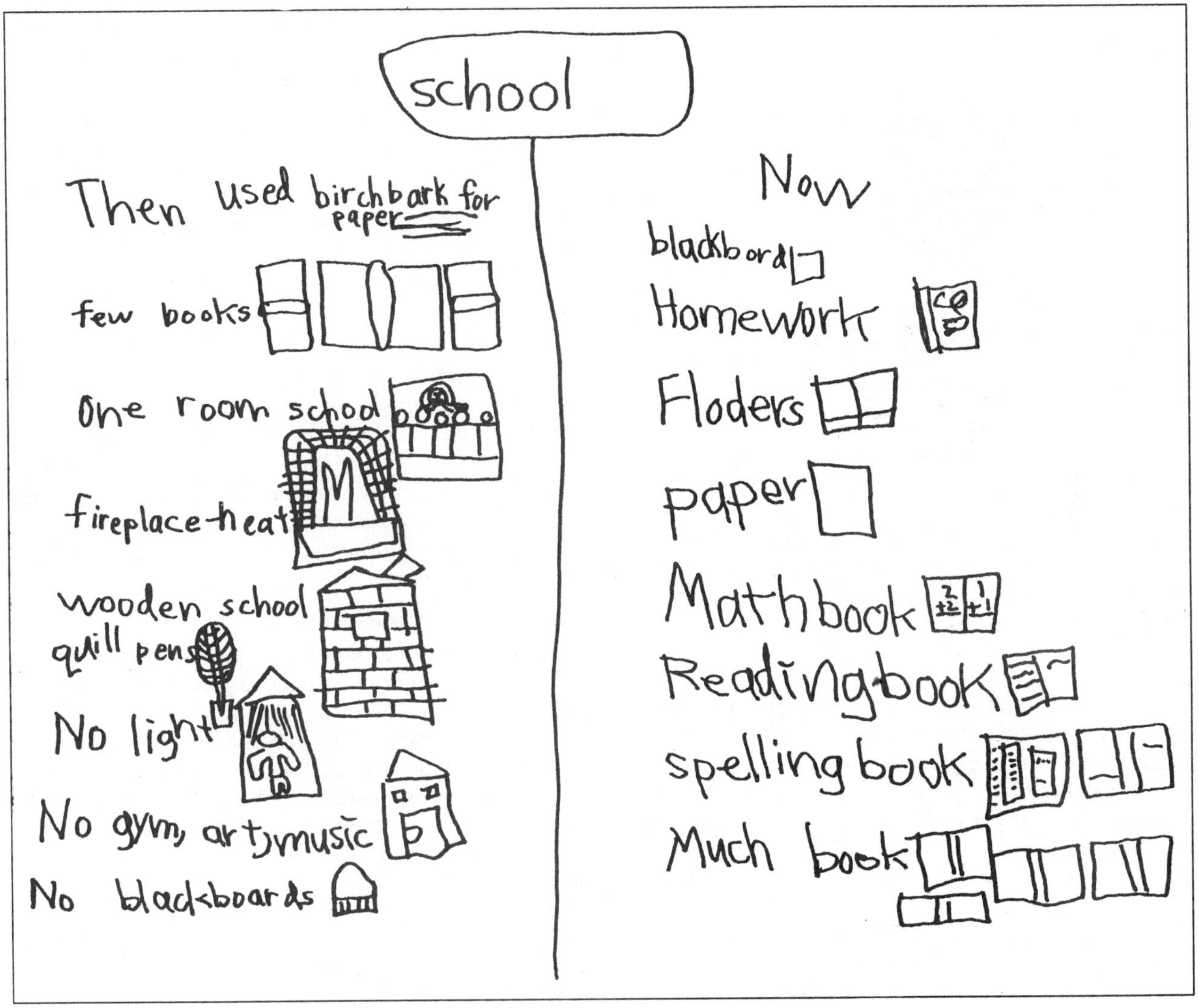

FIGURE 5-8 A content journal entry with information added at the end of a lesson.

dren move into the elementary grades, the journal may actually look more like a journal. It might be in the form of a composition book, a spiral bound notebook, or a looseleaf binder. At the early childhood level, it takes on a more informal appearance. It may be a shoebox, a folder, a mailbox, or a bin in which individual student papers are kept. The format, therefore, doesn't really matter. What matters is the fact that the journal will be a tool for helping children to learn.

Young children may keep a content journal by responding, in one way or another, to the learning experiences in which they are participating. After learning about the color red, the shape of a circle, or the concept of a truck, the child may draw pictures of red objects, objects that contain circles in their shapes, or various kinds of trucks. Rather than using single sheets of paper, the teacher may provide a large sheet of poster board to a group of children in order for them to jointly respond to the learning experience.

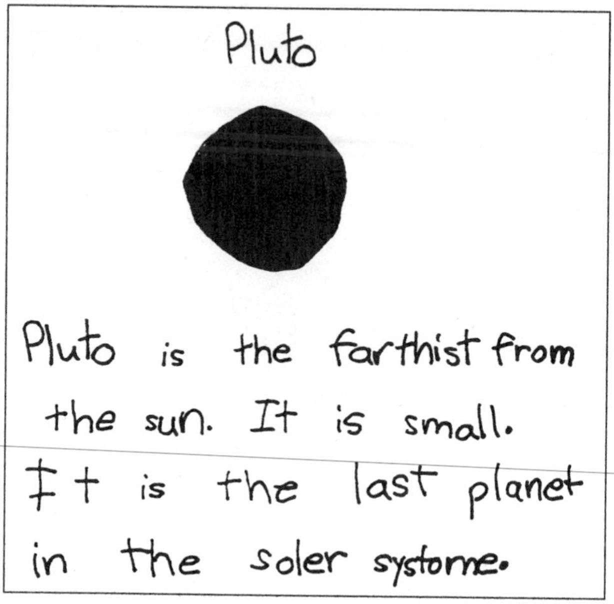

Pluto

Pluto is the farthist from the sun. It is small. It is the last planet in the soler systome.

FIGURE 5-9 Content journals can be used by children to keep new information of interest to them.

A content journal is not used only after a learning experience. An effective strategy for helping children acquire new information is to allow them to recall the ideas they already possess about a topic (Figure 5-6). Ask them to write or draw everything they can think of about the topic in their journal. They can even be encouraged to make guesses when they aren't totally sure about their information (Figure 5-7). After the lesson, they can return to their journals to make any changes they feel are needed in their original understandings. They can add additional pictures, words, or ideas to their journals at this time as well (Figure 5-8).

Using a content journal in a lesson provides several benefits. It does not really matter whether the content is a basic concept, science, mathematics, or music. When used prior to a lesson, a content journal helps children recall relevant ideas and knowledge to which new information and ideas can be related. A content journal can also be used as a tool for children to construct ideas that may or may not later prove to be valid. Encouraging children to return to the journal during and after a lesson can help them clarify their new knowledge and organize their ideas. This entire process enables children to see that their understanding of the world can and should change as new learning occurs. The content journal allows them to help learn new concepts. Whether the journal is a piece of drawing paper, lined paper, poster paper, clay, or a chalkboard makes no difference. The materials used will depend on the level of the child and the purpose of the task. The major idea to remember is that content journals are a language arts tool that can help children learn.

THEMATIC UNITS

The term *thematic unit* refers to an interdisciplinary approach to teaching that integrates many parts of the school day. It is quite different from a topical unit that focuses on a topic within a single subject. A topical unit is primarily based on the learning and understanding of factual material within a single subject area. A thematic unit may extend across many curriculum areas.

Focus of Thematic Units

A thematic unit integrates an idea, concept, or theme across all of the subject areas. It meaningfully relates a theme to all subject areas and strives for meaning on a variety of levels. Rather than a focus on acquiring a body of factual information, a thematic unit provides opportunities for a general understanding as well as the development of attitudes and values related to the theme. Keep in mind that no one can acquire all of the facts and knowledge about a given topic. With a thematic unit there is a stress on acquiring meaning, developing attitudes, and acquiring the ability to engage in additional learning dependent on the child's interests and motivations. Children are not viewed as empty pitchers to be filled to the brim with knowledge. They have a decision-making role in their learning that can be used to help them develop an emotional stake in their own learning.

A thematic unit developed from a whole language perspectives would include many of the characteristics found in a language arts program using a whole language approach. This might include the use of big books, independent reading, reading aloud, writing, and oral language. A child learning about clouds may begin by simply recording information in a content journal (Figure 5-10). However, this may be expanded into other areas such as art (Figure 5-11) and

IN SCIENCE

I talked about clouds. Clouds are in the sky. wan ther is no clouds it is sunny. Clouds are in the sky on rainny days. Clouds are white. I like clouds. clouds arepretty.

FIGURE 5-10 Content journal entry on the topic of clouds

oral language (Figure 5-12) if children are encouraged to create their own weather reports.

It makes sense to integrate content areas within an entire integrated day. There are times, of course, when the unit might focus primarily upon a literature component such as a specific type of book, an author, or an illustrator. This is to be expected and encouraged. Too often, educators fall into a routine where they feel that science, mathematics, social studies, and other subjects must be taught for a prescribed number of minutes on a daily basis. It is a trap to avoid. The needs of the children and the professional judgment of the teacher in relation to those needs should specify the when, what, why, and how of teaching in early childhood education.

MODEL UNIT

To illustrate a possible approach to providing content area instruction, a thematic unit on trees and forests is provided here. The items summarized focus mainly on the daily classroom routines that might be implemented. The details of planning such an overall unit, the instructional strategies and the evaluation are described in later units.

Unit Development

The development of a unit on trees and forests, or any other unit, should begin with the establishment of a rationale for teaching such a unit and learning goals for children. A rationale is simply an understanding of the importance for children to be exposed to such a unit. In this case, it is a set of reasonable answers to such questions as: Are the children able to grasp the concepts of tree and forest? How are trees and forests meaningful to the children? Is it important for children to learn about trees? Will the children be able to

THE WEATHER

tomorrow it will be sunny and not as cold in the afternoon. The high temperature will be 43 degrees. I listened to a radio. It is almost Spring and It is cold. This is fun and we like today It is St. Patrick's Day. It is March 17. It is Thursday and There are three more days till spring. In the Spring mothers get their babies

FIGURE 5-11 Child-created weather report

FIGURE 5-12 Child-created weather symbols for use in a weather report.

understand some of the new ideas we will be dealing with?

Developing Goals.

With a rationale for teaching a unit on trees and forests, the teacher can now form some general goals focused on student learning. That is, the teacher must have some idea of how students will benefit from participating in this unit. Student learning goals can be developed by answering questions such as: What new information do I expect children to possess as a result of this unit? What new understandings about the world will I expect children to form? Do I intend to alter the attitudes that children possess about their world? With answers to these questions, teachers can form realistic student learning goals.

Goal Statements.

For the purpose of this model unit, it is assumed that the teacher will be implementing the program with a group of children from four years to five years of age. The goals are related to the things children will have learned, developed, or acquired by the end of the unit. Possible goals for such a group might include, but not be limited to, such items as:

- The children will know that there are different kinds of trees.
- The children will be able to identify different kinds of trees.
- The children will know the basic life cycle of a tree.
- The children will be able to tell some examples of the value of trees.
- The children will understand some of the relationships between people and trees.
- The children will increase their vocabulary of words related to trees.
- The children will understand the relationship of trees to other things in the environment.

Some of these goals might sound more appropriate for elementary or secondary students. It must be understood that not all children will reach all of these goals or even any one of the goals to the same level as other children. Also, it must be understood that these are goals rather than mandates or guarantees. As children go through school, they will be exposed to instruction on trees and forests over and over again, sometimes within an integrated unit and sometimes within a single subject. There is no driving need to make sure that they acquire a specified amount of factual learning at this point in their education. Children will come to the classroom with some information and understanding of this topic. They will most likely complete this unit with their previous knowledge expanded. The task for the teacher is to provide meaningful learning for each individual student in a developmentally appropriate manner.

Planning Instructional Activities

Given the rationale and the student learning goals, the teacher can now focus on developing instructional activities that will enable the children to engage in learning that will help them progress toward achieving the goals. In developing activities, it is helpful to think in terms of the theme from a variety of angles related to different content areas: How does mathematics apply to trees? How do trees fit into our community life? Do trees have anything meaningful to do with music? What type of literature can I use within this unit? This last question is critically important. Searching for and collecting a variety of books will be extremely helpful not only in presenting important ideas and information but also in integrating the unit. On most topics, there are many books that quite naturally provide the integration within the story.

Figure 5-13 provides a planning overview for a tree unit. Note that the individual activities are grouped under content headings. This does not mean that each of these activities will be conducted separately. This is a planning chart. Its purpose is to insure that each of the areas is addressed so that each area can be integrated into the instruction. Most storybooks written for children are not bound by artificial content area boundaries. The discussion, reading, and writing of the children and the teacher need not be confined by these boundaries either.

Daily Schedule

The plan to include a focus on the theme of trees and forests might be implemented over a period of approximately two weeks. With young children, plans are constantly changing, so the plans need to be flexible. Any time schedule is always subject to change in much the same way that any activity planned can be moved up to an earlier time or delayed until another day. It is also important to note that a thematic unit does not need to take place in a two-week time period. A unit might be completed in as little as three days or as long as a month. The activities suggested here could be included in whatever daily time schedule the teacher is most comfortable using. The activities could be arranged in a different order. Activities might also be added or dropped in accordance with the needs of the group.

Day 1.

During the first five days, the unit might use a big book related to trees and forests as a unifying element. An excellent choice would be *In a Dark Dark Wood* (1980), a traditional tale retold by June Melser and Joy Crowley. It is available in a big book format and uses a recurring choral line to make the story more predictable for young readers and listeners. By pointing to each word as it is read, the teacher reinforces the concept that the words that we hear are the words that can be seen written on the page. When reading the book for the first time, the reader can pause and ask the children to predict what might be coming on the next page. Allowing children to look through this book in the reading area after the telling encourages a further activity of independent reading.

Each day should include stories on the theme of trees and forests to be read aloud. To increase motivation and to entice readers into the unit, one might choose humorous books related to trees for this first day. Oral language discussions, whereby children are asked to tell everything they know about trees, might precede the read-aloud story. A writing/drawing activity could be related to some of the personal knowledge children have about trees. The theme might also include nutrition by arranging to have apples for the morning snack. Children could be reminded that apples come from trees.

Day 2.

When reading the same big book on the second day, have children "echo read" along with the reader. That is, the reader reads the line and then the children repeat the line. Using different intonations can provide additional interest to this activity. It is not important with preschoolers to have them actually read the words from the page. The focus here is to build their confidence, allow them to feel the rhythm of the language and provide them with a sense of involvement. The read-aloud books for the second day might include both humorous books related to trees and factual books on the topic of trees and forests. The read-aloud books, the big book, and other related books can continue to be provided in the reading area for independent reading. If there is no set time in the daily schedule for independent reading, this might be a good time to initiate the practice. Starting with brief times of three to five minutes before moving on to the next activity might be appropriate. The time span can be increased to fit the interest and attention span of the children. The writing/drawing activity for this day may be a response to the read-aloud story. It may be a drawing of a tree seen in one of the books or it may be an illustration of a

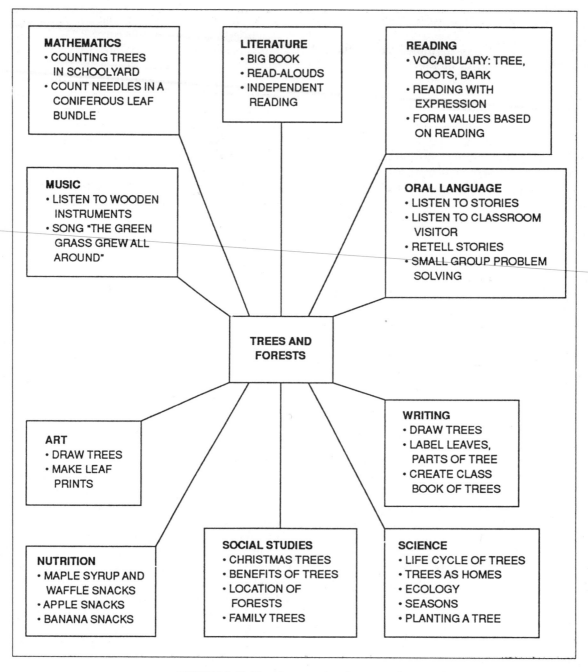

FIGURE 5-13 Planning overview for tree unit

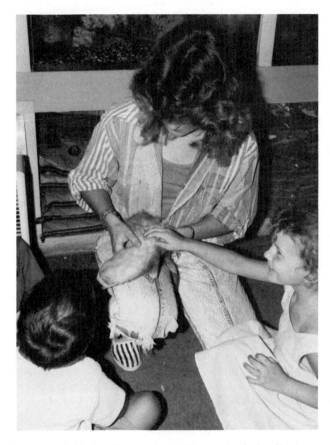

FIGURE 5-14 Children can learn about animals that live in or near trees.

character from one of the stories with the character's name written using invented spelling.

If the weather is nice, this might be a good day to take a stroll around the schoolyard or a walk to the park. Paper bags can be brought so that children can collect things associated with trees. This might include bark pieces, seeds, leaves, and twigs. As each of these is discussed by the group, the teacher might also introduce the idea that other living things are often associated with trees. Insects, squirrels, chipmunks, and birds might all be seen in the trees.

After returning to the classroom, the teacher could introduce the possibility of the group constructing a book similar to the big book that is being read daily. The children should be involved with both this decision and the plot line for the story. Titles, suggesting

the direction the story will take, might include "In a tall tall tree," "In the dark dark park" and "In the dark dark forest." The title and plot are of secondary importance. The real goal is to allow children to begin to use their knowledge of trees and to develop some control over the use of language. All of these points can be discussed over a morning snack of bananas, which also happen to grow in trees.

Day 3.

Continue with a third reading of the big book. When reading it this time, encourage the children to read along with the teacher when they know the words. Most big books contain memorable lines that children quickly recall. This book is no exception. Following this reading, it may be well to immediately attempt to create the related big book story by the class. As the story is being created by the children, the teacher may serve as the scribe. Ideas generated by the children can and should be discussed by the group in hopes of reaching a consensus as to the appropriateness of each new line. The teacher can periodically read what has been written to remind the children of the sense of the story. This writing activity can end for the day with the reading of the class created text.

The read-aloud stories for use on this day might include selections from folk tales, fairy tales, and fantasy fiction. There are numerous possibilities dealing with stories that take place in forests or that include a tree as an important part of the story. An additional oral language activity for the day might be one in which the teacher asks the children to describe the feelings they get as they view some of the pictures from the books. The teacher might display pictures that evoke feelings of happiness, foreboding, fear, and tranquility. A small group or whole class oral language activity would be sorting or classifying some of the materials collected on the previous day's walk. It is more important that children attempt to provide reasonable explanations of why they group objects in certain ways than that they arrange them in some predetermined way. There are often many possibilities for solving a single problem in life. It is not too often that there is only one correct answer. The activities might be concluded with a snack of applesauce, which originates in the apple tree.

FIGURE 5-15 Trees have been used to make many types of homes.

Day 4.

Use the original big book again, but this time allow the children to read it. Smaller size versions of the story may be used as well. The teacher must be tolerant of the "errors" the children may make when doing this reading. Focus on whether or not the children are creating a meaningful retelling of the story as opposed to the "correctness" of their version compared to the actual words written on the page. Independent reading on this day may be expanded to some of the other books that have collected in the reading corner from previous read-aloud sessions. The read-aloud books for today might include stories about trees as homes.

An oral language activity dealing with science and social studies can emerge from the read-aloud books that addresses the topic of trees as homes. While trees serve as homes for animals, insects, and other forms of life, they serve humans as well. Using pairs of children, small groups, or even the whole group, the class can generate ideas about how trees help people. Among the possibilities are shade, lumber, oxygen, food (e.g., maple syrup, apples, walnuts), windbreaks, and natural beauty.

A writing and drawing activity for the day can focus on the big book story the class developed on the previous day. The text can be read by the teacher and the group in order to help recall the story line. Using pairs of children or individual youngsters, illustrations are created for the pages of the story. The decision of how much of the text should go on each page can and should be decided upon by the group as much as possible. After all, it is the group's book. Illustration possibilities might also be discussed. When completed, the illustrations are placed on poster sized pieces of paper, the text lines are attached under the pictures, and the pages are bound into a book, complete with cover. This might be a good time to serve another tree-related snack such as oranges.

Day 5.

The fifth day, the mid-point of the unit, has a celebration flavor to it. It is a great day to invite visitors to the classroom to help celebrate. Visitors might include parents, the school director, community representatives, older siblings, senior citizens, and the building clerical and custodial staff. The visitors can be treated to a choral reading of the original big book by the children. If time allows, a reading of the big book created by the children can be done as well. This reading can also take place over the next several days of the unit. If one of the classroom visitors is an older sibling, perhaps that person might just happen to have something to show the children that is made out of wood. With a little luck, a visitor might be able to play a song for the children with an instrument made from wood. Such instruments include the guitar, banjo, violin, cello, viola, piano, and dulcimer. Other visitors who might be able to share an aspect of wood or trees with the children include tree service workers, landscapers, lumber yard owners, and garden club members.

Independent reading should continue on this day just like any other day. If it can be arranged ahead of time, a classroom visitor could become an honorary read-aloud story person for the day. Since the day may be an exciting one for the children, a more serious story might help to keep a balance. Realistic fictional stories focused on values, beliefs, and attitudes within the general theme of trees might constitute appropriate choices. The day's writing or drawing ac-

FIGURE 5-16 Maple trees are tapped to gather the sap.

tivity might be a personal response to some aspect of the read-aloud story. Discussion of some possibilities could be helpful to the children. While the teacher should participate in this activity and share the writing or drawing with the children, the latter can be delayed until later. Otherwise, some children might see the teacher's work as the only appropriate response, thus suggesting that they copy it as well as they can. To lend an elegant touch to the end of the first half of the unit, the day's snack might be waffles with maple syrup. A brief explanation of how maple syrup is made from the sap of the maple tree can be given (Figure 5-16). Classes located in areas where maple syrup is made might be fortunate enough to go on a field trip to a maple sugar house (Figure 5-17).

If the fifth day occurs on the last day of the school week, a home activity might be suggested for over the weekend. The activity could include such things as a walk to an area with trees, learning about the trees nearest the child's home, or the creation of a simple family tree using poster paper and photographs of family members. This latter activity could be especially fascinating for a young child. It could be done with the help of older siblings, parents, or grandparents. Confining the family tree to just two or three generations of immediate family members will keep the project manageable.

Day 6.

The second five days of the unit will be somewhat similar to the first five days in terms of some of the daily activities. A big book reading continues to serve as a central part of the unit. A different book will be used over the course of the five days. A good choice would be *The Old Oak Tree* (1987), by Jill Eggleton. It has a familiar, repetitive line that children will quickly recall on subsequent readings. As the story proceeds,

FIGURE 5-17 Maple sap is boiled to make maple syrup in a building called a sugar house.

FIGURE 5-18 At snack time, children learn that food can come from trees.

the reader meets three creatures with humorous nonsense names: a frabbit, a freeblie, and a frossil. Just as they came into the story, the three creatures depart as they go off to lunch, leaving only the narrator at the conclusion. As with the first day's reading of the previous week, the reader can pause at key points in the story and encourage children to predict the events that will follow.

To provide a lighthearted beginning to the week, the read-alouds for this first day might be chosen from the genre of fairy tales that take place in forests or wooded areas. A writing or drawing activity, in which children respond to the story, might take place right after this reading. Children could be encouraged to engage in independent reading as they finish their responses. The snacks for the second week can be similar to or variations of the snacks used for the first week. Possibilities might include coconuts, tropical fruits, olives, nuts, and other types of orchard fruits.

Several oral language activities could be conducted on this day. Those children who did tree or forest projects or activities over the weekend with their families could report on them. Children who bring in family trees can be encouraged to tell about the family members in the photographs. A second oral language activity is related to music. Children might learn the traditional song "The Tree in the Wood," which is also known by its refrain line "The green

grass grew all around." Like a big book story, it contins a repetitive story line that children quickly learn and enjoy. It is found in a number of sources, but is most readily available in folk song collections such as Tom Glazer's *Treasury of Folk Songs* (1964).

A third oral language activity would focus on helping children use some of their new knowledge by relating it to some of the things they already know. Using the ideas embedded in the discussion planning sheet illustrated in Figure 5-19, the teacher can lead a discussion that identifies the similarities and differences between trees and people. While the chart itself would not be used with four- and five-year-olds, the ideas within the chart can be explored by asking children relevant questions. What foods do people need? What foods do trees need? Do people get sick? Do trees become ill? What happens when each of these occur? The emphasis should be on divergent thinking where children generate a variety of possible responses to these questions.

Day 7.

The big book reading would have an echo reading format, and the reader would begin to include different intonations for various parts of the story. If some of the children can benefit, one might draw their attention to the apearance of and the sound made by the letters "fr-" that forms the initial part of the names of the three creatures met in the story. Independent reading would continue with the books being collected in the reading corner.

The read-aloud session might be preceded by a couple of other oral language activities. First, the children can be shown pictures of cross sections of trees in which the rings can be seen. Guesses about what the rings could mean are encouraged. The correct answer, which is that there is one ring for each year the tree has lived, can be provided by either a child or a teacher. This could lead into a review of the information generated by the discussion chart used on the previous day (Figure 5-19).

The read-aloud books could include a combination of humorous books and factual books about trees and forests. The writing and drawing activities could include responding to some of the ideas shared in the books used. Possibilities might include a drawing of a tree in a particular season, a collage made from some

Concept	Trees	People
Food What kind of food is needed and used? What happens if it is not available?		
Movement Does each move? How are the movements different from each other?		
Appearance What does each look like? How does each look in different seasons?		
Breathing What kind of air (i.e., oxygen / carbon dioxide) does each need? What kind does each produce?		
Illnesses and Hazards What kinds of things are dangerous for each? Why are they dangerous?		
Aging What happens to each as it grows and gets older? Do they look different as they get older?		

FIGURE 5-19 Discussion planning sheet on trees

of the leaves, and seeds collected on the previous week's field trip and any response related to factual information discovered in one of the books.

The song learned on the sixth day, "The green grass grew all around," is sung daily over this second five day time block. After it is sung, the teacher might introduce the idea of writing a book based on the song. The repetitive line used in the song, or a line similar to it, will make the book predictable and easy to learn for the children. It has the possibility of becoming a humorous, factual, or thought-provoking story.

Day 8.

Children should be encouraged to read along with the big book story if they know some of the words.

The actual writing of the class big book based on the big book being read might be introduced right after the reading. It could begin with the musical activity of singing the song, "The green grass grew all around." As in the first week, the group should discuss and develop each line cooperatively. The teacher can again serve as a scribe for the story. The illustrations can be done by individual students, pairs of children, or small groups. As with the text, a discussion of the illustrations to be created can be discussed by the group.

Independent reading in the reading corner and read-alouds would naturally take place. This might be a good day to use fairy tales that take place in forests. An oral language activity could include an art, mathematics, and science format. The activity could use the collection of bark, twigs, leaves, and seeds gath-

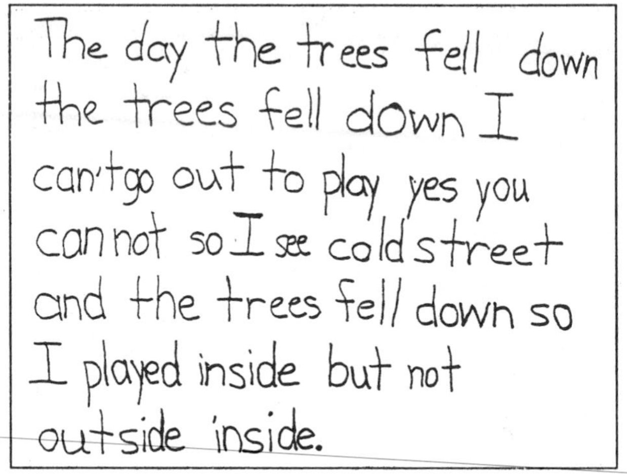

The day the trees fell down
the trees fell down I
can't go out to play yes you
cannot so I see cold street
and the trees fell down so
I played inside but not
outside inside.

FIGURE 5-20 A discussion of storms can be used to integrate science with the unit on trees. This story was written about storm damage to the trees near the child's home.

ered on the field trip earlier in the unit. Seeds and leaves could be classified according to a number of criteria: color, size, shape, and so forth. A counting activity could be based on the number of leaves of each shape or color. A discussion of how trees grow could be based on taking apart and examining some of the seeds from the collection. If some of the seeds are from a maple tree, this might be a good day to have pancakes and maple syrup for a snack.

Day 9.

The children might be encouraged to read the big book alone. They could use the actual big book or smaller size copies of the story. After singing the "green grass" song, the text and illustrations for the class big book based can be examined. Encourage the children to help put the large pages in the correct order and to match the appropriate illustration with each section of the text. The book can now be bound within covers and read for the first time in its finished format.

Factual science books might be good choices for reading aloud and independent reading. The oral language activity for the day is a discussion of the steps one must take in order to plant a tree. A classroom visitor, such as a florist or a member of a local garden club, might help with this activity. Factors

such as a sunny location, distance from other trees, preparation of the hole, and proper watering are major pieces of information to share. Part of this discussion could address the importance of planting trees and how they help other living creatures. An art and writing activity could be chosen from such possibilities as leaf pressing, leaf tracing, and charcoal rubbing of a paper with a leaf placed under it. The activities could conclude with a snack of apples and a singing of the song for the week.

Day 10.

On this final day of the unit, two choral readings of the big books will take place. The original big book could be first, followed by singing the song for the week and reading the big book developed by the class. It would be wonderful to have an audience present on this day. Perhaps parents, local government officials, or representatives of civic groups could be invited. After the readings the class could move outside to a preselected site in order to have a tree-planting ceremony. A tree would have been acquired previously. A gardening center, mail order house, outdoor center, or governmental conservation department are all possible sources for a low-cost or no-cost tree for the ceremony. A brief review of the steps for planting a tree is followed by the actual planting. Children should be selected from the group to help do the actual work. This might require a bit of preparation beforehand, such as loosening the earth where the hole will be made for the tree.

After the tree-planting ceremony the class could return to the room for a read-aloud story that would begin the conclusion of the entire thematic unit. A thought-provoking book about the importance of trees could be paired with a humorous one to give some balance to the unit. A final writing and drawing activity about the tree-planting ceremony would help to reinforce both the message of the read-aloud and the importance of trees. A tree-related snack feast would end the unit. A combination of such things as apples, bananas, walnuts, peaches, and waffles with maple syrup would provide a flavor of celebration to the unit.

Tree Unit Literature

The two big books provide a literature foundation for the unit on trees. They are predictable, enjoyable,

FIGURE 5-21 People plant trees to make their homes nicer.

and motivating for children. By themselves, however, they are insufficient in providing a literature-rich environment for young children. In addition to the big books, children should experience read-aloud books several times each day. All of these stories should be available for the children to return to during independent reading time. Books related to a unit on trees are described here in four general areas: factual science books, realistic, thought-provoking fiction, humorous stories, and stories that can best be described as fairy tales, folk tales, and fantasy tales. There is, of course some overlap. Some versions of fairy tales are quite humorous. Some of the factual science books are actually thought-provoking fiction that is scientifically accurate. In choosing books for sharing with children, it is important to make selections from each group. This will help to provide richness and balance.

Factual Science Books.

Books for young children geared primarily to presenting information are becoming much more appropriate. The language used is clearer than ever before. The illustrations and photographs are accurate and attractive. *The Hidden Life of the Forest* (1988), by David Schwartz, presents a picture of a northeastern forest. Appropriate for ages four to ten, its photographs present the forest environment in stunning detail.

Caroline Arnold's series book, *A Walk in the Woods* (1990), provides a nature walk through the ecosystem for ages three to six. Through the clear, simple text and Freya Tanz's colorful illustrations, children receive straightforward answers to their first questions about trees. How old are they? How do they grow? How do they help animals? How do they help people?

Trees (1988), by Andrew Langley, is a large format science book. It blends factual information with clearly detailed artwork and illustrative photographs. John Williams's *The Life Cycle of a Tree* (1989) is a science book with appeal to both young children and older children or adults. It is part of a series of books on life cycles. Its simple text, large print, and accurate illustrations provide a clear understanding of the life cycle of a tree to children. Smaller print information is also included to provide additional information to older children. Ron Hirschi's *Who Lives in . . . Forest?* (1987), also a series book, is designed for children aged three to seven. It uses full color photographs to capture the essence of early spring in the forest. Emphasizing the use of the senses, it provides a picture of what happens at that time of year to plants, rabbits, chipmunks, owls, squirrels, bears, and fish.

Some intriguing books about the natural environment are being published in other countries. From Australia comes Thelma Catterwell's *Aldita and the Forest* (1989). It introduces children to the creatures of the Australian woodland. It tells the story of a tiny white butterfly. Since this butterfly hatches after the others have migrated, it must face the world alone.

FIGURE 5-22 Trees give us shade to play in.

One category of science books on trees depicts them as homes for a variety of life forms. From England is Naomi Russell's (1989) *The Tree*. It traces the lifespan of an oak tree from its acorn stage to its death. During its life, the tree provides beauty, shade, and pleasure. After many years it is cut down for other uses. What is left behind? An acorn. The fold-out pages, although rendering the book more fragile, are a valuable part of the volume. Also from England is Helen Cowcher's *Rain Forest* (1989). It contains vivid pictures of a rain forest complete with the sloths, tapirs, anteaters, and Blue Morpho butterflies that inhabit it. Unfortunately, the rain forest appears to be doomed as the bulldozers of progress nibble away at its edges. Although momentarily saved from destruction, the animals wonder how long their home will survive. A startling picture of a howler monkey screeching a warning provides a heavy ecological warning. Suitable for kindergarten children is Bianca Lavies's *Tree Trunk Traffic* (1989). It provides much information about a family of squirrels living in a maple tree. Both the text and the photographs have some entertaining details.

Bordering on realistic fiction are several books that provide important information on how trees and the forest serve as homes. Natalia Romanova's *Once There Was a Tree* (1985) is a Russian tale of ecology. It concerns an old tree stump and the creatures who live within it and claim it as their own. The message to the reader is that the stump and the tree that springs from its decaying remains are part of nature and really belong to everyone. Laura Jane Coats's *The Oak Tree* (1987) is appropriate for three- to seven-year-olds. It covers a one-day period in which a mother robin tends her newly hatched birds. This is contrasted with other events such as the sun rising and children playing. For children aged five to eight, Peter Parnall's *Apple Tree* (1988) presents the story of a battered old apple tree as it goes through a cycle of seasons. It depicts the interdependence of tree and animals as the tree suffers through a cold winter. Among the other life forms the tree sustains are bumblebees, ants, bugs, chicadees, robins, woodpeckers, nuthatches, deer, and mice. Rosemary Wells's *Forest of Dreams* (1988) presents a similar tale. With illustrations by Susan Jeffers, the pictures and words depict the thawing of the forest with the approach of spring. As the story unfolds, a young girl discovers the har-

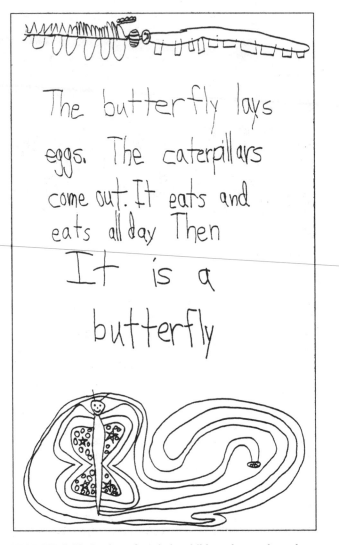

FIGURE 5-23 Stories often help children learn about how some animals use trees for homes. One child recreated this information in a story and a picture.

bingers of another aspect of spring: the stirring of field mice, the singing of birds, and an expectant doe.

Tejima Keisaburo's *Woodpecker Forest* (1989) shows the growth of a young woodpecker against the background of the changing seasons of the forest. The woodcut textures of the illustrations seem almost real. Young children will be able to identify with the fears of the young woodpecker. In the dark, even familiar sights and sounds can seem frightening to a young bird. Finally, Jane Yolen's Caldecott Medal winning *Owl Moon* (1987) captures the eery stillness of the forest at night. It is the story of a young child and a grandparent who venture into the evening forest in search of owls. John Schoenherr's stark watercolor illustrations capture the blue-black majesty of the nighttime forest.

Realistic Fiction.

Tejima Keisburo's *Fox's Dream* (1987), with its illustrative woodcuts by the author, will take the reader's breath away. Set in Hokkaido, the northernmost island of Japan, it provides a lonely picture of a young fox in the winter woods. The fox is cold and hungry as it measures its solitary walk in the forest. It wonders if spring will ever come, or if it will ever be a part of a family again. Poetic phrasing is a perfect complement to the intense winter forest images with their icy, snow-covered ground. A poem from a different era is given new life through Susan Jeffers illustrations in *Stopping by Woods on a Snowy Evening* (1978), by Robert Frost. Although young children may not appreciate the depth of this well-known poem, the pictures and words create a peaceful and serene picture of a forest in winter.

Realistic fiction often involves young children and their growing understanding of the woods. Such books can be quite inviting to young children, who see themselves in the place of the young characters within the story. Jeanne Titherington's *Where Are You Going Emma?* (1988) is appropriate for the very youngest readers. In the story, Emma wanders over the stone wall that borders her grandfather's meadow. The brook, pebble, flower, grass, and leaf that Emma finds are fascinating discoveries. When she realizes that she may have wandered too far, she hurries back to her grandfather's orchard. In Jean George's *One Day in the Woods* (1989), the reader accompanies Rebecca for a whole day in a northeastern deciduous forest. In search of the rare ovenbird, they observe flying squirrels, deer, and wood ducks. The book depicts the balance and harmony that exist both vertically and horizontally in the forest.

A book that is about a product from trees actually has a larger message about a reverence for nature and art. Claude Clement's *The Voice of the Wood* (1989)

is a haunting tale of an old instrument maker. The craftsman captures the harmony of nature to create a cello that combines the strength of the tree with the beauty of the song of the birds singing in the trees. There is only one musician who is worthy enough to play the instrument, and even he must do so with a sense of humility. Another book with a deep message is *Yonder* (1988), by Tony Johnston. Sometime in the past a farmer planted a plum tree. As the seasons pass and the farmer's family grows, the tree flourishes. Each time a child is born, another plum tree is planted. This eloquent story is a moving reflection of family, continuity, and the passing of time. A book of equal stature is the now classic *The Giving Tree* (1964), by Shel Silverstein. It is the story of a young boy and a young tree who grow up and grow old together. It is a wonderful story with many themes: relationships of man to nature, growing old, personal needs, friendship, selfishness, and love.

A number of books about trees are related to the Christmas season. *Apple Tree Christmas* (1984), by Trinka Hakes Noble, is the story of a young girl whose Christmas season is nearly ruined when an ice storm destroys her apple tree. *Uncle Vova's Tree* (1989), by Patricia Polacco, is a bittersweet story of contrasting cultures that spans successive holiday seasons. On the first Christmas, Uncle Vova, with laughter and singing, takes the children on a nighttime sleigh ride. The happiness continues as they all decorate the tree that Vova and his wife Svetlana planted when they first came from Russia to America. The next Christmas, Vova is gone. The miracle of his tree and the memories of him live on in this warm and happy story. Finally, Gloria Houston unfolds a wonderful story of Christmas during wartime in *The Year of the Perfect Christmas Tree* (1988). When Papa is called to war, Ruthie and her mother resolve to keep his promise to provide the town with its traditional Christmas tree. On Christmas Eve, they climb the hill, find the tree Papa had marked months earlier, and deliver it to the town. The ending to this story will have everyone smiling and crying at the same time.

Humorous Stories.

This unit has a factual basis centering around the theme of trees and forests; it is especially important in such a unit to keep in mind the age and nature of the

FIGURE 5-24 Toys have often been made from trees.

trip. The book shares the enjoyment of the family members getting away from it all for the weekend. Another story of friendship is James Marshall's *Three Up a Tree* (1986). Spider, Sam, and Lolly become engaged in some competitive storytelling in a treehouse. The fun is greatly enhanced by snappy dialogue and illustrations as only James Marshall can draw them.

A new version of an old Italian tale is presented by Inna and Robert Rayevsky in *The Talking Tree* (1990). In this story, a king spends much time searching for a talking tree that contains a lovely princess who has been placed within the tree by a witch's spell. Although he did not anticipate it, the king's search leads him to risk his life in an attempt to release the prin-

audience. Young children will not simply sit and listen to a barrage of facts about trees and forests. Such an approach does not take into consideration their developmental needs and interests. One way to vary the unit is to use realistic fiction and humor relating to trees and forests. Humor is almost always appropriate for children and adults alike.

The Little Old Lady Who Was Not Afraid of Anything (1986), by Linda Williams, presents a lighthearted look at how nature can become rather spooky as night falls and one is alone in the woods. The little old lady actually does become afraid in the story, but only until she understands what is making her afraid. In *Just Me and My Dad* (1977), Mercer Mayer enables the reader to follow the adventures of a youngster and his father as the two trek into the forest on a camping

FIGURE 5-25 Christmas trees are often found in children's literature.

cess from the spell. Just as the reader thinks that the king and the rescued princess will live happily ever after, a clever twist in the plot sends the king on one more adventure prior to the happy ending. A book that is somewhat related is *The Talking Tree; or, Don't Believe Everything You Hear* (1986), by John Himmelman. In this story, Skylar gets trapped inside an old apple tree. As he calls for help, various neighbors come to believe that the tree is actually talking. Skylar begins to enjoy the preposterous situation. Hilarious pictures are used to depict the reactions of the crowd to the words of the tree.

Fantasy, Folk, and Fairy Tales.

Always popular, these tales often take place in forests. In addition, trees often have a role of some sort in the story. One such story taking place in the deep dark woods is *Troll Country* (1980), by Edward Marshall, a pseudonym for James Marshall. In this tale, Elsie Fay encounters a smelly, ugly, not-too-smart troll. The battle of wits is not even close as Elsie Fay outwits the troll. It is a story told with fun and charm. Two other tales also told by James Marshall are *Goldilocks and the Three Bears* (1988) and *Red Riding Hood* (1987). Both of these classic fairy tales are retold with words and pictures in a humorous and irreverent manner.

On the more serious side, Steven Kellogg provides a wonderful narrative for four- to nine-year-olds in *Johnny Appleseed: A Tall Tale* (1988). In this story, Kellogg recounts the life of John Chapman, the original Johnny Appleseed. Chapman's love of nature, his kindness to animals, his physical fortitude, and his widespread planting of apple trees are all chronicled. In *The Great Kapok Tree* (1990), Lynne Cherry provides an ecological warning similar to that found in Helen Cowcher's *Rain Forest* (1989). The kapok tree is located in a South American rain forest where a man is attempting to chop it down. Because the tree is so large, the man quickly tires of his work, sits down to rest, and drifts off to sleep. While the man sleeps, the animals who use the tree as their home whisper their pleas to spare the tree. There are plenty of ecological messages here: the roots hold the soil in place; the trees prevent the land from becoming a desert; the trees provide beauty; the tree provides oxygen for the woodcutter's children; and the forest give the animals

a home. Finally, a child appears and asks the woodcutter to see the forest and the world in a new way. When the woodcutter awakens, he is surrounded by the animals and the lush beauty of the rain forest. The pleas have worked their magic. He drops his axe and leaves the forest. It is a powerful and serious book that plays to the compassionate nature of children. The artwork is gorgeous, and the story provides much information about rain forests.

SUMMARY

Using language as a tool to enhance learning in the content areas is a powerful approach to education. Since language is the basic tool for learning in schools, it makes sense to help children learn strategies to make their own learning more effective. To do this, teachers must break down the barriers that separate and isolate different subjects. When this is not done, children who later enter middle schools and high schools are at a disadvantage.

There are several content areas in early childhood education. They tend to be integrated at that level to a greater extent than they are in later schooling. Literature is a broad and basic content area that comprises a great amount of learning time in the early years. It includes a wide variety of genres including fables, myths, fairy tales, fiction, and so forth. Science includes topics such as the human body, health, and nutrition. Mathematics focuses on counting, numbers, time, money, and computation. Social studies includes such topics as self-esteem, family, community, and holidays. The arts are made up of music, art, and drama. Physical education includes both fine and gross motor skills as well as games and individual skills. Each has an important place in the child's development.

There are a number of reasons to support the integration of content areas. First, a number of educators over the past several decades have stressed how such integration can make learning more meaningful to children. Second, integrated units can more easily provide opportunities for positive social interactions while working toward common goals. Third, integrating content areas with language arts can help children come to a better understanding of how information is structured in the various subjects.

It is not necessarily an easy task to transfer a whole language approach to content subjects. Classrooms have been observed in which teachers showed some facility with the approach in language arts, but reverted to traditional methodology in content subjects. Continued training and feedback from fellow teachers is a key component to successfully making the transition.

Children's storybooks that support content areas are quite numerous. They are available in a variety of formats, appropriate for a wide range of age levels. Many of these books can be used in thematic units on topics such as community, ponds, and forests. Scientific and historical books are available that present information to young children at an appropriate level. In addition, it was found that humorous books, fairy tales, and realistic fiction all have a place within a content area subject.

The thematic unit was identified as a key tool for integrating content areas with the language arts. The thematic unit described in this unit included a rationale for presenting the unit, goals for students, instructional activities, and a schedule for implementation of the unit over a period of time. No specific amount of time is specified for completing a thematic unit. It depends on the theme being addressed. Units lasting from three days to one month are quite common.

An effective tool for learning in the content areas is the content journal or learning log. While it may be comprised of a number of formats, its purpose is always to help the child arrive at meaning. It is an informal place to write or draw ideas, hypotheses, and information learned from instruction. It can be used to make guesses about what happens to polliwogs or to draw a picture of the forest in the winter. It can be used before, during, or after instruction.

Questions and Activities for Review and Discussion

Multiple Choice

1. Instruction is most efficient when it
   a. is understandable to children.
   b. supports learning in other areas.
   c. is supported by learning in other areas.
   d. is all of the above.
2. Fairy tales are one part of the content area of
   a. art.
   b. music.
   c. literature.
   d. science.
3. Nonfiction books often include stories about people who
   a. exist only in the mind of the author.
   b. are animals who talk and dress like people.
   c. are imaginary but seem real.
   d. really lived.
4. A compare/contrast structure for organizing text materials
   a. shows how one thing causes another.
   b. describes similarities and differences.
   c. explains the order in which two things occur.
   d. all of the above

5. A task that is of interest to a child and that deals with a real problem in the eyes of the child is said to be
   a. artificial.
   b. isolated.
   c. incomprehensible.
   d. authentic.
6. Content journals can be helpful in the learning of
   a. terms.
   b. ideas.
   c. processes.
   d. all of the above
7. A thematic unit is basically
   a. a topical outline of a subject.
   b. a lesson focused on a single topic.
   c. an interdisciplinary approach.
   d. a section of a book.

True or False

T   F   1. Content area specialists have traditionally paid little attention to the way knowledge is organized in their disciplines.
T   F   2. Literature can be considered a content area.
T   F   3. Whole language strategies can generally not be applied to topics such as mathematics and science.
T   F   4. A content journal can be used to make guesses about a topic.
T   F   5. A thematic unit should generally not take more than three days to complete.

Essay and Discussion

1. Explain the problems young children face when asked to learn knowledge in isolated segments.
2. Describe what is included in the content area of literature in early childhood education.
3. Explain some of the ways in which the information in nonfiction texts is typically organized.
4. Describe some of the criticisms directed at teachers who are not well-versed in using a whole language approach across the curriculum.
5. Describe some of the ways content journals can be used to enhance content learning.

References

Applebee, A.N., J.A. Langer, and I.V.S. Mullis. 1989. *Crossroads in American education*. Princeton, N.J.: Educational Testing Service.

Armbruster, B.B., T.H. Anderson, and J. Ostertag. 1989. Teaching text structure to improve reading and writing. *The Reading Teacher* 43: 130–137.

Arnold, C. 1990. *A walk in the woods*. Westwood, N.J.: Silver Burdett.

Arnosky, J. 1989. *Come out, muskrat.* New York: Lothrop, Lee & Shepard.

Blegvad, L. 1985. *Anna banana and me.* New York: Margaret K. McElderry.

Carrick, C. 1984. *Dark and full of secrets.* New York: Clarion.

Catterwell, T. 1989. *Aldita and the forest.* Boston: Houghton Mifflin.

Cherry, L. 1990. *The great kapok tree.* New York: Harcourt Brace Jovanovich.

Clement, C. 1989. *A voice in the wood.* New York: Dial.

Coats, L.J. 1987. *The oak tree.* New York: Macmillan.

Cowcher, H. 1989. *Rain forest.* New York: Farrar, Straus & Giroux.

Dewey, J. 1966. *Democracy and education.* New York: Free Press.

Eggleton, J. 1987. *The old oak tree.* New York: Modern.

Foreman, M. 1987. *Cat and canary.* New York: Dial.

Frost, R. 1978. *Stopping by woods on a snowy evening.* New York: E.P. Dutton.

George, J. 1989. *One day in the woods.* New York: Crowell.

Glazer, T. 1964. *Treasury of folk songs.* New York: Grosset & Dunlap.

Hiebert, E.H., and C.W. Fisher. 1990. Whole language: Three themes for the future. *Educational Leadership* 47: 62–64.

Himmelman, J. 1986. *The talking tree; or, don't believe everything you hear.* New York: Viking Kestral.

Hirschi, R. 1987. *Who lives in . . . alligator swamp.* Spring Valley, N.Y.: Dodd Mead.

Hirschi, R. 1987. *Who lives in . . . the forest.* Spring Valley, N.Y.: Dodd Mead.

Houston, G.M. 1988. *The year of the perfect Christmas tree.* New York: Dial.

Johnston, T. 1988. *Yonder.* New York: Dial.

Keisaburo, T. 1987. *Fox's dream.* New York: Philomel.

Keisaburo, T. 1989. *Woodpecker forest.* New York: Philomel.

Kellogg, S. 1988. *Johnny Appleseed: A tall tale.* New York: Macmillan.

Langley, A. 1988. *Trees.* New York: Franklin Watts.

Lavies, B. 1989. *Lily pad pond.* New York: E.P. Dutton.

Lavies, B. 1989. *Tree trunk traffic.* New York: E.P. Dutton.

Marshall, E. 1980. *Troll country.* New York: Dial.

Marshall, J. 1988. *Goldilocks and the three bears.* New York: Dial.

Marshall, J. 1987. *Red riding hood.* New York: Dial.

Marshall, J. 1986. *Three up a tree.* New York: Dial.

Mayer, M. 1977. *Just me and my Dad.* New York: Golden Press.

McGee, L.M., and D.J. Richgels. 1985. Teaching expository text structure to elementary students. *The Reading Teacher* 38: 739–748.

Melser, J., and J. Crowley. 1980. *In a dark dark wood.* Auckland, New Zealand: Shortland.

Michels, T. 1989. *At the frog pond.* New York: Lippincott.

Munro, R. 1987. *Christmastime in New York City.* Spring Valley, N.Y.: Dodd Mead.

Noble, T.H. 1984. *Apple tree Christmas.* New York: Dial.

Parnall, P. 1988. *Apple tree.* New York: Macmillan.

Piccolo, J.A. 1987. Expository text structure: Teaching and learning strategies. *The Reading Teacher* 40: 838–847.

Polacco, P. 1989. *Uncle Vova's tree.* New York: Philomel.

Provensen, A., and M. Provensen. 1985. *Town and country.* New York: Crown.

Rayevsky, R. 1990. *The talking tree.* New York: G.P. Putnam's Sons.

Rockwell, A. 1985. *Come to town.* New York: Crowell.

Romanova, N. 1985. *Once there was a tree.* New York: Dial.

Rosenblum, R. 1988. *My block.* New York: Atheneum.

Russell, N. 1989. *The tree.* New York: E.P. Dutton.

Schwartz, D.M. 1988. *The hidden life of the forest.* New York: Crown.

Schwartz, D.M. 1988. *The hidden life of the pond.* New York: Crown.

Silverstein, S. 1964. *The giving tree.* New York: Harper & Row.

Stevens, J. 1987. *The town mouse and the country mouse.* New York: Holiday House.

Strickland, D.S., and L.M. Morrow. 1990. Integrating the emergent literacy curriculum with themes. *The Reading Teacher* 43: 604–605.

Titherington, J. 1988. *Where are you going Emma?* New York: Greenwillow.

Wells, R. 1988. *Forest of dreams.* New York: Dial.

Williams, J. 1989. *The life cycle of a tree.* New York: Franklin Watts.

Williams, L. 1986. *The little old lady who was not afraid of anything.* New York: Harper & Row.

Yolen, J. 1987. *Owl moon.* New York: Philomel.

Ziefert, H. 1987. *Jason's bus ride.* New York: Viking Kestral.

UNIT 6

The World of Children's Literature

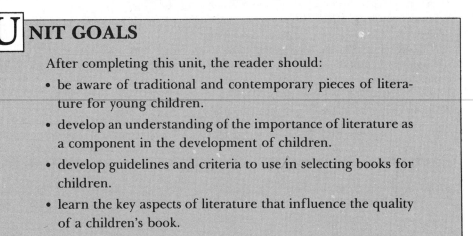

UNIT GOALS

After completing this unit, the reader should:

- be aware of traditional and contemporary pieces of literature for young children.
- develop an understanding of the importance of literature as a component in the development of children.
- develop guidelines and criteria to use in selecting books for children.
- learn the key aspects of literature that influence the quality of a children's book.
- learn procedures for telling and reading stories to children.

PREVIEW

Through the ages, people have enjoyed telling and sharing stories. At one time, storytelling was the dominant method for sharing a culture's heritage with the next generation. To a large extent, that role has been taken over by schools, books, newspapers, and the electronic media. To a certain extent, the traditional role of storytelling still survives. Many children experience some of their first understandings of the culture through the chants and nursery rhymes of their parents and early childhood caregivers. The appreciation of listening to or reading a good story is still with us, however. Most of us still enjoy stories throughout our lives.

Books for children provide a wealth of language and diverse experiences through literature. The stories found in books provide children with vocabulary,

language structures, and knowledge about the world. In addition to story reading in the home and in early childhood programs, other organizations strive to provide literature experiences for young children. Children's rooms in libraries often hold story hours for infants, toddlers, preschoolers, and primary grade children. These sessions are often held several times each week. Theatrical performance groups travel to many areas to stage productions that are often based on traditional favorites from children's literature. Country fairs and festivals held in both urban and rural areas usually have provisions for entertaining children. These often include puppet shows and theatrical presentations based upon stories found in literature for children.

To provide a comprehensive understanding of the role of children's literature, this unit explores a number of key ideas and concepts. These include the importance of literature, examples of quality literature covering a wide variety of subjects, and criteria for identifying good books for children. Also examined are the elements of character, setting, plot, theme, and the tools needed to become an effective reader or teller of stories.

INTRODUCTION

Over the past several decades there has been a significant amount of research on the influence of reading and literature in the lives of young children. Much of the research has been focused on children who enter school already knowing how to read, those who have actually learned how to read without ever being exposed to any formal reading instruction. Such children, referred to as natural readers, often arrive at school with a deep interest in stories, reading, language, and books. Their ability to learn reading independently is often traced to some key factors in their preschool years. They tend to have had an ample supply of books in their homes. They were frequently in the company of adults who read to them and who themselves read as a recreational activity. They had people to talk to and to answer their questions about books, reading, language, and literature.

On the other hand, many children arrive at school with serious deficiencies in language abilities. Jim Trelease (1989), a noted advocate on the importance of sharing books with young children, traces much of this problem to the many hours of television viewing engaged in by many children. The focus of the child's mental activity is the chief difference between literature and television.

In watching television, a child can assume an almost totally passive role. The message is both told through the television speaker and shown on the television screen. The messages need to be simplistic and straightforward in order to conform to the half-hour time slot or ten-second sound bite. The presentation requires little interpretation, since it will be fleeting and not subject to a second showing by the viewer.

In contrast to television viewing, reading or listening to a story requires the child to be intellectually active in order to derive meaning from the message. The story does not have to be simple enough to fit into a certain time slot. The author can depend on the audience to re-read portions of the text or to read more slowly at other points in the story in order to get the meaning of the message. Time to reflect on the meaning of a story is a key element in arriving at truth and understanding. Child psychologist Bruno Bettelheim (1976) states that finding meaning in life is the greatest need of any human being. He further believes that it is the most difficult thing to achieve for anyone at any age. Given that the purpose of literature is to help people arrive at meaning, it becomes a critical element in child development. Through literature, children learn about the world in which they live and about the people who inhabit that world. As they develop these understandings, they come to know themselves better as a part of the process.

Learning about the World

While most books for children are not intended to be informational books, they often do inform children about the world. Even when books do not fully explain every concept presented, they often spark the curiosity of children. After reading or hearing a story, children often ask questions or seek explanations about it. Anyone who has spent time reading books to children is familiar with having children stop the reader in the middle of a sentence in order to inquire about the meaning of a word.

Reading and books can serve both as a reinforcement to the knowledge children already possess and as a preliminary step in acquiring new knowledge. Learning is a process of relating new information and ideas to that which is already known. A story can introduce a child to something new. Later, as related activities and stories are used, they become meaningful in relation to the initial story. Similarly, if a child has had a certain experience, stories related to that experience can be more meaningful. They are more meaningful because the child is able to more easily make sense out of the stories by relating them to the initial experience.

As an example, consider how books might play a role for the teacher of a class of preschoolers planning a field trip to a pond. The pond might be located in an urban park or near a farm in a rural setting. The teacher might use books before, during, and after the visit. When the idea of the field trip is first discussed by the teacher, some of the children might

FIGURE 6-1 A classroom turtle can introduce children to the pond life that they will learn about in books and stories.

be familiar with ponds. They can be encouraged to offer information about them. The information can be supplemented with books such as David Schwartz's *The Hidden Life of the Pond* (1988), Tilde Michels's *At the Frog Pond* (1989), Jim Arnosky's *Come Out, Muskrats* (1989) and Bianca Lavies's *Lily Pad Pond* (1989). Some of these books might be used before and during the field trip as well. Fictional stories about animals related to pond life can be used at all points throughout the field trip experience. Good choices would include Leo Lionni's *Swimmy* (1963), Arnold Lobel's *Frog and Toad Are Friends* (1970) and Carol Carrick's *Dark and Full of Secrets* (1984). The preferred approach might be to intersperse the use of the books before, during, and after the field trip. Heavy-handed content lessons seldom work well with young children. Throughout their schooling, children will be exposed to this information. At this point, the emphasis should be on helping children learn what is meaningful about the book.

Learning about People

Literature can help fulfill the natural curiosity children have about all of the things they find around them. The world is full of people, all kinds of people. Children see people of different races, of different cultures, with different physical and personality characteristics, and of different sexes. While they may be drawn to some people and fear others, they are often curious about all. Many of the fears young children have of people who are different from themselves are based upon ignorance. Knowledge can eliminate much of that fear. Literature can play a major role in providing that knowledge.

Books can help provide information on nearly every kind of person the child might encounter. Children who are concerned about the new baby in the house can share in reading Russell Hoban's *A Baby Sister for Frances* (1960) or Martha Alexander's *Nobody Asked Me If I Wanted a Baby Sister* (1971). If they exhibit fears about a grandparent who has been stricken with Alzheimer's disease, Vaunda Micheaux Nelson's *Always Gramma* (1988) and Jonah Schein's *Forget Me Not* (1988) are useful tools for helping a child understand.

Children may have a curiosity or fear of people outside of their immediate family as well. This is particularly true when children meet people from different cultures or people who have a disability. *Watch Out for the Chicken Feet in Your Soup* (1974), by Tomie dePaola, takes a humorous look at a child's growing understanding of someone whose old world ways present quite a contrast with modern life. *Aunt Armadillo* (1985), by Robin Baird Lewis, illustrates the fine relaionship a child develops with her eccentric aunt. Superb stories involving people with physical handicaps can be found in Lorraine Henriod's *Grandma's Wheelchair* (1982), Curt and Gita Kaufman's *Rajesh* (1985), Joan Fassler's *Howie Helps Himself* (1975) and Bernice Rabe's *The Balancing Girl* (1981).

A growing body of children's books include minority children in positive natural roles. Black Americans are featured in Barbara Winther's *Plays from Folktales from Africay* (1976), Lucille Clifton's *The Boy Who Didn't Believe in Spring* (1973), and Jack Ezra Keats's *The Snowy Day* (1962). Books that focus on Hispanic Americans include *My Dog is Lost* (1960), by Ezra Jack Keats and Pat Cherr, and *Angelita* (1970), by Wendy Kesselmann. Books focused on people from Asia include Arnold Lobel's *Ming Lo Moves the Mountain* (1982) and Helena Clare Pittman's *The Gift of the Willows* (1988). Each of these books is a quality piece of literature because each effectively portrays the universal nature of experience.

Learning about Oneself

As children learn about the world and the people they find in it, they begin to make judgments about life and to develop values that will guide their decisions about life. As they develop and grow they acquire both helpful and harmful values. Teachers and parents can play a role in shaping these values by maintaining open and honest communication with children. Sharing books is an effective tool for fostering this communication. Books provide information and problem situations to be discussed. They enable readers and listeners to share the problems and discuss possible solutions. As they share the reading, parents and teachers can help children to reflect more upon why they would take certain actions in specific situations. These discussions can help children learn more about their own values and to refine those values as they grow.

Given the tremendous effect literature can have on the development of children, it makes sense to use care and thought in choosing books. To do this, three different things are needed. First, teachers must have some knowledge about literature. Recognizing a quality book along with having a basic understanding of character, setting, plot, and theme will help teachers develop appropriate criteria for selecting children's books. Second, teachers must possess a basic knowledge of books currently available. This includes traditional children's literature, nonfiction books, and contemporary fiction titles. Third, teachers must possess certain skills to effectively share books with young children. This is true of both oral storytellers and those who are reading books to children. Each of these three areas is explored in this unit. For a fuller analysis of any of these see *Growing Up with Literature* (1991), by Walter Sawyer and Diana E. Comer.

ASPECTS OF LITERATURE

The aspects of literature to consider when selecting books for children include characterization, setting, plot, and theme. These, together with components such as print and illustrations, provide ideas for developing criteria for book selection. Before considering any of these, however, teachers must take the children into consideration. A good book in terms of the technical aspects of literature may not be an appro-

FIGURE 6-2 Children have needs that help them choose books for different times and places.

priate selection for a particular child or group of children. Teachers must always be aware of the children's developmental needs, their interests, their ability to understand language, and their motivation for attending to books on certain topics. In addition, it is useful to consider the purpose for selecting a book as well. Is the book going to be used to introduce a topic in a science unit? Is the book going to be used to help children learn about the concept of sharing? Is the book going to be used solely for the sheer enjoyment of experiencing a good story? When there is a firm understanding of each of these, the next step is to examine the aspects of literature.

Characterization

In children's literature, people, animals, objects, and even pretend beings can make up the possible characters. Every story has at least one character. There should not be more characters than are necessary for the telling of the story. The characters who are the most memorable in stories are those with whom we seem to develop a relationship. They are characters who we can look at and say, "Yes, I know what that's like." Such characters are effective, because we care about them. Whether they are human or animal characters, they possess credibility and consistency.

Credible Characters.

Authors build their characters within the story. They let the reader know what the character is like. They share the character's personality and motivations with the reader. In doing this, authors enable readers to develop an emotional link with the character. As such, the reader can enter the character's world and share in the fun and adventure.

Credibility does not mean that the characters have to seem real. Rather, it means that within the context of the other aspects of the story the characters are believable. Take, for example, the characters created by the writer/illustrator team of Harry Allard and James Marshall. In their books *The Stupids Die* (1981), *The Stupids Step Out* (1974), and *The Stupids Have a Ball* (1978), they create a credible family whose last name is Stupid. In the topsy-turvy world presented in the books, the Stupid family is credible in spite of its incredibleness. Each member of the family acts in a manner that in ordinary circumstances would be seen as unbelievable. In the world of the Stupids, however, everything seems kind of normal. Readers relate to the characeters because everyone has done something foolish at one time or another.

Consistent Characters.

Characters should be consistent. That is, young readers find that they can relate better to characters when they are somewhat dependable. The character may change and grow over time, or within the context of the book. However, that change and growth should be consistent with the personality of the character. H. A. and Margaret Rey's books about Curious George the monkey are a good example. Norman Bridwell's books about Clifford the big red dog are also. The characters from both books seem to learn from their mistakes, but neither betrays its basic personality. Curious George will still be curious. Clifford will still cause problems with his size in the next book.

Bland characters who remain consistent do not work well. This does not mean that a character has to be special or in any way remarkable. Rather, it means that characters should not be stereotypical. It means that characters who are perhaps a little different can overcome an obstacle related to their difference. In Charlotte Zolotow's *William's Doll* (1982), readers meet a little boy who wants a doll of his own more than anything else in the world. His parents are reluctant to fulfill his request because of their own stereotyped thinking about the appropriate roles of the sexes. In Tomie dePaola's autobiographical story *The Art Lesson* (1989), the main character's patience and motivation help overcome many of the early obstacles found by anyone attempting to develop a special skill.

Animal Characters.

Animal characters are found throughout literature written for children. Those books provide much information about the characteristics of the animals in addition to other benefits for the reader. Most children in their early years have a great interest in animals. This interest is supported by books with animal characters even when the story is a fantasy or uses imaginary animals such as unicorns. Often, the animals display human characteristics in their speech and actions. Children readily accept this even though they frequently realize that animals do not really talk or dress like humans. Animal characters addressing a difficulty places the problem at a comfortable distance for the child. This allows children to more easily discuss topics they are concerned about.

Animal characters are particularly effective in portraying human characteristics when they retain some of the animal characteristics that render them unique. This, combined with the personality given to them by the author, renders such animal characters as truly memorable. Beatrix Potter was an early writer of modern children's books featuring animal characters. Her stories featured characters such as Peter Rabbit wearing clothes but retaining his animal instincts and activities. The widely popular Berenstain Bears series by Stan and Jan Berenstain moves the format closer to that of humans. While still retaining some of the characteristics of bears, such as liking honey and living in a hollow tree, the Berenstain Bears family encounters problems similar to those encountered by human families.

A variation of books featuring animal characters is the story that combines both animal and human characters. The development of an unexpected friendship between a human and a beast is featured in Susan Meddaugh's book *Beast* (1981). In Arthur Yorinks's *Louis the Fish* (1980), the main human character fulfills a lifetime yearning by actually turning into an animal character.

Setting

The term *setting* usually makes us think of the time and location of a story. This is basically correct, but setting can entail more than just time and place. Setting can include the cultural conditions in which the characters find themselves as well as the way characters live within that culture. A present day story would be different if it took place in a city in America than if it took place in a rural Australian township. The differences would not merely be in terms of geography and weather. The distinctions between the two locations would also be affected by those things that are held as important in the two locations. Family and community codes would also influence the story. If the story were moved to China, Siberia, or New Zealand, the story would once again be changed.

Since the possibilities for setting are nearly endless, so too are the variations for the moral, ethical, and social possibilities for stories. The reason for this is that characters are tied to setting. The characters in a story act within a setting. Just as in real life, individuals in stories are influenced by the environments in which they find themselves. If characters consistently act in ways that are not believable in the context, the story seems contrived. This does not mean that characters need to act in predictable ways. Deviations from what is predictable creates interest and excitement. An author must make a character consistent enough to be believable within the setting, but different enough to create interest.

Settings in children's literature vary widely. *Make Way for Ducklings* (1941), by Robert McCloskey, uses the very specific setting of the Boston Garden. The two towns suggested in Bernard Waber's *Ira Says Goodbye* (1988) are more vague, but clearly they are typical American small towns. *The Legend of Old Befana* (1980), by Tomie dePaola, uses a small village in medieval Italy as its setting. David McPhail uses a general setting in Africa for *Snow Lion* (1982).

Familiar Settings.

Stories that take place in familiar settings are often enjoyed by children. The story does not have to take place in a specific location familiar to the child, how-

ever. Settings that are obviously a home for a family, a characteristic schoolroom, or a typical childcare center all fit under the heading of familiar settings. Each can be a place for love, joy, excitement, and sadness. Ordinary objects found in any home take on totally new meanings when the child character awakens to find himself only a few inches tall in William Joyce's *George Shrinks* (1985). Sadness fills the home depicted in Tomie dePaola's *Nana Upstairs and Nana Downstairs* (1973) at the death of the child's grandmother. Terror turns to comfort in Nancy Carlson's *Witch Lady* (1985) when Louanne Pig discovers that the old lady who lives in the "haunted house" on the block turns out to be warm and kind. Patricia Reilly Giff, while dealing with real life childhood problems, creates a friendly and comfortable school setting in books such as *Happy Birthday, Ronald Morgan* (1986), *Today Was a Terrible Day* (1980) and *Watch Out, Ronald Morgan* (1985).

Nature Settings.

Natural settings are quite common in children's literature. This is true for two reasons. First, since many books contain animal characters, nature settings are the expected location for the story. Second, natural settings provide a variety of interesting locations, many of which can attract the curiosity of young children. *When I Was Young in the Mountains* (1982), by Cynthia Rylant, provides a nostalgic view of life in the mountains of West Virginia. Alvin Tresselt's *Hide and Seek Fog* (1965) provides a fine story that could only take place along the New England coast. There are many excellent books featuring animal characters that take place in the forest. Arnold Lobel's *Days with Frog and Toad* (1979) is but one example of such books.

Plot

The plot of a book is a guide to help the reader make sense out of the story. Since a plot is an artificial element, it may or may not unfold in chronological order. In developing a plot, an author selects a set of episodes necessary to tell a story. The function of the plot is to translate character into action (Thrall and Hibbard 1960). The plot begins by setting up interest for the reader. It often does this by presenting a problem within the story to which the reader can re-

FIGURE 6-3 Natural environments, such as Assateague Island in Virginia, have provided the settings for many children's books.

late. The conflict proceeds by presenting the character's attempts at solving the problem. It generally concludes with a climax, or a point in which the tension of the problem reaches a peak, followed by a resolution of the problem and a return to life as before.

Barbara Shook Hazen's book *Tight Times* (1979) provides an excellent example of a well-developed plot featuring a complex problem that is well understood by many children: poverty. The story begins by introducing the reader to the main character and the problem of the story, a young boy who very much would like to have a pet dog. The action rises with his parents explaining how they could not afford to have a pet right now. The illustrations in the book make it clear that the parents do not have well paying jobs and that their apartment is plain and small. While the child keeps his hopes alive, the situation worsens when the father comes home unexpectedly in the middle of the day, explaining to his son that he has lost his job. Later that day, the depressed child finds a small kitten in a trash barrel out on the sidewalk. A passing stranger explains that the kitten belongs to no one. The child quietly brings the kitten to his kitchen to give it some milk. The climax of the story occurs with the dropping of the milk container and the parents' discovery of the child's kitten. In a tearful scene, the child's mother and father agree to allow him to keep the kitten. The story ends with the family drawing closer together. While the father is still unemployed there has clearly been a refocusing by everyone on the important things in life.

Based on this example, it is clear that plot can address some sophisticated subjects with young children. The plot, however, needs to be believable and understandable. If it is confusing or boring, the child will lose interest in the story. As it unfolds, a plot should only hint at what is to come. If the adult reader can guess the final outcome of the plot on page one, the child is likely to be able to do the same. The focus should be on believable plots that capture and maintain interest.

Theme

Theme is an abstract concept. It refers to messages or ideas embedded in the story that the author suggests are important to the story. A theme cannot be identified as easily as if it were one of the main characters. In children's literature, the themes of growing, friendship, family, and self-esteem are common. While themes are abstract ideas, children can and do identify them. Lehr (1988) studied the ability of kindergarteners to identify themes in stories. She found that they could identify themes in both folktales and in realistic fiction, although it was stronger in the latter type of literature. The children's identification of themes differed from that of adults, but they were congruent with the texts. This suggests that young children may view themes differently from adults, but not incorrectly. Lehr also noted that children with a background that included early and frequent exposure to literature were better able to identify themes in stories.

Authors often use themes to help readers develop an awareness or sensitivity to an issue, event, or idea. There may be only a single theme in a book, or there may be several. A theme may be a major issue in a story or it may be a subtle, underlying idea. Whatever the case, themes usually add to the story. They provide issues and ideas for discussion. They help develop the conflict in the plot. And they are usually related to the motivations and actions of at least some of the characters in the story.

Friendship and human relations constitute a large proportion of the themes in childrens books. James Marshall explores these ideas over and over again in his George and Martha books about the two hippopotamus friends. In *Big Sister, Little Sister* (1966), Charlotte Zolotow explores the special friendship inherent in the relationships that develop among siblings. The special relationship between a child and grandparent is addressed by Patricia MacLachlan in *Through Grandpa's Eyes* (1980). In the story, a child learns to more fully appreciate both his own senses and his grandfather's friendship even though the latter's blindness prevents him from doing some things. The friendship that develops between people and their pets is often explored. In Susan Jeschke's *Perfect the Pig* (1980), a young woman and her pet pig overcome both hardship and separation in order to retire to a quiet life in the country. The sadness that overwhelms a child at the death of a beloved pet is presented by Holly Keller in *Goodbye, Max* (1987).

Components of Books

Besides the literary conventions described above, teachers must also be aware of the other components of books when making selections to share with children. While these concepts are described separately here, they are usually integrated with the others in any book. To make judgments about any of these concepts, consideration of the context in which it is found should always be taken. The components discussed here include text style, narrative style, illustrations, and anti-bias factors.

Text Style.

The size, color, and location of the print on a page comprise the text style of a book. While there are hundreds of possible type settings, care must be taken by a publisher in making the selection. The type setting can and should contribute to the unity between the words of the story and the illustrations used to illustrate the story. Small print set against huge illustrations can create a humorous effect as in *Veronica* (1969), by Roger Duvoisin. Dr. Seuss books often use type sizes to emphasize words and ideas in the story. In Eric Carle's *The Grouchy Ladybug* (1977), the size of the print increases as the story progresses in order to support the story's plot.

While most print is usually presented in black on a white background near the illustrations, this is not always the case with children's books. The contrast is frequently reversed when photographs are used to illustrate a book. This is seen in many of Tana Hoban's books such as *A Children's Zoo* (1985). Robert McCloskey uses the same sepia color for both the print and the illustrations in *Make Way for Ducklings* (1941). The location of illustration and text can vary as well. Books that contain poetry vary from the common paragraph form. Alphabet books such as Bill Martin, Jr. and John Archambault's *Chicka Chicka Boom Boom* (1989) contains both varying sizes of black text and large, colorful letters involved in the actual story plot.

Narrative Style.

Every writer has a distinctive voice and an individual style for telling a story. An author's style is reflected in the choice of words, the use of literary devices, and the rhythm of the language used. One author might use short words and a straightforward text to make the story as clear as possible. Another might choose to use a variety of vivid language to create a distinctive picture in the mind of the reader. A. A. Milne, the Brothers Grimm, Lewis Carroll, and Bill Martin, Jr. use a poetic style to enhance the light-hearted tone of their stories.

Repetition is a staple of literature for children. It is predictable, it invites young children to participate in the reading, and it is fun. Any child who has ever experienced the reading of Wanda Gag's classic *Millions of Cats* (1928) will most likely recall it with a special fondness. Another classic is Margaret Wise Brown's *Goodnight Moon* (1947), one of the best loved bedtime stories of all time. Its quiet, soothing illustrations are perfectly matched with the soft, repeating lines of the text. This is in sharp contrast, however, to Judith Viorst's smashingly upbeat classic *Alexander and the Terrible, Horrible, No Good, Very Bad Day* (1972). The repeating line of the title makes it a perennial favorite of both children and adults.

Illustrations.

For young children, the illustrations that accompany the text are as important as the text itself. They support, extend, and explain the narrative. As such they should be carefully integrated with the story. In addition, they should be of high quality, possess vividness, and contain appropriate and necessary details. The range of possibilities for creating illustrations for children's storybooks is wide. Perhaps the most commonly used medium is oil painting. Artists have also used watercolors, pen and ink, and colored pencil as mediums for illustrating books. Many accomplished artists have lent their hand to creating pictures for book illustrations over the years. Among the most popular are Maurice Sendak, Mitsamasa Anno, Gyo Fujikawa, Briam Wildsmith, Tomie dePaola, Steven Kellogg, Arnold Lobel, and Donald Carrick.

Readers of children's books can observe such varied techniques as woodcuts and linocuts by Don Freeman and Marie Hall Ets, charcoal and colored pencil by Susan Jeffers and Taro Yashima, and collage by Ezra Jack Keats and Eric Carle. Still other books use photographs as illustrations. The best known photographers for children's books are Tana Hoban and Roger Bester.

A key component of the illustrations used in a children's book is how well they are integrated with the text. After all, the major purpose of the illustrations is to help the reader obtain meaning from the book. The illustrations must also be integrated with each other. One picture must have a logical connection with the previous one as the story unfolds. A superb example of illustration and text being totally integrated is Leo Lionni's *Swimmy* (1963). The feeling for the enormity of the ocean is created as a contrast to the nearly insignificant size of the small fish. Donald Crews shares this ability to integrate illustration with text in *Freight Train* (1978). As the story progresses, the sense of increasing speed is derived equally from the text and the illustrations.

Anti-bias Factors.

Modern publishing companies do not generally accept or print works containing bias in areas of race, sex, age, national origin, religion, or disability. In most cases, publishing companies attempt to provide a forum for the diversity of modern society. However, in the past, this was not always the case. As a result, many school and public libraries still contain books that contain both overt and subtle negative bias toward minority groups. When selecting books from these sources to share with children, teachers should use special care to avoid choosing those with biased messages.

In choosing books for a classroom or center collection, it is important to not establish bias by omission.

FIGURE 6-4 Writer and illustrator Dave Ross has provided many favorite books for young children.

That is, when selecting books, it is important to include selections that will help children to become aware of and learn about all of the individuals who make up a society. There is no formula to use in determining percentages of different type of books to choose. Books should be primarily chosen because the stories in them are inviting and appropriate for young children. With over 4,000 titles for children being published each year, however, there are ample high-quality books reflecting the cultural diversity of society. For example, Patricia Reilly Giff provides a strong girl character, Emily Arrow, in her Polk Street School series. Carol Carrick's *Stay Away from Simon* (1985) provides a good look at the disabled child.

Criteria for Selecting Books.

While each of the above criteria is helpful in making story selections for children, teachers must keep in mind the needs, interests, and motivations of the children who will read or listen to the book. A purpose for sharing the book should also be identified. Perhaps it is to reinforce a unit on native Americans. It may be to introduce the concept of friendship. One of the best purposes, of course, is simply to help children experience the pleasure of reading a great story. An excellent activity for anyone seeking to become more involved with children's literature is to go to libraries and bookstores in order to read a wide range of books. Get to know the store owners and librarians. Let them know of your interests and to make suggestions to you. Librarians can provide a listing of the children's picture books that have won the award for the best book each year, the Caldecott Medal. Finding out the titles of books that experienced early childhood teachers recommend is also useful. It is helpful to keep track of good books by keeping notes or records on each book. Figure 6-5 provides a format for recording the information used for making judgments about specific books.

PICTURE BOOKS FOR CHILDREN

Most, if not all, of the books used in early childhood education programs are referred to as picture books. This is true even if they contain words, as most picture books do. There are, of course, picture books that do not contain any words. An example of this is *One Frog Too Many* (1975) by Mercer and Marianna Mayer. Picture books may also be referred to as tradebooks, which distinguishes them from textbooks. Textbooks for young readers are described elsewhere as basal readers. They will not be included here. While there is no right or wrong way to group picture books, the general categories of traditional stories, nonfiction and concept books, and contemporary fiction will be used here. They are grouped this way in order to facilitate this discussion. In a library or in a classroom they might be found mixed together or grouped differently. Also, there is an overlap between the different groups. Some classic children's books seem to be largely books about concepts. Some books about concepts or a content area also tell a realistic fictional story. In books, as in life, it is usually impossible to place everything into neat categories.

Traditional Stories

Traditional stories comprise the literature that has stood the test of time. They are stories enjoyed by one generation after another. They include Mother Goose, the Brothers Grimm, nursery rhymes, folk tales, fairy tales, and legends. Some of these stories are simple poems remembered from childhood and often recited orally to children from the memory of the teacher. At other times, they are incorporated into a picture book and presented as a read-aloud story. Collections of Mother Goose, Brothers Grimm, chants, rhymes, and other tales are also available. When using collections, teachers must decide if there are enough illustrations included to help the children maintain interest in and understanding of the story. Figure 6-6 provides a partial list of traditional rhymes and stories available in a variety of formats.

There are a number of Mother Goose collections available. Every early childhood classroom should have at least one copy available. A traditional favorite is *Brian Wildsmith's Mother Goose* (1964). Softly textured bright illustrations are included for each of the rhymes. A more recent addition is *The Random House Book of Mother Goose* (1986). Over 300 nursery rhymes were selected and illustrated by Arnold Lobel for this collection. Many of the lesser known rhymes are included in the volume.

Many rhymes and traditional stories are regularly published with new illustrations each year. Some of these stories are updated through their illustrations, others retain their old world charm, and still others take on a whole new look. Alice and Martin Provensen's *Old Mother Hubbard* (1977) presents the story in a modern day city with cars and trucks going up and down the busy street just outside Mother Hubbard's apartment. *The Three Billy Goats Gruff* (1984) retains an old world look, but Ellen Appleby's illustrations give it a decidedly comic appearance. Paul Galdone, who has illustrated a number of traditional stories, presents some wonderful chase scenes in his story *The Gingerbread Boy* (1975). The distinctive pictures of James Marshall are used to illustrate Freya Littledale's *The Boy Who Cried Wolf* (1975). Ed Young presents a different look at the Little Red Riding Hood story with a Chinese version titled *Lon Po Po* (1989). Finally, Ezra Jack Keats creates a world loved by thousands of children in his

Title:_____

Author:_____

Publisher / City / Date:_____

Who are the main characters?_____

Are the characters credible and consistent?_____

Type of characters (animal / human / both):_____

What is the setting for the story?_____

What is the basic problem described in the plot?_____

How is the problem in the plot solved?_____

What are some of the themes in the story?_____

What is the text style?_____

What is the narrative style?_____

What kind of illustrations are used?_____

How do the illustrations enhance the story?_____

Is the book biased towards any minority group?_____

Does the book include any portrayals of any minority group members?_____

    If yes, which ones?_____

For what age level would this book be appropriate?_____

What topics does this book relate to?_____

How could this book best be used?_____

Is this a high quality book appropriate for young children?

_____No

_____Yes

_____Yes, but only under certain conditions: _____

FIGURE 6-5 Record sheet for selecting children's books

A cat came fiddling	Old Mother Goose
As I was going to St. Ives	Old Mother Hubbard
Baa, baa, black sheep	One, two, buckle my shoe
Beauty and the beast	Over in the meadow
Cinderella	Pat–a–cake, pat–a–cake
Ding, dong, bell	Pease porridge hot
Georgie Porgie, pudding	Peter, Peter, pumpkin eater
and pie	Peter Piper
Goosey, goosey, gander	Peter Rabbit
Hey diddle diddle	Pussy cat, pussy cat
Hickory, dickory, dock	Puss in boots
Humpty Dumpty	Rapunzel
Hush–a–bye baby	Rumpelstiltskin
I saw a ship a–sailing	Seven in one blow
Jack and Jill	Simple Simon
Jack be nimble	Sing a song of sixpence
Jack Sprat could eat no fat	Sleeping Beauty
Little Bo–peep	Snow White
Little Boy Blue	Solomon Grundy
Little Jack Horner	Tales of Brer Rabbit
Little Miss Muffet	The boy who cried wolf
Little Polly Flinders	The elves and
Little Red Hen	the shoemaker
Little Timmy Tucker	The fisherman and his wife
London Bridge is	The frog prince
falling down	The hare and the tortoise
Mary had a little lamb	The house that Jack built
Mary, Mary, quite contrary	Three billy goats gruff
Monday's child	Three little pigs
Old King Cole	Ugly Duckling

FIGURE 6-6 Partial listing of traditional stories and rhymes

recreation of the Appalachian country rhyme *Over in the Meadow* (1971).

Nonfiction and Concept Books

Nonfiction books cover both content area topics, as described in unit five, and biographical books. The purpose of these books is to provide information to readers that is timely, accurate, and unbiased. Concept books for early childhood education ordinarily cover three areas: the alphabet, counting and numbers, and basic concepts.

Biographies.

Some nonfiction books border on fiction. This is particularly true with biographies written for chil-

dren. The reason for this is that children often attend to a narrative more easily than they attend to a subject matter book. Since no one knows exactly what conversations took place, authors often develop conversations and actions likely to have happened during the person's life. Such books are referred to as historical fiction, even though most of the information they present is true.

Jean Fritz has contributed greatly to the field by presenting young children with understandable biographical stories. Her books include *And Then What Happened, Paul Revere?* (1973) and *George Washington's Breakfast* (1969). Biographical stories of lesser known individuals are also available. The story of a strong female role model is presented by Eleanor Coerr in

FIGURE 6-7 The stories of "Snow White" and other traditional tales are often recreated in books for children. *From* The Child's Fairy Tale Book, *by Kay Chorao. Reprinted courtesy of E.P. Dutton.*

FIGURE 6-8 Mike Thaler, author of children's books, is an expert at involving children with language through riddles. *Used courtesy of Mike Thaler, "America's Riddle King."*

The Big Balloon Race (1981). It details the life of Carlotta Myers, a nineteenth-century balloonist.

Alphabet Books.

The visual symbols used in written language are found in the alphabet. While a large number of the letters can and should be learned through literature and stories, alphabet books are useful as well. Children enjoy the feeling of accomplishment that comes from identifying the letters as they appear on each of the pages of these books. It is best to refrain from placing pressure on children to memorize the letters and sounds of the alphabet at an early age. These books can be used simply as books to enjoy and as books to help children become more comfortable with the language.

As with traditional stories, many fine artists have produced inviting high-quality alphabet books. Humor is often used in the presentation of alphabet books. Edward Lear, in *An Edward Lear Alphabet* (1983), uses humorous verse in the presentation of the letters. Bill Martin, Jr. and John Archambault present a wonderfully happy song story in their alphabet book *Chicka Chicka Boom Boom* (1989). Combining concepts and the alphabet, Cindy Szekere uses each letter to present an emotion in *Cindy Szekere's ABC* (1983). Teri Sloat's *From Letter to Letter* (1989) places the illustrative pictures totally within the letters themselves. Although not really an alphabet book, Jack Gantos uses a fictional story to describe a cantankerous cat learning the alphabet in *Rotten Ralph's Show and Tell* (1989).

There are certain things to be aware of when choosing an alphabet book. The letter sound should be heard clearly in the word used to represent the letter. Each letter should be presented clearly whether or not it has an entire page devoted to it. The hard sound of the letter should be used for words beginning with the letters "C" and "G." The letters "S," "W," and "T" should be used in words in which they are not blended with other letters such as "H" and "R."

Counting Books.

Just as with alphabet books, many fine illustrators have lent their hand to counting and number books for children. Tana Hoban's *Count and See* (1972), Eric Carle's *1, 2, 3 to the Zoo* (1969), Ezra Jack Keats's *Over in the Meadow* (1972), and Amy Ehrlich's *The Everyday Train* (1983) are but a few examples. Suzanne Aker's *What Comes in 2's, 3's, & 4's* (1990) is a welcome variation to traditional counting books. It allows the children to relate the concept of numbers to their own lives. A similar opportunity exists for children reading Kate Spohn's *Clementine's Winter Wardrobe* (1989). Mary Serfozo's *Who Wants One?* (1989) provides a variation on counting books by accompanying each of the numbers with rhymes that ask questions.

When using counting books, the teacher might plan to use several over the course of time. They can be left in the reading area so that children can return to them. Sharing the book with a friend should be encouraged, as should recreating the numbers in the book with real objects.

Concept Books.

The concepts stressed in early childhood programs are often referred to as basic concepts. They include all of the labels and nuances of language that adults and older children take for granted. They may include name words such as dog, house, car, bicycle, baby, airplane, flag, water, and so forth. They may also include descriptive and directional words such as red, big, long, tall, between, in, near, over, under, in front of, above, below, and scratchy. When selecting concept books, the concept depicted should be presented in a clear manner that will be understood by children. The illustrations should be captivating and closely represent the concept being described. A good concept will motivate children to return to it over and over again.

Artists and storytellers alike have made valuable contributions to concept books over the years. Tana Hoban has used photographs to illustrate many concept books. Eric Carle uses imaginative illustrations for his color concept book *My Very First Book of Colors* (1985). Other artists who have developed imaginative concept books include Richard Scarry, Mitsumasa Anno, Brian Wildsmith, and Dr. Seuss. Some books address concepts through fictional stories. They can be used to add additional interest and motivation to the study of basic concepts. Robert Lopshire explores basic concepts in *The Biggest, Smallest, Fastest, Tallest* (1980). Seymour Reit helps children learn about the hospital and injuries in *Jenny's in the Hospital* (1984). Children learn more about their bodies through books such as Marc Brown's *Arthur's Nose* (1976) and *Arthur's Eyes* (1979). The concept of sharing is explored by Mercer Mayer in *Me Too!* (1983).

Concepts books are available for even the youngest children. True Kelley has written two books focusing on these children. *Let's Eat!* (1989) looks at food. The book presents a variety of food, where food comes from, good eating habits, and even tricks to be done with food. In *Look, Baby! Listen, Baby! Do, Baby!* (1987), Kelley explores the infant's senses of looking, listening, and trying to do things. Amanda Leslie uses shapes and colors to give clues for guessing in her picture books *Hidden Animals* (1989) and *Hidden Toys* (1989). Anne Miranda celebrates the expanding world of the toddler in her books *Baby Talk* (1987) and *Baby Walk* (1988).

The concept of a holiday is enjoyed by children and adults alike. Many holidays are closely tied to religion. Many are tied to historical events. Recognition of holidays should be broad whether or not they seem to affect children in the class or not. Children should be aware of the Jewish holidays whether or not there are any Jewish children in the class. Children should be aware of Martin Luther King, Jr. Day whether or not there are any minority children in the class. A growing number of books help celebrate these special days.

Christian holidays might include reading books such as Tomie dePaola's *An Early American Christmas* (1987), Emily McCully's *The Christmas Gift* (1988), and Gail Gibbons's *Easter* (1989). Jewish holidays could include readings of books such as Maida Silverman's *Festival of Lights: The Story of Hannukkah* (1987) and *Festival of Esther: The Story of Purim* (1989), Lynne Schwartz's book about Passover *The Four Questions* (1989), and Marilyn Singer's *Minnie's Yom Kippur Birthday* (1989). Other holiday units might include books such as Barbara Samuels *Happy Birthday Dolores* (1989), Caroline Bauer's *Halloween: Stories and Poems* (1989), Eileen Spinelli's *Thanksgiving at the Tappletons'* (1989), and Lillian Hoban's *Arthur's Great Big Valentine* (1988).

CONTEMPORARY STORYBOOKS

Every year increasing numbers of books are published for young children. The question is not whether there are enough books to share with young children. Rather, it is one of becoming familiar with these books in order to make intelligent choices in selecting books for sharing. The best way to become familiar is to read widely and often. Know the children with whom the books will be shared. Observe them at play, and listen to their language to help determine their interests. Follow the suggestions provided above for evaluating the quality of the books. Books are suggested here in the areas of humorous books, thoughtful books, and realistic fiction. This summary should serve as a beginning. Many books do not fit neatly into these categories. However, a tremendous number of books included have been shown to be loved by children.

Humorous Books

Most of us like to laugh and smile. Both adults and children enjoy the fun of a good story is filled with mirth. Mark Twain suggested that analyzing what makes something humorous usually proves deadly. He indicated that he didn't set out to be humorous in

his writings; the humor emerged through telling the story. Perhaps we should leave it at that. Let us just say that humor is "stuff" that is funny. Children, like adults, will know it when they hear it and when they see it.

Norman Bridwell has ceated an entire world of good natured fun around Clifford, the big red dog featured in his widely known series. Among some of the favorites in this series are *Clifford Gets a Job* (1965), *Clifford Takes a Trip* (1966), *Clifford, the Small Red Puppy* (1972), *Clifford's Halloween* (1966), and *Clifford's Tricks* (1969). Another good choice of a series is the one by H. A. Rey, beginning with the now classic *Curious George* (1963). From the same time period is Maurice Sendak's *Where the Wild Things Are* (1963). Although not a series, Dr. Seuss has consistently pleased young children with humorous stories, such as *Horton Hatches the Egg* (1940).

A contemporary series of related humorus stories has been compiled by Harry Allard featuring the Stupid family. Titles such as *The Stupids Die* (1981), *The Stupids Have a Ball* (1978), and *The Stupids Step Out* (1974) have delighted young audiences. The illustrator of the books about the Stupid family, James Marshall, has himself created a series of humorous stories about two hippopotamus friends with books such as *George and Martha* (1972) and *George and Martha Encore* (1973). He has also illustrated the books of other humorous writers such as Daniel Pinkwater's *Roger's Umbrella* (1982). Robert Munsch, a popular writer from Canada, consistently produces books that poke good-natured fun at people and common problems. His book on toilet training, *I Have to Go* (1987), is a favorite of adults and children. Another Munsch favorite is the hilarious *Pigs* (1989). The story describes some ridiculous consequences of not following the directions of your parents.

Children are frequently brought into the fun of the book through a humorous title. Judi Barrett's *Cloudy with a Chance of Meatballs* (1978) is just such a book. Other books that create the same sort of initial response include Adrienne Adams's *A Woggle of Witches* (1971), Steven Kroll's *Santa's Slam Bang Christmas* (1977), Daniel Pinkwater's *The Wuggie Norple Story* (1980) and Kathleen Stevens *The Beast in the Bathtub* (1985). *Bicycle Bear* (1983), by Michaela Muntean, is unique in this area. It is a humorous story with a wonderful surprise ending that will delight youngsters. It is told entirely in verse. A more subtle type of humor is found in a book like Arnold Lobel's *Ming Lo Moves the Mountain* (1982), in which a family discovers a unique way to solve what seems to be an insurmountable problem.

Thoughtful Books

In contrast to books that use humor, thoughtful books make the reader pause to think about something. It may be the idea of sharing, contemplating the wonder of a moonlit night, or feeling sad about the death of a pet. These books help children deal with a variety of topics on a very human level. It sometimes helps to discuss these issues in the context of a book rather than solely at a personal level.

One of the more serious events in a young child's life is the loss of something beloved. Several books address the loss of a favorite stuffed animal. They include Rosemary Billam's *Fuzzy Rabbit* (1984), Ron Maris's *Are You There, Bear?* (1984), and Ginnie Hofmann's *The Runaway Teddy Bear* (1986). Joan Hewett's *Rosalie* (1987), Yukio Tsuchiya's *Faithful Elephants* (1988), and Judith Viorst's *The Tenth Good Thing About Barney* (1971) present the issue of the aging and deaths of favorite animals and pets. The issue of survival in a sometimes hostile world is explored by Toshi Yoshida in *Elephant Crossing* (1989). Each of these books is written with a tremendous sensitivity that enables young children to deal with an emotional issue. One of the most traumatic events in a youngster's life is the death of a parent or grandparent. No book or discussion can ever make up for such a loss. A book and a discussion can help children to begin to understand the situation, however. Among the best choices of books to be used in such a situation include Tomie dePaola's *Nana Upstairs, Nana Downstairs* (1973), Vaunda Micheaux Nelson's *Always Gramma* (1988), and Jonah Schein's *Forget Me Not* (1988).

Friendship, the lack of friends, and the loss of friends are all concepts and events that can bring happiness or sadness to one's life. While young children tend to focus on themselves, they are aware of others and enjoy their time with acquaintances and friends. Friends for young people include both other people and inanimate objects. Frank Asch has developed a series of books surrounding the friendship between a young bear and the moon. Using the concept of hibernation, *Mooncake* (1983) describes a trip to the moon for the purpose of seeing how the moon tastes. In *Moongame* (1984), the little bear confronts the idea of the loss of a friend. During a game of hide and seek, the moon slips behind a cloud. The little bear is quite worried, but is relieved when his friend slips out from in back of the cloud. The joys of friendship and the pain created by its loss are beautifully portrayed in Bernard Waber's *Ira Says Goodbye* (1988). The ups and downs of friendship are explored in Stan and Jan Berenstain's *The Trouble with Friends* (1987), Miriam Cohen's *Will I Have a Friend?* (1967), and Bernard Waber's classic *Ira Sleeps Over* (1972).

The concept of self is explored by a number of thoughtful books for young children. The idea of self-reliance is addressed in *I Can Do Something When There's Nothing to Do* (1985), by Karen Erickson and Maureen Roffey. In this book the reader follows a toddler through a day when the child is forced into using the environment to develop enjoyable activities when there is no one else around. *Helga High-Up* (1987), by Marjorie Weinman Sharmat, addresses the issues of self-awareness and acceptance of self. In the book, Helga the giraffe comes to realize that she is taller than anyone else. She goes through periods of self-consciousness, of lowered self-esteem, and finally of liking and acceptance of herself.

Realistic Fiction

Stories that describe events that could actually occur are included in the category of realistic fiction. Sometimes the characters in the story are animals, but the events are always believable. The Berenstain Bear books are a good example of this type of story. The books in this group might be humorous or they might be thoughtful, so there is much overlap between categories of books. What distinguishes this group is that it is comprised of stories with strong characters and plots. The plots have situations and ideas that are real to young children. The resolutions are possible, and the feelings they evoke are very natural.

A wonderful book with a strong, memorable character is Anna Grossnickle Hines's *Grandma Gets Grumpy* (1989). In the story, Grandma plays a stereotypically kind, sweet role as she cares for her five grandchildren. One night, however, things get out of hand and the group has to work out a very real parenting problem. Another story dealing with the child/grandparent relationship is Holly Keller's *The Best Present* (1989), in which a child has to deal with the hospital rule of not allowing children under a certain age to visit inpatients. In Cynthia Rylant's *Mr. Griggs' Work* (1989), children are introduced to the idea that elderly people are still quite capable of leading useful, productive lives. Louise Goodman presents a very realistic look at strong child characters dealing with typical sibling relationships in *Ida's Doll* (1989).

Books about relationships involving strong characters hold a special interest for children who are in the process of learning about friendship and self-confidence. Charlotte Zolotow's *Some Things Go Together* (1969), Robin Baird Lewis's *Aunt Armadillo* (1985) and Anna Grossnickle Hines's *Don't Worry, I'll Find You* (1986) are all appropriate for young children. Friendship is explored in Jan Ormerod's *Making Friends* (1987), Aliki's *We Are Best Friends* (1982), Carol Carrick's *Stay Away from Simon* (1985), and Patricia Reilly Giff's *Happy Birthday, Ronald Morgan* (1986).

Children seek to establish their own identities as they grow up. They need to see that everybody is different. There are several books with realistic plots that can be used to point out human differences. Charlotte Zolotow's *William's Doll* (1982) lets children know that having a doll is a healthy need for both boys and girls. Tomie dePaola's *Oliver Button Is a Sissy* (1979) portrays a young boy who loves to dance more than anything else in the world. He perseveres with hard work, and, despite the taunts of others, finally gains acceptance and a right to be himself.

Poetry

Poetry is the most intense and imaginative type of literature. It addresses the world, emotions, life, and the individual person. It can make us laugh. It can make us cry. A poet selects each word in a poem with care and purpose. Poetry uses an economy of words to create a picture in the mind of the reader. Just as in prose, poetry for children has been written in many styles covering a range of topics. Poets use a number of language devices to create special effects in their poems. Onomatopoeia is the use of words, such as "pop" and "hiss," whose sounds suggest the meaning of the word. Personification is used when an inanimate object is given human qualities. A simile compares two things with the words "like" and "as" in phrases such as "The puppy bounced around the house like a rubber ball." A metaphor assigns atypical characteristics to something in phrases such as "The flashlight was a searchlight shining out across the blanket of ocean." Alliteration is the repetition of an initial consonant in a line such as "Bouncing baby boy."

Poetry for children should be selected more for its content than for the technical aspects of its rhyme scheme or meter. It should be rhythmic, vivid, alive, and clear. It should be read with feeling and always out loud. There is little reason to expect children to memorize poems, although they will sometimes do this with poems that strike them as particularly enjoyable. Poetry for children can be created by the teacher and the children. Such creations provide a unique opportunity for manipulating language in a meaningful and special way.

One of the best known and best loved writers of children's poetry is Jack Prelutsky. He has provided several books of poetry appropriate for use at holidays. They include *It's Christmas* (1980), *It's Thanksgiving* (1982), and *It's Valentine's Day* (1983). Other collections of his poetry include *Rainy, Rainy Saturday* (1980) and *The New Kid on the Block* (1984). They contain poems that can be used at any time at all.

There are poems for all occasions contained in any number of collections. Illustrator Tasha Tudor has collected traditional poems for children in *First Poems of Childhood* (1967). Myra Cohn Livingston celebrates the four seasons of the year with *A Circle of Seasons* (1982). Another of her collections, *Dilly Dilly Piccalilli* (1989), provides a varied group of poems for very young children to use in order to look at the world in new ways. Illustrator Nicola Bayley has collected a number of bedtime rhymes for very young children in *Hush-a-Bye Baby* (1986). Two books full of humorous nonsense poetry that will add humor to any day are Babette Cole's *The Silly Book* (1990) and X. J. Kennedy's *Ghastlies, Goops & Pincushions* (1989). Crescent Dragonwagon adds to the world of humorous stories told in rhyme with *This is the Bread I Baked for Ned* (1989). It describes, in clear verse, the preparation of a meal. The meal was planned for one, but the host is surprised to learn that Ned has brought along quite a crowd of friends as his luncheon companions.

Poems are meant to be read aloud. Jill Bennett provides a wonderful group to start with in *Noisy Poems* (1989). The twelve poems will be sure to leave children longing to recite them independently. Another group of great poems for reciting out loud is Joanna Cole's collection of jumprope rhymes, *Anna Banana* (1989). Whether children use them as jumprope rhymes or not, they will quickly become fascinated with the catchy phrases and rhythmic beat of these poems.

STORYTELLING

Storytelling is an art form people have long loved. In the days before general literacy, storytelling was the major way a culture's history and beliefs were transferred from one generation to the next. The storyteller held a place of great importance in most cultures. Today, people still enjoy the art of good storytelling, but there are many other media competing for a listener's attention. Television has become a major teller of stories, but because it must operate as a commercial media, it is not able to be the source of literature that books and storytellers can be.

In early childhood education, there are two major possibilities for storytelling. The first is reading aloud to children from books. Since younger children can ordinarily listen to stories with understanding at a higher level than they can read them independently, books that are read aloud broaden the range of possibilities for them. The other possibility is oral storytelling. This activity may use some of the same stories as reading aloud, but it is done without the book being read word-by-word to the children. A variation of oral storytelling is the use of such props as flannel boards and puppets in telling stories.

Reading Aloud

The New Read-Aloud Handbook (1989), by Jim Trelease, has become a key source for anyone interested in reading aloud to children. It provides a large, annotated bibliography of some of the best books to read aloud. Also included in the book is Jim Trelease's persuasive argument for reading aloud to children from the time they are infants. He contends that listening to the language and learning words and ideas is an important factor in the process of learning

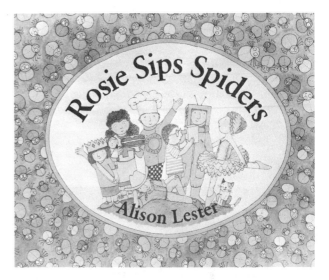

FIGURE 6-9 The list of good read-aloud books for young children is long and varied. *From* Rosie Sips Spiders, *by Alison Lester. Reprinted courtesy of Houghton Mifflin Company, nonexclusive and nontransferable.*

to read. Such reading and listening is a natural act that motivates the child to grow in language skills without pressure. Trelease is disturbed by the fact that as children progress through the grades, reading aloud decreases dramatically. By the time children finish secondary school, and often much earlier, reading aloud has ceased as a daily activity.

Reading a book aloud is not as easy as it sounds. A teacher should not simply pick up a book and read it to the children without considering both the planning of the reading and the delivery of the story. Reading books to young children should be a part of the everyday routine. Selected books should make sense for the children for that day. That is, books can be chosen to fit a particular theme being studied. They can be selected because they have something to do with the time of year or a holiday celebration. Books can also be chosen simply because they are wonderful stories the whole group should experience. In addition, the actual reading of the story should be done in a way that enhances the experience for the children. The reader should become familiar with the book before reading it aloud. Reading done with drama and enthusiasm both motivates the children to listen and makes the story more memorable. Varying the pace

A Hundred Hugs.

I Like the crecer Huggles
becouse he hags. he hugs a Lit of
pepple, he Like to hugs pepple

a Hundred Hugs.

FIGURE 6-10 Children frequently use read-aloud books as springboards to their own writing and drawing, as this child did.

and volume of the reading in keeping with the action of the story can add much to the activity of reading stories aloud.

Oral Storytelling

Telling a story orally can free the teacher from some of the constraints of reading aloud. When telling a story orally, the teller does not have to keep track of the spot on the page where the text is located, the behavior of the children, or whether or not all of the children can see the illustrations. When telling a story orally, all eyes are focused on the storyteller. The storyteller must therefore become everything important in the story. The storyteller must tell the story as well as use movement to dramatize the story. This does not mean that the teacher must act out roles, although that may be the case during some stories. Rather, the storyteller may use hand motions, body position, body movement, facial expressions, and voice to substitute for both the written text and the illustrations in the book. Obviously this is more

difficult than reading aloud, but the process is well worth the effort. A deeper communication can take place between the storyteller and the audience as well as the opportunity to allow children to see and practice some of the important skills used in oral language communication.

In oral storytelling, the presenter must choose works that are personally meaningful. The stories should be well liked by the storyteller because that attachment must be shared with the audience. Many storytellers select a certain type of story in which to specialize. Some choose African folk tales, some choose tall tales, and others choose stories about the sea. Whatever the choice, most storytellers develop a personal interpretation of a story before they use it. They decide what the story is really about, what we can learn from it, and why it is important. This helps the storyteller decide how to tell the story, including which parts to use, how to vary voice and movement to enhance certain parts, and how to best involve the audience in coming to an understanding of the story. Professional and amateur storytellers are often found in the community. They may be associated with a folk music organization, theater group, or church. Looking into some of these opportunities could lead to a classroom visit by a gifted storyteller with an enchanting tale to tell.

The use of certain props as part of storytelling is a motivating tool that can be use effectively with young children. Props such as flannel boards, flannel board characters, and puppets can help children visualize part of the action of the story. The imaginations of the children must fill in other parts of the tale being told. A flannel board is a flat surface, such as a piece of plywood, covered with flannel, felt, or other soft cloth. Flannel board pieces representing people, animals, furniture, trees, houses, and other parts of a story are placed on the flannel board as they are introduced in the story. These pieces are usually made from felt. The story can be a read-aloud or a story told orally. The pieces used to tell the story can be left in the reading corner after the telling so that children can retell the story themselves with the flannel board.

Children and adults both seem to enjoy using puppets. Puppets take on human qualities even though most children know that they are just puppets. Children will talk to them as though they are real, thereby creating the potential to involve children more in the saved for use at a later time or with another class. Homemade or commercially purchased hand puppets or finger puppets are a bit more sophisticated. They can be constructed with pieces of felt and quickly stitched together with needle and thread. Several books provide instructions on how to make such puppets. The most complex type of puppet is the marionette, or string puppet. Although these may be somewhat too difficult to use as part of the regular classroom program, there are often opportunities to have children see such puppet shows presenting some of the finest traditional children's stories.

When choosing stories to be told with a flannel board or with puppets, care should be taken. Certain stories are too complex to be told in this way. It is best to choose stories with simple plots and a limited number of main characters. A plot that unfolds gradually may be best for a flannel board. Such a story allows the storyteller to add pieces to the flannel board throughout the session. The number of characters is a major

FIGURE 6-11 Storyteller David Novak mesmerizes children with a dramatic oral retelling of "The Itsy Bitsy Spider." *Photo courtesy of David Novak, storyteller, dba A Telling Experience.*

FIGURE 6-12 Puppets can help tell a story.

activity of telling the story without the problems of rehearsal and practice. Puppets can be created in different styles. Cut out figures glued to craft sticks are the simplest type. The figures can be made from a photocopy of an illustration from the book containing the story. Appendix A provides some basic models of figures that can be used to create flannel board pieces or puppets. Characters and objects for specific stories can be created and used as needed. All should be concern when using puppets. Despite the effort expended to tell the actual story, a storyteller still has only two hands. Three or four characters might be the maximum number for an effective storytelling with hand puppets. As with flannel boards, the puppets can be left in the reading area after the story is told so that children can recreate the story at a later time.

SUMMARY

Books and literature are critically important factors in the language development of young children. Children who enter kindergarten already knowing how to read have frequently been found to come from language-rich environments. They have had access to books, people to read to them, and people to talk to about the books. In addition to helping children acquire literacy skills, literature helps children learn. Through books, youngsters learn about the world, the people in that world, and their own lives.

One of the most important tasks for a teacher of young children is the careful selections of books to be shared with those children. A number of factors should be considered in making selections. First, one should be aware of the children themselves. The teacher should know what interests and motivates the children. Second, one should have some idea of the purpose for sharing a book. This may be related to the topic being addressed in a class or for the enjoyment of literature.

When reviewing books for possible use, teachers should consider a number of characteristics of the books themselves. The literary characteristics generally revolve around the concepts of character, setting, theme, and plot. If these are carefully addressed by the author, the book will probably be of interest to a wide range of children. The presentation of the story within the books must be considered as well. Test style, narrative style, illustrations, and anti-bias factors must be analyzed. The whole purpose of a book is to bring meaning and understanding to the reader. Each of these characteristics is closely related to this purpose.

A world of literature waits for the creative teacher and the children under the care of that teacher. Thousands of books are published each year; there is no shortage of available books. Teachers, however, must develop a familiarity with available books in order to make wise selections. Traditional books include Mother Goose stories, nursery rhymes, fables, folk tales, fairy tales, and legends. Nonfiction books include alphabet books, counting and number books, basic concept books, informational books, and biographies. Contemporary books cover a wide range of genres and styles. They include humorous stories, thoughtful books, realistic fiction, and poetry.

Sharing stories with young children is something that should be carefully considered and planned. The two basic procedures to be used are reading the story aloud and telling the story orally from memory. Reading aloud, although the more common practice, still requires familiarity and planning on the part of the reader. Storytelling is more difficult, requiring the development of some theatrical skills to effectively present the tale. Variations of each of these methods use props such as puppets and flannel boards to bring an additional dimension to the storytelling.

Questions and Activities for Review and Discussion

Multiple Choice
1. Children who learn to read before coming to school are referred to as
    a. extremely intelligent.
    b. natural readers.
    c. high IQ children.
    d. proficient at mathematics as well.

2. Literature helps children learn more about
   a. the world in which they live.
   b. other people.
   c. themselves.
   d. all of the above
3. In selecting books to be read to an audience of young children, the first thing to consider is the
   a. plot.
   b. characters.
   c. theme.
   d. audience.
4. A character who seems believable within the context of the story is said to be
   a. consistent.
   b. human-like.
   c. credible.
   d. all of the above
5. Plot contains elements that build
   a. reader interest.
   b. conflict.
   c. problems.
   d. all of the above
6. The most commonly used medium to illustrate children's books is
   a. oil paint.
   b. watercolor paint.
   c. colored pencil.
   d. photographs.
7. Stories that have not actually taken place but depict a situation that could occur are referred to as
   a. realistic fiction.
   b. non-fiction.
   c. biography.
   d. fantasy fiction.

True or False

T F 1. Reading a book and watching a television show are quite similar activities.

T F 2. Books on a specific topic should only be shared with children after a lesson has been taught about that topic.

T F 3. Text style is not an important factor to consider when choosing children's literature books.

T F 4. Because watercolor paint is too soft and light, it is not used to illustrate books for children.

T F 5. Concept books can generally be used only with children who are at least four years old.

Essay and Discussion

1. Compare and contrast the activities of reading a book and watching a television show.

2. Describe character, plot, theme, and setting in literature.
3. Discuss the benefits of using books that feature animal characters.
4. Select a children's storybook and describe its narrative style.
5. Describe how a teacher might go about choosing an alphabet book.

REFERENCES

Adams, A. 1971. *A woggle of witches*. New York: Macmillan.
Akers, S. 1990. *What comes in 2's, 3's, & 4's?* New York: Simon & Schuster.
Alexander, M. 1971. *Nobody asked me if I wanted a baby sister*. New York: Dial.
Aliki (Brandenberg). 1982. *We are best friends*. New York: Greenwillow.
Allard, H. 1981. *The stupids die*. Boston: Houghton-Mifflin.
Allard, H. 1978. *The stupids have a ball*. Boston: Houghton-Mifflin.
Allard, H. 1974. *The stupids step out*. Boston: Houghton-Mifflin.
Appleby, E. 1984. *The three billy goats gruff*. New York: Scholastic.
Arnosky, J. 1989. *Come out, muskrats*. New York: Lothrop, Lee, & Shepard.
Asch, F. 1983. *Mooncake*. New York: Prentice Hall.
Asch, F. 1984. *Moongame*. New York: Prentice Hall.
Barrett, J. 1978. *Cloudy with a chance of meatballs*. New York: Atheneum.
Bauer, C. 1989. *Halloween: Stories and poems*. New York: Lippincott.
Bayley, N. 1986. *Hush-a-bye baby*. New York: Macmillan.
Bennett, J. 1989. *Noisy poems*. New York: Oxford.
Berenstain, S. & J. 1987. *The trouble with friends*. New York: Random House.
Bettelheim, B. 1976. *The uses of enchantment*. New York: Knopf.
Billam, R. 1984. *Fuzzy rabbit*. New York: Random House.
Bridwell, N. 1965. *Clifford gets a job*. New York: Scholastic.
Bridwell, N. 1966. *Clifford takes a trip*. New York: Scholastic.
Bridwell, N. 1972. *Clifford the small red puppy*. New York: Scholastic.
Bridwell, N. 1966. *Clifford's Halloween*. New York: Scholastic.
Bridwell, N. 1969. *Clifford's tricks*. New York: Scholastic.
Brown, M. 1979. *Arthur's eyes*. Boston: Little Brown.
Brown, M. 1976. *Arthur's nose*. Boston: Little Brown.
Brown, M.W. 1947. *Goodnight moon*. New York: Harper and Row.
Carle, E. 1969. *1, 2, 3 to the zoo*. New York: Collins World.
Carle, E. 1985. *My very first book of colors*. New York: Crowell.
Carle, E. 1977. *The grouchy ladybug*. New York: Crowell.
Carlson, N. 1985. *Witch lady*. New York: Viking Penguin.
Cole, B. 1990. *The silly book*. New York: Doubleday.
Cole, J. 1989. *Anna banana*. New York: William Morrow.
Carrick, C. 1984. *Dark and full of secrets*. New York: Clarion.
Carrick, C. 1985. *Stay away from Simon*. New York: Clarion.
Clifton, L. 1973. *The boy who didn't believe in spring*. New York: E.P. Dutton.
Coerr, E. 1981. *The big balloon race*. New York: Harper and Row.
Cohen, M. 1967. *Will I have a friend?* New York: Macmillan.
Crews, D. 1978. *Freight train*. New York: Greenwillow.

dePaola, T. 1987. *An early American Christmas.* New York: Holiday House.

dePaola, T. 1973. *Nana upstairs, Nana downstairs.* New York: Putnam.

dePaola, T. 1979. *Oliver Button is a sissy.* New York: Harcourt, Brace, Jovanovich.

dePaola, T. 1980. *The legend of Old Befana.* New York: Harcourt Brace, Jovanovich.

dePaola, T. 1989. *The art lesson.* New York: Putnam.

dePaola, T. 1974. *Watch out for the chicken feet in your soup.* New York: Simon and Schuster.

Dragonwagon, C. 1989. *This is the bread I baked for Ned.* New York: Macmillan.

Duvoisin, R. 1969. *Veronica.* New York: Knopf.

Ehrlich, A. 1983. *The everyday train.* New York: Greenwillow.

Erickson, K., and M. Roffey. 1985. *I can do something when there's nothing to do.* New York: Scholastic.

Fassler, J. 1975. *Howie helps himself.* Chicago: Albert Whitman.

Fritz, J. 1973. *And then what happened, Paul Revere?* New York: Coward-McCann.

Fritz, J. 1969. *George Washington's breakfast.* New York: Coward-McCann.

Gag, W. 1928. *Millions of cats.* New York: Coward-McCann.

Galdone, P. 1975. *The gingerbread boy.* New York: Clarion.

Gantos, J. 1989. *Rotten Ralph's show and tell.* Boston: Houghton-Mifflin.

Gibbons, G. 1989. *Easter.* New York: Holiday House.

Giff, P.R. 1986. *Happy birthday Ronald Morgan.* New York: Viking Kestral.

Giff, P.R. 1980. *Today was a terrible day.* New York: Viking Penguin.

Giff, P.R. 1985. *Watch out Ronald Morgan.* New York: Viking Penguin.

Goodman, L. 1989. *Ida's doll.* New York: Harper and Row.

Hazen, B.S. 1979. *Tight times.* New York: Viking.

Henriod, L. 1982. *Grandma's wheelchair.* Chicago: Albert Whitman.

Hewett, J. 1987. *Rosalie.* New York: Lothrop, Lee, & Shepard.

Hines, A.G. 1986. *Don't worry, I'll find your.* New York: E.P. Dutton.

Hines, A.G. 1989. *Grandma gets grumpy.* New York: Clarion.

Hoban, L. 1988. *Arthur's great big valentine.* New York: Harper and Row.

Hoban, R. 1960. *A baby sister for Frances.* New York: Harper and Row.

Hoban, T. 1985. *A children's zoo.* New York: Mulberry.

Hoban, T. 1972. *Count and see.* New York: Macmillan.

Hoffman, G. 1986. *The runaway teddy bear.* New York: Random House.

Jeschke, S. 1980. *Perfect the pig.* New York: Scholastic.

Joyce, W. 1985. *George shrinks.* New York: Harper and Row.

Kaufman, C. & G. 1985. *Rajesh.* New York: Atheneum.

Keats, E.J. 1971. *Over in the meadow.* New York: Scholastic.

Keats, E.J. 1962. *The snowy day.* New York: Vanguard.

Keats, E.J., and P. Cherr. 1960. *My dog is lost.* New York: Thomas Y. Crowell.

Keller, H. 1987. *Goodbye Max.* New York: Greenwillow.

Keller, H. 1989. *The best present.* New York: Greenwillow.

Kelley, T. 1989. *Let's eat!* New York: E. P. Dutton.

Kelley, T. 1987. *Look, baby! Listen, baby! Do, baby!* New York: E.P. Dutton.

Kennedy, S.J. 1989. *Ghastlies, goops, & pincushions.* New York: McElderry.

Kesselman, W. 1970. *Angelita.* New York: Will and Wang.

Kroll, S. 1977. *Santa's slam bang Christmas.* New York: Holiday House.

Lavies, B. 1989. *Lily pad pond.* New York: E.P. Dutton.

Lear, E. 1983. *An Edward Lear alphabet.* New York: Lothrop, Lee, & Shepard.

Lehr, S. 1988. The child's developing sense of theme as a response to literature. *Reading Research Quarterly* 23: 337–357.

Leslie, A. 1989. *Hidden animals.* New York: Dial.

Leslie, A. 1989. *Hidden toys.* New York: Dial.

Lewis, R.B. 1985. *Aunt Armadillo.* Scarborough, Ontario, Canada: Annick.

Lionni, L. 1963. *Swimmy.* New York: Pantheon.

Littledale, F. 1975. *The boy who cried wolf.* New York: Scholastic.

Livingston, M.C. 1982. *A circle of seasons.* New York: Holiday House.

Livingston, M.C. 1989. *Dilly dilly piccalilli.* New York: McElderry.

Lobel, A. 1979. *Days with frog and toad.* New York: Harper and Row.

Lobel, A. 1970. *Frog and toad are friends.* New York: Harper and Row.

Lobel, A. 1982. *Ming Lo moves the mountain.* New York: Scholastic.

Lobel, A. 1986. *The Random House book of Mother Goose.* New York: Random House.

Lopshire, R. 1980. *The biggest, smallest, fastest, tallest.* New York: Scholastic.

MacLachlan, P. 1980. *Through Grandpa's eyes.* New York: Harper and Row.

Maris, R. 1984. *Are you there, bear?* New York: Viking Penguin.

Marshall, J. 1972. *George and Martha.* Boston: Houghton Mifflin.

Marshall, J. 1973. *George and Martha encore.* Boston: Houghton Mifflin.

Martin, B., Jr., and J. Archambault. 1989. *Chicka chicka boom boom.* New York: Simon and Schuster.

Mayer, M. 1983. *Me too!* New York: Golden Books.

Mayer, M. & M. 1975. *One frog too many.* New York: Dial.

McCloskey, R. 1969. *Make way for ducklings.* New York: Puffin.

McCully, E. 1988. *The Christmas gift.* New York: Harper and row.

McPhail, D. 1982. *Snow lion.* New York: Parents Magazine.

Meddaugh, S. 1981. *Beast.* Boston: Houghton Mifflin.

Michels, T. 1989. *At the frog pond.* New York: Lippincott.

Miranda, A. 1987. *Baby talk.* New York: E. P. Dutton.

Miranda, A. 1987. *Baby walk.* New York: E. P. Dutton.

Munsch, R. 1987. *I have to go.* Toronto, Ontario, Canada: Annick.

Munsch, R. 1989. *Pigs.* Toronto, Ontario, Canada: Annick.

Munteau, M. 1983. *Bicycle bear.* New York: Parents Magazine.

Nelson, V.M. 1988. *Always Gramma.* New York: G.P. Putnam.

Ormerod, J. 1987. *Making friends.* New York: Lothrop, Lee and Shepard.

Pinkwater, D. 1982. *Roger's umbrella.* New York: E.P. Dutton.

Pinkwater, D. 1980. *The wuggie norple story.* New York: Four Winds.

Pittman, H.C. 1986. *The gift of the willows.* Minneapolis, Minn.: Carolrhoda.

Prelutsky, J. 1980. *It's Christmas.* New York: Greenwillow.

Prelutsky, J. 1982. *It's Thanksgiving.* New York: Greenwillow.

Prelutsky, J. 1983. *It's Valentine's Day.* New York: Greenwillow.

Prelutsky, J. 1984. *The new kid on the block.* New York: Greenwillow.

Prelutsky, J. 1980. *Rainy, rainy Saturday.* New York: Greenwillow.

Provensen, A. & M. 1977. *Old Mother Hubbard.* New York: Random House.

Rabe, B. 1981. *The balancing girl.* New York: E.P. Dutton.

Reit, S. 1984. *Jenny's in the hospital.* New York: Golden Books.

Rey, H.A. 1963. *Curious George.* Boston: Houghton Mifflin.

Rylant, C. 1989. *Mr. Griggs' work.* New York: Orchard.

Rylant, C. 1982. *When I was young in the mountains.* New York: E.P. Dutton.

Samuels, B. 1989. *Happy birthday Dolores.* New York: Orchard.

Sawyer, W., and D.E. Comer. 1991. *Growing up with literature.* Albany, N.Y.: Delmar Publishers Inc.

Schein, J. 1988. *Forget me not.* Toronto, Ontario, Canada: Annick.

Schwartz, D. 1988. *The hidden life of the pond.* New York: Crown.

Schwartz, L. 1989. *The four questions.* New York: Dial.

Sendak, M. 1963. *Where the wild things are.* New York: Harper and Row.

Serfozo, M. 1989. *Who wants one?* New York: McElderry.

Seuss, Dr. (pseud. for T. Geisel). 1940. *Horton hatches the egg.* New York: Random House.

Sharmat, M.W. 1987. *Helga high up.* New York: Scholastic.

Silverman, M. 1989. *Festival of Esther: The story of Purim.* New York: Little Simon.

Silverman, M. 1989. *Festival of lights: The story of Hannukkah.* New York: Simon and Schuster.

Singer, M. 1989. *Minnie's Yom Kippur birthday.* New York: Harper and Row.

Sloat, T. 1989. *From letter to letter.* New York: E.P. Dutton.

Spinelli, E. 1989. *Thanksgiving at the Tappleton's.* New York: Harper and Row.

Spohn, K. 1989. *Clementine's winter wardrobe.* New York: Franklin Watts.

Stevens, K. 1985. *The beast in the bathtub.* New York: Harper and Row.

Szekere, Cindy. 1983. *Cindy Szekere's ABC.* Racine, Wis.: Western.

Tsuchiya, Y. 1988. *Faithful elephants.* New York: Houghton Mifflin.

Thrall, W.F., and A. Hibbard. 1960. *A handbook to literature.* New York: Odyssey.

Trelease, J. 1989. *The new read-aloud handbook.* New York: Viking Penguin.

Tresselt, A. 1965. Hide and seek fog. New York: Mulberry.

Tudor. T. 1967. First poems of childhood. New York: Platt and Munk.

Viorst, J. 1972. *Alexander and the terrible, horrible, no good, very bad day.* New York: Atheneum.

Viorst, J. 1971. *The tenth good thing about Barney.* New York: Atheneum.

Waber, B. 1988. *Ira says goodbye.* Boston: Houghton Mifflin Company.

Waber, B. 1972. *Ira sleeps over.* Boston: Houghton Mifflin Company.

Wildsmith, B. 1964. *Brian Wildsmith's Mother Goose.* New York: Franklin Watts.

Winthner, B. 1976. *Plays from folktales from Africa.* Boston: Plays.

Yorinks, A. 1980. *Louis the fish.* New York: Farrar, Straus, Giroux.

Yoshida, T. 1989. *Elephant crossing.* New York: Philomel.

Young, E. 1989. *Lon Po Po.* New York: Philomel.

Zolotow, C. 1966. *Big sister, little sister.* New York: Harper and Row.

Zolotow, C. 1969. *Some things go together.* New York: Harper and Row.

Zolotow, C. 1982. *William's doll.* New York: Harper and Row.

Section 3

Emerging Language and Literacy

Bill Martin, Jr.

"Mother Goose is the best learning language course anyone ever has, and it's all apprehended (absorbed is a better word) without having to consider a rule. My Mother Goose is worn from constant reading and referencing."

Photograph and text courtesy of Bill Martin, Jr.

TO THE READER:

One of the most fascinating aspects of human development is the emergence and growth of language in children. Language is one of the primary things that separate human beings from other living things. While we do not fully understand exactly how young children come to learn language, there are a variety of intriguing ideas and theories about it. Educators, linguists, and psychologists around the world have studied the development of language in many different cultures. Young children seem to share certain aspects of language development as they acquire the ability to communicate through sounds, words, and longer connected texts. You will learn many of these aspects and concepts in this section.

Section 3 will provide you with a wide range of ideas about language and how it is used in the everyday life of young children. It is important that you understand the information provided in each of the units as you observe, plan for, and work with young children. As will become clear, you will especially need strong observation skills. This will enable you to better identify and understand a variety of childhood behaviors and how those behaviors are related to language growth and literacy.

You will develop a more comprehensive understanding of both the technical terminology dealing with language and some of the diverse theories, which can serve as a guide to understanding language growth. The purpose of this information is to provide you with the ability to both view some of the subtleties of language with understanding and confidence and to consider language from a variety of different perspectives. Culture will be seen as an influential factor in a child's language and view of the world. As society becomes increasingly multicultural, the ability to understand this will become increasingly beneficial.

Since young children spend so much time engaged in play and in the presence of other children, these two areas are particularly important to consider. Play is one setting in which language is present, useful, and growing. It provides an environment for children to use the new words and sentences they have acquired. The ability to communicate and cooperate with other children both during play and during educational programs is a meaningful skill for young children. The growth in educational theory and practice of the concept of cooperative learning as an effective instructional tool makes it an important area for early childhood educators. One of the keys to successful cooperation is clear, meaningful language. You will learn how the principles of cooperative learning can be used in an integrated language arts program to benefit young children.

UNIT 7

Views of Language Development

UNIT GOALS

After completing this unit, the reader should:

- understand that a whole language approach is not based on any one theory of language development.
- understand that a whole language approach is not based on the beliefs of any one individual.
- understand that whole language is influenced by a variety of discoveries from the study of language development.
- develop an overall grasp of the relevant key ideas of language development.
- understand some of the basic contributions of individuals such as Jean Piaget, Lev Vygotsky, Benjamin Lee Whorf, Roger Brown, and Marie Clay.

PREVIEW

From the earliest days of human existence, when language first emerged as a uniquely human attribute, nearly everyone has learned language to some extent. It is no mystery why people learn language; they do so in order to help satisfy their own needs and desires. Language helps people state what they want, don't want, like, and don't like. At a more advanced level, language enables people to better understand themselves and their world.

Children begin to learn language at an very early age. How they do this is still somewhat of a mystery. There is an even more fascinating question, however. Once children develop a minimal facility with lan-

guage, how do they continue to get better at using language? Obviously, something occurs within family structures, childcare situations, play groups, and other normal living environments that helps children improve their language skills. Continuing this development is a major responsibility of early education and elementary school programs.

It is not the intention of this unit to fully explore all of the diverse theories of language development that have emerged over the years. The purpose here is to provide an overview of some of the key ideas that have emerged from a number of sources related to a whole language approach. Four key ideas are explored. First, through the work of a number of individuals, the concept of how language develops is explored. Second, the relationship of language development to the child's environment is examined. Third, the role of social class and cultural background as factors in language development are considered. Finally, the reader will understand the inability of any one theory to fully explain language development.

INTRODUCTION

Language, the ability to laugh at a humorous story, and the ability of people to reflect and consider their own existence differentiate human beings from animals and other living things. Each of these characteristics is highly related to the others. The language of a humorous story causes laughter. It is only through the ability to recall some of the silly things we sometimes do that we can talk about those incidents with others, thereby causing others to laugh.

Many have proposed theories and conducted research in the area of language development; this is not the place for a comprehensive description of all these efforts. While there is no absolute consensus about how language develops, the work of the individuals described in this unit as well as the work of many others supports a whole language approach to teaching the language arts.

Many of the theories described in this unit were developed by studying language users in natural settings. This is in sharp contrast to much of the research on language development conducted over the past several decades, in which research was not conducted in natural settings, but was conducted using a behavioral scientific model. Such research is often done in laboratories or laboratory type settings with tightly controlled environments and narrowly defined variables. The environment is specifically controlled so that factors that might occur naturally do not have any effect on the variable being studied. The variables are narrowly defined so that they can more easily be reduced to a numerical value or test score.

As a result of the way much behavioral research is carried out, whole language teachers do not automatically assume that the findings and conclusions of such research are applicable at the classroom level. Such teachers clearly understand that environment and language do interact. Teachers have too frequently found that research findings do not seem to be applicable in

FIGURE 7-1 Much can be learned by studying children's language attempts in natural settings.

a natural setting. This has long been acknowledged as a very real problem. Several decades ago, John Carroll (1964) suggested that the differences between the psychological laboratory and the natural setting of the classroom are so deep that they go to the very basis of how teaching and learning are conducted in each environment. He indicated that the inductive, nonverbal learning investigated in the behavioral laboratory is incompatible with the deductive, verbal-explanatory type of teaching found in most classrooms and teaching materials. A whole language approach, with its use of child input, environment, and peer interactions widens the gap still further.

As a result of these characteristics of a whole language classroom, the traditional progression of theory leading to research and research leading to practice has been turned around. It is now the practitioners, the teachers in the classrooms, who are developing the most productive theories. These same teachers are often engaged in naturalistic research within their classrooms to verify their beliefs. This is not at all a negative situation. It is simply different from tradition. Those teachers, however, are working from some well-respected beliefs developed through a number of sources in the field of language development.

Five theorists and their contributions are representative of the many who have influenced this approach. Jean Piaget, a Swiss psychologist, is best known for his work in cognitive development. Lev Vygotsky, a Russian psychologist, was a contemporary of Piaget. Benjamin Lee Whorf was an amateur linguist who lived and worked in America. Roger Brown, an American linguist, concentrated on the study and learning of words and the emergence of language structure. Marie Clay, a New Zealand educator, is best known for her work in the area of reading and writing instruction. The work of each is described here with reference to their views on language and how those views are related to whole language.

JEAN PIAGET

Jean Piaget was a brilliant scientist whose talents flourished at an early age (Ginsburg and Opper 1979). Early in his career he became fascinated with natural science and focused particularly on the study of molluscs, earning a Doctor of Philosophy degree at the age of twenty-one. He studied psychology and the psychoanalytic work of Freud and Jung in Zurich. Later, in Paris, his work with intelligence tests at the Binet Laboratory led him more directly into his life's work of studying child development.

While testing for intelligence, the focus is normally on obtaining the one correct answer. Piaget, however, found that the wrong answers suggested an interesting pattern. In his work, Piaget noticed that the same wrong answers kept occurring and that different kinds of wrong answers seemed to occur at different age levels. Piaget concluded that intelligence was not a matter of the quantity of correct answers, but rather that the thinking of children differed with age. He therefore rejected the use of standardized test procedures as valid tools for studying children. As a result, he developed interview procedures that involved the child in the direction the process would take. Later, he added materials for children to manipulate as part of the study process. His focus was not on proving that his thoughts were correct but on following the lead of the child in order to attempt to learn the underlying rationale for the child's responses.

The continuation of this work led to Piaget's major publication on language and cognitive processes, *The Language and Thought of the Child* (1926). This book presented both naturalistic and experimental observations on how children use language. Among the findings Piaget described in this book is that the speech of the young child is primarily egocentric, or focused on the child. As children get older, Piaget observed a decline in this egocentric speech. Ginsburg and Opper (1979) caution that this egocentric behavior is not a negative characteristic. That is, the child is not egocentric at the expense of others. The child simply fails to take into account the views and needs of others. As children grow to the age of four, five, or six years, Piaget notes a decline in egocentric speech and an increase in communicative speech.

Three types of egocentric speech are identified by Piaget (1926): repetition, individual monologue, and collective monologue. In repetition, the child mimics the speech of adults or others. Piaget interpreted this as something the child did for the pleasure of using and playing with words. An individual monologue occurs when the child does not yet differentiate between a word and its corresponding action or object. It may also be used to achieve with words something the child cannot achieve in reality. An example of this might be when a child says "Stay up" when the blocks being stacked keep falling down. The child's language is used as a part of the child's action rather than as tools for communication. Collective monologues are quite similar to individual monologues except that they take place in groups of children. A child might speak a monologue and believe that others are listening, but because the speech is largely egocentric, it is not truly communicative. Communicative speech is distinguished from egocentric speech in that the former takes into account the interests of the listener and intends to transmit information to that listener.

A key belief of Piaget's approach to language is its relationship to thinking. According to Piaget, thinking does not depend on language. That is, only after the thought process is established can a child transfer the concept or principle into language. In addition, Piaget tended to underestimate the significance of the role experience plays in development. These Piagetian beliefs have become the subjects for much disagreement over the years. Indeed, a whole language approach, while embracing the naturalistic approach to observing children, challenges these latter points.

LEV VYGOTSKY

Lev Vygotsky was a Russian psychologist who lived from 1896 to 1934. His increasingly influential book,

Thought and Language (1962), was originally published in 1934 shortly after his death. It was reissued in 1962. Both Piaget and Vygotsky were aware of each other's work at the time and both understood that they took different positions in key areas of language development. The Soviet Union allowed Vygotsky's work to surface in 1956 after many years of neglect. His work is now a major influence in the field of language development.

In his book, Vygotsky makes it quite clear that his main unit of analysis is the "word." He describes the word as a microcosm of conscious human thought. He saw word meaning as the internal component of the word itself. He viewed word meaning as the point in which thought and speech united to form a verbal thought. Vygotsky viewed thought and speech as two independent processes, but ones that interacted with each other.

Vygotsky's theory of language development is interactionist. That is, he believed that over the course of their development, children participated in meaningful interactions with individuals in their communities. Through this interaction, an inner speech or inner language develops and becomes the basis of effective oral communication (Elsasser and John-Steiner 1977).

The concept of "inner speech" divides the theories of Piaget and Vygotsky. While both acknowledge the existence of egocentric speech, Vygotsky did not see its decrease with age as a sign that it is replaced with communicative speech. Vygotsky viewed the decrease of egocentric speech as a sign that it is going underground as intrapersonal speech. This intrapersonal or inner speech becomes a kind of semantic shorthand that serves as the basis for effective oral and written language. What begins as egocentric speech eventually becomes internal thought. Oral and written communications are seen as elaborated forms of inner speech. The elaborated form requires many more words to transmit the abbreviated sense of inner speech.

A central point in Vygotsky's analysis of language is the concept of internalization. His view contends that children are active learners, able to bring together several features of their experience in order to develop thoughts. Vygotsky's theory suggests that children engage in meaningful interactions with members of their communities. This interaction forms a

FIGURE 7-2 Children sometimes focus on a single word in their language, thinking, and drawing as a tool to help them learn the word.

foundation for competent use of language. Pflaum (1978) summarizes Vygotsky's position succinctly. First, language is a major driving force behind cognitive growth. Second, the strategies used to acquire language become major tools for the acquisition of thought processes. A preschool program based on Vygotsky's theories might place great emphasis on the importance of interaction between children and adults as well as between children and other language users.

This framework leads Vygotsky to suggest that language can lead cognitive development rather than follow it as Piaget would have suggested. In view of this, Vygotsky would be much more supportive than Piaget of the notion that instruction could influence the rate of cognitive development. The problem for education, therefore, is to provide instruction that enables children to master language.

Based on Vygotsky's theories, Berk (1985) provides several recommendations for early childhood classroom practices that are appropriate to a whole language approach. First, opportunities for play are especially important. Environments rich in social interaction opportunities provide an excellent medium for private speech to grow. An integrated approach would suggest the appropriateness of including children of different ages and abilities. Second, the environment should include good adult models who are perceptive about the private speech used by children. Through their observation, adults can structure their language in such a way that it can be subsequently used by the children to solve other problems they may encounter. Third, adults working with children should be constantly aware of the outer limit of a child's ability and experience. Fourth, learning environments can be provided that do not require children to work silently on tasks requiring a single correct answer. Adults must be tolerant of the need of children to be verbally active as they complete tasks and solve problems. Egocentric speech used by chil-

FIGURE 7-4 Vygotsky's beliefs support the concept of an integrated environment for children of different ages and abilities.

dren as they go about their work should be viewed as a tool children use to help them learn.

BENJAMIN LEE WHORF

In the 1930s Benjamin Lee Whorf began to be known for his hypothesis that language and culture were interrelated. He was, at the time, an amateur linguist who suggested that a key characteristic of language was that it served as a reflection of the culture. It helps to shape the culture. It is shaped by the culture. His theory suggests that words and objects are associated and that language is required as a social necessity. Few would argue with many of these points. However, he went beyond this by asserting that we understand a language only by understanding the culture from which it comes. The reverse of this was also seen as true.

Whorf felt that language is not merely an agent for voicing ideas. Language is itself a shaper of ideas. It is a guide for a person's thoughts, for analyzing concepts and for synthesizng ideas. Whorf's theory argues that we learn about our environment along lines suggested by our native language. Concepts, classifications, categories, and the ways that we organize thoughts are not in our minds naturally. In addition, the world does not come at us in neat categories, but hits us in random bits and pieces. From the moment

FIGURE 7-3 Vygotsky contends that children benefit from many opportunities to interact with adults.

a child first sees and hears, there is a wide range of sights and sounds: colors, objects, voices, mechanical sounds, noises and so forth. Whorf's theory further suggests that we categorize the reality of the world largely by the linguistic system in our minds. The linguistic system in our mind has generally been learned through the language of our culture.

Whorf based his theory on a careful study of language and culture of two very different populations. He engaged in an intense examination of Hopi Indians and compared their language and culture to that of the English-speaking population. Among some of his key findings was the fact that the Hopi language has no tenses. It has no nouns for time, days, or years. The Hopi tend to view life in terms of a continuous movement, of becoming. In English, on the other hand, there are numerous ways of marking and counting time. Time is so concrete a concept that it is almost as though days and hours are actual objects. The complexity of how English speakers view time goes even beyond that. There are numerous ways of speaking in terms of time. English speakers are constantly forced to choose correct terms and tenses when referring to time. As a result, English speakers come to view time in terms of a linear progression.

As a result of these findings, Whorf concluded that an individual's thought processes and perceptions are determined by the richness of the language learned. Taken to its logical conclusion, this suggests that language and culture can limit thought and restrain innovation. While some aspects of Whorf's theory may be questioned, there is some merit to his position.

Whorf's ideas have some implications for the early childhood educator. The first is that children from diverse ethnic backgrounds and children whose native language is other than English may not view the world in the same way as those who originate from the mainstream culture. It is necessary for the teacher of such children to contemplate how the world view of these children can best be utilized to help them learn. Such children should not be seen as having deficiencies. That is clearly not the case. Their backgrounds are simply different. A second implication is that working in a multi-cultural group can be a stimulating, positive experience for all of the children. Learning to see the world in a different way, sharing values from different cultures, and experiencing the diversity that makes people interesting are opportunities waiting to be used for the benefit of all the children.

ROGER BROWN

At about the same time that Whorf was studying the meanings and nuances of words between two cultures, Roger Brown was developing his hypotheses about how young children develop their understanding of the meanings of words. While Brown did some investigation among different languages and cultures, his primary interest was how children develop increasingly more sophisticated understandings of words.

Brown (1958) asserts that the most deliberate part of first language teaching involves telling children words for different things. Parents and caregivers of

FIGURE 7-5 The child that drew these pictures was engaged in learning the word and concept of a "tree."

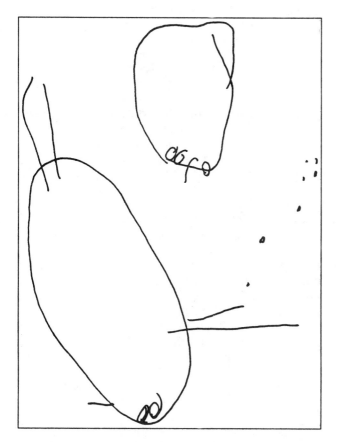

FIGURE 7-6 The child who drew these figures demonstrated the learning of size as a character trait by stating that the larger figure is a scary monster and that the smaller figure is a baby.

young children devote countless hours over a considerable number of years explaining both the meanings of words and which words are used to describe things in the environment.

Brown noted, however, that one object may have a variety of words that can be used to name it. A child might be told that a dime is money. However, it might also be called a dime, a coin, a 1988 dime, or a metal object. Roger Brown investigated names for things are determined. The answer to this has implications for the cognitive development of the child. While the culture demands that things have names or language labels attached to them, the culture also demands that other referants are needed as well. In some situations, referring to a dime as money works quite well. At

other times, it doesn't work nearly as well. When the amount of money needed to make a purchase is a quarter, a dime will simply not do even though it is money. Yes, it is money, but not the correct amount.

Some might think that children first acquire concrete language, and later more abstract. Brown (1958) discovered that this is not necessarily so. Many children do learn that dimes, pennies, and quarters are all referred to as money before they learn the specific names for each of the coins. That is, they learn the abstract term *money* prior to learning the more concrete term *quarter*. The same thing is observed when children learn the abstract term *fish* prior to the more concrete terms *bass* and *perch*. On the other hand, children learn the concrete terms *milk* and *water* prior to learning the more abstract term *liquid*. The same thing is observed when children learn the concrete terms *Mama* and *Dada* prior to the more abstract terms *parents* and *adults*.

Brown (1958) concluded that it is not true, therefore, that vocabulary is ordinarily acquired from the concrete to the abstract. He felt that the child's purposes and needs suggest that objects are learned first by what he described as their common name. Sometimes the common name is a more abstract label, while at other times it is a more concrete label. Corresponding to this is the way adults present the names

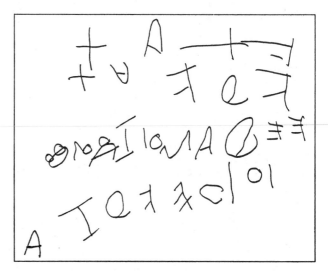

FIGURE 7-7 The child who created these figures may be attempting to form an understanding of a language rule.

of things to children. Brown found that adults tended to categorize and name things in maximally useful ways. That is, they gave the name that would be most useful to the child.

Brown was aware of the long-accepted fact that children tend to overgeneralize in their use of the names that they have learned (McCarthy 1946). Many of us have also heard young children referring to any four-legged animal as a dog. This, according to Brown, is an overgeneralization of the word *dog*. That is, the child associates the word with the image of a dog. When another image with similar features is observed, the word *dog* is used to name it. The other image may have many of the same characteristics of a dog such as four legs, a head, a tail, and a body covered with hair or fur. Horses, goats, cats, and cows all would fall into such a category. It was a common belief at the time that cognitive development in language is a process of increasing differentiations, greater distinctions, and more categories. Each of these categories was viewed as becoming smaller and more concrete as language was acquired (Lewin 1935).

It is Brown's belief that the sequence in which children acquire words and names is largely set by adults. The sequence may also be determined by the utility of the categorizations. That is, words that have the highest practical utility are learned first. The words with the least utility tend to be learned at a later time. In regard to the level of abstraction, it is possible that words with a middle level of abstraction might be learned first if they have a high degree of utility. If this is the case, words would be added from both directions: higher abstraction and greater concreteness.

Brown and Fraser (1963) and Brown and Bellugi (1964) studied and described how children develop the syntax and rules of language. They arrived at their conclusions through a study of the oral language errors that children make. Adult speech is seen as a key ingredient in the process. The models provided by adults are seen as undergoing a specific cognitive process by the child in order to develop rules about language.

According to Brown's findings, as children are growing up they hear a rather large sample of sentences. They hear this language sample from family, friends, television programs, and so forth. As children hear this mature speech over time, the regularity of some aspects of the language becomes more clear. From this regularity, children induce an implicit grammar. That is, they develop rules about how language should be put together to form sentences.

The process by which children form their rules follows four steps. The first step in the process takes place with children merely imitating the language they hear. For example, an adult might move a toy car along the floor and say, "The car goes vroom." The child might imitate the action with the car while saying the same exact sentence spoken by the adult.

On the other hand, Brown observed that sentences such as "I digged in the lawn" and "I saw sheeps" are not likely imitations of adult language. He felt that these errors indicated rules the children were following rather than imitations of adult speech. This led to his identification of the other three steps in the process: reduction, expansion, and progressive differentiation. Reduction is accomplished by the child by taking a normal sentence and omitting function words that carry little essential information. "I am very tall" becomes "I tall." It is as if the child reduces the sentence to a telegraphic form. Expansion takes place when the child generalizes the telegraphic sentence to new utterances such as "My tall" and "I very tall." What has happened is that the child has formed a rule that has a logic behind it and that is often demonstrated consistently by the child. Progressive differentiation occurs when the child revises and refines these initial rules and they become more and more consistent with a more standard form of English. Brown (1973) further investigated his hypotheses and conclusions about language by studying these concepts in other languages. He investigated how children developed a first language in twelve other languages. These investigations resulted in the verification of his original conclusions.

MARIE CLAY

Marie Clay is a New Zealand educator who has had an increasing influence on how educators view the way young children develop literacy. She is best known for her comprehensive assessment and remediation procedures known as the "Reading Recovery Program" (1979b). The program is designed to provide intense remediation for young children experiencing difficulty in learning to read. Clay bases the program on, among other things, the fact that a strong language base is critically important to helping children learn to read. She sees the strategy of prediction about language as a crucial tool children can use to aid their developing reading ability. The structure of language (syntax) and the meaning of language (semantics) are identified by Clay as the two powerful bases upon which prediction rests.

While Clay's work is primarily focused on reading, she has developed a clear view of how language develops in children (1979a). Her view begins with a stress on the importance of an emotionally involved adult in the child's early life. Between two and three years of age, the child develops a first "private" language that may or may not be consistently understood by the adult. However, the emotionally responsive adult persists in attempting to understand the child. This individual perfoms the task of keeping the child talking. By encouraging the child to talk, the listener is able to study and learn the frame of reference from which the child operates. By coming to an understanding of this, the adult is able to respond to the child more accurately.

The language responses by the adult reward the child and confirm the predictions upon which the expressive attempt was based. The fact that the communication was understood confirms for the child suc-

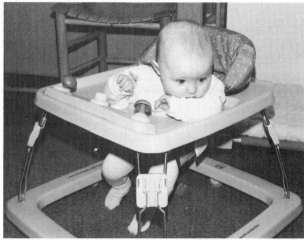

FIGURE 7-9 Children seek to learn, explore, and understand their world well before they can talk about it.

cess in the new way of expressing an idea. If the listener seems puzzled, the child tends to reject the hypothesis about language that helped form the utterance. Clay warns that it is particularly important for the adult to maintain a warm, supportive relationship with the child. When a child is experiencing difficulty with language, the adult must make even greater efforts to engage the child in conversation and to create more opportunities for genuine interaction.

According to Clay (1979a), while the language of other children may be helpful, it is the language of the responsive adult that is critical. This is because adults provide effective models of mature conversation, something other children are less able to do. One of the most common activities responsive adults engage in is the process of expansion. This occurs most often when a child makes a statement the adult may not quite understand. Rather than ignoring the child or responding with "What?", the adult will reformulate the statement in the form of oral feedback. As Roger Brown noted, children often reduce language structures to telegraphic speech. These forms tend to be used as they are originally understood and in expanded versions as the child matures in language skill. The adult's response helps both the child and the adult to check the understanding of the child's statement. Examples of this strategy include the following:

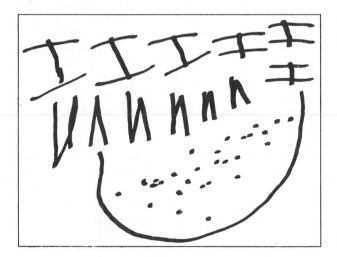

FIGURE 7-8 The child who creates art and language can be encouraged by a responsive adult who shows interest in learning more about the child's creation.

Child statement	Adult response
Me big.	Yes, you are big.
That truck.	Yes, that's a truck.
My up.	Yes, I'll pick you up.

Clay warns that children's errors should not be viewed as mistakes, but as indications that the child is experimenting and learning new language meanings and structures (1979a). At age three, a child may seem to speak without errors. A year later, the same child's language may seem to be full of errors. The errors are a result of the child moving into uncharted language waters. The child's language, at such times, again includes more hypotheses about how the language works. The child is again finding out if ideas can be expressed in certain ways that have not been previously tried. As a result of this, a correcting ap-

FIGURE 7-11 A popular Dr. Seuss story. From *The Cat in the Hat*, by Dr. Seuss. *Reprinted courtesy of Random House.*

proach to working with young children is not likely to lead to progress. In fact, it can inhibit language growth if the major interaction with the adult is based on informing the child that an error has been made. Constant correction may encourage children to continue using only safe language structures rather than risk failure by trying to learn and use new structures.

This same principle holds true for the acquisition of dialects, which are normally acquired in the preschool years (1979a, 1982). Dialects are not errors. Children who develop dialects are merely demonstrating that they are learning the rules and structures of the language that they find in the world around them. Clay suggests that dialectical speech should be respected and preserved. The teacher's role is to add some standard pronunciations to be used with some of the people the child will encounter in life and to open up the world of books to the child. She bases these beliefs on an understanding of the critical roles that both language and culture play in a child's life.

Clay is a firm believer in the importance of the home and the family as a part of a child's early education. She feels that parents should be invited to participate in the process of helping children develop oral language and

FIGURE 7-10 Children's book author Theodor Geisel, better known as Dr. Seuss. *Photo courtesy of Czeslaw Czaplinski. Reprinted by permission of Random House.*

FIGURE 7-12 Language plays a critical role in the life of a child.

literacy. Toward this end, she has provided two excellent resources: *Reading Begins at Home* (Butler and Clay 1987) and *Writing Begins at Home* (Clay 1988). In these books, Clay shows parents that the development of literacy is not a forbidding or mysterious process. On the contrary, the journey can be filled with pleasurable sharing between parents and children long before the latter begin to attend school. Children develop much language by such listening and talking about Dr. Seuss stories, Mother Goose tales, and other good literature.

SUMMARY

This unit provides an overview of some of the ideas and theorists who have influenced the whole lanugage

movement in the area of language development. It is clear that any view of language development is influenced by a variety of ideas concerning how children acquire language during their early years. This unit focuses on the work of five individuals who examined emerging language, the role of environment, and the influence of social class and culture on language. Through this examination, it is clear that a single theory of language development cannot adequately explain how children develop a first language. One must examine a number of findings and beliefs in order to obtain an adequate grasp of how young children develop language.

Jean Piaget was an Austrian scientist who was influenced by the psychoanalytic work of Freud and Jung. He became fascinated by the wrong answers children often gave on standardized tests he was using in his early work. While conducting this early work, he noted that there seemed to be patterns in children's errors and that the patterns changed with the ages of the children. He later came to reject the use of such standardized testing, preferring instead the interview and observational procedures he developed. He identified the early speech of developing children as egocentric speech, a behavior he believed was replaced by social speech as the children developed. Piaget contends that thinking does not depend on language; rather, language follows thought.

Lev Vygotsky was a Russian psychologist who was a contemporary of Piaget. The word, particularly word meaning, was the focus of much of his analysis of language. Words, for Vygotsky, represented the uniting of thought and speech to form a verbal thought. While thought and speech were seen as independent processes, they were viewed as interacting with one another. Vygotsky viewed the role of interaction with adults as critical to the language development of the child. In contrast to Piaget, Vygotsky viewed egocentric speech not as something that was replaced by social speech, but as something that was transformed into an intrapersonal or inner speech as children grew older. Also in contrast to Piaget, Vygotsky saw language as a major driving force behind cognitive growth. Classrooms influenced by Vygotsky's views would include children of different ages, a great deal of social interaction, and the conspicuous presence of perceptive adult language models.

Benjamin Lee Whorf, an amateur linguist, spent a

great deal of time studying and comparing the Hopi Indian language with the language of English speakers. His theories, based upon his research, suggest that a powerful link exists between language and culture. He concluded that we can fully understand a culture only by understanding the language of that culture. Conversely, we can fully understand a language only by understanding the culture from which that language emanates. Whorf felt that we not only learn through language, but that language in itself shapes ideas.

Roger Brown, an American linguist, studied how children develop an understanding of words and syntax. He noted that many objects or concepts often have a number of words and referents that are used to describe them. In studying this, Brown discovered that parents first teach, and children first learn, the common words for objects. These common words are those having the greatest utility to the child in daily life. The first words learned to describe objects are ordinarily learned without regard to their level of abstraction. In studying children's acquisition of the structure of language, Brown was able to outline a four-step process by which children listen to mature speech and then develop rules about how language works. The four steps of the process include imitation, reduction, expansion, and progressive differentiation.

New Zealand educator Marie Clay has enjoyed an increasingly elevated position in education due primarily to her innovative Reading Recovery Program for young children with severe reading difficulties. She has based her program on some very clear assumptions about how children develop language. Her view places great importance on the presence of an emotionally responsive adult in the life of the young child. This individual assists the child on the journey from a private language to a social language. The critical role of the adult during this time is to provide ample language opportunities for children as well as feedback that enables the child to verify or reject currently held hypotheses about how language works. As with Piaget and Brown, Clay studied the errors that children make. She interpreted many of these errors to mean that language growth was occurring. For Clay, errors indicate that the young child is forming and attempting to implement new language hypotheses.

Questions for Review and Discussion

Multiple Choice

1. Piaget preferred to obtain information about the thinking of children by using
   a. an interview process.
   b. standardized tests.
   c. intelligence tests.
   d. studies of their parents.
2. According to Piaget, when the child mimics the speech of an adult, the child is engaging in
   a. parallel speech.
   b. repetition.
   c. individual monologue.
   d. collective monologue.
3. In studying language, Vygotsky's main unit of analysis was the
   a. text.
   b. paragraph.
   c. sentence.
   d. word.

4. According to Roger Brown, the most deliberate part of first language teaching is
    a. teaching a child the alphabet.
    b. telling a child what things are called.
    c. helping a child memorize the alphabet.
    d. teaching a child to overgeneralize language rules.
5. When a child overgeneralizes, Brown would say that the child is
    a. hypothesizing a rule underlying language.
    b. making a careless language error.
    c. not attending to adult language models.
    d. using sequence incorrectly.
6. A comparison of the Hopi Indian language and the English language was used to support the views of
    a. Piaget.
    b. Vygotsky.
    c. Clay.
    d. Whorf.
7. Marie Clay suggests that one of the most critical people to a child's language development is
    a. a dependable friend or playmate.
    b. a caring older sibling.
    c. an emotionally responsive adult.
    d. another child of the same age.

True or False

T   F   1. Piaget was influenced by the work of Freud and Jung.
T   F   2. Vygotsky's beliefs about language and thought are nearly identical to those of Piaget.
T   F   3. A child saying "I eated the cookie" is overgeneralizing, according to Roger Brown.
T   F   4. Whorf contends that language is a shaper of ideas.
T   F   5. Clay does not view the role of adults as particularly important to the development of language in the child.

Essay and Discussion

1. Describe the three types of egocentric speech identified by Piaget: repetition, individual monologue, and collective monologue.
2. Compare and contrast the major views of Piaget and Vygotsky concerning cognitive thought and language.
3. Describe the differences Whorf found when he compared the concept of time between the Hopi Indian language and English.
4. Based on the ideas of Roger Brown, identify the various words and terms that might be used in place of a word such as *car*.
5. Summarize the role Clay would suggest for a parent or other adult in helping a child to develop language.

References

Berk, L.E. 1985. Why children talk to themselves. *Young Children* 40: 46–52.

Brown, R. 1973. *A first language.* Cambridge, Mass.: Harvard University Press.

Brown, R. 1958. How shall a thing be called. *Psychological Review* 65: 1, 14–21.

Brown, R., and U. Bellugi. 1964. The processes in the acquisition of syntax. *Harvard Educational Review* 34: 133–151.

Brown, R., and C. Fraser. 1963. The acquisition of syntax. In *Verbal Behavior and Learning: Problems and Processes,* ed. C.N. Cofer and B.S. Musgrove. New York: McGraw Hill.

Butler, D., and M.M. Clay. 1987. *Reading begins at home.* Portsmouth, N.H.: Heinemann.

Carroll, J.B. 1964. Words, meanings, and concepts. *Harvard Educational Review* 34: 178–202.

Clay, M.M. 1982. *Observing young readers.* Portsmouth, N.H.: Heinemann.

Clay, M.M. 1979. *Reading: The patterning of complex behavior.* Exeter, N.H.: Heinemann.

Clay, M.M. 1979. *The early detection of reading difficulties.* Exeter, N.H.: Heinemann.

Clay, M.M. 1988. *Writing begins at home.* Portsmouth, N.H.: Heinemann.

Elsasser, N., and V.P. John-Steiner. 1977. An interactionist approach to advancing literacy. *Harvard Educational Review* 47: 355–369.

Ginsburg, H., and S. Opper. 1979. *Piaget's theory of intellectual development.* Englewood Cliffs, N.J.: Prentice-Hall.

Lewin, K. 1935. *A dynamic theory of personality.* New York: McGraw-Hill.

McCarthy, D. 1946. Language development in children. In *Manual of child psychology,* ed. L. Carmichael. New York: John Wiley.

Pflaum, S. 1978. *The development of language and reading in young children.* Columbus, Ohio: Charles Merrill.

Piaget, J. 1926. *The language and thought of the child.* London: Routledge and Kegan Paul.

Vygotsky, L. 1962. *Thought and language.* Cambridge, Mass.: M.I.T. Press.

Whorf, B.L. 1956. *Language, thought and reality.* Cambridge, Mass.: John Wiley.

UNIT 8

Components of Language

PREVIEW

Language is a key component for leading a happy and healthy life. It enables us to form friendships as well as to secure the basic necessities of life: food, water, health care, shelter, and safety. Centuries ago this was so, even though much of the population was illiterate in terms of reading and writing. How could this have happened? The answer is simple: language is not merely sounds and symbols. Language primarily is a medium for meaning. Basic components underlie all language, whether it is oral or written. People have used an understanding of these components to help insure their survival. The understanding of these components and the role they serve is generally a tacit understanding. That is, in order to use lan-

guage we do not have to identify the rules of the language or explain how language works. The rules are assimilated from living in the culture. How this occurs is the focus of the study of linguistics. Several of the key components linguists ordinarily study are explored here. Among the key concepts and ideas examined in this unit are:

- How do the meanings implicit in language aid the language user?
- How does the stucture of language serve as a device for sending and receiving meaningful communications?
- How do the sounds of language help language users derive meaning from both text and oral language?

- How do the practical aspects, or pragmatics, of language help the users of language share meaning?

INTRODUCTION

An integrated approach to language arts using a whole language philosophy relies on the support of a number of assumptions. These assumptions have a sound basis in research, practice, and logical thought. Among these are beliefs about how language works. Many of these concepts have been investigated and described by theorists who have studied how language develops in children. A number of the assumptions are based on how language components function in everyday use.

An initial assumption is that nearly every child possesses, to some degree, a facility for learning both oral and written language. While there may be a very limited number of profoundly disabled children who do not seem to learn or respond to any language whatsoever, most children seem to develop some language ability. Even children who are seen as having language learning problems in elementary school have generally demonstrated their ability to learn and use sophisticated language structures in oral language.

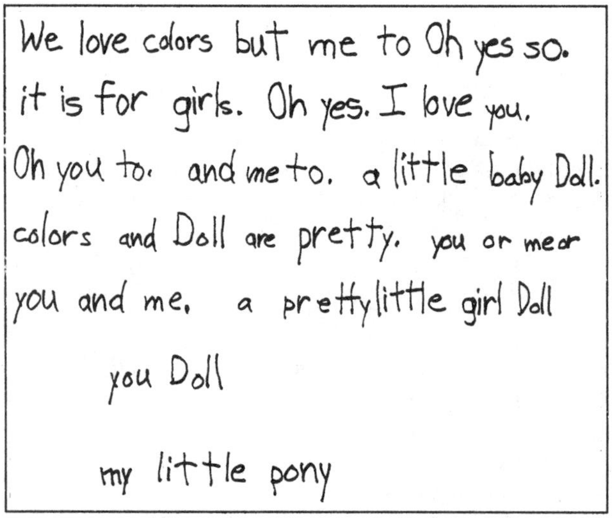

We love colors but me to Oh yes so.
it is for girls. Oh yes. I love you.
Oh you to. and me to. a little baby Doll.
colors and Doll are pretty. you or me or
you and me. a pretty little girl Doll
   you Doll

   my little pony

FIGURE 8-1 The child who wrote this is explaining words and concepts using written language.

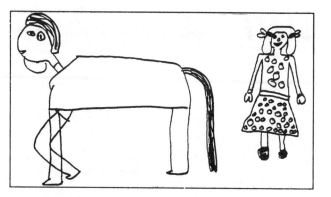

FIGURE 8-2 Illustration drawn by a child to accompany the written piece found in Figure 8-1.

Too often, cultural factors are viewed as language deficiencies. In addition, severely disabled children have often shown the ability to develop some language using alternative forms of communication even when professionals have suggested that this was not possible.

A second assumption is that language is a meaning focused process. Its main purpose is to enable us to share or obtain meaning from others in oral or written form. Language is not viewed as a set of skills to be mastered, because this would do little for the establishment of meaning. Rather, it is the individual, monitoring a variety of aspects or components of language over a period of time, who allows meaning to emerge.

The definition of a term, in conjunction with certain other words, spoken with a certain tone of voice, in the context of a specific situation creates meaning. Think about how many ways we can say the word *yes* as a response to a question. We can quickly see the need to view language as a process rather than as a set of skills. The term can be spoken in a monotone, with laughter, with anger, with fear, and with scorn, to name but a few ways. Each variation conveys a different meaning. Simply being able to say the word or words is only one part of the process of using language.

A third assumption, related to the second, is that language has a social component because of the listener/speaker and reader/writer relationship. These relationships have much to do with how well meaning is conveyed. A listener and a speaker are usually in close proximity to one another. A child and parent

FIGURE 8-3 Writers of children's books must establish social relationships based on their perceptions of children. *From Petunia,* by Robert Duvoisin. *Reprinted courtesy of Random House.*

are often only inches or feet apart as they communicate. Facial expressions, body language, tone of voice, and the selection of appropriate language all play significant roles in establishing meaning within the social relationship of parent and child.

On the other hand, the social relationship of reader and writer is quite different. A child listening to or reading a storybook will most likely never have met the author of the book. However, the child will often be able to relate quite well to the meaning of the story. The reason for this is that the author has taken pains to establish a social relationship from a distance. While the writer of a children's story book does not know each of the children who will read the book, the writer does usually have an understanding of children. Often, writers observe children, talk to them, study them, and find out what interests them. Writers are then able to establish a long distance social relationship based upon their perception of children who will probably be reading the books they write. This same idea holds true for most other books as well, including the book you are now reading. The author attempts to establish a social relationship with the reader based upon a perception of what that reader might be like.

A fourth assumption is that people establish mean-

ing through an integrated use of semantics, syntactics, phonology, and pragmatics. These four concepts are seen as key components of language in which children develop a facility that enables still further language growth (Hasenstab and Laughton 1982). This, in turn, enables them to become effective in both obtaining and conveying meaning through language. Further, it is primarily in whole pieces of text that these components interact in such a way that authentic meaning occurs. That is, while each of these can be examined in isolation, they tend to only be used in natural communication. As a result, it is from natural communication that most children develop their tacit understanding of how the components work.

SEMANTICS

The study of the meaning of words is referred to as semantics. It involves investigating the relationship

FIGURE 8-4 In whole pieces of text components of language interact to produce authentic meaning.

between names and concepts as well as the relationship between referents and names. Take as an example the concept of money. We often take our knowledge of money for granted. We all need it and use it, yet we don't think twice about just exactly what the idea of money means. To a young child, the concept of money is usually associated with the coins we use as change. As a concept for an adult, however, money represents the power to purchase things one may want or need. Money has a number of referents. These are terms and phrases that are related to money. Some of the referents are simply actual or slang terms that are used in place of the word *money*. Examples might include cash, dough, bucks, scratch, and dollars. Referents can often be in the form of phrases that add additional meaning to the concept of money. We refer to money as something we work hard for, the root of all evil, as something we shouldn't throw at problems, as something that doesn't grow on trees, and as something which shouldn't be taken for granted. These, too, all add additional meaning to the concept of money, particularly when the term is used in a certain context. It is within contexts that meaning emerges in terms of the total communication. Nevertheless, it is important that children develop a basic awareness of the words that refer to the meaningful objects and ideas in their environments.

Semantic Cues

Semantic cues are important for children in both oral and written language. They form clues that assist children in understanding the total communication. A semantic cue is evidence derived from the general sense or meaning of a written or oral communication that aids in the identification of an unknown word. Imagine that a certain child did not know the word *gobbled*. Imagine too that this same child heard or read in a story the line, "The hungry giant quickly gobbled down his dinner." Many children who know the other words in this sentence would determine that the word *gobbled* meant something along the lines of eating quickly. They would do this by using their knowledge of words such as *hungry* and *dinner*. These other words are semantic cues, from the context of the sentence, that provide clues about the meaning of the unknown word.

Schema Theory

A significant amount of interest centers around the use of schema theory as it relates to comprehension and the establishment of meaning through language. It is based on research in the areas of memory, comprehension, and intelligence (Bartlett 1932; Kintsch and Greene 1978; Piaget 1952). A schema is an image of reality held in thought. A schema is similar to a concept, but has a much wider applicability.

Pearson and Spiro (1980) have developed a model of reading comprehension that is based on schema theory. The model is explored in the context of classroom implementation by Pearson and Johnson (1978). Schemata are based upon the experience of the individual. The greater the experiences, the more schemata an individual is likely to possess. Schemata are somewhat like brief plays or dramatic sequences representing a variety of events, actions, and sequences. A child who has gone to a fast food restaurant develops a fast food restaurant schema. It might run in a sequence like this:

1. Walk up to the counter.
2. Get in a line.
3. Look up at the menu sign to decide on items wanted.
4. Place order.
5. Pay for food.
6. Pick up tray of food and walk to eating area.
7. Find an empty table.
8. Sit down and eat meal.
9. Put papers, containers, cups, and plastic utensils on tray.
10. Deposit trash in trash container and place the tray on top.
11. Leave restaurant.

This schema is basically the one followed by millions of people daily as they eat at fast food restaurants. It varies little no matter which restaurant we patronize. On the other hand, a very different schema is followed at a more formal and traditional restaurant. At such an establishment, items such as making reservations, being shown to a table, tipping, and leaving all of the dishes on the table at the end of the meal are part of this schema. Since understanding both oral and written stories depends on relating new information to that which is already known, a child is well

FIGURE 8-5 A visit to a farm can help children develop a schema for the concept of a farm.

served by possessing a wide range of schemata. If children listen to a story that takes place in a restaurant, they can recall their restaurant schema as an aid to helping them make sense of the story.

Story Grammar

A story grammar is a specific type of schema that can aid a young reader or listener to better understand stories. Most stories follow some variation of a fairly reliable sequence of events. A typical story might unfold along certain lines. As an example of this the classic children's book *The Little Engine That Could* (Piper 1930) is used to illustrate the pattern as follows:

1. A main character is introduced. While the little engine referred to in the title doesn't come along in the story until halfway through the book, the original train and its contents are introduced at the very beginning. Particularly noteworthy is the little toy clown.
2. A setting or scene is established. The setting is presented in words and pictures as the train meanders on the tracks through the countryside.
3. A problem is presented. When the original engine breaks down, the problem emerges. The train is carrying food and toys for the good little boys and girls in the city. Everyone realizes that this cargo must go through.
4. Other characters might be introduced. As the story progresses, the reader gets to know some of the occupants on the train as well as other passing engines.
5. Main character makes one or more attempts at solving the problem. In the story, several attempts are made at resolving the problem. A shiny new engine, a passenger engine, a freight engine, and a rusty old engine are all asked for help in pulling the train over the mountain. The tension mounts as each train refuses to help.
6. Main character solves problem. Finally, the little blue engine comes along. This engine does not have a great deal of faith in its ability to pull the train over the mountain, but agrees to help anyway.
7. The situation returns to normal. The little blue engine succeeds. As the goal is achieved, the little engine receives a boost in self confidence. All is well in the end, and life goes on.

While some of these steps may be interchanged, the basic format is fairly consistent for many stories written for young children. Learning this story grammar helps young children achieve a better understanding of any story. Such an understanding helps children make better hypotheses about the meanings of unknown words encountered. It also assists them in reconstructing the story either by retelling or through dramatizing it in play. Research strongly suggests the important role of story grammar as a tool for language understanding (Carnine and Kinder 1985; Idol 1987; Ryan and Short 1984).

SYNTACTICS

The grammatical relationship and function of word order in sentences is called syntax. Syntactics is the study of the arrangement and relationship between the symbols in syntactic sequences. Syntax helps us identify unknown words by observing how they are used in sentences. Just as with semantics, syntax can aid the reader in establishing meaning within a text. The language user is helped by attend-

FIGURE 8-6 Fairy tales have a particular story grammar that helps to identify them as a distinct type of story. *From* The Child's Fairy Tale Book, *by Kay Chorao. Reprinted courtesy of E. P. Dutton.*

ing to the syntactic cues found in the language. For example, a basic sentence structure might use the following types of words: noun—verb—noun. A sentence like "Sally likes cookies" fits this pattern. If a child does not recognize the word Sally in the sentence, the child could still predict that it is probably a noun because it is people who usually like cookies and people's names are nouns.

Syntactic Cues

A syntactic cue is evidence from knowledge of the rules and patterns of language that aids in the identification of an unknown word. The way the word is used within a sentence serves as a major clue to meaning. While a multitude of rules relate to the proper use of grammatical constructs, it is not ordinarily helpful for children to memorize them. Most rules are known by language users intuitively. They develop a tacit understanding of them from years of oral language use. Most four- and five-year-olds probably cannot recite even one rule of syntax. Yet their language conforms to virtually hundreds of such rules through their tacit understanding of them.

Knowledge of Syntax

A knowledge of syntax, whether it be a tacit or an actual knowledge of rules, provides language users with options for developing hypotheses concerning unknown words. Take, for example, the sentence, "The car skidded off the icy road and hit a _____ pole." If a listener or reader knew all of the words within the sentence with the exception of the word in the blank space, a limited number of possibilities could be formed. The fact that the word *pole* is a noun and is an object of the sentence suggests that the word in the blank must be a modifier.

Syntax is often not used by itself. It works in conjunction with other cues. In the above example of the car skidding, semantic information cues supplied by words such as icy, road, skidded, and hit suggest, in combination with the syntactic cue, that the word in the blank might be something like *utility* or *telephone*. The shorter the sentence, the less helpful syntax becomes as an aid to the reader. Consider the sentence "The girl is _____ ." Many possible words can fit into the blank in this sentence. As a matter of fact, even semantic cues are of little value in such a sentence. When such a situation occurs, one must remember to look to the greater context beyond the sentence for both semantic and syntactic cues. In authentic language situations, single, brief sentences such as this are seldom found. They are usually embedded in longer statements and paragraphs. Through the use of syntax, readers and listeners can monitor and verify the hypotheses they generate from cues.

A knowledge of syntax is a valuable tool for children participating in whole language classrooms. Many of the big books they encounter use the repetition of a syntactic pattern to make them more predictable. Even when children have not yet learned to recognize the words in print, the sound of the recurring familiar syntactic pattern enables children to recognize the pattern in oral language. This continues to build a tacit understanding of syntax, which serves as an aid to the process of learning to read.

PHONOLOGY

Phonology is the study of speech sounds and their functions in language. Through the use of phonic skills, children have still another tool to use in reading. The term *phonics* also refers to an approach used to teach beginning reading skills. The approach stresses symbol-sound relationships as well as a number of skills and activity sheets purportedly designed to develop phonic skills in children. With young children, speech articulation disorders can interfere with the ability to use phonics. Over-reliance on phonics can be an ineffective reading approach since it takes much longer to identify unfamiliar words than would an integrated approach using phonology, semantics, and syntactics.

Phonic Cues

A phonic cue is the evidence in a spelling pattern within a word that suggests speech sounds. That is, the letters within words represent speech sounds that can enable readers to identify words. Take, for example, the sentence "The _____ was sleeping." The sentence does not have enough meaning-rich information to enable a reader to effectively identify a word in the place of the blank space. There are too many possibilities for the person or thing that might be sleeping. Syntactic cues, while helpful, do not provide enough information either. The structure of the sentence indicates that the word in the blank space must be a noun of some sort. It also suggests that it is the subject of the sentence. However, it could be a baby, a mother, a bear, or even a more abstract entity such as a storm.

If the letters of the word in the blank are C-A-T, however, phonology can help a reader identify the word even if only some of the sounds of the letters can be established. Consonant sounds are much less variable than vowel sounds. Therefore, it is likely that a young reader might be able to identify the letters *c* and *t*. It is less likely that the reader can identify the correct sound of the vowel *a*. Since the word has to have a vowel sound of some sort between the first and last letters, the possible words include *cat, sat, cet, ket, cit, kit, sit, cot, set, sut*, and *cut*. There are other possibilities, but this list will do for our purpose. At this point the young reader can bring in a knowledge of semantics to further develop the hypothesis of what the word might be. While something may sleep on a cot, the cot itself does not sleep. Therefore, the word could not be cot. Other words could be rejected be-

FIGURE 8-7 Children can use many tools to interact with letters and sounds.

cause they make even less sense. While *kit* is a word, it is not even related to sleeping, which is also true of the word *cut*. The only possibility that makes sense is *cat*. A cat is an animal that children have seen and that they know also sleeps. In short, the child uses phonics to make hypotheses that are then narrowed down through the use of semantics. While this discussion is rather drawn out, such decisions are usually made quite rapidly. As children acquire increased skill decisions are made with a smooth, nearly subconscious fluency as the reading occurs.

Grapho-phonics

Grapho-phonics is a specific part of phonology. It refers to the relationship between the phonology (sounds) and the orthography (written symbols) of a language. It is based on the relationship between phonemes and graphemes. A phoneme is the smallest linguistic unit in spoken language in which a change in the meaning of a word can result from a change in a phoneme. For example, the sounds of *r, b,* and *c* are all phonemes because they all produce words that have different meaning when added to the front of the sounds represented by *-at*. A rat is different from a bat, which is different from a cat. A grapheme is simply the written representation of a phoneme. Often sounds are represented by a single letter, especially the consonants. Some sounds are represented by more than one written letter and at times by different combinations of letters. The long-O sound, for example, is represented by several spellings as seen in the words *note, boat, so*, and *know*. This does not mean, of course, that this procedure should be taught to young children. Many preschool children have difficulty learning and studying such linguistic units despite the fact thay they use them constantly in oral language (Kolinsky 1986; Lundberg, Frost, and Peterson 1988).

Phono-grapho, or sound to letter, correspondence is the relationship between a phoneme and its graphic representations. The sound of *s* is found in the words *sit, city*, and *grass*. It is a one-way relationship. The relationship cannot be reversed. This relationship is also true of grapho-phono, or letter to sound, correspondence.

Phonology by itself is not sufficient to learn to read. A knowledge of semantics, syntactics, and pragmatics is also necessary. In addition, phonology focused solely on letters is also insufficient as a solitary read-

FIGURE 8-9 There are many social contexts in which children can use language with peers and adults.

ing skill. Young learners need to become aware of syllabication, spelling patterns, and concepts about print as well.

PRAGMATICS

A most fascinating component of language is referred to as pragmatics. This is the study of meaning in language as it is influenced by the social, cultural, or intentional contexts in which the language is used. Each of these factors has an effect on the meaning of a communication that ranges from the subtle to the profound.

Social Context

The social context refers to factors present in the environment in which the communication takes place. The language used in a classroom conversation is different than the language used on the playground. The language used when tucking a child in for a nap is different than the language used when we see a child about to wander into a busy street. Relationships exist between language users in each of these environments. The language we choose to use in each of these is influenced by these social relationships.

Each language user in the social context acts with certain assumptions about the other's age, interests, motivations, and so on. This is true for both the message giver and the audience. A second variable is the

FIGURE 8-8 The child who wrote this proclaims, "I know my A - B - C's."

FIGURE 8-10 Children are continually learning language from their environment.

opportunity to respond. In oral language, there is a give and take throughout the conversation. In written language, the writer controls the direction of the message throughout the text. It is only at the end of the written text that the reader has an opportunity to respond. Also within the social context is the factor of the cohesion of the message. This refers to the relationship of one part of the message to other parts. In oral language, a speaker has the opportunity to provide elaboration, define terms that seem puzzling, and sequence an explanation in another way whenever a listener seems to need this type of clarification. In writing, forms such as the friendly letter help to provide cohesiveness to the message.

Cultural Context

The cultural context refers to factors within the social group to which the language user belongs. Children from financially impoverished backgrounds have different experiences from those of children from privileged backgrounds. Children from diverse ethnic backgrounds possess language that is influenced by those backgrounds. The culture of the Hopi Indians is different from the Hispanic culture. The culture of the African American is different from the culture of Americans of European backgrounds. The

way these cultures influence the language of the user provides a richness and diversity in the classroom that contributes to the educational and language growth of all.

Within most cultural contexts, children develop many understandings about language, reading, and writing at an early age. They develop an understanding that there are such things as books, that reading is important, and that stories are enjoyable. They observe people talking and reading as a regular part of daily life. They see that people use reading to get meaning and that fairy tales are fun. As they share stories within their culture, they build a wider range of schemata. They recall information previously learned and add new information to it.

Intentional Context

The intentional context refers to factors related to the goals and purposes of language users. Most young children quickly learn that language can be used as a tool for meeting their needs and wants. At an early age, children learn to use language with the intention of having something happen. A child who has fallen down and wants to be comforted has different needs from those of a child who has played all morning and is hungry for lunch. They tend to use

FIGURE 8-11 The intention of encouraging imagination can be enhanced by interacting with books. *From* The Stupids Step Out, *by Henry Allard, illustrated by James Marshall. Reprinted courtesy of Houghton Mifflin Company, nonexclusive and nontransferable.*

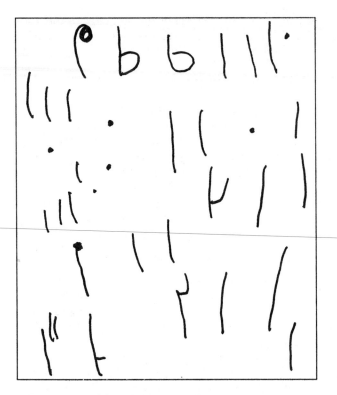

FIGURE 8-12 Although it may not be identifiable, the child who created this may have had a definite intention for it.

different language structures to satisfy these needs. The language structures may be reinforced by tone of voice, amount of eye contact, and body language. Intentions may be either explicit or implicit. An explicit intention is specifically stated as in "I want to tell you a story." An implicit statement is related to the child's purpose, but is not specifically stated. For example, the child might want you to laugh at the story being told, but not tell you that your laughing is the ultimate intention.

Functions of Language

Closely related to the intentional context, Halliday (1975) identifies seven functions of language. Children who tend to be shy may be limited in their functional use of language. That is, they may not be able to use the powers of language to effect changes in their situation in order to fulfill their needs and de-

sires. Halliday (1975) identifies the functions of language as:

Instrumental—I want
Regulatory—Do as I tell you
Interactional—Me and you
Personal—Here I come
Heuristic (problem solving)—Tell me why
Imaginative—Let's pretend
Informative—I've got something to tell you (p. 6)

SUMMARY

Language enables people to fulfill a variety of needs and wants. Even when people lack basic reading and writing skills, they are often able to deal with their surroundings through the use of oral language. By making use of their tacit understanding of language components, they are able to both send and receive meaningful communications. The most critical components, and those that interact with each other in general language use, are semantics, syntactics, phonology, and pragmatics.

Semantics is the study of the meaning of words. In this unit, it was seen that a single concept may have a number of words and referents relating to it. In addition, the context in which an unfamiliar word is used can supply clues as to the meaning of that word. These clues are referred to as semantic cues. They are helpful to users of both oral and written language.

Schema theory plays an important role in semantics. As children learn schemata, the sequences and little dramas that represent many life experiences, they become better able to derive meaning from communications. One type of schema, the story grammar, is particularly helpful. A story grammar is a general format in which most stories unfold and develop. A story grammar provides a framework to which information from a story can be related and rendered meaningful.

Syntactics is the study of the grammatical relationships and functions of word order in sentences. Like semantics, a knowledge of syntactics can aid the language user in deriving meaning from a text. Through syntactics, a language user can make predictions of the part of speech (e.g., noun, verb, adjective) where an unfamiliar word in a sentence might be. It is noted that children know many syntactic rules intuitively. Young children develop the ability to speak in grammatically correct sentences without having been taught any of the formal rules of syntax. In addition, the big books associated with whole language programs use this innate knowledge of syntax as a tool to enable the young child to more easily learn to read.

Phonology is the study of speech sounds. Many traditional early reading programs rely on the study of phonics as the sole or major tool for teaching young children to read. While the ability to make sound-symbol correspondences is a useful tool for young learners, it is not sufficient for teaching children to become effective readers. Phonics must be integrated with other language components in order for the child to become an effective reader.

Pragmatics is the study of how language is influenced by social, cultural, and intentional factors. Social factors are related to the environment in which communications take place. Cultural factors are related to the social groups to which the language user belongs. Intentional factors are related to the purpose for which the individual is using language.

Questions and Activities for Review and Discussion

Multiple Choice

1. Semantics refers to the study of
    a. speech sounds.
    b. meaning.
    c. structure.
    d. letters.

2. Evidence, based on meaning, that enables us to identify an unknown written word is known as a
    a. feature of orthography.
    b. sound-symbol correspondence.
    c. syntactic structure.
    d. semantic cue.

3. A syntactic cue is evidence, used to identify an unknown word, that has been derived from
    a. rules and patterns of language.
    b. the meanings of a word.
    c. the sounds of the letters in a word.
    d. all of the above

4. The use of repeated syntactic patterns makes some books for children
    a. more predictable.
    b. less understandable.
    c. more complex.
    d. less enjoyable.

5. Phonic cues provide readers with information about
    a. the meanings of unfamiliar words.
    b. the speech sounds of letters.
    c. the social context of a story.
    d. the structure of a word.

6. The smallest linguistic unit in spoken language in which a change can result in a variation of meaning is a
   a. grapheme.
   b. phoneme.
   c. grapho-phonic rule.
   d. phonological element.
7. The role played by social, cultural, and intentional factors in reading is referred to as
   a. semantics.
   b. phonology.
   c. syntactics.
   d. pragmatics.

True or False

T   F   1. Language is primarily composed of a set of discrete skills to be learned.
T   F   2. The components of language can effectively interact only in whole pieces of text.
T   F   3. A schema is similar to a concept, but it has wider applicability.
T   F   4. The shorter the sentence, the more efficient syntactic cues become.
T   F   5. Wanting a child to grasp the theme of a story being read is an intentional factor.

Essay and Discussion

1. Describe what is meant by schema theory and explain why it is useful for a language user.
2. Describe the key components of a schema for buying an article of clothing in a store.
3. Generate several examples of sentences in which syntax plays a role in helping the reader identify an unknown word. Generate several examples of sentences in which it does not play a significant role.
4. Describe the relationship between phonemes and graphemes.
5. Explain how the culture of the reader/listener can effect the meaning of a communication.

References

Bartlett, F. 1932. *Remembering.* Cambridge, Mass.: Harvard University Press.

Carnine, D., and B.D. Kinder. 1985. Teaching low-performing students to apply generative and schema strategies to narrative and expository materials. *Remedial and Special Education* 6: 20–30.

Halliday, M.A.K. 1975. *Learning how to mean.* New York: Elsevier.

Hasenstab, M.S., and J. Laughton. 1982. *Reading, writing and the exceptional child.* Rockville, Md.: Aspen.

Idol, L. 1987. Group story mapping: A comprehension strategy for both skilled and unskilled readers. *Journal of Learning Disabilities* 20: 196–205.

Kintsch, W., and E. Greene. 1978. The role of culture-specific schemata in the comprehension and recall of stories. *Discourse Processes* 1: 1–13.

Kolinsky, R. 1986. L'emergence des habiletes metalinguistiques. *Cahiers de Psychologique Cognitive* 6: 379–404.

Lundberg, I., J. Frost, and O. Peterson. 1988. Effects of an extensive program for stimulating phonological awareness in preschool children. *Reading Research Quarterly* 23: 263–284.

Pearson, P.D., and D.D. Johnson. 1978. *Teaching reading comprehension.* New York: Holt, Rinehart and Winston.

Pearson, P.D., and R. Spiro. 1980. Toward a theory of reading comprehension instruction. *Topics in Language Disorders* 1: 71–88.

Piaget, J. 1952. *The child's concept of number.* New York: W. W. Norton.

Piper, W. 1930. *The little engine that could.* New York: Platt & Munk.

Ryan, E.B., and E.J. Short. 1984. Metacognitive differences between skilled and less skilled readers: Remediating deficits through story grammars and attribution training. *Journal of Educational Psychology* 76: 225–235.

UNIT 9

The Importance of Play

U NIT GOALS

After completing this unit, the reader should:

- know what constitutes the concept of play.
- develop a knowledge of the developmental stages of play.
- understand the relationship that exists between language development and play.
- be aware of the benefits of play to the overall development of the child.
- know the potential effects of different factors that may or may not exist in the play environment.
- understand how to encourage play activities that are likely to stimulate language development.
- understand how to integrate literacy activities within play.

PREVIEW

Almost from the very moment of birth, children seem to involve themselves in play activities. Play is often described as the business of childhood. The fact that it is a self-initiated activity in which children are motivated to engage over long periods of time makes it a rich territory for language development activities.

As children grow older, their play becomes more complex. Rules are added to play activities through language interactions with others, and language itself takes on increasing importance as one of the aspects of play. As children grow into adults, play often continues, but in substantially different forms. Play becomes integrated with thinking, problem solving, social interaction, and many of the recreational aspects

of life. These activities might include art, music, movies, dance, and both informal and organized sports.

Children's play has been studied for many decades. Various stages have been identified, challenged, verified, and questioned. A substantial body of research has been conducted on the play of young children. Among the major ideas addressed in this unit are developmental theories of play, the importance of play in child development, the influence of the environment on play, and the relationship between literacy and play.

INTRODUCTION

Play may be described as the work of childhood. This is true not in the literal sense, but in a more

FIGURE 9-1 Play is the predominant activity in the lives of children.

symbolic sense. Since work may be seen more as something people have to do, play can be viewed as something fundamentally different because it is something most people freely choose to do. This does not mean, of course, that all work is tedious and all play is enjoyable. There is much work, particularly in the realm of early childhood education, that has a play component to it and is thoroughly enjoyable for children. On the other hand, some types of play require physical exertion and serious mental effort.

For children, play is the predominant activity of life. The very young child looking up from the crib at a colorful mobile is playing. The slightly older child building with blocks is at play. The preschoolers pretending that their tricycles are police cars and fire engines are at play. The child on a scout camping trip, the teenager going to a high school dance, and the adult involved in a game of bridge or bowling are all playing. It is evident that the social aspects of play become more complex and sophisticated as people grow older.

This unit provides an understanding of the stages of play through which children progress. The stages occur within a range of ages, but they often appear in a fairly predictable pattern. Because play is such a predominant activity of childhood, it is a natural place to enhance the development of language and literacy. There is a substantial amount of research on the activities and benefits of using play environments as

places to encourage language. While children initiate much of the activity of play, adults can provide models and structures that enable the play environment to become a more effective place for language development. The active roles adults can take are described.

UNDERSTANDING PLAY

Play springs from a number of different needs of children and has a variety of purposes, depending on the perspective taken. Behaviorists, Freudians, and developmentalists all view these factors somewhat differently. One of the longest held views on the rationale for children's play is that it is engaged in for the purpose of releasing excess energy. This view, first proposed by Spencer (1878), fit well with the nineteenth-century view of children as little more than wild animals and savages in need of taming.

A Freudian perspective holds that the purpose of play is to enable children to relieve emotions such as frustration, anger, hostility, and aggression (Morrison 1990). Freudians would tend not to introduce adult involvement into children's play since its primary purpose is therapeutic.

Behaviorists tend to focus on play based on the motivations of the child. They contend that arousal control suggests that organisms function best with a moderate amount of stimulation in the environment. When uncertainty is created by a lack of stimulation, the organism seeks more stimulation through an exploration of the environment. This exploration, designed to return the organism to a comfort level of arousal, is termed play behavior (Berlyne 1960; Christie and Johnsen 1983).

Definition of Play

A more developmentally appropriate and defensible definition of play includes the concept of the interrelationship between play and learning. Morrison (1988) defines play simply as self-motivated activity through which children learn. This view has a long history leading up to it. Karl Groos (1901), a pioneer in the study of children's games, felt that play had a great deal of importance for the development of the individual, preparing him or her for the tasks of life. Adler (1927) believed that play and games, beyond all else, serve as communal exercises that enable children to satisfy their social feelings. More recently, Bruner (1966) described games as artificial but powerful representations of reality. He claims that games involve children both in understanding language and in social organizations of the world.

Boundaries of Play

A view of play that includes learning, language, and social structure requires some specific parameters to separate it from other human activities. Johnson, Christie, and Yawkey (1987) identify five characteristic activities that constitute play. First, play activities are separated from other daily activities in such a way that actions are performed differently in play situations than in nonplay situations. Second, the motivation for play emanates from the child rather than from people or forces outside of the child. Children choose to play rather than have an adult direct them to engage in play. Third, the child's focus is primarily on the activity rather than on the end product or goal of the activity. Children focus on the process of molding clay, for example, as opposed to completing a sculpture within a set amount of time. Fourth, free choice is involved concerning the specific activity. If children wish to play a game rather than building with blocks, they do so. Fifth, pleasure with the activity is an intrinsic part of the situation. If children do not enjoy the activity they are involved in, it cannot be described as play. Arn (1986) extends these characteristics by viewing play, especially pretend play, as a process of communication. According to Arn, this type of play consists of two parts: what children say and the context of the play. The context of the play is the structure of the play situation in which children can use language to relate to one another.

STAGES OF PLAY

A number of models categorize the stages of play that children go through from birth through their school years. The model of stages developed by Parten (1932) is by far the most widely known and used by educators. She developed the stages based upon extensive observations of preschool children engaged in play activities. While ages can be applied to each of the stages, their can be considerable overlap between ages and stages. This can be due either to

FIGURE 9-2 Books can help connect play to learning by providing stories to recreate at play time. *Reprinted courtesy of Houghton Mifflin Company, nonexclusive and nontransferable.*

the rate of development of the child or the fact that some types of earlier play are engaged in long after the onset of later stages of play. Each of Parten's (1932) six stages is described with the approximate ages at which they are typically observed.

Stage 1: Unoccupied Behavior

Generally, children who are observed engaging in unoccupied behavior are under three-and-one-half years old and are usually the least talkative children. The children may not appear to be playing at all. Rather, they might simply gaze about the room or playground at whatever happens to be of interest at the moment. Children engaged in unoccupied behavior include those who, when there is nothing of interest occurring, play with their bodies, stand around doing nothing, repeatedly get on and off chairs, follow a teacher or parent around the room, or simply sit and gaze around at nothing in particular. Unoccupied behavior is usually seen in children from birth to two years of age. Usually little or no language or interaction is observed with this type of play.

Stage 2: Onlooker

Children who spend time watching other children or groups of children playing are engaged in onlooker play. Children may engage in some communication with those who are playing, but do not become involved in the activity itself. Rather, they might give suggestions, ask questions about the activity, or simply talk about unrelated topics. This type of play is distinguished from unoccupied behavior because children are focused on an activity rather than engaging with the environment in a frequently shifting, random manner. Onlookers station themselves within speaking distance of the activity and engage in some communication with the participants in a play activity. Onlooker play is usually seen in children aged two years and older.

Stage 3: Solitary Play

Children engaged in solitary play are focused on a specific activity. While they may play within speaking distance of other children, they make no attempt to communicate with those children. Additionally, they choose toys, games, or activities that have no relationship to those used by other children. Children choosing their own individual play activities at playtime, who make no attempt to communicate with or influence others around them, are said to be engaged in solitary play. Children tend to engage in solitary play at age two-and-one-half years and older.

Stage 4: Parallel Play

Closely related to solitary play is parallel play. In fact, due to the nature of the two types of play, the line between them often seems blurred in natural play situations. Children engaged in parallel play are engaged in independent activities. However, they choose activities that naturally bring them into the proximity of other children. For example, a number of children might be playing in the sandbox on the playground. The choice they have made, playing in the sandbox, has brought them into proximity with other children engaged in the very same activity. However, they play in the sand as they see fit. There is no attempt to communicate with other children, to influence the play activities of others, or to control the comings and goings of others into the area. Parallel play is not solitary because it occurs within a

FIGURE 9-3 Parallel play

group. On the other hand, it is independent play due to the lack of communication and influence with others in the group. In short, children play alongside of other children rather than with other children. The motivations of children for choosing parallel play over solitary play cannot be observed. The fact that such a choice was made designates parallel play as a more socialized form of play. Parallel play is usually first observed in two-and-one-half- to three-and-one-half-year-old children.

Stage 5: Associative Play

In associative play, children play with others. Their language is focused on the common activity in such a way that it is clear that the interest is centered more on the associations rather than the activity. A large amount of conversation about the common activity is heard from the group. For this reason, the interests of the individual group members maintain priority over the interests of the group. For example, if someone suggests that a sand castle be built, each child makes an individual sand castle rather than focus on one sand castle constructed by the group. In this type

FIGURE 9-4 A sandbox can provide an environment that encourages many levels of play.

of play, we may observe such things as sharing of materials, participation in trains or boats, and some attempts to control entry into and exit from the group. While all group members engage in similar or identical activities, there is no organizational structure to the group that suggests that everyone is working toward a common goal or product. The type of play is usually observed in children between three-and-one-half and four- and-one-half years old. It continues throughout childhood.

Stage 6: Cooperative Play

The most distinguishing factor between associative and cooperative play is that in the latter the goal of the group takes priority over individual interests. In cooperative play, the group is structured around a competitive goal, the attainment of some product, the playing of a team game, or the dramatization of a story or schema. Leaders emerge from within the group, and all group members share a sense of belonging or not belonging to the group. The very focus of the group necessitates that each member strive cooperatively within a designated role. The effort of each child is a piece of the coordinated effort of the group. As an example, consider a group of children dramatizing a restaurant schema. Some children may be assigned to make food for the meal out of modeling clay, others to cook the food, and still others to play the roles of hosts and customers. Children will comment on and criticize each other for their effectiveness or failure in fulfilling their roles. Some children are excluded from the activity by the leaders,

while those within the group are not permitted to leave. This type of play is often observed in children aged four-and-one-half years and older.

Play Norms

When Parten (1932) conducted her original study she developed norms coinciding with the ages at which children engage in the various types of play. She developed these norms based upon many hours of observation of children over the course of several months. A replication of Parten's research by Barnes (1971) resulted in findings that differed somewhat from those of Parten. Barnes found that children entering kindergarten and first grade were much less socially skillful than were the children observed by Parten nearly forty years earlier. He found children less able to engage in associative and cooperative play than did Parten.

Barnes (1971) suggested a number of explanations for the changes he observed in the social skills of young children. One possible reason cited is that modern preschool children spend much more time engaged with television and other mass media. This replaces past practices that involved children spending more time interacting through language and playing with peers. Modern toys were often cited as far more conducive to solitary play compared to the simpler, more symbolic toys of the past. Modern families tend to be smaller, thus providing fewer siblings with whom to interact and play. Finally, Barnes sug-

FIGURE 9-5 Conversation is common in associative play.

gests that contemporary parents provide more reinforcement to their children for engaging in independent activities than did parents in the past. In summary, Barnes concluded that times change. As the values and beliefs of society change, children's behaviors reflect those changes.

Teachers must exercise caution when using norms of any type with young children. While the investigations by Parten and Barnes provide valuable information about the play behaviors of children, they do not take into account many of the underlying values and attitudes that might drive those play choices and behaviors. It seems clear that as children get older they tend to interact more with peers and less with adults. Their play does seem to follow certain stages that may be influenced by such factors as physical and cognitive development. Other variables, however, may also influence the interactions of young children. These include the cultural and economic backgrounds of children as well as such factors as altruism and moral strength. Striking examples of these are found in the strengthening of peer relationships in the extreme circumstances of World War II concentration camps. Writers of children's literature such as Avi and Schleyer, who use historical events as the basis for some of their writing, are also aware of these environmental factors. Robert Coles, who has written about the moral fortitude of very young black children who have personally faced acts of outrageous racism, clearly illustrates the potential of children to be influenced by their own sense of ethics within their environments (Coles 1967).

Environmental Influences

Both obvious and subtle environmental factors can have an effect on the play behaviors of children. The type of toys, variety of equipment, peer group, and location of the play area can all have an effect on the play and language development of children. As noted above, the kinds of toys available at different times in history may have a critical influence on the play behaviors of children.

With the youngest children, teachers should carefully consider the play environment. Caruso (1988) offers three guidelines for developing and maintaining an appropriate play environment. First, the area should be open with numerous materials visible and

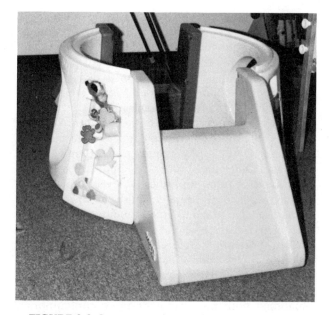

FIGURE 9-6 Common equipment found in a play area.

accessible to the children. Second, adults should provide guidance so that there is an appropriate match between the developmental age of the children and the toys and materials they select. Third, teachers should spend a considerable amount of time at the children's level. In this way, caregivers can guide and encourage children to help enhance their growing play skills.

Since our focus on play is related to language, it makes sense to consider the peers with whom children have an opportunity to interact. Educators have recognized the important role peers play in the development of social and cognitive skills (Hartup 1983; Shantz 1983). They have also come to recognize the value of peers in helping children overcome social and cognitive deficiencies (Cole 1986; Furman, Rahe, and Hartup 1979; Strain 1977).

Most of the studies on peer relationships within play environments focus on situations in which the children are the same age. This is probably partly because education has a tendency to segregate children based on age, sex, and disability. This is ironic, since most children grow up in families and communities where their peer groups are quite diverse (Ellis, Rogoff, and Cromer 1981). Diverse peer groups offer unique advantages. Young children like to imitate older children (Peifer 1972). Older children find it rewarding to be imitated by younger children (Thelen and Kirkland 1976). Older children also make the necessary speech and language adjustments in order to deal effectively with younger children (Turiel 1969). Mounts and Roopnarine (1987) found that classroom diversity enhances the experiences of all of the children. Younger and less able children tend to engage in more sophisticated forms of play that require more complex use of language. Older and more able children do not discontinue their more sophisticated levels of play when in the presence of younger children. Instead, they adjust their language to accommodate younger children. This has the effect of sharpening the language skills of those older children.

Outdoor play environments are an important extension of indoor classroom learning. However, most studies of children's play have focused on indoor play situations. With the advent of more contemporary playgrounds, teachers might wish to attend to the types of play observed on various types of playgrounds. Hart and Sheehan (1986) compared the physical activities and social interactions observed on both a traditional playground and a contemporary playground. Traditional playgrounds are those containing separate equipment areas for slides, swings, see saws, and climbing bars. Contemporary playgrounds are those that are primarily constructed with sand, concrete, and wooden pillars. Contemporary playgrounds emphasize novel forms and heights in aesthetic arrangements. Such playgrounds often have ramps, poles, automobile tires, swings, and slides incorporated into them. Hart and Sheehan (1986) found that children engaged in less unoccupied, solitary, and onlooker behavior on traditional playgrounds. They cautioned against reading too much into their results. Teachers need to be aware of the potential for differing amounts of verbal interaction as a function of the environment in which the children find themselves.

LANGUAGE AND PLAY

At a very young age, children enjoy and experiment with the sounds of language. Their early language play includes crying, cooing, and babbling. As early as two months old they attend to different voices. By six months they can respond to the tone of a speaker's voice. From one year on, receptive and expressive language grows rapidly.

Age, Language, and Play

In the early stages of development, a child's play tends to be either solitary or with an adult. This early play includes a general alternating of vocalizations and games such as "peek-a-boo" and "so-big." When the child begins to use words, at about one year old, a major milestone is reached. These words or holophrases often stand for sentences expressing such things as requests, commands, protests, and responses. At about eighteen months old, the child begins to use language to express needs and generally understands many words. It is at about this time that symbolic play emerges. The language play enjoyed by the child at this point includes poems, rhymes, fingerplays, and songs.

By two years old, the child is using two-word sentences and is engaged primarily in solitary and parallel play. When children do communicate in play situations it is sometimes a negative interaction. This is possibly because they may have some difficulty communicating, which can cause frustration. While children are able to convey complex concepts (e.g., possession, agent-action), they are still quite egocentric.

At about age three, when children are able to utter more complex sentences, associative and cooperative play become possible. Children gain the ability to use language more dramatically. Their ability to discuss ideas, concepts, and experiences assists their increasing socialization in play. Beyond the age of three, children acquire the ability to use their language to engage in dramatic play and games with an increasingly complex array of rules. Figure 9-9 outlines the ages at which both language and play behaviors typically occur. It is based on the work of Boone (1965), Branston and Dubose (1974), Glazer (1980), Kelly and Parsons (1975), McCandless and Trotter (1977), and Westby (1980).

An important element that relates play to literacy is the growing ability of children to make and use symbols (Dyson 1985). Oral symbols are spoken words and sentences. Visual symbols are written words and sentences. While it is most obvious in the develop-

FIGURE 9-7 This child uses play as a means to investigate the sounds he can make.

studies actually remove the children from the classroom in order to conduct their studies in more sterile laboratory surroundings. In this way, they hope to draw pure conclusions about children and their play. Since children develop and change dramatically over time, teachers should be careful when making generalizations about them based on a few research studies. Since young children are dramatically affected by their surroundings, this warning is more appropriate when experiemental studies are used. In naturalistic observation studies, this is not such a problem if the observer is unobtrusive within the classroom.

Using a naturalistic approach, Weir (1962) and Chukovsky (1971) identified the age of two years as the point in which children begin to engage in three types of extensive play with language. The first type of play deals with sounds. For example, a child may create a string of nonsense syllables together and repeat them in a sequence. The second type of play deals with syntactics. In this play, a child might substitute words from the same grammatical category for another word. The third type of play deals with semantics or meaning. This type of play involves a variety of possibilities in which the original meaning is distorted to create humor. Jokes and puns fall into this category of play. Cazden (1976) suggested that

ment of writing, all literacy development is interwoven with the child's growth as a symbol user and living social being (Vygotsky 1978; Dyson 1986, 1989). As they grow, children are constantly expanding the way they create and use oral and visual language symbols as they learn how and when such symbols are appropriate (Mathews 1984; Wolf and Perry 1989).

Research on Language and Play

Research on play has continued since Parten's original study (1932). Naturalistic research attempts to be primarily a procedure whereby the investigators spend a considerable amount of time observing the children engaged in play. They analyze their observations to develop theories and beliefs about the play of children. Experimental studies are also used to investigate play. Rather than observe, experimental investigators control the environment and the kinds of children in the research study. Many experimental

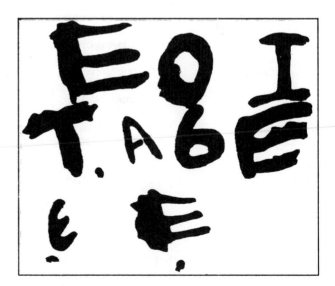

Figure 9-8 These letters were created with paint by a child during play time.

Age	Typical Play Activities	Language Used
1 month	watches mobiles, objects	cries
2 months	watches hands	attends to voice
3 months		alternating vocalizations
4 months	motor: hits, waves	cooing
5–7 months	uses toys: soft toys, music boxes, rattles, undoes things	responds to tone of voice, babbles
8–9 months	object permanence, gets wanted things	understands: No–No, Where's Daddy?
10–11 months	some appropriate use of toys, peek–a–boo	follows simple commands
1 year	trial and error toy use, toys: pots and pans, push and pull toys, dolls, clay, sandbox, etc.	word (holophrases), jargon, expresses (command, greeting, protest, etc.)
1-1/2 years	pretend play (e.g., eat and drink), uses dolls, combines toys	enjoys listening to words
2 years	represents experience—plays house, difficulty sharing	two–word sentences (telegraphic), 270-word vocabulary
2-1/2 years	represents more (store, doctor), toys (puzzles, wagons, trucks, boxes)	phrases, short sentences, uses questions, plurals, possessives
3 years	pretend (unplanned but in sequence), waits, takes turn, tries to conform, dresses up, role plays, toys (tricycles, guns, sorting toys)	understands some concepts (big/little) and prepositions, syntactical speech, tells own experiences
4–7 years	acting, interest in rules, plans ahead, takes turn, participates in groups, toys (puzzles, cars, costumes)	understands some major language rules, rhyming
7 years	pretends, collects, organized sports	adult structures

FIGURE 9-9 Age, play, and language

this type of play with language has two benefits. First, it allows children to practice and master different aspects of language. Second, it expands their knowledge about language. Through this play, children learn that they can use, misuse, and distort the rules and structures about language.

As noted in Figure 9-9, as children grow older they begin to engage in what is called socio-dramatic play.

Figure 9-10 This piece, "Jeremy and the Trucks," was created by a child during play time.

This is play in which children act out an event they have experienced or learned from some source or that they created themselves. It may be a re-creation of a story from a book that was read to them. Observational studies have supported this type of play as providing practice for language skills (Garvey 1974, 1979). Garvey observed two types of language being used by children engaged in socio-dramatic play. The first type was the language used by children in the roles they had undertaken. A child pretending to be a cowboy or a soldier acted and talked in a manner appropriate to the role. The second type of language use involved the structuring of the dramatic situation. This included the use of language for planning a story sequence, assigning roles to various children, and seeking children to cooperate in the activity.

Experimental studies have been conducted with socio-dramatic play to determine if it can lead to greater language achievement. Smilansky (1968), working with lower socioeconomic status Israeli children, concluded that play training led to higher quality play as well as gains in verbal fluency. Lovinger (1974) replicated Smilansky's study using children from the United States. She concluded that play training produced gains in the number of words children used in free play. Collier (1979) investigated Cazden's (1976) conclusion that language play leads to increased knowledge about how language works. The results

indicated that children could increase this skill by becoming engaged in language play. According to Christie and Johnsen (1983), however, flaws in the way each of these studies was conducted prevents acceptance of their findings. Among the flaws noted were the presence in the room of adults interacting with children and the lack of sufficient control groups. Control groups are groups of children similar to the children being studied. Control groups, however, are not given the special instruction provided to the other children such as how to play word games.

Play in which stories were reenacted was studied by Yawkey (1980). Young children were divided into two groups. While both groups were read a story, only one group was encouraged to act out the story following the reading. A test designed to measure the children's comprehension of the story was used at the completion of the experiement. The findings indicated that the group that acted out the story had a better understanding of the story than the group that had only listened to the story. Christie and Johnsen (1983) suggest that the results from such a brief investigation were not conclusive enough to warrant acceptance. They found that it is quite difficult to use experimental research methods with young children who perhaps do not see any value in conforming to the strict guidelines required by such research.

Story re-enactment requires children to use the same skills they use in sociodramatic play such as the ability to cooperate in shared make-believe (Bretherton 1984). Ishee and Goldhaber (1990) identify seven steps in a continuum of story re-enactment:

FIGURE 9-11 A box of old clothes can provide props for sociodramatic play.

observer, walk on, mime, mime plus, actor, actor/author, and narrator. Each of the steps builds on the one before it. An observer may occasionally glance at children involved in the story. The walk on moves into the action but makes no gestures and uses no language. A mime follows the model of others in making gestures appropriate to the story. A mime plus follows the model of others in both gestures and language. An actor makes gestures and uses dialogue with only rare prompts. An actor/author initiates and exhibits some control over the story. A narrator coordinates the entire story re-enactment with either toys or children.

As classrooms have increased the quantity and quality of reading and writing opportunities for young children, research indicates that children in those classrooms readily include material from that environment into their play (Christie 1990; Hall, May, Moores, Shearer, and Williams 1987; Isenberg and Jacob 1983; Roskos, 1988; Schrader 1989). Christie (1990) describes a number of the situations in which this has occurred. For example, in the housekeeping centers of early childhood programs, children have been observed writing notes to family members, using the "TV Guide" to look up programs, reading stories to dolls, reading recipes to make meals with toy foods, and glancing at newspapers. The observations do not end at the housekeeping center. Other children have been observed acting out doctor's office routines, banking procedures, and restaurant schemas.

PROMOTING LITERACY-BASED PLAY

According to Christie (1990), dramatic play does not emerge spontaneously. Children from lower socioeconomic status backgrounds tend to seldom engage in dramatic play situations without some type of intervention program (Dansky 1980; Saltz, Dixon, and Johnson 1977; Smilansky 1968). Even when children do engage in dramatic play without direction, it does not necessarily mean that rich language, the recreation of stories, and literacy activities will be included in that play without the proper equipment (Hall, May, Moores, Shearer, and Williams 1987). Christie (1990) suggests that in order to take full ad-

vantage of dramatic play activity for literacy development, the variables of setting, time allocation, and teacher involvement must be considered.

Settings

An absolute must for any nursery school, preschool, or daycare center is a housekeeping corner or center. This center should include an abundance of props that might be found in a typical home. Among the preferred items are replicas of kitchen furniture and appliances, dishes, utensils, dolls, doll accessories, telephones, ironing boards, brooms, baby carriages, and cradles (Johnson, Christie and Yawkey 1987). If literacy is going to be encouraged in such centers, it is important that reading and writing materials that might be found in the home be included in the housekeeping center. Among the preferred materials are pens, pencils, note pads, diaries, cookbooks, telephone books, picture books, magazines, catalogs, and newspapers (Christie 1990). These materials have been found to make it more likely that reading and writing will be incorporated into children's play (Hall, May, Moores, Shearer, and Williams 1987).

In addition to the housekeeping center, other centers with themes can also be set up in such a way that literacy activities are likely to result. Christie (1990) suggests a restaurant, post office, bank, grocery store, and doctor's office as excellent choices for additional centers. A doctor's office could be set up with a waiting area, an examination area, and an office area for paying bills. The waiting area could contain books and magazines related to visits to a doctor's office. The examination area could contain an alphabet eye chart, forms for writing prescriptions, and toy doctor's tools. The office area could contain a variety of pens, pencils, forms, and bills.

Morrow and Rand (1991) suggest a number of possibilities for centers that could be used in early childhood classrooms. A fast food restaurant, ice cream parlor, or bakery could be equipped with order pads, menus, a cash register, recipes, and lists of products. A post office might include all of the items necessary for children mailing letters. It might include paper, envelopes, stamps, lists of addresses, cash register, scale, and mailboxes. Morrow and Rand suggest some general guidelines for encouraging literacy activities in centers. First, reading and writing materials likely to

FIGURE 9-12 An animal center provides play opportunities.

stimulate literacy should be included in the center. This might include different sizes and types of paper, pencils, pens, markers, crayons, books, magazines, and newspapers. Second, materials should be organized in clearly labeled boxes or bins so that they can be easily recognized and put away. Third, teachers should model possible uses of the materials, suggest additional possibilities, and change the materials from time to time. Fourth, all levels of literacy development must be accepted and recognized as legitimate. Fifth, anecdotal records, observations, and examples of children's work should be kept to provide information for assessment (Morrow 1989; Schickedanz 1986). Morrow and Rand's (1991) reseach on these steps has provided support for their effectiveness.

Those who have successfully used such centers recommend introducing them one at a time and using them for a period of several weeks (Woodward 1984). At the end of that time, the center can usually be transformed into another center by using some of the materials and props in the new center. Woodward (1984) also suggests locating the centers near each other. In this way dramatic play can be carried out between centers. For example, a sick child might be brought from the housekeeping center to the doctor's office.

Time

It takes time to play. Dramatic play, in which children are acting out rich, elaborate schemas, takes even more time. Children need time to decide what the activity will be, who shall play which roles, how to include additional children who want to participate, and how to handle situations in which there are not enough children to fill all of the roles. If the play period comes to an end before the action can be played out, children are sent the message that less sophisticated forms of play that require less time, less imagination, and less language are those that meet the expectations of adults.

Research has shown that at the early childhood level, children are much more likely to engage in sustained dramatic play if play periods are longer rather than shorter. Christie, Johnsen, and Peckover (1981) suggest that such play periods should be for at least thirty minutes. Caution, of course, should be used when applying an arbitrary number of minutes to a play period. The important point to remember is that there are important social and language benefits to extended play periods. If that type of schedule is not in place, there should be an effort to arrange for such time periods. If shorter periods are currently scheduled throughout the day, they can be combined to provide longer periods of time. As children get older, there is a tendency for schools to decrease the number and length of play periods. When this occurs, it might be worthwhile to examine the curriculum to determine what can be combined, adapted, or omitted. As play is so critical for children's language, social, and overall growth, it would be difficult to justify a schedule that does not include enough time for children to play.

Teacher Involvement

Most of us have observed children at play. Some children seem to be constantly in the middle of the activity. Some are always involved on the periphery. Finally, some children, for a number of reasons, always seem to be on the outside of the play situation. Traditionally, teachers have kept their involvement in children's play confined to a custodial role. They supervised the group to insure the safety of the children, but did not participate in the play situation. An increasing body of research has suggested that appropriate teacher involvement is beneficial to the children in the play situation (Christie 1983; Smilansky 1968). The involvement helps outsiders become involved, helps insiders construct more elaborate dramatizations, and helps all children to incorporate literacy into the play.

The least intrusive form of teacher involvement described by Christie (1990) is observation. This is more than watching the children in order to ensure that no one gets hurt. It is a closer kind of activity in which the teacher both sends and receives messages. By providing attention and close observation, the teacher is telling the children that their play is both interesting and important. It can also help the teacher gather information to better understand the literacy development of the children. Observation can help the teacher develop ideas for immediate or future modifications to the centers and also to determine whether more involvement is needed. A number of sources suggest that teacher observation and an assessment of the child's literacy development can occur simultaneously (Goodman, Goodman, and Hood 1989; Morrow 1989; Morrow and Smith 1990). Vukelich and Valentine (1990) conducted an investigation in an early childhood classroom to validate the belief. Based on their study of children during free play periods, they concluded that such an environment both encourages literacy development and provides an excellent context for teachers to assess that development.

Outside and inside intervention are more intensive forms of teacher involvement in the play of children (Christie 1982; Smilansky 1968). With outside intervention, the teacher remains on the outside of the actual play situation, but takes actions designed to have an effect on children who are both inside and outside of the play activity. A child might be encouraged to, or be given a suggestion of how to, become more involved in the play activity. The teacher can provide suggestions to the children in the group that will enable them to vary their activity in order to make it more interesting. Possible literacy-related activities might be suggested when appropriate as well.

Inside intervention involves the teacher entering into the play situation, taking on a role, joining in an episode, and modeling desired behaviors (Christie 1990). For example, if a teacher observes children having difficulty understanding the roles involved in a store center, inside intervention might be appropriate. The teacher might model how to look through the store's sale circular, locate a product on a store

directory, count out the correct amount of play money, or write a check to pay for the item. Research has shown that children both enjoy and accept inside intervention by the teacher in their play activities (Smilansky 1968). In addition, play behaviors such as this are usually generalized and modified to fit new situations (Christie 1990). When using inside intervention, it is important for the teacher not to dominate the activity. Once the purpose for the inside intervention has been addressed, the teacher can withdraw to a less obtrusive type of intervention.

BENEFITS OF PLAY

There are numerous benefits of play. Children engage in different types of play. While each is important, it is clear that language and social interaction occur more frequently at higher levels of play. This does not mean that younger children should be forced to participate in levels of play that are neither appropriate nor meaningful to them. Rather, teachers and parents should be aware of the benefits for children within each type of play. Dramatic play, particularly, offers opportunities for literacy and social enhancement, especially when print becomes an integral part of play (Christie 1990).

Social Benefits

Play has long been found to have a positive social influence on young children. Charlesworth and Hartup (1967) found that social reinforcement was a key factor in providing benefits. Particularly in dramatic play, they observed a high degree of social reinforcement being provided by children to other children. The major impact of this was the continuation of the activity. This continuation was found to occur less frequently in lower levels of play.

The benefits of mixed age groups of young children have also been identified (Mounts and Roopnarine 1987). Children benefit from practicing skills they have just mastered. It gives them confidence and helps them to engage in activities with less effort. Therefore, it is a benefit for both older and younger children who find themselves within the same group. Younger children observe and emulate the activities

FIGURE 9-13 Teachers can extend play periods by encouraging children to recreate their play in pictures and stories.

Language Practice

In language learning, as in most other life activities, skills and strategies that have just been learned are not usually learned at a high level of mastery. Whether it is a young child learning how to wrap a peanut butter sandwich in waxed paper or an adult learning how to hit a tennis ball with a backhand stroke, practice is usually needed after the basics of the procedure have been acquired. The same thing is true for language skills.

Toddlers who have just learned to make the association of a toy truck as a representation of a real truck as well as what trucks do, often spend hours pushing a toy truck around a play area. They make the truck's sound, have the truck move from place to place, and admire their achievement for doing these things. Preschoolers who hear a fairy tale during story time often re-create the story through dramatic play. As they do this they practice dialogue, story plot, and the integration of language, movement, and lit-

of older children. Older children enjoy modeling more sophisticated forms of play for younger children.

Teachers have a responsibility to foster both the social and literacy benefits of play. Children naturally interweave their art, language, and play. Teachers should discuss this with children to help them reflect upon these processes (Dyson 1990). By helping them engage in this reflection, children can become more sensitive to the qualities of life that surround them (Feeney and Moravcik 1987; Rosenblatt and Winner 1989). To do each of these things takes time. Therefore, teachers need to provide time for children to explore their own lives and their social relationships with others (John-Steiner 1985).

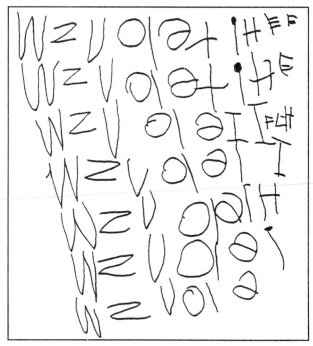

FIGURE 9-14 Early attempts to use language is a form of play.

erature. Each of these practice routines provides a better understanding to the child of how language works.

Language Hypotheses

Children are constantly attempting to determine how language works. To do this, they often make guesses about how words go together and try out those guesses on other language users. Depending on the responses they receive from other children, they are able to determine whether their languages guesses were correct or not.

Children might be observed making attempts at reading, drawing, and writing. Their attempted spelling of the words they use to accompany their illustrations is a form of play. Dramatizing new versions of stories they have heard and creating dramatizations of stories they have made up are often experiments to see if they can make sense. By encouraging these activities and infusing the play of children with literacy materials and activities, adults can increase the benefits of play.

SUMMARY

There have been several interpretations of children's play over the years. Freudians viewed play as a means of dealing with negative emotions. Educators of the Victorian era saw play as an outlet for excess energy, a belief that continues to this day among many. Behaviorists view play as a device for restoring equilibrium to the child.

In this unit, play is seen as an activity that is freely chosen by the student. The youngest of children engage in play. Play is different from the concept of work, although the two may share several characteristics depending on the specific activity involved. Play is seen as an activity in which children can increasingly make use of their growing social and language skills. Since play is the predominant activity of young children it is seen as a potential environment for literacy development.

Children progress through a set of stages or levels of play (Parten 1932). The six levels described here include unoccupied behavior, onlooker play, solitary play, parallel play, associative play, and cooperative play. The latter type is often seen in socio-dramatic activities of young children. Although the levels are hierarchical, children do not go through them in such a sequential fashion that one type of play ends as another emerges. Rather children stretch the boundaries of each level so that there is a substantial overlap between them. Some types of play continue into adulthood.

The environment in which children play is an important factor. In the classroom, teachers should set up theme areas and supply them with props and materials. The inclusion of language-related materials such as books, papers, markers, and pencils can increase the likelihood of literacy activities becoming a part of the play. Theme areas such as housekeeping, post office, doctor's office, and store comprise a good basic set. In order for children to effectively engage in socio-dramatic play, a sufficient amount of time is required. Outside play areas such as playgrounds enable children to re-create stories that demand more space for movement. Children of different age groups can play together both indoors and outdoors with benefits to each.

The teacher and parent have definite roles in the play of children. The role goes beyond a custodial task aimed at insuring the safety of the children. More attention to the play of children communicates the message that play is both interesting and important. Three levels of adult involvement in play are described. Observation is the least obtrusive. It can be used both for achieving a better understanding of children's development and for assessing the level of literacy development. Outside intervention and inside intervention bring the adult closer to and even within the play activity. Such involvement can influence the integration of literacy activities within the play structure.

Play has many benefits for children. It serves as an environment for increasing social growth. It does this by providing an unstructured opportunity for children to make social connections with other children. It also provides a place for children to practice many of the language skills they have learned, thus assisting children to create a fluency in their use of those language skills. Finally, play provides children with an opportunity to try out new hypotheses about language. It is an environment that can provide children with immediate feedback about the validity of their assumptions concerning language.

Questions and Activities for Review and Discussion

Multiple Choice

1. Freudians might identify the purpose of children's play as an activity for
   a. exploring the environment.
   b. developing language.
   c. getting rid of excess energy.
   d. the release of anger.
2. The motivation for a child to play tends to come from
   a. the child.
   b. parents.
   c. teachers.
   d. toys and games.
3. In parallel play, children can usually be seen
   a. conversing with others.
   b. cooperating in a common project.
   c. playing alongside of others.
   d. dramatizing a story.
4. When older children play in the same area as younger children, the older children usually
   a. adjust the level of language they use.
   b. enjoy being imitated by younger children.
   c. continue to engage in more sophisticated play.
   d. all of the above
5. Language play can involve
   a. the sounds of language.
   b. semantics.
   c. syntactics.
   d. all of the above
6. Socio-dramatic play seems to emerge best if play periods provide a time frame of about
   a. 10 minutes.
   b. 15 minutes.
   c. 30 minutes
   d. 60 minutes.
7. The most intensive form of teacher involvement in children's play is
   a. inside intervention.
   b. outside intervention.
   c. observation.
   d. onlooker behavior.

True or False

   T   F   1. All play is enjoyable, just as all work is tedious.
   T   F   2. Associative play is accompanied by a large amount of conversation.
   T   F   3. Cooperative play is never seen in children younger than five years of age.

T   F   4. Language play allows children to practice and master various aspects of language.

T   F   5. The least intrusive form of teacher involvement is inside intervention.

Essay and Discussion

1. Describe play as a developmental activity in a young child's life.
2. Define Parten's six stages of play.
3. Explain why the ages at which contemporary children engage in certain types of play might differ from those of children who lived at an earlier time.
4. Describe the play and language of a typical four-year-old child based upon the information in this unit. If possible, visit a daycare center or nursery school to verify your description by observing some four-year-old children.
5. Describe the three levels of teacher involvement in children's play as described by Christie.

References

Adler, A. 1927. *Understanding human nature*. Greenwich, Conn.: Fawcett.

Am, E. 1986. Play in the preschool: Some aspects of the role of the adult. *The International Journal of Early Childhood* 18: 2, 90–97.

Barnes, K.E. 1971. Preschool play norms: A replication. *Developmental Psychology* 5: 1, 99–103.

Berlyne, D. 1960. *Conflict, arousal and curiosity*. New York: McGraw-Hill.

Bretherton, I., ed. 1984. *Symbolic play: The development of social understanding*. Orlando: Academic Press.

Boone, D.R. 1965. Infant speech and language development. *Volta Review*, unpaged.

Bronston, M.B., and M.B. Dubose. 1983. Inner language. Paper presented at the annual meeting of the Council for Exceptional Children, New York.

Bruner, J.S. 1966. *Toward a theory of instruction*. Cambridge, Mass.: Harvard University Press.

Caruso, D.A. 1988. Play and learning in infancy: Research and implications. *Young Children* 43: 6, 63–70.

Cazden, C. 1976. Play with language and metalinguistic awareness: One dimension of language experience. In *Play D Its Role in Development and Evolution*, ed. J. Bruner, A. Jolly, and K. Sylva. New York: Basic Books.

Charlesworth, R., and W. Hartup. 1967. Positive social reinforcement in the nursery school peer group. *Child Development* 38: 993–1002.

Christie, J.F. 1990. Dramatic play: A context for meaningful engagements. *The Reading Teacher* 43: 542–545.

Christie, J.F. 1982. Sociodramatic play training. *Young Children* 37: 4, 25–32.

Christie, J.F. 1983. The effects of play training on young children's cognitive performance. *Journal of Educational Research* 76: 326–330.

Christie, J.F., and E.P. Johnsen. 1983. The role of play in social-intellectual development. *Review of Educational Research* 53: 93–115.

Christie, J.F., E.P. Johnsen, and R.B. Peckover. 1988. The effects of play period duration on children's play patterns. *Journal of Research in Childhood Education* 3: 123–131.

Chukovsky, K. 1971. *From two to five.* Los Angeles: University of California Press.

Cole, D. 1986. Facilitating play in children's peer relationships: Are we having fun yet? *American Educational Research Journal* 23: 201–215.

Coles, R. 1967. *Children of crisis: A study of courage and fear* 1. Boston: Atlantic-Little Brown.

Collier, R.G. 1979. Developing language through play. *Elementary School Journal* 80: 89–92.

Dansky, J.L. 1980. Cognitive consequences of sociodramatic play and exploration training for economically disadvantaged preschoolers. *Journal of Child Psychology and Psychiatry* 20: 47–58.

Dyson, A.H. 1986. Transitions and tensions: Interrelationships between the drawing, talking and dictating of young children. *Research in the Teaching of English* 20: 379–409.

Dyson, A.H. 1989. *Multiple worlds of child writers: Friends learning to write.* New York: Teachers College Press, Columbia University.

Dyson, A.H. 1990. Symbol makers, symbol weavers: How children link play, pictures and print. *Young Children* 45: 2, 50–57.

Feeney, S., and E. Moravcik. 1987. A thing of beauty: Aesthetic development in young children. *Young Children* 42: 6, 7–15.

Furman, W., D.F. Rahe, and W.W. Hartup. 1979. Rehabilitation of socially withdrawn preschool children through mixed-age and same-age socialization. *Child Development* 50: 915–922.

Garvey, C. 1979. Communicational controls in social play. In *Play and Learning*, ed. B. Sutton-Smith. New York: Gardner.

Garvey, C. 1974. Some properties of social play. *Merrill-Palmer Quarterly* 20: 163–180.

Glazer, S.M. 1980. *Getting ready to read: Creating readers from birth to six.* Englewood Cliffs, N.J.: Prentice-Hall.

Goodman, K.S., Y.M. Goodman, and W.J. Hood. 1989. *The whole language evaluation book.* Portsmouth, N.H.: Heinemann.

Groos, K. 1901. *The play of man.* New York: Appleton.

Hall, N., E. May, J. Moores, J. Shearer, and S. Williams. 1987. The literate home-corner. In *Parents and Teachers Together*, ed. P.K. Smith. London: Macmillan.

Hart, C.H., and R. Sheehan. 1986. Preschooler's play behavior in outdoor environments: Effects of traditional and contemporary playgrounds. *American Educational Research Journal* 23: 668–678.

Hartup, W.W. 1983. Peer relations. *Handbook of Child Psychology* 4: Socialization, personality and social development. New York: Wiley.

Isenberg, J., and E. Jacob. 1983. Playful literacy activities and learning. (ERIC Document Reproduction Service ED 238 577).

Ishee, N., and J. Goldhaber. 1990. Story re-enactment: Let the play begin! *Young Children* 45: 3, 70–75.

Johnson, J.E., J.F. Christie, and T.D. Yawkey. 1987. *Play and early childhood development.* Glenview, Ill.: Scott Foresman.

John-Steiner, V. 1985. *Notebooks of the mind: Explorations of thinking.* New York: Harper & Row.

Kelly, M., and E. Parsons. 1975. *The mother's almanac.* Garden City, N.Y.: Doubleday.

Lovinger, S.L. 1974. Socio-dramatic play and language development in preschool disadvantaged children. *Psychology in the Schools* 11: 313–320.

Mathews, J. 1984. Children drawing: Are young children really scribbling? In *Early Childhood Development and Care* 17, ed. R. Evans. New York: Gordon & Breach.

McCandless, B.R., and R.J. Trotter. 1977. *Children: Behavior and development.* New York: Holt, Rinehart, & Winston.

Morrison, G.S. 1988. *Education and development of infants toddlers and preschoolers.* Glenview, Ill.: Scott Foresman.

Morrison, G.S. 1990. *The world of child development.* Albany, N.Y.: Delmar Publishers Inc.

Morrow, L.M. 1989. *Literacy development in the early years.* Englewood Cliffs, N.J.: Prentice-Hall.

Morrow, L.M., and M.K. Rand. 1991. Preparing the classroom environment to promote literacy during play. In *Play and Early Literacy,* ed. J.F. Christie. Albany, N.Y.: SUNY Press.

Morrow, L.M., and J.K. Smith. 1990. *Assessment for instruction in early literacy.* Englewood Cliffs, N.J.: Prentice-Hall.

Mounts, N.S., and J.L. Roopnarine. 1987. Social-cognitive play patterns in same-age and mixed-age preschool classrooms. *American Educational Research Journal* 24: 463–476.

Parten, M.B. 1932. Social participation among preschool children. *Journal of Abnormal and Social Psychology* 27: 243–269.

Peifer, M.R. 1972. The effects of varying age-grade status of models on the imitative behaviors of six year-old boys. *Dissertation Abstracts International* 32: 6216A-6217A.

Rosenblatt, E., and E. Winner. 1989. The art of children's drawing. In *Art, Mind and Education: Research from Project Zero,* ed. H. Gardiner and D. Perkins. Urbana, Ill.: University of Illinois Press.

Roskos, K. 1988. Literacy at work in play. *The Reading Teacher* 41: 562–566.

Saltz, E., D. Dixon, and J. Johnson. 1977. Training disadvantaged preschoolers on various fantasy activities: Effects on cognitive functioning and impulse control. *Child Development* 48: 367–380.

Schickedanz, J. 1986. *More than the ABC's: The early stages of reading and writing.* Washington, D.C.: National Association for the Education of Young Children.

Schrader, C.T. 1989. Written language use within the context of young children's symbolic play. *Early Childhood Research Quarterly* 4: 225–244.

Shantz, C. 1983. Social cognition. In *Handbook of Child Psychology* 4, ed. E. M. Hetherington. New York: Wiley.

Smilansky, S. 1968. *The effects of sociodramatic play on disadvantaged preschool children.* New York: Wiley.

Spencer, H. 1878. *The principles of psychology.* London: Appleton.

Strain, P. 1977. An experimental analysis of peer social initiations on the behavior of withdrawn preschool children: Some training and generalization effects. *Journal of Abnormal Child Psychology* 5: 445–455.

Thelen, M.H., and K.S. Kirkland. 1976. On status and being imitated: Effects on reciprocal imitation and attraction. *Journal of Personality and Social Psychology* 33: 691–697.

Turiel, E. 1969. Developmental processes in the child's moral thinking. In *Trends and Issues in Developmental Psychology,* ed. S. Mussen, J. Langer, and M. Covington. New York: Holt, Rinehart, & Winston.

Vukelich, C., and K. Valentine. 1990. A child plays: Two teachers learn. *The Reading Teacher* 44: 342–344.

Vygotsky, L.S. 1978. *Mind in society: The development of higher psychological processes.* Cambridge, Mass.: Harvard University Press.

Weir, R. 1962. *Language in the crib.* The Hague: Mouton.

Westby, C.E. 1980. Assessment of cognitive and language abilities through play. *Language, Speech and Hearing Services in Schools* 6: 154–168.

Wolf, D., and M.D. Perry. 1989. From endpoints to repertoires: Some new conclusions about drawing development. In *Art, Mind and Education: Research from Project Zero,* ed. H. Gardiner and D. Perkins. Urbana, Ill.: University of Illinois Press.

Woodward, C.Y. 1984. Guidelines for facilitating sociodramatic play. *Childhood Education* 60: 172–177.

Yawkey, T.D. 1980. An investigation of imaginative play and aural language development in young children, five, six and seven. In *In Celebration of Play,* ed. P.F. Wilkinson. New York: St. Martin's Press.

UNIT 10

Cooperative Learning

UNIT GOALS

After completing this unit, the reader should:

- develop an understanding of the practices used in cooperative learning.
- understand the basic principles incorporated into any cooperative learning instructional program.
- identify the benefits of using cooperative learning as an instructional procedure with young children.
- recognize the obstacles that sometimes confront the implementation of cooperative learning principles.
- develop a repetoire of cooperative learning activities and strategies to be used with young children.
- identify the teacher's role when cooperative learning is used.

PREVIEW

Cooperative learning has had a long and comprehensive history in the field of education. Cooperative learning procedures have been developed both for general use and for use within specific curriculum areas. Cooperative learning has been used with students of all ages, from the very young to university level classes. It has been used with children of all ability levels and with children from differing cultural and socioeconomic backgrounds. As suggested by its name, cooperative learning involves communication between the participants.

Cooperative learning is particularly appropriate for an integrated language arts curriculum that takes advantage of so much of the natural language of children. By doing so, an integrated language arts program provides many opportunities for children to engage in meaningful social interactions that may require cooperative behaviors. Cooperative learning has long been shown to be an effective tool to facilitate use of social interactions to make learning more effective and enjoyable. In the process, cooperative learning builds interest in language itself. The satisfaction of achieving success through meaningful joint effort also tends to heighten the self-esteem of the children involved.

In this unit, key concepts of cooperative learning

are described. The basic elements found in most co-operative learning models are identified. This includes the role a teacher might assume in the process. In addition, research studies on the cognitive and affective benefits of cooperative learning are shared. The obstacles to the implementation of cooperative learning within organizations are described. Finally, the applications that make cooperative learning beneficial for children are explored.

INTRODUCTION

Most of us have heard or read in the news the lament of personnel managers who cannot find enough of the "right kind of people" to employ. According to the complaint, they are able to find workers who are intelligent enough, but those same potential workers don't seem to possess "people skills." The term *people skills* translates to mean the ability to work together as a team, to motivate others to be productive, and to maintain a team spirit in the workplace. At the same time, evidence suggests that many adults have a difficult time getting along with others or working together. Divorce rates are high, domestic violence is on the rise, and many people abuse drugs as a way to escape modern life. Each of these might be cited as potential evidence.

In actuality, it should come as no surprise that adults often lack the ability to work well together. Schools are traditionally places where individuals are encouraged to achieve all they can according to their ability. Competition pits student against student. Without it ever being mentioned aloud, everyone seems to have an implicit understanding of how the system works to continue a tradition of competition. If one individual goes up, another individual must stay the same or go down. If everybody goes up, someone in charge will change the system in order to reinstate the old order. There are certain accepted facts of life in many schools. Some children are winners. Some are losers. Some are also-rans. The outcome of the competition determines who falls into each category.

This is not to say that competition is bad or evil. Sometimes it is necessary. Used as the sole tool of schooling, however, it creates individuals who cannot cooperate. By the end of high school, graduates have often received thirteen or more years of training on how to survive in a competitive environment. By the end of college, the training has increased to seventeen years. With such a long period of training in a competitive environment, it is no wonder young workers lack the "people skills" needed to work in cooperative situations requiring the mutual support of co-workers.

All of this should not be taken to mean that cooperative learning should be used so that society can be provided with more productive workers. On the contrary, cooperative learning effects are beneficial to the whole person. The ability to work together can help build peer relationships as well as the self-esteem of the individual. In short, the ability to cooperate can help an individual be a better person.

This unit investigates the concept of cooperative learning. As with any idea that has such broad appeal, there are many approaches, types, and conceptualizations of cooperative learning. While there may be differing understandings of the approach, basic principles form a common foundation upon which most of the systems rest. The teacher's role tends to shift depending on the philosophy upon which the model rests, the composition of the class, and the content being addressed. Both the benefits and obstacles of cooperative learning are investigated as well. Finally, a number of cooperative learning activities and practical procedures are described that can effectively and efficiently be put into classroom practice. These should enable the reader to begin to implement cooperative learning in the classroom within an integrated language arts program.

DEFINING COOPERATIVE LEARNING

Most children will spend about thirteen years learning a variety of subjects in elementary and secondary schools. Many will extend their years of learning by attending trade schools, community colleges, and universities. A substantial percentage of children will begin their schooling prior to kindergarten in a variety of childcare settings ranging from informal daycare to structured preschool programs. These individuals will, in short, spend many years in a learning situation. Following all of this "preparation for life," many will enter adulthood facing situations and expectations for which they are not prepared. One of the most obvious of these expectationss is that they be able to work as part of a team structure. Many people, after years of survival in competitive education programs, find themselves facing a world that demands that they get along with others and function as part of a group with a common purpose.

According to Johnson and Johnson (1987b), three distinct teaching procedures can be used to engage groups of children in content learning: competition, individualization, and cooperation. While cooperation as an effective teaching procedure has a tremendous amount of research support (Johnson 1980; Johnson, Johnson, and Maruyama 1983; Johnson, Maruyama, Johnson, Nelson, and Skon 1981), it is the least used of the three approaches. Although content learning in specific disciplines is not the sole focus of early childhood education, it is addressed within the general area of language development. More important, however, is the fact that much of the groundwork that can help children work cooperatively with one another can be introduced, modeled, and reinforced with young children.

Competition

Competition is the predominant teaching/learning procedure used in schools. Although not always stated, there is an implicit assumption that there will be winners and losers. If one child obtains a goal, another child cannot obtain the same goal. This assumption enters a child's life early and pervades virtually all aspects of it. In school, there can only be one winner of the spelling bee, one valedictorian of the class, one student government president, one person with the highest class average, one child with the winning essay, and one line leader. The teacher is the primary source of information, structure, and rewards. Outside of school, competitive sports teams include such sports as baseball, gymnastics, soccer, football, hockey, and basketball. More often than not, the major emphasis is on winning, despite the often heard pronouncements to the contrary.

Several conditions operate in schools that maintain and perpetuate the competitive model. These include rigid and arbitrary grade level standards that children must meet to proceed to the next grade, group-

ing patterns that limit both the more and less able children, and an emphasis on standardized testing. Heterogenous grouping patterns, which comprise a mix of students of differing abilities, are becoming more typical in many schools. While this creates more opportunities for less able students, a highly competitive learning environment may also create new stresses. The less able will be highly unlikely to emerge as consistent winners due to the fact that the odds in such a learning environment are stacked against them. In addition, there is little incentive for more able students to assist the less able students. There is no reward, and it diverts the more able from reaching their goal, which is to be the winner. In addition, children are evaluated based on their achievements compared to the achievements of other children.

Individualization

The individualization model is a system that is also widely used in schools, although not as frequently as the competitive model. With individualization, each child is like a small island. Children strive toward their goals without any reference to other children. Objectives are set for each child to attain based on that child's skills and abilities. Other children may be working on entirely different objectives. With individualized programs, children often work in different work areas and with different materials from one another. The work is paced in accordance with the ability of each individual child. As with the competitive model, the teacher is the source of all information, structure, and rewards. Each child is evaluated based on the attainment of a goal set prior to the beginning of the instruction.

Like competition, individualization is firmly set within elementary and secondary schools. Often, entire programs are identified as individualized programs. Many are in curriculum areas such as reading and mathematics. A great number are federal- and state-funded programs for specialized populations such as the disadvantaged, disabled, gifted, and non-English speaking. State and federal lawmakers place great trust in individualization. The term itself suggests that money will be specifically targeted to the exact needs of the children for whom it is intended.

At the preschool level, the largest individualized

education program is that which serves children with disabilities. Federal laws and regulations specify that each disabled child will be served with a program that is individualized to address the specific needs of that child. Such children are often provided educational services in segregated programs in which all of the children are identified as disabled. Therefore, despite the fact that each child is receiving an individualized program, the fact that it is provided within a seemingly homogenous group often renders one child's program quite similar to the programs of all the other children.

Cooperation

The least used teaching procedure in education is the cooperative model. To be sure, students do need to learn how to participate in competitive situations. Competition with moderation and humor can be fun and motivating. The same is true for an individualized approach. There are certain times, subjects, and students that can be addressed effectively with an individualized approach. Therefore, all three procedures should be included within the repertoire of every teacher working with children.

With the cooperative model, children can reach their goals only when other children around them also achieve their goals. To accomplish these goals, students usually work in small, heterogenous groups in which there is positive interdependence between all of the group members. The teacher serves as a consultant or coordinator to the students as they work together to achieve a goal. All of the members of the groups are winners. All groups can be winners because it is the attainment of the goal, rather than demonstrating superiority over other students, that is the focus of the evaluation. There is an individual accountability because each member of the group must contribute to the task of the group. Unlike competition and individualization, there are ordinarily no structures within schools to maintain or encourage the cooperative model. On the contrary, there are obstacles to making use of such a model in schools. These will be discussed in this unit.

Limits of the Cooperative Model

While the cooperative model can be used to teach children within most curriculum areas, there are lim-

FIGURE 10-1 Sharing with others and helping each other are key elements of cooperative learning.

its to its effectiveness as well. Boring, inconsequential, and irrelevant subject matter does not assume any new value simply because it is taught with a cooperative structure (Sapon-Shevin and Schniedewind 1989/1990). As teachers begin to use the cooperative model it may be just as important to reconsider what is being taught while investigating how to teach it through this new procedure.

Using cooperative learning with other models may not be wholly effective unless a rethinking of how those other models are used takes place. The key to implementing cooperation with competition is to use moderation with the latter approach. In addition, care must be taken not to confuse children when using different models. Children who are asked to help each other at one moment and forbidden to do so the next are rightly justified in their confusion. Children must be part of the process in deciding where to use a cooperative model. They need to be involved in determining why cooperation should be used in one situation but not in another.

Cooperation can be thwarted by the tendency to want to combine it with the competitive model. That is, some may think that by pitting cooperative groups against each other, the best of both worlds will be had. This sends mixed messages to children (Sapon-Shevin and Schniedewind 1989/1990). It also eliminates one of the benefits of cooperative learning: developing an intrinsic sense of the value of working together. In the process, it reinforces a very unhappy message for children: in school there must be winners and there must be losers.

BASIC PRINCIPLES

As with any procedure, cooperative learning is based on a number of principles. Without the teacher understanding these, the implementation not only suffers, but often fails. In cooperative learning, concepts such as interdependence, social interaction, interpersonal skills, group process, and accountability are critical to the overall model. Understanding these concepts enables the teacher to make appropriate decisions when implementing cooperative learning.

Interdependence

The idea of students helping other students for the benefit of all as an expected part of the classroom routine may seem unusual to some students who have never participated in such an experience. Yet that idea is one of the cornerstones of cooperative learning. In order for the group to accomplish something, each member must understand that everybody else in the group must do their part. Let us suppose that a teacher plans to use a cooperative structure with a group of four-year-olds. The goal may be to undertake a craft project that requires a supply of autumn leaves of different colors. To accomplish this, the teacher might lead a group of children on a nature walk to the park. The task on the nature walk might be for one student to collect brown leaves, a second to collect yellow leaves, a third to collect red leaves, and a fourth to collect orange leaves. Each child knows that they all must find enough of each color leaves to do the project; therefore, they have an incentive to help the other children meet the expectations placed on them. In a competitive model, there might be some sort of reward for the child who gathers the most leaves or the one who gathers them the fastest. This would serve as a disincentive toward both helping others and considering the leaf gathering as a group goal with a group process.

The leaf collection example is only one approach to establishing the mutual dependence of group mem-

bers on each other. Joint rewards also encourage interdependence. For example, the group might not be able to make their craft projects unless all of the required colors of leaves are found. Sharing materials is another approach. A joint art project in which the group has one large sheet of paper on which to create one picture is an example of this. Since young children tend to focus on themselves, this can be an area of difficulty. For this reason, assigning roles can reinforce the concept. If the picture is supposed to be a farm scene, one child can be assigned to draw the barn, another the animals, another the farmer on the tractor, and so on. The roles will change depending on the task assigned.

Social Interaction

In order for interdependence to emerge, it is necessary for social interactions to occur. Each individual must understand the roles of each group member. It is through these interactions that much learning occurs as well. Groups should be carefully structured and the activities planned so that the desired social interactions are most likely to occur. Children need to have various types of interactions modeled regularly in order to understand their purpose and usefulness. Among the most important types of interactions are oral summarizing, giving and receiving directions, and relating what is being learned to previous learning (Johnson, Johnson, and Holubec 1986).

In the example of gathering leaves, the teacher and children can provide oral summaries by identifying the roles that each group member has been assigned. Children can be encouraged to give directions to each other that will help those other children accomplish their task. Children who receive those directions and respond positively to the directions can be reinforced for their actions by being told how that will help the group. Relating the task to previous learning can be done through a discussion recalling what leaves from trees look like and how they can be distinguished from twigs, seeds, and bark. Also, identification and review of target colors to be sought can be accomplished through a discussion.

Interpersonal Skills

Young children do not possess interpersonal skills by nature. For that matter, older students often do not possess them either. Many times teachers will try to use learning teams only to discard the process because the students do not seem to be able to work cooperatively. Children must be taught the skills needed to work effectively with others. Teachers need to understand how to teach these skills to children.

If children are going to work together, they need to develop four basic interpersonal social skills (Johnson 1986; Johnson and Johnson 1987a). First, children need to know each other and trust each other. Feelings of competition and distrust must be set aside. Each child needs to understand that the others in the group are working toward the same goal. Second, children need to talk to each other with accuracy and clarity. It is important that messages be clear. Third, children must learn to accept and support one another. All children have different strengths and weaknesses. Children need to understand that in group work it doesn't really matter who is quicker, more clever, or more artistic. They must understand that the goal is a group goal and that all will contribute to it as best they can. The ability to encourage the participation of others is a valuable life skill. Fourth, children need to learn how to resolve differences in ways that are neither negative nor destructive. They need to see that problems can be solved without one child being clearly the winner and the other child the loser.

Group Process

Johnson and Johnson (1989/1990) suggest a series of steps for teaching children the four key interpersonal skills. First, they get to the heart of the matter by clearly stating that children must be motivated to learn the skill by seeing a need to use the skill. The teacher can explain the skill by showing children what it looks like, telling them why it will be more helpful to have the skill than not to have it, and telling them that they will be reinforced for using the skill.

Second, children must learn what the skill is and when to use it. This is done by much teacher modeling. Third, the skill must be practiced again and again. This can be done in both role-playing situations and in real problem-solving situations in the classroom. When this is occurring, it is critical that the teacher provide feedback concerning how well the skills are being used. Fourth, the children must begin

FIGURE 10-2 Children need to learn to talk to others and to support the efforts of others.

to reflect on their ability to use the skills. Periodically, the groups should talk about the skills they are using, the ones they have not been using, and how they can improve how they are using the skills.

Children need to persevere in their attempts to use the skills. They need to go through the process of transforming the skill from a contrived, conscious action to one in which the skills are used automatically and naturally. This process does not happen overnight. Skills are often identified one at a time as the teacher sees the need for the group to focus on that skill. To attempt to teach all of the skills at once, especially with young children, is an impossible task. For many children, these skills will take years to be learned and to be refined for use in new situations. However, the longer learning these skills is delayed, the more difficult it will be to develop them.

Accountability

Cooperative groups are not successful until each member of the group has made an honest contribution to the goal of the group (Johnson, Johnson, and Holubec 1986). It is important for the teacher to stress the contributions and learning of each individual group member. While it is true that the group has a common goal, the aim is for all members to benefit from the totality of the project.

If one or two members contribute the bulk of the effort to a project while others are content to stand back, the process is breaking down. It may be that the members are not using all of the interpersonal skills they possess or it may be that there is a need to review those skills. The teacher needs to constantly assess this individual accountability. This can be done by asking individual group members about the progress of the project.

Also under the heading of accountability is the importance of self-assessment. This is done in reference to individual group members and to the group itself. Johnson, Johnson, and Holubec (1986) provide a set of questions to be used for each. In helping children to assess their contributions to the group, the following set of statements can be used:

1. I made sure that everyone got a chance to help.
    Yes   Sometimes   No
2. I listened carefully to everyone's ideas.
    Yes   Sometimes   No
3. I said so when I didn't understand something.
    Yes   Sometimes   No
4. I said so when I thought that someone's idea was good.
    Yes   Sometimes   No

The providing of the "Yes—Sometimes—No" responses is appropriate because the statements do not necessarily lead to a strictly yes or no type of response. As children go through the course of a project their interest may rise and fall, and events in the environment can have an effect on participation as well.

The statements developed by Johnson, Johnson, and Holubec (1986) for self-assessing the process of the group include:

1. We made sure that we all had a chance to help.
    Yes   Sometimes   No
2. We listened carefully to each other's ideas.
    Yes   Sometimes   No
3. We said so when we didn't understand something.
    Yes   Sometimes   No
4. We said so when we thought someone's idea was good.
    Yes   Sometimes   No

ROLE OF THE TEACHER

Some cooperative learning models are highly structured sets of procedures designed to ensure that students learn large amounts of content material efficiently. Such models are more correctly identified as classroom management tools. They are designed primarily to help the teacher manage the learning process. In an early childhood classroom, such an approach is developmentally inappropriate. In an integrated language arts program, such an approach does not adequately deal with the goals inherent in the program. It must be remembered that a major focus of an integrated language arts program is the inclusion of students in helping to shape the instruction. A major goal of such a program is to foster, at an early age, the concept that children need to share some of the responsibility for their own learning. The role of the teacher, therefore, is not that of a manager focused on producing a finished product in a timely manner. Rather, the teacher's role is that of a coordinator. The teacher serves as a guiding participant in the literacy development program, not the master who controls it. To be sure, decisions have to be made by the teacher. The professional responsibility rests with that individual. The decisions a participating coordinator must make are qualitatively different, however, from those made by a controlling manager. The decisions focus on planning the process, organizing the learning activities, monitoring and supporting students, and evaluating the process.

Planning the Process

Planning the process involves a good deal of decision making. There are decisions to be made about children and groups. Other decisions must be made about the learning being planned. Each of the decisions should be made with an understanding that one factor can easily affect another in the learning situation.

Young children will most likely be lacking in many cooperative skills. It will be necessary, therefore, to model cooperative skills and to begin with simple concepts before moving on to more complex ones. The teacher must make a number of decisions in order to complete these plans.

It is suggested that groups be no larger than two or three children to begin with. All members of the class need to be a part of a group, and all group members should be in very close proximity so that they can face each other. This will help them to communicate. It will be helpful to begin by assigning specific roles. Each role can and should be modeled by the teacher before children can be expected to do it. Roles can be activity-related or process-related. Activity roles have to do with the actual learning activity. If a poster is being created, children might have the roles of drawing objects, tracing letters, coloring background, and so on. Process roles have to do with creating a cooperative atmosphere. These roles might include encourager, praise giver, and checker to see if everybody is participating.

Decisions must be made about the learning activity itself. The teacher must decide on the academic objectives as well as the cooperative skill objectives. Is the objective to create a poster about spring? Is the objective to get children into the practice of recognizing and praising the efforts of other children? All of these considerations are important. All must be decided. When those decisions have been made, the teacher needs to decide on the materials to be used. This can be a key decision. If too much material is provided, it can circumvent the need of the group to share and cooperate. If the objective is for the group to construct a poster about the spring season, giving each child a sheet of poster paper defeats the purpose of the cooperative group and encourages activity that does not necessarily conform to the need of the group to work together. Therefore, materials should be provided in such a way that they tend to foster cooperative effort.

Organizing the Learning Activity

The decisions made to organize the learning activity have to deal with the learning activity itself as well as the cooperative aspects of group work. In regard to the learning activity, children need to understand

FIGURE 10-3 Learning activities can be planned to provide opportunities for cooperation.

where they are attempting to go. They need to know what they are supposed to be doing and how they are supposed to do it. They also need to know how to tell when they have accomplished whatever it is their group is attempting to accomplish. Modeling the processes, showing examples, and explaining ideas are all helpful activities here. How each of these is accomplished must be decided by the teacher.

Within the context of the learning activity, the teacher must decide how to develop and increase the ability of the children to function within cooperative groups. The first decision concerns how to make sure all children participate in the activity. This can be done through several steps. First, make sure that each of the children knows that they have a certain job to do and that they have a responsibility to help other group members do their job. This can help both children who are reluctant and those who might not fully understand what is expected of them, despite the explanations and examples provided by the teacher. Second, joint accountability can be used. This would involve the teacher asking any group member at random to explain what is happening at any point in time in the group. Third, shared materials and assigned roles can be used. This will necessitate sharing and cooperation in order to complete the activity. The possible roles young children might assume in a cooperative learning activity include:

Recorder	Artist
Writer	Reader

Gluer	Cutter
Checker	Paster
Encourager	Measurer
Checker	Speaker
Direction giver	Runner
Timekeeper	Collector
Questioner	Responder
Materials giver	Spokesperson

Any cooperative learning activity will lend itself more to some cooperative skills than other. The teacher must decide which ones they are and attempt to develop or increase them. It is important to let students know what skills are going to be most helpful to them in completing the project or activity. It should be clearly explained to the children that they are expected to help, listen, share, stay with the group, take turns, ask questions, use quiet voices, or whatever other skills are being developed. Once specific cooperative skills have been decided upon, they must be taught by the teacher. This would include explaining the need for the skill, describing it, modeling it, having children describe it, having children model it, having children use it, and reinforcing it when it is used within the group process.

Monitor and Support Students

Once students are engaged in the learning activity, the teacher must make sure to observe, understand, and record what is occurring within each of the groups. The activities observed will provide information on how well the learning is progressing and how well students are able to work together. This requires ongoing decision making on the part of the teacher.

Even with the best of instruction, some children have difficulty understanding what they are supposed to do. The teacher must constantly decide when this is the case and, if it is, what to do about it. In some instances the difficulty may lie with the group process not functioning effectively. When this is the case, attention must be given to re-teaching cooperative skills. On the other hand, when the problem is clearly with the task, the teacher must be ready to re-teach procedures, explain concepts, and provide information the student needs to know.

The teacher must be able to decide when intervention is necessary. Careful observation must be done to determine the areas where the process is breaking down. Are children talking to each other? Are they telling each other what they are doing? Are other children responding or ignoring those comments? Is anyone making sure that all group members understand what they are supposed to do? Is anyone praising the efforts of others? If all of these things are taking place, the teacher should provide feedback that they are using good group skills. If something critical is missing, the teacher must decide how to deal with the situation. Can a comment or suggestion to a single child correct the stiuation? Does the group need to pause, so that the teacher can clarify a specific cooperative skill? Whatever the case, the teacher must record the observations. This recorded information can be used to provide helpful feedback to the children at a later time. It can also be used to plan future activities.

Evaluate the Process

Any activity has certain objectives concerning student learning. This requires the teacher to decide whether the group accomplished what it was supposed to. Did the poster get completed? Did the food items get constructed from the colored modeling clay? Did the pages of the book get illustrated? Did the children acquire an understanding of what a farm is? Was each group member able to discuss the finished product? The answers to questions such as these enable the teacher to decide whether or not the learning objectives were achieved.

It is also necessary to evaluate the group processes. Did students participate? Did they stay with their group? Did they share? Did they take turns? Did they praise the efforts of others? Did they interact in meaningful ways about their project? Since children are all individuals, the answers to these questions will vary depending on the individual child. Teachers should consider each of these questions with reference to specific children or specific groups. In addition, the group should become familiar with the concept of self-assessment. They can ask themselves these questions in order to make decisions about areas they would like to improve. The teacher can bring the activity to a conclusion by briefly summarizing the entire activity, reviewing key ideas or completed projects, and identifying the important aspects of the cooperative goals of the project.

TYPES OF COOPERATIVE LEARNING

There are several structures or types of cooperative learning. Kagan (1989/1990) describes a structural approach to cooperative learning in which several dozen distinct cooperative learning formats are identified. The best known of these are: Jigsaw (Aronson, Blaney, Sikes and Snapp 1978); Student—Teams—Achievement—Divisions or STAD (Slavin 1980); Think—Pair—Share (Lyman 1987); and Group—Investigation (Sharan and Hertz-Lazarowitz 1980). Kagan identifies structures as being content free. Activities, he contends, while often designed to be cooperative, are tied to a specific curriculum area. He feels that the distinction is important since structures can be used across content areas and with children of different ages. Activities are specific to a particular content area as well as specific grade or age levels. From Kagan's (1989/1990) summary, five structures are identified as being applicable to children in early childhood education: Roundrobin, Match Mine, Three-step Interview, Think—Pair—Share, and Co-op Co-op. Each has differing academic and social functions.

Roundrobin

The Roundrobin structure is designed to build the concept of teams. The procedure might begin or be demonstrated at circle time or after children have been divided into smaller groups. Each child in turn shares something with the team or group. The topic is not important, but should be decided upon prior to the beginning of the procedure. Each of these structures can be used with several content areas. For example, if the class is beginning a thematic unit on dogs, each of the children might be asked to share something they know about dogs.

The academic goals of this activity include recalling information related to the topic being addressed, developing sentences to express ideas and opinions, and sharing information known about the topic. The social goals of the activity deal with individual roles and developing a concept of group participation. By having all contribute information, each child has an opportunity to participate. Children get to know the other children in the group, and they come to understand that each member has something to contribute to the learning group.

Match Mine

The match mine structure was developed to build the communication skills of individual children participating in the group. Ordinarily this procedure involves pairs of students. In the traditional way this structure is implemented, one student seeks to arrange a set of objects in the same manner as another student through the use of oral communication only. Therefore, it is an activity that focuses more on developing oral language communication skills than content areas. With young children, the set of objects may be shapes, trucks, or toy animals. They may be arranged by the first child by size, color, or some other characteristic. The second child would then attempt to arrange a second set of objects in the same way without being allowed to look at the first set. Only oral communication between the children is used.

The major academic focus for this structure is vocabulary development. Children engaging in a match mine procedure will need to recall, identify, interpret, and use object names and descriptive terms in order to achieve success. The social goals would include communication skills and role taking abilities. Children will need to think about the way they are giving and receiving oral directions. There is a need to be clear and to give the other child specific information. The child who is listening to the directions will need to attend closely to the oral language and follow the directions closely.

Three-step Interview

The three-step interview is designed to foster both language concept development and group process skills. It is a useful alternative to the Roundrobin structure at the beginning of a thematic unit. Consider again the example of a thematic unit on the topic of dogs. The three-step interview can be a useful tool for recalling relevant knowledge and sharing it with the group through oral language. In this structure, pairs of students interview each other: first one way and then the other. After the students interview each other, they share the information they have learned with the group.

The academic goals for this structure are wide and

varied, but they all enhance language development and comprehension. They may include sharing personal information, responding to a story, developing hypotheses about a natural scientific process, or drawing conclusions about an experiment. The social goals focus on the individual. The first goal is that of participation. In this structure, each child has an equal opportunity to participate. The participation is unpressured and enjoyable. Improving listening ability is another social goal. In order to share a partner's information with the group, children need to have listened and understood the information provided by that partner.

Think—Pair—Share

The think—pair—share structure, like the three-step interview, is designed to encourage language concept development and group process skills. It provides still another tool for recalling relevant information about a topic and sharing it with others. It offers the added benefit of providing the child with the opportunity to analyze the information and to revise it. The procedure begins by having the children think about a given topic. It may be a topic provided by the teacher or developed by the group in conjunction with the teacher. After children have had an adequate time to recall what they know or have learned about the topic, they pair up with another student in order to discuss it. After they have discussed it with the other student, they share it with the class.

The academic goals of this structure are the development of thinking processes and the ability to generate and revise language statements. Children often have a great deal of information. Their information, however, might not be totally accurate at all times. The discussion phase of this structure allows children the opportunity to clarify their knowledge by pooling it with the knowledge of others. They may still come away with information that is not totally accurate, but it will most likely be more accurate than it was. The social goal of this structure is individual involvement in a learning activity that uses oral language. Children are invited to participate. Their contributions are appreciated. They have the opportunity to think about their information and to change it as they acquire new information and ideas from their partners.

Co-op Co-op

The co-op co-op structure has a number of functions within most content areas. Variations of the procedure are used with all ages of students. The gist of the procedure is that children work in a group in order to produce something. The thing produced may be a picture, poster, classroom storybook, model, or display. Whatever the product, it is shared with the total group when completed. Each student within the group producing the product makes a particular contribution to the completion of that product. The contribution may be some aspect of the actual construction of some part of the product, or it may be a group role such as encouraging the other children or organizing the activities of the group.

The academic goals that might be included under the co-op co-op structure vary. Learning and sharing materials and information in whatever curricular area the structure is used in is a major goal. When the procedure is used, it is often used as a tool for helping children use language to acquire information and to understand processes. Other academic goals might include analysis, application, synthesis, and evaluation of the material being learned. The specific goals are related to the content, the age level of the participants, and the reasons for selecting this structure. The social goals of this structure include resolving conflicts that arise within groups and presentation skills. While most conflicts that arise within groups are not violent, they do need to be dealt with in order for the group to continue to function. Children need to practice cooperative skills that they have learned in order to help the group operate smoothly. Children also need to communicate with each other in order to determine the best manner in which to share the finished product with the rest of the class. Again, group members must negotiate with each other in order to proceed successfully. None of this happens easily, of course. It takes place over time by means of careful teacher modeling, instruction, guidance, and feedback.

BENEFITS OF COOPERATIVE LEARNING

There are two major benefits of cooperative learning. The first is in the area of achievement. Many cooperative learning structures focus on learning subject matter content. Since the 1970s substantial number of research studies have investigated the ability of students to master content materials through cooperative learning. The second general area of benefit is in the social skills area. This area includes such diverse concepts as self-esteem, attitude toward students with disabilities, intergroup relations, and the ability to work cooperatively. A substantial number of research studies have assessed these areas as well.

Achievement

Slavin (1991) summarized the results of nearly seventy studies that investigated the achievement effects of cooperative learning. Significantly greater achievement was found to be related to cooperative learning in 61 percent of those studies. No achievement difference was found in 37 percent of the studies comparing cooperative learning and traditional instruction. Only one study found traditional instructional methods to result in greater achievement than the cooperative learning instruction.

Slavin identified two critical elements found in the studies supporting the use of cooperative learning: group goals and individual accountability. This finding is related to the fact that simply giving and receiving answers without explanation is negatively related to achievement (Webb 1985). Group goals and individual accountability motivate children to give explanations and take seriously the learning of all group members. According to Slavin (1991) this process works with high, average, and low achievers. There is no research support for fears that cooperative learning will hold back high achievers. Equal or superior achievement for all types of students has been found using cooperative learning compared to more traditional instruction.

Social Skills

Some of the earliest research on cooperative learning found that peope who cooperate learn to like each other (Slavin 1977). Later studies have consistently validated the earlier findings (Slavin 1991). This is important for all children. It is even more important in multicultural classrooms because ethnic separateness in schools does not naturally diminish over time

FIGURE 10-4 Some types of equipment can encourage cooperative play that leads to growth in social skills.

(Gerard and Miller 1975). Allport's (1954) Contact Theory, the dominant theory on intergroup relations, suggests that positive intergroup relationships only arise from school desegregation if children participate in cooperative, school-supported activities. Follow-up studies of peer relationships following cooperative learning activities have found that positive results transfer to out-of-school activities as well as other school activities (Slavin 1991).

Disabilities are an even greater barrier to friendship than ethnicity (Slavin 1991). For decades, children with disabilities have been segregated from their non-disabled peers in programs designed to meet their unique individual needs. Although such policies might have been well intentioned, their effect has been the near elimination of opportunities for children with moderate and severe disabilities to participate in regular education programs together with their non-disabled peers. Mainstreaming programs, which provide opportunities for participation during parts of the day, have helped alleviate this problem to some extent. Total inclusion programs, in which children with disabilities receive all of their special education services in the schools and classrooms they would normally attend, hold immense promise for extending the rights of these children to participate in regular school programs. Studies investigating the effects of cooperative learning for classes that include disabled and non-disabled children found that all children demonstrated increases in achievement, self-esteem, and acceptance of differences (Madden and Slavin 1983; Johnson, Johnson, and Maruyama 1983).

The self-concept and self-esteem of children can be fragile. Children need to see themselves as successful in order to feel good about themselves. Constantly being reminded of their failures has a debilitating effect on children that is increasingly difficult to overcome, especially by the time they enter their pre-adolescent years. Cooperative learning has been found to be effective in building self-esteem in children (Blaney, Stephan, Rosenfeld, Aronson, and Sikes 1977; Slavin 1991). As children view themselves as successful in their dealings with others as well as with academic tasks, they tend to view learning in a positive light (Schultz 1989/1990). Concerns are sometimes raised about the benefits of using cooperative learning with gifted children. Research shows that gifted children not only maintain their achievement levels, but also learn to work with others as they extend their learning on an individual basis (Augustine, Gruber, and Hanson 1989/1990).

OBSTACLES TO COOPERATIVE LEARNING

Cooperative learning is unlike many other educational innovations. It has a firm base of research support, varying types and structures, and a great many teachers who enthusiastically support its use. This does not guarantee its implementation over a long period of time, however. Many other innovations possessing many of these same characteristics have come and gone. Slavin (1989/1990) cites four reasons why this is not likely to occur with cooperative learning. First, its research base suggests that it will most likely be found to be successful whenever it is correctly used. Second, its characteristics make it a method unlikely to be forced upon teachers. Third, many new teachers have received training in its classroom uses. Fourth, it makes teaching and learning more enjoyable. Still, there are certain obstacles to the long term inclusion of cooperative learning in classrooms.

Resistance to Innovations

Most people become comfortable in routines. They like familiarity and come to value predictability. In many ways, routines are helpful to all of us as we go about our daily lives. They help us to get to work or school on time. They enable us to know how to order food in restaurants, wash our laundry, and do chores around the house. On the other hand, they can sometimes be a cause for resistance to change. This has been known to occur with cooperative learning as well as with other innovations.

Steinberg (1989) has identified three obstacles to the use of cooperative learning. The first obstacle is that opponents charge that children cannot use cooperative learning effectively because they do not know how to be productive and responsible group members. Proponents of cooperative learning acknowledge that this is true for many children who have had no experience in cooperative learning. They counter, however, with the belief that these skills, developed through the proper implementation of cooperative learning, are some of the most critically important skills that any child can learn. Through cooperative learning, children learn to deal appropriately with conflict and develop the crucial language skills of negotiating with others.

A second charge is that unless ability grouping is used, assignments will be too easy for some and too difficult for others. As was noted in the section on benefits of cooperative learning, students of all ability levels can benefit from its use. In addition, it is best for children to become familiar with the strengths, interests, and styles of others. Classroom teachers can structure groups so that at times they are more homogenous while at other times they are more heterogenous. In addition, there is a lack of evidence supporting homogenous grouping patterns as producing greater achievement.

The third charge is that the time it would take to teach children the social skills necessary to become productive group members decreases the time that could be used to learn curriculum material. The research simply does not support such a charge. Learning to work together to learn the material requires students to work with the content in a variety of ways. As a result they tend to learn the material successfully.

Ineffective Implementation

A second obstacle to the effective inclusion of cooperative learning in classrooms is incorrect use of the strategy. If teachers who are not knowledgeable in cooperative learning procedures attempt to use it, it can produce chaos and failure in the classroom. The fault is not with cooperative learning. The problem with the failures of incorrect use of cooperative learning can usually be traced to improper training of those attempting to implement it.

Several strategies and procedures can be used by teachers to guard against the failure of incorrect attempts to use cooperative learning. First, teachers should be aware that cooperative learning involves more than placing students in groups and giving them a common assignment. Second, teachers should combine cooperative learning as an instructional method with other instructional tools. Third, teachers should remember that cooperative learning does contain structure. Fourth, teachers need to be aware that cooperative learning structures can and should be acquired and assessed over time. These structures can vary in effectiveness, depending on the children and the curriculum. Finally, teachers need to provide the necessary materials, social skill training, and support to make cooperative learning successful for the children.

PRACTICAL BEGINNING CONSIDERATIONS

Like any other effective teaching strategy, cooperative learning takes time to learn and implement. Edwards and Stout (1989/1990) contend that it takes two to three years for teachers to fully incorporate it into their teaching styles for the recommended 60 percent of the teaching day. They suggest pacing the introduction of the approach. Begin by becoming familiar and comfortable with the background of cooperative learning. Adcock and Segal provide an excellent model for cooperative learning in early childhood programs in *Play Together, Grow Together* (1983). For kindergarten through grade two, a good source is Loma Curran's *Cooperative Learning Lessons for Little Ones* (1990).

Follow the initial familiarization period by introducing cooperative learning within one lesson in a single topic or subject area. Teachers need to constantly monitor, revise, assess, and model different aspects of the approach in order to determine what works best with the group. Modeling is particularly important for young children. They need to see and hear what they are expected to do. Teachers contemplating the use of cooperative learning can rely on some basic, practical suggestions as well as some initial activities for beginning cooperative learning with young children.

Practical Suggestions

The practical aspects of using cooperative learning are not altogether different from those for any instructional tool. Edwards and Stout (1989/1990) outline several areas for consideration that they have found to be helpful. Their suggestions pertain to primary grades and older children. For younger children, some of these suggestions can be adapted or eliminated. Each is described here.

Arrange Groups Efficiently.

It is suggested that children be grouped in clusters for the entire day. This is done whether children use tables, desks, or the rug as instructional areas. If whole class explanations are being given, children can simply turn toward the teacher for those parts of a lesson. If this does not work out, teachers need to be willing to consider the variables and experiment with other arrangements.

Define Group Size.

While different purposes might suggest different group sizes, it is best to start small. Especially with young children, groups of two are a good starting point. As youngsters develop more social skills, their ability to work with larger groups increases.

Decide on Time Length for Groups.

With older children, teachers often have the same groups work together for six to eight weeks. With kindergarteners and younger children, a more realistic target might be to have two children work as a group for a single lesson, a day or a week. Teachers need to strike a balance between children working together because they want to and working together because they need to. While the teacher might avoid putting two children together who are unlikely to cooperate with each other, there is the need for chil-

Class News.
Emily made bread.
Abel went to Disney world.
Bobby is going to go.
Moira is a new girl in our class.

FIGURE 10-5 Language activities can help children become aware of the needs and interests of others.

dren to understand the importance of being able to work with many different people.

Develop Team Concept.

Whenever groups are formed, it is important for the children in the group to get to know the other children in the group in order to develop a sense of being part of the group. Activities for doing this might include children telling about themselves, identifying similarities with other members, and choosing a group name.

Divide Group Responsibilities.

While an ultimate goal is for the group to decide how it will divide responsibilities among the members, young children will frequently need assistance in understanding the roles of other group members. One simple procedure for doing this is to place different colored stars or circles at different places on the carpet or on different chairs around the table. In this way, children can be assigned roles according to the color: red stars pass out papers, paints, glue, and crayons to the group; blue stars draw the turkey; yellow stars color the illustration, and so on.

Decide When to Use.

As noted earlier, cooperative learning can be used for different learning situations. It should not be the only instructional tool, however. Teachers need to carefully consider which activities and topics are best suited for cooperative learning. Among the activities

for which cooperative learning strategies are often helpful are brainstorming ideas, solving problems, learning new concepts, creating stories and artwork, and higher order thinking activities.

Initial Activities

A number of beginning activities have been developed by Johnson, Johnson, and Holubec (1988) for teachers wishing to employ cooperative learning. The activities can be used quickly and without a great deal of preparation. While they do not demonstrate the full power of cooperative learning, they do provide opportunities for children to become aware that they can work with others in ways that are mutually beneficial. Several of these activities are appropriate for young children.

Learning Partners.

Children using the learning partners activity get into pairs after something has been taught or after a learning activity has occurred. They take turns telling the other child what was learned, what they observed, or some other aspect of the lesson. The activity is not intended to be a re-teaching. It is simply a quick reinforcement as well as an opportunity to share the learning through language.

Drill Partners.

This activity also involves children working in pairs. It ordinarily takes place after factual material has been taught. This might include the numbers one through six, the primary colors, a set of basic shapes, or kinds of vehicles. Whatever it is, it should be something that there is a fundamental need for children to know well. Each child takes turns drilling the other on this factual information using words, pictures, or cards. While the academic goal is to learn the material, it is probably more important that children develop a sense of using language as a tool for learning and an understanding of how to help others learn.

Story Buddies.

With younger children, each child can be asked to tell something about a favorite story to another child. Kindergarteners and older children can read to each other. They may use stories from picture books or

FIGURE 10-6 Many stories illustrate the concept of cooperation. *Reprinted courtesy of Houghton Mifflin Company, nonexclusive and nontransferable.*

stories that they have created on their own. They may also share their responses to stories.

Problem Solvers.

Using groups of two or three children to solve a basic problem can be a bit more challenging. To do this, the teacher might assign an appropriate problem of some sort to the group. The group members can either be assigned roles or select the roles on their own. Each member of the group, however, is expected to be able to explain the solution to the problem. Problems might include picture puzzles, a matching activity, or a science experiment.

SUMMARY

There is a great need for people who can work well together in life. It is also believed that it is simply good for the people themselves to be able to work together cooperatively. Traditionally, education instructional programs have operated under competitive and individualized models. Neither one focuses on the development of social skills as a part of the learning process. The cooperative learning model is an instructional system in which children can reach goals only when the others around them also reach the same or similar goals. This can only occur when children work together.

There are five basic principles that establish a foundation for cooperative learning. These basic principles are interdependence, social interaction, interpersonal skills, group process, and accountability. Each of these must be understood by teachers in order for them to teach, model, monitor, and assess their presence as cooperative learning is integrated into an instructional program. Through the development of these principles, children learn to help and encourage others as a normal part of the learning process. It has been shown that this sense of teamwork and responsibility can have powerful affective results. Research and theory support the contention that cooperative learning can help reduce prejudices in integrated settings and can provide a social bridge between children with disabilities and their non-disabled peers. In addition, cooperative learning has been shown to lead to increases in self-esteem and positive attitudes toward school and learning.

The roles of teachers and children are different in cooperative environments than they are in competitive settings. In competitive settings, the teacher tends to be the manager of the learning. In cooperative settings, the teacher's role is that of a coordinator, much like the role described for the teacher in a whole language program. The teacher needs to be effective in modeling, monitoring, observing, and evaluating strategies used in the process of learning. Children using cooperative learning in an early childhood program are seen as active participants with definite roles. The roles fall into two types. Activity roles are related to the actual activity taking place and may include such things as paster, illustrator, or writer. Process roles are related to the process of working as a group. These roles include such things as encourager, praiser, and listener.

Several cooperative learning structures are available for use by early childhood educators. They range from very basic structures such as round robin, in which pairs of children develop the ability to take turns sharing information, to more complex structures such as co-op, co-op, in which small groups assume diverse roles in order to accomplish a task. Other structures that fall between these two ends include match mine, three-step interview and think—

pair—share. Each of these structures can be used within different curriculum areas.

There are obstacles to making cooperative learning a regular part of the classroom instructional program. One obstacle involves the typical human resistance to change. Some teachers might resist a new approach simply because they are comfortable with the approaches that have been used for years. They may attempt to discredit the new approach or they may simply ignore it. Another obstacle to cooperative learning is insufficient training and expertise for those who do attempt to use it within the instructional program. While teachers can begin to use cooperative learning fairly soon after some initial training, a one-day workshop does not provide adequate knowledge about the strategy. The strategy itself must be constantly monitored and adjusted to make it effective for a particular classroom. It is estimated that it takes about two years of study and effort in order to make cooperative learning a significantly effective part of a teacher's classroom instructional program.

Finally, a number of practical considerations should be addressed when first attempting to include cooperative learning in an instructional program. The initial decisions should be made based upon teachers' knowledge of the children in their care. These decisions will need to be reviewed and revised constantly as the structures, the children, and the curriculum areas change. The initial decisions to be made include such things as the size of groups, the activities, the configuration of the groups, and the length of time groups should work together.

Questions and Activities for Review and Discussion

Multiple Choice

1. *People skills* is a term used to refer to
   a. the ability to give orders to others.
   b. the ability to work with others.
   c. an understanding of human intelligence.
   d. an ability to identify personality types.

2. Interpersonal skills include
   a. knowing and trusting others.
   b. providing clear information to others.
   c. accepting and supporting others.
   d. all of the above

3. According to Johnson and Johnson, the first step in helping young children learn an interpersonal skill is to have them
   a. see a need for the skill.
   b. learn a definition of the skill.
   c. practice the skill.
   d. identify examples of the skill.

4. The concept of having the teacher ask any group member to explain what is happening in the group is known as
   a. competitive evaluation.
   b. skill testing.
   c. joint accountability.
   d. social skills assessment.

5. When monitoring the cooperative learning process, the teacher should always

    a. record the observations.
    b. provide additional directions.
    c. intervene.
    d. participate in the group's activities.
6. The cooperative learning structure that includes a mechanism for encouraging children to think about and revise their thoughts concerning something is
    a. round robin.
    b. think-pair-share.
    c. three-step interview.
    d. all of the above
7. Cooperative learning can probably be fully implemented in an instructional program in approximately
    a. six weeks.
    b. four months.
    c. two years.
    d. five years.

True or False

T   F 1. Cooperation is the most frequently used teaching procedure in traditional instructional programs.

T   F 2. The concept of students helping other students is referred to as interdependence.

T   F 3. Children who are assigned cooperative learning process roles will focus primarily on the actual activity.

T   F 4. Evaluation of the effectiveness of the cooperative learning activity is confined to the accomplishment of the learning objectives.

T   F 5. Cooperative learning can do little to break down barriers caused by race and disability.

Essay and Discussion

1. Identify the major principles of the cooperative learning model.
2. Describe the interpersonal skills that are the most critical for a cooperative learning environment.
3. Describe the decisions a teacher must make when planning the use of cooperative learning as a part of the classroom instructional program.
4. Describe the two areas within cooperative learning that should be evaluated for effectiveness.
5. Describe why cooperative learning is likely to overcome obstacles to its integration in instructional programs.

REFERENCES

Adcock, D., and M. Segal. 1983. *Play together, grow together*. Mount Rainier, Md.: Gryphon House.

Allport, G. 1954. *The nature of prejudice*. Cambridge, Mass.: Addison-Wesley.

Aronson, E., N. Blaney, C. Sikes, and M. Snapp. 1978. *The jigsaw classroom*. Beverly Hills, Calif.: Sage.

Augustine, D.K., K.D. Gruber, and L.R. Hanson. 1989/1990. Cooperation works! *Educational Leadership* 47: 4–7.

Blaney, N.T., S. Shephan, D. Rosenfeld, E. Aronson, and J. Sikes. 1977. Interdependence in the classroom: A field study. *Journal of Educational Psychology* 69: 121–128.

Curran, L. 1990. *Cooperative learning lessons for little ones.* San Juan Capistrano, Calif.: Resources for Teachers.

Edwards, C., and J. Stout. 1989/1990. Cooperative learning: The first year. *Educational Leadership* 47: 4, 38–41.

Gerard, H.B., and N. Miller. 1975. *School desegregation: A long range study.* New York: Plenum.

Johnson, D.W. 1980. Group processes: Influences of student-student interactions on school outcomes. In *School Psychology of School Learning,* ed. J. McMillan. New York: Academic Press.

Johnson, D.W. 1986. *Reaching out: Interpersonal effectiveness and self-actualization.* Englewood Cliffs, N.J.: Prentice-Hall.

Johnson, D.W., and R.T. Johnson. 1987a. *Joining together: Group therapy and group skills.* Englewood Cliffs, N.J.: Prentice-Hall.

Johnson, D.W., and R.T. Johnson. 1987b. *Learning together and alone: Cooperative, competitive and individualistic learning.* Englewood Cliffs, N.J.: Prentice-Hall.

Johnson, D.W., and R.T. Johnson. 1989/1990. Social skills for successful group work. *Educational Leadership* 47: 4, 29–33.

Johnson, D.W., R.T. Johnson, and E.J. Holubec. 1986. *Circles of learning: Cooperation in the classroom.* Edina, Minn.: Interaction Book Company.

Johnson, D.W., R.T. Johnson, and E.J. Holubec. 1988. *Cooperation in the classroom.* Edina, Minn.: Interaction Book Company.

Johnson, D.W., R.T. Johnson, and G. Maruyama. 1983. Interdependence and interpersonal attraction among heterogeneous and homogeneous individuals: A theoretical formulation and a meta-analysis of the research. *Review of Educational Research* 53: 5–54.

Johnson, D.W., G. Raruyama, R.T. Johnson, D. Nelson, and L. Skon. 1981. Effects of cooperative, competitive and individualistic goal structures on achievement: A meta-analysis. *Psychological Bulletin* 89: 47–62.

Kagan, S. 1989/1990. The structural approach to cooperative learning. *Educational Leadership* 47: 4, 12–15.

Lyman, S. 1987. Think-pair-share: An expanding teaching technique. *MAA-CIE—Cooperative News* 1: 1–2.

Madden, N.A., and R.E. Slavin. 1983. Mainstreaming students with mild academic handicaps: Academic and social outcomes. *Review of Eduational Research* 53: 519–569.

Sapon-Shevin, M., and N. Schniedewind. 1989/1990. Selling cooperative learning without selling it short. *Educational Leadership,* 47: 4, 63–65.

Schultz, J.L. 1989/1990. Cooperative learning: Refining the process. *Educational Leadership* 47: 4, 43–45.

Sharan, S., and R. Hertz-Lazarowitz. 1980. A group investigation method of cooperative learning in the classroom. In *Cooperation in Education,* ed. S. Sharan, P. Hare, C. Webb, and R. Hertz-Lazarowitz. Provo, Utah: Brigham Young University Press.

Slavin, R.E. 1980. *Using student team learning.* Baltimore, Md.: The Center for Social Organization of Schools, The Johns Hopkins University.

Slavin, R.E. 1989/1990. Here to stay—Or gone tomorrow? *Educational Leadership* 47: 4, 3.

Slavin, R.E. 1991. Synthesis of research on cooperative learning. *Educational Leadership* 48: 5, 71–81.

Steinberg, A., ed. 1989. Cooperative learning: Making it work. *Education Letter* 5: 1–4.

Webb, N. 1985. Student interaction and learning in small groups: A research summary. In *Learning to Cooperate: Cooperating to Learn,* ed R. Slavin, S. Sharan, S. Kagan, R. Hertz-Lozarowitz, C. Webb, and R. Schmuck. New York: Plenum.

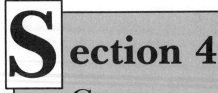

Section 4
Components of a Program

Dave Ross

"As a primary school student who struggled mightily with language arts, I fully endorse any effort to make reading fun for children."

Reprinted courtesy of Dave Ross.

TO THE READER:

Working with young children is an exciting, tiring, powerful experience. The characteristics of energy, patience, ability to observe, thoughtfulness, resourcefulness, and organization are required by all involved: teachers, parents, teacher aides, and assistants. The children provide many rewards for this hard work and diligence. They produce miracle after miracle over the years by acquiring the ability to talk, listen, read, and write. The most sophisticated and powerful computers can not begin to compare to the language learning capabilities of young children.

Providing an environment in which language learning is enhanced does not happen by accident. Nor does it happen by strictly following the directions of a commercially manufactured early childhood language learning program. An integrated language arts program, which supports the efforts of children to learn, understand, and use language, comes about through careful planning, implementation, and evaluation of a coherent instructional program focused on the needs of children as individuals. This section introduces you to these three parts of an effective program.

In planning a program you will see the importance of understanding the foundations of a whole language approach that you learned in the early part of this book. You will use that knowledge to make decisions about what can and should be included in an instructional lesson or unit. Much of this planning occurs outside of the classroom prior to the instructional lesson. You will learn the process for setting realistic goals for the children and the program. A number of tools are provided to enable you to develop effective plans efficiently.

Implementation of the program occurs in the classroom. While it ordinarily follows the planning process, teachers need to continually adjust and expand their plans depending on the children's response to the lesson or unit. You will learn how to follow the plan you have developed using numerous instructional strategies. You will also learn about characteristics and strategies of effective teachers that have been identified through years of research. Developing these characteristics and strategies as part of your own teaching style can help you become a more effective teacher of young children as you implement your planned instruction.

Evaluation occurs at all points in the lesson or unit. This might sound strange, since evaluation has traditionally only occurred at the end of a lesson or a unit. In an integrated language arts approach, however, evaluation is a necessary and important part of both the planning process and the implementation of the program. The evaluation stage of a program should include a number of people. You will learn about the important roles of teachers, children, parents, and others in the evaluation process.

UNIT 11

Planning a Program

UNIT GOALS

After completing this unit, the reader should:

- develop a systematic approach to planning a literacy development program for young children.
- develop the ability to use numerous instructional planning tools.
- identify specific aspects of an instructional program that need to be carefully considered and planned.
- develop the view that planning is a comprehensive process that must address all phases of a program.
- identify and make decisions about the critical components of an educational plan.
- develop the ability to plan a total early childhood literacy program.

PREVIEW

Planning for young children is somewhat akin to predicting New England weather in the springtime. No matter what the conditions are at any given time, they are likely to be much different a short while later. Does this mean that planning for young children is of little value? No, not at all. Planning is of great value. The point to keep in mind is that teachers must allow for flexibility within the plans.

Even if a plan does not work out as expected, a plan with flexibility built in is far better than attempting to teach a unit or even a lesson with no plan at all. There are valid reasons for this view. A plan serves as a guide as the teacher works toward goals. A plan should always be seen as something that can be revised as needed. The plan can and should have provisions for situations in which the plan does not seem to be working. Finally, a plan encourages one to focus on what could occur or what should occur in the classroom.

Attempting to teach without a plan is like trying to get from New York City to Los Angeles without a compass, money, or map. We might eventually get there, but it will be as much by luck as by design. In addition, there will be a great deal of wasted resources and effort. In the process, we run the risk of bringing about frustration and discouragement in those who are traveling with us.

INTRODUCTION

Most people like to have some idea of where they are going and how they are going to get there. This is usually true of teachers as well. It gives them confidence and a sense of purpose. While children may not articulate it, they tend to like some structure that responds to their needs. They like to have an understanding of the purpose of what is happening. Plans for instruction serve this purpose even though they may need to be revised, recycled, or even discarded along the way. However, plans must first be developed based upon the best information available at the time.

There are a number of tools and strategies to help the teacher plan. The first thing teachers need in this process is an understanding of exactly how to go about planning. Many do not naturally know how to plan or even what should be included in a plan. A good organizational framework for planning will need to account for many things. It will need to provide an understanding of how to plan, a knowledge of what process is best for planning a particular unit or lesson, and a means to identify the point to actually begin developing a plan.

No one operates in a total vacuum. While this may seem like a trite statement, it is important for teachers to constantly keep this concept in mind. Teachers do not find themselves in generic classrooms with generic materials and generic children. All teachers find themselves in specific classrooms with specific children and finite resources. There are boundaries to every teaching situation. It is well worth the effort for teachers to conduct an inventory of these boundaries. Such an inventory helps to develop the parameters of any plan.

Three general program areas need to be planned. The first is the curriculum. This is comprised of the goals and objectives of the program. The curriculum ordinarily specifies the desired outcomes of the program in terms of the development of the child. Curriculum statements answer questions such as: What do I want children to know, feel, and do as a result of this program?

The second area that needs to be planned is the implementation of the program. It refers to the in-

struction provided to children. It may be for a single lesson, a thematic unit covering two weeks, or an entire year. Each of these time spans must be planned by making a multitude of decisions. Implementation plans answer questions such as: What will be done tomorrow in the classroom? How will it be done? How can children be interested in this topic? How can the home environments of children be used to encourage literacy development?

The third area to be planned is evaluation. In an integrated language arts program, an adequate evaluation is much more involved than simply giving children a test or marking off skills attained on a checklist. Such approaches tend to address only cognitive learning. It is crucial to plan evaluation so that the totality of the learner is addressed.

ORGANIZING FOR PLANNING

Anyone who has ever visited a well-run early childhood program cannot help but be impressed by the sense of efficiency, the well-thought-out activities, and the diversity of instruction being provided. Day (1983) describes such a program, created with the development of children in mind, as being evident even before you enter the building. In the play yard there are gardens, various types of equipment, and children of different ages engaged in a variety of activities. There may be cages in which animals are kept as well as chairs and benches for children to sit and read storybooks. You may even see children with paper and pencil drawing, writing, or recording what they see.

In the classroom, Day (1983) describes a scene in which there are few, if any, individual student desks. Instead, there are tables, centers, and work areas at which children participate in numerous activities. Some of these activities are done with a teacher or parent volunteer. Some are done independently or with other children. The activities may include lying on the carpet reading a book, doing a science experiment, learning about kittens, or participating in a tea party. It is evident that the children seem to be quite content, yet actively interested and purposeful in their activities.

A scene such as this does not happen by accident. It occurs only after careful planning has taken place and those plans have been put into practice by a thoughtful, well-organized teacher and staff. Where do teachers begin to create such plans? Actually, an effective planning process begins well before the actual classroom plans are developed. Teachers must organize for planning. This means that it is helpful to have some specific ideas about how to go about the process of planning. Trial and error won't do. Too many things can go wrong, and too many false starts can lead to a chaotic situation. The best way to get ready to develop a plan is with some planning tools that help the teacher address the many factors to be considered when developing an effective program for young children. We begin by identifying several strategies and tools to help the teacher.

Semantic Maps

The first tool that is quite helpful in developing plans is the semantic map. Semantic maps are also known as semantic webs or simply as webs. While writers from elementary school through higher education have become accustomed to using semantic maps to plan their writing, these maps can be used to plan many other things as well. Sawyer and Comer (1991), for example, demonstrate how these webs can be used to plan literature units with young children.

Semantic maps came out of the work in which scientists studied artificial intelligence. As the scientists attempted to program computers to simulate the actual workings of the human mind, they had to develop a theory of how human beings learn things. They concluded that people learn new things by relating them to things or ideas they already know (Pearson and Johnson 1978). The semantic map was developed as a model of how things are known. As new information is perceived, the individual attempts to fit it into the map of what is already known in such a way that it makes sense. The map is not seen as something that is made up of a number of information building blocks. Rather, it is a whole entity. It contains specific parts, but they have importance not only to themselves but in their relationship to other parts as well.

To illustrate how to develop a semantic map as a tool for planning a program, imagine that a teacher wishes to develop a unit on the concept of growing for a group of children. The age range of the children would suggest the depth or complexity of the information that might be shared with them, but it would not affect the process of using a semantic map as a planning tool. Let us imagine that the age range

of the children in this case is a group of three- to five-year-olds.

Brainstorm.

The first step in developing a map is to brainstorm all of the possible ideas that may be relevant to such children under the general idea or theme of growing. Some things like trees, flowers, and one's own body come immediately to mind. In stretching our minds, we might also come up with some less obvious concepts such as the role that seasons play in plant growth and the contribution of the sun to growing. Figure 11-1 summarizes a list of possible ideas under the heading of growing. While the list might seem impressive, it is rather random and disorganized. Something more needs to be done with it to make it useful in planning a unit.

Categorize.

The second step in the process involves categorizing the information. To do this, we need to scan the list in order to determine the ideas and terms that seem to be related. The original list has been categorized in Figure 11-2. It might be noted that not all of the original words and ideas are included under the categories. It also might be noted that some new ideas are included for the first time. This is to be expected. As new ideas that fit the theme occur to the teacher, they should be included. Decisions about whether or not to include everything that was originally generated must also be made as the process continues.

Create the Map.

The third step is to transfer the information listed under each of the categories onto a semantic map. Here too, new ideas can be added while other ideas may be deleted from consideration. Figure 11-3 illustrates a semantic map for the concept of growing. Here, the reason for the use of the terms *map* and *web* becomes obvious. The illustration produced appears to resemble a road map or a spider's web. The big city, or central part of the map, is simply the concept of growing. The villages and suburbs comprise the categories identified from the original random listing. Dotted lines, showing relationships between certain ideas and concepts, can be added to help keep in mind the existence of these relationships. For example, we

trees	play
flowers	babies
getting old	getting bigger
mother	going to school
doctor	dentist
children	horses
food	grandparent
religious ceremonies	bushes
air	pets
plants	springtime
kindergarten	lambs
sisters	animals
illness	sun
pediatrician	changes
grandmother	forests
planting seeds	ponds
people	birthdays
brothers	families
gardens	fish
farms	home
water	lambs
grownups	autumn
father	

FIGURE 11-1 Growing: Brainstormed list of ideas and possibilities.

might draw a dotted line between the word *plants* and the word *garden* as well as between the word *plants* and the category circle *needed for growing*. It should be remembered that the illustrations depicted here are only examples. There is no one correct size or style of semantic map. The individual using it determines its correctness.

Expand the Map.

There is one final step in using the web. It might become obvious at this point that the concept of growing might encompass too large a topic for a unit with young children. It may be a bit too abstract as well. For example, a teacher might wish the theme to be more concrete by focusing on just fast-growing items such as beans, kittens, and grass. To address these concerns, the fourth step is to select aspects that are most appropriate and to expand the map. This is done by adding new topic information and by adding

the instructional components that might be needed to create a focused unit. For our example (see Figure 11-4), the category of "Children" from the "Things That Grow" circle in the upper left hand corner of Figure 11-3 has been selected. In addition, the categories "Needed for Growing" and "People Who Help" have been combined into one category called "People and Things to Help." New elements have been added as well. These include the language, literature, related subjects, and activities needed for an instructional program. The map can and should be

Things that grow	trees	bushes
	people	sisters
	flowers	fish
	pets	animals
	brothers	plants
	lambs	children
Needed for growing	water	
	sun	
	food	
	air	
Places for growing	gardens	
	farms	
	forests	
	ponds	
	families	
	home	
People who help	mother	
	father	
	doctor	
	families	
	grandparents	
	dentist	
Markers of growth	getting older	springtime
	doctor visit	being grown up
	changes	religious
	play	ceremonies
	birthdays	getting bigger
	kindergarten	going to school
		no more diapers

FIGURE 11-2 Growing: Categorization of ideas.

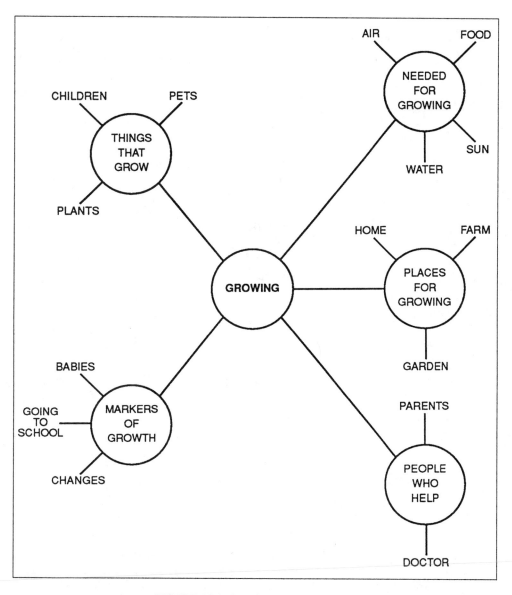

FIGURE 11-3 Growing: Creating a map.

expanded further at this point. Specific titles of books, actual play activities, songs for transitions, and names of possible classroom visitors might be added. When this is completed, the teacher will have an over-all view of the boundaries and possibilities for such a unit. At that point the concrete planning of classroom instruction can take place. Using the information de-veloped in the semantic map, planning charts for in-struction are a most useful tool.

Charts

Another powerful planning tool is the chart. It can be used for many purposes at varying points in the instructional process. A chart can be a simple outline

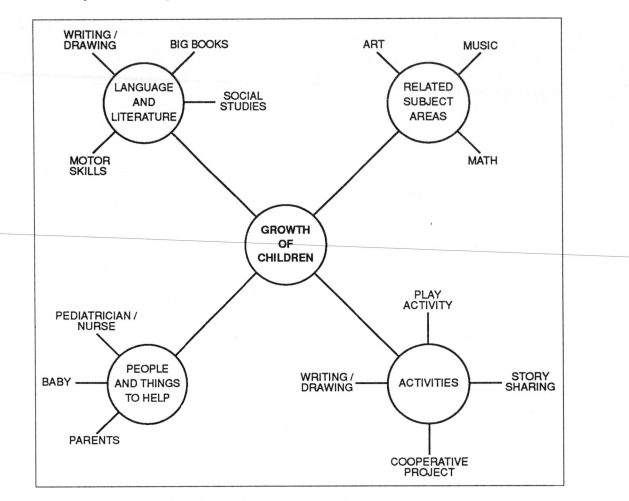

FIGURE 11-4 Growing: Expanding the map.

of information. It can also be a diagram, a table, or an illustration. The purpose of any chart is to organize information. For our lesson on the growth of children, several charts might be helpful. The primary chart might be an instructional planning chart. The information included in this chart will be the practical information represented in the map in Figure 11-5. While the semantic map organizes useful information to consider in developing the unit, the planning chart translates this information into a plan of instruction. There are different ways of developing a planning chart. The important thing is to include all of the key characteristics needed for teaching the unit.

One of the first things the planning chart requires is a statement of the goals and objectives of the unit. That is, what will the students know, believe, and do as a result of participating in the unit? It might be useful to think of these statements in reference to what the children knew, believed, and did before the unit. What instruction attempts to do is to change the knowledge, beliefs, and abilities of children in some way. For example, a goal might be for four-year-olds to understand the idea that different things happen in their lives as they get older. They learn to swim, they go to kindergarten, they reach religious milestones, and so forth.

Theme / topic:_____   Time span: _____

Goals / objectives:_____

Related subject areas:_____

Resources
Big books: Book titles: Poems / songs: Art / writing supplies: Audio–visuals:

Schedule of activities

Activity type	Title / description	Group	Day / time
Big book			
Read–alouds			
Silent reading			
Poems / songs			
Art / writing			
Cooperative project			
Play			
Audiovisual			
Visitors			
Field trips			
Other			

Evaluation

Goal / objective	Assessment tool / strategy	Results / comments
#1 #2 #3 Instructional Plan	 What worked well? What did not work well?	

FIGURE 11-5 Planning chart

The resources and activities comprise what will happen in the classroom and with what materials, in order to help children achieve the goals. In an integrated language arts curriculum, the teachers will want to make a great deal of use of authentic literature, oral discussions, songs, and student created writings and drawings as materials. Obviously, there may be other resources as well such as parents, volunteers, classroom visitors, films, and pictures. The schedule of activities in the chart provides a means for making decisions about the sequence in which things will occur in the unit. The schedule of activities in Figure 11-5 is for illustrative purposes. When actually planning a unit, it is helpful to make decisions about what will happen on each of the days over which the unit will extend. This enables teachers to make plans concerning when to invite classroom visitors, what materials are needed on specific days, and when to begin cooperative projects. It also reminds teachers that some things such as reading aloud, songs, and play activities should occur every day.

The evaluation is a process of comparing what has happened by the end of the unit with the original goals. Two things need to be addressed here. First, have the goals been achieved? Did children learn some of the things expected? Are they able to do the new things mentioned in the goals? Are different children at different levels?

Second, an assessment of the instructional plan itself should be made. Did the activities and materials seem appropriate for the purposes? Did they seem to enhance the opportunities for students to learn new things? What didn't work as well as expected? Why not? How can those things be improved for the next time this unit is done? In many ways the evaluation of the goals of the lesson and the evaluation of the instructional plan are interrelated. The reason for this is that most things done after the goals have been established are done in reference to those goals.

Files and Timelines

Two additional tools for organizing instructional plans are files of information and timelines for accomplishing different aspects of a unit or its plan. Files of information should be kept by all teachers. Anyone teaching young children must become a collector of sorts. There is no end to the number of possible things that might be needed to develop a unit. As we have seen previously, there is a range of content area subject matter that might be addressed in an early childhood education program. It is wise for teachers to develop files or folders of miscellaneous materials related to each of these. Examples of materials that might be found in a file on the growth of children might include: pictures, photographs, height and weight charts, poems, song sheets, names and addresses of people who will come to the class to talk about the topic, reviews of books on the topic, names of big books on the topic, and a list of field trip destinations related to the topic.

In addition to these files, a file should be kept for each unit developed. This will aid in future planning. No unit or lesson ever turns out perfectly. There is always room for improvement. There are always different children in next year's class. Whenever a unit is going to be used again, careful consideration should be given to the notes on the evaluation of last year's presentation of the unit. Before trying the unit again, new ideas can be added, procedures that caused difficulty the last time can be changed, and activities that didn't work the last time can be discarded or used in a different way.

Timelines are planning tools that begin well before the unit is used with children and end sometime after the unit ends. Timelines include the who, how, what, where, and when of the unit. While they do not need to have a lot of detail, they serve as a guide to the teacher for accomplishing things on time. A timeline would include the dates for accomplishing all aspects of the unit, who will accomplish it, and how it will be accomplished. For example, if a pediatric nurse is going to be invited to speak to the children about nutrition and growth, the teacher (who) must telephone (how) that person one or two weeks beforehand (when) to set the date for the classroom visit. Following the visit, the nurse should be thanked for taking the time to visit with the children. Therefore, the teacher (who) will probably want to write a brief thank-you note to the nurse (how) the day after the visit (when). Each of these things can be done with a learning purpose in mind. Writing a thank-you note models an appropriate social behavior. Having the visitor in the first place demonstrates that we can get information from other people.

There are a number of ways to set up a timeline. Some prefer different parts of a unit listed on different sheets of paper, while others prefer a long, horizontal piece of paper. Depending on what the teacher feels comfortable using, horizontal and vertical rows can be created with the headings for who, what, when, where, and how.

INSTRUCTIONAL PLAN COMPONENTS

A number of factors should be included in an instructional plan. They can be grouped and classified in a number of ways. There is usually a sizable overlap between any two methods of classifying them. Therefore, one system should not be seen as correct while others are viewed as being wrong. Developing a consistent approach with a clear rationale supporting it is what is most important. A system for developing an instructional plan that consists of four components is described here. The four components are identified as givens, goals and objectives, implementation, and evaluation. The implementation, particularly, includes both long- and short-term factors. Each of these must be taken into consideration when developing a plan for instruction as each has an influence on the effectiveness of the unit.

Givens

The givens of an instructional plan comprise all of the factors and influences surrounding the classroom. They often include personal resources and the community. Givens usually cannot be changed or can only be changed slightly. They include the children in the room, the teacher, the parents of the children, the physical aspects of the classroom, and the community.

Children.

It is important to keep in mind that all children share a common humanity. It is equally important to recognize and accommodate their tremendous diversity. The children a teacher plans for may possess different abilities, socioeconomic backgrounds, cultural backgrounds, religious beliefs, and native languages. They also possess a diverse and often change-able set of likes and dislikes. In terms of school and learning, children are motivated by and toward diverse topics. They are influenced by differing types of rewards and possess experiences that have differing influences on their learning.

This diversity cannot be ignored. It must be planned for. While it is beneficial for children to work together on interesting tasks and activities, teachers should not expect the same responses or degree of learning from all children. Some will need more background building than others. Some will need explanations a second time and with more concrete examples. Others will seem to absorb the learning more quickly. Plans to address these issues through individual sessions, cooperative learning, and small group activities must be considered.

Teacher.

While the teacher might be seen as someone who can quickly change, the essence of a teacher remains fairly constant over a long period of time. The essence of a teacher does change, but it changes gradually rather than in dramatic shifts. For example, teachers possess beliefs formed over many years of being a student, teacher, and/or parent. They possess many beliefs about children: what makes them the way they are, why they do or do not appear to be interested in classroom activities, and what motivates them. Teachers possess attitudes toward the subject matter they teach. One teacher may believe in the value of learning to recite the alphabet and numbers at an early age, while seeing storybooks as an extra activity. Another teacher may believe in immersing children in a wide range of language and print opportunities, encouraging language skills to emerge through that immersion.

Teachers vary in their skills and abilities both in and out of the classroom. Some teachers seem to be able to keep the children purposeful for longer periods of time. Some teachers are capable of generating a great deal of enthusiasm and participation in parents. Some teachers are able to generate one creative activity after another for the instructional program. It is important for teachers to take a step back and to identify their own particular capabilities. In that way they can use their strengths effectively while continuing to develop professionally in other areas.

Parents.

Parents and families are just as varied as children. Gone are the days of the nuclear family with a father who worked outside the home, a mother who stayed at home, 2.3 children, a dog, a cat, and a white picket fence. While that was never totally the norm, society has moved even further away from it. Nearly one-half of all children are reared in single-parent households. In some of those households, the parent does not work outside the home. In many other families, it has become necessary for both parents to work in order to make ends meet. In still other families, both parents have chosen to pursue careers.

It is inappropriate to draw moral conclusions about the family arrangements of any of the children. The fact is that children come from different family situations. This fact must be taken into consideration in the instructional program. Can parents be used as resources to enhance the program? Will some be able to reinforce some of the activities at home during the evening or on weekends? Will some be able to help with projects during the week? Do some parents have jobs or talents that would make them appropriate classroom visitors for some units?

Classroom Environment.

While the teacher interacting with the children creates the affective environment in the classroom, there are also the physical aspects of the classroom to consider. An inventory of the room is a useful starting point. What are the dimensions of the room? Is it a square, rectangle, or some other shape? What books, supplies, and materials are contained in the room? What kind of equipment and furniture does it contain, and can the pieces be moved easily?

When an inventory has been completed, decisions can be made to make changes so that an appropriate layout of the room can be created. There is no single best way of arranging a room. Every space is different. The location of doors, lights, traffic patterns, sink, and windows all play a part. In a program that stresses an integrated language arts approach, the language and literature area plays a major role. Such an approach makes great use of such things as centers, play areas, housekeeping areas, and so forth. Figure 11-6 illustrates a classroom layout that places the literature cen-

ter in a central point in the classroom. In Figure 11-7, on the other hand, the language area is found in the reading corner. The choice is partly a function of the teacher's beliefs and the characteristics of the children in the classroom. A number of other possibilities can be developed for other layouts.

Community.

Every community has different things to offer. There are no communities with nothing to offer. Rural, suburban, and urban areas all provide unique possibilities. Urban areas tend to have more cultural potential with such things as libraries, museums, and governmental centers. Suburban areas tend to have more shops and markets. Rural areas tend to have more potential for exploring such topics as farms and natural settings. An inventory of the community should be made so that teachers can make decisions about how to best use that community for the benefit of the learning of the children.

The community can be brought to the children by means of classroom visitors. Farmers, feed store owners, supermarket produce managers, shopkeepers, firefighters, doctors, and museum curators are but a few of the possibilities. The children can also be taken into the community for valuable learning experiences. In rural areas, the children might visit a dairy farm. In suburban areas, the visit might be to a grocery market or computer store. In urban areas, children might visit a museum or a park. It all depends upon the unit being studied and the opportunities available in the community.

Goals and Objectives

Goals are broad general ideas of what is intended for the children to attain as a result of their participation in the program. Goals tend to be less measurable due to the lack of specificity in the statements that describe them. The language used in goal statements can be interpreted in several ways depending upon the values and beliefs of the individual reading them. For example, consider the goal statement: Children will understand that language is a tool for communication. While most would agree that such a goal is worthwhile for young children, there could be differing opinions as to its meaning. Does it mean that children will demonstrate the ability to listen? Does it

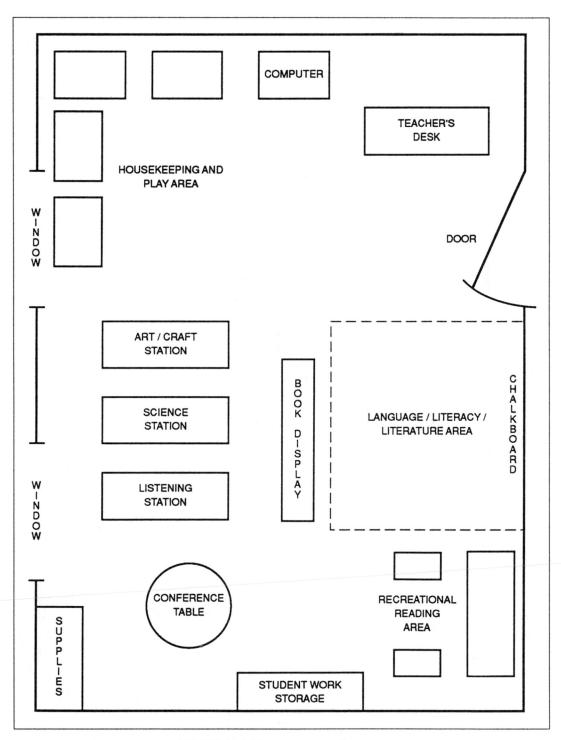

FIGURE 11-6 Literature center classroom

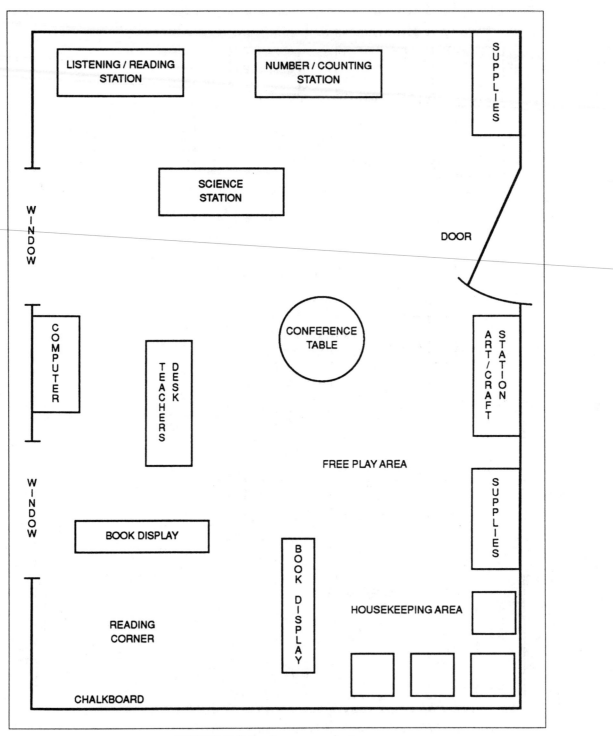

FIGURE 11-7 Reading corner classroom

mean that children will acquire certain reading skills and abilities? Does it mean that children will use language to have their needs met? It could mean each of these things or still others.

Objectives are more specific statements of what is intended for the children to attain as a result of their participation in the program. Objectives can have varying degrees of specificity. Many educators feel that behaviorally stated objectives are absolutely necessary in order for student progress and accountability to be addressed. Behaviorally stated objectives include a statement of the behavior the child will demonstrate (e.g., writing one's name), the conditions under which it will be done (e.g., when given a piece of paper and a crayon), and the criteria indicating the acceptability of the performance (e.g., using both capital and lower case letters). This objective might be phrased something like, "Given a crayon and a piece of paper, children will write their names using both capital and lower case letters."

Demands for behaviorally stated objectives peaked with the curriculum movements of the 1960s. They are still seen by many teachers as critically important. They give an impression of precision, accountability, and an aura of scientific correctness. The major problem with attempting to use them with a language arts program is that it breaks down language skills into bits and pieces that frequently have little or no meaning. Language does not exist in small, isolated bits and pieces that can be taught and learned in isolation. Such learning, devoid of context, has little meaning for the child.

Does this mean that teachers should not have objectives for children? No, this is not defensible. Teachers must have a sense of the kinds of things children need to know about language as well those abilities children need to acquire in using language. The objectives for young children need to be more specific than goals, but without the artificial specificity of behaviorally stated objectives. Use of the broad objectives identified in units two, three, and four can serve as a guide. The unit on evaluation will aid in determining how to assess the attainment of these objectives. In addition, an integrated language arts program strives to develop important values and attitudes toward language and literature. The acquisition of values and attitudes cannot be placed in a behaviorally stated objective with any certainty of validity.

Appropriateness.

Objectives for young children should first be developmentally appropriate. By virtue of this belief, it is likely that there may be different objectives for different children in the program. It is also possible that there will be some objectives for all of the children. An inventory of the characteristics of the group will serve as a useful guide in making these decisions.

Language Objectives.

Every unit should include language and literacy objectives. These include oral language, writing/drawing, and reading/literature objectives. In many cases, certain objectives will be carried from unit to unit for longer periods of time. This is because some language abilities take a longer time to develop than others. Consider your own ability to write a letter to another person. You may have done this with pen pals in the second or third grade. That did not mean, however, that you had accomplished everything there was to achieve in the area of letter writing. As you became more proficient with language, your letter writing became more sophisticated. You added variations, such as business letters and letters to the editor. The same thing is true for the language learning of young children. They develop meaningful language abilities over extended periods of time.

Social Objectives.

Social objectives refer to the learning children do in reference to their abilities to function within social settings. Since language is a key social tool, it is quite likely that any integrated language arts unit will include social objectives as well as language objectives. Social objectives may be addressed through the storybook being read, during free play, and during cooperative learning projects. They are often integrated with language, so that both language and social objectives are addressed at the same time or during a single activity.

Content Objectives.

Since language and content learning are likely to be integrated, most units will also contain content objectives. That is, if the theme of a unit is frogs and toads, it is likely that the teacher will have developed some ideas concerning what the children ought to learn about these animals. It might be something about the similarities and differences of frogs and toads, the places they live, or how they help people. It will often be a combination of both lower and higher order cognitive learning. Lower order cognitive learning is comprised of factual rote learning. An example might be the learning of the names of three different types of frogs. Higher order cognitive learning deals with the meaningfulness of the content. Examples might include understanding the life cycle of a frog, comparing and contrasting frogs and toads, and determining whether certain bodies of water would be adequate to support the lives of frogs. Teachers need to be careful in choosing objectives here. Essential knowledge should be the focus. When selecting content objectives, teachers might question the importance of those things children are being asked to learn. The learning should be meaningful, useful, and interesting to the child.

Planning the Implementation

Planning the implementation deals with coordinating all of the instructional aspects that will lead to the attainment of the goals and objectives within the parameters of the givens. There are several procedures for assisting the teacher to do this. It may be helpful to use a process similar to the one illustrated in Figures 11-1 through 11-5. Certain key considerations should be kept in mind when planning the instructional program. They include both long-term and short-term factors.

Long-term Factors

The long-term factors to consider when planning the implementation include activities, motivation, and the roles of the participants. Each of these is important in relation to the others.

Activities.

The activities used should, of course, be related to the goals and objectives of the unit. However, many decisions must be made concerning these activities. First, the activities must be appropriate for the developmental level of the children. Second, the activities

FIGURE 11-8 Teachers need time to plan integrated language activities.

need to be chosen to provide a wide array of experiences for the child. Using a single type of activity or even a limited number of activities will make a program seem tedious to young children.

Large group activities need to be interspersed with activities designed to be used with small groups, pairs of children, and individual children. Play activities as well as cooperative projects should be a part of the program. Based upon the theme and goals of a unit, teachers should select activities that include literary, art, music, and motor skills.

Motivation.

It is important that children be motivated to participate in the activities that will help them learn. Motivation for learning can be provided in a number of ways (see Sawyer and Comer 1991). Using a magic trick associated with the content, showing how the learning can be enjoyable, and engendering an excitement for the activity can all provide children with the motivation to learn.

Moving from one activity to another can sometimes be confusing to young children. Transitional activities can be useful tools. They can help children to move from one activity to another, to understand the connection between the two activities, and to motivate the child for the second activity. Fingerplays and rhymes provide an excellent way to make these transitions, particularly if they involve the participation of the children.

Participant Roles.

In thinking ahead toward the instructional part of the program, the roles of the individuals taking part in the program should be clearly identified. In an integrated language arts program for young children, it is critical to recall that the role of the teacher is quite different from the role of the teacher in a traditional language arts program. The tasks for the teacher must be clearly identified. How will the teacher serve to coordinate certain activities? To what extent will the teacher participate in play and cooperative projects?

The roles of children, parents, and classroom visitors must be considered as well. Has the classroom visitor been contacted for a specific time and date? What will the children learn from the visit? What new social skills will the children be provided in order for them to be successful on their cooperative project? What expectations are there for parents? Will materials be sent home so that parents can reinforce what is happening in the classroom?

Short-term Factors

The short-term factors to consider when planning the implementation include pacing and materials. As with long-term factors, these are important in relation to each other as well.

Pacing.

Setting the pace for the day might seem like a fairly routine concept, but it has a number of ramifications. The pace at which instruction takes place must be flexible. Some children will achieve the learning quickly while others will take substantially longer. Some will tire of the activity and choose not to continue. They may not understand the activity or they may simply need to do something different.

Children with disabilities in the classroom may need additional support to have a meaningful experience with the activity without regard to the pace. Non-English-speaking children may be comfortable with a pace similar to native language speakers as long as the process of the activity is clearly demonstrated in a visual format. Each child will have a different pace, but for different reasons. The teacher must be prepared to accommodate these differences to determine the best time to move on.

FIGURE 11-9 Adequate space and materials are necessary for planned activities.

Content Materials.

Planning the use of the materials requires a well-organized teacher who is able to keep track of a number of details. In most types of thematic units, a wide range of materials will be required. They must be decided upon beforehand and acquired by the time the lesson occurs. It is highly likely that many of the materials will not be found in the classroom. The teacher, therefore, must develop sources of materials outside the classroom. Among these might be the school library, the public library, local bookstores, parents, fellow teachers, and local businesses.

Most thematic units will have a strong literacy component; therefore, teachers will need to have rich sources of language-related materials. Since oral language discussion and tales for storytelling are important parts of an integrated program, teachers might wish to obtain personal copies of resource materials. This might include books on thematic units, volumes of folk tales and fairy tales, and anthologies of chants, rhymes, and fingerplays.

While books may comprise a substantial portion of the needed material, it is likely that other media and supplies might be needed as well. If the unit relates to science, supplies for experiments might be needed. These may include aluminum pie plates for holding water, measuring cups, wooden objects, rulers, and egg cartons. Teachers need to plan for this by identifying sources for these materials.

Planning the Evaluation

Evaluation is much more than a test of student learning or a check of how many new concepts the

FIGURE 11-10 Common objects found in the classroom can add reality and motivation to an activity.

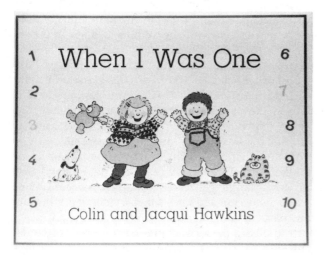

FIGURE 11-11 Literature will be found in most well-planned thematic units. *From* When I Was One, *by Colin and Jacqui Hawkins. Reprinted courtesy of Viking Penguin.*

children have acquired. Evaluation is systematically gathering information to be used to make decisions. As such, it needs to be done more frequently than at the end of a lesson or unit. Important events occur throughout the entire program. In fact, important events are occurring even as the teacher is planning a unit. Therefore, it makes sense to evaluate not just the child's learning, but the plan for that learning as well. In addition, it is valuable to evaluate the process

of the child's learning as the instruction is taking place, rather than only at the end. As a result, there are two focal points for evaluation, the unit itself and the learning of the child.

Unit Evaluation.

All aspects of the instructional unit should be assessed. This includes the plan, the implementation, and the evaluation. To begin with, it must be decided whether the different components of the unit plan were reasonable. That is, were the activities developmentally appropriate, sufficient for increasing learning, and successful in fostering language skills and cooperative social behaviors? Were they manageable in terms of acquiring materials, setting up activities, and monitoring the behavior of children participating in them?

The implementation of the plan in the actual classroom is a key area for evaluation. It is here that deficiencies in any plan clearly emerge. Therefore, one

FIGURE 11-12 Evaluation of the child's learning should be done using the natural processes and products of the learning activities.

may wish to ask whether or not the plan was implemented in the way expected. If yes, to what can problems be attributed? If no, were the unexpected occurrences a negative factor? What can be done in the future to improve this plan?

Learning Evaluation.

Just as all parts of the unit should be evaluated, all aspects of students' learning should be evaluated as well. This means that the evaluation of the child as a learner needs to be broad and comprehensive. It does little good to know that a child has achieved or not achieved something. That type of information is but a picture of something frozen in time. It does not tell us why such a situation exists or how to improve on the situation.

Evaluation of the child's learning needs to take place throughout the unit. Even before the instruction begins, teachers need to have some evaluative information concerning the knowledge, skills, beliefs, and abilities of the children. It is important to keep in mind that understanding is largely a process of relating new information to information that is already known. Teachers who know their children well are in a good position to help them understand new learning. Procedures need to be planned to gather this kind of information.

As the unit is progressing, the process of learning needs to be evaluated. Children need feedback as they make guesses and hypotheses about the validity of their views of the world. Perceptive teachers constantly seek to understand the views of their children and to provide feedback that enables the children to make decisions about the validity of those views. Observational procedures and information-gathering techniques need to be used by teachers to both keep track of the learning processes of children and to provide feedback to the children.

The learning of the children at the end of the unit should be addressed as well. Traditionally, this has been the sole focus of evaluation. The evaluation at this point should determine whether or not the original goals and objectives have been achieved. Were the language objectives achieved? The social objectives? The content objectives? While this information can be shared with parents and children, it should only be one part of the evaluation information shar-

ing. It is only partially meaningful to know what a child has accomplished. It is equally important, and perhaps more meaningful, to understand how the child has been able to learn and what kinds of things can be done to enhance that learning. This information will help teachers to improve the learning of children in the future.

SUMMARY

In order to plan instruction successfully, teachers need to develop an organized approach to planning. Such an approach will serve as a useful guide and help to make the instruction more efficient. Given the nature of young children, however, teachers must not assume that everything will proceed according to plan, no matter how carefully the plan was developed.

Teachers can use several tools to help them engage in effective planning. The first tool is the semantic map. It involves brainstorming ideas, classifying those ideas, and creating a map or web that depicts those ideas in an organized manner. As specific parts of the map are targeted, those sections can be expanded to include a number of additional factors related to planning a thematic unit for young children.

Other useful tools for organizing instruction include charts and timelines. Charts are any type of illustration, diagram, or table of information used by the teacher to prepare an instructional program. Charts can be used to translate the different components of a lesson that originated in a semantic map into an instructional plan. Timelines ordinarily comprise a period of time beginning before a unit is begun and ending some time after the unit is concluded. They are helpful to the teacher in identifying the different things that need to be done to make a lesson successful and when to accomplish those things.

A planning process was described that identified four critical areas to consider. Each area can be identified and studied by itself. However, it is important to realize that each of the four areas is related to each of the other areas. Without the four areas being integrated into a whole, an effective instructional program does not exist.

The first area refers to the givens within a program. Everything in life operates within a certain context. An early childhood classroom is no different. Children possess a range of characteristics, capabilities, motivations, and interests. Teachers arrive in the classroom with both strengths and weaknesses. In addition, they also possess beliefs about how children learn and what constitutes effective instruction. The physical environment of the actual classroom also plays a role. Any facility will have certain equipment as well as certain possibilities. Whatever they are, the teacher must operate within these boundaries. The parents of the children and the community possess unique characteristics. Each of these factors represents boundaries within which the program must operate as well as possibilities for the program to explore.

The second area concerns the goals and objectives of learning. Within an integrated language arts program, we would expect to find reasonable and developmentally appropriate objectives that address the areas of language, social development, and content learning. Both lower order and higher order cognitive objectives might be included. Lower order objectives include those learnings that simply require the rote learning of pieces of information. Higher order objectives include those learnings that deal with the understanding, analysis, application, and evaluation of information and concepts.

The third area concerns the actual implementation components. This area describes the plan for presenting the instruction to children. It is comprised of long- and short-term factors such as classroom activities, motivational procedures, roles of the classroom participants, content materials, and pacing of instruction. While these features are integrated with the others and directed toward helping children learn, the activities of the classroom are of prime importance. The range of children's needs must be addressed. One activity, or even a few activities provided in a rigid manner, will simply not do. The diversity of children in a classroom is usually far too great to enable such a limited program to be successful. In addition, the activities should provide opportunities for social development, language development, play, and group projects.

The fourth area concerns evaluation. Two parts of the evaluation must be planned. The first part is an assessment of the unit plan itself. In order to conduct such an assessment, the teacher must reconsider what took place during the unit. Care must be taken to review deviations from the plan and the effect of those on the students. Ideas for improving the unit for the future should also be considered. Finally, the child's learning should be assessed. This takes place before, during, and after the instructional unit. The child's incoming abilities must be known in order for the teacher to provide the best instruction for that child. Constant monitoring and assessment should take place during the instruction in order to assess the ability of the child to make sense out of what is happening and, more importantly, to provide feedback to the child concerning the learning. Assessment at the end of the unit is closely related to the objectives upon which the entire unit is based.

Questions and Activities for Review and Discussion

Multiple Choice
1. The first general program areas to be planned are the
   a. activities.
   b. instructional procedures.
   c. goals.
   d. tests.
2. A semantic map contains components that are
   a. not ordinarily related to each other.

      b. facts and ideas isolated from one another.

      c. sometimes related to a theme.

      d. parts of an integrated whole.

3. Charts can be helpful in translating information from a semantic map into

      a. a plan of instruction.

      b. a curriculum.

      c. a classroom floor plan.

      d. a testing tool.

4. Timelines for instructional planning are used to plan components of a lesson that occur

      a. prior to classroom instruction.

      b. during classroom instruction.

      c. after classroom instruction.

      d. all of the above

5. In instructional planning, factors such as the children, the teacher, and the classroom environment are referred to as

      a. goals.

      b. givens.

      c. teacher variables.

      d. motivation factors.

6. In an integrated language arts program, curricular objectives should

      a. be reasonable.

      b. include language objectives.

      c. include social objectives.

      d. all of the above

7. Children's learning should be evaluated as the unit is progressing in order to

      a. test their ability.

      b. determine if they are motivated to learn.

      c. provide feedback to them.

      d. all of the above

True or False

T   F 1. Since young children are so unpredictable, it makes little sense to plan an actual program of learning for them.

T   F 2. Semantic maps are basically illustrations of isolated ideas and pieces of information.

T   F 3. Diagrams, tables, and illustrations can all be used as planning charts.

T   F 4. When developing instructional plans, it is best to assume that all children are basically alike.

T   F 5. Evaluation consists primarily of testing students to determine whether or not they have learned the material that was taught.

Essay and Discussion

1. What are some reasons for planning instruction for young children?

2. Explain the process for developing a semantic map. Use illustrations if needed.

3. Describe the components that a teacher might include in an instructional planning chart.

4. Draw an original diagram of an early childhood education classroom floor plan that could be used with an integrated language arts program.
5. Describe the factors that may affect the pacing of instruction.

References

Day, B. 1983. *Early childhood education: Creative learning activities.* New York: Macmillan.

Pearson, P.D., and D.D. Johnson. 1978. *Teaching reading comprehension.* New York: Holt, Rinehart and Winston.

Sawyer, W., and D.E. Comer. 1991. *Growing up with literature.* Albany, New York: Delmar Publishers Inc.

UNIT 12

Implementing a Program

U NIT GOALS

After completing this unit, the reader should:

- understand some of the major points researchers have concluded constitute effective instruction.
- develop an awareness of effective teaching characteristics.
- acquire a number of effective instructional activities to be used to implement a program.
- develop an understanding of how to manage the daily aspects of a classroom.
- develop skills to use in understanding and managing the classroom behaviors of children.

PREVIEW

As we have seen, careful planning is somewhat analogous to a road map. Just as a road map can help us more efficiently arrive at our travel destination, a well-developed plan can help and guide children as they go about the task of achieving growth in literacy. After traveling a certain route in a vehicle a few times, there is often less need to use the map. The route is more familiar, road names and numbers are committed to memory, and landmarks are recognized during the trip. On each succeeding trip, we are more confident of our way. We begin to notice opportunities to take shortcuts, vary the roads, time our travel for certain periods of the day, and merge into the correct lanes of traffic well before it is time to make our turns. In short, we have developed the confidence to be experts in our ability to travel to our destinations.

Implementing an instructional program is similar to the travel analogy described above. The first time a class or program is taught, teachers rightly feel somewhat anxious and tentative. As time passes, confidence builds. Teachers becomes more familiar with the needs, interests, and personalities of the children. The effectiveness of activities becomes known. Different strategies are used more effectively, and time is used more efficiently. This does not mean, however, that the travel/instruction analogy is consistent at all times. Children are not roads, they are people. A teaching activity is not an automobile, it is a process in which human beings engage. In short, as with any activity in life, things can go wrong. This is why any plan should have provisions for the unexpected. Becoming knowledgeable about effective teaching is one of the ways teachers can gain strategies to deal more confidently with the unexpected.

FIGURE 12-1 The teacher is of tremendous importance to the literacy development of children.

While trial-and-error may lead to some useful information about teaching, it is better to start with a foundation gained through an analysis of the literature on classroom instruction. In this unit key ideas and concepts to be discussed include research findings on classroom instruction, characteristics of effective teaching, classroom tested activities, and procedures for managing a classroom program.

INTRODUCTION

The purpose of this unit is to familiarize the reader with ideas, activities, and procedures that are effective in providing instruction in the classroom. While an integrated language arts program places much emphasis on developing learning independence, pupil choice of reading and writing tasks, and natural language, teachers still must provide instruction. The instruction tends to be with individuals and small groups rather than with the whole class. During such activities as story time, circle time, and discussion groups with young children, however, the instruction is provided to the whole class. More often than not, instruction tends to be based on student needs rather than on the directions stated in an instructor's manual. The role of the teacher may be different, but the task remains the same. The job of the teacher is to foster student learning.

Over the past several decades, much research has been conducted on the process of classroom teaching. Virtually every aspect has been addressed from the tone of the teacher's voice, to the size of the group, to the verbal reinforcement used by the teacher, to the time spent on practicing the material that was taught. Much of this research came to the same conclusions. Nevertheless, substantial amounts of it came to alternate conclusions. Some of the key concepts emerging from this research are summarized in this unit.

Much of the research on classroom learning uses the learning of content information as the criterion for success. This further compromises how easily generalized the conclusions are to early childhood education. In language arts, many of the goals are focused on such aspects as positive attitudes toward learning, curiosity about language, and willingness to take language risks. These are more complex than the simple acquisition of information.

Many time-tested and classroom-tested activities can be helpful in implementing an early childhood language arts program. Some have been mentioned previously, while others may be new. They are discussed here as key tools the teacher can and should become expert in using. They can form a core set of tools with which to provide an effective instructional program. Some require more long-term planning than others. Some can be used on an immediate basis given the teacher's assessment of the needs of the children at a particular time.

Managing the classroom is a long-term process. It is a task that will require variations over the years as different materials, needs, and children come and go. Some of the tools are directed at handling the physical aspects of the room. Others are aimed at managing the behavior of children. Still others, such as using available resources, are a combination of planning and implementation.

EFFECTIVE TEACHING RESEARCH

Teaching as a profession has had a long and rocky history. One of the central characteristics of a profession is an agreed upon knowledge base. That is, there are core ideas and beliefs about what is included and what is not included. Medicine uses the knowledge bases of such disciplines as human biology and chemistry. The legal profession possesses a base of laws and court decisions. Teaching, because of the contradictions found in much of its research, has not possessed the luxury of such a knowledge base. The field of psychology, while helpful to teaching, does not comprise an a sufficient knowledge base for teaching. Does this mean that teaching should not be considered a profession? Absolutely not. To consider it less than a profession eliminates the status that it rightfully deserves. At one time medicine contained much myth and error. As time went on, truths and principles replaced the misinformation.

Early Research on Teaching

Research on teaching has not been neglected. It has been conducted for many years, although many of the findings of earlier research have subsequently been rejected. Coleman and his colleagues (1966) and Jencks and his colleagues (1972) created small revolutions in education with the conclusions of their research released in national reports. They asserted that neither schools nor teachers had a significant effect on student achievement.

As a result of reaction to these reports and President Lyndon Johnson's Great Society programs, massive curriculum development efforts were launched in the 1960s. They were led by subject matter specialists, particularly in mathematics and science. These programs were based on the belief that greater achievement could be brought about by greater expenditures. "Teacher proof" materials were developed with the view that teachers were weak links to be worked around or as technicians to be programmed (Porter and Brophy 1988). These efforts did not lead to educational improvement and have been largely discarded.

Focus on the Teacher

Since the early 1970s, the concept that the teacher possesses a central role in the improvement of education has emerged. An array of elaborate observation procedures, interview techniques, and data collection tools have been developed (Porter and Brophy 1988). In general, the emphasis has been on linking teaching behaviors with improved achievement.

Two general principles have resulted from these efforts. First, students who receive active instruction from their teachers and who are supervised and monitored in their work achieve more than students who spend most of their time working on their own with curriculum materials (Brophy and Good 1986). This only makes sense. When the teacher does not teach, students do not learn as much. The second principle states that much of the active instruction provided by teachers is a result of professional planning, thinking, and decision making by teachers (Clark and Peterson 1986). Each of these principles is compatible with an integrated appoach to language arts instruction.

The Institute for Research on Teaching at Michigan State University has developed a model of what they describe as good teaching (Porter and Brophy 1988). In their model, teaching is viewed as encompassing factors within an interactive process. Factors include such things as student aptitude, social norms, teachers' beliefs about instruction, resources available, and so on. All of these factors, in combination, influence the immediate responses of students to the instruction. Good teachers use this feedback to adjust both their current instruction and future instructional planning. The best teachers attend to all of the factors influencing the process. The sheer complexity of attending to all of the factors while teaching, however, makes it necessary for most teachers to simplify the task by selecting certain factors to address and by introducing routines and procedures to make the task possible. In any case, given the number of children teachers work with on a daily basis and the limitations of resources found within most schools, many of the factors cannot be adequately addressed at the classroom level. Using professional judgment, teachers must make the best decisions that circumstances permit (Lampert 1985). Nevertheless, it is important for teachers to be aware of characteristics that have been identified as relevant to effective teaching. This knowledge helps the teacher make critical choices during the implementation of a planned program.

CHARACTERISTICS OF EFFECTIVE TEACHERS

Given the tremendous complexity of the task, it is helpful for teachers to be aware of the characteristics that are consistently observed in effective teachers. This knowledge can help teachers make better decisions even though it is known that they are seldom able to attend to all of the factors involved (Clark and Peterson 1986). The Institute for Research on Teaching has identified eleven characteristics of effective teachers (Porter and Brophy 1988). Each is discussed here. It is important, however, to keep in mind that a mere summation of these characteristics does not equal an effective teacher. These characteristics are interactive. They have an effect on and are affected by each of the other characteristics. Therefore, it is important to see each of the characteristics in terms of how well it fits into an overall view of teaching.

Ability to Set Clear Goals

As seen in the planning process, relevant, meaningful, developmentally appropriate goals are particularly important. More than anything else, the teacher needs to always keep in mind the goals for the students in the program. These goals must be made clear and understandable to the children. Most people appreciate having some idea of what they are attempting to accomplish and why it is important to accomplish it.

In language arts, as in many other areas, the teacher must choose from a wide range of possible goals. It is not reasonable to address or work toward every potential goal all of the time. The task of the teacher is to decide on both the appropriate goals for children and an appropriate number of such goals. If too few goals are chosen, the classroom program becomes too focused and lacks diversity and appropriate challenge. In such a situation, the program is compromised (Sedlak, Wheeler, Pullin, and Cusick 1986). On the other hand, the program should not have too many goals. If too many goals are attempted, the program becomes too crowded and critically important goals are given less and less attention (Armbruster and Anderson 1984).

Integration with Other Subjects

Because teachers tend to be people-oriented individuals who are intensely interested in the development of children, they do have a tendency to incorporate added goals into their programs without deleting other goals (Flooden, Porter, Schmidt, Freeman, and Schwille 1981). Care must be taken when adding additional goals.

An integrated approach to language arts can often deal with increased goals more successfully than a program that stresses isolated tasks and subject matter. For example, Prawat (1985) found that teachers who stressed both social and academic goals were more successful than teachers who included both sets of goals but put different priorities on each. Schmidt, Rohler, Caul, Diamond, Cianciolo, and Buchmann (1985) found that teachers who used an integrated approach to teach language arts skills within the context of another subject area were successful in achieving goals in both areas.

Knowledge and Strategies

Effective teachers possess several types of knowledge, all of which help them to teach their students. First, they are knowledgeable about the subjects they teach. At the early childhood level, teachers should have a comprehensive knowledge of language and language development. In addition they need to have a basic but accurate knowledge of such subjects as mathematics, science, social studies, humanities, physical development, and the arts. Second, teachers must also possess a knowledge of their children and what those children bring to the learning situation. Just as teachers have varying degrees of knowledge about different subject fields, children possess different levels of knowledge and information about many different topics. Teachers need to develop the subtle awareness that tells them why children are or are not taking advantage of the literacy opportunities available to them (Fielding and Roller 1992).

In addition to possessing certain knowledge, teachers must use that knowledge to develop effective strategies for helping children learn. Some children may know a wide range of animal names, while others

FIGURE 12-2 The effective teacher uses a variety of instructional strategies.

may possess only a few of those names. Teachers presenting a unit on animals need to develop and implement strategies for dealing with such a situation. They need to make decisions about whether to employ small group discussion, cooperative learning, read alouds, or field trips to address the different needs of children.

Anticipating Misconceptions

Related to this is the concept of conceptual change teaching (Anderson and Smith 1987). The strategies of conceptual change teaching focus on the fact that some children may possess information that is inaccurate. An integrated language arts approach stresses the need to relate new information and ideas to that which is already known to the child. But what if the child possesses misinformation or partial understandings? If these are not identified, children may complete the current learning activity with the original misinformation intact (Eaton, Anderson, and Smith 1984).

Does this mean that the teacher must take on the role of pronouncing children right or wrong in terms of their pre-existing knowledge? While this is a traditional approach, there are more powerful and positive ways to teach. Porter and Brophy (1988) suggest confronting children's misinformation by contrasting it sharply with the accurate information. In this way

children can both recognize the differences between the two sets of information and come to the understanding that views and positions held can be altered. Children will have done this frequently already as they have tried out different language structures.

Communicate Expectations

Effective teachers are clear in their explanation of expectations to students. In an integrated language arts program, it is desirable to include the children in developing goals and expectations. This provides them with a sense of ownership over what is occurring in the program as well as the motivation to work toward goals that they helped to set. Not all children participate in this process to the same extent. In this case the teacher's task is twofold. First, efforts must be made to encourage all children to participate in the development of goals and expectations. Second, the teacher must make certain that all children clearly understand the goals.

In addition to understanding the goals of a unit on such topics as animals, friendship, community, or shapes, children need to know why the goals are important and relevant to themselves. Effective teachers help children see how the learning will have an impact on their lives beyond the boundaries of the educational program. It has been found that such an understanding fosters both personal and social responsibility as well as cognitive learning (Anderson, Anderson, and Prawat 1985; Anderson and Prawat 1983; Anderson, Brubaker, Alleman-Brooks, and Duffy 1985).

Expert Use of Materials

No one should be engaged in reinventing the wheel. Therefore, when high quality instructional materials are available, they should be used. The work schedule of most teachers does not ordinarily provide a sufficient amount of time to develop all of the materials that might be needed (Ball and Feiman-Nemser 1986). On the other hand, much of the commercial material available in the language arts has been widely criticized for a lack of literary quality (Anderson, Hiebert, Scott and Wilkinson 1985; Leinhardt and Smith 1985; Shulman 1986).

An integrated language arts approach makes extensive use of such materials as trade books, paper,

FIGURE 12-3 Television can be an effective tool if it is used with restraint and expertise.

writing tools, crayons, pencils, and markers. This is in sharp contrast to more traditional language arts materials often described as "reading readiness" materials. These latter materials fall into the category of commercial materials that have been criticized for their quality in terms of literacy and instruction. Using established criteria for selecting material (see Sawyer and Comer 1991), teachers can obtain high quality material for their language and literacy program. The use of this material allows teachers to devote more time to the other aspects of instruction (Porter and Brophy 1988).

Strategies for Independence

Helping children share responsibility with their teachers is a valuable characteristic of the effective teacher. To do this, children need to learn that they are capable of taking some of this responsibility. Teachers help them acquire this by modeling and providing instruction in how to make sense of things, comprehension, problem solving, and metacognitive strategies for focused learning (Duffy, Roehler, Book, Meloth, Vavrus, Putnam, and Wesselman 1986; Palincsar and Brown 1984; Raphael and Kirschner 1985).

This does not mean, of course, that children should be totally responsible for their own learning. The teacher must judge whether there is too much supervision, which limits the learning potential of the child, or too little supervision, which leads to confusion (Navarro, Berkey and Minnick 1986).

Higher Level Objectives

For years, language arts programs that focused on "reading readiness" objectives attempted to have children achieve mastery over the visual and auditory surface features of language. Much time was spent in such activities as learning to recite the alphabet, learning the sounds of the letters, printing the letters, and identifying rhyming words. This kind of learning, which depends primarily on memory and recall (also known as rote memory) is referred to as lower level cognitive learning. While these can be useful skills, they can be learned indirectly by immersing children in a rich literary environment with books, drawing, and writing.

Effective teachers understand the need to have children master not only lower level learning, but higher level learning as well. Higher level learning includes such things as understanding the meaning of messages, creating language communications, learning to apply language that has been learned in practical situations, and developing the ability to evaluate and respond to oral and written communications. An integrated approach to language arts includes all of these characteristics within its boundaries.

Regular Constructive Feedback

Most people do not enjoy doing tasks in which they are never quite sure about whether or not they are being successful. In many situations in life, we can see that we are making progress. The goal is clear and precise. We can determine for ourselves how close we are to achieving it. In developing literacy, children are traveling in unchartered waters. As we have seen, they are constantly making hypotheses about language that they attempt to use in new situations. They depend on the feedback they receive to determine the validity of their hypotheses.

Regular feedback to children is necessary not only in literacy situations, but in all learning situations. This requires the teacher to be aware, through constant monitoring, of what each child is doing so that no child spends a long period of time in a frustrating situation. The feedback should be constructive. A simple statement of right or wrong is often insufficient. It is more useful to provide feedback that encourages children to think of alternative possibilities. In this way, they will be taking more responsibility for their learning by discovering truths more independently.

Acceptance of Responsibility

The first and most basic responsibility of any teacher is for the health and safety of the children. The second responsibility is to provide a rich and meaningful program to the children. Effective teachers go beyond both of these, however, by assuming responsibility for the learning of all of their students.

Accepting this responsibility is not always easy. Some children present teachers with continuing problems of personal adjustment and behavior. Nevertheless, teachers who are viewed as more successful tend to see such difficulties as something to be corrected rather than as something to be endured (Porter and Brophy 1988). Such teachers might seek help from program directors and social workers while they attempt to deal constructively with the student. They would not, however, confine their efforts solely to attempts to control the behavior of the student through demands and punishments (Rohrkemper 1981). Rather, they would strive to identify, recognize, and build on the student's strengths as well.

Reflective Practitioner

Effective teachers have been found to be individuals who tend to frequently reflect upon themselves and their roles in the lives of children. While teachers are not totally autonomous individuals, they do determine to a large extent what will happen in their classrooms. They do not confine their thoughts merely to the activities they will conduct with the children entrusted to their care. In addition, they reflect upon and monitor all aspects of their roles as teachers. They make conscious decisions about the value of the materials they use. They self-evaluate their instruction, seeking ways in which to improve it. They consider their responsibility to enable all of their children to learn. Finally, they reflect upon their responsibility as one of the most important adults in the life of each child in their classroom.

ACTIVITIES FOR LEARNING

When considering activities to be used during instruction, it is important not to see them simply as activities without regard to their connection to other aspects of the program. An activity that is done because it sounds enjoyable may not accomplish much. There is a great need, of course, to engage children in enjoyable activities. Much learning can and should occur through enjoyable activities. The task of the teacher, however, is to select activities that will be helpful to student learning, motivating and enjoyable. Three types of activities are described here. While some have been mentioned previously, others are discussed as well. They include activities related to stories that are read to, read by, or written by the children. General activities that can be used with a wide range of subjects are described as well. Finally, social activities that combine language and play are described.

Story Activities

Several activities related to stories are discussed in units two, three, and four. They are, of course, particularly applicable here. Those that comprise some of the mainstays of early childhood programs include the activities of reading aloud, oral storytelling, flannel board stories, puppetry, and conferencing.

Reading Aloud.

Reading aloud is one of the most productive parts of a language arts program. It should be done several times each day. It can serve several purposes: introducing a theme, motivating the children, teaching about the reading process itself, and teaching about a subject. It can also be used to summarize or conclude a day, a unit, or a lesson. There are several excellent sources for selecting read-aloud books. The best

FIGURE 12-4 A classroom visitor reads a book aloud.

source might be the librarian at the school or the local public library. Another useful source is *The New Read-aloud Handbook* (1989), by Jim Trelease. This book recommends the best stories for reading aloud. It contains sections on predictable books, wordless books, picture books, and short novels for young children.

Oral Storytelling.

Oral storytelling is particularly well suited for use with young children. It requires the person sharing the story to know the story well and to love the story. It has the advantage of not having to manipulate a book, enabling the teller to focus more on the children and involving them completely in the tale.

There are several benefits derived from oral storytelling. First, children are introduced to and encouraged to participate in an enjoyable and motivating oral language activity. As they begin to engage in this activity on their own they develop an awareness of story sequence, confidence as oral language users and a wider range of vocabulary. Bettelheim (1976) has suggested the possibility that oral storytelling helps children create more mental images. By not having

the pictures from a storybook to look at as the story unfolds, children create mental images or pictures in their minds to accompany the tale.

Flannel Board Stories.

Flannel board stories may be re-creations of stories from literature or they may be stories created in the classroom by the teacher and/or children. Each can be valuable as part of a language or literature unit. To engage in flannel board stories, the storyteller needs to know the story well, have the necessary flannel board characters, and a flannel board for telling the story. Stories that work best with a flannel board are those with relatively few characters and with a plot that progresses gradually throughout the tale. Excellent choices include Audrey Wood's *The Napping House* (1984), Ann McGovern's *Too Much Noise* (1967), and Tomie dePaola's *Stega Nona* (1975). If there are two many characters and objects the flannel board becomes crowded. If the plot does not unfold throughout the tale the flannel board remains as only a single picture.

Although commercial products are available, flannel boards are relatively easy to construct. A flannel board is basically a piece of flannel, felt, or other fuzzy type of material that uses a rigid backing of some type. Flannel board characters and objects are placed on the board as a story is told. A metal backing can be used if magnetic characters and objects are used. Figure 12-5 provides an illustration of a number of flannel board construction possibilities.

Puppetry.

Puppets can be used in numerous activities with young children. They can tell a story, carry on a conversation with a single child, be good listeners, and participate in a discussion with a group of children. Puppets are entertaining, motivating, and expressive. Through puppets, teachers and children can assume many characteristics in terms of personality and human behaviors. They can assist the child in being creative, in attempting language structures, and in telling stories.

Puppets can be special friends to children. They enable children to express emotions and fears that they might otherwise not be able to share. They do

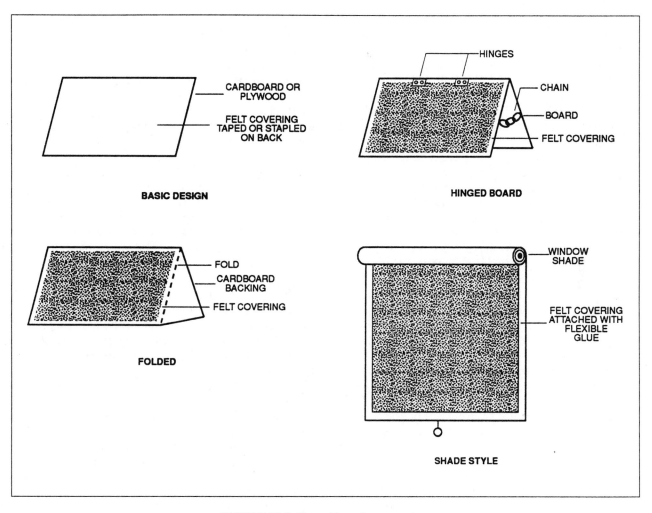

FIGURE 12-5 Flannel board construction

this by providing an intermediary through which the child can express these emotions. This allows children to say things they would ordinarily not be comfortable saying. Included in this area is the need for children to express anger and hostility. Puppets can provide an outlet for these feelings in a socially acceptable manner. They do this by allowing the child to transfer these negative feelings to an emotionally neutral puppet.

Children do not automatically know how to use puppets. They may seem like toys, so if no instruction or modeling is provided, children may tend to play with puppets only as toys. Teachers need to show children how to use puppets effectively. They can do this by demonstrating how to hold the puppet, move its arms, and make it talk. The instructional plan for each unit should be reviewed so that specific parts of the program can be identified as being particularly appropriate for a puppet activity. It is not necessary to be a ventriloquist. When not done expertly, such attempts seem contrived and distracting. Children are accepting when teachers use their regular voices to make the puppets talk. As puppets are introduced, they should maintain a consistent personality. When well-known puppets are used, they will already possess a distinct personality.

Using puppets regularly will model the appropriate use of the puppets. Teachers may wish to avoid the violent behavior associated with "Punch and Judy" puppet plays. Discussions and language activities should be acknowledged and reinforced. Opportunities for seeing puppets outside of the classroom should be encouraged. Arts programs and public libraries often stage puppet shows for children. Taking children to these events and encouraging parents to do likewise is a worthwhile effort. Creating additional puppets is a good in-service or parent volunteer activity. *Creative Teaching with Puppets* (Rountree, Shuptrine, Gordon, and Taylor 1981) is an excellent source of ideas and information for these activities.

There are a number of types of puppets. Stick puppets are the simplest to make. They can be created simply by gluing a picture of a character onto a craft stick. Puppets can also be made from paper bags, socks, and boxes. Characters from well-known contemporary and classic children's literature are popular with children. New characters and creative puppet designs allow teachers the freedom to endow their puppets with distinct personalities.

When using puppets, teachers may wish to construct a puppet stage from a large packing carton or by draping a cloth over a piece of rope. A stage, however, is not necessary. Children accept the idea of puppets attached to the hands of the teacher. When demonstrating how to use a puppet, teachers should use slow, deliberate movements rather than waving the puppet excitedly. Conversations between puppets can be very motivating to children. It will both model the use of puppets as well as give children ideas about creating conversations between themselves.

Conferencing.

The process of conferencing occurs when two individuals meet to discuss and learn. A conference may include a child and teacher, a child and another child, a teacher and a small group, or a small group of children. The purpose of the conference is to give individuals an opportunity to talk about their learning and to learn more about a topic. A teacher may use a conference to teach a small group a language strategy or skill. Pairs of children may engage in a conference in order to share their knowledge about turtles.

A teacher may engage a child in a conference in order to provide the child with a trial audience to tell about a picture or language response that was created in relation to a story read in class. The teacher may use this situation as a valuable teaching tool. It can provide the opportunity to give feedback to the child that encourages additional thinking. Questions that encourage additional thinking and language are those that cannot be answered with a single word or a simple sentence. Examples include:

- Why did the little bunny run away?
- Did something like that ever happen to you? Would you tell me about it?
- What do you think might happen next?
- How can you tell that the baby felt sad?
- What would you do if you were the puppy?

Whenever teachers engage in conferencing with children, much useful information can be learned concerning literacy development. By being a responsive listener, teachers can encourage children to share an insight into their development as readers, writers, and oral language users. It is an opportunity for informally assessing language growth and development. For this reason, it may be helpful to use charts and anecdotal records to collect this valuable information. Figure 12-6 provides an example of a format that may be used to collect information about a child's development as a reader. It provides an open-ended format. The teacher can use it to write anecdotal records and the comments of both the children and the teacher.

Figure 12-7 provides an example of a format for use in collecting information about a child's development as a writer. The format is a check-off system that requires little comment or writing by the teacher. It is quicker to use, but does not allow for anecdotal information. These are examples; there are many possibilities. Much will depend on the development of the child in the group, the beliefs of the teacher, and the availability of staff to allow for instruction, monitoring, and record keeping to occur at the same time. Perhaps a combination of the two, a checklist with room for anecdotal notes, would best serve the purposes of some teachers. When using these formats, it is important to refrain from becoming an interrogator. That is not the purpose of these tools. Their pur-

Student	Book title or topic	Child's response to the book or story	Comments

FIGURE 12-6 Reading/literature conference record sheet

pose is to gather information in an unobtrusive way so that planning future instruction can be improved. While the information may be useful for assessing individual children and the program as well, it should still be gathered informally.

General Activities

In addition to the story-related activities that might be used to implement a plan of instruction, general activities have proven to be successful in early childhood programs. They have a wide range of applicability beyond thematic units and language arts areas, although most content can be introduced and learned within the context of language arts thematic units. Among these activities are the thematic approach, classroom centers, discussion groups, and transitions.

Thematic Approach.

While not a specific activity, the thematic approach has long been seen as a useful tool for organizing curriculum and content. It enables teachers to help children learn ideas and concepts within a general framework. The purpose of the thematic approach is to help children make sense of what they are learning and to recognize that most aspects of life and learning are related to other aspects.

The theme should be something that emerges naturally. For example, a math activity that is contrived and meaningless but is included because it has some remote relationship to the theme has little value for children. If adults are not able to identify the relationships, children are not likely to see them either. Activities and instruction in content areas within the theme should be selected for their meaningfulness and usefulness to understanding the overall theme.

Classroom Centers.

A center is a table or other area in the classroom where a specific activity is engaged in or where there are special materials and supplies available for use by children. Some centers such as an art center, a listening center, a craft center, or a writing/drawing center might stay fairly constant over a long period of time. The activities for these centers should change according to the theme being used currently. For example, in a unit about trees, an art project using tree leaves

may be done at the art center. During the next theme, the art center might be used simply as a free choice activity.

Other centers may only be used for a specific period of time before they are replaced by a totally different type of center. In the tree unit, a tree planting center could be created, with each child planting a maple seed in some earth in a styrofoam cup. When the trees sprout in a few weeks, some might be planted outside. During the next unit, which may be on the topic of the growth of children, the tree planting center might be converted to a center on the topic of nutrition, where children have opportunities to learn about the four food groups.

Discussion Groups.

While discussion groups can be described here as a separate activity, in actual practice they are often combined with other activities. A discussion group occurs whenever members of the class meet to learn new concepts, share ideas, or solve problems. They may or may not include the teacher. They may include the total class or only a portion of the class.

Discussion groups provide the teacher with the opportunity to teach or model new skills and strategies for certain children or for the entire class. They can be used before, during, and after other activities such as read alouds, cooperative projects, play periods, and flannel board stories. The best approach to these groups is to keep them brief and frequent rather than longer and less frequent. In this way difficult skills or strategies can be modeled more frequently. Shorter discussion group periods can be less tedious to young children as well.

Transitions.

Transitions can be combined with other activities or used independently. They are devices used to end one activity while redirecting the attention of the children to a new activity. They can be fun and motivating to children. Using transitions embodied in songs, chants, rhymes, and fingerplays can help ease children into a change in activity. Sawyer and Comer (1991) describe several ideas for transitions. Among them are songs, rhymes, magic wands, and fingerplays. For example, the teacher may create a simple

Student	Topic / subject	Characteristics of child							
		Engages in global planning	Attempts to tell related story	Able to tell a related story	Attempts to draw related picture	Able to draw a related picture	Attempts to write related words	Writes related words	Exhibits a sense of ownership

Code: + = Yes   — = No

~ = Sometimes   0 = Not appropriate for this topic

FIGURE 12-7 Writing/drawing conference record sheet

fingerplay with a two-line poem that children will come to recognize as the signal to put away the toys and move to the carpet for story time.

Social Activities

Early childhood is a period of emerging social skills as well as emerging literacy. Often the two are intermingled so much that it is difficult to determine what is taking place at any one time. While young children are often focused on their own needs and interests, they do enjoy participating in social activities with other children. This interest serves as a powerful motivation to use social activities to further the development of both language and social skills.

It is beneficial to keep a continuum of social activities in mind when planning instruction for young children. Activities range from those that are more independent to those that require a fair amount of cooperation and turn taking. Games, free play, and circle time represent the range of activities in this area. There are, of course many others. Each of these three can be combined with the others or with general or story activities if the teacher's purpose suggests the appropriateness of such a combination.

Games.

As discussed in the unit on play, games appeal to people of all ages. They require some degree of co-operation and can be used for a number of different purposes. Guessing games, Simon Says, and Copy Me are but a few of the possibilities that have been used successfully with young children. It is helpful to have a book of games on hand in the classroom.

While games can be used as enjoyable activities by themselves, they can and should be used as possibilities for use within thematic units. For example, Simon Says can be used within a unit about animals. The commands can request the children to make sounds, hold up pictures, or produce actions representative of various animals. Guessing games that use riddles can help children or pairs of children to learn things as diverse as seasons, vehicles, and buildings.

Free Play Periods.

The possible uses of play have been discussed in the unit on play. Activities involving play are among the

FIGURE 12-8 Room for play and social activities is an important part of the instructional program.

most powerful for developing language and social skills. Since play is such an influential part of the lives of young children, it should never be forgotten as an activity with potential for learning.

Circle Time.

Perhaps the most structured social activity of the day for young children is circle time. Often used as the initial activity for introducing and organizing the day, it has potential for other purposes throughout the day as well.

Circle time usually begins with a quiet pause while everyone finds their place in the circle and gets ready. An audible signal such as a small bell is sometimes used. Names, colored circles, or stars taped to the floor can be used to help children find their places. This might be followed by a song or a fingerplay to get all of the children focused on a common activity. It is also common to have each member of the group make a comment, say "Good morning," or be recognized in some way. This helps children see themselves as important, contributing members of the circle.

The circle might end at this point or it might incorporate an activity related to the unit being used at the time. The teacher must proceed with enthusiasm and keep the activity moving along so that it is completed before interest wanes. A clear expectation of what is to be done should be communicated at the beginning, followed by the teacher modeling some appropriate responses. Each child should have an opportunity to take a turn at participating in the activity. If a unit is being presented on the four food groups, for example, each child might have an opportunity to name a favorite food and to name its food group.

Ending a circle time activity should be done with care. If the activity has been a particularly exciting one, this is especially important. If circle time simply ends at this point, chaos could descend upon the room. A quiet group activity such as a fingerplay or chant could be used to help children regain some control over their excitement and to aid in the transition to a new activity. Dismissing a part of the group at a time is effective, especially if the children can then be directed to certain parts of the room or to subsequent activities.

FIGURE 12-9 A visit to the post office needs to be included in the instructional scheduling.

MANAGING THE PROCESS

It should make sense to the teacher that a well-defined plan can be of immense help in implementing the classroom instructional part of a program. It provides the teacher with the goals, materials, and instructional activities that are most likely to benefit the learning of the children. A teacher's command of a range of activities and a classroom that is set up to accommodate the needs of the program can also play important roles in effective instruction.

Several other factors can help create a smooth-running instructional program. The way the teacher manages the classroom can help make the routines of the day more predictable and assuring for children. The systematic procedures a teacher uses to share new ideas and concepts with the children also reassure them. Consistent, predictable procedures for dealing with disruptions can help provide a feeling of safety for all children. The expert use of available resources can help to provide interest and diversity to a program in a relaxed and absorbing manner.

Classroom Management

Managing the day-to-day program requires the development of certain patterns in the day. Children and teachers need to know what is going to happen so that they can be prepared for changes in activities and events throughout the day. In general, the proce-

dures outlined above will constitute the major portion of the instructional day. However, when teachers need to present specific information and concepts, they need to be consistent in using effective, explicit instruction. Attending to these two additional functions, scheduling and explicit teaching of information and concepts, can also assist the teacher in managing the classroom.

Scheduling.

Young children are comfortable with routines. This does not mean that teachers should do the same things every day. It does mean, however, that making sure that certain things happen when they are supposed to happen can be reassuring to children and make them feel comfortable in the classroom. For example, many teachers like to begin the day with circle time. They can use this activity to greet the children, acknowledge the presence and importance of each child, conduct a warm-up activity, and share what is going to happen that day. Within this framework, teachers can provide great variation in terms of acknowledging children, the warm-up activity, and the day's schedule. The fact remains that the children can still look forward to participating in circle time shortly after they arrive.

A sample of a daily schedule is provided in Figure 12-10. It should be viewed as only one of many possibilities. It covers a period of six hours. Many early childhood programs provide daycare services that extend the child's day on both ends. Many nursery school and kindergarten programs have children attend for only half the day. In some programs, children attend only two or three days per week. The schedule must be tailored to the needs of the children, the goals of the program, and the developmental level of the members of the class group.

Explicit Teaching.

The term *explicit teaching* refers to a pattern of instruction that is useful to teaching a specific body of content, concepts, or skills (Rosenshine 1986). It contains procedures that are applicable to any well-structured discipline (Simon 1973). Reading, writing, language, and social skills do not constitute a specific body of well-structured information, as do history, biology, and mathematics. Therefore, patterns and practices of explicit teaching are far less applicable (Spiro and Meyers 1984).

With this caveat, several principles can be helpful to teachers when they are engaged within a thematic unit in teaching specific information as described by Rosenshine (1986). First, begin the lesson with a brief statement of goals. This principle is, in fact, a valuable device for use with almost any type of teaching. Second, review previous learning that is relevant to the new information. Third, present the new information in small steps with clear explanations. Fourth, provide opportunities for all students to engage in some type of practice using the new information. Fifth, continuously check for whether or not the children are understanding the information. Finally, provide systematic feedback and clarification to all of the children. Other principles might include such things as providing regular practice of the new material and guiding the students as they go about their learning.

As can be seen, these procedures would have certain uses with young children as well as several shortcomings. Teachers might wish to employ these strategies with some bodies of information. They might include learning colors, names of animals, or the identification of shapes. Short sessions using explicit teaching would be appropriate. On the other hand, much of what we learn in life is not well defined and well structured. This includes much of the material in

a language arts program as well as the social skills we learn in order to participate in group activities. While explicit teaching has been used as the principle method of teaching in some reading programs (Reid 1978), its use is generally confined to a limited number of skills. Although it has a place, such an approach is generally inappropriate for most components of an integrated language arts program.

Disruptive Children

As with children at all educational levels, some children experience more difficulty in participating appropriately than others. There is nothing necessarily wrong with either the teacher's method of teaching or the child's development when this occurs. It is a natural part of being a child. When young children are actively engaged in activities and projects, they are far less likely to engage in disruptive behaviors. As a result, disruptions are more likely to occur at other times in a language arts program. Teachers are are likely to encounter common disruptions during circle time, discussion groups, and story time. A variety of types of disruptions and strategies for both preventing and addressing them have been discussed in the literature (Machado 1990; Sawyer and Comer 1991). Several of these ideas and strategies are described here.

Common Disruptions.

There are a number of predictable types of disruptions that teachers can ordinarily expect from young children. Interrupting either the teacher, who might be reading a story, or another child, who might be sharing an idea orally, is a common occurrence. Children sitting too close, particularly if on a carpet or at circle time, can cause bumping and mild pushing that would not occur if more space were available. Acting out with tantrums or destructive behavior is a more serious disruption that often cannot be ignored. Finally, teachers sometime note inappropriate peer relationships such as name calling, hitting, pinching, or shoving. In looking at each of these disruptions, it is clear that some are more serious than others.

Responding to Disruptions.

Teachers will experience a continuum of types of disruptions, from mild to more severe. There is also a

9:00	Circle time activities
	1._____ 2._____ 3._____
9:20	Thematic unit activities
	1._____ 2._____ 3._____
9:45	Free play period
10:15	Thematic unit centers
	Instruction:_____

Stations	Groups	7–10 minute rotation
Listening	A	
Art / craft	B	
Writing / drawing	C	
Science	D	

(A) ──→ (B)
↑   │
│   ↓
(C) ←── (D)

11:00	Free play period
11:30	Clean up and lunch
12:30	Story time in Literacy Center
	Title:_____
1:00	Nap time or quiet time
2:00	Outdoor activity or outdoor play period
2:40	Story time
	Title:_____
3:00	Circle time to conclude day
	1._____ 2._____ 3._____

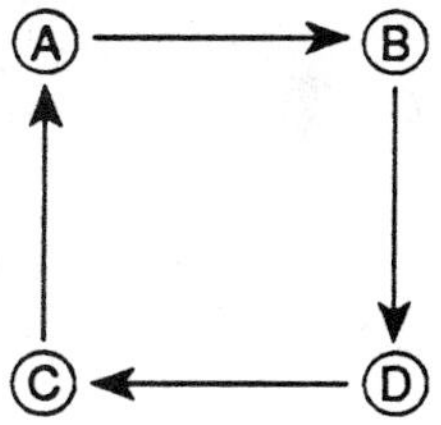

FIGURE 12-10 A sample daily schedule

continuum of strategies for dealing with disruptions from mild to more severe. On the mild end of the continuum is the response of ignoring the disruptive behavior. On the more severe end of the continuum is removing the child from the room and/or holding a case conference to develop an entire program to deal with a serious behavioral problem.

If the behavior is not something that can be ig-

FIGURE 12-11 The local firehouse can be an important instructional resource.

larly if the child interrupted with an idea that is relevant to the story. Other teachers feel that such children are capable of following certain classroom procedures such as speaking at appropriate times. They might respond by acknowledging such children and by reminding them to wait until the end of the story to share their ideas. At other times, it might be a positive idea to build relevant comments made during interruptions into the flow of the story. The teacher must make these decisions consistently, based on a knowledge of the children and a rational view of the instructional situation.

Sometimes the best response to problems is to prevent them from happening in the first place. In order to give children enough space so that they do not bump into each other at story time, procedures for seating can be planned beforehand. The names of children can be taped to the floor where each child is to sit. This can provide enough space between children while building recognition of children's names in print. For younger children, colored circles or stars can be used to designate a spot for each child to sit. Another way of dealing with this is to have children stand in such a way that they cannot touch any other

nored, the teacher must determine the best course of action for dealing with the disruption. A key principle in dealing with the disruption is to respond in such a way that the least amount of additional disruption is created. That is, the response by the teacher should be sufficient to address the problem without drawing unnecessary additional attention to it. Sometimes just looking directly at the child will cause the disruptive behavior to stop. At other times, a mild active response is needed.

The first step in using a mild response to deal with an interruption that cannot be ignored is to determine whether or not the interruption can serve a useful purpose. That is, will the comment by the interrupting child add something to the story or discussion or will it break the flow of the activity? Some teachers feel that preschoolers are not ready to use the hand raising rule or to wait until the end of the story in order to say what is on their mind. These teachers might suggest that it is better to keep the language flowing even if the story is never finished, particu-

> Ore Farm Trip. We met the farmer.
> We saw big middle size and baby cows. We saw the milking parlor and the milk house.
> Next we petted the calves and went on a hayride.
> Then we had ice cream and petted Kittens. it was a fun day.

FIGURE 12-12 One child created this piece following a scheduled field trip to a farm as part of a thematic unit.

FIGURE 12-13 Children's book author Patricia Reilly Giff visits a classroom.

child before they sit down. This will help assure enough space between children. Of course, teachers should use positive reinforcement to acknowledge appropriate behavior. The opportunity to receive praise is valued by young children.

Another response that can be taken beforehand is to make sure that children who are more likely to cause disruptions are sitting near the teacher or an aide. Actively involving the child is often effective. For example, the teacher reading a story might bring a child back into more appropriate behavior patterns by including that child's name in the story. The same

thing can often be accomplished by moving directly in front of the child and reading a line or two of the story while looking directly into the child's eyes. Only as a last resort should the child be physically removed from the group or the room. This would only occur when a child is unable to be controlled in any other way.

While these strategies can be helpful, there are also some things that the teacher should refrain from doing. Yelling is something that does little good in a language arts situation. It sends the message that the teacher is unable to use ordinary language to deal with behavior that is viewed by the children as normal and natural. Accusing children of being willfully disruptive is not a proper response either. Threatening to take actions that will not be carried out sends a message of untruthfulness to the children. They can become confused and distrusting as a result. Finally, the purpose of intervention is to help the child regain self-control and a positive sense of self. Avoid any strategy that would humiliate the child.

Available Resources

It is important to make expert use of whatever resources are available to the program. To do this, teachers must make efforts to become aware of what resources are available and to make decisions concerning how to include their use in the classroom program. Three different types of resources are generally available: materials, equipment, and people.

Materials for a program include all of the books, magazines, toys, manipulative objects, art supplies, household objects, and miscellaneous donations that teachers might ordinarily find in a classroom. The list does not stop there, however. There are a number of sources to supplement these supplies. Commercial sources for educational supplies abound. While the prices sometimes seem high, they may be the only sources for certain items. Other sources include the families of the children, local business establishments, libraries, garage sales, thrift stores, and flea markets.

Equipment refers to the larger items of long-term use in the room. This includes tables, desks, chairs, computers, filmstrip projectors, dividers, and book shelves. These are more costly items that are held on a permanent basis in the classroom. This does not

FIGURE 12-14 Basket makers from the community can create a facinating classroom visit.

mean that teachers must be satisfied by what is currently available in the classroom. Other staff members may have a need for some of your equipment items in their rooms and be willing to trade equipment. Donations from commercial establishments and the families of the children can be sought as well.

People who the classroom teachers might see as resources include the children themselves, the teachers, parents, siblings, grandparents, and community volunteers. They can serve as volunteer story readers, craft organizers, classroom visitors who share their occupations or experiences with the children, and extra hands for conducting classroom projects. To include these individuals it is most helpful to make personal contacts in order to extend invitations to participate in the classroom program.

SUMMARY

The successful implementation of a well-developed instructional plan begins with an understanding of the history of effective teaching. In the past, research on effective teaching has changed its focus periodically. At one point, the teacher was viewed as a possible impediment to learning. Materials were developed that were seen as "teacher proof," an indication that the developers saw the teacher as being irrelevant to the learning of children. More recently, the teacher has come to be viewed as an essential key to effective instruction. The planning, thoughtfulness, knowledge, and decision-making abilities of teachers are seen as being closely tied to effective instruction.

Research has revealed a number of principles that tend to guide the most successful teachers. These include establishing clear instructional goals, a knowledge of content and strategies, an ability to communicate expectations, a keen understanding of children, and the ability to make expert use of materials. In addition, effective teachers provide children with metacognitive strategies, address higher and lower cognitive learning, provide constructive and instructive feedback, integrate instruction with other content areas, and accept responsibility for the learning of all of the students in their program. Finally, effective teachers take the time to reflect upon their role and their practice. They are aware that they are not able to employ all of these principles all of the time. Nevertheless, they are aware of all of them and make diligent efforts to address each of them.

In addition to those described in Units 2, 3, and 4, there are established activities that are regularly used in early childhood language arts programs. Well-established story activities include reading aloud, oral story telling, conferencing, flannel board stories, and puppetry. More general activities include the thematic unit approach, classroom centers, discussion groups, and transitional procedures. Social activities include games, circle time, and free play.

Managing the entire instructional process is a key area of implementing an instructional plan. Planning is a major factor. A well-organized approach to the operation of the classroom is another key variable. This includes the development of a regular set of routines that the children come to know and expect. In addition, when specific information is being taught, some of the principles of explicit teaching can provide helpful ideas for making the instruction effective. The use of consistent procedures for handling disruptions and disruptive children can provide a common set of tools for helping teachers and children deal with the unpredictability of early childhood needs. Finally, the expert use of all available materials is needed. Teachers should not be confined by what is available within the classroom. The world is full of other possibilities waiting to be discovered.

Questions and Activities for Review and Discussion

Multiple Choice

1. Research reports produced by Jencks and Coleman concluded that, in regard to student achievement, teachers and schools
    a. are the most critical factors.
    b. do not have a significant effect.
    c. interact to produce learning.
    d. are most successful in language arts learning.
2. A general principle coming from the research on teaching suggests that much of the effective active instruction provided by teachers is a result of
    a. planning.
    b. thinking.
    c. decision making.
    d. all of the above
3. Many commercial materials available in the area of language arts have been criticized primarily for their
    a. poor teacher's manuals.
    b. high cost.
    c. literary quality.
    d. lack of colorful illustrations.
4. Information provided by the teacher that tells children both how they are doing and how they can do even better is called
    a. an instructional goal.
    b. a learning task.
    c. feedback.
    d. a lower cognitive function.
5. A traditional story activity that can still be used effectively in an integrated language arts program is
    a. reading aloud.
    b. oral storytelling.
    c. the flannel board story.
    d. all of the above
6. When two or more individuals meet for the purpose of discussion and learning, it is called a
    a. conference.
    b. lesson.
    c. evaluation session.
    d. tutorial.
7. Explicit teaching procedures generally do NOT include the following:
    a. statements of the goals of a lesson.
    b. discussions of the beliefs of the student.
    c. opportunities for students to practice the material.
    d. systematic feedback and correction.

True or False

T   F   1. Most research on classroom teaching can be directly applied to an early childhood education language arts program.

T   F   2. An integrated language arts program can often deal with an increase in goals better than a program that stresses the learning of skills in isolation.

T   F   3. Early childhood education teachers can and should develop the majority of their classroom language arts materials.

T   F   4. A classroom center can be just about any table or space that contains special materials to be used in a specific activity.

T   F   5. Explicit teaching is a system that is not well suited as the primary component of language arts instruction.

Essay and Discussion

1. Describe some of the factors that may prevent research on teaching from being valid for an early childhood education integrated language arts program.

2. Describe the various types of knowledge needed by language arts teachers working with young children.

3. Explain the difference between lower and higher cognitive learning and give an example of each from a language arts curriculum.

4. Describe some of the traditionally effective story activities for the early childhood langue arts program.

5. Identify a specific body of information applicable to early learning and describe the explicit teaching steps teachers might use to teach the information.

REFERENCES

Anderson, A.C., L. Anderson, and R. Prawat. 1985. *Socialization into the student role: Teacher and student influences*. Research Series No. 160. East Lansing, Mich.: Michigan State University, Institute for Research on Teaching.

Anderson, C.W., and E.L. Smith. 1987. Teaching science. In *The Educator's Handbook: A Research Perspective*, ed. V. Kowhler. New York: Longman.

Anderson, L., and Prawat. 1983. Responsibility in the classroom: A synthesis of research on teaching of self-control. *Educational Leadership* 40: 5, 62–66.

Anderson, L., N. Brubaker, J. Alleman-Brooks, and G. Duffy. 1985. A qualitative study of seatwork in first-grade classrooms. *Elementary School Journal* 86: 123–140.

Anderson, R., E. Hiebert, J. Scott, and I. Wilkinson. 1985. *Becoming a nation of readers: The report of the Commission on Reading*. Washington, D.C.: National Institute of Education.

Armbruster, B.B., and T.H. Anderson. 1984. Structures of explanations in history textbooks or so what if Governor Sanford missed the spike and hit the rail? *Journal of Curriculum Studies* 16: 181–194.

Ball, D.L., and S. Seiman-Nemser. 1986. *Using textbooks and teachers' guides: What beginning elementary teachers learn and what they need to know*. Research Series No. 174. East Lansing, Mich.: Michigan State University, Institute for Research on Teaching.

Bettelheim, B. 1976. *The uses of enchantment.* New York: Knopf.

Brophy, J., and T.L. Good. 1986. Teacher behavior and student achievement. In *Handbook of Research on Teaching,* ed. M. C. Wittrock. New York: Macmillan.

Clark, C.M., and P.M. Peterson. 1986. Teachers' thought processes. In *Handbook of Research on Teaching,* ed. M.C. Wittrock. New York: Macmillan.

Coleman, J.S., E.Q. Campbell, C.J. Hobson, J.J. McPartland, A.M. Mood, F.D. Weinfield, and R.L. York. 1966. *Equality of educational opportunity.* Washington, D.C.: U.S. Government Printing Office.

dePaola, T. 1975. *Strega Nona.* Englewood Cliffs, N.J.: Prentice Hall.

Duffy, G., L. Roehler, C. Book, M. Meloth, L. Vavrus, J. Putnam, and R. Wesselman. 1986. The relationship between explicit verbal explanations during reading skill instruction and student awareness and achievement: A study of reading effects. *Reading Research Quarterly* 21: 235–252.

Eaton, J., C. Anderson, and E. Smith. 1984. Students' misconceptions interfere with science learning: Case studies of fifth-grade students. *Elementary School Journal* 84: 365–379.

Fielding, L., and C. Roller. 1992. Making difficult books accessible and easy books acceptable. *The Reading Teacher* 45: 678–685.

Floden, R.E., A.C. Porter, W.H. Schmidt, D.J. Freeman, and J.R. Schwille. 1981. Responses to curriculum pressures: A policy-capturing study of teacher decisions about content. *Journal of Educational Psychology* 73: 129–141.

Jencks, C., M. Smith, H. Acland, M.J. Bane, D. Cohen, H. Gintis, B. Heyns, and S. Michelson. 1972. *Inequality: A reassessment of the effect of family and schooling in America.* New York: Harper and Row.

Lampert, M. 1985. How do teachers manage to teach? Perspectives on problems in practice. *Harvard Educational Review* 55: 2, 178–194.

Leinhardt, G., and D. Smith. 1985. Expertise in mathematics instruction: Subject matter knowledge. *Journal of Educational Psychology* 77: 247–271.

Machado, J. 1990. *Early childhood experiences in language arts.* Albany, N.Y.: Delmar Publishers Inc.

McGovern, A. 1967. *Too much noise.* Boston: Houghton Mifflin Company.

Navarro, R.A., R. Berkey, and F. Minnick. 1986. The art of becoming an instructional leader. Paper presented at the annual meeting of the American Educational Research Association, San Francisco, Calif.

Palincsar, A., and A.L. Brown. 1984. Reciprocal teaching of comprehension-fostering and comprehension-monitoring activities. *Cognition and Instruction* 1: 117–175.

Porter, A.C., and J. Brophy. 1988. Synthesis of research on good teaching: Insights from the work of the Institute for Research on Teaching. *Educational Leadership* 45: 8, 74–85.

Prawat, R.S. Affective versus cognitive goal orientations in elementary teachers. *American Educational Research Journal* 22: 587–604.

Raphael, T.E., and B.M. Kirschner. 1985. *The effects of instruction in compare/contrast text structure on sixth-grade students' reading comprehension and writing products.* Research series No. 161. East Lansing, Mich.: Michigan State University, Institute for Research on Teaching.

Reid, E.R. 1978. *The reading newsletter.* Salt Lake City, Utah: Exemplary Center for Reading Instruction.

Rosenshine, B.V. 1986. Synthesis of research on explicit teaching. *Educational Leadership* 43: 7, 60–69.

Rountree, B.S., M.B. Shuptrine, G.E. Gordon, and N.T. Taylor. 1981. *Creative teaching with puppets*. University, Ala.: The Learning Line.

Sawyer, W.E., and D.E. Comer. 1991. *Growing up with literature*. Albany, N.Y.: Delmar Publishers Inc.

Schmidt, W., L. Roehler, J. Caul, B. Diamond, D. Solomon, P. Cianciolo, and M. Buchman. 1985. The uses of curriculum integration in language arts instruction: A study of six classrooms. *Journal of Curriculum Studies* 17: 305–320.

Sedlak, M.W., C.W. Wheeler, D.C. Pullin, and P.A. Cusick. 1986. *Selling students short: Classroom bargains and academic reform in the American high school*. New York: Teachers College Press.

Shulman, L.S. 1986. Those who understand knowledge growth in teaching. *Educational Researcher* 15: 4–14.

Simon, H.A. 1973. The structure of ill-structured problems. *Artificial Intelligence* 4: 181–201.

Spiro, R.J., and A. Myers. 1984. Individual differences and underlying cognitive processes. In *Handbook of Reading Research*, ed. P.D. Pearson, R. Barr, M.L. Kamil, and P. Mosenthal. New York: Longman.

Trelease, J. 1989. *The new read-aloud handbook*. New York: Viking-Penguin.

Wood, A. 1984. *The napping house*. New York: Harcourt, Brace, Jovanovich.

UNIT 13

Evaluating a Program

UNIT GOALS

After completing this unit, the reader should:

- develop a basic understanding of the processes and products of evaluation.

- develop a set of beliefs underlying educationally appropriate evaluation practices for early childhood education.

- develop the ability to engage in essential evaluation activities.

- identify the critical aspects of early language learning and communication to be evaluated.

- understand the strengths and deficiencies of formal tests and assessments systems used in early childhood education.

- understand the proper uses of evaluation information and the appropriate audiences for this information.

PREVIEW

Accountability in education has often been cited as a goal by public officials. It is seen as a tool for improving and maintaining more effective educational programs at all levels. There are three ways government and other societal forces have traditionally attempted to improve learning in educational programs. First, the funding of special programs is used to address specific needs or specific children. The federal government's Headstart program for disadvantaged preschool children is an example of this. Funding is directed at providing such children with a learning program that enables them to be more suc-

cessful when they enter elementary school. Second, public officials attempt to improve education by enforcing standards to be met by teachers and schools. State agencies that license daycare centers and set guidelines for training and certifying teachers are engaged in this type of standard setting.

The third approach, and by far the most popular, is that of setting standards to be met by children. It is the most popular because it gets much positive publicity for those who propose it. It is also relatively inexpensive. The approach often involves using standardized tests. Even the most elaborate tests do not cost a great deal of money on a per child basis. It is certainly less costly than providing that same child with an effective educational program over the course of a year. Tests are appealing because they give the impression of exactness and precision. The premise that tests are able to reduce the complexity of language learning to a single number is quite attractive and too often not questioned. For this reason, the number of tests children are subjected to from the time they enter kindergarten or nursery school until the time they graduate from high school has grown enormously.

Evaluation seeks to provide information about how well a program is operating. While accountability may be one of the purposes of evaluation, it is not the sole purpose. Evaluation is not the same thing as giving a test. Tests cannot measure everything that should be evaluated. The younger the child, the less effective any test becomes. The more integrated a language arts program, the greater the focus on processes, meaningfulness, active learner involvement, cooperative learning, and social development. As these aspects of a program increase, the less valid any standardized test designed to measure the learning of factual information becomes.

In order to address the topic of evaluation of an early childhood education program, it is necessary for teachers to step back and acquire a grasp of what needs to be assessed: Why do such things need to be assessed? How will they be assessed? What will the information be used for? Critical ideas related to this are discussed in this unit. They include the concept of evaluation as both a process and a product, a philosophy of evaluation in early childhood programs, record keeping procedures, types of records to collect, the testing of young children, and the uses of evaluative information.

INTRODUCTION

This unit first identifies the concept of evaluation as a process. It is described primarily as a data gathering process geared toward helping people make decisions. The decisions made using this information might involve such things as beliefs about the learning of children and conclusions about the procedures used to gather the information. Tests and other assessment procedures are identified in this context.

Evaluation has special meaning in early childhood

education. Young children go through so many changes; therefore, teachers must develop a certain philosophy concerning the need for evaluation. In an integrated language arts program, language skills are not broken into isolated bits and pieces for children to learn. Therefore, teachers must decide exactly what learning should be assessed.

Assuming that there are some legitimate areas of learning to assess in an early childhood integrated language arts program, the task becomes one of developing procedures to gather information. Traditional approaches will not be appropriate or effective for this task. A contemporary method, sometimes referred to as authentic or natural evaluation, is described as a more realistic tool for the task. Other assessment systems that may have some uses are described as well.

Finally, the use of the information gathered in the evaluation is discussed. A number of questions can be raised in this area. Is the information of use to administrators and governing boards? How can teachers best use the information? How shall the information be shared with parents? How shall the information reflect on the children themselves? For each of these, the notion of time should be considered as well. Young children change so quickly over a period of a few months; teachers must make decisions about how long the information derived from an evaluation will remain valid. Will the information on a specific child be accurate three months from now? What decisions will the information be used to make that might have an effect on a child one year from now? Will decisions made about a program based on a certain group of four-year-olds be valid for the next group of four-year-olds? Since these decisions affect lives, they must be made with the utmost care.

WHAT IS EVALUATION

Evaluation is a normal part of any educational endeavor. It is often a part of other human endeavors as well. It helps to tell us whether or not our efforts have been successful or not. In education, evaluation is seen as a process that occurs according to a certain schedule for a number of different purposes. Traditional evaluation models have relied primarily on tests to measure student achievement at the conclusion of a program. An integrated language arts programs cannot be evaluated using such a traditional evaluation model. Instead, a more dynamic approach, often referred to as authentic assessment, is more appropriate. Each of these concepts and approaches is considered here.

Process

Evaluation is itself a process. That is, it refers to certain activities conducted over time. The starting point of any evaluation is the curriculum. Teachers must be clear about what they wish the children to accomplish before attempting to determine if such a goal has actually been reached. The question to ask is, what are the objectives of the curriculum?

With this knowledge, the second step is to gather information related to this. The question to ask at this point is, therefore, what have the children accomplished? While gathering this information can be a challenging task, let us assume for now that such information has been collected.

The third step is to compare the intended accomplishments (the objectives of the curriculum) with the actual accomplishments (what the students have actually mastered). When this is done, we may have discovered a number of possibilities. The students may have accomplished exactly what we had hoped. On the other hand, the students may not have accomplished anything that we had intended. There is the possibility, of course, that the students attained something between the two alternatives.

The fourth step in the process is the formation of a judgment. The judgment relates to our satisfaction or dissatisfaction with the comparison between the learning that was intended and the learning that actually occurred. Did the children learn enough of what was intended to deem the lesson, project, or program successful? How great a discrepancy was there? Was it within acceptable bounds?

Purpose

The purpose of evaluation is directly related to decision making. The ultimate use of evaluation information is to help make decisions. Consider the possibility previously described in which the actual accomplishments of the children did not closely match the intended results of a program. The evaluator has a responsibility to analyze both the evaluation process and the procedures being evaluated to determine possible reasons for the gap between the intended and actual learning. Are the objectives of the curriculum unrealistic for the children? Were the procedures used to gather information about the accomplishments of the children adequate and accurate? Was there sufficient instruction? Was the instruction provided to the children appropriate?

The evaluation should always be considered in light of whether or not it is appropriate to the given situation. This is particularly important for an early childhood program. Traditional approaches to evaluation do not necessarily fulfill the needs of an early childhood program evaluation.

Schedule

There are a number of points in time when different types of evaluation activities may occur. In general, they can occur before, during, and after a lesson, unit, or program. They can occur at each of these times for different purposes, although they tend to follow the general format of the steps of the evaluation process that have already been described.

At the initial stages of instruction, the evaluation that occurs is referred to as diagnostic evaluation. At this point, a teacher may attempt to determine such things as the previous knowledge children may have about a topic, the oral language skills possessed by the children, or the ability of the children to recall information related to a certain topic. Each of these details is sought for a specific purpose or there would be no point in gathering the information. The information is sought to help the teacher make decisions about the instruction or activities to be used with the children.

Evaluative information collected during the unit of instruction is identified as formative evaluation. The information collected during this stage is used by the teacher in a number of ways. First, it provides some ideas as to whether the children are progressing toward the goals that have been set for them. Second, the information can help the teacher determine whether the instruction being provided is effective or not. Third, the information can be used to help the teacher provide feedback to the students concerning their progress.

At the conclusion of an instructional unit, still more

evaluative information is gathered. This is the most familiar type of assessment and is generally referred to as summative evaluation. The purpose at this point is to determine the effectiveness of the entire instructional unit. Without the other two types of evaluation, this latter type is of limited value. It is important to understand the children's abilities and needs as they begin a unit as well as the areas in which they do or do not experience success as they proceed through a unit. Summative evaluation alone cannot answer many of the questions that may be raised when a unit is not as successful as we would have liked it to be.

Traditional Evaluation Model

The traditional model of educational evaluation relies heavily on tests in general and on paper and pencil tests in particular. A test is usually defined as a device or tool designed to measure something in an objective and standardized manner. Tests are used for a number of reasons. They are relatively inexpensive and easy to administer. This accounts for much of their popularity with cost-conscious legislators who wish to appear visible as educational reformers. Tests are such a familiar part of education that most people cannot imagine school without them. They are so familiar that their value is seldom questioned. Tests are seen by many as the best way, if not the only way, to measure children's learning.

In early childhood education, the tests most frequently used include intelligence tests, tests of development, speech and language tests, school readiness tests, and school achievement tests in the areas of language arts and mathematics. Most companies marketing these tests attempt to assure the user of the soundness of their tests. The two principal characteristics that determine the technical soundness of a test are validity and reliability.

Validity.

The validity of a test refers to whether or not a test measures what it claims to measure. This might sound like a simple thing to demonstrate, but in actuality it is not. Furthermore, the rapid changes of the early childhood years often render the degree of validity of many tests unacceptable. The validity of a test designed for use with young children might be demonstrated in a number of ways. One way is to gather a group of educators with expertise in the field of early childhood and ask them to examine and verify that a test is valid for its stated purpose. Another way might be to compare the results of a new test with the results of an already widely accepted test. If the results are similar, a certain amount of validity might be claimed for the new test. Still another way is to see from visible outcomes if the test actually measures what it claims to measure. Take, for example, a new test of school readiness for children entering kindergarten. The test ought to identify those children who will be successful in kindergarten and those children who will not meet with success. A test maker might give the test to a number of children and wait a year to see how well the test predicted the degree of success of the children. If the test was highly accurate in predicting the successes and failures, the test can claim a certain amount of validity.

Reliability.

Reliability refers to whether a test measures something consistently over time. That is, does the test measure the same thing each time it is used, and does it measure the same thing with different children? As with validity, there are a number of ways for a test maker to attempt to demonstrate the reliability of a test. One way is to give a group of children a test on two different occasions in order to see if similar results are found during each testing. Another way is to divide the test in half and give both parts to the same group of children. The test may be split into two parts in a number of different ways: odd questions versus even questions, first half of the test versus second half of the test, two different forms of the same test, and so forth. Whichever method is selected, the goal of the test maker is to demonstrate that the same thing is found each time the test, or part of the test, is used with a child. Using the school readiness test example, a test that shows that a child has a high probability of being successful in kindergarten no matter how the test is divided and administered would be considered reliable.

Authentic Assessment

Many of the ideas and assumptions that form the basis for faith in a traditional model of evaluation are questioned within the framework of an integrated language arts program, particularly a program designed for young children. A traditional approach to assessment has much in common with what is known as the "empty vessel" approach to learning. That is, at one point children were viewed as little more than empty vessels or containers to be filled up with knowledge and learning. The main focus was on product. The goal seemed to be only to increase the quantity of new information that the child learned.

It is true that children need to learn new ideas, concepts, and understandings. It is also true that it is valuable for teachers to know how much children have learned at certain points in a program. However, reconsider the fact that the ultimate purpose of evaluation is to provide information that can be used to make decisions. What kind of reasonable decision can be made with the knowledge that some children learned some information while other children did not? Obviously teachers cannot do a great deal with such information. Teachers need to gather evaluative information that can truly be used to make instructional decisions to directly benefit the children.

The fundamental factor that distinguishes authentic assessment from a traditional approach to evaluation is that the former addresses the process of learning in a much more substantial way. While authentic assessment includes gathering information to indicate the kinds of things children have learned, it does so in relation to the process by which they have or have not learned. This enables the teacher to better understand the conditions surrounding how children seem to best acquire new understandings, ideas, and values. Authentic assessment grew out of the whole language approach largely because of the need to integrate evaluation within the processes of the classroom. Just as knowledge cannot be broken down into neat little bits and pieces to be learned, the assessment of that learning cannot focus on those bits and pieces in isolation from the context in which it was learned.

AUTHENTIC ASSESSMENT WITH YOUNG CHILDREN

As teachers implement a whole language approach to literacy and language learning, they have to deal with the issue of assessment. Teachers have traditionally been expected to use certain evaluation proce-

FIGURE 13-1 Authentic assessment uses the reading and writing that children do on a continuing basis.

dures in their classrooms. In a traditional skills-based program, the assessment tools that have been widely used have seemed reasonable and valid. Teachers of language have, for a long time, taught specific skills in isolation from contexts; the assessment tools followed this pattern as well. These assessment tools do not validly or reliably assess the learning that occurs within a whole language approach.

Philosophy

With a whole language approach, teachers begin to feel uneasy about using the tests and assessment tools they have used in the past. It has been suggested that this uneasiness is caused by the profound differences that underlie whole language and traditional assessment procedures (Cambourne and Turbill 1990). On a practical school and classroom level, differences can be traced to contradictions between philosophy and policy; they can be revealed by asking a set of questions related to philosophy and policy (Linek 1991):

- Are individual needs stressed in both school philosophy and policy statements?
- Is school achievement, based on norm-referenced tests, a major force in forming philosophy or setting policy?
- Are individual needs stressed in philosophy while standardized testing and grading stressed in policy?

FIGURE 13-2 Traditional paper and pencil tests are inappropriate for young children.

A school's philosophy and policy may be written or implied. That is, teachers might actually find each written down in some document or each may be simply the unstated rules by which everyone seems to operate. A school's philosophy can often be found in such documents as brochures, parent newsletters, and mission statements. The philosophy usually discusses the hopes and beliefs about children that guide the school. The policy of a school, on the other hand, is often revealed through such documents as board of education minutes, rules developed by the board of directors, and directives developed by the administration. A contradiction occurs when the school philosophy stresses the importance of the needs of the child while the policy stresses the need to have students achieve certain levels on standardized tests.

Natural Learning

Whole language asserts that the most powerful and effective language learning is based on a theory of "natural learning" (Cambourne 1988). This assertion emerged from research conducted in natural settings that showed how language learning occurs in the day-to-day lives of children interacting with their environments (Cambourne 1988; Cambourne and Turbill 1987; Halliday 1975; Holdaway 1979). Teachers who use a natural learning approach create classrooms in which learners are valued participants in the literary environment. Children are encouraged to take language risks, make approximations, and take control of their own language learning in real contexts.

This view differs greatly from a traditional approach that views literacy as a single skill made up of many separate subskills, each of which exists, and can be measured, without reference to the other subskills (Cambourne and Turbill 1990). Using a skills-based assessment within a whole language program is like trying to place a nut on a bolt with a different thread; it can be done only with force, and even then the fit is incorrect (Johnston 1986).

Natural Theory of Assessment

To develop a natural theory of assessment, Cambourne and Turbill (1990) looked to the first teachers of young children: the parents. They noted that parents and others who have an interest in children's lives are constantly assessing development. In making these assessments, parents were found to observe, react, intervene, and participate in the activities of their children. When called upon to make judgments about their children's development, they could synthesize their observations and give accurate reports. They were also found to be quite capable of using their information to make sound decisions about what to do next for their children.

Three things were identified that seemed to explain how parents came to be such expert evaluators of their children's development. First, they spend large amounts of time interacting and observing their children. Second, they possess an implicit understanding of what makes up "growth" and how it should proceed. Third, they seem to know what to look for. That is, as they become more expert, they develop a more and more sophisticated set of markers or indicators of growth. These markers include such things as learning to walk, learning to talk, being able to use a telephone, and riding a bike.

The use of a natural assessment of young children's learning is much more appropriate for a whole language approach. Also referred to as responsive evaluation (Guba and Lincoln 1981), natural assessment is based on several assumptions. First, a standardized procedure or test is assumed to be inappropriate for assessment in natural settings. Second, it assumes that people can evaluate as effectively and validly as tests. Third, it assumes that those engaged in evaluating can and should be involved in the program being evaluated. This third assumption requires teachers to work together more closely and with more openness than they may be accustomed to doing. Furthermore, teachers must be willing to compare their observations with those of others and to have their observations verified by others (Lincoln and Guba 1986).

Learnings to Assess

Over the past several decades, the curriculum of the primary grades has been pushed downward through the grades. The result of this is increased expectations, even for children entering kindergarten from nursery schools, preschools, and daycare centers. The force behind this "shove down" of the curriculum is the ever-increasing number of minimum competency tests mandated by many state governments for the primary grades. These tests tend to drive the curriculum. That is, they encourage teachers to teach to the test rather than teach what is developmentally appropriate for children. Another factor is the increasing expectation of parents for an academically oriented kindergarten program that fulfills the needs they perceive for their children (Simmons and Brewer 1985). Many have expressed concerns about this pressure for academic success and these unrealistic expectations placed on young children (Elkind 1981; Uphoff and Gilmore 1986; Martin 1985; Davis 1980).

Traditional Evaluation Model.

Despite the warnings concerning the unrealistic academic expectations placed on young children, kindergartens continue to be places where paper and pencil academic tasks have replaced many of the op-

portunities for exploration and curiosity. In their investigation of kindergarten report cards, Freeman and Hatch (1989) found that those language arts areas that most frequently appear include such skills as recognition of upper/lower case letters, child prints name, associates letters and sounds, recognizes likenesses and differences, expresses ideas clearly, recognizes rhyming words, recognizes names in print, demonstrates left to right progression, orders events in sequence, shows interest in stories and books, understands positional vocabulary, writes upper/lower case letters, and classifies objects. Some of these areas have relative importance within an integrated language arts program. However, most of these skills are surface and mechanical features of language. While these skills may be addressed on traditional standardized readiness and achievement tests, they do not, in themselves, deal with the significant aspects of meaningful communication and literacy. This is not an isolated situation. Studies similar to this have produced the same findings (Kamii 1985; Smith and Shepard 1987).

Responsive Evaluation Model.

When whole language teachers attempt to evaluate the learnings of children in their programs, they find that they need to apply the same level of thinking to assessment as they do to instruction. They find that in order to determine what they need to assess, they have to begin by identifying the aspects of literacy. One group of teachers defined these aspects as ownership, reading comprehension, writing process, word identification, knowledge of language and vocabulary, and voluntary reading (Au, Scheu, Kawakami, and Herman 1990). Another group of teachers, guided by Cambourne and Turbill's (1990) concept of identifying broad markers of language growth, developed a set of seven general categories that addressed both oral and written language. These included:

1. A sense of audience when communicating. This includes whether the child demonstrates an awareness of the background of the audience, chooses words for a specific audience, and explains pronoun referents (e.g., he, she) when telling a story.

2. Use of conventions appropriate to the language context. In written language, this includes accurate spelling, punctuation, usage, and handwriting. In spoken language, it includes accurate pronunciation, grammar, diction, and expression.

3. Use of a range of registers/genres. This includes the use of form and vocabulary appropriate for a given audience and recognition of the form and style being used.

4. Acquisition and use of vocabulary appropriate to context. This includes the use of a range of synonyms, new words (writing and speaking), precise terms, and a more sophisticated use of vocabulary (e.g., using vocabulary from one context to another, for special effects, etc.).

5. Use of a range of grammatical options. This includes the appropriate use of tenses, pronouns, conjunctions, and prepositions. It also includes an absence of overgeneralizations (e.g., runned), paraphrasing ability, logical sentence construction, and the use of longer and more complex sentences.

6. Confidence in using language in different contexts. This includes a willingness to share, question, answer, volunteer, and attempt new language tasks in different wettings and for different purposes.

7. Comprehension of language heard or read. This includes an ability to answer questions, retell, and generalize about something that was experienced, heard, or read.

Each of the seven areas identified can be expanded into several possibilities. It should be noted that they closely correspond to the objectives outlined in the units describing oral language, reading, and written expression. This is logical, since the evaluation should closely match the goals of a program. Just as teachers cannot attempt to achieve all possible goals for a group of children at any given time, they cannot assess all possible markers of growth at any given time. Clearly, teachers need to identify the objectives they are working toward and choose the key aspects of those markers in order to validate growth toward those objectives. With this accomplished, teachers can consider the practical aspects of gathering the appropriate information to evaluate the program.

PRACTICAL PROCEDURES

Early childhood educators tend to work in a demanding environment; therefore, they need systematic and accurate procedures for collecting assessment information on individual children. It is important to keep in mind the fact that insufficient or vague information is of no more value than no information at all. The key, therefore, is to devise procedures and tools that will enable the teacher to collect critical and useful information in a manner that is neither too time consuming nor too cumbersome. Two specific areas need to be addressed in order to develop such tools. The first is record keeping, which refers to a means of collecting information that enables the teacher to make decisions about learning and instruction. The second is the portfolio, which is a device or tool for storing information in a way that can be meaningfully used to chronicle the growth and development of children over time.

Record Keeping

Record keeping refers to collecting information that documents the language abilities, attitudes, and skills of children over time. This information describes the ways that children use language, how they value language, what strategies they use to solve problems with language, and what they understand about their own language skills. It is important for record keeping to take place over time. In that way, the teacher will have a continuous record of growth and change. By continually recording data, the teacher will also have a constant supply of information to use in making instructional decisions.

Various people can be involved in record keeping. The first person who comes to mind is, of course, the teacher. By virtue of the position, the teacher must be involved in collecting information about children and in recording that information. Much of the information will be gathered through constant child observation, or "kid watching." As described in the initial units, "kid watching" is one of the cornerstones of a whole language approach. Teacher aides might also collect and record information. They will need to be trained in regard to understanding what to look for and how to interpret some of the things they see children doing, saying, drawing, reading, and writing. Parents are a valuable source of information as well.

They have spent many years observing and interacting with their children. They are often some of the most expert "kid watchers" of all. Finally, the children themselves can and should be involved in record keeping. This will begin in a fairly basic manner, but the goal will be to clarify the concept of self-monitoring their own language abilities.

The record keeping devices used by any of these groups will vary over time. They will also vary depending on who is doing the record keeping. Recording devices such as audio tape machines or video cassette recorders (VCRs) might be used during classroom activities and play times. Surveys, questionnaires, and interviews might be used with parents and individual children in order to obtain both general and more specific information about language. Observations using a written or coded format might be done by the teacher at key times within the program. Notes and observations from parents can also serve as record keeping devices. Finally, the children produce drawings, writings, and retellings that serve as valuable record keeping devices.

The question might now be asked: Exactly what kind of information should teachers be looking for? In general there are five broad groupings of information that teachers tend to find most beneficial (Cambourne and Turbill 1990):

1. Strategies used by children as they read, write, and use oral language.
2. The degree of understanding children have about the processes they are using to deal with language.
3. Attitudes toward different language arts.
4. Interests and background of the learners.
5. Control that children demonstrate over language.

Information about the first four of these is generally quite descriptive since each is ordinarily observed or the information is gathered through questioning. For the fifth area, teachers need to use the descriptions contained within the categories of broad markers described earlier. Figure 13-3 provides an example of a literacy assessment recording form that uses some possible broad markers to describe the child's reading development. It is basically a coded sheet somewhat similar to a checklist. Figure 13-4 provides a different approach, one in which comments and anecdotal notes can be recorded in broad categories under the general topic of writing development.

Portfolios

A portfolio is a container of some sort that chronicles the history of a child's language development. It is bigger than a file folder and smaller than a packing crate. In short, it is difficult to explain exactly the size or shape of a portfolio. Practically, it has to be large enough to contain the materials that teachers and children select to be included in it. On the other hand, it has to be small enough to be stored in an easily accessible classroom location throughout the duration of the program. It might be used to contain any of the devices or tools for collecting record keeping information. While this is usually in the form of papers and forms, it might also include audio tapes, notebooks, VCR tapes, and art projects. The key is to include indicators of learning that can be used by parents, teachers, students, and administrators to form an accurate view of a child's language development (Valencia 1990).

Observations.

Teachers, aides, and parents can record observations to be placed in a portfolio. Not every anecdotal record or emergent reading checklist needs to be placed in a portfolio, however. There should be a reason for placing it there. For example, teachers might decide to include anecdotal records about a child's ability to retell a story on a bimonthly basis. While such records might be collected weekly, the bimonthly records would demonstrate growth over time by presenting three or four sets of anecdotes. The same procedure might be used for notes from parents and interviews with students concerning their current interests. A single audio or video tape can be used to collect several months worth of information. It can be added to without the need to create more space in the portfolio.

Work Samples.

A second category of material is work samples produced by the child. Reading response logs, drawings, and written stories might be included. Not every piece of student work needs to be placed in a portfo-

Name:			
Native Language:		Code { A – Accomplished / B – Beginning / C – Not observed	

Literacy Marker	Date	Date	Date
Writes first name			
Writes last name			
Draws recognizable pictures			
Talks about own drawings			
Talks about book illustrations			
Draws print–like figures			
Recognizes name in isolation			
Recognizes name in context			
Writes some letters			
Writes some words			
Writes some sentences			
Uses invented spelling			
Uses conventional spelling			
Reads environmental print			
Reads some words in books			
Reads pattern books			
Reads own writing			
Relates print to illustration			
Chooses to do reading			
Chooses to do writing			
Predicts events in story			
Re-creates stories in play			

FIGURE 13-3 Sample emerging literacy assessment record sheet.

Name:_____	Native Language:_____		
Literacy Marker	Date	Date	Date
Global aspects			
• Planning activity			
• Content development			
• Organization			
• Ownership			
• Voice			
• Ability to discuss own writing			
• Willingness to take risks			
Drafting aspects			
• Has a point of view			
• Uses sentences			
• Reviews and revises			
• Language (vocabulary)			
Conventional aspects			
• % of conventional spellings			
• % of invented spellings			
• Punctuation use			
• Language (usage)			
• Capitalization			
• Handwriting			

FIGURE 13-4 Sample written language assessment recording sheet.

One time I went
don a hill. I got
a snow bren. It
herta lot. Then we
went to McDonelds.
we had fun!.

FIGURE 13-5 Portfolios should include a range of a child's work.

lio. An exception to this might be a listing of all the books a child has read. The key is to select a representative sampling of the child's work (Jongsma 1989). At the early ages, some of the selections of children's work should be made by the teacher, some by the student, and some by the parents. It is important to include the student as much as possible in the selection process. Discussions of why something is significant helps develop self monitoring and self assessment, both long-term learning goals. The portfolio might also include some of the materials produced outside of school. As with observations, a decision might need to be made concerning the frequency of adding materials to the portfolio. If too many materials or extremely bulky materials are continually added, the portfolio becomes too unwieldy to use in making decisions about a child's language development.

Informal Measures.

By either using the broad markers described previously, or by using other assessment tools, teachers will want to develop a set of interview forms, schedules, and checklists to collect objective information about a child's growth and development in the language arts. Different versions or different forms of these measures will most likely be used over time. Some of these records will also be included in a child's portfolio. In addition, teachers may see the need to use some of the more formal evaluation systems that are somewhat more appropriate than standardized tests in an integrated language arts program. These can be included in a portfolio. On the other hand, a portfolio is definitely not the place for standardized achievement test reports or any kind of classroom test. The portfolio must remain a place where both teachers and children can go to reflect on current learning and growth in order to help decide on future learning directions.

FORMAL EVALUATION SYSTEMS

Formal evaluation systems include any of the tools for measuring learning, behaviors, and attitudes that have been developed and made available for wide use by educators. The most common of these are the standardized readiness and achievement tests marketed by large, commercial publishing companies. Lesser known, but more appropriate for an integrated language arts program, are procedures developed by national education systems and early childhood literacy specialists. The problems inherent in standardized tests are considered here. This is followed by discussions of some of the more promising evaluation systems.

Standardized Tests

Those who are familiar with how literacy emerges and how language works for children who are attempting to learn it understand why standardized tests can be criticized both for their limitations and for the potential harm they can cause (Pikulski 1990). In spite of this, standardized test use continues to grow, with over 100 million being administered annually to children in the United States alone (Neill and Medina 1989).

Among the most commonly used standardized tests in language arts are readiness and reading tests. Most have two or three parts. One part might assess children's word recognition or knowledge of vocabulary. Another part might measure a child's ability to sound out or decode words. Still another part might attempt to measure a child's ability to understand something read. With young children, this is usually done by presenting the child with a brief passage, after which the child is required to answer a brief series of multiple choice questions.

The scores children receive on standardized tests are compared to a geographically distributed national reference group of children who took the test prior to it being placed on the market. There is great pressure on schools to have as many of their students score above the national average as possible. Many schools and most states boast that their students are scoring above the national median on these tests. Such a boast is illogical, of course. By definition, a median means that about half of the group is above it while the other half has to be below it. Since the tests are used year after year, and since teachers are under pressure to teach to the test, it is hardly surprising that after a few years of use far greater than half of the students taking these tests score above the median. This is but one of the problems associated with standardized tests. There are several others.

The dissatisfaction with standardized tests is not limited to the United States. Noted New Zealand educator Marie Clay (1990) identifies three areas in which she feels standardized tests have limitations. First, they tend never to measure well the earliest stages of learning nor the stage where children develop competency. Second, standardized tests focus on the products or outcomes of learning. They do not address the processes that have led up to the learning. The results provided by the tests, therefore, do not offer any guidance to the teacher about how to improve children's learning. Third, the tests themselves have to be limited to include only items that are simple and straightforward so that they might easily convert the child's learning to a number. Because of this limitation, standardized tests do not address the partial successes children attain as they engage in the process of learning.

British educator Myra Barrs (1990) identifies several additional problems with standardized tests. First, she argues, is the problem of context. It has long been known that children are likely to perform more poorly when assessed with material that lacks interest and meaning. Children perform better when they are dealing with materials, perhaps self-selected, that are interesting and motivating to them. In order to maintain objectivity, most standardized tests use language and passages that are dull and bland. Certainly they do not use well-loved passages from quality children's literature. This means that the tests do not show how representative the students' performance is compared to their normal work. Second, Barrs contends that most standardized tests are biased. Since boys tend to perform better than girls on multiple choice tasks as compared to free response tasks, the tests tend to discriminate against girls.

A third criticism identified by Barrs, and perhaps the most significant, is that most standardized tests are based upon theories that simply don't stand up to the knowledge about language available from psycholinguistics and the research on emerging literacy. Standardized tests in the language arts continue to view literacy as a single skill made up of many subskills that have little or no effect on the others. Tests are designed this way because such an approach serves to quantify learning and to translate it into a single number. The tests measure only what can be measured. As a result, such an assessment tool ignores what is most important (i.e., the process) and individual (i.e., the strategies used by the child to get at meaning) about reading and literacy.

These arguments are not lost on the manufacturers of tests. There is an effort to make the tests seem more natural, interactive, literature-based, and process-oriented (Pikulski 1990). This new generation of tests sometimes comes packaged to look like a series of short paperback books. They often include colorful illustrations and photographs of children taking the tests. Despite these surface changes, such tests still tend to be standardized against discredited theories of word recognition. Teachers who actively engage in authentic assessment will learn far more about children's learning than they will from a standardized test score. The children will benefit as well. Research has shown that engaging in a dynamic assessment of children, even children with disabilities, raises the teacher's expectations of the assessed child (Delclos 1987).

Social interaction and natural communication play a strong role in the development of language arts abilities of young children, and mention should be made of standardized tests designed to assess these social interactions. While such tests are much less frequently used, it is important to point out that they suffer from many of the problems of other standardized tests. In addition, they neither adequately identify social interaction problems nor do they provide any framework for helping the teacher plan approaches to address a problem.

Storybook Classification

Given the inappropriateness of most paper and pencil tests for assessing the language arts abilities of young children, early childhood educators need to become familiar with alternative assessment tools. Authentic assessment is a particularly useful informal approach. There are a limited number of more formal tools that follow many of the guidelines of authentic assessment for young children. One of the assessment instruments that does follow some of the guidelines is the "Classification Scheme for Emergent Reading of Favorite Storybooks," developed by Elizabeth Sulzby (1985, 1988). It can be used to evaluate children on a day-to-day basis as well as to maintain a history of a child's development over time.

Assumptions.

The storybook classification scheme is based on four assumptions (Sulzby 1985, 1988; Sulzby and Teale 1987). The assumptions follow a typical behavioristic approach, which limits the use of the instrument. Still, the approach has some merit. First, it makes the assumption that literacy begins prior to the time that children are reading from print, but that the process can be observed through the children's explorations with print. Of course, this latter point may or may not be a valid assumption. Some of what constitutes emergent literacy may not be visually observable because language development is predominantly a thinking process. Second, the approach assumes that social interactions with parents and teachers are the foundation for emergent literacy. Here again, this may or may not be a totally valid assumption. Children also interact with other children and re-create stories on their own. These activities cannot be disregarded as having no importance to literacy development. Third, the approach assumes that oral and written language are acquired

That night the witch returned to the tower. She fastened Rapunzel's braids to the hook in the window frame, and when the Prince came and called,

> Rapunzel, Rapunzel,
> Let down your hair,

she let the braids down.

FIGURE 13-6 Story books have an important role in the evaluation process. *From* The Child's Fairy Tale Book, *by Kay Chorao. Reprinted courtesy of E.P. Dutton.*

simultaneously and in combination with each other; as such, children are continually learning the relationship between oral and written language. A more prudent statement here might be that children are repeatedly engaged in hypothesis testing with language in attempting to learn these relationships. Fourth, the approach assumes that children acquire all aspects of conventional literacy in an emergent manner and re-establish them in an integrated system that allows them to learn print independently.

Classification Scheme.

The storybook classification scheme was designed to be used with familiar storybooks, those that children request that parents and teachers read over and over again. The scheme cannot be used with pattern books, books that children memorize verbatim, or books that aren't storybooks (Valencia 1991). To use the system, the teacher must become familiar with either an eleven point classification scheme or an abbreviated five point scheme that describes the manner in which a child attempts to retell or read a storybook to an adult who has requested the retelling from the child. Both scales are described and illustrated by Sulzby (1985, 1988). The five-point scale, which most will find adequate for daycare, preschool, and kindergarten age children is summarized here.

The first point on the scale is described as "Attending to Pictures, Not Forming Stories." This means that it appears that the child is doing the retelling primarily by looking at the pictures. Rather than providing a connected narrative, the child is simply talking about the pictures on the page that is open at the time.

The second point on the scale is described as "Attending to Pictures, Forming Oral Stories." This means that the child is telling a story by looking at the pictures, but that the story is more of a narrative that connects one page with another. The language and tone of the child is like that of someone telling a conversational story or like that of someone who is reciting the story.

The third point on the scale is described as "Attending to Pictures, Reading and Storytelling Mixed." Here, the child is using the pictures to tell the story, but the language and tone differ from previous categories. At this level, the child's speech moves between that of an oral storyteller and that of an actual reader. At some times the story sounds like a conversation, while at other times it has the intonation of someone actually reading a text.

The fourth point on the scale is described as "Attending to Pictures, Forming Written Stories." In this category, the child is using the pictures to tell the story but the listener no longer needs to see the pictures to understand the child's telling of the story. Both in language and tone, the child's speech sounds like reading to the point that if the listener were not watching the child it would be assumed that the child was actually reading the text.

The fifth point on the scale is described as "Attending to Print." There are a number of subcategories contained in this stage. They are similar in that they all relate to the child actually attempting to do something with the printed text as well as with the pictures illustrating the story. At the most basic phase, the child attends to print but does not use it as a tool to help read the story. This progresses through phases where the child makes increasing use of the print on the page as an aid to reading and finally to conventional reading.

Obviously, there are limitations to this system of storybook classification. It approaches language learning in a manner that is more behavioristic than holistic. This limits its use to what is observable through hearing and seeing. Secondly, it creates an artificial situation in which the child is asked at several points over time to retell a story to an adult in a manner that would not come about naturally. Finally, the system is applicable to only a fairly narrow range of books. It excludes many of the types of books children often find quite useful in developing literacy. The chief contribution of the system may be its descriptions of how children go about the task of attempting to pick up a book and read it. These descriptors may prove rather useful as a possible base for teachers to use in describing children's attempts to read. Figure 13-7 provides an example of how the categories might be incorporated within a format for collecting information about a child's emerging reading ability.

Primary Language Record

The Primary Language Record Handbook (1989) outlines a multidimensional assessment program that is used throughout England and Wales. It is a more general formal evaluation system, which is available to educators in early childhood education programs. It was developed in response to national education reforms that stressed the need for formative evaluation that helps shape teaching by addressing the "how" as well as the "what" of children's learning (Barrs 1990). The Primary Language Record, or PLR as it is known, places great emphasis on observation of children, or "kid-watching." It stresses the need to observe and record information about children on several occasions, over a period of time, in different contexts, using different recording and measurement techniques (Barrs 1990). Through this approach, it is believed that valuable feedback will be provided to

Name:_____ Native Language:_____

Code {
1 – Attending to pictures; not forming stories
2 – Attending to pictures; forming oral stories
3 – Attending to pictures; reading / storytelling mixed
4 – Attending to pictures; forming written stories
5 – Attending to print

Date	Storybook	Classification	Notes

FIGURE 13-7 Sample record form for Storybook Reading Classification Scheme.

teachers that can then be used to guide teaching. There are seven aspects of the PLR that need to be understood in order to gain a fuller understanding of its multidimensional approach: parent involvement, structured observation, samples, error analysis, conferencing, teacher judgment scales, and cumulative records (Barrs 1990).

Parent Involvement.

Besides the involvement of all teachers who work with a child, the PLR also involves the parents of the child in the assessment procedures (Barrs 1990). The first two components of the PLR involve discussions. One of these discussions is with the parents. The PLR recognizes that parents have many years of experience in observing the development of their child. Parents have a right and an important role to play in contributing their perceptions of their child's language and literacy development to the school records. The second discussion involves the child. This discussion about children's literacy development encourages children to reflect on the learning of language.

Structured Observations.

Structured observation includes recording critical information about a child over time. In the PLR, observations are collected under the three headings of reading, writing, and talking and listening. No preconceived checklist is used that identifies those aspects likely to be noted and important. The types of information and the intervals of time in which information is collected vary depending on the child. A bilingual child's oral language might necessitate a different type of observation than a native language speaker learning to read predictable books. On the other hand, the resulting observations of both would have an immediate effect on teaching. The information recorded would allow teachers to base their instruction on direct observation concerning the child's needs. While there is no checklist of what will likely be seen, there is a need to grid or chart the circumstances surrounding the observations. Teachers understand the importance of recording the social and curricular circumstances in which observations occur.

Figure 13-8. Observing a child's literacy by watching and listening.

Samples.

The term *sample* refers to an in-depth look at a specific child's reading or writing as a regular part of that child's literacy development. It may be a thorough analysis of the process a child uses to draw, write, and tell a story. It may be a close observation of the strategies a child uses when attempting to read a book the teacher has just shared with the class. Whatever the case, the analysis often uses a schedule or a set of broad markers as a guide to understanding the child's progress. The sampling also includes provisions for the teacher to record anything that seems significant within the particular context from which the sample is taken.

Error Analysis.

Whenever teachers observe a child reading or writing, a number of factors are usually apparent. These may include fluency, word recognition, articulation, and the ability to self-correct errors. Recording the errors and the strategies the child uses while engaged in a language activity provides the teacher with much useful information. It allows the teacher to identify the kinds of errors a child is making. It provides an illustration of the child's understanding of the reading or writing process. It identifies the strategies a child uses to address apparent errors. Each of these provides information on which to design instruction to meet the child's needs.

Conferencing.

A conference within the PLR format is an in-depth interview with the child. The conference has a number of different purposes, all of which are aimed at creating information for the benefit of both the child and the teacher. Through careful questioning and listening, both the teacher and the child can develop a better understanding of the child's literacy development. Through this process, children come to a clearer sense of themselves as readers, writers, and language users. By reflecting on their own learning, they begin to identify areas in which they are doing well and those in which they may need some help. Being aware of this information also helps children monitor their own progress. Obviously, this same information will suggest to the teacher the strategies that will best enable the child to continue language growth.

Teacher Judgment Scales.

The PLR contains scales for evaluating the progress and development of children as emerging readers. They identify broad markers as indicators of reading growth along a continuum from dependence to independence. They are designed for use over a long period of time. A key aspect of the scales is that they provide information to help the teacher make decisions about what type of instruction the children need to progress further.

Cumulative Records.

Traditionally, cumulative records comprised little more than a folder with the child's name, address, test scores, report card grades, health report, and an occasional note from home. In the PLR, the cumulative record comprises the reports, structured observations, interview notes, scales, and samples of the child's writing and drawing. It is quite similar to a portfolio. The commentary accompanying the records allows both

the teacher and the child to review and contemplate both the achievements and the needs of the child. The information developed through the PLR, together with samples of the child's work, comprises a total picture of the child's literacy development over time.

Reading Recovery

The term *reading recovery* actually refers to a tutorial intervention program developed by Marie Clay that is used throughout New Zealand and in many areas of North America. The program is described in Clay's book, *The Early Detection of Reading Difficulties* (1985). It is a highly successful program that is used with first grade children who are having difficulty learning to read. While several of the procedures of Reading Recovery are not appropriate for the very young child, it is included in this unit on evaluation due to the fact that it combines a structured but natural evaluation system with a teaching system. Through a year-long training period, Reading Recovery changes the way teachers look at and assess children. It evaluates the children's reading ability in such a way that the evaluation always provides information that can be used to make instructional decisions.

Assessment Surveys.

The Reading Recovery assessment system includes a set of six independently administered procedures that are used to provide a detailed description of a child's knowledge of reading and writing (Pinnell 1987). The surveys evaluate several areas of reading and writing, many of which are fairly self explanatory. For example, different surveys determine a child's ability to recognize individual letters and frequently used words. Writing is assessed by analyzing a child's writing samples. Several samples are used to determine the child's language level (e.g., use of letters, words, sentences, and paragraphs), message quality (e.g., recording of ideas, repetition of sentence patterns, etc.) and directional principles (e.g., left to right directional pattern, word spacing, etc.). Other parts of the writing assessment include a written vocabulary test in which the child writes as many words as are known and a dictation test. A concepts about print test, which was described more fully in an earlier unit, determines the child's knowledge about basic features of books and printed language.

Running Records.

One of the most important features of the Reading Recovery system is the assessment tool called running records. A running record is a systematic coding of a child's strengths and weaknesses observed when the child is attempting to read materials of varying difficulties. When the child is reading easier material, the running record will reveal the child's strengths and strategies used to deal with new or unfamiliar text. When the child is reading more difficult material, the running record will reveal a child's weak areas where effective strategies need to be acquired. The running record, also referred to as a mis-cue analysis, provides information that guides the teacher in forming subsequent instruction.

To take a running record of a child's reading, the teacher might ask the child to read several 100- to 200-word pieces of text of varying difficulty. For younger children who are reading books with a limited number of words, the passages will be less than 100 words. The teacher, using a copy of the text the child is reading, records the child's reading using a system of codes. Figure 13-9 provides a sample of the coding that can be used to take a running record. A teacher might wish to develop a different code. This is acceptable, as long as all of the child's reading miscues or errors are collected for study. Following the collection of the running record, the child's accuracy rate and self correction rate are computed. These can be compared over time. The errors that the child has made are analyzed so that instructional decisions can be made to address the child's needs. The Reading Recovery program spends many months training teachers to make appropriate instructional decisions based on the observed errors of children.

REPORTING EVALUATION RESULTS

Up to this point, the stress has been on the process of evaluation rather than on the product. The documented observations, anecdotal records, running records, audio tapes, video tapes, writing samples, literacy checklists, and so forth constitute some of the products of the evaluation. They might be kept in portfolios or files and shared with several possible audiences. These products might be used as the basis for developing still other products of evaluation such as reports to administrators, agencies, other teachers, children, and parents. Depending on the recipient of the information, the evaluation product would be developed differently. In each case, it would be closely linked to the purpose for which the evaluation information is needed.

Reporting to Administrators

Administrators may include a number of different individuals. The administrator may be the director of a daycare center, a board member, a principal, or an administrator of an agency such as a state department of education. Each individual or institution might have different needs. The familiarity of the administrator with an integrated language arts program would have an impact on the usefulness of the information as well. Individuals without knowledge and understanding of a whole language approach may not understand the evaluation products that result from authentic assessments. Such individuals are probably more comfortable with the norm-referenced information that can be derived from standardized readiness tests despite the limited value of such information.

Many administrators, of course, have become familiar with a whole language approach to literacy. They will be comfortable with the products derived from authentic assessment and be able to make great use of portfolio information describing language growth processes. They may also wish to have summary information representative of a class or instructional group as well. Depending on the purpose or need, this information can probably be generated in an acceptable format. For example, an administrator may wish to know the numbers of children in a group who have demonstrated certain literacy behaviors associated with a critical language development marker. This information can be readily obtained by examining individual children's portfolios.

Reporting to Teachers

The informational products developed through authentic assessment practices are particularly rele-

Error or miscue	Written text	Student reads this	Teacher records this
No error, √ for each word	The cat plays.	The cat plays.	√ √ √
Word substitution	The dog barks.	The doll barks.	√ / doll / √
Multiple attempts	The house is white.	The h– h– home is white.	√ / h– h– home / √ √
Self-correction	My bike is red.	My bit–bat–bike is red.	√ / bit–bat / SC √ √
No response	She is a funny girl.	She is a .... girl.	√ √ √ _____ √
No response; child is told word	Bill is strong.	Bill is	√ √ / TOLD /
Repetition of word or phrase (not an error if words are corrected)	Mary is so silly.	Mary is so sally. Mary is so silly.	▼√ √ √ / R / SC /

FIGURE 13-9 Sample codings for recording running record mis-cues.

vant to teachers. With appropriate training and knowledge, they can use the information just as it exists in a student's portfolio. It can be used to provide feedback to students as well as guide the teacher in making instructional decisions. Other teachers can make use of information from portfolios, although it may need to be condensed and presented in a summary format through checklists and summary sheets such as those illustrated in Figures 13-3, 13-4, and 13-7.

Teachers in other buildings and in other schools may need to receive this information. For example, the teacher in the next level the child is moving to in

a preschool will learn much about the literacy development of a group of children by studying the authentic assessment products in their portfolios. For those five-year-olds leaving an early childhood program, the elementary school kindergarten teachers will greatly benefit from studying the children's literacy portfolios. Teachers tend to focus on individual children; they will most likely not need the kinds of group summary information that administrators might require from time to time. An exception to this might be when teachers are planning major changes to their instructional approaches or curriculum. They might wish to make judgments concerning certain in-

FIGURE 13-10 Teachers need to understand and explain the reactions of children to an author's style and to the literature.

structional strategies or curricular objectives based on their effect on the learning of the children.

Reporting to Parents

For years, parents of elementary-school-aged children have been indoctrinated to expect report cards with letter grades (e.g., A, B, C, D, F), number grades (e.g., 100, 95, 90, 85) and coded letters (e.g., S for satisfactory, N for needs improvement). These reports have been used so pervasively that most parents seldom question their usefulness or validity. Such reporting systems, though used less frequently, are not unheard of at the pre-kindergarten level. Unfortunately, reporting devices such as these can do harm while at the same time providing little useful information to parents. The harm they cause is to establish a belief that learning is basically something that can be reduced to a letter or number. This fosters the view that learning is a product, a collection of information that the child has mastered with the aid of the teacher. In addition, many come to believe that they really know what a number or letter grade means. Yet, few have a clear explanation of what a grade of "B" on the subject of word identification represents. Such a concept misses the point of what evaluation is really all about. Some have suggested that authentic assessment tools such as holistic ratings of student

writing can be converted into traditional letter and number grades (Linek 1991). This approach is discouraged since it mainly gives credence to a system that has little usefulness or validity. In addition, the approach also takes something that is potentially informative and renders it uninformative and misleading.

For parents, especially, evaluation should be useful and timely. Evaluation information that is useful will provide a clear picture to parents of the literacy development of their child. It will explain the things the child can do well and what things seem to be difficult at the present time. Useful evaluation information will provide parents with the larger picture of literacy development and where their child's current development fits into that picture. This means that the information must explain what is meant by such terms as "retelling a story," "developing a voice in writing," and "responding to an author's style." The information must also explain why these are important literacy development strategies and abilities for children. Evaluation information needs to be provided to parents on an ongoing basis rather than through quarterly reports. Frequent communication does not mean that a formal report card needs to be issued every two or three weeks. Timely information means that communication should take place whenever anything of note occurs. At the early childhood level, this often means on a daily basis. A notebook that comes and goes on a daily basis with the child can provide a means for timely evaluative information.

Notebooks and folders that go back and forth between school and home with evaluative information invite feedback. This is important at all levels of schooling, but particularly at the early childhood level. It should be remembered that parents spend years as observers of their children. As their children emerge into literate human beings, they can provide teachers with a wealth of information concerning the extension of literacy abilities beyond the classroom. It is quite relevant for a teacher to know whether or not children select reading and writing at home and on weekends as recreational activities. The comments and observations of parents can help teachers make decisions about the future instructional needs of the students in a way that is not altogether different than the comments and observations of the teacher. An added benefit to this type of communication is that it

FIGURE 13-11 A parent sent this button-filled vest to school. Her child had designed the vest in response to a reading of a story about missing buttons by Arnold Lobel.

involves parents in the formal education of their children in a manner that is active, responsive, and meaningful.

SUMMARY

Evaluation is a process. It entails gathering information, comparing that information to something else, and then making a decision about how closely the two match. There are three different points in the instructional program where evaluation activities occur. At the beginning of instruction, diagnostic evaluation may be conducted to determine such things as the language and literacy levels of the children. During the instruction, formative evaluation is done to both determine the progress children are making in their learning and to provide feedback that is helpful to them. Following instruction, summative evaluation seeks to determine the actual outcomes of the entire instructional lesson or unit.

The purpose of evaluation is to help make decisions. Teachers need evaluation information in order to make decisions about the instructional strategies and procedures they are using or that they intend to use. Children need evaluation information in order to develop an awareness of themselves as learners. Parents need evaluation information in order to keep informed about their child's development. This infor-

mation also allows parents to participate in their child's education beyond the instructional program.

Traditional evaluation models tend to focus primarily on summative evaluation. Furthermore, they tend to rely on standardized tests as the primary tool for providing assessment information. At the early childhood level, language arts programs have often used reading readiness and reading achievement tests. There are a number of different problems associated with using standardized tests with young children. Children change quite rapidly in their development during the first few years of their lives. The tests do not take this into account. Standardized tests also need to quantify learning so that the test results can be analyzed arithmetically. Learning does not translate very easily into a single score on a test. Standardized tests in the language arts tend to be based on theories of language and reading that have been shown to lack validity. They make the assumption that literacy is a single skill that can be broken down into discreet and isolated subskills. This view makes it easier to test these skills, but it does not make the assumption valid.

An evaluation system that came out of the literature on whole language is much more responsive to the needs of an integrated language arts approach. It is known as authentic assessment, responsive assessment, and natural evaluation. It assumes that evaluation should take place in a natural environment, use real literature and materials, and involve the teacher interacting with the child. The system uses such tools as parent interviews, child interviews, multiple observations, child work samples, teacher/child conferences, and a host of information-gathering formats. Most of this information is compiled in a portfolio that is accessible to the teacher, the parent, and the child.

Besides informal types of authentic assessments, there are several more formal versions that follow many of the principles of natural assessment. The storybook classification scheme was developed in the United States by Sulzby (1985, 1988). Although it takes more of a behavioristic approach, it does provide a tool that may be useful in identifying some of the language markers associated with learning to read. *The Primary Language Record Handbook* (1989) was developed in England in response to the need to evaluate the literacy development of children in a more valid manner. The Reading Recovery program was developed in New Zealand by Clay (1985) as a combined teaching and assessment program for young children experiencing severe difficulty in learning to read. Each of these tools has much to offer a teacher looking for ideas and formats for implementing authentic assessment as part of an integrated language arts program.

The actual reports, observations, work samples, and anecdotal records collected are the products of evaluation. They have different uses and different purposes, depending on the audience with whom they are to be shared. Administrators often need evaluation information comprised of summary statements. Teachers need specific information that is directly related to classroom instruction. They need information that serves as a guide to current and future instruction. Children need information that helps them to see themselves as learners. Parents need information that is meaningful and ongoing. Letter and number grades are not necessarily useful even though they are quite familiar to most parents. Information that helps parents better understand their children's literacy development is much more meaningful. Such information also invites responses from parents that helps to involve them in the formal education of their children.

Questions and Activities for Review and Discussion

Multiple Choice

1. The first step taken in an educational program evaluation process is the identification of the
   a. intelligence levels of the children.
   b. instructional approach used.
   c. curriculum objectives.
   d. tests to be used.

2. The ultimate purpose of educational evaluation is to provide information for people to
   a. make decisions.
   b. pass or fail children.
   c. provide funding for a program.
   d. determine the ability of children.

3. Teachers attempting to determine the oral language levels of children at the beginning of a program are engaged in
   a. diagnostic evaluation.
   b. formative evaluation.
   c. summative evaluation.
   d. standardized testing.

4. The concept of a test measuring something consistently over a period of time is known as
   a. validity.
   b. reliability.
   c. the norming sample.
   d. norm-referenced measurement.

5. A means of collecting information that documents the ability, attitudes, and skills of children over time is called
   a. record keeping.
   b. summative evaluation.
   c. a standardized test.
   d. computer assisted instruction.
6. A major criticism of standardized tests is that they only measure
   a. actual reading ability.
   b. what can be easily measured by a test.
   c. the reading ability of older children.
   d. all of the above
7. The process of coding and recording the oral reading of a child in the Reading Recovery program is called
   a. the child interview.
   b. summative evaluation.
   c. storybook classification.
   d. running records.

True or False

T   F 1. Evaluation seeks to provide information about how well a program is operating.

T   F 2. Evaluation that occurs during the instructional part of the program is called summative evaluation.

T   F 3. Authentic assessment emerged from the development of the whole language approach.

T   F 4. Interview techniques are of little value as a language evaluation tool for young children.

T   F 5. The Primary Language Record involves both the child and the parents as participants in assessing literacy development.

Essay and Discussion

1. Describe the four steps contained in any evaluation process.
2. Explain why formative evaluation information is particularly important for a classroom teacher.
3. How do parents become good evaluators of the development of their children?
4. What is a portfolio, and what does it contain?
5. Describe the type of evaluation information that needs to be shared with parents.

REFERENCES

Au, K.H., J.A. Scheu, A.J. Kawakami, and P.A. Herman. 1990. Assessment and accountability in a whole literacy curriculum. *The Reading Teacher* 43: 574–578.

Barrs, M. 1990. The Primary Language Record: Reflection of issues in evaluation. *Language Arts* 67: 244–253.

Cambourne, B.L. 1988. From guinea pigs to coresearchers. Brisbane, Pre-Conference Institute, World Reading Conference.

Cambourne, B.L., and J.B. Turbill. 1987. *Coping with chaos.* Sydney: Primary English Teachers Association.

Cambourne, B.L., and J.B. Turbill. 1990. Assessment in whole language classrooms: Theory into practice. *Elementary School Journal* 90: 337–350.

Clay, M.M. 1985. *The early detection of reading difficulties.* Portsmouth, N.H.: Heinemann.

Clay, M.M. 1990. Research currents: What is and what might be in evaluation. *Language Arts* 67: 288–298.

Davis, H.G. 1980. Reading pressures in the kindergarten. *Childhood Education* 57: 76–79.

Delclos, V.R. 1987. Effects of dynamic assessment on teachers' expectations of handicapped children. *American Educational Research Journal* 24: 325–336.

Elkind, D. 1981. *The hurried child.* Reading, Mass.: Addison-Wesley.

Freeman, E.B., and J.A. Hatch. 1989. What schools expect young children to know and do: An analysis of kindergarten report cards. *Elementary School Journal* 89: 595–605.

Guba, E., and Y. Lincoln. 1981. *Effective evaluation: Improving the usefulness of evaluation results through responsive and naturalistic approaches.* San Francisco: Jossey-Bass.

Halliday, M.A.K. 1975. *Learning how to mean.* London: Arnold.

Holdaway, D. 1979. *The foundations of literacy.* Sydney: Ashton-Scholastic.

Jongsma, K.S. 1989. Portfolio assessment. *The Reading Teacher* 43: 264–265.

Johnston, P. 1986. The process of assessment in language arts. In *The dynamics of language learning: Research in reading and English*, ed. J. R. Squires. Urbana, Ill.: NCTE/ERIC.

Kamii, C. 1985. Leading primary children toward excellence: Beyond worksheets and drill. *Young Children* 40: 3–9.

Lincoln, Y., and E. Guba. 1986. *Naturalistic inquiry.* Beverly Hills, Calif.: Sage.

Linek, W.M. 1991. Grading and evaluation techniques for whole language teachers. *Language Arts* 68: 125–132.

Martin, A. 1985. Back to kindergarten basics. *Harvard Educational Review* 55: 318–320.

Neill, D., and N. Medina. 1989. Standardized testing: Harmful to educational health. *Phi Delta Kappan* 70: 688–702.

Pikulski, J.J. 1990. The role of tests in a literacy assessment program. *The Reading Teacher* 43: 686–688.

Pinnell, G.S. 1987. Helping teachers see how readers read: Staff development though observation. *Theory Into Practice* 26: 51–58.

The Primary Language Record Handbook. 1989. London: Center for Language in Primary Education.

Simmons, B., and J. Brewer. 1985. When parents of kindergarteners ask "Why?" *Childhood Education* 61: 177–184.

Smith, M.L., and L.A. Shepard. 1987. What doesn't work: Explaining policies and retention in early grades. *Phi Delta Kappan* 69: 129–134.

Sulzby, E. 1985. Children's emergent reading of favorite storybooks: A developmental study. *Reading Research Quarterly* 20: 458–481.

Sulzby, E. 1988. A study of children's early reading development. In *Psychological Bases of Early Education*, ed. A. D. Pellegrini. Chichester, N.Y.: Wiley.

Sulzby, E., and W.H. Teale. 1987. *Young children's storybook reading: Longitudinal study of parent-child interaction and children's independent functioning*, Final Report to The Spencer Foundation. Ann Arbor, Mich.: University of Michigan.

Uphoff, J.K., and J. Gilmore. 1986. Pupils' age at school entrance D how many are ready for success? *Young Children* 41: 2, 11–16.

Valencia, S.W. 1990. A portfolio approach to classroom reading assessment: The whys, whats, and hows. *The Reading Teacher* 43: 338–340.

Valencia, S.W. 1991. Assessment of emerging literacy: Storybook reading. *The Reading Teacher* 44: 498–500.

Section 5
Special Needs

Mike Thaler, "America's Riddle King"

"All children are citizens of the most powerful nation in the world: IMAGI—NATION."

Photograph and text courtesy of Mike Thaler.

TO THE READER

One of the most fascinating aspects of working with young children is experiencing their diversity. Yes, children have many similarities. They tend to reach certain developmental milestones such as self-feeding, walking, talking, and toileting within certain ranges of ages. Each child, however, is a unique individual. This is a benefit, since this diversity makes the work of early childhood teachers both exciting and engaging.

Children with special needs, like all other children, share a common humanity. Such children are described as children with special needs mainly because their differences seem to go beyond the range we would generally observe in a group of young children. The differences, however, aren't the important thing. What is important is the fact that their needs might be more intense than those of other children.

As you shall see, there are many needs these children might demonstrate. Some may need to learn English as a second language. Some may need intensive speech and language therapy. Some may need more exposure to basic concepts and books. Some may need physical assistance, technological supports, or environmental adaptations. Some may need the services of a special education teacher. Some may need greater challenges in different areas due to their advanced capabilities.

In this section, you will learn about the various types of special needs children may have. Related to this, you will learn why children with disabilities should be included in regular early childhood programs rather than placed in special treatment facilities. Strategies for working with children who have special needs are described. In addition, you will learn about numerous children's books that can be used to help the entire class learn about various types of disabilities.

Also in this section, you will learn how to adapt a regular early childhood literacy program to include children with special needs. Traditionally, children with disabilities were segregated in specialized programs. Federal and state laws have gradually begun to change in the direction of integration over the past couple of decades, although much still needs to be done. Among the challenges of including children with disabilities in regular early childhood education programs is the need to develop positive attitudes in all individuals. Teachers may not be used to working with children with disabilities in the regular classroom. Many children may have biases against or fears of children with disabilities. Such attitudes are usually the product of ignorance. Included in this section are a number of strategies for developing positive attitudes for all involved.

UNIT 14

The Exceptional Child

UNIT GOALS

After completing this unit, the reader should:

- identify different types of children who might be identified as exceptional children.
- become familiar with disabilities that may affect a child's ability to learn spoken or written language.
- develop an understanding of children from diverse cultural backgrounds.
- develop an understanding of the gifted and talented child.
- build a set of strategies and procedures for making early childhood education programs accessible to all children.
- develop a familiarity with books for young children that address the child with disabilities and the multicultural child.

PREVIEW

The world is becoming smaller, not in a geographical sense, but in a cultural sense. People from different nations and backgrounds are increasingly finding themselves living in multicultural neighborhoods. There is also a tendency to identify children as gifted and talented at an earlier age. The question must be raised: How can the needs of all of these children be met in a regular educational program? In addition to this, children with disabilities are being integrated into regular educational programs in ever-increasing numbers. Previously, these children tended to be educated in separate special education programs, iso-lated from children without disabilities. As a result of these shifting patterns, the early childhood educator must assume the responsibility of becoming aware of the exceptional child, whether the child is from a different culture, possesses a disability, or is gifted and talented.

Providing appropriate services to all children is a responsibility of all members of the educational community. It is both an ethical and professional responsibility. In the case of children with disabilities, it is a legal right for such children to receive an appropriate, integrated, educational program. Public Law 94–142 guarantees educational services to all children with disabilities through age twenty-one. Including culturally diverse children, youngsters with disabilities, and children who may be gifted and talented in a regular early childhood educational program provides benefits to all children. We live in a society comprised of people with diversity. Growing up together can help us learn toleration, patience, respect, empathy, and friendship for each other.

To include children with such diversity within a single program dictates that teachers not provide a single type of instructional program with the hope that everyone will learn equally well. Rather, it demands that teachers plan with the needs and strengths of these children in mind. An integrated language arts program is particularly well suited as it supports a respect for and belief in children as learners. Beyond the provision of an instructional program is the need for teachers to become active advocates for including and meeting the needs of all children in an integrated language arts setting. The key ideas and concepts explored in this unit that will help teachers achieve these goals include the identification of various disabilities, an understanding of cultural diversity, the identification of the gifted and talented, and procedures for making programs accessible.

INTRODUCTION

For many years the child with disabilities was shut out or turned away from regular educational programs. They were partly served either by a number of publicly and privately supported alternative institutions or not served at all. In the latter case they either remained in their homes during their educational years or they were warehoused in several types of settings. The settings that housed children with disabilities ranged from mental institutions to juvenile detention centers. The passage of Public Law 94–142 in 1975 changed much of this situation. It mandated, among other things, that children had a right to receive a free, appropriate, publicly supported education in the least restrictive environment. This meant that parents and families of children with disabilities could not be made to pay for the education of their children. It also meant that children should receive an education in a regular educational program to the greatest extent possible. For the elementary and secondary school years, it meant that unless there were

particularly extenuating circumstances, children with disabilities should be educated in the school they would normally attend if they did not possess disabilities.

This unit explores the different types of children with disabilities who might be found in any educational program. In order for educators to participate in educating exceptional children in regular classroom programs, it is necessary that teachers understand various disabilities and the types of diversity a child can possess. Children who are not from the mainstream culture are increasingly included in regular education programs. While they may also receive specialized services designed to meet their specific needs, there is a pressing need to insure that they effectively participate in the regular educational program. Children who are gifted and talented may have special needs that should be addressed within the regular educational program as well. It also must be recognized and stressed that they possess much in common with all of the children they meet in a regular educational program.

Finally, the need to help all children participate in a regular early childhood education program is explored in this unit. The emphasis here is on developing a program that welcomes and supports children both initially and throughout their early childhood years. It includes strategies for developing awareness, providing a social framework, and increasing understanding and tolerance. Specific procedures and strategies for supporting the curriculum and instructional environment are discussed in a later unit.

THE CHILD WITH DISABILITIES

The passage of Public Law 94–142, and subsequent revisions of this law, created a new era for the child with disabilities. For the first time, children with disabilities had the right to an education at no cost to their families. Furthermore, the spirit and the language of the law stated that the education should be provided in the least restrictive environment to the greatest extent possible. This meant that such children should be educated in their home school; that is, they should receive their education in the school they would attend if they did not have a disability. There was no mention of the severity of the disability in this provision. Therefore, the intent of this law is clear: It indicates that to the greatest extent possible all children with disabilities should attend their home school.

The fact that the law supported greater inclusion of children with disabilities in regular education programs did not insure that inclusion. There has been both active and subtle resistance to such programs. This is not surprising, since schools have traditionally maintained whole-class, teacher-directed, age-graded, instructional programs with largely homogeneous groups of children (Goodlad 1983). Nevertheless, both logic and court decisions have continued to expand the placement of children with disabilities in programs with nondisabled children and to provide appropriate services within those programs (Giangreco and Putnam 1991).

Public Law 89–313 extended similar rights to infants, toddlers, and preschool children with disabilities. Since many states do not operate preschools, nursery schools, or daycare centers, they have elected to fund services to private providers of educational services for children with disabilities. Fiscal requirements dictated by state and federal funding agencies have often made it difficult for these service providers to educate children with disabilities in an integrated setting. The trend is changing, as evidenced by recent court decisions in cases involving both preschool and school-age children (Giangreco and Putnam 1991). The trend for the future is for greater inclusion of all children with disabilities in regular instructional programs at all levels of education.

The first step a teacher can take to bridge the gap from exclusion to inclusion is to become familiar with the types of disabilities a child might possess. In considering the possibilities, it is important to keep three things in mind. First, a disability does not eliminate the possiblity of meaningful learning, either in the language arts or in any other content area. In fact, a disability might not impede cognitive learning at all. Many highly gifted people also happen to possess a disability. Second, disabilities are not an either/or condition. There is often a wide range of potential strength in any one of the ten disabilities described here. Third, using a classification or a label as the primary descriptor of a child cannot help but diminish that child's sense of worth. This is something that all need to guard against. A person is first and foremost a human being. As a member of the human

FIGURE 14-1 All children have a right to participate in regular education programs.

family, we need to know and to learn about that child as a person. It can be argued that classifying children with disabilities has the potential to do more harm than good. The classifications used in education laws and regulations are described here so that readers become informed of the terms used to describe children with disabilities. It should also be noted that a condition that is viewed as a disability is not necessarily an educational disability. The regulations that govern this point out that the disability must adversely affect a child's ability to learn in order to be considered an educational disability.

Speech Impaired

In all likelihood, the disability that early childhood educators will enounter most frequently is speech impairment. The classification covers a wide range of speech and language difficulties within which there is a wide range of severity. Children experiencing difficulties articulating the sounds associated with language are placed in this category, as are children with no speech or with unintelligible speech. It should be noted, however, that there is a developmental progression in which children seem to acquire the ability to articulate the various sounds. A young child who has difficulty with the sounds associated with the letters *l, r, s,* and *f* is not necessarily speech impaired. At some point between birth and adolescence, all children go through the process of learning to articulate these sounds.

While some children may be able to articulate sounds and words adequately, other language difficulties impair their learning. They may have difficulty understanding how language works, the meanings of words, or how to use language in social, educational, and problem-solving situations. These children are also grouped under the category of speech impaired. Other difficulties experienced by children that can result in a speech-impaired classification include voice disorders and stuttering. Each of these areas usually requires the services of a speech and language therapist to work in conjunction with the regular teacher.

Visually Disabled

Children who have vision difficulties that adversely affect their ability to learn may be classified as disabled. Those children whose vision problems can be corrected to restore normal learning ability are not classified under this category. It is used, instead, to classify those children whose learning is still affected even with the best corrective lenses and other technology. Blind children are also classified here.

There are a number of potential strategies and procedures to address the needs of these children. Large print books, books on tape, specially designed instructional materials and strategies are only a few of the possibilities.

Hearing Impaired

This classification is also described as hard of hearing. It refers to those children with permanent or fluctuating hearing impairments that adversely affect their educational performance. It does not include those children who are classified as deaf. Children classified as hearing impaired can sometimes be assisted with sound amplification devices such as hearing aids. They may also need the services of sign language interpreters, speech therapists, and special education teachers.

Deaf

The term *deaf* refers to hearing impairments so severe that the individual is impaired in processing language either with or without amplification devices. A number of amplification devices, including hearing aids, are often used to partially assist the child. Other services and materials include the provision of speech language therapists, sign language interpreters, the learning of sign language, and special education services.

Deaf-blind

Children classified as deaf-blind are experiencing both hearing and visual impairments that are so severe that they cause communication, developmental, and educational problems that cannot be adequately accommodated in programs designed solely for deaf or blind children. While such children might be viewed as too severely disabled to function within a regular program, teachers should focus on abilities as well as disabilities. Deaf-blind children often possess perfectly normal abilities to touch, taste, smell, think, and love. There is no reason why they cannot receive the services they need to address their disabilities in a classroom with their non-disabled peers. The key is to provide the necessary services to enable this to become a reality.

Mentally Disabled

Mental disability is also referred to as mental retardation. Here too, a wide range of severity exists within the classification. To be classified under this category, children must be found to possess general intelligence significantly below average as well as similar deficits in adaptive behavior observed during their developmental period. Adaptive behavior refers to life skills such as the onset of language, toilet training, walking, and developing peer relationships.

The deficiencies in intelligence and adaptive behavior must adversely affect the child's educational performance in order to justify a classification of mental disability. This is not always the case. Many higher functioning children whose intelligence falls into the mentally retarded range on a standardized intelligence test are motivated and encouraged to function within so-called normal limits, well above their seeming potential. When this occurs, it is inappropriate to classify a child as mentally disabled. The fact that intelligence scores have traditionally been found to be rather unreliable with young children suggests that great caution be used in assigning this classification.

Learning Disabilities

Until the 1960s there was no such classification as learning disabilities. The term was invented in an attempt to explain the inability to learn of children who did not seem to possess another more obvious disability. The laws and regulations that describe it state that it is a disorder in a psychological process related to the learning and use of written or spoken language or of mathematics. The term includes a wide range of other conditions such as perceptual disabilities, brain injury, minimal brain dysfunction, dyslexia, and developmental aphasia, all of which are difficult if not impossible to identify or diagnose. The term excludes children who have learning problems due to physical, mental, or emotional problems as well as children whose learning difficulties are the result of environmental, cultural, or economic factors.

The vagueness of the standards and criteria for using the classification of learning disabilities has caused its use to be both unclear and not uniformly applied. This has resulted in large numbers of misclassifications using the learning disabilities category (Algozzine and Ysseldyke 1986; Sawyer 1989). The vagueness of the standards make learning disabilities, more than any other classification, a judgmental disability. That is, the label is given to a child because someone makes a judgment that the child will be better off with it and the programming that accompanies it than without it (Moore, Hyde, Blair, and Weitzman 1981).

While learning disabled has become the most widely used label to classify children as disabled, early childhood education teachers are not likely to see many children labeled as such in their programs. This is because the laws and regulations rely primarily on individual standardized tests to identify educational achievement. Since there are really few or no tests in reading, writing, and mathematics at the early childhood level, there is a lack of evidence for classifying children as learning disabled at that level.

Orthopedically Impaired

The term *orthopedically impaired* refers to several severe orthopedic impairments that adversely affect a child's educational performance. Some orthopedic impairments are caused by congenital factors: clubfoot, absence of some member, and other causes. Others are caused by disease: polio, tuberculosis, and others. Still others have different causes: cerebral palsy, amputations, fractures, and burns. Children with these disabilities often possess average or even above average learning ability. While they may need special educational services to function within a regular program, they also often need the services of speech therapists, physical therapists, and occupational therapists.

Other Health Impaired

Two subcategories fall under the heading of other health impaired. The first is autism. While it is often manifested by severe communication, developmental, and educational problems, autism is a puzzling disability. Contrary to popular belief, a wide range of people are autistic or possess many autistic tendencies. The most common notion is that of a totally noncommunicative child who is isolated from all human communication and is often self-destructive. Continuing research has found that, despite years of belief to the contrary, children on the more extreme end of the autistic range do respond in differing degrees to education and therapy; they often do improve their abilities with appropriate educational services. Facilitated communication is opening new frontiers to some people with autism by showing them to have unsuspected intelligence and understandings.

On the other end of the spectrum are those individuals with milder autistic behaviors. They are particularly puzzling because they often appear as nondisabled in many ways. As a result they are often misunderstood and treated as socially maladjusted, with no provisions for their disability. This does these children a great disservice. They do need special programming, and they do need to function in an environment that meets their needs. Children with autism often require the services of special education teachers, speech therapists, social workers, and psychologists. There is a growing awareness that the best possible setting for autistic children is within a program of non-disabled peers. This is in direct contradiction to the traditional, isolated, residential special education centers in which such children have historically been placed.

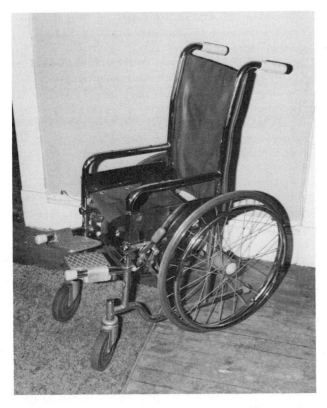

FIGURE 14-2 Some people may need special equipment to help them participate.

The second subcategory of other health impaired includes individuals who possess limited strength, vitality, or alertness due to chronic or acute health problems. These problems are the result of several factors: heart condition, tuberculosis, rheumatic fever, nephritis, asthma, sickle cell anemia, hemophilia, epilepsy, lead poisoning, leukemia, and diabetes. It should be noted that the health problem must adversely affect the child's educational performance in order to be considered an educational disability. Services required for this subcategory are similar to those for orthopedically disabled. The needs of the individual child determine the specific services that should be provided.

Multiply Disabled

Children classified as multiply disabled include those who have two or more disabilities. In addition,

the severity of the impairment must be such that it causes educational problems that cannot be adequately addressed in special education programs designed for one of the impairments. The term does not include deaf-blind children.

Emotionally Disturbed

The classification of emotionally disturbed does not generally include children who are overactive, inattentive, or socially maladjusted. Rather, it is used to identify children who exhibit, over a long period of time and to a marked degree, one or more characteristics associated with emotional difficulties. Five different factors ordinarily serve as a basis for the classification:

- An inability to learn that cannot be explained by intellectual, sensory, or health factors
- An inability to develop appropriate personal relationships with peers and adults
- Inappropiate feelings or behaviors under normal circumstances
- A general unhappiness or depression
- The development of physical symptoms or fears associated with personal or school problems

The term also includes children who are schizophrenic, although such a classification is ordinarily not given until adolescence. As with learning disabilities, the classification of emotional disturbance borders on the category of judgmental disabilities. Great care should be taken when using this classification. Children often manifest some of the behaviors listed above. Misclassifications can have devastating effects on children and their families.

THE CULTURALLY DIFFERENT CHILD

As nations become more multicultural, it becomes increasingly important for educators and childcare workers to develop both a better understanding of multicultural issues and an ability to effectively include children from different cultures in programs. Two different types of culturally diverse children are discussed here, although there may be considerable overlap between the characteristics of the two groups.

Children who are not native speakers of English comprise one group. Children who are native English speakers but who grow up in non-mainstream cultures form another group. As the number of multicultural children in early childhood education programs grows, it becomes more critical for teachers to develop certain attitudes and strategies for meeting their needs.

Non-English Speakers

The term *non-English speakers* is perhaps somewhat misleading. Even if new immigrants have never heard or seen a word of English prior to entering the country, they are immediately surrounded by the sounds and sights of English. This experience is quite similar to the one experienced by newborn children. Shortly after birth, they are surrounded by language as well. Therefore, most children will have some experience with English, although it will often be insufficient to enable them to fully participate in a program that uses only English. Children may originate from many countries. Therefore, children with diverse native languages may be found in a program. Among the more likely languages are:

Albanian—spoken in Albania

Amharic—spoken in Ethiopia

Arabic—spoken in Saudi Arabia, Jordan, Lebanon, Syria, Iraq, Egypt, and parts of northern Africa

Burmese—spoken in Burma

Chinese—spoken in China

Farsi—spoken in Iran

French—spoken in France and Canada

German—spoken in Germany, Switzerland, and Austria

Greek—spoken in Greece

Haitian/Creole—spoken in Haiti

Hebrew—spoken in Israel

Hindi—spoken in India

Italian—spoken in Italy

Japanese—spoken in Japan

Khmer—spoken in Cambodia

Korean—spoken in Korea

Lao—spoken in Laos

Malayalan—spoken in India

Polish—spoken in Poland

Portugese—spoken in Portugal and Brazil

Romanian—spoken in Romania

Serbo-Croatian—spoken in a number of Slavic countries

Spanish—spoken in Spain, Mexico, Puerto Rico, and a number of South American countries

Tagalog—spoken in the Philippines

Turkish—spoken in Turkey

Thai—spoken in Thailand

Urdu—spoken in Pakistan and India

Vietnamese—spoken in Viet Nam

Children who have very little skill with English and are functionally non-English-speaking will have the greatest needs. Those children with some ability to use English, who might be described as limited English proficient, will have nearly as great a need as non-English speakers. They will need assistance in developing language skills and strategies to deal with non-routine activities as well as help in enlarging their repertoire of English language skills. Those children who have become fluent or proficient speakers of English will still have needs, although they will be less obvious than previously. They will need assistance with cultural understandings, idioms, figures of speech, and other culture-related language.

Regardless of the level of proficiency, non-English-speaking children will share certain needs as they are integrated into regular early childhood programs (Thonis 1990). The first and foremost need is not a language need, but a security need. Such children will in many cases be affected by the fact they are not able to communicate with other children. Their immediate need will be to develop a sense of security in the surroundings in which they find themselves. Teachers need to be sensitive to this loneliness. When this need is met, teachers will be able to provide meaningful language experiences within the context of the child's feeling of well being. To meet this need, teachers must view cultural diversity as a source of pleasure and potential rather than as a hurdle to be overcome. One of the best places to begin is to forge a bond with the child's parents, first language, and heritage. These are the meaningful influences in the lives of children. The ways in which people use language in their culture are closely tied to other patterns within their culture (Heath 1983). Many minority cultures teach their children through stories and tales. Such children may have difficulty dealing with the majority culture's practice of relating facts and beliefs explicitly and without an explanatory story (King and Goodman 1990). This does not mean that the teacher must learn the languages of the non-English-speaking children in a program. It does mean that teachers should make an attempt to learn some of the key terms as well as some of the more powerful beliefs and influences in the child's culture.

The needs of a child to bridge the language gap are best met within an environment that includes supportive peers and a teacher who respects the cultural origins of the children. When providing language opportunities, teachers must remember to follow many of the same guidelines they would use for English-speaking children. Attending to the level of difficulty of the task, the rate of presentation, and the allotment of time for learning are all important. Special attention will need to be given to the relationships between speech and print; English is full of exceptions and inconsistencies. Teachers need to be realistic about the amount of written language non-English speakers will be able to deal with initially. This does not mean that oral and written language should be used in isolation from each other, however.

English Language Speakers

While many children grow up in an English language environment, they may demonstrate significant cultural differences from the majority culture. They may have grown up in a Hispanic-American culture, in an African-American urban community, on a rural native American reservation, or in a rural Appalachian environment. While most of these children may speak English, they may speak a particular dialect of English. The structure, vocabulary, and sounds of their language may be recognizably different from Standard English.

Since our society compels most adults to use Standard English when appropriate, there is a tendency to want to help children change their language or dialect to Standard English. The urge to do this should be resisted, according to Eller (1989). Instead, she suggests that we examine our own biases and avoid the tendency to classify such children as verbally deficient because their language does not conform to our perception of language correctness. Rather than viewing a dialect or language pattern as a deficit, Eller maintains that it should be seen as a language competence that can be built on with diverse opportunities to interact in meaningful situations. This does not mean that children should not develop the ability to use Standard English when it is needed. Rather, it means that we should not view our role as that of replacing a child's natural language with Standard English.

The view of language dialects as deficits emerged in the 1960s and 1970s. Linguists such as Bernstein (1986) argued that the more "elaborate" language used by middle class families was more useful in school settings than the "restricted code" of language used by working class and minority cultures. This view was refuted by research that demonstrated that children from minority and lower socioeconomic cultures are highly competent language users when they are permitted to use their own language and maintain control (Labov 1985). The situation in which language is used has a tremendous influence over the ability of the language user to demonstrate language competence (Halliday and Hasan 1985). The fact that Standard English has long been associated with the upper class encourages the perpetuation of the deficit theory, and hence Standard English has a higher status in our schools (Rosen 1979; Stubbs 1980). In actuality, the deficit of some children may simply be that their language is perceived as deficient (Eller 1989).

The needs of children from English-speaking non-majority cultures can best be met through an integrated language arts program. The first need such children have, much like non-English speakers, is for security. They need to know that they are important and valued participants in the classroom. Teachers need to become familiar with some of the differences of both language and their culture. This can be done by forming a strong bond between child, parent, language, and culture. There is a popular notion that children need to become culturally literate as well as functionally literate (Hirsch 1987). This view holds that those who are not familiar with a traditional Euro-American view of our society are culturally illiterate. While there is, in fact, a need for many common understandings among the peoples of a nation, such a view results in a perceived deficiency rather than an actual deficiency (Eller 1989). We create the myth of a deficiency when we raise the false expectation that only knowledge of the dominant culture has value in school or society.

Another need of these children is to be immersed in language activities that can build upon their inherent competencies with language. This can best be done by examining the context in which language is used in the classroom and our expectations for the participation of children. Quite often, conversation and dialogue does not require that responses be given in complete sentences. Yet, we often expect children to respond in complete sentences when a word or a phrase will do (Golden and Pappas 1987). It is necessary for early childhood educators, therefore, to provide opportunities for children to build upon their language competence through the use of new and diverse ways of using language. This can best be done through situations that encourage children to collaborate, cooperate, and negotiate with each other through language.

Effective Teachers

Teachers who are familiar with a whole language approach will possess many of the characteristics needed to be effective with students who are culturally diverse or who come from minority backgrounds. Since the range of possible language backgrounds that non-English-speaking children bring to the classroom is so great, it is likely that most teachers will not be fluent in the child's language. While it would be helpful to be fluent in the child's native language, it is not a realistic expectation for teachers. Several other characteristics effective teachers of children from diverse cultures and minority children have, however, been identified by Thonis (1990). Some of the characteristics relate to teacher attitudes, while others relate to knowledge and skills.

Attitudes.

The most basic attitude that a teacher must possess is a faith in the children as learners. The teacher must believe that minority children can learn English. The teacher must view the cultural differences of such children as a positive enhancement to the classroom. Teachers must possess the ability to appreciate the social and cultural diversity different children bring to the classroom. The children's background and culture can be included as a source of enrichment to the other children; while at the same time, it should be afforded the respect it deserves. Finally, teachers

need to have an empathy with those children who may have a sense of bewilderment when they find themselves in a strange place, with strange people, talking a strange language.

Knowledge and Skills.

The most important knowledge teachers need to possess is a knowledge of language. They must understand how language is acquired, how it works, how it is integrated in the culture, and how one language is related to another language. Teachers must also be skilled in a number of instructional strategies for helping children learn a second language. They need to understand the role that natural language plays in the instructional situation as well as specific strategies for promoting word recognition and comprehension of communications. They need to be expert in managing the classroom and in keeping it a place for growth and language experimentation. Finally, they need to be skilled at assessing the needs and the growth children demonstrate.

GIFTED AND TALENTED CHILDREN

For some young children, learning and acquiring new skills seem to require little effort. Other children may be particularly skilled at some activity, such as art or music, at a very young age. Such children are often categorized as gifted and/or talented. Several questions emerge regarding these children. How high an I.Q. does the child have? Should the child be in a special program? Should the child be placed with older children? Each of these questions may have a range of answers depending on who is speaking. Teachers may have one view. Parents may have another. Child development specialists may have still another. The ultimate question explored here is, what is in the child's best interest from the perspective of providing a developmentally appropriate education to that child?

Intelligence

As described in previous units, the administration of standardized tests to very young children is suspect. Children change rapidly at that age, and the tests may not be measuring what they claim to be measuring. An intelligence test generally provides an ability score, often referred to as an I.Q., or intelligence quotient. Numerically, average I.Q. is usually defined as a score of 100 on an intelligence test. Scores within fourteen or fifteen points above and below 100 are usually considered to be in the average range. Depending on the test, a gifted individual may be defined as somebody who scores well above the average range.

The problem with this way of approaching intelligence is that it diminishes children to reduce them to a single number. Some intelligence tests break down a single score into two to fifteen subscores. While that may seem reasonable, given the multiple intellectual abilities a child might possess, it still reduces the child to a number. Furthermore, the number represents an ability that a test maker feels is definable by a single number. The ability may or may not be demonstrated consistently in a day-to-day, natural environment.

Talents

In addition to intellectual giftedness, some children are identified as particularly talented in a skill or motor ability. A young child may have developed a high degree of skill in playing a musical instrument or in drawing pictures. Other children, despite having seemingly average intelligence, may have developed an early ability to read or use numbers. While such skills are to be encouraged, the talent may have been as much a product of the environment as an inate talent.

In considering both intelligence and talents, teachers should consider whether the special skills such children seem to possess are produced or inherent. It is becoming more and more routine for parents to hold children out of school an extra year in order to make them more "ready" a year later. Elementary school teachers and administrators routinely advise parents to keep children who score low on school readiness tests out of school for an additional year. Parents are often told that the extra time will help their children be more "ready" for school next year. Of course, one year later, these children will have an extra year of life experiences as compared to those who will enter kindergarten with them. As a result, such children can seem to be gifted and talented by comparison when they do enter kindergarten. The position taken here continues to be that it is not the responsibility of the child to be ready for the school's

program. It is the responsibility of the school to be ready for the child by providing a program into which virtually all children can enter and learn.

Special Programs for the Gifted

There is a long history of developing and providing specialized programs any time a specific group of children is identified. This has occurred to a great extent with disadvantaged children and children with disabilities. To a lesser extent, it has also occurred with children who appear to be gifted or talented. While there are arguments on both sides of the issue, the bulk of evidence suggests that including all children in an integrated program is more beneficial for all of the children involved.

There are many benefits for gifted and talented children when their needs are met within a regular program. First, they often have the same needs as their peers. Just because a four-year-old may be able to read at a level comparable to that of a second or third grader does not mean that the child is just like an eight- or nine-year-old. Such children are usually quite like other four-year-old children in terms of their social development and play needs. Young children often resist being removed from their peers for the purpose of receiving special instruction related to their special talents. Second, all children need to learn to relate to and cooperate with children who may be less able than themselves. Placing them in an artificial situation with others of high ability can provide and reinforce an unrealistic view of both themselves and the world.

In addition to benefits for the gifted and talented child, there are advantages for the average and less able child in meeting their needs in an integrated setting. More able children can provide good models of language behavior for other children. This provides a source for learning and using new vocabulary and language constructs for all children. In addition, integrating special needs children into a program helps teach all children in that program to learn and cooperate with others different from themselves (Donder and Nietupski 1981; Stainbeck, Stainbeck, and Hatcher 1983).

MAKING PROGRAMS ACCESSIBLE

The position held here is that all children should be integrated into a single, integrated, language arts program. This does not mean, of course, that one approach or teaching method should be used with the entire group. An integrated approach is based on the belief that children come to a program with different strengths, and that those strengths should be acknowledged and valued. In short, the idea is not to change children to fit the program, but to modify the program to welcome and fit the needs of children. Whether the children are gifted, disabled, or from diverse cultures, they can all benefit from participating in the program. Such a belief suggests the need to ensure that the program is accessible to all children. Artificial roadblocks such as entrance requirements prevent this accessibility. Such roadblocks should be replaced by beliefs, strategies, and materials that welcome all children into a program. Several of these are described here.

FIGURE 14-3 Children can become sensitive to the needs of people with disabilities through social interaction, books, and toys.

Circle of Friends

The concept of a "circle of friends" is described as a tool for including children with moderate and severe disabilities within a regular classroom program (Perske 1988). The fundamental characteristics of it are quite familiar to most early childhood educators who have established classrooms where children are encouraged to be caring, supportive members of their group. There is much overlap between a circle of friends and cooperative learning. They both involve caring, cooperative relationships, support for the efforts of others, and working and playing together in a natural environment.

When children with disabilities are placed in programs that are segregated from their nondisabled peers, they are denied the opportunity to practice social skills and to form social relationships that are a normal part of the development process. In addition, with the exception of their families, their relationships are primarily with adults who are paid to be with them. This is not a normal environment. In a regular education program, the teacher can place children in varied groups. The members of the group can be taught how to support the efforts of all other group members just as would be done in a cooperative learning project. Peer responses, peer tutoring, and peer modeling all play a role for the circle of friends. Peers can provide effective support for a child with a disability whether that child is engaged in the same curriculum, an alternate curriculum, or a parallel curriculum. Only

when all children are allowed to be together can they can develop friendships and support each other. The futures of all children do not only depend upon the skills they achieve, but also on the acceptance and support they receive from their peers.

There are two purposes for providing services by special education teachers, speech therapists, and teacher aides in the regular classroom. First, these teachers need to teach critical skills required by the child. Second, they need to support and assist the child's integration. By providing assistance and support to all children in the group who may need it, they demonstrate that there are more similarities than differences between children.

Involving Families

Families need to feel that their child with disabilities is welcome in a regular early childhood program. Depending on the organization that operates a program, the details of involving a child with disabilities can range from the very routine in some programs to a bureaucratic nightmare of red tape in others. Staff members of a program can actively aid and encourage the inclusion of children from diverse backgrounds and children with disabilities in integrated programs. These efforts involve outreach, identification, and communication of rights.

Parents are unaware of the existence of all of the possible programs to which their child might gain access. Early childhood centers can help solve this problem with specific outreach efforts aimed at publicizing the availability of their program. Public service announcements through newspapers, television, radio, and community bulletin boards are a good way to start. Another approach is to make representatives from the school available for informational presentations at churches, community centers, and multicultural events.

Helping to identify children who may have exceptional characteristics is also needed. Locating bilingual individuals to help explain the program to non-English-speaking parents can aid in making the program more accessible to multicultural children. Making contact with local, state, and federal agencies that assist individuals and families with disabilities can help make the program more accessible to children with disabilities. The same approach can be taken when contacting pediatricians, clinics, and public health agencies in the community.

Helping parents and families understand the rights of children to participate in publicly funded programs is still another way of supporting accessibility. Federal law supports the rights of children with disabilities to receive services in support of their educational needs. Helping parents use these rights can be promoted by early childhood program staff by sharing and interpreting information and documents that describe the child's rights.

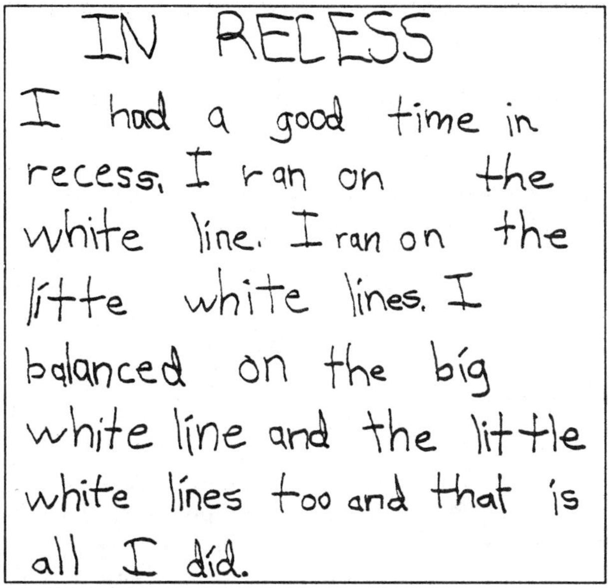

Least Restrictive Environment

The term *least restrictive environment* comes from the federal legislation supporting the education of children with disabilities. These children have a right to receive publicly supported educational services in the least restrictive environment. This means that children with disabilities should receive educational services in regular education programs along with non-disabled peers to the maximum extent appropriate. That is, children with disabilities should be removed from a regular education program only when the nature and severity of the disability is such that supplementary aids and services cannot be provided in the regular education environment. Placing children in separate classes or in separate schools in order to take advantage of specific services provided in those separate facilities is not a satisfactory reason for removing the child. Those services should be moved and provided in the regular educational program. States

FIGURE 14-4 According to Marsha Forest, all children have a need for fun, freedom, friends, and control.

and localities nearly always have explanations of the rights of children with disabilities available for parents in clear, non-technical language. In many cases, they are available in Spanish and other languages. Even with this, however, parents may need assistance in dealing with the paperwork involved in securing the rights of their children with disabilities.

Recognizing Needs

All children have certain basic and not-so-basic needs. This is true for gifted, disabled, average, and multicultural children. They need, to some degree, to have fun, freedom, friendships, and control (Forest 1986). The role of parents and educators is to work together to establish this as a principle for all children. Certain educational myths that impede the acceptance of this principle have been identified by Forest (1986). Becoming aware of them can prevent our succumbing to them.

First is the myth of credentials. Being a qualified or certified teacher does not give the right to use that credential as a rationale for denying a child any of the basic needs. The second myth is the myth of fixed intelligence. Teachers should never predict the present or future performance or behavior of a child based upon an intelligence test score. Stating that a child will never have the intellectual ability to form a meaningful friendship is indefensible. The third myth is the myth of the value of grouping. Stating that a child with a disability needs to be placed in a small group that proceeds at a slower pace and only includes other children with disabilities and a special education teacher is insupportable. It is both a denial of a child's right for friendships and an admission that the regular program is so rigid that a significant number of children are not having their needs met.

USING LITERATURE

As a reflection of our changing society, many high-quality children's books are being published that address the fact that there is a great diversity among children. Many of the more recently published children's books celebrate that diversity in an honest and straightforward manner to which young children will easily relate. These include books dealing with ethnic diversity, multicultural issues, and disabilities.

When selecting such literature, several things should be kept in mind. First, be aware of how the book will be used. Will it be used for a single reading, or will it be part of a themed unit on disabilities or Hispanic culture? Why is this book being used? Is it because it relates to the cultural background of the children? Is the purpose of using the book to make children aware of the culture of others or of certain disabilities? What other activities will be used in connection with the book? Second, make sure the book is a high-quality piece of literature appropriate for the children with whom it will be used. A confusing book about a deaf child that includes themes and ideas too sophisticated for the children will be of little value. A story should be selected, first and foremost, because it is a good story. Without that quality, children will be less likely to be motivated by it. With these questions answered, teachers are much more likely to make wise and considered children's book selections.

Multicultural Literature

Using books that reflect the traditions and values of other cultures helps to strengthen the understanding of the world as a community. The stories contained in

them will often be loved by children for their intrinsic value. They are the stories of humanity, family, love, friendship, community, and the natural world. For minority and immigrant children, these books can be a comforting reflection of their lives. The stories contained within them can validate their cultures and experiences (Cox and Galda 1990). With a little effort, teachers can locate some fine literature for young children that relates to a diversity of cultures.

African-American.

Several classic and contemporary books that focus on family relationships of African-American peoples are well worth considering. Tony Bradman uses a repeated text structure in *Wait and See* (1987) to accompany the portrayal of a Saturday morning shopping trip in an urban setting. Jeannette Caines captures a moment of fantasy imagined by a young boy in *I Need a Lunchbox* (1988). In this story, a young child plays out a competition with his sister with his dream of a different new lunchbox for each day of the week. In a wonderful story of intergenerational love in an extended family, Eloise Greenfield captures the curious imagination of a young child in *Grandpa's Face* (1988). Frightened by her actor grandfather's angry face during a rehearsal, Tamika plots a way to find out if Grandpa will ever use that face on her. Using some hilarious child antics, Tamika comes to realize that Grandpa's face will never show anything but love for her. Herschel Johnson depicts the same theme in *A Visit to the Country* (1989). In this book, Romare Bearden's illustrations depict the classic textures of a summer in the rural South. Finally, this same theme is developed in a story by Nigel Gray in *A Balloon for Grandad* (1988) that takes place in North Africa.

A realistic picture of family love is shared by Sonia Appiah in *Amoko and Efua Bear* (1988), a story based on firsthand experiences in the Ghanian culture of West Africa. Amoko is a young Ghanian girl who experiences the loss and recovery of Efua, her beloved teddy bear. The rhythms of African-American storytellers is captured by Angela Johnson in *Tell Me a Story, Mama* (1989). Humor and action are wrapped around the intergenerational love shared by mother and daughter in this recollection of favorite stories.

Two books that depict turn of the century African-American traditions give young readers a fascinating historical view of black culture. In *Mirandy and Brother Wind* (1988), Patricia McKissack shares an event from the lives of her own grandparents. It is the story of Mirandy's plan to win a cakewalk contest with Brother Wind as her partner. Another story set in the same time frame, and also by Patricia McKissack, is *Nettie Jo's Friends* (1989). It is the story of how a kindness given is often returned to the original giver. Scott Cook's dazzling illustrations capture both the history of the time and the imagination of the tale.

Caribbean Culture.

Arnold Adoff's *Flamboyan* (1988) takes the reader on an imaginative dream voyage of Culebra Island, Puerto Rico. While traveling with Flamboyan, a young Puerto Rican girl whose hair is the red color of the blossoms of the Flamboyan tree, readers learn about the beauty of her island home, its people, and its culture. They meet pelicans and silverfish through the poetic language of the story and the brilliant illustrations. In *The Chalk Doll* (1989), Charlotte Pomerantz weaves a tale that ties the generations together with childhood stories from Jamaica. Rose learns of the tremendous poverty her mother endured as a child as the latter tells stories of her childhood on the lush island.

Hispanic and Native American.

Both pre-Columbian and more modern settings are found in books for young readers about native Americans. The geography of the stories covers the north, central, and southern sections of the western hemisphere. In addition to stories, there are collections of wonderful music, games, and fingerplays that bring these cultures to young readers and emerging readers. A must for every early childhood program is Lulu Delacre's *Arroz con Leche: Popular Songs from Latin America* (1989). A similar collection of Native American chants and songs is available in Virginia Driving Hawk Sneve's *Dancing Tepees: Poems of American Indian Youth* (1989).

Three books by Deborah Nourse Lattimore bring three pre-Columbian civilizations to life. In *Why There Is No Arguing in Heaven* (1989), she provides young readers with the creation myth of the Mayan culture. Her previous stories include an Aztec tale titled *The Flame of Peace* (1987), and a Minoan story titled *The*

Prince and the Golden Ax (1988). Ellen Alexander provides young children with an Incan version of the story of the great flood in *Llama and the Great Flood* (1989). Another myth for young children is found in Flora's *Feathers Like a Rainbow* (1989). It is the brilliantly illustrated retelling of an Amazon Indian tale that explains how the birds of the tropical rain forests acquired their splendid colors.

Native American Indian stories are also well represented in the literature for young children. Four different books by Paul Goble are well worth considering. The Cheyenne legend explaining the origin of the big dipper is told with a quiet subtlety in *Her Seven Brothers* (1988). *Beyond the Ridge* (1989) explores the Plains Indians' depiction of death. It illustrates, through chants and prayers, the contrast of the joys of the spirit world and the grief shared by the family members left behind in this world. Goble brings us two interactive humorous stories about the Lakota Sioux trickster Iktomi in *Iktomi and the Boulder* (1988) and *Iktomi and the Berries* (1989). The telling of each of these stories encourages and even requires group participation.

Asian Culture.

A traditional Japanese tale is recounted in Dianne Snyder's *The Boy of the Three-Year Nap* (1988). It is the story of a young man who anticipates a life of leisure when he marries the daughter of a wealthy rice merchant. His dream evaporates when he is tricked into going to work for the merchant. A Japanese folk tale extolling the virtues of perseverance and reverence for all living things is retold in Helen Clare Pittman's *The Gift of the Willows* (1988). An original story set in Japan is told in David Wisniewski's *The Warrior and the Wise Man* (1989). It is a story of contrasting approaches to the meaning of life. Two brothers, a warrior and a wise man, are each undertaking a quest for the five elements. The cut-paper collages used to illustrate the story form a striking contrast to more traditional illustrations.

China of long ago is the setting for Moira Miller's *Moon Dragon* (1989). It is a folk tale about Ling Po, the most pompous man of the village. As might be expected, his bragging gets him into a predicament that gives the rest of the inhabitants of the village a good laugh. Moving to India, Kristina Rodanas brings us a fine tale of generosity in *The Story of Wali Dad* (1988).

Wali Dad, a poor grasscutter, is overwhelmed by the extravagant gifts sent to him by the Princess of Khaistan following his sending of a simple but charming gift to her.

Literature about Disabilities

There is a growing awareness on the part of authors who write books for children that disabilities are a natural part of life. They understand that children possess disabilities, have friends and family members with disabilities, are curious about disabilities, and have an ability to accept disabilities. Whether a classroom has a child with a specific disability is irrelevant. The focus should be on helping children to understand that disabilities are a part of life and that people should not be judged based on their disabilities or lack of disabilities. Many of the books that include children and adults with disabilities as major characters can help provide information to children. With information comes understanding. With understanding comes acceptance. Stories that involve disabled characters should not be used simply because of that factor. The stories should be selected because they are good pieces of literature and because the stories serve a useful purpose in the instructional program. Stories can be found that deal with disabilities related to physical problems such as orthopedic problems, blindness, and deafness. Other books are available that deal with intellectual abilities to learn, such as mental retardation, learning disabilities, and language impairments.

Physical Disabilities.

In *The Balancing Girl* (1981), Berniece Rabe clearly demonstrates that a physical disability in no way diminishes the person. Although Margaret is confined to a wheelchair, she is as typical as a child can be. She enjoys her friends, her school, and the opportunity to participate in a class project. Only jealous Tommy, who is not disabled, has difficulty accepting Margaret's skill at being able to intricately balance objects. With kindness and humor, Margaret deals with Tommy in a way that both guides and teaches him to become more human. In *I Have a Sister, My Sister Is Deaf* (1977), Jeanne Whitehouse Peterson helps young children to understand the concept of deafness. She also helps young readers to understand that

FIGURE 14-5 Children need to develop a positive self-concept.

children with disabilities have needs, wants, and families who love them. Another storybook on deafness is Ada Litchfield's *A Button in Her Ear* (1976).

Children with disabilities possess the need to be as independent as they possibly can be. This message comes across quite well in Joan Fassler's *Howie Helps Himself* (1975). Howie is confined to a wheelchair and has greatly diminished strength. The story is an account of his efforts to do something for himself that requires tremendous physical effort. The pride he feels in accomplishing his task draws the reader into a feeling of sharing and liking. In *Anna's Silent World* (1977), Bernard Wolf takes the reader, through text and photographs, into the world of a deaf child. The reader becomes aware of both the similarities and differences of Anna, who was born deaf. While learning to speak and to understand the world around her was a tremendous challenge for Anna, she shows us that she is like any other young child in terms of her needs to have family, friends, pets, and fun. A story about a blind child that also has a multicultural basis is *The Seeing Stick* (1977) by Jane Yolen. It is a modern legend set in ancient China. The child is the emperor's daughter who learns about her world through her relationship with a wise old man and his "seeing stick."

Physical disabilities are also explored in Lorraine Henriod's *Grandma's Wheelchair* (1982), Susan Jeschke's *Perfect the Pig* (1980), and Curt and Gita Kaufman's *Rajesh* (1985). Visual disabilities are explored in stories such as Ezra Jack Keats's *Apartment Three* (1983), Ada Litchfield's *A Cane in Her Hand* (1977), Ellen Raskin's *Spectacles* (1972), Miriam Cohen's *See You Tomorrow, Charles* (1983), and Patricia MacLachlan's *Through Grandpa's Eyes* (1980).

Intellectual Disabilities.

In *Sherman Is a Slowpoke* (1988), Mitchell Sharmat introduces the very young child to the concept that everybody is different. Using animal characters, Sharmat shows that we should be open to new friends and new experiences even if they are perhaps a little scary at first. In a touching story, Joe Lasker explores the relationship of siblings who have a family member with disabilities in *He's My Brother* (1974). The exact disability is never revealed, and it is not important. It could be mental retardation, autism, or learning disabilities. What is revealed is that the child has a life. He draws, gets dressed, plays, loves, and cries. He is also loved by his family. This story will provide much for young children to talk about. Harriet Sobol's *My Brother Steven Is Retarded* (1977) is a story drawn from the author's actual life. The book uses photographs of her family living with, learning with, and loving a disabled child who obviously loves them back.

Although not specifically about individual disabilities, several other books deal with characters who are

FIGURE 14-6 Children's book author Jean Marzollo.

different in one way or another. They can be used to lead into awareness and acceptance activities with young children. They include Miriam Cohen's *First Grade Takes a Test* (1980), Tomie dePaola's *Oliver Button Is a Sissy* (1979), and Charlotte Zolotow's *William's Doll* (1972).

SUMMARY

A well-designed integrated language arts program is the ideal educational environment to meet the needs of a wide variety of young children. Children "identified" either as disabled, gifted and talented, or both do not need to be sent out to specialized programs to have their needs met. An integrated language arts program, as its name implies, integrates people, language arts, and oral and written language in a natural, meaningful context. This includes children with disabilities and children with multicultural backgrounds. Early childhood educators need to develop an awareness of concepts, understandings, and ideas associated with diabilities and multiculturalism in order to help children benefit from access to programs.

There are a number of different classifications under which a child might be identified as disabled.

Some of the classifications for children with disabilities are related to physical difficulties. Among these are deafness, blindness, orthopedic disabilities, and other health impairments. Other disabilities may be related to learning or intellectual difficulties. These might include learning disabilities, speech impairments, and mental retardation. Still other children might be classified as emotionally disturbed when it is determined that the behaviors are not representative of social maladjustment.

An integrated language arts program would seek to include children with disabilities within the context of the regular program. This would be true even when children need the services of special education teachers, speech therapists, occupational therapists, and psychologists. There is a growing awareness that these services can be integrated within the regular educational program. Special or separate programs for children with disabilities, though long used in education, are seen as less effective, especially given the need of children to be with their peers. In addition, federal and state regulations specify that unless there are particularly extenuating circumstances, children with disabilities should be educated in the schools they would attend if they did not possess a disability. This concept is often referred to as the need to educate children in the least restrictive environment.

Children from multicultural backgrounds are found much more frequently in early childhood programs. Some of these children are recent immigrants, while others live in communities characterized by cultures that are different from the mainstream. It is important for teachers to view children from other than mainstream backgrounds as bringing enrichment to the program. For many years, these children were characterized by unjustified linguistic theories as being language deficient. More recent studies have shown this not to be so. Possessing different language does not constitute a deficiency. Quite often, the only deficiency was a perception of a deficiency by those who lacked a comprehensive knowledge of the purpose and function of language.

Teachers need to develop the skills and attitudes that will enable them to work effectively with multicultural children or children with disabilities. A welcoming, supportive attitude is critical. This can be expressed to the children in a number of different ways. A teacher can develop a strong initial bond by immediately getting to know the parents, the child, and some of the values and traditions of the child's culture. A teacher can become familiar with the disability a child might possess as well as disabilities in general. It is also important for a teacher to have an understanding of how language works and how children tend to learn language. A teacher needs to keep an open mind and an open classroom. Involving parents and the children themselves can help all connected with the class develop some new understandings and an appreciation for the diversity of people we find in our society.

A great many books written for children deal with an assortment of disabilities and cultures. New titles are published each year. Books often use children with disabilities as characters. Disabilities addressed in the literature for young children include deafness, blindness, orthopedic impairment, and other classifications. Books on multiculturalism deal with places around the world. Books on African-Americans and Hispanic-Americans are becoming much more available. In addition, a number of recent publications focus on Native Americans, Asian cultures, and Caribbean cultures.

Questions and Activities for Review And Discussion

Multiple Choice
1. The disability that early childhood educators are most likely to see in a program is
   a. deaf.

b. speech impaired.
c. mentally retarded.
d. learning disabilities.

2. Which of the following disabilities would be most likely to need the services of an occupational therapist?
a. learning disabilities
b. deaf
c. orthopedically impaired
d. emotionally disturbed

3. Non-English-speaking children in an early childhood education program might be found to have an oral language ability to use which of the following languages?
a. Spanish
b. Chinese
c. Urdu
d. any one of these

4. A child might be identified as gifted or talented because of
a. an ability to play the piano at age four.
b. a high intelligence level.
c. an early reading ability.
d. any one of these

5. An effective social tool for integrating children with moderate or severe disabilities into an educational program is a
a. circle of friends.
b. behavior modification system.
c. separate program for children with disabilities.
d. none of the above

6. The concept of educating children with disabilities in the school they would attend if they were not disabled is called the
a. home school rule.
b. non-segregation theory.
c. least restrictive environment.
d. distance law.

7. The first and foremost reason for selecting a multicultural book to share with a class is that the story
a. is a quality piece of literature.
b. is at the reading level of the children.
c. is based on the cultures of children in the program.
d. uses mostly pictures to tell the story.

True or False

T   F   1. Speech impaired is a classification that refers only to a child's ability to articulate language sounds.

T   F   2. To be classified as mentally retarded, a child must demonstrate significant delays in both intellectual ability and adaptive behavior.

T   F   3. Working class children and children from low socioeconomic status homes typically come to school with significant language deficits.

T   F   4. Talented and gifted children have special needs that can usually only be met in programs specially designed to serve such children.

T   F   5. The concepts of least restrictive environment and "circle of friends" could not be used together.

Essay and Discussion

1. Compare and contrast the disabilities of spech impaired and mentally retarded.
2. Explain why an integrated language arts early childhood classroom can be an appropriate placement for a child with a disability.
3. Explain why it is appropriate to view African-American and Hispanic-American children as possessing language competence.
4. Explain the advantages of educating talented and gifted children in an integrated language arts program rather than in a separate program developed only for such children.
5. What are the three educational myths identified by Marsha Forest that can impede the child's needs for fun, freedom, friendship, and control?

REFERENCES

Adoff, A. 1988. *Flamboyan*. San Diego, Calif.: Harcourt Brace Jovanovich.

Alexander, E. 1989. *Llama and the great flood*. New York: Crowell.

Algozzine, B., and J.E. Ysseldyke. 1986. The future of the LD field: Screening and diagnosis. *Journal of Learning Disabilities* 29: 394–398.

Appiah, S. 1988. *Amoko and Efua bear*. New York: Macmillan.

Bernstein, B. 1986. A sociolinguistic approach to socialization; with some reference to educability. In *Ethnography of communication*, ed. J. J. Gumpery and D. Hynes. New York: Basil Blackwell.

Bradman, T. 1987. *Wait and see*. New York: Oxford.

Caines, J. 1988. *I need a lunchbox*. New York: Harper.

Cohen, M. 1983. *See you tomorrow, Charles*. New York: Dell.

Cohen, M. 1980. *First grade takes a test*. New York: Dell.

Cox, S., and L. Galda. 1990. Multicultural literature: Mirrors and windows on a global community. *The Reading Teacher* 43: 582–589.

Delacre, L. 1989. *Arroz con leche: Popular songs and rhymes from Latin America*. New York: Scholastic.

dePaola, T. 1979. *Oliver Button is a sissy*. New York: Harcourt Brace Jovanovich.

Donder, D., and J. Nietupski. 1981. Nonhandicapped adolescents teaching playground skills to their mentally retarded peers: Toward a less restrictive middle school environment. *Education and Training of the Mentally Retarded* 16: 270–276.

Eller, R.G. 1989. Johnny can't talk either: The perpetuation of the deficit theory in classrooms. *The Reading Teacher* 42: 670–674.

Fassler, J. 1975. *Howie helps himself*. Chicago: Albert Whitman.

Flora. 1989. *Feathers like a rainbow*. New York: Harper and Row.

Forest, M. 1986. Making a difference: What communities can do to prevent mental handicaps and promote lives of quality. In *Volume III: Helping Children Live,*

Learn and Grow in Their Communities. Toronto: National Institute on Mental Retardation.

Giangreco, M.F., and J.W. Putnam. 1991. Supporting the education of students with severe disabilities in regular education environments. In *Critical Issues in the Lives of People with Severe Disabilities,* ed. L.H. Meyer, C.A. Peck, and L. Brown. Baltimore, Md.: Paul H. Brookes.

Goble, P. 1988. *Her seven brothers.* New York: Bradbury.

Goble, P. 1988. *Iktomi and the boulder.* New York: Orchard.

Goble, P. 1989. *Beyond the ridge.* New York: Bradbury.

Goble, P. 1989. *Iktomi and the berries.* New York: Orchard.

Golden, J.M., and C.C. Pappas. 1987. A sociolinguistic perspective on retelling procedures in research on children's cognitive processing of written text. Paper presented at the National Reading Conference, St. Petersburg, Fla..

Goodlad, J.J. 1983. A study of schooling: Some findings and hypotheses. *Phi Delta Kappan* 64: 462–470.

Gray, N. 1988. *A balloon for Grandad.* New York: Orchard.

Greenfield, D. 1988. *Grandpa's face.* New York: Philomel.

Halliday, M.A.K., and R. Hasan. 1985. *Language, context, and text: Aspects of language in a social-semiotic perspective.* Victoria, Australia: Deakin University Press.

Heath, S. 1983. *Ways with words: Language, life, and work in communities and classrooms.* Cambridge, N.Y.: Cambridge University Press.

Henriod, L. 1982. *Grandma's wheelchair.* Chicago: Albert Whitman.

Hirsch, E.D. 1987. *Cultural literacy: What every American needs to know.* Boston: Houghton Mifflin Company.

Jeschke, S. 1980. *Perfect the pig.* New York: Scholastic.

Johnson, A. 1989. *A visit to the country.* New York: Harper and Row.

Johnson, A. 1989. *Tell me a story.* New York: Orchard.

Kaufman, C. & G. 1985. *Rajesh.* New York: Atheneum.

Keats, E.J. 1983. *Apartment three.* New York: Macmillan.

King, D.F., and K.S. Goodman. 1990. Whole language: Cherishing learners and their language. *Language, Speech, and Hearing Services in Schools* 21: 221–227.

Labov, W. 1985. The logic of nonstandard English. In *Language and Social Context,* ed. P.P. Giglioli. New York: Viking Penguin.

Lasker, J. 1974. *He's my brother.* Chicago: Albert Whitman.

Lattimore, D.N. 1987. *The flame of peace.* New York: Harper.

Lattimore, D.N. 1988. *The prince and the golden ax.* New York: Harper.

Lattimore, D.N. 1989. *Why there is no arguing in heaven.* New York: Harper.

Litchfield, A. 1976. *A button in her ear.* Chicago: Albert Whitman.

Litchfield, A. 1977. *A cane in her hand.* Chicago: Albert Whitmen.

MacLachlan, P. 1980. *Through Grandpa's eyes.* New York: Harper and Row.

McKissack, P.C. 1988. *Mirandy and Brother Wind.* New York: Knopf.

McKissack, P.C. 1989. *Nettie Jo's friends.* New York: Knopf.

Miller, M. 1989. *Moon dragon.* New York: Dial.

Moore, D.R., A. Hyde, K. Blair, and S. Weitzman. 1981. *Student classification and the right to read.* Chicago: Designs for Change.

Perske, R. 1988. *Circle of friends.* Nashville, Tenn.: Abingdon Press.

Peterson, J.W. 1977. *I have a sister, My sister is deaf.* New York: Harper and Row.

Pittman, H.C. 1988. *The gift of the willows.* Minneapolis, Minn.: Carolrhoda.

Pomerantz, C. 1989. *The chalk doll*. New York: Lippincott.

Rabe, B. 1981. *The balancing girl*. New York: E. P. Dutton.

Raskin, E. 1972. *Spectacles*. New York: Atheneum.

Rodanas, K. 1988. *The story of Wali Dad*. New York: Lothrop.

Rosen, L. 1979. An interview with William Labov. *English Journal* 68: 16–19.

Sawyer, W.E. 1989. Attention deficit disorder: A wolf in sheep's clothing . . . again. *The Reading Teacher* 42: 310–312.

Sharmat, M. 1988. *Sherman is a slowpoke*. New York: Scholastic.

Sneve, V.D.H. 1989. *Dancing teepees: Poems of American Indian youth*. New York: Holiday.

Snyder, D. 1988. *The boy of the three-year nap*. Boston: Houghton Mifflin Company.

Sobol, H. 1977. *My brother Steven is retarded*. New York: Macmillan.

Stainbeck, S.B., W.C. Stainbeck, and C.W. Hatcher. 1983. Nonhandicapped peer involvement in the education of severely handicapped students. *The Journal of the Association for Persons with Severe Handicaps* 8: 39–42.

Stubbs, M. 1980. *Language and literacy: The sociolinguistics of reading and writing*. Boston: Routledge and Kegan Paul.

Thonis, E.W. 1990. Teaching English as a second language. *Reading Today* 7: 6, 19.

Ward, B. 1977. *Anna's silent world*. New York: Lippincott.

Wisniewski, D. 1989. *The warrior and the wise man*. New York: Lothrop.

Yolen, J. 1977. *The seeing stick*. New York: Crowell.

Zolotow, C. 1972. *William's doll*. New York: Harper and Row.

UNIT 15

Adapting Programs for Special Needs

PREVIEW

In nineteenth century America, debtors were often imprisoned for not paying their bills. Many individuals spent several years in jail, most for owing sums of less than twenty dollars. They could not free themselves because the only way they could get out of jail was to pay their debts. In jail, they had no ability to earn money to pay those debts. In short, society had placed these individuals in a position where they had no options. Similar treatment was afforded to the mentally ill at that time. They were often warehoused in institutions that did little or nothing to provide them with increased life options. In many cases, their treatment was inhumane. While reform for imprisoned debtors occurred in the nineteenth century, similar reform for people with disabilities did not occur until well into the twentieth century.

Public Law 94-142 went into effect in 1975. It provided a legal framework for integrating the disabled into society. While change has occurred, much still remains to be done with integrating children with disabilities into regular education programs. Too often, such children continue to be served in separate programs. This both isolates them from their non-disabled peers and removes them from their communities. Similar procedures are often followed in the case of other groups of children with special needs.

Multicultural, non-English-speaking, and gifted and talented children are often served in programs isolated from mainstream education opportunities. On the other hand, an integrated approach to special services maintains life options for children. It provides them with the opportunity to both remain in their community and to participate in programs with their peers. The approach enriches the lives of all involved. The major concepts discussed in this unit focus on developing an understanding of classroom-based special services and strategies for adapting a language arts program for children with special needs.

INTRODUCTION

This unit builds upon assumptions established previously. First, it is assumed that language ability is best developed in a naturalistic setting. Second, it is assumed that the environment must provide many opportunities for children to use language in meaningful ways. Third, language development is viewed as a process in which children grow by taking risks as they make attempts to communicate and to develop their control over language.

This unit begins by examining the concept of classroom-based special services. This refers to the procedures in which specialists provide services within regular educational programs. This is opposed to a more traditional approach of either placing students with special needs in other settings or removing such children from regular programs for the purpose of providing the services. There are many possibilities for delivering such services to children within the program. In addition, there are many advantages to consider with this approach. The goals and objectives of this approach must be carefully designed. In developing goals, teachers need to be aware of a number of practical considerations.

The major portion of the unit describes strategies to be used by teachers to adapt a regular program for students with special needs. Some of these strategies deal with providing an appropriate environment while others deal with the need to relate the program to the experience of the children. The major portion of the discussion of strategies deals with the need to adapt language and social interactions between teachers, children, and their peers.

CLASSROOM-BASED SPECIAL SERVICES

While different types of services might be provided to children with special needs within a regular program, there is considerable overlap between the actual activities used. A speech therapist might address the language needs of a speech-impaired child in a manner similar to the way a teacher of English as a second language might address a limited-English-speaking child. A special education teacher may work with children on social interaction skills in a manner strikingly similar to the approach used by the early childhood language arts teacher. Therefore, with good communication between all of the teachers involved, children with special needs can be effectively included in regular programs.

Types of Services

The types of services provided to children with special needs can range from those that are totally unobtrusive to those that are very intensive. The decision on the services needs to be based on the specific needs of the children in question. Specialists, parents, and early childhood educators need to work collaboratively to make decisions about the level and intensity of services.

Staff Development.

The least intense form of service is through staff development with the regular program staff (Miller, 1989). Rather than working with specific children within a program, a specialist might provide in-service workshops that enable the regular program staff to better serve the children with special needs. Such training programs may address curriculum, instruction, modeling, evaluation, and feedback. By employing this approach, the specialist influences the attitudes, policies, and practices used for children with special needs (Damico 1987). Therefore, it is important for administrators, teachers, aides, and parents to be involved in this important information-sharing process.

Consultation.

Due to the recognition of language as a naturally occurring process that can best be addressed in a social setting, consultation is increasingly used as an approach to providing services to children through program adaptation (Marvin 1987). The consultant may be a speech therapist who has expertise in a particular language development area. Consultants address the needs of the children by collaboratively planning a program with the regular teacher or caregiver. Parents should participate in this collaboration whenever possible. The relationship between the individuals is collegial rather than supervisory. They share information, goals, and responsibility for the growth of the children.

The consultant who does not work with individual or small groups of children is said to be providing indirect consultant services. The consultant who actually works with individual or small groups of children is said to be providing direct consultant services. Depending on the needs of the child, direct service, indirect service, or a combination of the two may be used. Consultation is a particularly appropriate model because of this concept. It affords the flexibility to provide services to children whose needs range from mild to intensive. Becauses it is a service provided totally in the regular classroom, it is a naturalistic and meaning-based strategy.

Team Teaching.

The team teaching approach shares some of the characteristics of the consultation model, but it tends to maintain more of an equal division of teaching and responsibility. The consultant may be involved in a range of responsibilities with the regular teacher. The team teachers, whether they are speech therapists, special education teachers, or regular education teachers, jointly develop the program. Together they develop objectives, provide instruction, monitor progress, and evaluate the program. At any time, either teacher may provide instruction or work in some way with individuals, small groups, or the total group.

One-to-one Intervention.

For some students, it may be appropriate to have a specialist work with a child on a one-to-one basis (Miller 1989). When this is the case, the specialist uses the materials and activities that are normally provided within the regular program in order to address

FIGURE 15-1 Special services provided in a regular classroom often require that two or more teachers work collaboratively.

the specific needs of the child. Areas that might be addressed using this approach include understanding of vocabulary, oral language, reading, development of writing ability, and teaching of specific content areas. The specialist needs to keep in close contact with the regular teacher in order to tailor the services to the needs of the student within the regular program. In order to make this approach effective, it is often necessary for the specialist to spend time observing the child both in the classroom and in less structured situations in order to plan and assess needs. The one-to-one approach can be used by itself. It can also be used in combination with other approaches. Successful classroom-based intervention programs using one-to-one intervention in combination with other approaches have been identified and described by Nelson (1986).

Multilevel Curriculum.

For students with more severe disabilities, a multi-level curriculum approach may be appropriate. This approach involves the use of alternate goals and objectives for individual children. However, the goals and objectives are within the same curriculum area, and the teaching is done within the same program as the other children (Campbell, Campbell, Collicott, Perner, and Stone 1988; Giangreco and Putnam 1991). A student with severe disabilities might be integrated into a regular program that is focused on a theme of "the farm," for example. While some of the non-disabled children might be learning the growth process of corn or bean plants, the child with severe disabilities might be learning such concepts as recognition of corn and beans or the words that correspond to pictures of corn and beans. This approach enables children who are more severely disabled to acquire knowledge and skills in the least restrictive environment of the regular classroom.

Curriculum Overlapping.

For some children with severe disabilities, there may be academic areas and topics that are not relevant to the child's needs. The content may be determined to be non-essential to the needs of the child or beyond the cognitive capabilities of the child. When this occurs, the child can still participate in shared group activities with goals and objectives developed from other curriculum areas. This approach is described as curriculum overlapping (Giangreco and Meyer 1988). For example, a child with severe intellectual disabilities might be included in the unit on "the farm" but without the objectives associated with plants and how they grow. Instead, the objectives for this child might be in the area of socialization, attending to a speaker, and developing an understanding of participation in a group.

Advantages of Classroom-based Services

Most educators clearly recognize the need for early education. The federal Head Start program as well as other early intervention programs for children from disadvantaged backgrounds have for quite some time demonstrated the effectiveness of early intervention (Harris 1986; Hunt 1982). While many of the advantages of integrating children with special needs into regular early childhood education programs are obvious, others may be more subtle.

By providing services within the context of a regular program, several benefits occur for children with special needs. First, children do not miss parts of the classroom program by being out of the room while important activities, stories, and projects are taking place. Second, there are fewer problems of carryover. *Carryover* refers to how well a child is able to transfer learning that takes place out of the classroom setting back into the classroom. Children have frequently been removed from the classroom in order to receive specific special services. The special services were often provided using totally different materials and without any connection to what was happening in the regular program. As a result, children have tended to be unable to transfer the learning back into the regular classroom. A major factor related to this problem is the possibility that the special instruction may have had no relevance to what was occurring in the classroom.

Providing special services to children with disabilities within the context of the regular program has still other benefits. First, it conforms to both the letter and the spirit of the least restrictive environment provision of Public Law 94-142. The approach enables children to attend programs they would attend if they were not disabled. Second, it maintains a belief in the ability of children to function within society. Third, it maintains high expectations for children. While it is unwise to set expectations unrealistically high, teachers must guard against setting expectations so low that there is no challenge for the child or striving for the teacher. If we hold that a child can accomplish nothing, the child will most likely live up to that expectation. Finally, integration within a regular program keeps children's life options open. Segregating children with disabilities into programs specifically set up for them narrows the options for those children. The longer children are maintained in segregated programs, the more narrow the options become.

Goals and Objectives

When services are provided to children with special needs within an integrated language arts program, the goals and objectives for the child should reflect

- Describing the activity being engaged in
- Calling attention to an activity
- Using color, size, and attribute words to tell about a toy

If the special services provided are developmentally appropriate, they will include the use of objects and activities within the regular environment. The special services will deal with the activities taking place within the regular language arts program, and they will utilize the objects and experiences that make up the child's daily life. The instruction will not focus on individual skills such as simply labeling objects or actions. Rather, the focus would be on communication. This means that the emphasis would be on relating meaning and ideas to other children in a diversity of contexts.

Practical Considerations

Making integration work requires both the regular teacher and the teacher providing services to students with special needs to work closely together no matter which model is used. Dividing the responsibility should be guarded against. When both teachers are

FIGURE 15-2 Providing special services in a regular classroom provides opportunities for all children to interact.

the philosophy of the approach. Our discussion here is primarily limited to the consideration of services related to the language development of children. The goal of the services would be to enable language to emerge parallel to growth in play, problem solving, social development, and other contexts in which language is used (Norris and Hoffman 1990). In early childhood education, a more specific goal would be for the child to grow from the ability to label objects and actions in egocentric play to the ability to describe actions and states involved in social interactions and cooperative play (Norris and Hoffman 1990).

The objectives identified for individual children would be more specific than the goals of the intervention program, but would continue to be general enough to apply over a range of activities and growth periods. Examples of objectives might include:

- Producing relevant utterances (for example, two, three, or four words in length) in a play setting
- Requesting objects and activities in a play situation

FIGURE 15-3 Integrated special education services enable children with disabilities to benefit from the literacy activities that can only happen in a regular classroom.

jointly responsible for a program, a pattern tends to develop in which one teacher takes responsibility for some aspects of the program while the other teacher assumes responsibility for others (Christensen and Luckett 1990). When this occurs, the teacher not taking direct responsibility might be tempted to use the time to attend to clerical functions, prepare other materials, or use it as preparation time. If this occurs, the system has broken down. It is important to involve both teachers in the planning and implementation of the program to the greatest extent possible.

To make the best possible use of both teachers, a few guidelines may be helpful. First, both teachers must be involved in designing activities that make maximum use of the availability of both teachers. This may mean dividing the group in two for an activity. It may also mean that one teacher runs the activity while the other observes and makes anecdotal notes on specific targeted children. Second, the teachers need to develop and maintain schedules together so that each knows what the other is doing and when it is being done. Third, each teacher should observe the other teacher so that effectiveness and follow-up activities can be discussed after a lesson.

STRATEGIES FOR ADAPTING A PROGRAM

There are many useful strategies for adapting a regular early childhood language arts program to meet the needs of integrated students with special needs. In fact, many of the characteristics of an integrated approach to the language arts constitute adaptations that support the inclusion of children with disabilities, multicultural, and non-English-speaking children. The strategies described here focus mainly on ways in which teachers can address the language development of children with special needs. These strategies are generally used in an integrated approach whether children with special needs are found in those programs or not. When such children are present, the teacher must focus more carefully on using these strategies, using them more intensively and perhaps using them more frequently.

Contingent Responses

The concept of contingent responses comes from studies that examined the interactions occurring between mothers and young children. Contingent responses are the consistent reactions of the mother or other caregiver to the behaviors and utterances of the child (Snow 1981; Tiegerman and Siperstein 1984). It has been found that these reactions or responses seem to help children develop communication skills (Harding 1984; Scoville 1984). These responses also help children learn other aspects of effective communication such as eye contact, gestures, and vocalization (Bakeman and Adamson 1986; Harding 1984). As more and more infants and toddlers with disabilities are integrated into regular early childhood programs, it is imperative that teachers be aware of this powerful and effective oral language strategy (Rhyner, Lehr, and Pudlas 1990).

In a study investigating teachers' use of contingent responses with children with disabilities it was found that the frequency of contingent responses by teachers was actually quite low (Rhyner, Lehr, and Pudlas 1990). This underscores the need for teachers of integrated children with disabilities to be particularly aware of this function of the teaching role. Since nothing is as effective as a speech act that works as intended (Muma 1978), nonresponsiveness by teachers could actually decrease the language risks that children are willing to take. Quality contingent responses, on the other hand, can encourage children to take the next turn or to take further risks associated with the development of oral language.

Repeated Contexts

It is a well established principle of learning that opportunities for developing language must be repeated so that the child can go from the familiar to the unfamiliar (Nelson 1985; Piaget and Inhelder 1969). Too often, intervention programs for both preschool and school-age children have provided children with activities of short duration that have little to do with what occurs before or after the activity (Norris and Damico 1990). An integrated language arts program contains a number of opportunities for repeated contexts that can be emphasized for students with special needs.

Theme Building.

Using themes, a teacher can provide related opportunities in play, stories, reading, art, music, snacks, drawing, storytelling, and dance. This allows children to become quite familiar with the theme and to proceed to unfamiliar language structures and vocabulary as a result. A story from a familiar fairy tale can provide opportunities to discuss characters, clothing, the actions of the characters, and their feelings. The children's writings, play, and drawings associated with that story provide many repeated contexts that can be used to continue the discussion about the story. As the ideas and information become known to the children they can move on to other components of language such as increased vocabulary, more abstract ideas, and more complex language structures (Norris and Damico 1990).

Collaborative Activities.

The use of themes encourages the use of collaborative activities such as art, music, and dramatic recreations of the story (Harste, Woodward, and Burke 1984). These activities provide children with the opportunity to generalize concepts they are learning beyond the immediate context in which they are learned. If the children have listened to the story of "The Three Little Pigs" the teacher might wish to explore the concept of hiding (Norris and Damico 1990). Activities might be developed in which children hide toys during free play, play "hide-and-go-seek," and hide objects within their drawings and artwork.

Scaffolding.

Language activities should be designed so that they include both authentic use of language and opportunities for others to facilitate the use of language (Norris and Damico 1990). When adults provide these two things for young language users they are furnishing children with a scaffold (Feuerstein 1980; Langer and Applebee 1986). This is done when adults provide models, prompts, and invitations for the child to use language. Any time teachers provide the necessary means to help children use language, they are providing scaffolds. The amount of support that needs to be provided depends on the individual child's language development. The teacher must constantly make decisions about this. In reading the story of "Cinderella" a teacher might direct the attention of

FIGURE 15-4 Some activities, such as the oral storytelling of "Beauty and the Beast Storytellers" Martha Hamilton and Mitch Weiss, need no adaptations to benefit a wide range of children. *Photograph courtesy of Peter Carroll. Reprinted courtesy of Martha Hamilton and Mitch Weiss, P.O. Box 6624, Ithica, N.Y.*

the children to the illustrations in the book and provide scaffolds with the following comments:

"How does Cinderella look in this picture?"
"What do her clothes look like?"
"Why do her sisters treat her like that?"
"What colors do you see here?"
"How is the castle different from your house?"

It should be noted that scaffolding does not tend to elicit language from children in brief or one word responses. It invites divergent responses that allow for an assortment of language uses. As adults use scaffolding, they come to discover that they are doing less "talking at" children and more "talking with" them. This type of interaction tends to continually provide children with models and structures of language use that are new to them. As children become accustomed to hearing these structures used, they are able to incorporate them into their own repertoire of language forms (Vygotsky 1978).

Adults can use specific cue words as part of their

FIGURE 15-5 Snack time provides both an opportunity and an invitation to use language.

interaction with children. These cue words help children identify what type of additional information is needed (French and Nelson 1985; Nelson 1985). These cue words include:

and . . .	next	when
after	because	so
but	except	if
what	who	why
until	which	then

By embedding these words in questions and comments, adults provide scaffolds that help children determine what information is needed next. Examples include: "What happened next?" "If he keeps it, what will happen?" "What do you think she will do after she gets to the town?"

Over time, the adult attempts to shift more and more of the responsibility for the communication to the child. This is done by collaborating with the child. This involves helping the child communicate effectively with a third person such as another child, another adult, or a puppet (Norris and Hoffman 1990). This process is in keeping with the metaphor of a scaffold as described by Bruner (1978). He explains that in constructing a building, a scaffold is initially built to support the wall. As the wall becomes more structurally complete, the amount of scaffolding can be decreased and gradually removed. Eventually the building stands on its own. People and language, of course, are more complex. The amount of scaffolding needed by children may increase or decrease over time depending on the child and the complexities of the language tasks and social situations. Therefore, teachers must be committed to playing an active role in this process. It has been shown that without this active involvement, children with special needs are less likely to benefit from being placed in an integrated program (Ekholm and Hedin 1984).

Provide Positive Feedback

When children engage in language communications they need to know whether or not they were successful in their attempt. Those who receive the communications need to make constant decisions about the degree of success of the communications. Giving information to children about the success of their communications is referred to as feedback. The feedback, of course, should be directly related to the communication itself. Teachers need to keep in mind

The corefole QUTRE

ONE day amannn had a colrfole qutre . BOY was it a waudferl coen . THERIRNO NO Sijust thng hsa a coen liek taht .

the end

FIGURE 15-6 With the appropriate scaffolding and the use of a typewriter, a five-year-old wrote and illustrated the story, "A Colorful Quarter."

the relative level of a child's language ability when making decisions about the success of a child's communication attempt. With young children, this feedback will primarily be in the form of oral responses.

When a child successfully communicates, the teacher can provide feedback that confirms, expands, or extends the child's language (Norris and Hoffman 1990). A child's communication can be confirmed by repeating the child's message (Child: "I'm hungry." Teacher: "I'm hungry too.") or by using nonverbal responses such as facial expressions or gestures. An expansion can translate the child's message into a more complex language structure (Child: "Car red." Teacher: "That's right, your car is red."). An extension adds new ideas to the topic, thus inviting additional interaction from the child (Child: "Read book." Teacher: "Yes, let's read a book. What book would you like to read?").

Seek Revisions

Another type of feedback is used when the child's communication attempt is not successful. This feedback is not negative and does not tell the child that the language attempt was wrong. Rather, it tells the child that either the communication is not true or that the communication needs to be repaired (Corsaro 1979; Schegloff, Jefferson, and Sacks 1977). The purpose of this is not to get the child to say something correctly according to adult standards, but to help the child discover the difference between the intended communication and the actual communication (Norris and Hoffman 1990).

When indicating to a child that something in the communication is not true, the feedback should indicate both what is untrue and how the statement is communicating false information (Norris and Hoffman 1990). For example, if a child said "Cookie eat Suzy," the teacher might respond with "No Suzy, the cookie didn't eat you. You ate the cookie."

When it is determined that the intended message does not coincide with the actual message, the teacher can request revisions in a number of different ways. A request might be made for more specific information (Corsaro 1979): "Do you mean that you already ate lunch or that you are going to eat lunch?" A teacher might also model a revision that states what the child intended (Corsaro 1979): "Oh, you mean you are

hungry and want to eat lunch now." A teacher might also use the occasion to introduce or reinforce a new word or concept: "Oh, you mean you are so hungry that you want to eat a 'feast' just like the king did in our story today." Whatever the revision, the child should revise the original communication and repeat it before the interaction continues. This helps the child make meaningful adjustments to the language based on natural feedback (Duchan 1984).

Relevant Activities and Materials

Minority and multicultural children are historically over-represented in special needs programs. It has been suggested that "cultural discontinuity" may be a major reason for this (Reyhner and Garcia 1989). Cultural discontinuity is a concept that is used to describe the internal conflict children face in having to choose between the home's and the school's language and culture (Cooter 1990). Teachers must respond to this need by helping children learn to deal with both languages and cultures by using materials and activities that help children create bridges between the two.

Several practices have been identified as being particularly effective with minority and multicultural children (Reyhner and Garcia 1989). First, teachers need to understand the close connection between oral language and reading. Teaching reading without addressing the oral language needs of the children will tend to be a frustrating and nonproductive exercise. Second, materials should be used that reflect the children's culture and experiences. Both commercially available tradebooks and classroom created materials can be used. Third, small interactive groups working collaboratively enhance the needed support for the language risk taking of children. Fourth, teaching reading and writing in coordination with each other enhances the development of each. Fifth, providing experiences such as field trips and role playing in which language is highly contextualized helps children make language connections (Sutton 1989). All of these practices, of course, are clearly within the realm of an integrated language arts program.

Teach Strategies

As has been established for all students, the teaching of isolated language arts skills does not add up to a literate learner. While skills must be developed within contexts, it is particularly important to teach strategies. Skills are helpful in controlled language situations. Strategies enable the child to deal with unpredictable situations. Skill instruction focuses on a child's deficits. Strategies focus on a child's strengths and competencies by developing and strengthening them. While skills deal with the "what" of language, strategies deal with the "how to" of language. Strategies enable the child to perceive relationships, construct meaning, apply background knowledge, and deal with the unpredictable aspects of oral and written language.

A number of strategies are particularly helpful for multicultural children who are just learning English (Sutton 1989). They include helping children establish a purpose for listening, reading, and writing;

FIGURE 15-7 Many storybooks are relevant to almost all children and cultures. *Reprinted courtesy of Houghton Mifflin Company.*

Planting bushes
First I got some water
Then I put some Pet moss in.
Then I put water on.
Then I put the tree in.
Then I put dirt around it.
Last I got mulch and put it on the trees.

FIGURE 15-8 Using oral retelling and concrete experiences, a child was able to describe a sequence of events in words and illustration.

familiarizing children with different types of books; introducing self-monitoring abilities; developing problem-solving procedures; and using learning strategies. Learning strategies useful for young children include predicting, questioning, and retelling.

SUMMARY

An integrated language arts program stresses the desirability of classroom-based interventions for children with special needs. This occurs when teachers with specific specialties come into the program rather than removing the children from the program in order to provide special services. Teachers who are likely to provide these services in the area of language development include speech therapists and special education teachers.

A number of models may be used to provide special services to children within a regular program. The models range from those useful for helping children with less severe disabilities to those that are useful for helping children with more severe disabilities. Staff development and consultation might be quite appropriate for serving children with milder needs. Consultation is also an effective tool that can be used with children who have more severe disabilities. For the children with the most severe disabilities, the models of overlapping curriculum and multilevel curriculum should be considered. The model used depends on the needs of the children. It may also be helpful to combine various aspects of different models when the needs of children suggest such an organization. Whatever model is used, it is almost always beneficial to provide services to students with special needs within the regular program.

There are many strategies that regular teachers and specialist teachers working together can use to assist children with disabilities within the regular language arts program. Among these are contingent responses, repeated contexts, positive feedback, revision requests, and the use of relevant materials and activities. Some of these are particularly useful for multicultural children, while other are geared more for use with children with disabilities. Most, however, have a general applicability.

A special relationship must exist between the teachers providing services to children with special needs integrated into a regular program. There must be a sense of teamwork and shared responsibility. When this is assumed, the benefits are great. Having additional adults in the room provides increased opportunities for observing children, the use of the specific expertise of different individuals, and the ability to develop and implement a program in a collaborative manner.

Questions and Activities for Review and Discussion

Multiple Choice

1. Services provided to children with disabilities in regular educational programs are called
   a. pull-outs.
   b. classroom-based.
   c. segregated.
   d. alternative education centered.
2. A teaching model in which the early childhood teacher and a special education teacher jointly plan, teach, and evaluate a program is called
   a. team teaching.
   b. a pull-out approach.
   c. one-to-one intervention.
   d. a resource program.
3. When the regular curriculum is beyond the cognitive ability of a child with a disability, the most appropriate model for instruction might be
   a. curriculum overlapping.
   b. multilevel curriculum.
   c. staff development.
   d. team teaching.
4. The objectives of a language development program for children with special needs should

       a. focus on communication.
       b. relate to objectives and activities in the regular program.
       c. be general enough to cover a range of growth periods.
       d. all of the above

5. Repeated contexts refer to procedures that help children go from
       a. one skill to another skill.
       b. the familiar to the unfamiliar.
       c. the general to the specific.
       d. all of the above

6. Scaffolding is particularly useful for helping children to
       a. answer questions correctly.
       b. determine the correct answer.
       c. continue an oral language interaction.
       d. develop convergent thinking.

7. In order to help a child see the difference between an intended and an actual communication, a teacher might ask a child for
       a. an explanation.
       b. a revision.
       c. a negation.
       d. an extension.

True or False

T   F   1. Speech therapy services can be effectively provided within an integrated language arts program.

T   F   2. Consultation requires little communication between the different teachers providing services to children with special needs.

T   F   3. Providing educational services to children with disabilities in programs isolated from the regular education program decreases rather than increases their life options.

T   F   4. Scaffolding is an appropriate strategy for helping children expand their oral language abilitity.

T   F   5. Cultural discontinuity can refer to the differences between the language of the home and the language of the school.

Essay and Discussion

1. How can staff development be used as a service for children with special needs?
2. Describe how a multilevel curriculum approach might be used in an early childhood education language arts program.
3. Describe the relationship that should exist between teachers providing services to children with special needs within a regular early childhood education program.
4. Describe one type of repeated context that might tend to occur in an early childhood education integrated language arts program.
5. Explain the three different types of feedback that can be given to a child who is successful in an oral language communication.

REFERENCES

Bakeman, R, and L.B. Adamson. 1986. Infants' conventionalized acts: Gestures and words with mothers and peers. *Infant Behavior and Development* 9: 215–230.

Bruner, J.S. 1978. Learning how to do things with words. In *Human Growth and Development*, ed. J.S. Bruner and R.A. Gorton. Oxford, United Kingdom: Oxford University Press.

Campbell, C., S. Campbell, J. Collicot, D. Perner, and J. Stone. 1988. Individualized instruction. *Education New Brunswick* 3: 17–20.

Christensen, S.S., and C.H. Luckett. 1990. Getting into the classroom and making it work. *Language, Speech, and Hearing Services in Schools* 21: 110–113.

Cooter, R.B. 1990. Learners with special needs. *Reading Today* 8: 28.

Corsaro, W.A. 1979. Sociolinguistic patterns in adult-child interactions. In *Developmental Pragmatics*, ed. E. Ochs and B.B. Schieffelin. New York: Academic Press.

Damico, J.S. 1987. Clinical discourse analysis. In *Communication Skills and Classroom Success: Assessment of Language Learning Disabled Students*, ed. C.S. Simon. San Diego, Calif.: College-Hill.

Duchan, J.F. 1984. Language assessment: The pragmatics revolution. In *Language Science*, ed. R.C. Naremore. San Diego, Calif.: College-Hill.

Ekholm, B., and A. Hedin. 1984. *Mainstreamed children and ordinary children in twelve daycare centers: An observational study*. Linkoping, Sweden: Pedagogiska Institute.

Feuerstein, R. 1980. *Instrumental enrichment: An intervention program for cognitive modifiability*. Baltimore, Md.: University Park Press.

French, L., and K. Nelson. 1985. *Young children's knowledge of relational terms: Some ifs, ors, and buts*. New York: Springer-Verlag.

Giangreco, M.F., and L.H. Meyer. 1988. Expanding service options in regular schools and classrooms for students with severe disabilities. In *Alternative Education Delivery Systems: Enhancing Instructional Options for All Students*, ed. J. Graden, J. Zins, and M. Curtis. Washington, D.C.: National Association of School Psychologists.

Giangreco, M.F., and J.W. Putnam. 1991. Supporting the education of students with severe disabilities in the regular education environment. In *Critical Issues in the Lives of People with Severe Disabilities*, ed. L.H. Meyer, C.A. Peck, and L. Brown. Baltimore, Md.: Paul H. Brooks.

Harding, C. 1984. Acting with intention: A framework for examining the development of the intention to communicate. In *The Origin and Growth of Communication*, ed. L. Feagans, C. Garvey, and R. Golinkoff. Norwood, N.J.: Ablex.

Harris, S. 1986. Evaluation of a curriculum to support literacy growth in young children. *Early Childhood Research Quarterly* 1: 333–348.

Harste, J.C., V.A. Woodward, and C.L. Burke. 1984. *Language stories and literacy lessons*. Portsmouth, N.H.: Heinemann.

Hunt, J.M. 1982. Toward equalizing the developmental opportunities of infants and preschool children. *Journal of Social Issues* 38: 163–191.

Langer, J.A., and A.N. Applebee. 1986. Reading and writing instruction: Toward a theory of teaching and learning. *Review of Research in Education*. Washington, D.C.: American Educational Research Association.

Marvin, C.A. 1987. Consultation services: Changing roles for SLTs. *Journal of Childhood Communication Disorders* 11, 1: 1–16.

Miller, L. 1989. Classroom-based language intervention. *Language, Speech, and Hearing Services in Schools* 20: 149–152.

Muma, J.R. 1978. *Language handbook: Concepts, assessment, and intervention.* Englewood Cliffs, N.J.: Prentice-Hall.

Nelson, K. 1985. *Making sense: The acquisition of shared meaning.* New York: Academic Press.

Nelson, N.W. 1986. Individual processing in classroom settings. *Topics in Language Disorders* 6, 2: 13–27.

Norris, J.A., and J.S. Damico. 1990. Whole language in theory and practice: Implications for language intervention. *Language, Speech, and Hearing Services in Schools* 21: 212–220.

Norris, J.A., and P.R. Hoffman. 1990. Language intervention within naturalistic environments. *Language, Speech, and Hearing Services in Schools* 21: 172–84.

Piaget, J., and B. Inhelder. 1969. *The Psychology of the Child.* New York: Basic Books.

Reyhner, J., and R.L. Garcia. 1989. Helping minorities read better: Problems and promises. *Reading Research and Instruction* 28: 84–91.

Rhyner, P.N.P., D.H. Lehr, and K.A. Pudlas. 1990. An analysis of teacher responsiveness to communicative initiations of preschool children with handicaps. *Language, Speech, and Hearing Services in Schools* 21: 91–97.

Schegloff, E.A., G. Jefferson, and H. Sacks. 1977. The preference for self-correcting in the organization of repair in conversation. *Language* 53: 361–382.

Scoville, R. 1984. Development of the intention to communicate. In *The Origin and Growth of Communication*, ed. L. Feagans, C. Garvey, and R. Golinkoff. Norwood, N.J.: Ablex.

Snow, C.E. 1981. Social interaction and language acquisition. In *Child Language D An International Perspective*, ed. P.S. Dale and D. Ingram. Baltimore, Md.: University Park Press.

Sutton, C. 1989. Helping the nonnative English speaker with reading. *The Reading Teacher* 42: 684–688.

Tiegerman, E., and M. Siperstein. 1984. Individual patterns of interaction in the mother-child dyad: Implications for parent intervention. *Topics in Language Disorders* 4: 40, 50–61.

Vygotsky, L.S. 1978. *Mind in society.* Cambridge, Mass.: MIT Press.

UNIT 16

Developing Positive Attitudes

UNIT GOALS

After completing this unit, the reader should:

- understand the importance of helping young children develop positive attitudes about learning, themselves, and their peers.
- understand the relationship between positive attitudes and the development of language and literacy.
- develop the ability to implement strategies and activities designed to enhance positive attitudes in young children.

PREVIEW

Nothing succeeds like success. How many times have we heard that statement? It's an old cliche, but it does have validity. It can be observed throughout the world. Consider the winning team that seems to get better with each victory. Players who were just average a couple of weeks ago now seem to play better. The team makes fewer mistakes. The players' confidence builds, and they begin to play with more poise. In the process, they develop team spirit. They support each other. They help and encourage each other. They try to keep negative feelings out and positive feelings in. When a teammate makes an error, no one gets upset. Everyone accepts it, and the team moves on together. In short, their current success is partly due to their past success.

This is similar to the way language develops. It is often a product of a cooperative group process. By supporting each other, children are helping both themselves and others develop valuable language

skills. Early childhood educators can do many things to enhance this process. In this unit some of the major ideas related to this issue are addressed. They include the development of an awareness of the relationship between attitudes and language learning, improved social acceptance of children with disabilities, and the development of a classroom environment with a tone of acceptance and encouragement.

INTRODUCTION

Think back to your own childhood and recall something you wanted to learn or something in which you wished to participate. It may have been learning to ride a bicycle, play checkers, roller skate, or construct a specific craft project. As you acquired the skills and abilities necessary to do any of these things, you probably began to feel better about engaging in the process. As you made fewer mistakes, you began to enjoy the process more. The supportive people around you, whether they were friends, siblings, or parents, provided support and encouragement. As you experienced success, you looked forward to still more success.

Each of these descriptions parallels the process by which children acquire the ability to use language. Since language is an ability that mainly serves to link us with other human beings, it is quite natural that anyone developing the ability to use language is surrounded by people. In many cases, children find themselves surrounded by other children. This peer group must often serve as the support network for children taking risks with language and learning language. The acceptance, support, and recognition from others is a powerful motivating force for children. It is important for children to understand that they have a role to play in helping others grow by recognizing both the achievements and human characteristics of others.

All people need recognition. Some are comfortable with a moderate amount of recognition. Larger amounts make some children and adults feel self-conscious. Others may need more reassurance before they believe that they are valuable members of the group. Sometimes children seem to need constant recognition. This is frequently related to a poor self-image and a lack of confidence on the part of those children. At times this lack of a positive self-image is displayed through hostile behavior toward those who are perceived as less able. The children who are the recipients of the hostility are often children who are less able, disadvantaged, from minority cultures, or disabled. This behavior is ultimately destructive for both children.

There is a close relationship between language learning and social interaction. Children need to develop the ability to interact with many different people. Early childhood programs that include multicultural, talented, non-English-speaking, and children with disabilities provide an environment that is much like the one the children will live in for the remainder of their lives. A well-structured program uses this diversity to enrich the lives of all of the children involved. This unit describes several beliefs and strategies that can help set the stage for these benefits. The benefits that can spring from positive attitudes about self and language learning are explored. This is followed by a description of procedures for fostering

FIGURE 16-1 Each child needs to be recognized as an individual.

positive attitudes among children. Some of the procedures are general, while other are specific to developing positive attitudes toward children from multicultural backgrounds and children with disabilities.

ATTITUDES AND LANGUAGE LEARNING

There is a close relationship between attitudes and learning. Attitudes refer to an individual's beliefs and feelings toward other people, ideas, and things. When the attitude is positive, there is an increased chance of growth occurring. The reason for this is that a positive attitude is closely related to the motivation for dealing with that person, idea, or thing. Children can have positive or negative attitudes toward both themselves and other people. When they are positive toward themselves we refer to that as a good self-concept. When they have negative feelings about themselves we refer to that as a poor self-concept. When children view other people in positive ways it might be referred to as an accepting attitude. When it is negative, it might be seen as hostile, closed, or rejecting.

Social Interaction

As we have learned, language learning is enhanced through the opportunity to meaningfully interact with numerous individuals in natural situations. If children experience the opportunity to interact with other children from an early age, they will feel comfortable with those children. It will not matter if the other children possess disabilities or do not possess native English language skills. The positive attitudes developed will encourage children to interact with

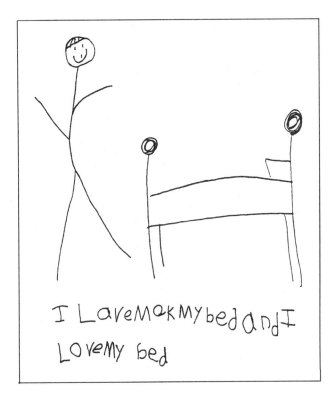

I LaveMakMybedandI LOveMy bed

FIGURE 16-2 Positive attitude, language, and learning are all related.

nicating. As their successes accumulate they become more confident about their abilities to use language. As they become more confident they feel more comfortable taking risks and in turn use new language structures. Their successes lead to more success.

By integrating all children within a regular program, young children grow up understanding that such things as race, gender, intelligence, and physical limitations are concepts that might be used to describe people but need not separate us as human beings. This alone should be enough to warrant an integrated approach. Beyond that, however, there are other benefits. By enabling children to learn about differences in people in a natural and nurturing environment, they grow up with fewer fears of the unknown. They are not fearful when they meet someone who does not see or who may not speak the same language. Finally, children can benefit from the opportunity to experience the richness of the lives of others. Children from other countries and other ethnic backgrounds bring with them fascinating cultures, experiences, and stories that can be shared. Children with disabilities bring intelligence, creativity, and friendship to relationships just as any other children would. By successfully communicating with each other, all children can gain positive self-concepts and feelings of competence with the language.

each other using their language abilities and the language models available to them. Children with more English language ability will need to attend to their language use more closely in order to make themselves understood by those who possess less ability in the language. They will also need to listen more attentively, and they will discover the need to provide clear feedback to other children to let them know that they understand the communication.

Risk Taking

As children engage in language use with other children they will see where their language attempts work and where they do not. As they gain in skill at communicating, they will understand this through the feedback they receive from those who are communicating with them. This feedback provides language users with the information they need to understand when they have been successful at commu-

STRATEGIES FOR POSITIVE ATTITUDES

Placing children with differing needs within a regular program does not insure that the benefits of the regular program will occur (Gresham 1982). The program sometimes needs to be restructured in some way in order to benefit children with different needs. Many of the possibilities for restructuring aimed at developing positive attitudes by and toward children with special needs would be beneficial to programs no matter which children are served by them. Van Manen (1986) outlines a number of characteristics of an educational program that comprise what he calls the "tone of teaching" that occurs within the program. Some strategies such as peer tutoring by children with disabilities are specifically aimed at improving the self-concept of such children (Custer and Osguthorpe 1983). Some of these strategies work primarily

FIGURE 16-3 Each individual child adds something special to the classroom.

through improved peer social interactions (Gresham 1982), while others use simulations, celebrations, and presentations to help children feel a kinship with children with special needs. Each of the approaches has benefits.

Classroom Tone

According to Van Manen (1986), every classroom has a tone or an atmosphere. In every classroom teachers can ask: What does this room say to children? Does the room say that it is a place for children? Does it say that this is a place for cozy sharing of ideas and stories? Does it say that this is a good place for children to play and to be together? Does it say that this is a happy place? Does the teacher's voice always say that each child is important and that the teacher is glad they are here?

When the teacher is talking or reading a book to the children, more than the story's message is being conveyed. The teacher's voice and body language tell much about the classroom tone. Genuine enthusiasm about the story being read is contagious and obvious. Clearly the story is being shared not just because it is story time, but because the teacher loves the story and feels a genuine part of what is being taught.

The teacher's voice is not the only clue to the classroom tone. Information abounds in other features of the typical early childhood classroom. What characteristics should teachers examine? Are the decorations and displays minimal and obligatory? Or, do they capture a sense of the magic of childhood? Do they celebrate childhood? Do they say that the efforts of children here are truly important and worthwhile? Does the room give a sense that the teacher is able to see the world from the child's perspective?

Seeing the Child

While it may seem like an overly simplistic bit of advice, educators truly need to see the child. Professionals have a tendency to see a child in terms of their professional training and background. As a result, it is easy to fall into an unfortunate pattern of seeing children by their characteristics rather than as individual children. It is quite easy to see a Down's syndrome child rather than a child who happens to have Down's syndrome. The same is true for a child who is language delayed, or a child who is non-English-speaking. Van Manen (1986) contends that while we want to help children grow, we must also want them to savor their own existence and their own childhood. This is a subtle interpretation of how we look at children, but it is an important one. Children observe how teachers act toward different children. If they see teachers acting in different ways with different children, they model those tendencies, for good or ill. Obviously there are occasions when teachers must act differently toward different children or to different behaviors. On the other hand, the models we demonstrate toward different children must be carefully considered.

Hello and Goodbye

Each day as the children enter and leave the classroom, it is important for the teacher to acknowledge each individual child (Van Manen 1986). Van Manen (1986) provides some important suggestions for doing this. As children enter the room, have something to say that shows genuine interest in how they are

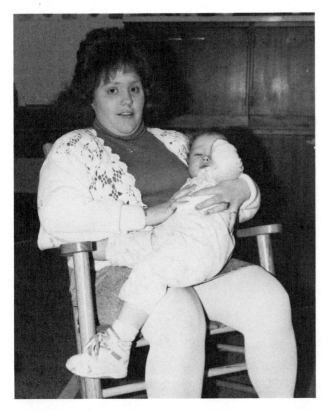

FIGURE 16-4 Each child needs to sense that he or she is seen as important and valuable.

arriving. Recognize the fact that a child is bringing in a favorite book from home to share with the class. Notice the new shirt or the toy that the child is bringing in for show and tell. When saying goodbye at the close of a day, make that same human connection with each child. End the day with a hug or a handshake, and say something to each of the children to show them that their presence on that day was meaningful and worthwhile. This is a good time to note activities that were socially appropriate. It is a good time to reinforce the child's behaviors that were extended to accept and make friends with other children who may have differences. This applies to children with or without disabilities. Each of them needs to feel worthwhile.

When a parent is waiting to speak with you, remember that the children must come first. Explain this to parents at the beginning of the program so that they will understand that you are not ignoring them when you focus exclusively on the children during these transition periods. This approach of building a positive self-concept is used widely in a number of situations in which the importance of self-concept is acknowledged. In the Reading Recovery program, for example, it is clearly assumed that the most powerful teaching builds on children's competencies rather than their deficits (Pinnell, Fried, and Estice 1990). Much of what occurs in the program is based on that belief. Therefore, building a child's sense of confidence is of utmost importance.

Assigning Responsibility

Children sense whether we believe in them. While they are comfortable with the structure we provide for them, they also seek a certain amount of responsibility as they grow. The ability to take responsibility provides children with valuable feedback about their own competence. Giving children tasks, chores, and jobs around the classroom tells them that we see them as capable individuals. Their accomplishment of the job provides them with a sense of self-confidence. Beyond this, children need to be given some responsibility to set expectations for themselves and to experience the consequences of that decision-making process. As teachers we need to be willing to accept the decisions children make, unless the decisions present a clearly dangerous situation. For the most part, decisions children make do not produce a potentially harmful situation. In the area of language, for instance, children are constantly making decisions, testing the results of the decision, and accepting the consequences. This helps them develop greater control over their language.

A fascinating use of providing responsibility to children with disabilities has resulted in the provision of a unique strategy to develop positive attitudes for all children. By using a high structure and clear expectations, Custer and Osguthorpe (1983) illustrated a creative approach to social interaction by the use of peer tutoring. By learning a three-step approach of demonstrating a skill, observing how well another child learns the skill, and giving helpful feedback, children with mental disabilities were able to successfully participate in a peer tutoring experience. Through the experience, the non-disabled children who were tutored developed a sense of respect, admiration, and a belief in the competency of their former tutees. A key part of the tutorial situation was the integration of music into the learning situation, a device that serves early childhood education particularly well.

Systematic Modeling

The concept of modeling, or demonstrating an appropriate procedure, is a powerful tool to help children learn. At times, however, children need to be specifically directed to the modeling if it is to be effective. If the children to whom the modeling is being directed are not attending, the effectiveness of the tool is lost. Some valuable guidelines for systematic modeling have been identified by Gresham (1982). They deal primarily with social interaction for children with disabilities, but are applicable to other areas as well.

When demonstrating inappropriate behaviors to be avoided, teachers should use a child who seems to have a high status among peers. Teachers should consider using a child with special needs as a positive model. Direct the attention of all of the children to the model. Reinforce the appropriate behaviors that have been modeled when they are used by the children in the natural environment. Re-create the model periodically. It helps children better understand the appropriate behaviors and demonstrates that they are important.

Social Initiations

It is the reponsibility of the teacher to restructure the regular program so that social acceptance of students with special needs is more likely. A couple of different activities can be used to help children become more comfortable with, as well as more accepting of, children with differences. The first activity involves helping children become aware of differences and seeing them for what they really are. When disabling conditions are a concern, teachers can invite somewhat older children or adults into the classroom to help children learn about disabilities. For example, a deaf child and a sign language interpreter could explain and demonstrate how communication can take place either with or without the sounds of language being present. A blind adult could explain life

FIGURE 16-5 Children can learn to accept differences as a natural part of life.

without sight, the challenges of daily living, and the use of braille to experience the beauty of literature. Such visits provide young children with a structure in which to initiate conversations with people with disabilities.

A second procedure is actually a strategy by which teachers can introduce and continue social interactions with all children. Depending on the disability, different approaches must be modeled for communicating with them. Children without disabilities may need to monitor their language more carefully or perhaps use some sign language to engage children with cognitive, physical, or emotional differences. Teachers need to be sure that children understand the communication demands of the situation. As children are successful, teachers can reinforce the behaviors that made the communication effective. This serves as both a language tool and a social device.

A third approach is through the use of simulations. A simulation is a small drama in which an actual situation is acted out. The purpose of the simulation is to give the participants a feeling for actually being in the real situation. An example of this would be using a blindfold to give children the feeling of what it is like not to have sight. A physical disability might be simulated by being confined to a wheelchair for a brief period of time. Through such simulations, children can experience the tremendous challenge that daily life can present for those with disabilities. For a person with such a disability, preparing food, getting dressed, and using a bathroom are often both difficult and challenging. Discussions about feelings following simulations can provide both empathy and respect for people with diabilities.

Cultural Celebrations

A strategy similar to social initiation that can be used to assist non-English-speaking children is the cultural celebration. Since books with multicultural themes are becoming more available, this can easily fit into a number of possible themed units. The initial assumption for using the activity is that all children have unique competencies. This is, of course, true for children who have not yet learned how to speak English.

The teacher needs to know something about the children's cultural background and then elicit the assistance of another adult or older child who shares the cultural background of those children being integrated into the regular program. During a classroom visit, children will be able to assist the visitor by demonstrating competencies about the culture being studied. The children might be able to demonstrate their competence by preparing specific food items, demonstrating a craft, or dramatizing a folktale from the culture. The multicultural children might also teach the other children some of the important words from the culture or something about a current holiday celebration.

Reshuffle the Deck

A variation of the cultural celebration approach is a strategy called reshuffling the deck. It can be used to address the needs of a number of children with special needs, including children with disabilities. The

FIGURE 16-6 Folktales such as "The Ants That Pushed on the Sky" can be used as part of a Native American cultural celebration. *From* The Child's Fairy Tale Book, *by Kay Chorao. Reprinted courtesy of E.P. Dutton.*

same assumption, that all children possess unique competencies, holds for this procedure as well. Because of its flexibility, it can easily fit into numerous themed units in an integrated language arts program. The purpose of the procedure is to help all children become aware of the competencies of children with special needs.

Reshuffling the deck refers to a key feature of the process. The focus of the process is something other than the learning that is usually expected in academic type tasks. In this way the playing field is made more accessible for all. For example, using play, cooperative learning, and social interaction, a teacher can have children assume the roles of characters in a familiar story such as "The Three Bears," "Little Red Riding Hood," or "Hansel and Gretel." The teacher's reading of the story sets the stage for natural social interaction. Later, when the story is re-created independently by the children, children with special needs will more frequently be included.

Variations on this procedure can focus on a number of other areas in which children generally have competencies without regard to their academic abilities. Using activities that include music, art, and sports can be helpful here. Homemade instruments can be brought in from home in Appalachian Mountain areas. Native American music, dances, and folktales can be used in many parts of the country, particularly the West and Southwest. Ethnic music, folktales, and dances can be used throughout the country. In each case, all of the children will become aware of the unique competencies of others. The children who share this expertise will see that they have something quite valuable to share with other children. The teacher can reinforce both the positive feelings and the social interactions that emerge from the activities.

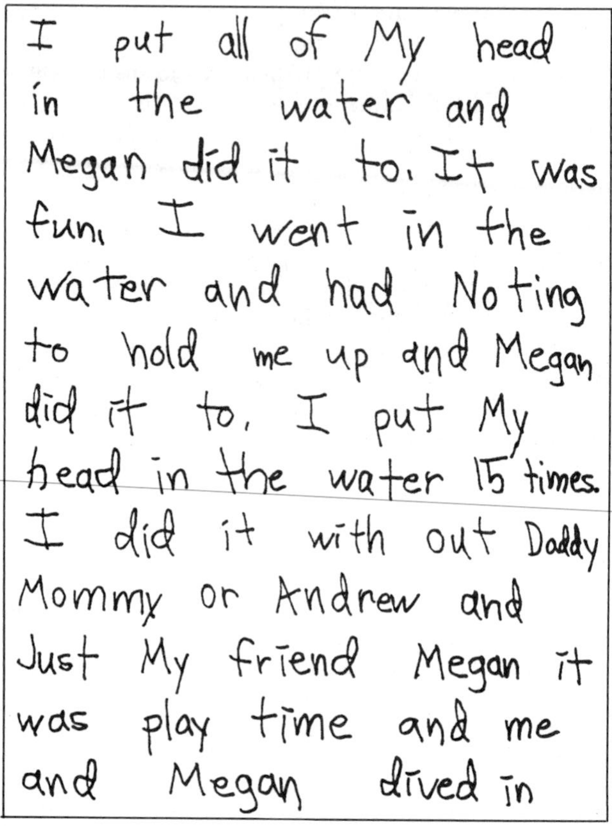
I put all of My head
in the water and
Megan did it to. It was
fun. I went in the
water and had Noting
to hold me up and Megan
did it to. I put My
head in the water 15 times.
I did it with out Daddy
Mommy or Andrew and
Just My friend Megan it
was play time and me
and Megan dived in

FIGURE 16-7 All children need to develop a sense of independence and accomplishment like that of this young writer.

Assume Giftedness

An interesting variation on working with students with special needs, assuming that they are gifted and talented, is provided by Salzer (1986). The rationale for the approach is based on a belief that too often educators tend to focus on the inabilities and deficiencies of children with special needs. The children become aware of this as the programs they are provided often focus exclusively on those things they have difficulty doing. On the other hand, tests are not used to guide the teaching of the gifted as much as they are with children with special needs because such instruments are seen as lacking reliability (Roedell, Jackson, and Robinson 1980).

Instructional programs for gifted children often stress the development of curiosity, creativity, independence, sensitivity, and self expression (Maker 1982). If young children with special needs are included in regular classrooms, and it is assumed that they are gifted, they will frequently benefit from activities directed toward developing these abilities. Their classroom experiences will include free play (independence and curiosity), drawing and writing (creativity and self expression), and music and story dramatization (sensitivity) (Salzer 1986). What child would not benefit from these kinds of experiences?

Opinion Requests

Another strategy that assumes that all children possess unique competencies is called opinion requests. It seeks to help children develop belief in themselves as having worthwhile ideas and opinions. This procedure focuses on the emergence of critical thinking and its relationship to language. Its flexibility enables it to be used with a number of themed units, as well as different books, stories, toys, pictures, and activities. To use the procedure, the teacher might engage the children in two or three similar activities over the course of the day. This might include story reading, games, the use of new toys, or discussions about pictures. Following this, all of the children are given a card with their name on it. After lining up the books, pictures, or toys in front of the room, the teacher asks the children to choose one item and to place their cards face down in front of one of them. Children might be asked to place their card in front of the one they thought was the funniest, best, most fun, etc.

When this has been completed the group can investigate which children selected which item. The discussion that follows allows children to give opinions that are accepted and valued by the teacher and the group. The emphasis is not on picking a winning category. The stress is on giving children an opportunity to explain why they selected an item. There is no right or wrong selection. Everybody, regardless of ability or need, has a right to express personal preferences. These preferences all have equal value.

Bibliotherapy

Bibliotherapy is particularly useful for helping young children develop positive attitudes about themselves and others. The term *bibliotherapy* comes from the Greek words that mean *using books to heal bodily disorders*. Several decades ago, bibliotherapy was identified as a potential tool for assessing personality and monitoring adjustment (Russell and Shrodes 1950). Years later, bibliotherapy was recognized more as a tool for helping children deal with several issues including such areas as attitudes about self and others (Cianciolo 1965). More recently, bibliotherapy has been described as an effective tool to use within language arts programs at the early childhood level (Sawyer and Comer 1991).

A number of benefits are associated with the use of bibliotherapy. First, bibliotherapy provides information through the use of books. Information can dispel myths and untangle a young child's misconceptions. Second, through books, children can find that others have a mutual understanding of a common problem. This helps children feel less alone in their fears and worries. It also helps them discuss problems, because they can feel that it is the character in the book who is really having the problem. Third, stories can illuminate childhood worries and help young children gain greater insight into their personal behavior. By using books, children gain a sense of control and mastery

FIGURE 16-8 Children can develop a sense of pride and acceptance through the use of books and toys.

over their feelings, worries, and problems. When this occurs, they are better able to deal with them and in the process can feel better about themselves.

While bibliotherapy can be a powerful tool, it should not be used only when teachers decide to help children develop more positive attitudes about some specific idea or group of children. It should be integrated within the program in such a way that it can be used in a natural manner as the program progresses through the year. That is, there should always be certain recurring ideas that surface in thematic units as the year progresses. In early childhood programs, teachers tend to stress the need to feel good about ourselves, to accept others, and to be a contributing member of a group. Using books and discussions about the stories to illustrate these themes should be blended within the program.

While adults may feel that some of the concerns that children have about themselves are inconsequential, they are often quite real and worrisome to the children who possess them. Children might worry about whether they run as fast, look as pretty, or draw as well as other children. Children who have learning difficulties do not always understand that they are having difficulty. However, they do sometimes understand these problems. Other children who may recognize these difficulties may taunt and tease the children with the worries. This further decreases any positive feelings such children may have about themselves. Bibliotherapy can be used to address some of these issues.

FIGURE 16-9 Children can worry about a sick pet and grieve over the loss of a pet.

Books that are worth considering for this purpose include Robert Kraus's *Leo the Late Bloomer* (1971), Patricia Reilly Giff's *Happy Birthday, Ronald Morgan* (1986), Miriam Cohen's *First Grade Takes a Test* (1980), and Berniece Rabe's *The Balancing Girl* (1981).

SUMMARY

Self-concept is an important part of language and literacy development. A child who feels comfortable and confident as a learner is far more likely to engage in the risk taking and curiosity about language that will stimulate growth. When children have special needs, it is important to integrate them into rich language environments. The most appropriate learning environment for children with special needs is seen as the regular educational program that they would ordinarily attend if they did not have special needs. When they are placed in regular classroom environments, however, it is important for the teacher to adjust the environment so as to be a welcoming place for all children. The tone of the classroom can be sensed by both adults and children. The tone will play a major role in helping children see themselves as competent and worthwhile learners.

Children with special needs who can benefit from inclusion in regular early childhood programs include multicultural children, non-English-speaking children, and children with disabilities. Simply placing children into such programs, however, does not automatically insure that benefits will accrue to the child. Teachers need to work together to be sure that the activities developed for children and the strategies used by teachers are designed to foster social interaction, language growth, and positive feelings.

A wide range of procedures and strategies are available to teachers to help them integrate students with special needs into regular classrooms. Many of the strategies can be used in a general way, while others are designed for use with specific children. Strategies such as "opinion request," "bibliotherapy," and "Hello and goodbye" may be used effectively with all children. A strategy such as "reshuffling the deck" is designed specifically for children with disabilities. The "cultural celebration" is most useful for children from diverse cultural backgrounds.

Questions and Activities for Review and Discussion

Multiple Choice
1. Risk taking in language learning is often fostered by a child's
   a. lack of a high level of intelligence.
   b. positive self-concept.
   c. ability to memorize letter sounds.
   d. all of the above

2. The atmosphere established in a classroom that characterizes that classroom is referred to as its
    a. size.
    b. color.
    c. tone.
    d. floor plan.
3. Giving children the responsibility of classroom tasks tells them that they are seen as
    a. needing things to do.
    b. capable individuals.
    c. inexpensive helpers.
    d. none of these
4. Young children are seen as constantly making decisions in the area of
    a. language.
    b. money.
    c. time management.
    d. clothing selection.
5. A dramatic play activity designed to give children a sense of the challenge of possessing a disability is called a
    a. simulation.
    b. story map.
    c. semantic web.
    d. story outline.
6. Reshuffling the deck is a procedure that refers to
    a. a card game.
    b. placing children with and without disabilities on an equal footing.
    c. asking questions in random order.
    d. a simulation of a social problem.
7. A useful tool for encouraging the validity of personal preferences is
    a. peer tutoring.
    b. skill demonstration.
    c. opinion request.
    d. cultural celebration.

True or False

T   F   1. Self-concept has little to do with a child's growth in the ability to use language.

T   F   2. Professionals can sometimes tend to see a child in terms of the disability rather than as a child who happens to have a disability.

T   F   3. If children are comfortable within an environment, they will often seek some responsibility as they grow.

T   F   4. Inviting people with disabilities into the classroom is not a recommended approach to helping children become aware of disabilities.

T   F   5. The opinion request procedure is a good tool for having children elect the best book read on a given day.

Essay and Discussion

1. Describe how a positive self-concept is related to language growth in the young child.

2. Describe a procedure for greeting and saying goodbye to the children in a program. Explain how such a procedure can create positive attitudes.
3. Explain some of the benefits that can occur when young children are given some responsibilities.
4. Design a simulation of a disability to be used with young children. Describe what would be done and the concepts developed in a discussion with the children following the simulation.
5. Describe an activity that would use the opinion request procedure as a tool for enhancing children's self-esteem.

REFERENCES

Cianciolo, P. 1965. Children's literature can affect coping behaviors. *Personnel and Guidance Journal* 43: 897–901.

Cohen, M. 1980. *First grade takes a test*. New York: Dell.

Custer, J.D., and R.T. Osguthorpe. 1983. Improving social acceptance ty training handicapped students to tutor their nonhandicapped peers. *Exceptional Children* 50: 173–174.

Giff, P.R. 1986. *Happy birthday, Ronald Morgan*. New York: Viking Penguin.

Gresham, F.M. 1982. Misguided mainstreaming: The case for social skills training with handicapped children. *Exceptional Children* 48: 422–433.

Kraus, R. 1971. *Leo the late bloomer*. New York: Simon and Schuster.

Maker, C.J. 1982. *Curriculum development for the gifted*. Rockville, Md.: Aspen Systems.

Pinnell, G.S., M.D. Fried, and R.M. Estice. 1990. Reading recovery: Learning how to make a difference. *The Reading Teacher* 43: 282–295.

Rabe, R. 1981. *The balancing girl*. New York: E.P. Dutton.

Roedell, W., N. Jackson, and H. Robinson. *Gifted young children*. New York: Teachers College Press.

Russell, D., and C. Shrodes. 1950. Contributions of research in bibliotherapy to the language arts program. *School Review* 58: 335–392.

Salzer, R. 1986. Why not assume they're all gifted rather than handicapped? *Educational Leadership* 44: 74–77.

Sawyer, W.E., and D.E. Comer. 1991. *Growing up with literature*. Albany, N.Y.: Delmar Publishers Inc.

Van Manen, M. 1986. *The tone of teaching*. Portsmouth, N.H.: Heinemann.

Section 6
Enhancing Creativity

Jack Prelutsky

"It's tough being a kid. People are telling you what to do. Grown ups are always bossing you around. Life is very earnest and difficult. Bigger kids pick on you. Teachers tell you what to do; you have homework, you have tests. You need a friend to help you see the funny side of all the things that are happening to you."

Photograph and text courtesy of Jack Prelutsky, Sylvia Vardell, and The New Advocate, *published by Christopher Gordon Publishers, Inc. Photo courtesy of Evergreen Studios.*

TO THE READER:

The next time you watch a young child draw, color, or work with clay, try to simply observe what is taking place. Don't ask for an explanation of what is being done. Don't try to guess what the picture is about. Don't offer suggestions for improvement. Simply sit and watch as the child creates. What you will see is one of the finest creative acts on earth. If you could locate that same child fourteen or fifteen years later you would find a young adult who most likely no longer engages in what could be called creative activities. Why this happens is no mystery. It is one of the more critical education problems of our time.

This section includes three units dealing with the concept of creativity in education. The first unit discusses creativity as both an abstract concept and a factor to be considered when planning instruction for the young child. One of the key ingredients in creative activities is the willingness to take risks. For young children developing language abilities, the willingness to take risks is a natural part of life. As we have seen, it is through this that children are able to expand their language competence.

The second unit focuses on creativity as experienced within the arts. Music, art, drama, literature, and storytelling are art forms where creativity is both encouraged and expected. Language plays an important role in all of them. With young children, the focus is not on developing skills and techniques associated with the various art forms. Instead, the purpose of a program is to establish possibilities, provide opportunities, and encourage risk taking.

The third unit investigates some of the factors in traditional language arts programs and in rigid school programs that tend to inhibit children's creativity. While there are many exciting new educational practices available, schools tend to be places where change comes slowly. The result is a tendency for schools to continue to see the function of education as dispensing knowledge. This leads to a focus on a correct set of answers to a specific set of questions. An integrated language arts programs breaks out of this mold and enables the child to grow in language ability in creative new ways.

UNIT 17

The Concept of Creativity

UNIT GOALS

After completing this unit, the reader should:

- develop an understanding of the concept of creativity.
- distinguish between the myths and facts of creativity in young children.
- identify some of the major factors often found to characterize creative individuals.
- form a set of beliefs about how to encourage creative behavior in children.

PREVIEW

Life is full of problems. We can agree with this because everyone we know constantly faces an array of problems. Some of those problems are minor. They crop up many times each day, are often solved quite quickly, and are then forgotten. Other problems may seem quite large. They can, at times, seem so complex that they have no solution. They can stretch out for days and weeks and cause us stress and anxiety.

Problems are not confined to grown-ups. Even the youngest children have problems that they must attempt to solve. They may want food and there is none to be found. They may want company but they seem to be alone. Observe a group of young children at play and watch how they address the various problems they are confronted with over a period of time. Think back to one of your own childhood problems. It may have been building a car from a model kit, acquiring a desired toy, or learning to ride a bicycle. Consider how you solved the problem at the time. Were creative approaches used to solve any of the problems?

Think about the great inventions of recent history. Consider the great pieces of art, music, dance, and drama created over the past few hundred years. How did each of these things come about? Why did people create them? Why didn't other people create them or works like them? What was the difference between the great inventors and creators and the rest of the population?

This unit explores the fascinating concept of creativity. It examines how and why great inventions and creations have come about over time. There are several important questions to ask while exploring this unit. When does creativity emerge? Are some people naturally creative? Is creativity genetic or learned? How can we become more creative?

INTRODUCTION

Most adults tend to have certain beliefs about creativity, how it comes about, and who possesses it. Some of these beliefs may be correct. Others may be quite misguided. The latter case is more likely, since creativity is often viewed as a kind of magical gift some people naturally possess that is totally denied to others.

This unit begins by examining what creativity is not. That is, the myths about creativity are explored. This is done for two reasons. First, a few misconceptions about creativity are widely believed to be valid. It is important to identify these for the myths that they are. Second, understanding what creativity is not allows teachers to see more clearly just what does comprise creativity.

The discussion then focuses on several factors that have been found to form a foundation for creativity. It is important for early childhood education professionals to be aware of these factors and how they are revealed in young children. This awareness can help teachers set up opportunities and environments that will enhance creativity.

Finally, a description of how to encourage creativity in young children is provided. This part of the unit clearly links the powerful role that a whole language approach to literacy can play in enhancing the creative behavior of young children. The beliefs and activities found within such an approach are comparable to those that are suggested as supportive of creative behavior in children.

FIGURE 17-1 A child created these designs after playing with fabric scraps.

MYTHS OF CREATIVITY

Several myths surround the concept of creativity. Some are less well known than others. Those myths more widely identified and accepted as valid tend to have a kind of reasonableness to them. The thinking behind them sounds logical, so people tend to accept the explanation as true.

The first myth about creativity is that it is caused by high intelligence. Researchers have actually found that intelligence does not correlate well with creativity (Barron 1969; Wallach 1976a, 1976b). This is not to say that intelligence does not play a role in creativity. Intelligence is a helpful factor in creative behavior. However, it cannot be said that creativity is caused by intelligence alone. Many very intelligent people are not at all creative. On the other hand, some creative individuals possess only average or slightly above average intelligence. Also, some individuals with mental

disabilities have demonstrated the ability to be creative in certain fields.

A second myth surrounding the concept of creativity is that idea production is a characteristic of a creative individual. Idea production is a term used to describe the ability to produce a large number of unusual ideas. As with intelligence, idea production by itself has not been found to correlate particularly well with real world creative accomplishments (Crockenberg 1972; Mansfield and Busse 1981; Wallach 1976a, 1976b).

A third myth about creativity is that talent is a necessary condition for creative behavior in a field of study or an artistic endeavor. Yet it is not unusual to find individuals in various fields with a high degree of technical talent who are not very creative (Perkins 1984). Granted, in the arts a certain amount of technical skill is helpful to the creative person. An individual who knows nothing about playing music is not likely to develop an exciting new piano concerto. On the other hand, the technical ability to play the piano beyond a certain level may be of little value in composing a new piano concerto to an individual who is not creative.

CREATIVITY

Most dictionaries define creativity as the ability to create things that are not borrowed or imitative of something else. This type of definition is of little value to teachers because creativity is better understood when viewed as a process rather than as a collection of products. The myths of creativity help us see what creativity is not. This knowledge can help develop a better understanding of what comprises true creative behavior in both children and adults. First, creativity should not be seen as an either/or characteristic, but as a range of behaviors along a continuum (Perkins 1984). This means that there are more or less creative individuals. If creativity were something people either had or did not have, then all artists could be clustered into two groups. One group would be comprised of the creative geniuses. The other group would be made up of people who could draw or paint but who showed absolutely no imagination in their work. We all know that the world is not like that. There are famous artists, lesser known artists, unknowns, and so forth. The same is true for other areas of art as well as many other fields such as science, mathematics, and business.

Individuals constantly display various degrees of creativity as they go about the business of solving problems. This display of creativity helps to better define just what creativity is. Creativity is thinking that leads to creative results in a given area of endeavor. What are creative results? Basically, creative results are appropriate and original solutions to problems. This is true for art, music, dance, and drama. After all, writing a new piano concerto is basically a problem to be solved. The composer's problem is to create a new or original piece of music that has never been written or played before. The composer must also write a piece of music that is appropriate. Concertos have certain requirements. Pianos are capable of producing certain notes and chords. Certain combinations of musical elements are pleasing to the lis-

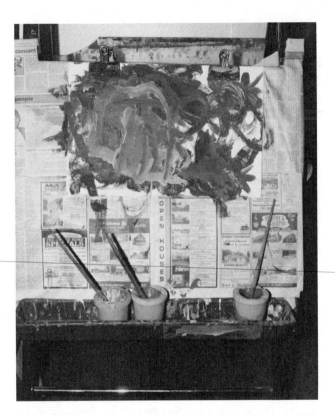

FIGURE 17-2 Easel and paints for exploring creative possibilities

tener. All of these things require the creative composer to produce a musical composition that is original and appropriate. To do this, creative individuals tend to be driven by their values, focus, objectivity, and personal motivation. The strength of these forces tends to determine the degree of creativity an individual is able to demonstrate.

Values and Focus

One of the characteristics that distinguish creative individuals is that they seem to possess certain values. They tend to value something and work diligently toward achieving something related to it (Getzels and Csikszentmihalyi 1976; Perkins 1981). For example, a composer might have a great love for music and work long and hard to compose a song. A poet has a reverence for the power of language and is willing to focus much time on the creation of a new poem. This

FIGURE 17-3 The kindergarten child who created this drawing and story did so with focus and perserverence.

characteristic can be observed as it emerges in children. Young children are intensely interested in their world and themselves. Their "work," which we usually refer to as play, is primarily directed toward learning about themselves and their world. As a result they can be seen working hard at learning about, exploring, and mastering various aspects of their world.

Another characteristic of creative individuals is an intense focus on purpose. They often see the problem they are working on in a way that is fundamentally different from the way less creative individuals would view it. Creative people tend to focus on their goals, explore alternative approaches, and develop a deeper understanding of the nature of the problem. They attempt to comprehend what is required to solve the problem. They are willing to redefine the problem. They are willing to adjust their approach to solving the problem as the situation warrants (Perkins 1984). Less creative individuals tend to approach problems in a logical but rather linear manner. They often perceive problems in terms of their literal surface features rather than in terms of their possible solutions. They seem to be less able to view problems with a depth of understanding (Chi, Feltovich, and Glaser 1981; Schoenfeld and Herrmann 1982).

Objectivity

Another area that distinguishes creative individuals is their ability to maintain a view of problems in an objective manner. They do not buy into a single approach and refuse to budge from it because it is the approach that they developed. Instead, they find it easier to move to other possible solutions. They look at problems in different ways, moving from the abstract to the concrete and back again to the abstract. Creative individuals seem more able to view problems from different roles: inventor, viewer, consumer, reader, writer, and so on (Perkins 1984; Schoenfeld 1982). This ability provides these individuals with more information upon which to act as they go about developing possible solutions to the problem.

The ability to operate in this objective manner requires a couple of different qualities. First, teachers need to be able to accept confusion, uncertainty, and a risk of failure. Each of these is part of the learning

FIGURE 17-4 These people figures were created by a child who perceived the subject from various viewpoints.

process. Creativity is not a clean and precise business. It often requires children to be messy. Second, children need to be able to test ideas and use the feedback to make improvements (Perkins 1981). It is not necessary for each idea to work out as anticipated. The important thing is to try something, see what happens, and learn from the results.

Personal Motivation

Another characteristic that differentiates creative individuals is a sense of personal motivation and personal control over the course of events. Creative people tend to believe that they, rather than others, cause events. They do not see things occurring primarily as a result of luck, chance, or circumstances. In addition, they have a sense of seeing a problem as something they can solve and as something they want to solve (Amabile 1983). In short, they see solving a problem as a worthwhile personal activity for themselves.

Each of the characteristics described seems to play an important role in creative activity. However, each interacts with the others. No one characteristic alone appears to be totally sufficient for developing creativity. In addition, the individual needs to have the intellectual ability to gain a basic understanding of the problem. This does not mean that the individual must be intellectually gifted. It means that an individual must know that the problem exists and have some idea of what the solution to the problem could possibly mean.

ENCOURAGING CREATIVITY

Now that a concept of creativity is established, it is necessary to explore the role of the early childhood educator in fostering creative behaviors in young children. No set of instructions, teacher's manual, or collection of curriculum materials and activities can do this. Commercial materials are available that purport to teach creativity to children of different ages. Training in creative thinking, however, has not been found to be productive (Mansfield, Busse, and Krepelka 1978). This might be because creativity and creative thinking do not exist as isolated abilities. Children and adults are not simply creative; they are creative artists, creative writers, and individuals who think creatively about solving problems in their environ-

ment. Perkins (1984) suggests that the best approach to encouraging creativity is by supporting the attitudes and beliefs that characterize individuals who are seen as more creative. Again, the focus is on values and focus, objectivity, and personal motivation.

Values and Focus

Children need to be acknowledged for their efforts and their values. They need to know that people share their belief in their work. Providing feedback concerning their efforts to fully comprehend a problem informs children that they are doing something of value and that they are seen as competent individuals.

Adults who wish to support the values and focus of children should patiently observe children in numerous tasks and activities. Creativity is not confined to the arts. It is found in all fields: the arts, science, mathematics, language, and so forth. Adults should point out the beauty and helpfulness of the created results and products in each of these fields. In so doing, it is important not to focus solely on the product to the exclusion of the process. Without the creative process employed to solve the problems encountered, there would be no creative product.

Objectivity

Children need to participate in activities where they can develop a sense of objectivity about problems. To do this, teachers and other caregivers can provide opportunities and encourage children to identify problems and projects that require that choices be made. By giving them space and opportunity, children can be encouraged to make decisions. This can be done in both language arts and other curriculum areas.

In committing to this process, teachers need to be willing to let the interests of the children drive the curriculum. Creativity can be a disorderly thing. Teachers must not constantly try to control the situation. Young children, especially, are often not interested in the content provided in a rigid traditional curriculum. Therefore, the group needs to communicate about what is important, about what is worthwhile, and about what project should be undertaken. By participating in these group discussions, children

FIGURE 17-5 A play is created by two children using masks.

see that there are a number of ways of seeing a problem or a project.

Personal Motivation

A sense of personal motivation can be encouraged as well. An understanding of how to approach this can often be achieved through the communications used in developing a sense of objectivity. By learning about the direction of the children's interests, teachers can provide developmentally appropriate tasks and activities that contain a reasonable amount of challenge. This enables children to see the activities as both worthwhile and solvable by them.

When proceeding in this direction certain things should be avoided. The first thing to avoid is a focus upon mechanical tasks. This includes tasks that do not involve any thinking on the part of the child. Such things as lining up a set of blocks, repetitious behaviors, and copying letters do not address the need for the development of personal motivation. Another thing to avoid is tasks that rely on convergent thinking. Convergent thinking is thinking that focuses on developing a single correct answer. In view of this,

traditional programs and texts in language arts or other content areas will be of little value here. The emphasis must be on doing things rather than on learning or memorizing things.

Children need to be encouraged to engage in divergent production. That is, they need to understand that it is perfectly acceptable to create things that are different, things that don't look like anyone else's creations, and things that may have new uses and appearances. To engage in this process requires children to develop creative, fluent, flexible thinking. Providing children with opportunities to engage in this type of thinking helps them understand that the process is both acceptable and valued. When this type of thinking is a normal part of a child's approach to life, there is a natural transfer of this approach to language activities. Children feel more comfortable engaging in activities such as choral speaking, talking about books, role playing, and the integration of arts into the language arts (Parsons 1992). An example of this is book creation. Johnson (1992) describes a comprehensive process for encouraging young children to create books by learning how to incorporate such

> Cousin Maureen
> How many holes do you have in your ears? four How many earrings do you have on your right ear? one
> How many earrings do you have on your left ear? zero what color eyes do you have? green what color hair do you have? brown

FIGURE 17-6 This dialogue between a child and an adult was recreated by the child after a conversation.

FIGURE 17-7 Fabric teddy bears constructed by children while observing the teacher create a model.

pects of the product. How will the story be recorded so that it can be remembered? Who will record it? At this point, children might need to identify certain activities that can be accomplished through cooperative learning groups. Rather than give assignments to children, the teacher might inquire about who will be responsible for certain things. What materials are needed? Who will get them? Who will draw the illustrations? Who will put the actual wording of the story together?

The key role of the teacher in this situation is that of an organizer, an encourager, a provider of opportunities, and a believer in the ability of children to solve problems. Will everything proceed smoothly in such a situation? Most likely it will not. Remember, creativity is an experimental process. There may be

diverse activities as writing, page design, illustration, binding, and the study of paper technology.

Model Activity

Now that a general sense of how to encourage creative behavior has been described, it might be useful to see how it can be applied to an early childhood language arts activity. Imagine a group of four- or five-year-olds in an early childhood program. It is circle time, and the children have been sharing information about the pets that they either own or would like to own. The teacher, sensing an opportunity to encourage a creative activity, asks the children if they would like to create a story, poem, or play about some of the pets. When the children respond positively to this idea, the teacher helps them generate questions related to the task, but neither gives nor expects specific answers.

The teacher might first help the children come to the realization that certain general parameters need to be established. Will it be a humorous story? A serious story? A story about caring for a pet? Who will write the story? Will it be an oral story rather than a written story? When these decisions have been made, the teacher might guide, not lead, the children to the point where they make decisions about the content of their story. Whose pets will be in the story? Where will the story take place? Will there be a problem or plot in the story? Will there be people in the story? The next step might be to help the children identify as-

FIGURE 17-8 This child is learning to solve an artistic problem while tie-dyeing a shirt.

many false starts, some seemingly wasted time, some duplicated effort, and a fair amount of confusion. The teacher must model appropriate behaviors for dealing with all of these things. The emphasis is on involving children in decision making and in seeing themselves as competent problem solvers. It should be clear at this point that many of the characteristics related to the development of creativity in children are similar to the beliefs underlying an integrated approach to language arts. Both have the goal of developing children as independent learners with a sense of competence and personal worth.

SUMMARY

Several myths surround the concept of creativity. Intelligence, idea production, and talent in a particular field are often thought of as being closely correlated with creativity. Research has not found this to necessarily be the case. While each of these may be somewhat helpful to a creative individual, creativity cannot be attributed solely to any of them.

Creativity is described as thinking that leads to creative results. While some people might be identified as creative individuals, the ability to be creative is best seen as something that operates along a continuum. That is, it is not something that people either do or do not possess. It is something that may be possessed in degrees. In addition, creativity usually emerges as people address problems in their lives. The problem may be learning to draw a teddy bear, how to ride a bicycle, or how to compose a piece of music.

Three different characteristics believed to enhance creative behavior are frequently observed in creative people. The first is values and focus. Creative individuals see their work and their achievement as having value. They also have the ability to focus on their purpose and goals. Second, creative individuals possess a sense of objectivity. While they are emotionally committed to their tasks, they do not cling to a single possible solution while rejecting other possibilities. They accept the uncertainty that is often found when attempting to look at a problem from differing perspectives. Third, creative individuals possess personal motivation. They believe that they, rather than luck, chance, or others, control events in their environment.

Developing creative behavior is viewed as a process of recognizing and supporting young children when they demonstrate the three characteristics described. Teachers can provide situations and activities that tend to make it more likely that these characteristics will emerge. Children should be helped to see that creativity transcends a number of fields of endeavor, not just the arts. The process by which creative results come about is critically important. Acknowledgement of the finished product is fine, but children need to be aware of how they accomplished what they did. Children can be assisted in becoming more aware of the process by involving them in the decision-making process that is used as the process continues.

Finally, a model activity was described. The activity demonstrated how a teacher might bring in knowledge about creativity while engaging children in a language development activity. A key factor was observed in the fact that the teacher kept using questions that required divergent answers. That is, there was not a right or wrong answer to the teacher's questions. Any number of possible answers would have been acceptable.

Questions and Activities for Discussion and Review

Multiple Choice
1. Creativity has been found to be consistently and highly correlated with
    a. intelligence.
    b. idea production.

    c. technical talent.

    d. none of the above

2. Creativity is a

    a. thinking process.

    b. tangible product.

    c. a special kind of intelligence.

    d. all of the above

3. A willingness to redefine a problem is a characteristic of an individual who tends to be

    a. more creative.

    b. less creative.

    c. more intelligent.

    d. less intelligent.

4. Less creative individuals tend to see problems

    a. more abstractly.

    b. from different perspectives.

    c. from different roles.

    d. more concretely.

5. In terms of their environment, more creative individuals tend to feel that things occur

    a. because others want them to occur.

    b. through their own efforts.

    c. by chance.

    d. by being lucky.

6. Creativity can be seen as an important part of

    a. art.

    b. science.

    c. mathematics.

    d. all of the above

7. The most appropriate problems and projects for encouraging creativity are those that

    a. require that choices be made.

    b. have a single correct solution.

    c. require a specific problem solving approach.

    d. all of the above

True or False

T   F   1. Creativity is basically the same as intelligence.

T   F   2. Creativity is not an ability that people either do or do not possess.

T   F   3. Creative individuals tend to value something and work toward achieving something related to it.

T   F   4. Less creative individuals tend to believe that events are controlled primarily by others or by chance.

T   F   5. Children need a large number of activities that follow a careful, step-by-step procedure in order to develop creativity.

Essay and Discussion

1. Identify and discuss an individual who has demonstrated creativity without possessing a high degree of technical talent.

2. Explain the difference between idea production and creative thinking.
3. Explain the differences between less creative and more creative individuals.
4. Describe the way more creative individuals tend to see their ability to control their environment.
5. Observe a group of preschool children and identify the activities and behaviors believed to demonstrate creativity.

REFERENCES

Amabile, T.M. 1983. *The social psychology of creativity.* New York: Springer-Verlag.

Barron, F. 1969. *Creative person and creative process.* New York: Holt, Rinehart & Winston.

Chi, M., P. Feltovich, and R. Glaser. 1981. Categorization and representation of physics problems by experts and novices. *Cognitive Science* 5: 121–152.

Crockenberg, S.B. 1972. Creativity tests: A boon or a boondoggle for education? *Review of Educational Research* 42: 27–45.

Getzels, J., and M. Csikszentmihalyi. 1976. *The creative vision: A longitudinal study of problem finding in art.* New York: John Wiley & Sons.

Johnson, P. 1992. *A book of one's own.* Portsmouth, N.H.: Heinemann.

Mansfield, R.S., and T.V. Busse. 1981. *The psychology of creativity and discovery.* Chicago: Nelson-Hall.

Mansfield, R.S., T.V. Busse, and E.J. Krepelka. 1978. The effectiveness of creativity training. *Review of Educational Research* 48: 517–536.

Parsons, L. 1992. *Poetry, themes, & activities.* Portsmouth, N.H.: Heinemann.

Perkins, D.N. 1981. *The mind's best work.* Cambridge, Mass.: Harvard University Press.

Perkins, D.N. 1984. Creativity by design. *Educational Leadership* 42: 18–25.

Schoenfeld, A.H. 1982. Measures of problem-solving performance and of problem-solving instruction. *Journal for Research in Mathematical Education* 13: 31–49.

Schoenfeld, A.H., and D.J. Herrmann. 1982. Problem perception and knowledge structure in expert and novice mathematical problem solvers. *Journal of Experimental Psychology: Learning, Memory and Cognition* 8: 484–494.

Wallach, M.A. 1976a. Psychology of talent and graduate education. In *Individuality in Learning*, ed. Samuel Messick & Associates. San Francisco, Calif.: Jossey-Bass.

Wallach, M.A. 1976b. Tests tell us little about talent. *American Scientist* 64: 57–63.

UNIT 18

Integration of the Arts

UNIT GOALS

After completing this unit, the reader should:

- recognize art, music, dance, and drama as powerful artistic and communication forms.
- understand the benefits of integrating the arts into a language arts program for young children.
- develop a set of instructional activities that integrate the arts with language.
- become aware of the children's literature that can be used within the process of integrating the arts and language.

PREVIEW

Think for a moment about those positive aspects of a culture from which pleasure is derived. It does not matter which culture. There is a commonality between all of them. The arts, though they may take different forms from culture to culture, stand out in their importance. The arts embody beauty, emotion, and creativity. Those who excel in the arts are usually held in high regard in any culture. Most people enjoy the arts as providers, as audience, or as both.

The arts do not exist apart from a culture. This is also true for language. They are both closely tied to the culture from which they emerge. African dance, Native American art, Japanese drama, and Latin American music are all meaningfully connected to their cultures. They all contain a certain beauty. They all deal with the emotional aspects of human existence. They all convey a meaningful message within that culture.

As teachers consider these relationships, certain ideas and questions may come to mind. This unit develops and addresses some of these concepts and questions: What are the benefits of integrating the various art forms with an early childhood language arts program? What is needed for young children to meaningfully participate in these art forms? How does a teacher integrate these art forms into classroom instruction and activities? Are there any books for young children that can be used to help make the experience meaningful for young children?

INTRODUCTION

This unit extends the examination of encouraging creativity in young children. The arts provide a particularly useful opportunity for children to explore creative possibilities. They are traditionally areas that are accepting of diversity and divergent thinking.

FIGURE 18-1 Face painting is an art form that is both fun and understandable.

Two general subjects are presented within this unit. The first is an investigation of the relationship between the arts and language. People develop an awareness of both the arts and language at a very young age. This awareness can remain a lifelong area of growth.

The second subject is an examination of four artistic formats. These include music, art, drama, and dance. Each is addressed in terms of the benefits of integrating them with the language arts. Activities for integrating them are discussed. Finally, numerous books for young children that address that particular artistic realm are described. Literature and storytelling, in fact, can be considered art forms as well.

The fact that each artistic area is discussed separately does not mean that they should be separated in early childhood programs. They are all related to culture, to language, and to each other. Different art forms are often combined. Opera is a combination of literature, drama, and music. Songs comprise the art forms of music and literature. Ballet combines drama, music, and dance. Modern dance combines art, music, drama, and dance. Each of these formats, much like language, is focused on creating meaningful communication between two individuals. The ballet dancer tells a story to the audience. The musician seeks to inspire a particular feeling or emotion in the listener. The lives of all who are involved in the arts, whether as artists or audience, are richer for the experience.

LANGUAGE AND THE ARTS

An underlying assumption of an integrated language arts program is that language is integrated in most of life's experiences. This is true for the arts as well. Just as language is intertwined with various art forms, the arts are closely connected with the everyday life of the world of children. Musical notes are read much like the words of a story, and oral language has a natural rhythm much like that of a song (Smardo 1984). With even very young children, studies have shown that the cries of babies consist of twelve sounds that are accompanied by specific rhythms such as those of sucking, babbling, and sneezing (Fridman 1973). Other studies show that babies have perfect timing as well as the ability to learn to match pitch (Gordon 1979; Miller 1981). It is not surprising, therefore, that music is frequently an integral component of many methods for teaching children to read (Fitzgerald 1983).

The arts are an important segment of the informal parts of an early childhood program as well. During free play children explore the possibilities of musical toys as instruments and musical instruments as toys. As they play, they sing, chant, hum, play homemade and pretend instruments, and participate as an audience for others (Lamme 1990). The use of music as an accompaniment to work and play is presented in stories for children. *The Piney Woods Traveler* (Shannon 1981) describes a peddler who sings a chant as he walks along the road. *Busy Monday Morning* (Domanska 1985) is a picture book that shares a chant sung by Polish farmers to help make their toil seem lighter.

FIGURE 18-2 Art and literature are combined in this story of "Cinderella." *From* The Child's Fairy Tale Book, *by Kay Chorao. Reprinted courtesy of E.P. Dutton.*

Without realizing it, young children often integrate the arts and language in a natural manner. Smardo (1984) described such an occurrence that began at circle time. A young girl dramatized a recent ride on a merry-go-round for the rest of the children. She created a picture in the mind of her audience through the use of drama and storytelling. The teacher followed this child's lead by later sharing the book *Carousel*, by Donald Crews (1982). This integrated literature and art into the environment. This was followed by children listening to a tape of calliope music while they created pictures of a merry-go-round.

Another example described by Smardo (1984) illustrates the integration of language, art, music, and dance. It begins at a weekly preschool story hour at the public library. For this session, the librarian has selected the book *Boom-de-Boom,* by Elaine Edelman (1980). It is the story of a jolly lady who dances all around the town while accompanied by her dog, cat, and a red geranium. At first the people who see her stop and stare. Then they join the parade as it continues around the town. By the time the book ends, joggers, children, policemen, and the mayor have all joined the parade. Following the reading of the story, the children re-created the experience by parading around the room while chanting "1–2-3, boom-de-boom" and playing rhythm band instruments.

Different cultures possess unique artistic forms that are integrated with language as well. Suskind and Phillip (1984) describe such an example as they relate their work with the Yupik-speaking Eskimos in Alaska. Oral storytelling is an important part of this culture. Children learn at an early age to engage in this format by integrating it with art. While telling the story, the child sketches figures in mud with a plastic ceremonial knife. This simultaneous drawing and storytelling is similar to children telling stories with puppets or a flannelboard. The increased focus of children on the storytelling and drawing decreases their inhibitions while at the same time allowing them to practice their language skills.

MUSIC

When we think of the arts and young children, music is perhaps the first area that comes to mind. Everyone remembers the chants, songs, and jumprope rhymes of childhood. Children seem fascinated by music and are usually eager to participate in this art form. Early childhood educators should be aware of the benefits, activities, and literature that can help them integrate music into a language arts program.

Benefits

Perhaps the most important benefit to using music is that it involves the opportunity to learn and use language. Songs are learned. Songs are sung. As children's language ability increases, songs can be created and shared with others. Music is also an important tool for encouraging sharing and cooperative behavior. It requires children to speak, sing, and listen carefully. To increase the pleasure and success of the experience, children need to become aware of the roles that they and others have in the activity.

Activities

It is important for children to focus specifically on music. This is often done in a special music class where children learn basic information about songs, rhythm, and instruments. The most practical approach for young children, however, is integrating music within the rest of the curriculum through thematic units (Gamberg, Kwak, Hutchings, and Altheim 1988; Lamme 1990; Moss 1990). This can be approached in three ways (Lamme 1990). The first approach would feature a thematic unit on music. Such a unit might include learning about musical instruments, singing, performance, and how music makes us feel. A second approach occurs when teachers integrate music into other thematic units of content area study. Such units might include science (sound), social studies (cultural songs), mathematics (rhythms), and language arts (lyrics, reading music). A third approach results when music is integrated into other thematic units where it can play a meaningful role.

Performances are another activity for integrating music. Children enjoy performing and participating as an audience for the performances of others. Younger children can perform using rhythm instruments. Older siblings who have learned to play an instrument can be invited to perform as well. These performances provide an opportunity for children to develop the schema for performances as a literacy event (Lamme 1990). In preparation for the performance, the group can print tickets, draw advertising posters, and learn about the person who composed the music. Books related to the musical instrument can be used to prepare the children for the performance.

A science unit on sound provides still another activity to help children integrate music. With young children, using music as a tool for developing an initial understanding of sound is particularly appropriate. Concepts such as pitch, tone, and volume can be discussed by older children. Younger children will enjoy learning about the different sounds animals

FIGURE 18-3 Peter Amidon, performer/teacher, shows children how creativity, music, literature, and storytelling can be combined. *Reprinted courtesy of Peter Amidon, 6 Willow Street, Brattleboro, Vt.*

make. All children can relate to the different sounds they hear in nature. Night animals, the weather, the wind, and the ocean all make distinctive sounds that are naturally integrated into our very existence.

Literature Related to Music

There are probably more books for young children related to music than to any of the other arts. They cover a range of topics including performance, instruments, child musicians, singing, and music related to other arts and topics.

Singing.

Many book titles are related to song and singing. Every early childhood program should have one or more songbooks containing a large number of traditional and contemporary children's songs. They can be used as a resource for thematic units, activities, and transitions. Children's books about singing in-

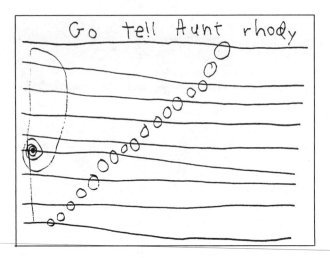

FIGURE 18-4 This drawing was created by a child who understood that music has both an oral and visual part.

clude *Sing, Pierrot, Sing* (dePaola 1983), *The Brementown Musicians* (Grimm and Grimm 1980), *The Little Moon Theater* (Haas 1981), *The Cat Who Loved to Sing* (Hogrogian 1988), *Looking for Daniella* (Kroll 1988), *Bravo, Minski* (Yorinks 1988), *Airmail to the Moon* (Birdseye 1988), *Jolly Mon* (Buffett and Buffett 1988), and *Granpa* (Burningham 1984).

Other books that address the enjoyment of singing include *Chester and Uncle Willoughby* (Edwards 1987), *The Maggie B* (Haas 1975), *Alfie Gives a Hand* (Hughes 1983), *By the Light of the Silvery Moon* (Langner 1983), *Lizard's Song* (Shannon 1981), and *Follow the Drinking Gourd* (Winter 1988).

Types of Music.

A number of picture books are available related to various types of music. Karla Kuskin's *The Philharmonic Gets Dressed* (1982) provides a humorous look at how the musicians in an orchestra prepare for a concert. Other books dealing with orchestral music include *Pages of Music* (Johnston 1988) and *I Like Music* (Komaiko 1987). An effective way to introduce young children to orchestral music is to combine playing the music with a reading of Prokofiev's *Peter and the Wolf* (1985). *Song and Dance Man* (Ackerman 1988) is a touching and nostalgic look at vaudeville. Band and dance band music are portrayed in *The Bunny Play*

(Leedy 1988), *Frog Goes to Dinner* (Mayer 1974), and *The Relatives Came* (Rylant 1985). Old time and ragtime music are an integral part of *Ragtime Tumpie* (Schroeder 1989) and *Ty's One Man Band* (Walter 1980). Young children will quickly identify the carousel music featured in *Up and Down on the Merry-Go-Round* (Martin and Archambault 1988).

Instruments.

Musical instruments are also depicted in many picture books for young children. Violin and fiddle are featured in *The Moon's Revenge* (Aiken 1987), *Zoo Song* (Bottner 1987), *The Maggie B* (Haas 1975), *Katie Morag and the Two Grandmothers* (Hedderwick 1985), and *Barn Dance* (Martin and Archambault 1987). Other string instruments that are acknowledged in books include the guitar in *Looking for Daniella* (Kroll 1988) and the mandolin in Tomie dePaola's *Sing, Pierrot, Sing* (1983). Woodwind and brass instruments are found in *The Paper Crane* (Bang 1985), *The Little Moon Theater* (Haas 1981), *Elbert's Bad Word* (Wood 1988), *All in the Early Morning* (NicLeodhas 1963), and *Ben's Trumpet* (Isadora 1979). Harmonicas are used in *The Scarebird* (Fleischman 1987) and *Apt. 3* (Keats 1971). Piano music forms a basis for the stories in *Dear Daddy* (Dupasquier 1985), *Rondo in C* (Fleischman 1988), and *A Piano for Julie* (Schick 1954). Even accordian music is a part of Vera Williams's *Music,*

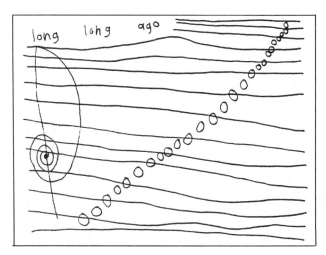

FIGURE 18-5 Song "created" by a young composer

Music for Everyone (1984) and *Something Special for Me* (1983).

Nature.

The first sounds children hear are those from their environment. As described previously, nature provides natural sounds, rhythms, and beats. Many books can be used when integrating this part of science into an integrated language arts unit. Among the possibilities are *Georgia Music* (Griffith 1986), *17 Kings and 42 Elephants* (Mahy 1987), *Listen to the Rain* (Martin and Archambault 1988), *Nicholas Cricket* (Maxner 1989), *Nightdances* (Skofield 1981), *Sophie's Knapsack* (Stock 1988), and *The Song* (Zolotow 1982).

ART

The world of art includes all of the visual arts such as drawing, photography, painting, and sculpture. Drawing is the art form children find particularly engaging. As we have seen, it is an important part of the language arts, particularly as it is related to emerging writing. Sculpturing with clay, sand, and mud can also provide young children with a unique opportunity for self-expression. As with music, there are a number of benefits, activities, and books associated with art for young children.

Benefits

One of the critical benefits of using art with young children is that it can encourage positive attitudes and values. Creating with pencil, crayon, or paint can provide children with a sense of control over both the medium and their environment. Art provides many opportunities for developing and practicing fine motor skills. Children must constantly use their hands to control pencils, crayons, scissors, paint brushes, and clay. It affords children an additional outlet for expressing themselves. Ideas or events that cannot be put into words can sometimes be put into pictures. This enlarges the possibilities young children have for expressing themselves.

Art is also fun. It is an activity that has many possibilities for parallel play and cooperative play. It can be used as an effective tool for fostering communications between children in a natural play setting.

Engaging in artwork furnishes children with an op-

FIGURE 18-6 Art can be a cooperative activity with social interaction opportunities.

portunity to engage in creative behavior. The creation of any piece of artwork is basically a problem to be solved. The creative act allows each of us to look at problems from different perspectives. Children can attempt to solve these problems in several different ways. They can create alternatives and make decisions about how they will proceed.

Activities

Aesthetic decision making is a powerful activity that can help children see the possibilities of creative expression. It can be used with young children to show them that there is often no single correct way to create art. Rather, art has different meanings and values for different individuals. To set up the activity, place several pieces of artwork around the border of the room. The actual number should be based on how many pieces the teacher feels the children can deal with at a given time. For three-year-olds, three pieces of art might be sufficient. For five-year-olds, up to ten pieces might be used. More important than numbers is that several different pieces are used. The first time this activity is used, it will be helpful not to include five pictures of trees, for example. At a later point, such a display might be considered.

When the pieces of art are in place, the teacher explains to the children that they are going to try to

FIGURE 18-7 Self-portrait by a preschooler. Note the name written in dots.

decide some things about each of the pieces of art. This is done by giving children a set of cards that have various symbols on one side of them. The number of cards should be based on the teacher's perception of how many cards the children can handle. The children then place each of their cards face down in front of the piece of art they feel the card goes with best. For example, a smile face on a card might mean "This piece of art makes me feel happy." A picture of a dollar bill on a card might mean "I think that this piece of art would cost a lot of money." A picture of a clock on a card might mean "I think it took a long time to draw or paint this piece of art." A picture of a sad face on a card might mean "This piece of art makes me feel sad."

When all of the cards have been placed face down in front of the different pieces of art, the teacher and children move from piece to piece. At each piece of artwork, the cards are turned over and the ideas are discussed. For example, if a single piece of art has many smile face cards in front of it, the group can discuss why the artwork seems to make many people feel happy. If there are no cards with clocks on them, the group might discuss why it might not take a long time to create that piece of artwork. It should be

noted that cards with the message of good versus bad are not used. Instead, cards that will encourage children to think and justify their attitudes and beliefs are used. This will help children understand that art is more than good or bad. Art has many qualities, and the creative process has a number of different possibilities.

There are many opportunities for engaging children in art activities within the language arts. The most obvious of these are drawing and writing. Children can use art to draw stories, to illustrate stories they have written, to respond to stories that have been read to them, and to accompany their own oral telling of stories. Teachers need to model and encourage each of these possibilities.

It is important to provide ample materials for chil-

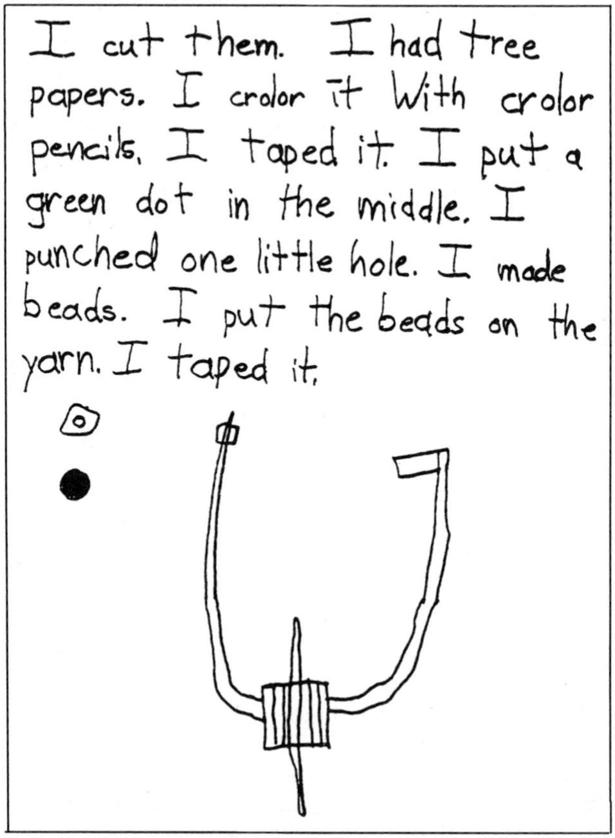

I cut them. I had tree papers. I crolor it with crolor pencils. I taped it. I put a green dot in the middle. I punched one little hole. I made beads. I put the beads on the yarn. I taped it.

FIGURE 18-8 Recollection of the creation of a necklace, written by a young child.

dren to use. Adults must step back from traditional notions of art and art materials and recognize that there are an untold number of possibilities for using non-traditional materials. These materials should be made available to children. It is not necessary to provide all materials all of the time, but it is helpful to rotate materials so that new possibilities are always available. Scraps from other projects and activities are one possibility. This might include construction paper, pipe cleaners, glue, paste, craft sticks, glitter, buttons, and beads. Natural objects that might be provided include acorns, leaves, peanut shells, pebbles, sand, twigs, seashells, and seaweed. Another possibility is a collection of packaging materials such as yogurt containers, styrofoam packing, cereal boxes, and cardboard containers. It is not necessary to show children how these can be used. If they are shown an example, children might tend to view that as the only possibility. There is no right or wrong way for children to use leaves or pieces of macaroni in a piece of art. If they use them in any way that is constructive or pleasing to themselves, they have used them well.

Literature Related to Art

One of the finest picture books on art is Tomie dePaola's *The Art Lesson* (1989). It is particularly useful because it transcends all of the arts. In an autobiographical tale, it clearly brings forth the creative aspects of the artist. It exemplifies the purposefulness, the values, the motivations, and the frustrations of the young artist. The book shows the need for adults to respond to the creative needs of young children by allowing them to be messy, by encouraging their attempts at creating meaning through art, and by tolerating and accepting differences in children who may be a bit different. Such values are clearly appropriate for anyone working with young children regardless of their talents and limitations.

Another book by Tomie dePaola, describing how the Indian paintbrush wildflower got its name, is *The Legend of the Indian Paintbrush* (1988). It tells the story of how Little Gopher brings the vibrant colors of the sunset to the earth. Using watercolors to create the stylized illustration, Tomie dePaola also uses the tale to introduce children to native American folklore. In *The Chalk Box Kid* (1987), Clyde Bulla portrays the role that a child's artistic vision and imagination play

FIGURE 18-9 A spinner could be a welcome classroom visitor who introduces children to yarn as a medium for creative activities.

as they lead to both acceptance and friendship. Another book that celebrates the unique vision of the individual artist is *Alice the Artist* (1988), by Martin Waddell. While Alice is creating her painting, she is influenced by the remarks of each passerby to change her picture. Finally, she declares her intention to have her work reflect her vision and is clearly happy with the results of her decision.

Children will empathize with the sense of self-esteem felt by Gregory the dog in *Frosted Glass* (1987), by Denys Cazet. Often viewed as a bit different from the others, he is justifiably proud when he is recognized for his artistic and imaginative creations. Another art related book with an animal as the main character is *Oh, What a Mess* (1988), by Hans Wilhelm. Franklin the pig's talent as a painter provides him with a way to develop friendships despite his concern over the mess in which his family and his home are usually found.

Concepts are frequently introduced and depicted in books related to art. The concept of color is developed in M. B. Goffstein's *Artists' Helpers Enjoy the Evening* (1987). Using both French and English, the story personifies five different crayons and takes the reader along on their after-dark adventures. The concept of a museum as a place to view great works of art is introduced in Posy Simmonds *Lulu and the Flying Babies* (1986). The story combines fantasy, art, and the work of the master artists. Another book that depicts a visit to an art museum is Laurene Krasny Brown's *Visiting the Art Museum* (1986). The illustrations cover art periods from the primitive to the era of pop art.

The visual and literary arts are often combined in children's literature. Vera Williams does this in *Cherries and Cherry Pits* (1986) by having the girl in the story tell and draw stories about four of her neighbors. Cynthia Rylant accomplishes this as well in *All I See* (1988). In her story, she depicts the growing friendship between a shy boy and a lakeside artist that results in the celebration of the creative potential in all of us. Both of these books contain evocative watercolor illustrations.

Since art is a universal concept, it provides a natural basis for introducing children to other cultures. An excellent selection to begin this is Barbara Steiner's *Whale Brother* (1988). The story is about Omu, an Inuit boy who wishes to become a master carver. He is frustrated by his efforts because the small animals he creates in ivory seem to lack life. When he spends time nursing a dying killer whale he learns of the patience he must develop to breathe life into his carvings.

DRAMA

Drama encompasses a number of different forms. For adults it can mean a television situation comedy, a broadway musical, a play performed at a local theater, or an opera. It is easily recognized that these examples make use of other art forms such as literature and music. The forms that drama assumes for children are equally varied and often related to those aimed at adults. Puppet shows, musical shows, plays, and creative dramatics can be effectively used with young children.

Benefits

Because there is a certain amount of entertainment value in a dramatic presentation, children are often attentive to short plays and theatrical productions. As a result, they are able to learn a variety of ideas and concepts (Goldberg 1982). The cultural content of the play pervades any production. The audience can learn things about the history, psychology, and culture depicted in the play's content. The conventions of the theater are reinforced as well. This might include such things as the curtain going up, the fact that actors and actresses talk to each other, and the applause of the audience at the conclusion of the show. Children can also further develop their own sense of ethics as a result of theater. In most cultures, theater often involves a depiction of right and wrong behavior for that culture.

Language development is another direct benefit of using drama with young children. By involving children directly in dramatic activities, oral language development is encouraged (Stewig 1982). By providing opportunities for participation, children can be challenged to create oral dialogue spontaneously, to develop a tolerance for dialects, and to explore the expressive qualities of their voices. Listening skills are enhanced through dramatic activity as well. Basic listening skills are used and practiced in order for the dramatic dialogue to continue. Children also receive valuable feedback concerning the effectiveness of their own utterances by listening to the responses of other children.

Children learn about the nonverbal components of communication that account for a large percentage of the communicated message through involvement in dramatic activities (Lefevre 1970). Most of us use gestures, facial expressions, arm movements, and eye movement as part of our communication repertoire. However, we tend not to use them consciously. We can challenge children to incorporate them in their oral language by asking them specific questions. How would the little kitten look when it saw the big dog? How would the monster say that? Having different

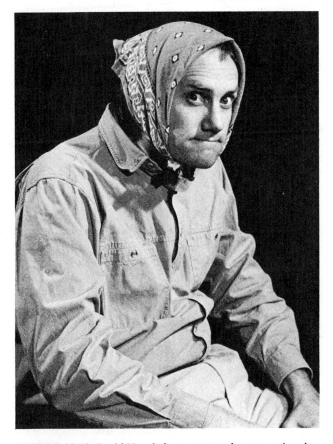

FIGURE 18-10 David Novak demonstrates the connections between storytelling, drama, and literature. *Reprinted courtesy of David Novak, dba A Telling Experience, P.O. Box 620327, San Diego, Calif.*

individuals respond to these questions can help children avoid stereotypes.

Another benefit of dramatic activities for young children, related to non-verbal aspects of communication, is the opportunity to become more aware of their bodies in space. Children are always in one environment or another, but they do not tend to focus on viewing themselves from a detached position. As a result, they may not think about the effects their movements might have on others. Through activities such as creative dramatics, children can begin to develop a sense of their physical relationship to their world.

The non-verbal aspects of language can be partic-

ularly important when including children with disabilities in the program, particularly when those children are deaf. Special education teachers often use sign language when working with children with disabilities. The approach is sometimes referred to as a total communication method. This means that as many of the senses as possible will be used within the communication process. Dramatic activities are particularly effective for incorporation of sign language (Brown 1988).

Activities

For most young children, the possibility of producing and putting on a play may be somewhat unrealistic. It should be remembered, of course, that the purpose of using dramatic activities with young children is not to produce plays on stage. The purpose is to help children broaden their opportunities for language growth. Given this, the most appropriate activities are probably found in what is called creative dramatics.

Creative dramatics should not be viewed so much as a thing but as a process through which children communicate (Sawyer and Leff 1982). Whether it is a message, feeling, or emotion, the environment for creative dramatics should be free from grades and criticism. The process is fundamentally different from putting on a play. Play production is imitative, while creative dramatics is creative.

Pantomime.

The pantomime is the most basic element of creative dramatics. While it may look relatively simple when done by an expert mime, it provides a task that has tremendous room for growth. When using pantomime with children, the focus should be on developing a sense of self and objects. Children can be exposed to the sense of size, weight, shape, position, and texture of both themselves and objects in their environment. The teacher can be involved in the process as both a model and as a participant when working with pairs or small groups of children.

Modeling the use of pantomime helps children see that they communicate by both their language and their actions. Pantomime uses only physical actions. The activity requires concentration as part of the enjoyment. Children learn that they must attend to the message their bodies are sending if they are to be understood. For example, they must learn that when they pantomime the opening of a door, the doorknob will be found at a certain height. They will learn that a basketball is carried differently than a suitcase. They will learn that they look different when moving a chair than when moving a handful of raisins.

Improvisation.

Another element of creative dramatics is improvisation. Its use of voice makes it more sophisticated than pantomime. This allows a wider range of possible messages to be communicated. With both pantomime and improvisation it is best to begin simply and then move to more sophisticated tasks. With improvisation, teachers may wish to begin with character improvisation. A child may want to assume the role of a favorite literary character, for example, and portray that individual for a minute or two. Following this, improvisation of a thought or a feeling might be tried. This might include the feelings of happiness, sadness, fear, and excitement. Eventually improvisations using two or more children portraying familiar events might be developed. These may include buying candy at the store, getting a measles shot at the doctor's, and eating breakfast.

Materials.

Creative dramatics can be encouraged by providing an environment that contains a number of props and materials that can be used for improvisation. A number of these props will ordinarily be found within many early childhood education programs. Teachers can encourage creative dramatics activities by collecting these materials into a single location and by modeling some of their uses in an improvisation.

Schickedanz (1982) identifies four different themes and some of the materials that might be included for each. For a house theme, the materials include various pieces of child-size furniture, a tablecloth, flowers, dolls, blankets, clothing, plastic fruits and vegetables, cooking utensils, play telephones, play-dough, and writing materials. Materials for a fire station theme include firefighter hats, old shirts, boots, a bell, play telephones, flashlights, maps, a short piece of

garden hose, and a large cardboard box to serve as a house or station. A doctor's office theme would need materials such as white shirts, toy stethoscopes and other medical props, a flashlight, a telephone, dolls, an appointment book, an eye chart, and a poster showing the parts of a body or a skeleton. A grocery store theme would include materials such as shelving units, empty food boxes, plastic fruits and vegetables, small grocery carts, a toy cash register, paper bags, play money, old shirts, a kitchen scale, newspaper grocery advertisements, and writing materials.

Literature Related to Drama

Drama is naturally a component of literature. It is often performed on stage, but it is conceived in an author's mind and committed to paper well before it arrives on the stage. Some drama, of course, is not necessarily meant to be performed. Chris Van Allsburg's *The Z Was Zapped* (1987) is a case in point. Although it may be a bit too violent for some, this play in twenty-six acts presents each letter of the alphabet as the recipient of some unpleasant fate. The reader is encouraged to guess what has happened to each of the letters as they are presented in dramatic black-and-white drawings.

Books about children in plays are available as well. In *The Berenstain Bears Get Stage Fright* (1988), Stan and Jan Berenstain illustrate how different children can feel more or less inhibited about their ability to perform before an audience. In ironic fashion, the authors show how quickly those feelings can be reversed from the time of rehearsal to the time of the actual performance. A similar book, to which young children will easily be able to relate, is Miriam Cohen's *Starring First Grade* (1985). The fear and helpfulness of the children in the story are handled with care and thoughtfulness. In *The Bunny Play* (1988), Loreen Leedy provides an excellent overall view of what happens in the production of a play. In this story, the bunnies put on a performance of "Little Red Riding Hood" from the moment of tryouts until the final performance. A glossary of theater terms is provided for vocabulary development.

The concept of drama as illusion is developed in Eloise Greenfield's *Grandpa's Face* (1988). In this book, designed for preschoolers, Tamika experiences the powerful effect an actor can have upon an audi-

FIGURE 18-11 A children's librarian and a theater director combine talents to help children experience a theatrical reading of a story.

ence. While watching her grandfather prepare for an acting role, she is frightened by the genuine frightfulness he is able to project. Sensing her fear, the grandfather reassures Tamika of his unending love and caring for her. A similar look into the world of acting is presented from a child's viewpoint by Brooke Goffstein in *An Actor* (1987). Using crayon drawings and a brief text, the book explores the life of an actor.

DANCE

While dance may initially seem like a purely physical activity, there is a communication aspect to it as well. Ballet and modern dance both attempt to communicate with the audience. They might tell a story such as "Swan Lake" or express an emotion such as happiness, fear, or love. Dance is nearly always accompanied by music that helps to communicate the message. Besides being one of the most creative forms of self-expression, it is also one of the most natural (Carlson 1989).

Benefits

For young children, there are a number of benefits to integrating dance into an early childhood program. The first benefit is that it provides an orga-

nized activity to develop gross motor skills. It helps children examine the possible movements they are able to make with their bodies. They have an opportunity to follow directions and coordinate their movements with those of other children. Second, they can explore the possibilities of communication through dance. This is somewhat similar to the activity of using pantomime to communicate an emotion, but this activity will be accompanied by music. The attempt to communicate an emotion through dance forms a starting point for identifying feelings. A third benefit is that dance provides a medium for developing language. Concepts such as heel, toe, arm, leg, head, forward, backward, up, down, turn, left, right, walk, run, skip, fast, and slow can all be used. The teacher can introduce and model each of these concepts. The teacher can reinforce an understanding of each as they are generalized by the children.

Activities

A simple activity for a small group of children is the re-creation of a children's book through dance. Using simple books with a limited number of characters works best. Books chosen should be selected for their clarity of emotion. Children can assume the characters within the story and use music to create freeform dances appropriate to the story. The teacher can read the story as the children perform the dance. Books and music that could lead to inappropriate or unsafe behaviors should be avoided.

Since many youngsters take dance lessons, these children can show other children some of the basic steps a dancer uses. This type of activity helps these young dancers see themselves as competent individuals. It also provides an opportunity for children to express and share their knowledge with others.

Older siblings who may have learned to square dance in school can be invited to both demonstrate this form of dance and to teach the younger children a basic dance. This exercise helps to involve family members in a cooperative activity that is both fun and meaningful.

Although not actually a dance, marching is a movement activity that shares many of the same benefits as dance. Marching activities, whether they be in the classroom or as a parade on the playground, create an atmosphere of celebration and an opportunity to explore movement and rhythm.

Literature Related to Dance

Two books about marching and parades that delight children aged two to five years are Donald Crews's *Parade* (1982) and Elaine Edelman's *Boom-de-Boom* (1980). An innovative retelling of the tale of the fox and the rabbit is presented in George Shannon's *Dance Away* (1982). In this retelling, the rabbit uses dancing as a way to outwit the fox as they approach the bank of the river. The rabbits celebrate this victory as they dance and sing their way home.

Square dancing is celebrated in *Barn Dance!* (1988), by Bill Martin, Jr. and John Archambault. The fantasy story depicts a young child getting up in the middle of the night to join the farm animals in a barn dance. Another book related to square dancing is Cynthia Rylant's *The Relatives Came* (1985). It is the simple story of a family reunion and how dancing weaves all of their lives together. Another story about a family for whom dancing has a special importance is Karen Ackerman's nostalgic *Song and Dance Man* (1988).

Freya Littledale provides a wonderful retelling of a story by the Grimm brothers in *The Twelve Dancing Princesses: A Folk Tale from the Brothers Grimm* (1988). The illustrations depict all of the joy and movement of dance.

A fictionalized story of the childhood of Josephine Baker is portrayed in the book *Ragtime Tumpie* (Schroeder 1989). Reading this book to young children while playing ragtime music in the background will surely motivate them to want to get up and dance. It is a good book to use to introduce children to the importance of music in their lives as well. A similar story that depicts the historical importance of dance in black culture is Patricia C. McKissak's *Mirandy and Brother Wind* (1988). Another story about the importance of dance in the lives of children is Tomie dePaola's *Oliver Button Is a Sissy* (1979). This story demonstrates the importance of creativity as a personal characteristic in the arts. The little boy in the story wishes to spend his days learning to dance. Neither the suggestions of his father nor the taunts of bullies can dissuade him from following this interest. While it requires careful preparation prior to sharing, it is the perfect story for demonstrating the role of perseverance and motivation. In Jean Richardson's *Clara's Dancing Feet* (1987), children are presented the story of a little girl who develops stage fright at her dance recital. The resolution of the problem is warm and believable.

SUMMARY

Just as the language arts are naturally integrated with much of life, the fine arts are integrated with language and other areas of life. Language and music are combined in the creation of a song. Music and dance are combined to produce ballet. Drama, music, and language are integrated in a Broadway musical production. The arts provide an excellent medium for the development of both communication skills and creativity. By introducing the arts to young children, teachers can also provide youngsters with the vocabulary common to each of these schemas. Music, art, drama, and dance are each explored. The benefits, activities, and literature related to them are described.

Music is a natural part of the world of childhood. It encompasses many of the characteristics common to language. Used as an accompaniment to activity or as the focus of the activity, music is something that children can enjoy at a very young age. It is found throughout the world and in the world of nature as well. It can serve as a bridge between cultures.

Art is closely related to language as a form of early writing. Children use it to express ideas and to further illustrate ideas that they have written or spoken about. The activity described as aesthetic decision making can be a powerful tool to help children understand that the arts can tolerate divergent thinking and personal creativity. Use of art in early childhood education should combine a wide range of possibilities and materials.

Drama as an early childhood education tool will generally take two forms. The first is pantomime. This helps children develop an awareness of their bodies in the environment as well as a sense of movement. They can use it to become more aware of how different situations require different movements. The other form is improvisation. It is somewhat like pantomime but incorporates both language and more than one person. Improvisation, like pantomime, can be used to describe emotions and ideas. It can also be more easily used to recreate experiences and stories.

Dance can serve as a tool to heighten a child's sense of feelings and aesthetics. It is an exercise that can involve other members of a child's family in a cooperative and enjoyable activity.

Questions and Activities for Review and Discussion

Multiple Choice

1. Research has shown that small babies can be taught to
    a. play an instrument.
    b. sing a simple song.
    c. match pitch.
    d. all of the above
2. Language learning can be used to integrate
    a. music.
    b. art.
    c. drama.
    d. all of the above
3. Helping young children to learn about music should mainly be done through
    a. separate special music classes.
    b. singing lessons.
    c. instrument lessons.
    d. integrated lessons.
4. A primary goal for integrating art in the language arts program is to provide young children with an opportunity to
    a. express ideas.
    b. improve their coloring skills.
    c. learn the names of a broad range of colors.
    d. learn the names of great artists.
5. An activity that can be used to integrate art and oral language development is
    a. the tracing of animal stencils.
    b. sorting different color crayons.
    c. aesthetic decision making.
    d. drawing animal pictures.
6. The benefits of using dramatic activities with young children include
    a. learning the schema of the theater.
    b. providing opportunities for oral language practice.
    c. learning the non-verbal aspects of communication.
    d. all of the above
7. Dance can be used to develop and reinforce
    a. basic concepts.
    b. communication skills.
    c. gross motor skills.
    d. all of the above

True or False

T   F   1. One of the similarities between musical notes and written language is that they can both be read.

T   F   2. There are relatively few children's books available that are related to the topic of music.

T   F   3. One of the benefits of using art with young children is the development of a sense of control over materials.

T F 4. Children should not be encouraged to dramatize scenes or events from stories that have been read to them.

T F 5. Dance can be used both to tell a story and to express an emotion.

Essay and Discussion

1. Describe one of the ways in which the arts and language are related.
2. Select a children's book related to music and discuss how it could be used in an integrated language arts program.
3. Observe an early childhood classroom. Record and describe the visual art and art activities observed in the program.
4. Explain the difference between putting on a play and using improvisation.
5. Select a children's book and explain how it might be used as a basis for a dance activity with young children.

REFERENCES

Ackerman, K. 1988. *Song and dance man.* New York: Alfred Knopf.

Aiken, J. 1987. *The moon's revenge.* Westminster, Md.: Alfred Knopf.

Bang, M. 1985. *The paper crane.* New York: Greenwillow.

Berenstain, S., and J. Berenstain. 1986. *The Berenstain bears get stage fright.* Westminster, Md.: Random House.

Birdseye, T. 1988. *Air mail to the moon.* New York: Holiday House.

Bottner, B. 1987. *Zoo song.* Jefferson City, Mo.: Scholastic.

Brown, L.K., and M. Brown. 1986. *Visiting the art museum.* New York: E.P. Dutton.

Brown, V. 1988. Integrating drama and sign language. *Teaching Exceptional Children* 21: 4–8.

Buffett, J., and S.J. Buffett. 1988. *Jolly mon.* New York: Harcourt, Brace, Jovanovich.

Bulla, C. 1987. *The chalk box kid.* Westminster, Md.: Random House.

Burningham, J. 1984. *Granpa.* New York: Crown.

Carlson, D.L. 1989. May I interest you in a dance. In *Learning from the Inside Out,* ed. S. Hoffman and L. Lamme. Washington, D.C.: Association for Childhood Education International.

Cazet, D. 1988. *Frosted glass.* Riverside, N.J.: Bradbury.

Cohen, M. 1985. *Starring first grade.* New York: Greenwillow.

Crews, D. 1982. *Carousel.* New York: Greenwillow.

Crews, D. 1983. *Parade.* New York: Greenwillow.

dePaola, T. 1979. *Oliver Button is a sissy.* New York: Harcourt, Brace, Jovanovich.

dePaola, T. 1983. *Sing, Pierrot, sing.* New York: Harcourt, Brace, Jovanovich.

dePaola, T. 1989. *The art lesson.* New York: G.P. Putnam's Sons.

dePaola, T. 1988. *The legend of the Indian paintbrush.* New York: G.P. Putnam's Sons.

Domanska, J. 1985. *Busy Monday morning.* New York: Greenwillow.

Dupasquier, P. 1985. *Dear daddy. . . .* New York: Bradbury.

Edelman, E. 1980. *Boom-de-boom.* Westminster, Md.: Pantheon.

Edwards, P.K. 1987. *Chester and Uncle Willoughby*. Boston: Little Brown.

Fitzgerald, S. 1983. The gift of song as entree to beginning reading. Paper presented at the sixth annual North Texas State University Early Childhood Symposium, Denton, Tex.

Fleischman, P. 1988. *Rondo in C*. New York: Harper and Row.

Fleischman, S. 1987. *The scarebird*. New York: Greenwillow.

Fridman, R. 1973. The first cry of the newborn: Basis for the child's future musical development. *Journal of Music Education* 21: 264–269.

Gamberg, R., W. Kwak, M. Hutchins, and J. Altheim. 1988. *Learning and loving it: Theme studies in the classroom*. Portsmouth, N.H.: Heinemann.

Goffstein, M.B. 1987. *An actor*. New York: Harper & Row.

Goffstein, M.B. 1987. *Artists' helpers enjoy the evening*. New York: Harper & Row.

Goldberg, M. 1982. Theatre in education: A summary of benefits. In *Learning through Dramatics: Ideas for Teachers and Librarians*, ed. N.H. Brizendine and J.L. Thomas. Phoenix, Az.: Oryx Press.

Gordon, E. 1979. *Manual: Primary measures of music audiation*. Chicago, Ill.: G.I.A. Publishers.

Greenfield, E. 1988. *Grandpa's face*. New York: Philomel.

Griffith, H. 1986. *Georgia music*. New York: Greenwillow.

Grimm, J., and W. Grimm. 1980. *The Bremen town musicians*. New York: Greenwillow.

Haas, I. 1975. *The Maggie B*. New York: Macmillan.

Haas, I. 1981. *The little moon theater*. New York: Atheneum.

Hedderwick, M. 1985. *Katie Morag and the two grandmothers*. London: The Bodley Head.

Hogrogian, N. 1988. *The cat who loved to sing*. Westminster, Md.: Alfred Knopf.

Hughes, S. 1983. *Alfie gives a hand*. New York: Mulberry.

Isadora, R. 1979. *Ben's trumpet*. New York: Greenwillow.

Johnston, T. 1988. *Pages of music*. New York: G.P. Putnam's Sons.

Keats, E.J. 1971. *Apt. 3*. New York: Macmillan.

Komaiko, L. 1987. *I like the music*. New York: Harper & Row.

Kroll, S. 1988. *Looking for Daniella*. New York: Holiday House.

Kuskin, K. 1982. *The philharmonic gets dressed*. New York: Harper & Row.

Lamme, L.L. 1990. Exploring the world of music through picture books. *The Reading Teacher* 44: 294–300.

Langner, N. 1983. *By the light of the silvery moon*. New York: Lothrop, Lee, & Shepard.

Leedy, L. 1988. *The bunny play*. New York: Holiday House.

Lefevre, C. 1970. *Linguistics, English and the language arts*. Boston: Allyn & Bacon.

Littledale, F. 1988. *The twelve dancing princesses: A folk tale from the Brothers Grimm*. Jefferson City, Mo.: Scholastic.

Mahy, M. 1987. *17 kings and 42 elephants*. New York: Dial.

Martin, B. Jr., and J. Archambault. 1986. *Barn dance!* Salt Lake City, Ut.: Henry Holt.

Martin, B. Jr., and J. Archambault. 1988. *Listen to the rain*. New York: Henry Holt.

Martin, B. Jr., and J. Archambault. 1988. *Up and down on the merry-go-round*. New York: Henry Holt.

Maxner, J. 1989. *Nicholas Cricket.* New York: Harper & Row.

Mayer, M. 1974. *Frog goes to dinner.* New York: Scholastic.

McKissack, P.C. 1988. *Mirandy and Brother Wind.* Westminster, Md.: Alfred Knopf.

Miller, S. 1981. Edwin Gordon, music psychologist for our time: A critique. *Southwestern Musician* 49: 20–24.

Moss, J.F. 1990. *Focus units in literature: A handbook for elementary school teachers.* Katonah, N.Y.: Richard Owen.

NicLeodhas, S. 1963. *All in the morning early.* New York: Holt.

Prokofiev, S. 1985. *Peter and the wolf.* New York: Viking Kestral.

Richardson, J. 1987. *Clara's dancing feet.* New York: G. P. Putnam's Sons.

Rylant, C. 1988. *All I see.* Danbury, Ct.: Orchard.

Rylant, C. 1985. *The relatives came.* New York: Bradbury.

Sawyer, W., and A. Leff. 1982. Elementary school dramatics: Coming to your senses. In *Learning through Dramatics: Ideas for Teachers and Librarians,* ed. N.H. Brizendine and J.L. Thomas. Phoenix, Az.: Oryx Press.

Schick, E. 1954. *A piano for Julie.* New York: Greenwillow.

Schickedanz, J. 1982. You be the doctor and I'll be sick: Preschoolers learn the language arts through play. In *Learning through dramatics: Ideas for teachers and librarians,* ed. N.H. Brizendine and J.L. Thomas. Phoenix, Az.: Oryx Press.

Schroeder, A. 1989. *Ragtime Tumpie.* Boston: Little Brown.

Shannon, G. 1982. *Dance away.* New York: Greenwillow.

Shannon, G. 1981. *Lizard's song.* New York: Greenwillow.

Shannon, G. 1981. *The piney woods peddler.* New York: Greenwillow.

Simmonds, P. 1988. *Lulu and the flying babies.* Westminster, Md.: Alfred Knopf.

Skofield, J. 1981. *Nightdances.* New York: Harper & Row.

Smardo, F.A. 1984. Using children's literature as a prelude or finale to music experiences with young children. *The Reading Teacher* 37: 700–705.

Steiner, B. 1988. *Whale brother.* New York: Walker.

Stewig, J.W. 1982. Drama: Integral part of the language arts. In *Learning through dramatics: Ideas for teachers and librarians,* ed. N.H. Brizendine and J.L. Thomas. Phoenix, Az.: Oryx Press.

Stock, C. 1988. *Sophie's knapsack.* New York: Lothrop, Lee, & Shepard.

Suskind, D., and A. Phillip. 1984. Yupik Eskimo folklore and children's play activities. Paper presented at the Annual Convention of the National Association for the Education of Young Children, Los Angeles, Calif.

Van Allsburg, C. 1987. *The Z was zapped: A play in twenty-six acts.* Burlington, Mass.: Houghton Mifflin Company.

Waddell, M. 1988. *Alice the artist.* Bergenfield, N.J.: E. P. Dutton.

Walter, M.P. 1980. *Ty's one-man band.* New York: Scholastic.

Wilhelm, J. 1988. *Oh, what a mess.* New York: Crown.

Williams, V.B. 1986. *Cherries and cherry pits.* New York: Greenwillow.

Williams, V.B. 1983. *Something special for me.* New York: Greenwillow.

Williams, V.B. 1984. *Music, music for everyone.* New York: Greenwillow.

Winter, J. 1988. *Follow the drinking gourd.* New York: Alfred Knopf.

Wood, A. 1988. *Elbert's bad word.* New York: Harcourt, Brace, Jovanovich.

Yorinks, A. 1988. *Bravo, Minski.* New York: Farrar/Straus/Giroux.

Zolotow, C. 1982. *The song.* New York: Greenwillow.

UNIT 19

Problems in Traditional Programs

PREVIEW

Toads cause warts. Breaking a mirror will give you seven years of bad luck. We have all heard such sayings. There is no real truth to them, but sometimes people want to believe in them anyway. This is because, in our culture, we are so familiar with these sayings that they have a life of their own. Familiarity seems to give these ideas a certain amount of credibility even though we know there is no truth to them. It is likely that these sayings began as attempts to explain certain occurrences. Throughout history, such myths developed; most people believed in them because they became so familiar and so commonly accepted.

In education as well, many attitudes, beliefs, and practices have evolved in a similar way and are often believed in and adhered to even when they have no basis in fact. These faulty beliefs and attitudes can give rise to ineffective practices that are often at odds with the foundations supporting an integrated language arts approach. As a result, they tend to limit both literacy development and the individual creativity of children. Critical ideas discussed in this unit include the concept of time for instruction, the structure of the curriculum, the relevance of curricular activities and materials, the validity of the uses of standardized tests, the view of parent participation, and commonly used grouping practices.

INTRODUCTION

Education in general, and teaching in particular, require teachers to constantly make decisions. This is especially true in the early childhood education classroom where the teacher must always expect the unexpected. The decisions that need to be made may concern certain children, the curriculum being implemented, the instructional strategy being used, or the assessment procedure that will be employed. As teachers go about the affairs of the classroom, many of the decisions made are logical, well thought out, and based upon solid evidence. Other decisions, however, may be based upon theories or beliefs that do not hold up well to scrutiny. In fact, many traditional practices of schools continue simply because things have always been done in a certain way. These practices and beliefs have often become such a standard part of schooling that no one even thinks to question them. The beliefs often sound somewhat logical and are often well intentioned. The inability of schools to examine and change such beliefs and practices might be referred to as institutional inertia.

Early childhood programs have historically advocated forcefully for developmentally appropriate educational practices. In doing so, they have been able to avoid many of the faulty beliefs and practices that have characterized elementary and secondary schools. There are two reasons for this. First, early childhood teachers tend to hold predominantly child-centered sets of beliefs. This naturally focuses their attention toward the most important part of education, the child. Second, young children, because of their constantly changing natures, do not allow teachers to cling to rigid beliefs. As educational and political pressure increases to force the elementary school program, curriculum, materials, and tests down into early childhood classrooms, it is important to resist their accompanying practices and beliefs that are detrimental to children.

In this unit, beliefs that lack evidence and support as well as the practices that result from them are examined. It is vital that teachers understand these beliefs and practices so that they don't accept them simply because they are part of the prevailing view of things. Many of these practices are actually harmful to children. They not only fail to encourage, but can actually discourage, the natural curiosity, creativity, and willingness to learn that most children bring to the classroom.

This unit is not a call for educational anarchy, where all of the traditional practices of schooling are rejected. Those who fail to understand an integrated whole language approach sometimes accuse those who practice one of advocating such a position. Clear

limits must be established for young children. Many traditional practices are of great value and should clearly be continued. Whole language teachers, however, are reflective individuals. They study and investigate all that they do. They think about the effects that their beliefs and practices have on children. Questioning the continuation of harmful practices that are based upon faulty beliefs is the responsibility of anyone who works with young children.

BELIEFS AND ATTITUDES

The meaning of the terms *beliefs* and *attitudes* refers to an acceptance of the truthfulness of something. People come to accept the truthfulness of something in several ways. First, they may have something presented to them in what seems to be a logical explanation. The presentation seems to make sense. A second method is to have something presented as an article of faith, as is done within religions. A third way is to have the idea presented in conjunction with evidence that supports the truthfulness of the idea. In education, it is usually best to develop beliefs that are based upon both the first and third types of presentation. That is, the idea should make sense, and it should be able to prove itself over time. While there are a number of ways of organizing faulty beliefs, they are grouped here under the headings of time, views of the child, structure, faith in tests, and the myth of the professional.

Time

While it may seem to be a simple abstraction, the concept of time in education generates a wide range of possibilities. The first questions, when referring to young children, might begin with the word *when*. When should certain ideas be introduced? When should a child begin nursery school? When should parents enroll their children in kindergarten? All of these questions imply that a definite answer can be found for each question. Since this is the expectation, there is no shortage of theories and beliefs that purport to respond to each of the questions with authority.

Such debate is a superficial cover for the real question: when should a child begin to engage in learning certain academic tasks (Karweit 1988)? That is the real question behind all of the other questions. Are four-

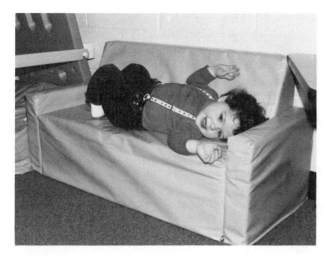

FIGURE 19-1 Children need time in which nothing is planned for them.

year-olds ready to learn from academic instruction? How about five- and six-year-olds? The issue is not whether, but when, to provide academic instruction.

In literacy instruction, the issue of time is of particular concern to those who work with four-, five-, and six-year-olds. While few states actually require children to attend kindergarten, most states offer such programs, and most children do attend them. In addition, most children entering kindergarten have also attended some type of preschool or daycare program as well. The most significant change in the kindergarten program over the past few decades is that it has become increasingly academic. Competency tests and other social factors have resulted in a downward push in the curriculum. What used to be part of a first grade program is now often found in kindergarten. What used to be part of a kindergarten program is now found at the preschool level.

Time for Learning.

Another factor related to time is the length of time children may need to learn. Because kindergarten and the early grades are based on the traditional school calendar, it is logical for parents and teachers to come to believe that a certain amount of learning should take place during each of the years a child spends in a program. Since programs have been developed and marketed for each of the early levels by commercial materials publishers, it is also logical for parents and teachers to assume that those materials represent an appropriate amount of learning for children at those levels. While each of these beliefs might seem logical, there is little support for either of them. For one thing, the traditional school calendar is based upon the agricultural growing season from colonial times. At that time children were needed during the summer to help on the farms. Thus the traditional school year has little relationship to the time children need to acquire certain literacy skills and abilities. For another, commercial materials publishers tend to base their products on market considerations rather than on developmental appropriateness.

Beliefs abound about the ideal length of the school day, the school year, and the number of days per week a child should be in school. The problem of kindergarteners not being ready for first grade is being addressed by many schools through a change from half-day to full-day kindergartens. Other schools believe that alternative programs will better meet the needs of such "unready" children.

School Entrance Time.

Schools tend to place faith in chronological age as the criteria for entrance. In general, five years old is usually seen as the "right age" to enter kindergarten. In the past, children were frequently required to be five years old by December or January of their kindergarten year to gain admittance. That is changing. Schools are now moving the criteria for kindergarten admittance to five years old by September or October of the kindergarten year (Karweit 1988). This is being done because of a belief that children who are older will be more "ready" for kindergarten. School officials are not alone in this belief. Parents are increasingly voluntarily holding their children out of kindergarten for an extra year (Shepard and Smith 1985). These practices provide schools with kindergarteners who are, in reality, older than the kindergarteners of the past. This in turn encourages the belief that these children are "ready" for more academic tasks.

Time and Child Diversity.

None of the beliefs about time mentioned to this point is supported by a definitive body of evidence. In fact, time is a superficial smokescreen to the most important consideration: the diversity of children. No matter when the criteria of age for kindergarten entrance is set, the entering children will possess a number of differences in ability, language skills, and knowledge about the world. Increasing the age requirement will certainly not help since some very young children will continue to enter the kindergarten while other older children will be held out by their parents for an extra year. The result of this is that many kindergartens now include children with age ranges of up to two years. The diversity of such a group is then far greater than it would have been if all of the children had simply entered when they were eligible.

The central problem of all of this, however, is not one of age or time. The central problem is the inability of inflexible traditional programs to meet the challenge of students with a range of diversity. A related problem is a seeming belief on the part of many that this inflexibility is appropriate or at least should not be questioned. Too often, kindergartens are seen as places and programs where children are expected to master a set amount of material in a set amount of time. Children who do not measure up are assumed to not be ready. There is no evidence to support these beliefs.

The focus should not be on whether or not the child is ready for the program. The focus should be on making the program flexible enough to meet the needs of a diverse group of children. Traditional programs need to question their focus and beliefs concerning the quantitative aspects of time that lead to such superficial questions as: Is the child the appropriate age to enter the program? Should our program be half day or full day? When should each new bit of instruction be introduced? Instead, traditional programs need to refocus their beliefs on the qualitative aspects of children by asking more relevant questions such as: what instruction is most appropriate to address this diversity of strengths and areas of need? How can we empower these children with language abilities and knowledge that will be meaningful to them?

View of the Child

A traditional view of the child that persists in many quarters even to this day is based on the "empty ves-

sel" model. This view sees the child as an empty container. The task of education, according to the model, is to fill up the container with knowledge. The child is not seen as bringing anything of value to the learning situation.

This belief about children leads to other attitudes that tend to decrease opportunities for children to develop their own language and creativity. For example, if teachers see children as not bringing anything to the learning situation, a natural outgrowth is the belief that any knowledge the children come to possess in terms of language, creativity, and problem solving must be provided to them. In the classroom, it would have to be concluded that only the teacher can fill this need. Since children are not seen as bringing anything of value to the learning situation, they surely cannot be expected to learn much from each other.

The result of this view is that children tend to be perceived in terms of how much of the curriculum they have absorbed at various points in time. The curriculum in classrooms with this view of the child tends to be prescriptive. That is, it is filled with lists of the knowledge and skills that children are supposed to acquire. Those who do acquire the knowledge, or fill their empty vessel to a prescribed level, are sorted into a higher status group. Those who fail are often assigned to a lower status group. The whole system tends to be based on the child learning a large number of correct answers.

Structure

The beliefs about structure in traditional programs generally focus on the areas of curriculum and instruction. The curriculum is a set of intended learning outcomes for children. The learning outcomes may be in the areas of language arts, mathematics, visual arts, or cooperative social skills. Although many consider it as such, the curriculum should not be perceived as a set of materials, a set of oral directions, a stack of dittos, a kit of learning materials, or a series of texts and workbooks. These materials are instructional materials. Instruction refers to an interaction between the methods and strategies used by the teacher, the materials, and the child. The purpose of instruction is to assist the child in attaining the learning within the curriculum. In a traditional program,

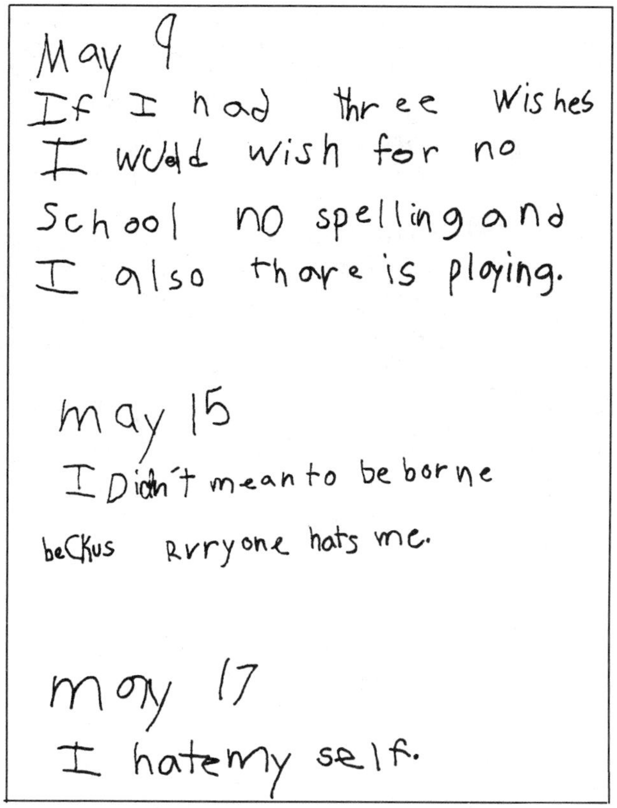

May 9
If I had three wishes
I wudd wish for no
school no spelling and
I also thare is ploying.

may 15
I Didn't mean to be borne
beckus Rvryone hats me.

moy 17
I hate my self.

FIGURE 19-2 This child's journal reveals the frustration and poor self-concept of a pressure-filled education program that resulted in school failure.

both curriculum and instruction tend to be rigid and unintegrated.

The traditional early childhood language arts program is characterized by a lengthy set of isolated curricular objectives. These are often referred to as reading readiness skills. The belief is that children need to master a number of things at a pre-reading stage before they are able to benefit from a traditional instructional program of beginning reading. A number of different approaches are found in traditional reading readiness programs. Some are phonetically based, while others tend to be based more on sight words and visual recognition. Still others are comprised of skills, such as auditory memory and visual perception, that some believe to be the basis of learning to read. The structure of all of these programs tends to be a collection of small, isolated bits and pieces that it is assumed will form a foundation for reading when they are all attained by the child.

While some of the traditional reading readiness programs may address certain important aspects of print, they tend to be ineffective for a number of reasons. First, the isolated bits and pieces do not fit together particularly well. Children can learn them with enough practice, but they often have great difficulty applying them in real world literacy situations. Second, the approaches largely ignore the concept of comprehension. Language and communication are meaningful only if they make sense. Too often, traditional programs do not make much sense to young children. Third, the narrowness and inflexibility of the programs take away the underlying social base of language that can foster risk taking, creativity, and problem solving. Language is reduced to a collection of correct answers devoid of real meaning.

The instructional approach often used with a traditional program follows a highly structured model. The belief system of the curriculum sees the skills of reading readiness as being of primary importance. Correspondingly, the belief system surrounding the instruction of such a program sees the acquisition of isolated reading readiness skills as the goal of the instruction. As a result, instruction tends to be teacher-centered and behavioristic. There is an emphasis on competition and extrinsic rewards. The teacher-centered focus is used because only the teacher knows what the reading readiness skills are and in what sequence they will be learned. A behavioristic approach is frequently used since it is an efficient procedure for acquiring information structured in the way that reading readiness skills are arranged. Extrinsic rewards are used in abundance since there is frequently little motivation on the part of children for learning such a collection of isolated pieces of information. Competition is used as a motivational tool as well.

Faith in Tests

During the past several decades schools seem to have fallen in love with tests, particularly the standardized tests that have been developed by commercial publishers and state departments of education. The tests themselves are carefully designed by professional test makers using sophisticated statistical procedures supposedly to insure that the instruments are valid and reliable. Legislators are also quite fond of tests. Tests enable them to demonstrate that they are doing their part to improve education by voting to mandate still another rigorous test designed to make the schools accountable. Tests are also quite inexpensive when compared to the development of newer or more effective programs. Many educators look favorably upon tests. The published versions are glossy, colorful, and attractive. They are easy to obtain, give, and score. They yield a wide range of numbers with such descriptors as standard scores, age equivalents, national percentile ranks, and normal curve equivalents. Whatever it is that they claim to measure, tests provide a score for that characteristic down to a single point or even a tenth of a point.

The kind of precise information that tests seem to be able to provide about children is extremely appealing. For the most part, large numbers of schools believe that tests can provide this precision. As a result, schools have placed far too much faith in tests. Schools have developed policies, justified the continuation of certain programs, and routinely made placement decisions about children based largely on test scores. In short, many schools accept the claims of the test developers that the tests are valid and reliable.

The major problem with using standardized tests with young children, particularly in the area of literacy development, is that tests are not able to meaningfully measure literacy development. It must be remembered that most tests are developed from a behavioristic perspective. That view places primary emphasis on what can be observed or seen. In literacy development, the most important aspects are those that cannot be seen: a willingness to take risks, an ability to reflect upon inherent abilities, an ability to adjust subsequent language attempts based on feedback, a desire to become independent in language, and a sense that meaning is at the core of language and communication. None of these characteristics can be adequately measured by the typical standardized test, no matter how many statistical procedures it has undergone.

Karweit (1988) identifies the major weakness of tests designed to measure early reading skills as their unjustified emphasis on language mechanics. Since the surface mechanical features of language comprise the bulk of what such tests can measure, program

FIGURE 19-3 Many aspects of a child's learning cannot be evaluated with standardized tests.

success tends to become equated with good test results that measure only those features of language. As a result, the curriculum becomes a set of activities designed to insure continued good test results. Thus, the more important standardized test results become for a program, the more superficial the program tends to become.

Myth of Professionalism

For years teachers and other educators have sought the recognition and respect that is usually accorded to people in high-status professions. The term *profession* has a number of possible meanings. In the world of work, a professional is usually described as an individual within a group of workers who possesses such qualities as an agreed upon body of knowledge, the ability to control entry into the profession, a certain degree of autonomy, and the ability to discipline its own members. Doctors, nurses, lawyers, dentists, and accountants are typical of the workers who are seen as belonging to a profession. People have respect for these workers that they often don't have for others, including those who teach.

Teaching is a noble career. Few jobs require the dedication, hard work, and energy that a good and effective teacher brings to the position. What excellent teachers in any society need is a sense of respect rather than the title of professional. With some educators, this idea seems to be lost. Those who demand the designation of "professional" often confuse the stereotyped trappings of the job with the concept of respect. They might tend to act much like a doctor or attorney with the expectation that such actions will garner respect. As a result, such individuals acquire or use a number of different devices to make themselves appear "professional." They may overdress for their positions. They may develop an air of aloofness with parents. They may gravitate toward increased use of such devices as standardized tests in order to employ the specialized vocabulary associated with these tools. They may even develop a belief that these behaviors will gain them respect in the eyes of parents and others. Nothing could be further from the truth. Such individuals make the mistake of believing the myth that professionalism is a matter of appearance and test data that suggest superiority. Parents who are concerned about the literacy development of their children care little for any of these things. They are more interested in learning about the information contained in the literacy portfolios of their children. They seek information that is clear, timely, and informative.

The reason that the myth of professionalism is a problem inherent with many current school programs is that too many educators believe in the myth. Those who attempt to create an air of professionalism through superficial behaviors tend to attract attention. They may come to believe in their authority so much that their actions eventually steer the school or program away from beliefs and attitudes that are actually most valuable. If in seeking recognition as professionals educators lose their credibility with parents, any recognition as a professional is meaningless.

PRACTICES

Many schooling practices continue long after the reason or the foundation for such practices has disappeared or become irrelevant. Unfortunately, a significant number of the beliefs and reasons for certain practices within schools continue to be cited long after they have been either disproved or replaced by improved reasoning. As a result, a number of traditional practices found in schools have little or no rational basis. Each of these practices has the potential to serve

as a barrier to the growth and creative potential of the child. A number of these practices are described here.

Time Practices

Inaccurate beliefs about time lead to several practices that are based upon a narrow view of how time ought to affect a child's life and learning. The practices are all based on the assumption that the program itself is correct: if the child doesn't learn on schedule, then there must be something wrong with the child. Few educators would actually make this admission in so many words, but it is at the heart of a number of indefensible practices related to time.

Entrance Time.

One of the most hotly debated practices is the cut-off date for kindergarten entrance. Years ago it was five years old by January first. Little by little it is edging toward September first. Even where it has reached that point, many argue that even this date is too late, especially for boys. The desire by educators advocating these changes is to enable all children to start off on a relatively even level. Parents do not always choose to keep younger children out of school an extra year. Some parents keep very able children out of kindergarten for an extra year in the hope that these children will be labeled as gifted. Even using achievement test data, however, the oldest and youngest children are only a few percentile ranks apart. By the end of third grade there is no difference whatsoever (Smith and Shepard 1986, 1989).

Pacing.

Some instructional models are based on a belief that having children engaged in academic tasks for longer periods of time will lead to better learning. While there is some truth to the belief that time on task enhances learning, a blind use of this principle can be destructive to the interest young children have in learning. A number of teaching models, usually referred to as "direct instruction" models, incorporate a rigid behavioristic approach that attempts to engage children in academic learning tasks using a rapid rate with skill activities for extended periods of time. As a result, teacher-directed activities, rather than play or child-centered activities, dominate the instructional day (Karweit 1988).

Retention.

By far the most harmful of the practices related to time is that of retention in grade. It is also one of the most prevalent practices. Despite decades of research outlining the negative effects of this practice, American schools retain a far higher proportion of children in kindergarten and the early grades than countries such as Japan, England, and Germany (McGill-Franzen and Allington 1991). Smith and Shepard (1986, 1989) summarize the short-term problems associated with retention in the early grades. The evidence is quite clear that the achievement and self-esteem of retained children are nearly always worse than comparable children who were promoted.

Retention is often disguised by calling it something different. Many schools do refer to it for what it is: retention. The child simply repeats kindergarten for a second year. At other times, different classes are set up that add another year to the child's school life. It may be called junior kindergarten, developmental kindergarten, or pre-first grade. The name doesn't really change anything. Children are removed from a group of peers and are very aware that the group is moving ahead without them.

McGill-Franzen and Allington (1991) report a number of startling findings about the long-term effects of retention. Since retained children rarely catch up to their peers, they reach their teenage years old for their grade and still behind academically, usually in literacy skills. These are the two most powerful predictors of dropping out of school. As a result, children who are retained in the early grades have only a 20 percent chance of graduating from high school (McGill-Franzen and Allington 1991).

Artificiality

The term *artificiality* refers to a wide range of practices that place children in language situations that are contrived. That is, there is little likelihood of the children ever being in such a situation in real life. Examples include pull-out programs, grouping together the children who are experiencing difficulty, and the use of language materials that have no counterpart in the real world. As such, much of the learn-

ing that might occur is not transferred because real language situations are so different from artificial ones. These artificial situations seem to persist largely because of schools' inertia. In other words, the practices are done simply because they always have been done. To the uncritical eye, they almost seem natural because adults have seen them in operation for so long. Several examples of artificiality are discussed here.

Behavioristic Instruction.

When teachers hear the term *behaviorism*, they often are reminded of studies of pigeons learning to do tricks in order to get a reward in the form of food. It is true that animals can learn to do certain tasks and perform certain procedures using this system. Many educators continue to believe that this approach is well suited to teaching young children as well. Little mention is made of the fact that the pigeons in most of the experiments are tremendously motivated to perform tasks for food. They develop this motivation because they are frequently starved to 80 percent of their natural weight prior to the training sessions.

Schools do not use this starvation approach with young children, fortunately. On the other hand, instruction that relies on a behavioristic approach must include some other reward system for the system to function. Typically, the rewards include stickers, stars, smile faces, stamps, and candy. Children are taught to see these rewards as worth striving for. With this in place, the system is continued. The learning that occurs is devoid of meaningfulness in regard to the communication needs of the child. Children have a need to be able to communicate effectively. They have interests that can be used to foster language exploration and risk taking. Replacing these needs with piles of stickers and collections of stamps simply ignores the role of the child in language learning.

Materials.

Many of the traditional materials used in early childhood literacy and language instruction bear little resemblance to real world language. Traditionally, children in kindergarten and the early grades are buried under an avalanche of ditto sheets, workbook pages, flash cards, and task cards from learning kits.

FIGURE 19-4 A comfortable reading area is one of the key materials for an inviting environment.

Nearly every piece of language is presented in isolation with little or no reference to how it relates to the central purposes of language. With many repetitions, children do learn many of the isolated bits, language rules, and segmented components of language. The major problem is that the knowledge is too abstract for young children to easily transfer to real world language situations. In view of this lack of meaningfulness to the child, much of this learned information is quickly forgotten until it is later retaught in another grade.

Structure

The various structural aspects of traditional programs are largely related to the concept of artificiality in education. Schools have great difficulty in changing. Even when systems within them no longer serve their original purpose, the underlying structures of these systems tend to take on a life of their own. They bend in order to attempt to address the changing needs, but they also maintain themselves. As a result many of the structures within schools tend to contradict many of the basic beliefs the school contends that it holds. School philosophies, goals, organizational patterns, and child opportunities are all areas where these contradictions emerge.

Philosophical Discrepancies.

To see how this can be a problem, teachers can simply compare the mission statement or stated philosophy of a school with actual classroom practices. Each should be carefully examined. What teachers often find is that the two do not coincide. As times change, the stated philosophies of schools change, but the actual classroom practices tend to remain the same. For example, most elementary schools that include kindergarten and the primary grades probably have a mission statement that sounds very child-centered. A look in the classrooms might reveal something completely different, however. Frequently teachers will encounter a program that is quite teacher or subject centered.

Misleading Goals.

Closely related to philosophical discrepancies is the existence of misleading goals. Here, also, the best way to detect this situation is to compare the stated goals of a program with actual classroom practices. Often schools have developed goals that sound quite appropriate to the needs of young children to learn language. However, in the actual classroom the program goals often seem to be replaced by the teacher's goals for presenting the instruction at a certain rate. The goals now seem to include such things as getting through the material and developing the skills necessary to pass the readiness test at the end of the term.

Lack of Opportunity.

When traditional classroom practices remain intact even in the face of changes in philosophical statements and goals, children suffer from a lack of opportunities. In a traditional subject-centered or teacher-centered literacy program, children lose the opportunity to engage in behaviors and activities that

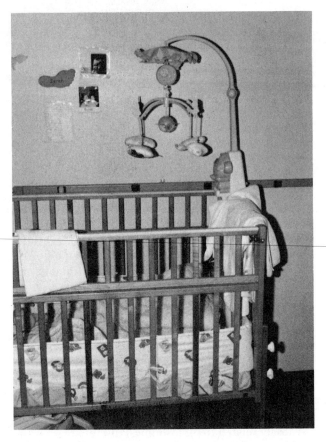

FIGURE 19-5 A look at the inside of a school can sometimes reveal much about the philosophy and goals of a program.

are necessary for meaningful language growth. First, the children lose the opportunity to take risks. The teacher is the holder of all knowledge. The role of the child is to respond correctly rather than experiment with new language attempts. Second, children lose the opportunity to be creative. It is difficult for children to be creative when they are given a ditto sheet containing a capital letter "A" and told to color it carefully. Third, the children lose the opportunity to make choices. In a teacher-centered program there is only one choice: follow the directions and the lead of the teacher.

Faith in Tests

When educators, the general public, and legislators come to believe in the validity of test results as ade-

quate measures of the abilities of young children, a number of alarming practices can result. These are usually based on what abilities or characteristics the tests claim to measure in the young child. Some tests claim to measure achievement in reading. Others claim to measure reading readiness skills. Still other tests claim to measure a wide range of skills and abilities that may or may not have much to do with literacy or a child's ability to develop literacy. They are often used, however, because of claims that the test results have some value for decision making. It is this last concept, the idea that tests produce information for decision making, that makes test use with young children particularly dangerous. Two questions need to be asked. Should instructional and program decisions about children rely primarily upon information derived from standardized tests? What erroneous decisions occur when tests are used as the sole or primary source of information?

Grouping

One of the primary end results of the use of standardized tests is grouping. One way or another, chil-

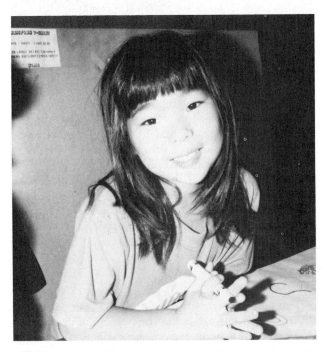

FIGURE 19-6 Children need opportunities to take language risks.

dren are often assigned to various groups as a result of how well or poorly they did on standardized tests. The usual effect is an attempt to create a set of homogeneous groups. That is, children are placed in groups with other children who scored similarly on the same test. The practice is based on a competitive model that is often justified as preparation for life. In reality, it is a device that creates winners and losers at a very young age. The winners are those who are placed in the high groups. The losers are those who are placed in the low groups. Children quickly figure out to which group they belong. The damage it does to their self-esteem can be considerable. While homogeneous grouping tends to help those children who are already more advantaged, it creates further barricades to the disadvantaged while promoting segregation.

Labeling

Closely related to grouping children is labeling children. One of the largest growing subgroups of young children is those with disabilities. Invariably, the decision to label a child in this way is largely a result of how that child scored on one or more standardized tests. Many would argue that this is justified as a means of obtaining needed special educational services. Such a justification would have more validity if the special education services were provided in an integrated setting, within the regular education classroom, and in conjunction with the regular educational program. This is, unfortunately, not often the case.

Most children who are labeled as possessing a disability are provided special education services in segregated settings, programs, and even buildings. In addition, they often disappear from public view. This is forcefully brought out by the findings of Lipsky and Gartner (1989). In attempting to determine what ultimately becomes of the millions of children who are labeled at an early age, they discovered that no one really knows. No federal governmental agency regularly collects information about whether these children ever return to mainstream education programs, graduate from school, become literate, or get jobs. Surely, this is not a service to such children. In addition, it deprives children without disabilities from developing friendships with and understanding of all children.

Parental Exclusion

A final unjustified practice of traditional programs is parental exclusion. While parents may be accepted within the schools on a regular basis, they are often barred from participating in many of the important activities of the school. Parents are often asked to serve as room parents, bake sale participants, party helpers, and parent-teacher organization officers. Ordinarily no written school policies prevent parents from being more fully involved, but usually no policies encourage parents to become more meaningfully involved, either. Rather, the lack of involvement stems from a tradition of not including parents as true partners in children's education. There is an often unstated but generally understood policy that the teacher is solely in charge of the child's education. This eliminates an important role for the parent in the child's education. It is critical that this not be allowed to enter early childhood education.

SUMMARY

A number of problems are found within traditional early childhood literacy programs. These problems often prevent children from experiencing the meaningfulness of language. In addition, they can serve as a barrier to the need of the child to take risks and to be creative with language. The problems are ordinarily the result of ineffective practices that are based on faulty beliefs. Early childhood education has historically advocated developmentally appropriate practices. Social and political pressures to push elementary school curriculum and practices down into early childhood programs can threaten these beliefs.

The faulty beliefs that often operate within elementary and secondary schools are comparable to myths that are created to explain things that can not be explained in any other way. The problem occurs when the beliefs are maintained after they are disproved. Five general areas of belief were discussed within the unit.

The beliefs surrounding the concept of time are numerous. Many of the concerns are based more on superficial than substantive ideas. For example, there continues to be much discussion about the best cutoff date for kindergarten entrance. This simply diverts attention from the real issue. The central problem is not the cutoff date but the inability of rigid kindergarten programs to meet the diversity of needs found within any group of entering kindergarteners. Other issues related to time include time on task and the appropriate time to begin academic learning.

Other beliefs concern a view of the child and the structure of the program. An inappropriate way of perceiving a child is as an empty container waiting to be filled up with information. This view ignores the fact that all children come to the learning environment with varying degrees of relevant information that can be used as a basis for learning. The structure of many traditional programs is far too rigid to help children see language as a meaningful tool. Such programs are based on a behavioristic approach that teaches readiness skills as isolated skills in a competitive manner. Children are motivated in these programs by a desire to earn stickers as rewards rather than a desire to communicate.

Other faulty beliefs are the myth of the professional and a misplaced faith in tests. While educators are truly deserving of great respect, the field of early childhood education must guard agains the invalid practices that are frequently found in many elementary and secondary schools. To do this, early childhood education teachers must focus on developing inner rather than outer qualities of the professional. Finally, too much faith is placed in the usefulness of tests. While they may appear to be handy and precise tools, they tend to ignore the key characteristics of language learning.

Faulty beliefs and attitudes have enabled many ineffective and questionable practices to continue at some levels of education. Some of these practices, such as philosophical discrepancies and misdirected goals, tend to serve as barriers to progress in schools. Others such as retention, grouping, and labeling are actually harmful to children. Still others such as behavioristic instruction tend to both stifle the creativity of children and prevent them from experiencing the meaningfulness of language.

Questions and Activities for Review and Discussion

Multiple Choice

1. Most practices found in any educational program are followed because of teachers' and administrators'
   a. beliefs.
   b. certifications.
   c. diplomas.
   d. all of the above
2. A traditional belief about young children and their ability to learn language is that there is a specific point in time that children are
   a. willing to learn.
   b. ready to learn.
   c. selecting language as an interest.
   d. both a and c
3. Seeing a child as a container to fill up with knowledge and information is known as the
   a. sponge paradigm.
   b. behavior modification theory.
   c. empty vessel theory.
   d. cognitive theory.

4. In traditional approaches, the key individual who has ordinarily been excluded from the classroom instructional process is the
   a. child.
   b. parent.
   c. teacher.
   d. classroom aide.
5. A major problem associated with using standardized tests to assess the language learning of young children is
   a. the validity of the tests.
   b. obtaining the tests.
   c. scoring the tests.
   d. administering the tests.
6. Using stickers and candy as rewards for student learning is often seen as an important part of
   a. a behavioristic approach.
   b. a whole language approach.
   c. a child-centered approach.
   d. an integrated approach.
7. A heterogeneous class is comprised of children whose abilities are most likely to be
   a. high.
   b. low.
   c. similar.
   d. mixed.

True or False

T   F   1. Most traditional practices in early childhood language instruction have a well-defined base of logic and research support.

T   F   2. Retention in an early school grade has been found to be an effective tool to help children catch up academically to their more able peers.

T   F   3. The stimulus-response-reward approach to learning is characteristic of behavioristic learning theories.

T   F   4. The only logical role for parents in the classroom is that of room parent.

T   F   5. Grouping less able children in a single classroom enables the teacher to help such children catch up to the more able children.

Essay and Discussion

1. Describe the relationship that exists between beliefs and practices in any educational program.
2. Explain why retention in kindergarten or the early grades is used so often in education.
3. Interview parents concerning their beliefs about any current practice in early childhood education. Summarize their reasons for holding that belief.
4. Describe some of the possible ways parents might be included in the instructional component of an early childhood program.
5. Describe some of the problems with basing decisions about a young child on the results of standardized tests.

REFERENCES

Karweit, N. 1988. Quality and quantity of learning time in preprimary programs. *Elementary School Journal* 89: 119–133.

Lipsky, D.K., and A. Gartner, eds. 1989. *Beyond separate education: Quality education for all.* Baltimore, Md.: Brookes.

McGill-Franzen, A., and R.L. Allington. 1991. Every child's right: Literacy. *The Reading Teacher* 45: 86–90.

Shepard, L.A., and M.L. Smith. 1986. Synthesis of research on school readiness and kindergarten retention. *Educational Leadership* 44: 78–86.

Shepard, L.A., and M.L. Smith. 1989. *Flunking grades.* Philadelphia, Pa.: Falmer.

Section 7

Parent and School Partnerships

Norman Bridwell

"I can't imagine a world without books for children. I spent a lot of time at the library when I was a boy. In the depression days, books were not easy to come by for me. I read a lot of fantasy.

"I think children should be allowed to read anything they enjoy. Reading should be an enjoyable experience. I would not try to force classics on a child. They will reach these books through the joy of reading."

Reprinted courtesy of Norman Bridwell.

TO THE READER:

Most educators readily admit that parents are a child's first teachers. However, this view doesn't really tell the whole story. Parents are more than a child's first teacher. They are a child's most important teacher. They are a child's most enduring teacher. They are a child's most influential teacher.

As educators, we need to be more aware of this critical role played by parents as teachers. We need to see that it is essential to continue to involve parents in their children's education. In fact, the involvement must go beyond the traditional types of parent involvement. Many of those roles, such as room parent and parent group member, have relegated parents to areas outside of the educational decision-making process. As a result, parent involvement in the education of their children decreases rapidly as children go through the elementary and secondary school grades.

This section contains two units that address a wide range of issues related to parent involvement. The first unit describes the historical, societal, and cultural barriers to parent involvement. Strategies for fostering greater involvement in the early childhood classroom are provided. Activities for fostering involvement are identified.

The final unit in the book addresses the need for parent involvement outside of the boundaries of the classroom. Most parents are deeply interested in encouraging their children's learning. Parents desire and welcome support for their participation efforts. Ideas for supporting parent involvement in education beyond the walls of the classroom are provided.

In many ways, this section is the most important one in the book. The cooperation that can and should develop between the school and the home is a bridge that integrates the child with all of life. A home and a family are a much more natural part of a child's life than are a school or a center. No matter how welcoming a school is, it cannot replicate the warmth and bonds of a family. The school is created to support the work of the family and the home in helping the child become a self-fulfilled, productive member of society.

UNIT 20

Parent Participation in the Classroom

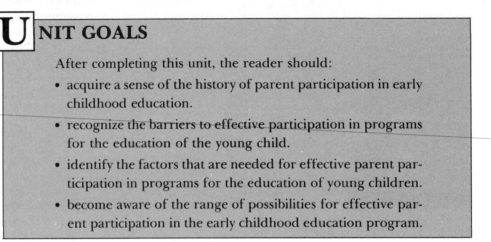

UNIT GOALS

After completing this unit, the reader should:

- acquire a sense of the history of parent participation in early childhood education.
- recognize the barriers to effective participation in programs for the education of the young child.
- identify the factors that are needed for effective parent participation in programs for the education of young children.
- become aware of the range of possibilities for effective parent participation in the early childhood education program.

PREVIEW

While some might disagree, we begin with the assumption that all parents want their children to be successful in school and in life. There is ample support for the belief that parents from all social classes hold similar educational and life goals for their children (Brantlinger 1985; Seginer 1983). Further, parents are usually willing to help their children toward success. On the other hand, not every parent feels comfortable as a participant in the education of their children. This can be due to many factors. Parents may not feel they have the skill to participate. They may lack the confidence to become involved. Remembering negative school experiences of their own might discourage them from participating in the education of their children. Still other parents may simply not have the time or inclination to become involved.

While the reasons for parents not becoming involved in their child's education may be many, parents are far too important for schools to exclude as active partners in the education of their children. Schools frequently give lip service to parent involvement with statements about open door policies, beliefs that a parent is a child's first teacher, and invitations to attend parent-teacher association meetings. If this is the extent of a school's parent involvement opportunities, however, then that school's commitment to parent involvement is suspect. Ample evidence supports the powerful effects of parent involvement.

A number of important ideas and concepts are discussed in this unit. They include the history of parent involvement, barriers to involvement, ways of increasing involvement, and opportunities for parents in the early childhood education program.

INTRODUCTION

The unit begins with a brief look at the history of parent involvement over the past two centuries. While parent involvement in teaching and bringing up children has always been evident in human history, these two centuries were selected for specific reasons. Understanding the involvement of parents in their children's literacy and social development education during the past two centuries is particularly important to understanding current practices. Parent involvement was fostered by certain beliefs and was driven toward certain goals. While some of those factors have faded, remnants of them can still be seen today. Some of those factors are helpful influences, while others remain as barriers to improving parent involvement.

The second section of the unit addresses some of the barriers to improving parent involvement in early childhood education programs. While some of the barriers have a historical base, others are the result of detrimental attitudes and characteristics. Some of these attitudes are held by parents. Others are held by teachers. Understanding what they are can help the early childhood educator recognize and overcome them.

The third part of the unit is a description of the practical elements of successful parent involvement. There is no magic formula for successfully involving every parent, but a number of steps can be taken to encourage many more parents to become active in this area. Knowing these steps and understanding how to take them can go a long way in meeting parent involvement goals.

The final part of the unit describes a number of possible opportunities for parents during the day in an early childhood instructional program. This discussion describes the practical aspects of making the best use of parents in a program. While classrooms always need traditional types of involvement such as room parents and bake sale coordinators, there are many other opportunities as well. Many of these are both more helpful to the teacher and more satisfying to the parent.

HISTORY OF PARENT INVOLVEMENT

Understanding history may or may not prevent us from making the mistakes of our predecessors. An understanding of our past, however, can help us to understand the way we are today. While beliefs about parent involvement have changed over the years, certain beliefs tend to last in some form well past the time when they are the predominant view.

Nineteenth Century

According to Brim (1965), one of the earliest formal programs of parent involvement in the United States began in Portland, Maine, in 1815. Like many other social issues of the time, the basis for the movement was centered in the Calvinistic religious tradition. The view of children at the time was based on a belief in the depravity of the infant. That is, children were seen as inherently evil. The role of parents was to provide strict discipline to help children overcome their natural inclination toward evil and depravity. "Spare the rod and spoil the child" was the guiding rule. In 1815, a group of Portland, Maine, mothers banded together to develop systematic plans for disciplining and breaking the wills of their children.

By the end of the nineteenth century, the child depravity theory had weakened considerably. It was now overshadowed by the influence of individuals such as Rousseau, Pestalozzi, and Froebel, who viewed the child as basically good (Froebel 1887). During this period, family care and love were viewed as important factors in helping children understand the world. Froebel viewed parents as an integral component of early kindergartens. As a result, parents were regularly involved in kindergarten programs.

Twentieth Century

The twentieth century has seen the effects of many influences due to the increased pace of world events. These societal changes, in conjunction with the rise of different educational beliefs, have resulted in decided shifts in views of parent involvement throughout the century. In the early part of the century a flood of immigrants entered the country. The emphasis was on mainstreaming people into the culture. Parents supported the work of the school in helping their children become acculturated by learning the language and ways of the new country.

During the first half of the century, the view of child rearing shifted back and forth between different positions. At times, the emphasis was placed on being gentle with children. At other times, the emphasis adopted was a strict approach with a heavy emphasis on discipline. Parent involvement in early childhood education during this period often took the form of parent education. That is, the emphasis was on teaching parents how to raise their children meaningfully, by including parents in early childhood education programs.

The latter half of the twentieth century saw an increasing government influence in involving parents in education. While education is generally seen as a state responsibility, the federal government has established itself in the provision of programs for populations who need additional support to fully benefit from the regular education programs supported by the state. These populations include children who are disadvantaged, disabled, and non-English-speaking. Federal programs for these young children include PL 99–457 programs for preschoolers with disabilities as well as Head Start, Follow Through, and Chapter 1 programs for the disadvantaged. Each of these programs requires the agencies administering them to engage parents at all levels, including the policy-making level.

Inherent in the federal programs were several themes concerning the role of parents in the education of their children. Gordon (1977) describes these themes in terms of parent roles, the environment, and lifelong human development. The first theme is the belief that the early years are critical to the lifelong development of the child. Positive or negative factors at that point in a child's life can have positive or negative effects on that child throughout life. The second theme is an acceptance of the concept that the home is an important environment for fostering the development of the child. The third theme is that parents need help and support both in creating a positive home environment and in fostering the development of their children.

While it should not be generally assumed that the parents of children who are disadvantaged or disabled require help in creating positive home environments for their children, it should be recognized that the requirement for parent involvement in federally supported programs has served a positive good. It has led to an understanding among many that parents both desire and are able to become more active in the more formal aspects of the education and devel-

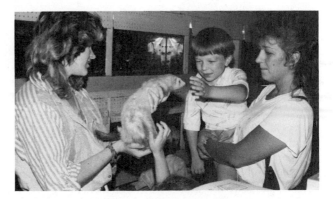

FIGURE 20-1 Parents organized and guided this field trip to a farm and pet store.

opment of their young children. While parent involvement may cause anxiety for some educators, it is important that it continue. Parents generally spend more time with their children at those ages than anyone else. Not using their resources during this period makes no sense. Both parents and educators have much to learn from each other when they begin to work cooperatively (Gordon 1977).

BARRIERS TO PARENT INVOLVEMENT

Why are parents not more active in their child's school or center? Why do parents become less active in schools as their children grow older? There are a number of reasons for this. Some of the reasons deal with economic difficulties that demand that both parents work. Some of the reasons deal with stresses such as health problems facing some families. Some of the problems deal with attitudes of teachers and parents about each other. Greenwood and Hickman (1991) identify several specific barriers to parent involvement. Among these are the attitudes of parents and educators, work and health, abilities needed for involvement, and school structure. Each barrier presents specific problems.

Characteristics and Abilities

Some people believe that parents do not have the characteristics or abilities needed to be effective in the educational program. The belief suggests that there is

FIGURE 20-2 Parents should feel welcome to participate in their children's educational programs.

something extraordinary about people who know how to work effectively with children. It further suggests that much specialized knowledge is needed in order to participate in the education programs of their children. The belief also contends that parents do not possess the social or administrative skills necessary for classroom or policy-making involvement. These views, frequently held by both parents and educators, are generally false. Schools have an obligation to support the confidence that parents need to have in themselves to help their children develop literacy. All parents have unique and valuable strengths; extraordinary abilities are not necessary. While some parents may truly be incapable of involvement, that number is probably much smaller than might be expected. The problem is suspected to be more a perception of ability than actual ability. When the class decides to engage in a creative activity such as a play or pageant, it is quite common for many parents to willingly and eagerly participate in the endeavor. This is especially true when it is clear that the participation will be both enjoyable and beneficial to the children.

Attitudes of Parents

Closely related to the problem of perceived inability is the problem of negative attitudes on the part of parents. While most parents do see the value of many

aspects of education, particularly the value of gaining literacy, some parents do not understand the value of other aspects of education. Although it does not justify this attitude, it must be admitted that a fair amount of what is included in many traditional elementary and secondary programs does seem rather irrelevant to the development of children. The traditional approach of having children learn large amounts of information is becoming impossible at best. The amount of information available today is increasing at a relentless pace. The point is not that children should not learn information. The point is that memory should not be the focus and that education needs to be far more selective about what information and facts are most important for children to learn. In addition, it is not at all clear that all children need to learn the same things. Depending on the child, the child's environment, and other social factors, one child's needs may be substantially different from another child's needs. Parents can easily develop a sense of powerlessness to deal with this kind of a situation effectively. Rather than try, they often tend to simply withdraw from the process. Without a sensitive approach to this taken by educators, it is understandable that the value of certain aspects of educational programs might be questioned by some.

Another source of parents' negative attitudes is the school life experienced by those parents. Adults who were failed by a rigid education system that did not meet their needs are not inclined to be particularly supportive if their children are enrolled in a similar type of system. As children, these parents most likely felt a sense of powerlessness to either participate in or change the system to make it more relevant for themselves. Those same attitudes can continue into adulthood.

Work and Health

Changing economic and social policies often require more families to have larger incomes to meet basic needs. This might be accomplished through both parents working the same or different hours. It may also require a single parent to work at more than one job. Whatever the case, the hours of work often conflict with the hours that children attend early childhood education programs. Many employers do not have flexible leave policies that enable parents to participate in the educational programs of their children. This is an unfortunate reality, because it places further stress on families that may be already overburdened.

Other parents are not able to become involved in their children's educational programs due to health reasons. Chronic illnesses, physical barriers at inaccessible buildings, and other health factors may make participation unrealistically difficult for parents. Some creative thought on the part of educators might help to alleviate this problem. It may not be necessary for parents to be physically present in the early childhood center. Some activities described in this unit can be accomplished in parents' homes.

Attitudes of Educators

The desirability of parental involvement in the education and the literacy development of their children has much support (Durkin 1977; Goldfield and Snow 1984; Greaney 1980; Henderson 1988; Topping 1987). This importance is readily acknowledged by both teachers and parents (Williams and Stallworth 1983–1984). Problems become apparent when each group describes its perception of the boundaries of parental involvement (Rasinski 1989). Parents may see their involvement as including instruction and policy development. Educators tend to see the appropriate involvement of parents as outside of the school curriculum, in roles that parents have traditionally held. These traditional roles include room parents, serving on the parent-teacher organization, running bake sales, and serving refreshments at open house night.

In his work with teachers, Rasinski (1989) has noted that parents are generally viewed negatively. They are seen as the cause of many problems. They are frequently seen as pushy, resistant to teacher recommendations, neglectful of their children, and difficult to contact. Rasinski describes a number of reasons cited by teachers for excluding parents from the program: they are not qualified; they do not understand the language development process; they are unfamiliar with instructional strategies and materials; over-qualified parents who may also be teachers exert too much pressure on the teacher; and, they make unreasonable demands or suggestions. Some of these reasons are cited due to previous experiences of teachers. While each of these charges may contain some truth, it is unfair to generalize such characteristics to all parents.

An informative look at parents' perceptions on this issue is presented in Goldenberg's (1989) study of parent involvement in the literacy development of young, at-risk children. The prevailing view among teachers noted by Goldenberg was that parents, particularly low-income, minority parents, are not capable of helping their children develop literacy. However, it was found that neither lower-income, lower-education, nor language minority status were barriers to parents' ability or motivation to help their children develop literacy. Goldenberg found that teachers tended not to notify these parents of their children's difficulties because they felt that it would do no good. There was an assumption that such families were so pressured by other factors that they would be unable to help their children. On the other hand, parents expressed dismay that they had not been told that their children were experiencing difficulty. Many parents who were made aware of a problem demonstrated the ability and perseverance to help their children, often with much success. Clearly, this prevailing attitude on the part of teachers leads directly to a state of fewer opportunities for such children to develop necessary literacy skills. It also lessens the motivation of parents to participate in the school and its educational programs.

ELEMENTS OF SUCCESSFUL INVOLVEMENT

The key factor to successfully involving parents in both the school and the literacy development of their children is empowerment. This refers to the idea of allowing individuals to have a voice in determining their roles in the process. It suggests that individuals need to be active and responsible in regard to their efforts in the educational process. This, of course, is a basic feature of a whole language approach: children and teachers are given increased choices, independence, and responsibility for learning and instruction. The extension of this concept to parent involvement is a natural part of an integrated language arts approach. If avenues for parent involvement are limited to those dictated by the school to parents, there is little reason to expect parents to be invested and committed to the process in the long term. If the programs are developed by parents, or jointly with parents, this will better insure the active participation and commitment of parents. Schools need to work together with parents to create the elements of successful involvement. Among those elements are a supportive policy, administrative support, a partnership approach, communication, and evaluation.

Policy

Slogans about a school being a community are well intentioned. They do not go far enough to insure parent involvement in the school program, however. A slogan is not a policy. It gives a hint of how things should be, but does not provide the practical framework for achieving parent involvement. The first critical step toward parent involvement is a written policy that addresses the central issue (Williams and Chavkin 1989). This policy should not be developed solely by teachers and administrators. Parents should be included at the beginning of this key step. Cochran and Dean (1991) suggest that a policy development team begin by coming to a consensus of understanding about some crucial parent involvement questions:

- What do I mean by parent involvement?
- What does this school or center mean by the phrase *parent involvement*?
- How do parents participate in decision making?
- What barriers to parental involvement currently exist?

The answers to these questions might be surprising to both teachers and parents. However, they do need to be answered. This enables both parents and teachers to have a common frame of reference concerning the words they are using. The answers to these questions have two outcomes. First, they provide an understanding of what contributions parents can make in the program. Second, they provide guidelines for the group to use as they develop written policies designed to encourage parent involvement. The goal of this step in the process is to produce written policy statements that specify the who, when, where, and how of parent involvement. The policies might deal with issues related to decision making, curriculum,

instruction, evaluation of staff, and learning assessment. These statements should be clearly written and approved by the policy-making board of the school or the center. This will help to make it clear that parent involvement is considered an important and serious part of the program.

Administrative Support

One of the most consistent findings of recent effective schools studies is that the best schools have effective leaders. For any educational program or activity to be successful, administrative support must be present (Berninger and Rodriguez 1989). If the leadership of the school or center appears to be ambivalent about parent involvement, the rest of the staff will tend to be less concerned about it. Administrative support can be demonstrated in a number of practical ways. First, the administration needs to make parent involvement a priority by making it a visible part of the program. It should be addressed in some way at every staff meeting, in every newsletter, and in each building. This tends to build high expectations for parent involvement. Second, the administration can acknowledge on a regular basis the importance of parent involvement to the program. This can be done through attendance at meetings at which parent involvement issues are on the agenda and by modeling some possible opportunities from within the classrooms. Third, the administration can and should also serve on any of the board or policy groups on which parents participate. Finally, the administration can take the lead in setting up opportunities for parents to discuss the school and provide ideas for consideration about the operation of the school. One way of doing this is by participating in parent-teacher conferences.

Partnership

The term *partnership* is used often when educators discuss the relationship between home and school. Often, however, the term is used to mean something less than a true partnership. A true partnership is when both parties have equality with, and a mutual respect for, the other. This is not how the term is ordinarily used in education when parent involvement is discussed. Generally, it is used to mean that the school will do the important work of providing instruction while parents make sure that they provide children with a good breakfast, that they read regularly to their children, and that they run bake sales profitably.

The key ingredient in a true partnership is equality. This idea can be somewhat unnerving to teachers who have become accustomed to being the authority figures in the educational program. When a belief in the concept of equality between parents and teachers is absent, the commitment to partnership is lacking. Studies clearly demonstrate that parents want to be treated as equals; they do not want a "professional-client" relationship (Lindle 1989). This does not mean that teachers must give up the authority that their training and experience give them. It does mean that teachers need to feel comfortable with parents in the classroom. It also means that teachers must begin to see parents less as consumers of education and more as colleagues in discussing the literacy needs of the young children in the classroom. Parents and teachers need to discuss what experiences might be most beneficial for helping children acquire literacy skills. Out of these discussions can come clear ideas of what parents can do for their children and how this will support the classroom instruction.

Parents can demonstrate support for the literacy programs of the schools by providing information and feedback on their children's out-of-school literacy development. This can enable the teacher to better plan for the child. On the other hand, the teacher can help parents become more skilled at gathering information to provide to the teacher. This procedure can be a teaching activity as well. By showing parents how to collect information about good beginning reading behaviors, for example, the teacher is also reviewing good adult behaviors to use with emerging readers. Using the work of Edwards (1989) and Resnick (1987), a series of questions can be used to serve as a tool for assessing parent-child storybook reading sessions. Questions might include whether the parent or other adult:

- Sits next to the child?
- Maintains a physical closeness?
- Prereads the story book?
- Allows the child to hold the book?
- Allows the child to turn the pages?
- Talks about the words and pictures?

FIGURE 20-3 Story and illustration by a child based on a weekend family activity.

- Connects the book to the child's life?
- Reads with drama and excitement?
- Shows enjoyment with reading?
- Answers questions about the story?
- Repeats the child's utterances?
- Expands upon the child's utterances?
- Pauses for the child to talk about the book?
- Comments positively about the child's interest?

Positive answers to each of these questions represent appropriate adult roles for reading books with children. The survey can be used to discuss the child's behaviors with regard to each of these. The survey can also be shared with other parents. Such a survey may be used as a theme for a parents night or included in a newsletter.

Communication

Without frequent communication, there is little possibility of building and maintaining parent involvement. Goldenberg (1989) illustrates clearly the result of a lack of communication: potential parent involvement is needlessly decreased. She describes a situation in which teachers decided not to contact parents concerning the learning difficulties that a group of minority children from low-income homes were experiencing. Interestingly, a few of these parents noted the difficulties on their own and responded appropriately by tutoring their children at home. Other parents were dismayed that they were not told about the difficulties until late in the year. The majority of these parents were found to possess both the ability and willingness to foster their children's learning.

Communication must be multifaceted. First, it should be a two-way street. It should not be a matter of the teacher giving instructions to the parents and the parents simply following those instructions. Second, communication also needs to take place at various points surrounding components of the instructional program. That is, communication should not be confined to notification of parents once a child is seen to be having difficulty. Communication needs to come well before such a situation arises. One of the best ways to help a child avoid difficulty is to identify the areas where problems are likely to occur. When that is done, teachers and parents can develop plans to address and, ideally, eliminate many of those difficulties. Third, the communication needs to include the concept of networking. Networking refers to the formal and informal connections that people make with others. Mechanisms should be in place that allow parents to meet and discuss issues with other parents, groups of teachers, and groups comprised of both parents and teachers.

Evaluation

Assessment of literacy development is a particularly important part of the whole language approach. The use of procedures such as standardized tests, traditional report cards, and the teacher as the sole evaluator of learning are greatly reduced if not eliminated altogether. This is just as well, since the misconceptions about such scores as percentile ranks, standard scores, and stanines often make the issue more cloudy than clear. It is quite natural that parents participate in the assessment procedures used with their children both at home and in the classroom. Parent involvement can be used as an opportunity to help them learn more about the growth of literacy in their children. At the same time, it can help parents appreciate the progress their children are making.

Three guiding principles for involving parents in the assessment process are suggested by Fredericks and Rasinski (1990). First, parent involvement should be an integral part of the program. That means that it should not be seen as an activity that was developed primarily to give parents something to do. Second, assessment procedures should take place in a comprehensive manner. They should not occur only once or twice a year. Assessment should be viewed as an ongoing part of the program. The information should be used to make decisions about the curriculum and the instruction. Third, parent involvement in assessment should be a systematic process. Although it requires some time and training, it does not have to be overly elaborate or sophisticated. It should be done on a regular basis with time for communication between teachers and parents built into the process.

IN-SCHOOL OPPORTUNITIES

Given positive attitudes toward parent involvement, teachers and administrators can organize the school or center to include the elements of successful parent involvement. The decisions about the opportunities for involvement will need to be made in some type of priority-based order. The policy-making board, which should have broad parent membership, will need to develop priorities. Certain resources and needs will have to be considered when developing these priorities. Such things as the number of parents, the needs of the staff, the needs of the children, the expectations of parents, and the focus of the program will all be considered. While it is by no means exhaustive of the possibilities, a number of potential in-school parent opportunities are described here.

Demonstrators

The possibilities for demonstrations that a parent might become involved in should be generated from the curriculum content. The demonstrations should be an integral part of the instruction for a particular unit. For example, a parent who plays a guitar might visit the classroom to sing a story about trees during a unit on forests. It should be made very clear that an older sibling, grandparent, relative, or friend could also substitute for the parent.

Teachers need to learn about the potential resources parents can provide. A simple survey in a

FIGURE 20-4 Older siblings as well as parents can provide valuable classroom demonstrations and presentations.

parent newsletter can provide the teacher with a wealth of resources. The survey need only ask parents about their interests and whether or not they would be able to share or demonstrate those interests with the children. The survey can also inform parents of topics or potential topics for the year and ask for ideas. When this procedure is used, it often triggers ideas that parents are more than willing to share.

Reading Partners

One of the best roles for parents is that of reading partners. This entails modeling or discussing, with parents, effective strategies for reading storybooks to children. Since such reading is constantly being done as part of any early childhood literacy development program, parents can participate at different points during the day.

It does require some training and preparation to become an effective reading partner. Like teachers, parents cannot simply pick up a book and have it be a motivating and exciting experience for the children. A good reader understands the things that a storyteller must do to create interest and excitement. The story should always be read by the reader beforehand. The reader must practice using voice and intonation to create different emotions appropriate to the plot of the story. The reader must learn how to actively include the children in the story reading. That may include both movement and thinking responses to the story. While it is not overly difficult to learn to be a good oral reader, it is important to learn and use these skills. It will make the experience more effective and rewarding for both the children and the parent.

Evaluators

Evaluation is an ideal ongoing process for parent involvement. Parents can do this both at home and in the classroom with their own children. They can also assist the teacher in this critical activity with other children in the classroom. As with reading partners, it requires some time and training to develop the process effectively.

An effective procedure for involving parents in assessment has been developed by Fredericks and Rasinski (1990). First, all parents should be surveyed early in the year about their expectations for their children's literacy development. These records should be kept in pupil folders and referred to regularly. Second, parents should work with the teacher to develop a series of parent surveys and recording sheets to be used both at home and in the classroom on a regular basis. A survey to be completed by parents at home might seek information about the child's feelings and attitudes toward language and literacy that the parent observes. Items on the survey might include questions such as:

- Does the child understand the stories being read?
- Does the child like to have stories read?
- Does the child seek to have family reading time?
- Does the child make guesses about words?
- Can the child retell the story to you?
- Does the child ask for more books?
- Does the child ask to go to the library?

- Does the child draw pictures about storybooks?
- Does the child write about the stories read?

Space on the survey should be left for additional comments from parents. They might be asked to indicate the strengths and needs they see in their children. They might also write any questions they have about their children's literacy development.

An observation sheet might be used in the home or classroom as well. It can be taken from the tools described in the unit on evaluation, or it can be developed in addition to those suggested. Items that can be responded to by parents by marking with a check might include:

- The child chooses to use a variety of printed matter.
- The child freely chooses to read or look at books daily.
- The child seeks to have stories read aloud.
- The child talks about the stories read.
- The child appears to understand the story.
- The child can retell a story that has been read aloud.
- The child attempts to read the story independently.

Here too, space should be left on the bottom of the page to allow parents to comment on other concerns or observations. Copies of each of the sheets or surveys should be returned to parents with the teacher's responses on them. The original sheets should be kept in the child's folder to be used to further assess growth over time.

A third step in this process is to keep additional information flowing between parents and teachers. Parents can be asked to make notes of things their children learn through reading as well as things their children didn't understand in the stories. This information should be gathered and responded to on a regular basis throughout the year.

The final step is to provide plenty of opportunities for parents to observe their children in the classroom. Ask them to observe and record their observations and perceptions concerning how well their children seem to function within the program and how this compares with behaviors observed at home and in other settings. Respond to these observations, and

FIGURE 20-5 Parents and grandparents can become valuable resources for a program.

record both the parent's perceptions and the teacher's comments in the pupil's folder for use in future assessment. Teachers should also seek parent ideas based on their observations and assessment of children and the program.

It is clear that the involvement of parents in the evaluation process is a valuable activity. The purpose is not to convert parents into evaluation specialists. Rather, the goal is to enable them to expand their meaningful participation in the literacy development of their children. Such involvement will benefit the parent, the child, and the teacher.

Trainers

Some parents may have more time available than others. Many of these parents can be used as trainers for other parents. This will enable these parents to assume an additional key role while allowing the teacher to devote more time to the instructional program. A school or center might consider establishing a person or group of individuals as coordinators of parent involvement. This individual or group could help to foster still greater parent involvement. Additional parent contacts could be made by telephone to recruit other parents. Improvements to the already existing means of communication could be made. For example, the classroom or school newsletter could be expanded. Additional articles about classroom events, photographs of classroom events, and reports of survey results could be added.

Tutors

Another possibility for parents is that of tutoring individual students in the program. This work need not include the intensive instructional tutoring that is often associated with the role. That type of activity is often not appropriate with young children. The parent tutor of young children might serve in the role of supporting a child's language attempts in a number of situations. In play, the tutor would try to increase the child's language at whatever level it happens to be. The tutor would need to be a good listener and have some knowledge about how to respond to the child. This requires some time for training and sharing goals for a specific child. Tutors might also serve all levels of exceptionality in the program. With both developmentally disabled and gifted children, the role is to expand the language and thinking of the child so as to enable the child to continue to move to a more independent level of language use.

Responder

The role of responder might seem odd at first, but it is particularly important to language growth. A parent who assumes this role performs a critical part of the role of the teacher. It is important to remember that the teacher will tend to function as a participant in the literate environment rather than the individual in charge of that environment.

The role of responder is particularly important in oral language, reading, and writing/drawing. Here the responder's purpose is to help children think about and monitor their learning. When a child draws a picture as a response to a story, the responder might ask the child a number of divergent questions about the picture. Such questions would tend to begin with the words *tell me about, why,* and *how,* rather than with the word *what.*

Planner

The role of planner, while it is usually for an in-school activity, requires much effort prior to the in-

FIGURE 20-6 Parents can help plan a thematic unit on travel by arranging a trip to an airport and by making contacts with airline personnel.

structional part of the program. Developing upcoming thematic units takes much research, materials collection, and materials production. As a planner, parents might work closely with the teacher to develop outlines of potential thematic units for use over the course of the program. Topics, learning goals, books, and songs must all be chosen well ahead of time. Following this, the books must be collected from the library, other classrooms, garage sales, and so on. Arts and craft materials must be collected from classroom supplies and donated materials. Samples of art projects need to be tested to identify potential areas of difficulty for the children. Potential classroom visitors must be contacted and scheduled. Parent involvement in this activity will prove invaluable to the teacher and the children.

SUMMARY

It is essential that parents be included in the education of their children. Over the past two centuries, parent involvement has gone through a number of phases. In the early nineteenth century, a Calvinistic theory held that children were inherently evil. The role of parents was to provide strict discipline so as to break the will of the child. As the century drew to a close, the work of early childhood educators such as Froebel had reversed the earlier view. During the twentieth century, the view of children changed as did the perception of the role of parents in education. Toward the close of the century, the federal government exerted pressure on educational programs by mandating parent involvement at all levels of education in federally sponsored programs. While the structure of parent involvement changed, some of the traditional beliefs about parent involvement continued.

Traditional beliefs as well as contemporary social needs have tended to create a number of barriers to parent involvement in education. Parents sometimes feel that they have neither the ability nor the social skills necessary to participate in their children's learning. Some parents have negative attitudes about schools that prevent them from seeking to be involved. Some parents feel powerless to influence events in the schools. For still other parents, the stress of family health problems and the demands of work interfere. The attitudes of educators also constitute a major barrier to parent involvement. Many teachers and principals do not wish to include parents in other than a narrowly prescriptive way. They prefer parents to restrict their involvement to reading to their children at home and running school bake sales.

Several elements can be put into place to enhance parent involvement. The critical first step is to bring educators and parents together for the purpose of developing written school policies to be used as a guide and a foundation for parent involvement. With this in place, schools can more easily develop several other elements for successful parent involvement. These include administrative support, the development of teacher/parent partnerships, increased communications, and evaluation.

The possibilities for parent involvement are nearly endless. This is especially true when parents participate in all phases of the educational program. Although parent involvement in classroom instruction has not been a traditional area of participation, it is a particularly effective one. In the classroom, parents can serve as demonstrators, reading partners, tutors, parent trainers, responders, and planners. The benefits of this involvement will affect teachers, children, and parents themselves.

Questions and Activities for Review and Discussion

Multiple Choice

1. A Calvinistic view of children was based on an assumption of
    a. the inherent goodness of the child.
    b. family care and love.
    c. infant depravity.
    d. the need for cultural mainstreaming.
2. Froebel's views in the nineteenth century saw parents as an integral part of
    a. the kindergarten program.
    b. grades one and two.
    c. the need to use strict discipline.
    d. the Calvinistic world view.
3. Some parents do not become involved in school programs because
    a. they do not feel intellectually capable.
    b. they had negative school experiences.
    c. their work schedule doesn't allow it.
    d. all of the above

4. Allowing parents or others to have a voice in determining roles is referred to as
   a. power surrender.
   b. empowerment.
   c. transfer of authority.
   d. election by design.

5. A written parent involvement policy can specify that parents should be involved in
   a. curriculum.
   b. instruction.
   c. evaluation.
   d. all of the above

6. The best time for a teacher to communicate with parents is when
   a. the child is experiencing difficulty.
   b. the child is experiencing success.
   c. the teacher senses that the child might be about to experience learning difficulties.
   d. all of the above

7. Parents are best employed in the assessment process to
   a. administer diagnostic tests.
   b. collect information through observation.
   c. administer standardized tests.
   d. report test results to parents.

True or False

T   F   1. Calvinistic doctrine stated that young children are inherently good.
T   F   2. The federal government has played a leading role in involving parents in policy-making in regard to the education of their children.
T   F   3. Teachers and parents have tended to disagree on the types of involvement parents should have in the schools.
T   F   4. A written policy does little to establish a commitment to parent involvement.
T   F   5. There is no training needed for a parent to become involved as an effective reading partner.

Essay and Discussion

1. Describe the influence of Calvinism on the involvement of parents in the education of their young children.
2. Describe the influence of the federal government in parent involvement in education programs for children.
3. Explain why teachers tend to communicate less frequently with parents who are language-minority, less-educated, or lower-income.
4. Describe the things that effective teacher/parent communications should include.
5. Discuss one of the assessment activities a parent could become involved in within the classroom.

REFERENCES

Berninger, J.M., and R.C. Rodriguez. 1989. The principal as catalyst in parent involvement. *Momentum* 20: 32–34.

Brantlinger, E.A. 1985. What low-income parents want from schools: A different view of aspirations. *Interchange* 16(4): 14–28.

Brim, O. 1965. *Education for child rearing.* New York: Free Press.

Cochran, M., and C. Dean. 1991. Home-school relations and the empowerment process. *Elementary School Journal* 91: 261–269.

Durkin, D. 1977. Facts about pre-first grade reading. In *The Kindergarten Child and Reading*, ed. L.O. Ollila. Newark, Del.: International Reading Association.

Edwards, P.A. 1989. Supporting lower SES mothers' attempts to provide scaffolding for book reading. In *Risk Makers, Risk Takers, Risk Breakers*, ed. J.B. Allen and J.M. Mason. Portsmouth, N.H.: Heinemann.

Fredericks, A.D., and T.V. Rasinski. 1990. Involving parents in the assessment process. *The Reading Teacher* 44: 346–349.

Froebel, F. 1887. *The education of man*, ed. W.T. Harris and trans. W.L. Hailmann. New York: Appleton.

Goldenberg, C.N. 1989. Making success a more common occurrence for children at risk for failure: Lessons from Hispanic first graders learning to read. In *Risk Makers, Risk Takers, Risk Breakers*, ed. J.B. Allen and J.M. Mason. Portsmouth, N.H.: Heinemann.

Goldfield, B.A., and C.E. Snow. 1984. Reading books with children: The mechanics of parental influence on children's reading achievement. In *Promoting Reading Comprehension*, ed. J. Flood. Newark, Del.: International Reading Association.

Gordon, I.J. 1977. Parent education and parent involvement: Retrospect and prospect. *Childhood Education* 54: 71–77.

Greaney, V. 1980. Factors related to the amount and type of leisure reading. *Reading Research Quarterly* 15: 337–357.

Greenwood, G.E., and C.W. Hickman. 1991. Research and practice in parent involvement: Implications for teacher education. *Elementary School Journal* 91: 279–288.

Henderson, A.T. 1988. Parents are a school's best friends. *Phi Delta Kappan* 70: 148–153.

Lindle, J.C. 1989. What do parents want from principals and teachers? *Educational Leadership* 47: 12–14.

Rasinski, T.V. 1989. Reading and the empowerment of parents. *The Reading Teacher* 43: 226–231.

Resnick, M.B. 1987. Mothers reading to infants: A new observational tool. *The Reading Teacher* 40: 888–895.

Seginer, R. 1983. Parents' educational expectations and children's academic achievement: A literature review. *Merrill-Palmer Quarterly* 29(1): 1–23.

Topping, K. 1987. Paired reading: A powerful technique for parent use. *The Reading Teacher* 40: 608–614.

Williams, D.L., and N.F. Chavkin. 1989. Essential elements of strong parent involvement programs. *Educational Leadership* 47: 18–20.

Williams, D.L., and J. Stallworth. 1983–1984. *Parent involvement in education project.* Austin, Tex.: Southwest Educational Development Laboratory.

UNIT 21

Parent Involvement Outside the Classroom

NIT GOALS

After completing this unit, the reader should:

- understand the need to empower parents for participation outside the classroom.
- develop an awareness of the need to foster parents' empowerment.
- develop an awareness of policies and opportunities designed to maintain and support parent involvement.
- identify meaningful roles for parents to assume outside of the classroom.

PREVIEW

To understand how to effectively build parent involvement over the long term, it is helpful to compare it to a garden. A garden does not occur naturally. It is created as a result of a carefully carried out process. While it helps to begin with fertile soil, that is not always possible. Sometimes, the soil must be nourished with compost, peat, and other organic components. This provides a good foundation on which to develop healthy, productive plants. Once this foundation is in place, the area must be cleared of weeds so that seeds can be planted in an organized and careful manner. Once the seeds are planted, the garden must be tended regularly in order for the plants to sprout, grow, and produce flowers or fruit. This care might entail keeping the area free of weeds, providing additional nutrients, watering the plants, and cultivating the soil. If any of these things are neglected, the garden is likely to become overgrown with weeds and disappear. A carefully tended garden, however, can produce flowers and fruit that sustain life and make the environment a better place.

Parent involvement, like a garden, must be built on a good foundation. The good foundation is a feeling of mutual trust and respect. Just as some gardens can produce with little attention from a gardener, many families are capable of fostering learning with little help from schools and educational programs. Teachers need to recognize that parent involvement must

FIGURE 21-1 Parents provide much of a child's early learning.

be maintained and supported. Without that it will wither and die just as the plants do in a neglected garden. With care and tending, the involvement of parents produces benefits to all who strive to maintain it. Parent involvement greatly benefits a school program and enhances the emotional and educational lives of children. This unit further describes the development and maintenance of parent involvement in the education of young children. Key ideas discussed include recognizing the important contributions of families, extending empowerment to all parents, acknowledging the importance of activities and policies for parent involvement, and clarifying key roles for parents.

INTRODUCTION

The importance of involving parents in the literacy development of their children can and should go beyond the classroom. While involving parents in the actual classroom program is quite important, it cannot be seen as the only place for that involvement. Parents should feel comfortable becoming involved in other areas as well. They should be confident about serving on advisory groups and boards associated with their children's school or center. They should be provided with the resources necessary to extend literacy development beyond the boundaries of the classroom. This extension may consist of both the home and the community.

This unit begins with a description of a process for extending the empowerment of parents. While it is important to attempt to include the parent in the

classroom, schools should foster or reinforce the idea that parents have the competence to work with their children independent of the classroom program as well. They also need to reinforce the idea that they have something worthy to contribute to the policy making of the school or program. They need to send the message to parents that their ideas are both welcome and worthy of careful consideration.

Following the description of the empowerment building process, specific procedures to develop and maintain parent involvement are provided. Both policy issues and practical ideas that can be put in place to encourage parent involvement are described. Parents who have been historically underrepresented in this area are the parents of disabled children. Such parents, due to the additional demands associated with caring for their children, are often more isolated and feel greater stress in their lives. It is particularly important to extend efforts to include these parents. Their involvement can have a profound effect on the literacy development of their children.

Finally, the various roles that parents can assume are identified and described. The general roles of decision maker, advocate, and teacher are discussed. Each of these important roles requires different characteristics and capabilities.

EXTENDING EMPOWERMENT

It has been shown that the more parents are empowered to become involved in the education of their young children, the better those children do academically (Cochran and Dean 1991). This is a powerful concept; this reason alone makes the empowerment of parents a worthwhile pursuit. However, the benefits of parental empowerment are not restricted to their own children. Through increased empowerment, it has been demonstrated that parents themselves develop an increased ability to initiate activities and carry out projects that benefit teachers, children, and parents (Chavez 1989; Hamilton and Cochran 1988).

Using over a decade of research on parent involvement, educators have identified a set of steps that seem to describe the process of parent empowerment (Cochran 1987; Cochran and Henderson 1985; Cochran and Dean 1991). The first step in the process is changing any negative perceptions that parents may have of themselves. When those negative perceptions decrease over time, parents acquire a sense of belief in themselves. The second step in the process occurs when parents extend their relationships. They extend those relationships not only within the family, but with neighbors and friends outside of the family. The third step in the process occurs when parents begin to take action on behalf of the child. This includes joining neighborhood groups, becoming actively associated with the schools, and establishing more interactions with other institutions and organizations in the community.

This view of empowerment requires that educators accept certain assumptions concerning parents. The first assumption holds that a deficit model of parent involvement is inappropriate. That is, it cannot be assumed that parents fail to become active in the community because there is something wrong with them. This leads to a second assumption that holds that all parents and families have strengths and that they have the ability to contribute positively to both the learning of their children and to the community. Single-parent families, extended families, two-parent families, black families, Asian families, and Hispanic families all have the ability to contribute something positive. Finally, it is assumed that all family members have an important role in helping children to develop literacy. Often, the mother is seen as the single family member who has a legitimate role. Fathers, grandparents, and siblings are increasingly recognized as having important roles in child development.

OPPORTUNITIES FOR INVOLVEMENT

Just as parent participation in the early childhood classroom doesn't simply occur, effective participation in other parts of the school and program is less likely to occur without encouragement. Schools and center staff members have many opportunities to encourage parent participation. While it is not simply a matter of scheduling a few open houses or parent nights, it is not so difficult that it cannot be effectively accomplished with the ordinary resources found in most programs. It is more a matter of will, planning, organization, and perseverance than anything else.

FIGURE 21-2 The child who created this piece senses the importance of family by writing: "I fold laundry with my Grandma."

Human relationships often do not thrive if left unattended. Therefore, efforts directed toward parent participation do need to be ongoing in order to sustain the involvement. As can be seen from the description of extending empowerment, once involvement is established, the focus might change. At that point, the focus might shift from establishing the involvement to maintaining and extending the involvement. The focus now falls into two categories: policy setting and functional activities.

Policy Setting

Policy setting refers to the development of guidelines used to operate a school or a program. Policies serve to provide answers to teachers and administrators concerning questions that arise in the day-to-day operation of the program. Three basic policy areas related to parental involvement are identified as having particular importance. They deal with communication, planning, and parent support.

FIGURE 21-3 Parents fill a number of different roles for their children.

Communication.

Policies related to communication largely deal with a schoolwide effort to make the school or center an open and inviting environment. Classrooms, hallways, and offices need to be warm and comfortable. Early childhood education centers should not have an institutional appearance. Formality and rigidity has a chilling effect on parents who venture into such areas. There are no fixed rules for creating a comfortable atmosphere. Teachers need to put themselves in the place of a parent and ask, "Would I feel comfortable coming here?"

A second aspect of good communication is honesty. Parents should not be mislead about what is happening in the program. For example, proposing that a child be placed in a segregated special education program as a short-term placement designed to help the child catch up to the rest of the children is not honest. Segregated special education placements are seldom short term. Such placements rarely enable children to catch up to their peers. Parents may accept such a placement at first, but over the years they will come to the conclusion that they were not told the truth.

Planning.

A second policy area for encouraging involvement is developing a procedure for planning the involvement. One of the best ways to do this is through establishment of a formal planning group. This group, comprised of teachers and parents, is established for the sole purpose of identification and coordination of opportunities for parents. The group should function in a collegial manner. While teachers may begin the process by leading the group, it would be best to turn this leadership role over to parents as soon as they are comfortable with such a role. The group should meet on a regular basis, have an agenda, keep records of its work, and communicate regularly with the administration and the policy-making board of the program or school. Among the tasks that this group can address are collecting information related to needs, identifying resources, and matching needs with resources. Information related to needs can mean a number of different things. The group can survey staff members to determine whether they need materials or people for planned or special projects. The group can identify resources by initiating and maintaining contacts with all parents, local businesses, and other community resources.

As specific needs are identified, they can be matched with available resources. For example, suppose a teacher in a toddler program needed certain art or craft materials related to an upcoming project as well as preparation of the materials prior to the date the project is to be undertaken. The group should be able to identify several parents, local business people, or community workers who could possibly meet this need. Even if a parent is employed during the hours that a child is in a program, this type of need could still be met. The parent does not always have to be present in the classroom to help with a project.

Support.

Many times parents can feel overwhelmed with the tasks of rearing young children. Long days and short nights can drain parents of the energy to take on any more responsibility than is required. A possible outcome of this is social isolation. The sense of isolation can lead to a further sense of being overwhelmed.

FIGURE 21-4 Parent mailboxes are an aid to communication at an early childhood center.

This can lead to still further isolation. For this reason, it is important to make any outreach efforts to parents both meaningful and supportive. Ritualistic open houses that merely provide superficial program information do not lead to further parent involvement (Wolfendale 1986). Parents need substantive opportunities to learn about the program in a way that is meaningful to them.

Particularly important is support for parents of children who are disabled, non-English-speaking, or from a minority culture. When supporting the efforts of these parents, it is important to avoid blaming the home environment for any difficulties the child might be experiencing. Professionals have traditionally focused their efforts on attempting to provide direct rather than empowering services to parents. Such efforts have tended to create a sense of passivity and dependence rather than active involvement and independence (Simpson 1988).

Parents of children with disabilities should receive support for their efforts and activities. Such parents tend to be more isolated and under greater stress than other parents (Brantlinger 1991; Sexton 1989;

Turnbull 1988). The severity of a child's disability is not necessarily an accurate guide for determining the support needed by the parents. More subtle disabilities such as mild autism and language delays are frequently associated with much higher levels of stress than might be commonly thought. For parents of these children it is particularly important to institute as many functional activities for parent involvement as possible.

Functional Activities

Functional activities for parent involvement include the practical day-to-day functions of a school or center that enable parents to participate in the program. There are two areas of focus for involving parents in

FIGURE 21-5 Parents extend the language of children through such activities as a trip to the ocean.

materials are being developed, it should be made clear to parents why the materials are needed and how they are going to be used. Parents need to have an opportunity to offer input about the materials. Without this opportunity for input, there is no emotional stake in the participation. Parents will justifiably feel that they are less than equal partners and interest will wane. If a workshop involves learning ideas to reinforce classroom instruction, the communication needs to flow in both directions. Parents should be invited to give their ideas about the issue, and those ideas should be given dignity and consideration. By doing this, both parents and staff will grow.

Accessibility.

A major barrier to parent involvement is a lack of accessibility. While this may include both physical and attitudinal barriers, there are some very practical barriers as well. Many of these barriers can be removed with a bit of careful planning and flexibility. For example, transportation can sometimes be a difficulty for parents. At times, parents simply have no way to get to the school or center to participate in an activity. Arranging for transportation can greatly help these parents. This does not mean that a car or bus needs to be purchased for this purpose. Transportation can often be provided by staff, public means, or other parents. The key is to find out who can provide transportation and to link those individuals with parents who need transportation. An alternative to this would be to provide the opportunities for parent participation in locations other than the school or center. A program can be held at someone's home, a meeting room in a local library, or at a community center. There is usually no cost for such an outreach program, and it could eliminate transportation problems.

The schedules of school programs often conflict with family schedules. Keeping the schedules of parent participation activities flexible can help overcome this difficulty. Offering opportunities at different times during the day and evening can address this need. The same opportunity could be offered more than once, but at different times during the day or evening. Related to this is the issue of childcare. While a family may have one child in a program, there may be other children at home who cannot be left on their own. Scheduling some opportunities in the late after-

FIGURE 21-8 There are many meaningful ways to include parents in a unit that uses books and field trips. *Reprinted courtesy of Troll Associates, Mahwah, New Jersey.*

noon and evening can allow spouses and older siblings to help with childcare duties. Providing childcare for children who are not in a program while their parents avail themselves of participation opportunities is another possibility. This occasional childcare service can be provided with paid employees or with volunteers. It provides a very real service to parents who otherwise could not become involved in the program.

ROLES FOR PARENTS

Since children have the best chance of success in educational programs when the home and school work in close cooperation, it makes sense to identify roles that parents can assume. Potential roles should include those that have been shown to be most effective. The federally funded Follow Through program has been the subject of over two decades of both quantitative and qualitative research on the topic of parent involvement. According to the Department of Health, Education, and Welfare (1977), Follow Through is a program that is intended to continue and expand upon the benefits of early childhood programs such as Head Start. As with most federal programs it contains a provision for strong parent and community involvement. Research has shown that the parent involvement component of the Follow Through program was generally more successful than nearly all other federal educational programs (Burns 1982; Olmsted 1991). The Follow Through research identifies three distinct roles in which parent involvement was particularly effective: advocate, decision maker, and teacher (Olmsted 1991).

Parents as Advocates

An advocate is an individual who pleads for a cause or supports the needs of another. As advocates, parents will plead the cases of their own children or their schools. In advocating for their schools, the parents' efforts are typically focused in two directions. First, parents might advocate within the schools. They might attend policy board meetings in order to learn about the funding and policies of the school. Parent efforts directed outside of their schools will generally seek to benefit their schools. Parents might undertake to learn about funding sources and policies of government offices. In each of these cases, parents might then attempt to exert influence in such a way that their efforts benefit the school or center attended by their children.

Parents also serve as advocates for their children. To do this, they attend meetings about their children, sit on school and center committees, and attend in-service workshops. Frequently, they seek answers concerning why things occur in addition to simply learning about what occurs. This is an especially important role for parents of children with disabilities. While some progressive programs include children with disabilities, many educational programs continue to place these children into segregated special education settings. Increasingly, parents are learning to advocate for their children to be placed in the school they would attend if they were not disabled.

Parents as Decision Makers

As effective decision makers, parents serve on school or center policy-making boards. While it is a commitment of time and energy, it is a critical role for parents. Schools and centers are created for the common good. Having parent representation on policy-making boards is in keeping with this purpose. Policy-making boards deal with several critical elements of program operation. These boards make decisions about hiring administrators and teachers. They make budget decisions. They make decisions about how the program will operate. None of these areas are to be taken lightly. Serving on these boards can be one of the most important areas of participation for those involved.

Parents as Teachers

While parents do not necessarily view themselves as teachers, they truly are teachers every time they talk or play with their children. Much of this teaching is done in the home. Since this is such an important role for parents, it makes sense to help them develop a view of themselves as teachers and to provide them with additional teaching strategies. The emphasis of

```
Our Trip
    Today I went to Williamstown.
I climbed The mountain. It was big.
I walked up and down.
I ate in a restaurant. I read in a
bookstore. I played in a playground.
They were all together. I had a
good time.
```

FIGURE 21-9 Journal entry by a child following an outing with a parent.

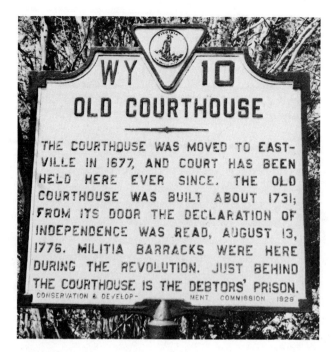

FIGURE 21-10 Parents often provide exposure to language on family outings.

these strategies should not focus on homework types of tasks. Instead, the strategies should enhance the program by attempting to increase the verbal interaction between the child and other family members.

Parents can use several strategies and guidelines in their roles as teachers. Establishing the environment of the home as a place for learning is important (Morrow and Weinstein, 1986; Stanovich 1986). Identifying a time and place can be beneficial. The time should be regular and the place comfortable. An example of how this can be done is the family read-aloud. Each day a children's storybook related to the topic of the classroom could be read. The entire family should participate. Either one person reads while other family members listen, or individual family members can take turns reading. Making a tape recording of the story can enable the child to listen to the story again and again. Answering questions about books and talking about books has been found to be closely linked to the development of early reading ability (Durkin 1966). Parents can also develop skills in oral storytelling and the sharing of favorite children's books.

One of the most powerful things parents can do as teachers is to help their children develop a sense of their competence as literate individuals. There are several ways to help this sense of self-esteem develop. Active involvement by parents with their children's literacy development has positive benefits (Henderson 1988). Parents can begin by holding realistic but high expectations for their children. This is furthered by modeling positive attitudes toward literacy. Engaging in the same activities as the children can demonstrate that parents see literacy as meaningful and rewarding. Working with children to create original picture books is meaningful and rewarding to both children and their parents. Writing and drawing responses to stories helps children see the importance of becoming actively involved with printed language. Parents who keep scrapbooks, write in a journal, and keep a diary model the connection between living, literature, and language.

SUMMARY

In addition to involvement in the early childhood classroom instructional program, parents can and should be meaningfully involved in other areas of a center or school. The first step in helping parents to achieve this goal is through supporting and extending their empowerment. This involves developing and maintaining positive views of themselves as well as improving their relationships with the individuals and institutions that are a part of their lives.

Parental empowerment does not usually emerge by itself. It grows if it is supported by concerned individuals who understand the value of helping parents to further participate in their children's education. School and center staff can take several actions in supporting parent involvement. These actions generally address policy and functional matters. Policy issues deal with such things as understanding the added stresses that children with disabilities can create, reducing the social isolation of parents, and establishing schoolwide efforts to support parent involvement. Functional activities include working to eliminate the practical barriers to parent involvement. A lack of communication is often seen as a block to parent involvement. This can be addressed through a number of mechanisms such as establishing regular communications and sharing meaningful information through these communications. Accessibility is another functional barrier. Scheduling time is a key issue. Structuring opportunities for parent involvement in a flexible manner can do much toward eliminating this barrier.

Finally, identifying the most effective roles for participation can do much to make parent involvement worthwhile. These roles include parents as advocates, parents as decision-makers, and parents as teachers. There is much evidence to support the importance of each of these roles. All three can be achieved with a flexible approach that requires, for the most part, a commitment to establishing such participation.

Questions and Activities for Review and Discussion

Multiple Choice

1. Parents can be involved in the education of young children
   a. in the classroom.
   b. in the home.
   c. at the school or center.
   d. all of the above
2. Parent empowerment is best described as a
   a. process.
   b. trait.
   c. skill.
   d. ability.
3. Parents who can become empowered are found in
   a. black families.
   b. single-parent families.
   c. Asian families.
   d. all of the above
4. The relationship between teachers and parents in a parent involvement planning group should be
   a. adversarial.
   b. collegial.
   c. formal.
   d. hostile.
5. A disability of a child that often causes a greater amount of stress for parents than might be commonly thought is
   a. spina bifida.
   b. deafness.
   c. mild autism.
   d. mental retardation.
6. An activity that centers can provide to parents to enable them to become involved is
   a. offering childcare pamphlets.
   b. providing childcare services at the center.
   c. sending a written summary of a project.

d. scheduling all activities during the morning.
7. It is particularly important to support the role of parent as advocate with parents of
   a. children with disabilities.
   b. boys.
   c. girls.
   d. gifted children.

True or False

T F 1. The only logical place for involving parents in the education of their children is in the home.

T F 2. A critical characteristic of parent empowerment is a sense of self-esteem.

T F 3. Parent involvement can be accomplished by scheduling a few open houses and parent meetings during the year.

T F 4. In parent involvement activities, the communication should flow from teacher to parent and from parent to teacher.

T F 5. Parents of young children should be provided with teaching strategies that will primarily focus on helping children with homework.

Essay and Discussion

1. Describe the three steps that have been found to lead to parent empowerment.
2. Explain why policy setting is important in a program designed to increase parent participation.
3. Discuss some of the guidelines that might be followed by a parent involvement planning group.
4. Describe some of the things that a school or center might do to improve communications with parents in regard to upcoming opportunities for parent involvement.
5. Interview a parent and a teacher of an early childhood education student about the role of the parent as an advocate. Summarize the findings.

REFERENCES

Brantlinger, E. 1991. Home-school partnerships that benefit children with special needs. *Elementary School Journal* 91: 249–259.

Burns, G. 1982. *Executive summary: The study of parental involvement in four federal education programs.* Washington, D.C.: U.S. Government Printing Office.

Chavez, M. 1989. *Risk factors and the process of empowerment.* Unpublished paper prepared for the Bernard van Lear Foundation, College of Education, University of New Mexico, Albuquerque.

Cochran, M. 1987. The empowerment process: Building on family strengths. *Equity and Choice* 4(1): 9–23.

Cochran, M., and C. Dean. 1991. Home-school relations and the empowerment process. *Elementary School Journal* 91: 261–269.

Cochran, M., and C. Henderson. 1985. *Family matters: Evaluation of the parental empowerment program.* Final report to the National Institute of Education. Ithaca,

N.Y.: Cornell University, Department of Human Development and Family Studies.

Department of Health, Education, and Welfare, Office of Education. 1977. Rules and regulations, Follow Through program. *Federal Register* 42(125): 33146–33155.

Durkin, D. 1966. *Children who read early.* New York: Teacher's College Press.

Hamilton, M.A., and M. Cochran. 1988. *Parents, teachers and the community: Building partnerships for the child.* Unpublished evaluation report. Ithaca, N.Y.: Cornell University, Department of Human Development and Family Studies.

Henderson, A.T. 1988. Parents are a school's best friends. *Phi Delta Kappan* 70: 148–153.

Morrow, L.M., and C.S. Weinstein. 1986. Encouraging voluntary reading: The impact of a literature program on children's use of library centers. *Reading Research Quarterly* 21: 330–346.

Olmsted, P.R. 1991. Parent involvement in elementary education: Findings and suggestions from the Follow Through program. *Elementary School Journal* 91: 221–231.

Sexton, D. 1989. Working with parents of handicapped children. Paper presented at the Institute for the Study of Developmental Disabilities, Bloomington, In.

Simpson, R.L. 1988. Needs of parents and families whose children have learning and behavioral problems. *Behavioral Disorders* 14(1): 40–47.

Stanovich, K.E. 1986. Matthew effects in reading: Some consequences of individual differences in the acquisition of literacy. *Reading Research Quarterly* 21: 360–407.

Turnbull, A.P. 1988. The challenge of providing comprehensive support for families. *Education and Training of the Mentally Retarded* 23(4): 261–272.

Wolfendale, S. 1986. Routes to partnership with parents: Rhetoric or reality? *Educational and Child Psychology* 3(3): 9–18.

Appendix A

FLANNEL BOARD AND PUPPET MODELS

The illustrations on the following pages may be used for the creation of flannel board pieces and puppets. The figures cover a number of topics generally found in stories and literature for young children. The figures can be duplicated on a photo copier so that they may be used as either patterns or actual figures. This will allow the teacher to create flannel board figures or stick puppets. In addition, the illustrations can be used as props for oral story telling, bulletin board figures, and parent newsletter illustrations.

Woman

Child (girl)

Child (boy)

Man

Tree (deciduous)

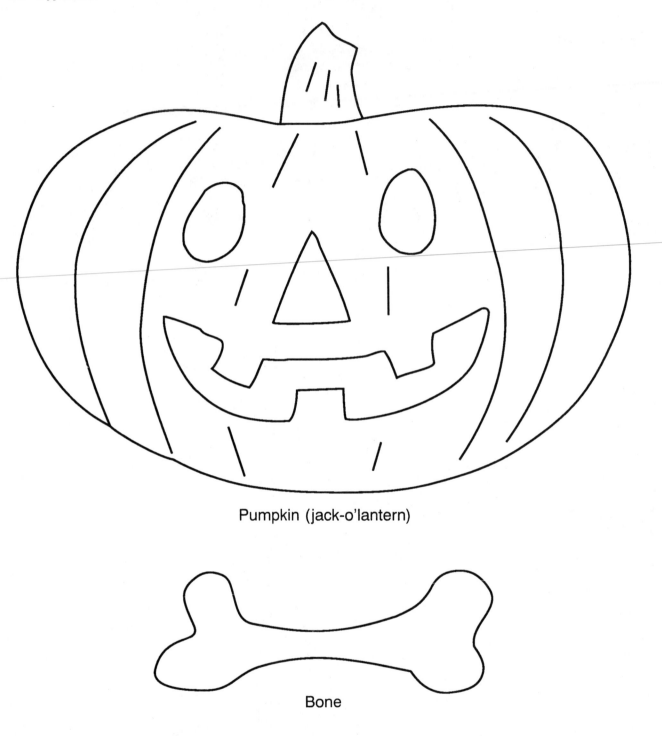

Pumpkin (jack-o'lantern)

Bone

Mushroom/Toadstool

Tree (coniferous)

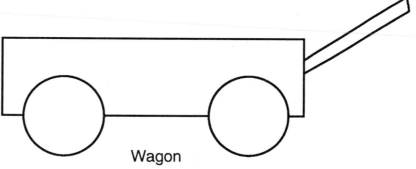

Wagon

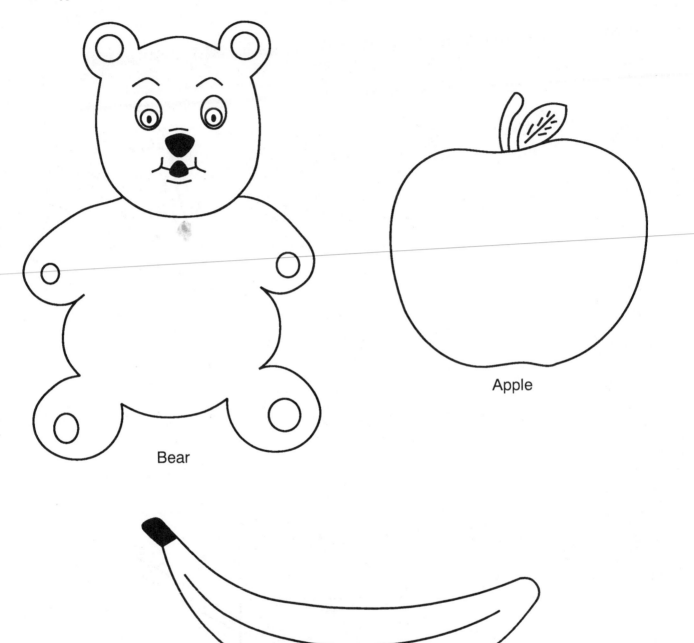

Bear

Apple

Banana

Mouse

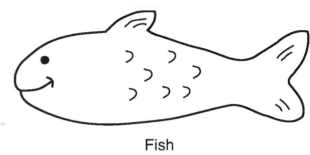

Fish

Bird

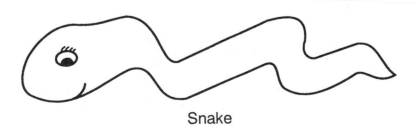

Snake

Rabbit

Cat

Dog

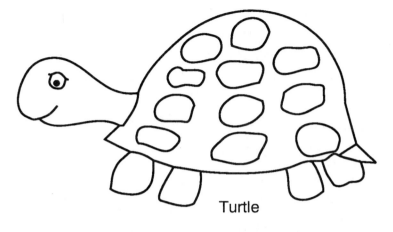

Turtle

Frog

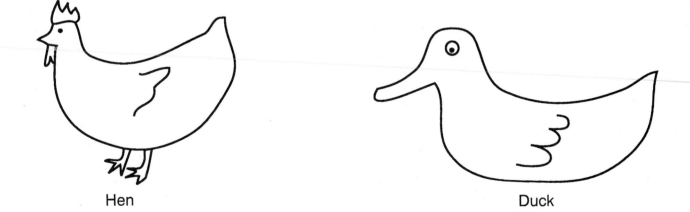

Hen

Duck

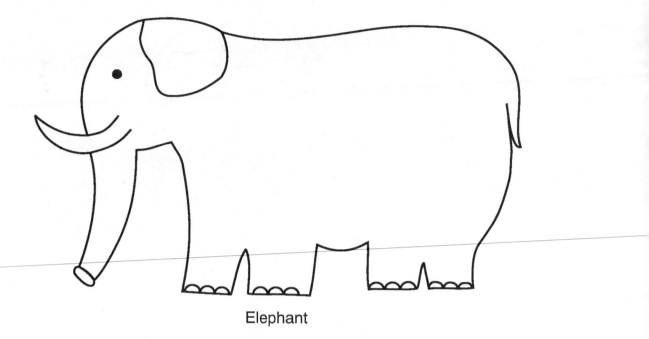

Elephant

Goat

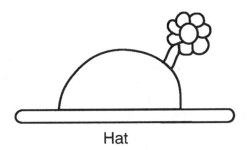

Hat

Hat

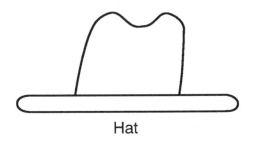

Hat

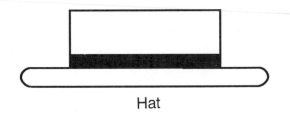

Hat

House

Horse

Cow

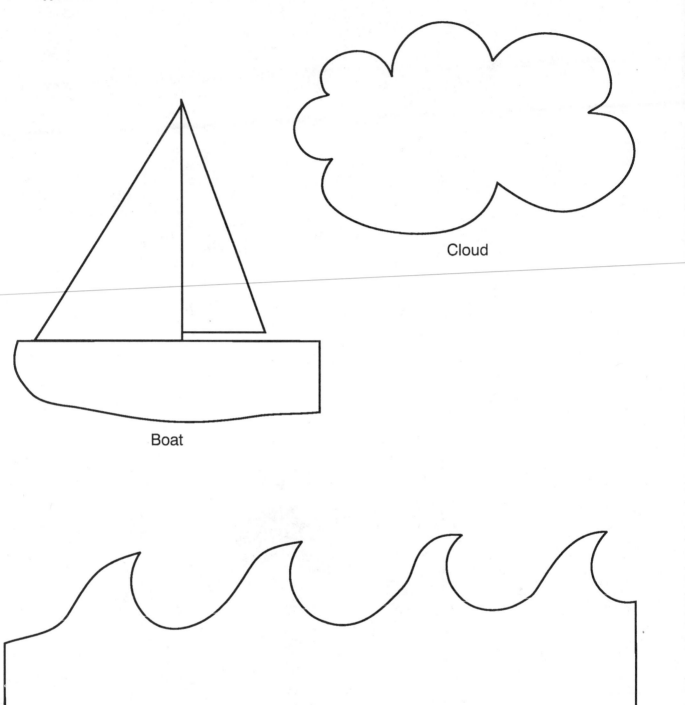

Cloud

Boat

Ocean

Tiger

Shoe

Candle

Mitten

Appendix B

THEMATIC UNIT OUTLINE FOR INFANTS AND TODDLERS
"SOUNDS"

The purpose of a unit at this level is to create an awareness of and an interest in sound, language, and the world. Therefore, the materials used will often be drawn from the environment. Children of this age benefit from sense stimulation and opportunities to explore their physical world. This thematic unit outline provides possibilities for the teacher to consider in developing objectives, activities, books, poems, songs, and parent activities related to the theme of "sounds."

Objectives

Children should:
- associate sounds as a part of language.
- attend to the sources of sounds.
- associate sound with meaning.
- develop the ability to create sounds
- begin to associate words with objects and actions.

Activities

Teachers should:

1. Use language constantly, particularly basic vocabulary associated with objects and actions familiar to very young children.
2. Respond in a meaningful way to the sounds and language of the children.
3. Demonstrate how to make sounds with both the voice and with toys used by young children.
4. Encourage children to create sounds by striking, with a rubber mallet or spoon, common objects such as pots, pans, bells, gongs, wet sponges, and wooden blocks.
5. Use words with distinctive sounds when the objects, people, or actions are present (e.g., Mommy, cookie, dog, truck, etc.).
6. Regularly use chants, nursery rhymes, songs, beginning storybooks, and poems with the children.
7. Provide soft or plush animal toys to use when demonstrating the sounds that animals make. Provide opportunities for children to use these toys during free play.

Books

Adams, P. 1990. *Old Macdonald had a farm.* Singapore: Child's Play International.
Allen, P. 1988. *Fancy that!* Danbury, Conn.: Orchard.
Dyer, J. 1986. *Moo, moo, peekaboo.* New York: Random House.
Isadora, R. 1985. *I hear.* New York: Greenwillow.
Seuss, Dr. (pseud. Theodor Geisel). 1963. *Hop on Pop.* New York: Random House.
Shannon, G. 1988. *Oh, I love!* Riverside, N.J.: Bradbury.
Wilde, I. 1986. *Baby's farm animals.* New York: Grosset and Dunlap.
Zeifert, H., and S. Taback. 1990. *Noisy barn.* New York: Harper and Row.
Zelinsky, P. 1990. *The wheels on the bus.* New York: E. P. Dutton.

Poems

From: *Poetry place anthology.* 1983. New York: Scholastic.
  "My drum," by Dorothy Z. Seymour
From: Prelutsky, J. 1980. *Rainy, rainy, Saturday.* New York:
  Greenwillow.
  "Tick Tock Clock"
  "Whistling"
From: Prelutsky, J. 1986. *Ride a purple pelican.* New York:
  Greenwillow.
  "Justin Austin"
  "Rumpitty Tumpitty Rumpitty Tum"
  "Molly Day"
  "Pennington Poe"
  "Timmy Tat"
  "Betty Ate a Butternut"
  "Cincinnati Patty"
  "Hinnikin Minnikin"
  "Kitty Caught a Caterpillar"
From: Prelutsky, J., ed. 1983. *The Random House book of poetry for children.* New York: Random House.
  "Fishes Evening Song," by Dahlov Ipcar
  "Sing a Song of Subways," by Eve Merriam
  "Sing a Song of People," by Lois Lenski
  "Hug O' War," by Shel Silverstein
  "Bubble Gum," by Nina Payne
  "I Am Rose," by Gertrude Stein
  "Toot! Toot!" by Anonymous
  "The Purple Cow," by Gelett Burgess
  "Clickbeetle," by Mary Ann Hoberman
  "The Yak," by Jack Prelutsky
Carle, E. 1989. *Animals, animals.* New York: Philomel.
  This anthology of poems about animals makes dramatic use of color and design. It uses a large format, with most of the illustrations covering a double page. Poems from Ogden Nash, the Bible, Shakespeare, and Lewis Carroll are perfectly integrated with the illustrations.
Carlstrom, N. W. 1989. *Graham cracker animals 1–2-3.* New York: Macmillan.
  This book contains fourteen poems in couplet form. The poems relate to the everyday adventures of young children. The topics include hats, shoes, pockets, wheels, and so on. Mother Goose D There are many volumes available.

Songs and Chants

From: Nelson, E.L. 1984. *The funny song book.* New York: Sterling."The Alphabet Song"
From: Grayson, M. 1962. *Let's do fingerplays.* Washington, D.C.:
  Robert B. Luce.
  "Bumblebee"
  "Choo-choo Train"
  "Christmas Bells"
  "Clap Your Hands"

"Down by the Station"
"Eeny, Meeny, Miney, Mo"
"Good Morning"
"Kitty Kitty"
"Let Your Hands Clap"
"Peas Porridge"
"Pitterpat"
"Shiver and Quiver"
"The Train"

From: Rubin, R., and J. Wathen. 1980. *The all-year-long songbook.* New York: Scholastic.
"Barnyard Song"

From: Wirth, M., V. Stassevitch, R. Shotwell, and P. Stemmler. 1983. *Musical games, fingerplays, and rhythmic activities for early childhood.* West Nyack, N.Y.: Parker.
"Old Macdonald Had a Farm"
"She'll Be Comin' Round the Mountain"
"Georgy Porgy"

From: Raffi 1982. *Raffi: Rise and shine (record).* Universal City, Calif.: Troubadour.
"Rise and Shine"
"Wheels on the Bus"
"Row, Row, Row"
"Ducks Like"

Parent Activities

Teachers should:

1. Keep parents informed about daily program activities.
2. Encourage parents to use the program activities, books, songs and poems at home.
3. Suggest that the family take trips to the zoo or a farm.
4. Invite parents or siblings who play a musical instrument to give a brief demonstration for the children.
5. Remind parents to point out sounds from the neighborhood on walks and outings.
6. Share the benefits of using correct or precise language at home for familiar objects, people, and actions.
7. Ask parents to refrain from using "baby talk" with the children.
8. Stress the importance of modeling the fluent use of language in all aspects of home life.
9. Help parents explore making various sounds with the children.

Appendix C

THEMATIC UNIT OUTLINE FOR PRESCHOOLERS
"BEARS"

The purpose of a unit for three- and four-year-olds is to expand opportunities to use and acquire language. To do this, there should be an increased emphasis on reading stories that have simple plots in them. This enables children to develop a sense of story while it reinforces their understanding of the power of language. Stories provide ideas for play. Children frequently re-create scenes from within the stories. While an objective may be for children to learn information about bears from this unit, many other important language goals can be realized. Oral language skills grow rapidly during these years. Children may seek to retell parts of the stories and to share some of their own background that is relevant to the stories being read to them. The thematic unit outline presented here includes objectives, activities, poems, songs, and parent activities related to the central theme of "bears."

Objectives

Children should:

- develop an understanding of the concept of bears.
- acquire information about kinds of bears (e.g., grizzly, teddy, polar) and where they might be found.
- draw or write a scene from a book related to bears.
- retell or re-create a concept or an idea from a story related to bears.
- function in a developmentally appropriate way as a part of a group being read a story.

Activities

Teachers should:

1. Lead a discussion about bears. Elicit information from the children to help them see that they already have some knowledge about bears. Possible ideas for inclusion in the discussion include kinds of bears, homes, habits, hibernation, colors, and size.
2. Help children engage in a creative dramatics activity based on the story of "Goldilocks and the Three Bears."
3. Read aloud books related to bears on a regular basis. Ask children to guess or predict what will happen at different points in the story.
4. Count the number of different kinds of bears discovered in the books read.
5. Make cookies in the shape of teddy bears. Eat the cookies at snack time. For an alternative use a recipe for a snack from the *Teddy Bear's Picnic Cookbook* (Darling and Day 1991).
6. Have children bring in their favorite teddy bear from home. Give the children an opportunity to talk about their bears at circle time.
7. Engage children in a cooperative project (e.g., constructing a mobile or a chart) related to bears.

Books

Asch, F. 1985. *Bear shadow*. Englewood Cliffs, N.J.: Prentice-Hall.
Asch, F. 1982. *Happy birthday, moon*. New York: Prentice-Hall.
Berenstain, S. and J. 1966. *The bears' picnic*. New York: Beginner Books.

Berenstain, S. and J. 1988. *The Berenstain bears: Ready, get set, go!* New York: Random House.
Bohdal, S. 1986. *Bobby the bear.* Salt Lake City, Ut.: North-South Books.
Brett, J. 1987. *Goldilocks and the three bears.* New York: Dodd, Mead.
Butler, D. 1989. *My brown bear Barney.* New York: Greenwillow.
Carlstrom, N. W. 1990. *It's about time, Jesse Bear.* New York: Macmillan.
Darling, A., and A. Day. 1991. *Teddy bears' picnic cookbook.* New York: Viking-Penguin.
Dunbar, J. 1987. *A cake for Barney.* Danbury, Ct.: Orchard.
Freeman, D. 1976. *Bearymore.* New York: Penguin.
Freeman, D. 1968. *Corduroy.* New York: Viking.
Glen, M. 1991. *Ruby.* New York: G. P. Putnam's Sons.
Graham, T. 1987. *Mr. Bear's chair.* New York: E. P. Dutton.
Graham, T. 1988. *Mr. Bear's boat.* New York: E. P. Dutton.
Hall, D. 1985. *Polar bear leaps.* New York: Alfred A. Knopf.
Hayes, S. 1986. *This is the bear.* New York: J. P. Lippincott.
Heller, R. 1985. *How to hide a polar bear and other mammals.* New York: Grossett and Dunlap.
Hofmann, G. 1986. *The runaway teddy bear.* New York: Random House.
Hofmann, G. 1978. *Who wants an old teddy bear?* New York: Random House.
Hissey, J. 1990. *Jolly tall.* New York: Philomel.
Johnston, T. 1991. *Little bear sleeping.* New York: G. P. Putnam's Sons.
Maris, R. 1984. *Are you there, Bear?* New York: Viking Penguin.
Marshall, J. 1988. *Goldilocks and the three bears.* New York: Dial.
Martin, Jr., B. 1967. *Brown bear, brown bear, what do you see?* New York: Holt, Rinehart, and Winston.
Marzollo, J. 1989. *The teddy bear book.* New York: Dial.
McCarthy, R. 1985. *Katie and the smallest bear.* New York: Alfred A. Knopf.
McCue, L. 1987. *Corduroy on the go.* New York: Viking-Kestral.
Minarik, E. H. 1957. *Little bear.* New York: Harper and Row.
Morgan, M. 1988. *Edward loses his teddy bear.* New York: E. P. Dutton.
Muntean, M. 1983. *Bicycle bear.* New York: Parents Magazine.
Murphy, J. 1984. *What next, baby bear!* New York: Dial.
Penny, M. 1991. *Bears.* New York: Franklin Watts.
Phillips, J. 1986. *Lucky bear.* New York: Random House.
Riddell, C. 1986. *Ben and the bear.* New York: J. P. Lippincott.
Ross, K. 1987. *Bear island.* New York: Random House.
Rylands, L. 1989. *Teddy bear's friend.* New York: E. P. Dutton.
Stoddard, S. 1985. *Bedtime for bears.* Boston: Houghton Mifflin Company.
Tolhurst, M. 1990. *Somebody and the three Blairs.* New York: Orchard.
Wahl, J. 1987. *Humphrey's bear.* New York: Henry Holt.
Yeoman, J. 1987. *The bear's water picnic.* New York: Atheneum.
Yektai, N. 1987. *Bears in pairs.* New York: Bradbury.
Zalben, J. B. 1988. *Beni's first Chanukah.* New York: Henry Holt.
Ziefert, H. 1986. *Bear all year: A guessing game book.* New York: Harper and Row.

Poems

From: Alexander, R. 1983. *Poetry place anthology.* New York: Scholastic.
  "Bear Weather"
From: Prelutsky, J. 1986. *Ride a purple pelican.* New York: Greenwillow.
  "Grandma Bear"

From: Prelutsky, J., ed. 1983. *The Random House book of poetry for children.* New York: Random House.
  "Grandpa Bear's Lullaby," by Jane Yolen
  "Polar Bear," by Gail Kredenser
Hague, K. 1984. *Alphabears.* New York: Henry Holt.
Johnston, T. 1991. *Little bear sleeping.* New York: G. P. Putnam's Sons.
Blankenship, J. 1984. *Teddy beddy bears.* New York: Random House.
Goldstein, B. 1989. *Bear in mind: A book of bear poems.* New York: Viking-Kestral.
Martin, Jr., B. 1983. *Brown Bear, Brown Bear, what do you see?* New York: Henry Holt.

Songs

From: Charette, R. 1983. *Where do my sneakers go at night?* (record). Windham, Me.: Pine Point Records.
  "Baxter the Bear"
From: Nelson, E. L. 1984. *The funny song book.* New York: Sterling.
  "The Bear Song"
  "Fuzzy Wuzzy (was a bear)"
From: Grayson, M. 1962. *Let's do fingerplays.* Washington, D.C.: Robert B. Luce.
  "The Bear Went over the Mountain"
From: Recker, P., and R. Packard. 1984. *Peanutbutterjam (record).* Hartford, Conn.: Peanutbutterjam Records.
  "Lullaby for Teddy-o"
From: Rosen, G., and B. Shontz. 1988. *Rosenshontz: Family vacation* (record). Brattleboro, Vt.: RS Records.
  "Party Teddy Bears"
From: Rosen, G., and B. Shontz. 1984). *Rosenshontz: It's the truth* (record). Brattleboro, Vt.: RS Records.
  "One Shoe Bear"
  "House at Pooh Corner"
From: Rosen, B., and B. Shontz. 1986. *Rosenshontz: Rock 'n' roll teddy bear* (record). Brattleboro, Vt.: RS Records.
  "Rock 'n' Roll Teddy Bear"
From: Wirth, M., V. Stassevitch., R. Shotwell., and P. Stemmler. 1983. *Musical games, fingerplays, and rhythmic activities for early childhood.* West Nyack, N.Y.: Parker.
  "Teddy Bear Chant"
Blankenship, J. 1984. *Teddy beddy bears.* New York: Random House.

Parent Activities

Teachers should:

1. Remind parents of the benefits of reading aloud books with bear characters and bear themes.
2. Encourage parents to reread, at home, the books that were read aloud at school.
3. Suggest that parents listen to the child orally retelling a story that was read in school.
4. Help parents to locate a toy store in order to look at the teddy bears on display. Talk about the different teddy bears (e.g., colors, size, attractiveness, similarities).
5. Encourage parents to make up a story about a teddy bear.
6. Suggest that the family visit a zoo to see live bears.
7. Share the benefits of a visit a library to take out books about bears.
8. Share songs about bears and teddy bears.
9. Ask parents to visit a museum to view an exhibit about bears.
10. Encourage playing with teddy bears with the child. Talk about what is being done. Encourage the child to talk about what is happening.

11. Suggest that families make cookies with a teddy bear cookie cutter.
12. Share activities such as making a sculpture of a bear using clay or play-dough.
13. Suggest that parents invite other children to have a teddy bear picnic in the park. Bring bear-shaped cookies, juice, and teddy bears.

Appendix D

THEMATIC UNIT OUTLINE FOR EARLY ELEMENTARY
"FRIENDS"

There are many purposes for implementing a thematic unit in language arts with five-, six-, and seven-year-old children. There is a need to continue the development of oral language skills. This extends the development of articulation, vocabulary, and a sense of schemas. At the same time, it is important to encourage children to demonstrate more control and independence in written language. Children may be introduced to stories and texts of varying lengths. Longer stories will help them to begin to develop a sense of story schemas. Opportunities to write and to use language as a social tool should be abundant. The thematic unit outline on "Friends" includes objectives, activities, books, poems, songs, and parental activities.

Objectives

Children should:

- develop the ability to tell about the concept of friends and friendship.
- recognize that friendship can take several forms.
- draw and/or write something related to the concept of friendship.
- use appropriate intonation when telling of an incident involving a friend.
- acquire and use vocabulary related to the concept of friendship.
- use relevant and accurate information to describe a friend.

Activities

Teachers should:

1. Read aloud books dealing with the concepts of friends and friendship. Support discussions related to friendship: What is a friend? What do you do with friends? Who are your friends?
2. In later discussions, expand the concept of friendship. Ask: Who can be a friend (e.g. dog, mother, teacher, teddy bear)? Why can each be a friend? How can they be friends?
3. Develop and support activities that require children to work in pairs. After the activities, help children to talk about the ideas of helping and joint effort.
4. Encourage children to talk about other issues related to friendship: Do you always want to be with a friend? Why or why not? When do you want to be with a friend?
5. Encourage children to draw a picture and/or write a story about a friend. Tell about the picture or story to another child or to the group.
6. Help children use creative dramatics to recreate a scene from a story related to friendship.
7. Provide opportunities to pantomime ideas related to friends (e.g. being alone, meeting a friend on the playground, telephoning a friend).
8. Discuss the emotions related to friends: Can a friend make us happy? Sad? Angry? How?
9. Provide toy telephones so that children can simulate conversations with friends during free play.
10. Describe and use creative dramatics to simulate personal feeling related to friendship: How do you act when you see a friend? How do you act when you disagree with a friend?

Books

Aliki. (1984). *Feelings*. New York: Mulberry.
Aliki. (1982). *We are best friends*. New York: Mulberry.

Barrett, J.D. (1989). *Willie's not the hugging kind*. New York: Harper and Row.

Carlson, N. (1983). *Loudmouth George and the cornet*. New York: Viking Penguin. Carlson, N. (1985). *Louanne Pig and the witch lady*. New York: Viking Penguin.

Cohen, M. (1967). *Will I have a friend?*. New York: Macmillan.

Cuyler, M. (1989). *Freckles and Jane*. New York: Henry Holt.

Delacre, L. (1988). *Nathan's fishing trip*. New York: Scholastic.

dePaola, T. (1974). *Watch out for the chicken feet in your soup*. New York: Simon and Schuster.

Fox, M. (1989). *Night noises*. New York: Gulliver/Harcourt, Brace, Jovanovich.

Giff, P.R. (1989). *Spectacular stone soup*. New York: Dell.

Hayes, G. (1984). *Patrick and Ted*. New York: Scholastic.

Henkes, K. (1988). *Chester's way*. New York: Greenwillow.

Hest, A. (1984). *The crack-of-dawn walkers*. New York: Macmillan.

Keller, H. (1987). *Lizzie's invitation*. New York: Greenwillow.

Lobel, A. (1970). *Frog and toad are friends*. New York: Harper and Row.

Marshall, J. (1972). *George and Martha*. Boston, MA: Houghton Mifflin.

Marshall, J. (1988). *George and Martha round and round*. Boston, MA: Houghton Mifflin.

Marshall, J. (1990). *The cut-ups carry on*. New York: Viking Penguin.

Marshall, J. (1987). *The cut-ups cut loose*. New York: Viking Kestral.

Marxhausen, J. (1990). *Some of my best friends are trees*. St. Louis, MO: Concordia.

Mayer, M. (1988). *Just my friend and me*. Racine, WI: Western.

McPhail, D. (1982). *Great cat*. New York: E. P. Dutton.

Munsch, R. (1984). *Millicent and the wind*. Scarborough, Ontario, Canada: Firefly.

Paige, R. (1988). *Some of my best friends are monsters*. New York: Bradbury.

Phillips, J. (1986). *My new boy*. New York: Random House.

Rabe, B. (1981). *The balancing girl*. New York: E. P. Dutton.

Rey, M. & H.A. (1984). *Curious George goes sledding*. New York: Scholastic.

Rogers, F. (1987). *Making friends*. New York: G. P. Putnam's Sons.

Ross, P. (1981). *M & M and the big bag*. New York: Viking Penguin.

Rossner, R. (1987). *Arabba Gah Zee, Marissa and Me!*. Chicago, IL: Albert Whitman.

Sadler, M. (1983). *Alistair's elephant*. Englewood Cliffs, NJ: Prentice-Hall.

Sharmat, M. (1988). *Sherman is a slowpoke*. New York: Scholastic.

Sundgaard, A. (1988). *The lamb and the butterfly*. Danbury, CT: Orchard.

Waber, B. (1988). *Ira says goodbye*. Boston, MA: Houghton Mifflin.

Waber, B. (1972). *Ira sleeps over*. Boston, MA: Houghton Mifflin.

Zolotow, C. (1961). *The three funny friends*. New York: Harper and Row.

Poems

From: Prelutsky, J. (1980). *Rolling Harvey down the hill*. New York: Greenwillow.

"My four friends"
"Harvey always wins"
"The fight"
"Nobody calls him Jim"
"Lumpy is my friend"
"Harvey never shares"
"No girls allowed"
"Tony and the quarter"

From: Prelutsky, J. (1984). *The new kid on the block*. New York: Greenwillow.

"The new kid on the block"
"Alligators are unfriendly"
"The neighbors are not fond of me"
"My dog, he is an ugly dog"
"My mother says I'm sickening"
"I'm the single most wonderful person I know"
From: Wise, W. (1971). *All on a summer's day.* New York: Pantheon.
"A secret"
"Lonely"
Charles, D. (1989). *Paddy Pig's poems.* New York: Simon and Schuster.

Songs

From: Charette, R. (1983). *Bubble gum and other songs for hungry kids* (record). Freeport, NY: Educational Activities.
"Oh, you're my friend"
"Yesterday I gave my brother away"
From: Charette, R. (1987). *Where do my sneakers go at night?* (record). Windham, ME: Pine Point Records.
"My dog"
"When I'm with my Dad"
From: Grayson, M. (1962). *Let's do fingerplays.* Washington, DC: Robert B. Luce.
"Aiken Drum"
"People"
"Playmates"
From: Paton, S., & Paton, C. (1975). *I've got a song* (record). Sharon, CT: Folk Legacy.
"Move over"
"You can't make a turtle come out"
From: Recker, P., & Packard, R. (1984). *Peanutbutterjam* (record). Hartford, CT: Peanutbutterjam Records.
"A book is a wonderful friend"
From: Rogers, F. (1981). *Won't you be my neighbor?* (record). Pittsburgh, PA: Family Communications.
"Won't you be my neighbor"
"Sometimes people are good"
"It's you I like"
From: Rosen, G., & Shontz, B. (1984). *Rosenshontz: It's the truth* (record). Brattleboro, VT: RS Records.
"A good friend"
From: Rosen, G., & Shontz, B. (1986). *Rosenshontz: Rock 'n' roll teddy bear* (record). Brattleboro, VT: RS Records.
"Little light of mine"
"The best that I can"
From: Wirth, M., Stassevitch, V., Shotwell, R., & Stemmler, P. (1983). *Musical games, fingerplays, and rhythmic activities for early childhood.* West Nyack, NY: Parker.
"Join in the game"
"Ten little Indians"
"The cookie jar chant"

Parent activities

Teachers should:

1. Share the benefits of reading aloud books with friendship themes.
2. Ask parents to listen to child retell stories read in school about friendship theme.

3. Suggest that parents develop a list of friends with the child. Identify the special relationships each has with the child (e.g. neighbor, playmate, pet).
4. Suggest that parents tell the child a story about a childhood friend of the parent.
5. Have a parent come to the classroom to read aloud a story about friends and friendship.
6. Encourage parents to allow children to invite a friend over on the weekend for a special activity (e.g. make cookies, play in a wading pool, go to the beach).
7. Suggest that families make a list of the things the child likes in a friend (e.g. humor, creativity, loyalty, fairness).
8. Encourage both parent and child to draw a picture of a special friend and tell the other about it.
9. Remind the parent to tell the child about the things that make him or her a friend to the parent.
10. Encourage families to learn and sing songs about friendship.
11. Remind the parents of the importance of teaching the child to dial the telephone number of a friend and to have a conversation on the telephone.

Glossary

ability — the power or competence to do a mental or physical task

abstract — a generalization that describes the qualities of an idea or object rather than identifying a specific concrete object

achievement — a demonstrated proficiency on a task

achievement test — a measurement device, ordinarily using pencil and paper, to determine what has been learned

affective — referring to feelings or emotions

allegory — a story in which the characters and plot represent or demonstrate ethical values

alphabet book — a picture book that presents the letters of the alphabet in sequential order

anecdotal record — notes or descriptions of actual behaviors observed

appreciation — an awareness of and positive reaction to the good qualities of something, such as a piece of literature

assessment — the process of gathering information or data in order to understand and make judgments about something

auditory — having to do with the sense of hearing

babbling — the stage of early language acquisition in which children, usually three- to six-months-old, produce and play with a variety of sounds

basal reader — one of a series of texts in a commercially produced reading instructional program

behavior — an overt, covert, or unconscious physical or mental act

behaviorism — a view of psychology that contends that only observable behaviors should be studied

bilingual — referring to the ability to use a second language in addition to the native language

Caldecott — a medal awarded on a yearly basis to the artist who illustrated the most distinguished American picture book for that year

character — the totality of an individual depicted in a piece of literature

child-centered — emphasizing the developmental needs of the child

classic — a piece of literature that has continued to appeal to readers over a long period of time

cloze — a procedure in which an individual restores missing oral or written information by using the context of the communication

cognitive — referring to intellectual functions

communication — the process of sharing information

competence — the ability to perform a task

comprehension — the process of acquiring the meaning of something

concept — the general meaning of an abstract idea

concrete — something that is real or literal as opposed to abstract

contemporary — in literature, referring to works produced during the present time period

content area — an organized body of knowledge, such as science or social studies, that is reflected in its specialized vocabulary

context — the language that surrounds a specific language unit

convergent thinking — the intellectual process of a person using information and ability to arrive at a specific conclusion

creative — the power to identify new problems and develop new solutions or ideas related to them

critical — the process of making judgments

culture — the patterns and products of a social group

curriculum — referring to the objectives, topics, or experiences of a school program

cursive — type of handwriting in which the letters of a word are connected

data — a collection of information

decode — the process of changing language symbols into meaningful communication

developmental — referring to the stages of physical, mental, and social growth

diagnosis — the process of identifying strengths and

weaknesses, particularly for the purpose of planning instruction

dialogue — a conversation between two or more individuals

disability — the loss or lessening of a physical, intellectual, or emotional function

disabled — referring to an individual who may have needs for additional services to participate in classroom activities due to physical, intellectual, or emotional factors

divergent thinking — the intellectual process of generating new ideas or alternate interpretations

drama — a story performed or told as a play

dyslexia — a term used to refer to a reading disability; its overuse has rendered the term rather meaningless for educators

eclectic — any process that borrows processes and activities from a variety of sources

egocentric — a focus upon oneself and an indifference to others; it is not necessarily selfishness in young children

emotional — referring to the ability to function within the environment

empathy — an identification with and an understanding of another person's thoughts and feelings

encode — the process of changing meaningful communication into language symbols

enrichment — additional experiences that supplement and support the regular classroom experiences

environment — all of those things outside of an individual that can affect the individual

essay — a written piece of text giving the author's view of something

evaluation — the process of collecting information and making judgments about something

fable — a prose or poetic story using animal or inanimate characters for the purpose of teaching something

fairy tale — an elaborated folk story that deals with real problems but includes imaginary characters and magical happenings

fantasy — a fanciful story told in a make-believe environment

fiction — imaginative narrative writing intended to entertain the reader

figure of speech — a use of language that is not literal

fine motor — the small voluntary muscles used in such activities as writing and cutting with scissors

fluency — a clear, effortless expression of oral or written language

folk tale — a simple story whose origin has been lost through repeated storytelling

genre — a type of literary work such as a realistic novel or poetry

goal — a general target to be attained

grammar — the morphology and syntax of a language

grapheme — the written representation of a phoneme

gross motor — the large voluntary muscles used in such activities as walking and jumping

hearing — the sense used to discern sound

heterogeneous — a grouping of students that includes those of differing levels of ability or achievement

holistic — an approach that assumes that the whole is greater than the sum of its parts

homogeneous — a grouping of students that includes only those of similar ability or achievement

idiom — an expression that does not use the literal meaning of the words included in it

implicit — something that is suggested rather than specifically stated

integration (inclusion) — serving all children within a regular educational program

intellectual — referring to mental abilities

interpret — the process of going beyond the literal meaning of a communication

kindergarten — a school or class, typically for five-year-olds

knowledge — a general familiarity with certain facts or ideas

learning — the process of changing behavior due to instruction and experience rather than through development

lexical — relating to words and word meaning

linguistic — having to do with the study of language

literacy — the ability to use language at a level that

enables the individual to meaningfully participate in society

literal — the meaning that can be explicitly understood from the words used

main idea — the central thought in a passage

mainstreaming — providing educational services to exceptional children within the regular classroom

manuscript — writing in which each of the letters are formed and printed separately from the others

miscue — in oral reading, a response by the reader that differs from that which would be expected, given the text being read

model — a standard or example that can be imitated or used to demonstrate something

myth — a story designed to explain a physical phenomenon

narrative — a piece of writing that tells a story

native language — the language a child first learns to speak

nonfiction — writing designed to describe, explain, or persuade rather than to tell a story

objective — a learning target at which instruction is directed

oral — referring to spoken language

orthographic — referring to spelling

peer group — a group of people in which an individual is a social equal

phoneme — the smallest spoken language unit that can result in a meaning difference

phonetic — referring to speech sounds

phonics — an approach to teaching reading that stresses sound-symbol correspondence

picture book — a book in which the illustrations are as important as the text to the telling of the story

process — a series of actions or activities directed toward some end

product — an outcome of a process

research — the systematic study of a problem

retelling — describing what occurred in a piece of writing after having read it

rote — exact recall of information with little regard for understanding

self-correction — recognition and correction of one's errors

semantics — the study of word meanings

sight word — a word that is recognized immediately without the need for decoding or the use of context

standardized test — a test with specific tasks and norms that enable test givers to make comparisons of the learning of a specific group of children with the learning of children from other geographical areas

standard language — the dominant language in a culture

storytelling — the art of sharing stories orally

syntactics — the study of the relationships and functions of sentence parts

tall tale — a humorous, exaggerated story

telegraphic speech — a stage in language development in which the speaker uses only the essential words of an utterance

test — a set of tasks that enable the test giver to quantify the performance of the individual taking the test

transfer — the carryover of learning from one situation to another

verbal — having to do with words or language

visual — having to do with the sense of sight

word identification — the process of determining the pronunciation and meaning of an unknown word

wordless book — a picture book that has no text

workbook — in reading, a paperbound book, usually one of a series to accompany basal readers, containing practice exercises of specific language skills

NAME INDEX

Complete bibliographical information for children's books and reference articles is provided at the end of the unit in which the book or article appears.

SUBJECT INDEX